W9-CDW-641

The American Express
International Traveler's Pocket
SPANISH
Dictionary and Phrase Book

The American Express
International Traveler's Pocket
SPANISH
Dictionary and Phrase Book

Simon and Schuster
New York

List of abbreviations

abbrev	–	abbreviation	*num*	–	numeral
adj	–	adjective	*pl*	–	plural
adv	–	adverb	*pref*	–	prefix
art	–	article	*prep*	–	preposition
conj	–	conjunction	*pron*	–	pronoun
excl	–	exclamation	*vi*	–	intransitive verb
f	–	feminine noun	*vr*	–	reflexive verb
m	–	masculine noun	*vt*	–	transitive verb
n	–	noun	*vt/i*	–	transitive/intransitive verb
nt	–	neuter			

The asterisk * denotes an irregular verb, to which the reader is referred in the list of irregular verbs in the grammar section.

Cross-reference letter keys occur in brackets after main section headings. Phrases are numbered in sequence following each main heading. Phrase words are cross-referenced in the English-Spanish dictionary section by letter and number to their relevant phrases.

Collins Publishers

Editor
Nicholas Rollin
with
Lorna Sinclair
Carmen Billinghurst
Assistant Editors
Susan Dunsmore
Valerie McNulty
Lesley Robertson
Managing Editor
Richard H. Thomas

Mitchell Beazley Publishers

Editors
James Hughes
Christopher McIntosh
Designer
Philip Lord
Executive Art Director
Douglas Wilson
Production
Julian Deeming

Edited by William Collins Sons & Co Ltd
and by Mitchell Beazley International Ltd
Designed by Mitchell Beazley International Ltd
87-89 Shaftesbury Avenue
London W1V 7AD
© Mitchell Beazley Publishers 1983
© William Collins Sons & Company Ltd 1983

Published by Simon and Schuster
A Division of Gulf & Western Corporation
Simon & Schuster Building
Rockefeller Center
1230 Avenue of the Americas
New York, New York 10020

Library of Congress Cataloging in Publication Data
Main entry under title:

The American Express international traveler's pocket dictionaries and phrase books, English/Spanish.

Includes index
1. Spanish language—Conversation and phrase books. I. American Express Company. II. Mitchell Beazley Ltd.
PC4121.A55 1983   468.3'421   82-19637
ISBN 0-671-47028-0

Typeset by Coats Dataprint Ltd, Inverness

Printed in Great Britain by William Collins Sons & Co Ltd, Glasgow

Contents

Pronunciation

English spelling gives only an approximate idea of how Spanish sounds. But Spanish is almost completely regular – the spelling matches the pronunciation. The letters whose pronunciation may give trouble are: the letter *r*, which is always rolled, especially at the beginning of a word (as is *rr*); the letter *c* before *e* or *i* and the letter *z*, which are pronounced like the *th* in *thin*; the letter *g* before *e* or *i* and the letter *j*, which have the guttural sound heard in the Scottish word *loch*, shown here as *kh*; the letter *h*, which is never pronounced; the letters *ll*, which are pronounced like the *lli* in *million*; the letter *v*, which is pronounced as a *b*: *vino* is pronounced *bee·no*.

Vowels: in Spanish, vowels are usually single sounds. When two occur together (e.g. *día, creer*) both are pronounced in quick succession: **dee·a**, **kre·er**. But vowel sounds are run together in words such as *viene* (**bye·ne**), *veinte* (**beyn·te**), *estación* (**es·ta·thyon**), and this is clearly shown in the dictionary section.

In southern Spain and Latin America *ci, ce* and *z* are usually pronounced as *s*, and final *s* may be silent or almost silent. Another major difference is that *ll* is pronounced as *y*.

Stress

Words ending in a vowel, *n* or *s* are stressed on the penultimate (second last) syllable; otherwise the stress falls on the last syllable. All exceptions are indicated by a written accent. The written accent may also distinguish between words spelled *and* pronounced alike, e.g. *solo* (alone) and *sólo* (only).

Punctuation

Questions and exclamations are punctuated at the beginning as well as at the end, with the first question mark or exclamation mark inverted:

¿Dónde está la estación?	Where is the station?
¡Cómo hace calor!	How hot it is!

The pronunciation given here is that used in Spain itself. In Latin America it is rather different, but European Spanish pronunciation is perfectly understood in Latin America.

Spanish spelling	Closest English sound	Shown here by		Example	
a	father	*a*		padre	**pa·dre**
e	pet	*e*		pero	**pe·ro**
i	feed	*ee*		litro	**lee·tro**
	yet	*y*		tiene	**tye·ne**
o	thought	*o*		dónde	**don·de**
u	moon	*oo*		algún	**al·goon**
	or quick	*w*		cuando	**kwan·do**
y	you	*y*		yo	**yo**
c	before a, o, u				
	cat	*k*		caja	**ka·kha**
	before e, i				
	thin	*th*		centro	**then·tro**
g	before a, o, u				
	got	*g*		gato	**ga·to**
	before e, i				
	loch	*kh*		gente	**khen·te**
j	loch	*kh*		jueves	**khwe·bes**
ll	million	*ly l·y*		calle	**kal·ye**
ñ	onion	*ny n·y*		niño	**neen·yo**
qu	quay	*k*		queso	**ke·so**
r	rolled	*r*		ropa	**ro·pa**
rr	carrot	*rr*		cerrado	**the·rra·do**
v	bat	*b*		vino	**bee·no**
z	thin	*th*		zumo	**thoo·mo**

The syllable to be stressed is shown in *heavy type*

Introduction

The Spanish language

Spanish is the mother tongue of more than 450 million people in various parts of the world, including some 40 million in Spain itself. Millions more speak it as a second tongue. It is an expressive language and one which is reasonably easy for the beginner to understand as its pronunciation follows such regular rules. Although Castilian Spanish is the national language of Spain, the Basques of northern Spain speak their own unique tongue; the Catalans of northeastern Spain speak Catalan, a language similar to Provençal; and the Galicians of the northwest speak Galician, a Portuguese dialect. Pronunciation varies greatly outside Castile and in the Spanish-speaking nations of Latin America.

How the book works

This is a combined phrase-book and dictionary, designed primarily for the needs of the traveler. It enables you to find easily and quickly just the phrase you need, whether you are buying a suit or trying to tell a garage mechanic what is wrong with your car. The Spanish is accompanied in all cases by an instant guide to pronunciation.

Many of the phrases listed consist of a basic group of words which can be linked up with different subsidiary words to produce variations, in the way that a power tool can be fitted with extensions. With phrases of this kind the basic "tool" is shown on one side and the "extension" on the other, with a dash in between. Alternative combinations are either indicated by an oblique stroke or shown on the line below. More phrases and expressions are to be found in the dictionary section at the back of the book. These also serve as a cross-reference index to the phrases.

Here is an example. If you look up the word "toll" in the dictionary, you will find "el peaje" and a cross-reference to Section T (Travel). Here you will see, against the number shown in the cross-reference, the kind of phrase you might need in using this word. With practice you will be able to express yourself with flexibility and confidence, and what you learn from this book can open the door to the whole Spanish language.

Understanding what you hear

This book not only tells you what to say but also helps you to interpret some of the things that will be said to you. For example, the section on "Finding the way" anticipates the sort of directions you may be given. But to understand what you hear it is necessary to attune your ear to sounds and intonations that may be unfamiliar. So read, listen, learn and practise. Even a limited competence in Spanish will bring you great satisfaction as you travel. So have a good trip or ¡Buen viaje!

Basic equipment (B)

Here are some of the words and phrases which make up the basic coinage of Spanish and which it is useful to have in your pocket for a wide variety of situations. You would be well advised to read through this whole section before starting your trip. If you can memorize any of it, so much the better.

Some essentials

Yes	You're welcome
Sí	De nada
see	*de na·da*
No	No thank you
No	No, gracias
no	*no gra·thyas*
Please	You are very kind
Por favor	Es Ud muy amable
por fa·bor	*es oos·ted mooy a·ma·ble*
Thank you	I am very grateful
Gracias	Se lo agradezco mucho
gra·thyas	*se lo a·gra·deth·ko moo·cho*

Greetings and exchanges

Bear in mind that the Spanish can be rather formal when they address each other. They are very sparing in their use of the familiar "tú" (*too*: you) — you should use this only when you are speaking to somebody you know really well. The normal form of *you* is "Usted(es)" (*oos·ted(·des)*) (usually written Ud(s)), which takes the third person form of the verb. The Spanish also use "Señor", "Señora" and "Señorita" a great deal.

Let us say that you are greeting a "Señora Rodríguez" whom you do not know, or whom you may have met only a few times. The correct form is "Buenos días, Señora" or "Buenos días, Señora Rodríguez". The use of "hola" would be rather impolite. If you are greeting a good friend called Juan, then "Hola Juan" is acceptable. If you are unsure, stick to "Buenos días . . .". Remember that handshaking is normal both on meeting and taking leave, and is not restricted to the first introduction.

1 Good morning/afternoon — (*to a man*)
   Buenos días/Buenas tardes — Señor
      bwe·nos dee·as/bwe·nas
         tar·des — *sen·yor*
                  (*to a lady*)
            — Señora
            — *sen·yo·ra*
                  (*to a girl*)
            — Señorita
            — *sen·yo·ree·ta*

2 Good evening
   Buenas tardes/Buenas noches
   bwe·nas tar·des/bwe·nas
   no·ches

3 Good night (*parting or going to bed*)
   Buenas noches
   bwe·nas no·ches

4 Hello
   Hola (*informal*)
   o·la

5 Hello (*by telephone*)
   Dígame
   dee·ga·me

6 Goodbye
   Adios
   a·dyos

7 How do you do?
   Encantado(a)
   en·kan·ta·do(a)

8 I'm very glad to meet you
   Encantado(a) de conocerle(a)
   en·kan·ta·do(a) de
   ko·no·ther·le(a)

9 See you soon
   Hasta pronto
   as·ta pron·to

10 See you later (in the day)
Hasta luego
as·ta lwe·go

11 What is your name?
¿Cómo se llama Ud?
ko·mo se lya·ma oos·ted

12 My name is . . .
Me llamo . . .
me lya·mo

13 How are you?
¿Cómo está Ud? (*formal*)
ko·mo es·ta oos·ted
¿Cómo estás? (*informal*)
ko·mo es·tas

14 I am very well thank you
Estoy muy bien
es·toy mooy byen

15 I'm sorry/I beg your pardon
Perdón
per·don

16 Excuse me, please
Oiga, por favor
oy·ga por fa·bor

17 That's all right/It doesn't
matter/Don't worry
No importa/No se preocupe
no eem·por·
ta/no se pre·o·koo·pe

18 With pleasure
Con mucho gusto
kon moo·cho goos·to

19 Just a minute
(Un) momento
(oon) mo·men·to

20 What did you say?
¿Qué dijo Ud?
ke dee·kho oos·ted

21 I understand
Comprendo
kom·pren·do

22 I don't understand
No comprendo
no kom·pren·do

23 Do you understand?
¿Comprende Ud?
kom·pren·de oos·ted

24 I don't speak Spanish
No hablo español
no a·blo es·pan·yol

25 I don't speak Spanish very well
No hablo muy bien el español
*no a·blo mooy byen el
es·pan·yol*

26 Please repeat that
Por favor repita eso
por fa·bor re·pee·ta e·so

27 Please speak more slowly
Por favor hable más despacio
*por fa·bor a·ble mas
des·pa·thyo*

28 Could you please write that
down?
¿Puede Ud escribirlo?
pwe·de oos·ted es·kree·beer·lo

29 Do you speak English?
¿Habla Ud inglés?
a·bla oos·ted een·gles

30 I am American
Soy norteamericano(a)
*soy nor·te·a·me·ree·
ka·no(a)*

31 I don't mind
No me importa
no me eem·por·ta

32 Agreed/fine
De acuerdo
de a·kwer·do

33 OK!
¡Vale!
ba·le

34 Isn't it?/Don't you agree?
¿No es así?
no es a·see

35 Do you follow?
¿Entiende?
en·tyen·de

36 Really?
¿De verdad?
de ber·dad

37 That's true
Es verdad
es ber·dad

38 You are right
Tiene razón
tye·ne ra·thon

Common questions and statements

Many of the things you will need to ask will involve the following groups
of words. You will notice that there are two ways of putting questions.
You may turn the statement around as in, Ud podría . . . (*oos·ted
po·dree·a*; you would be able . . .), to make the question as in, ¿Podría
Ud . . .? Alternatively questions are often asked by making a statement in
a questioning tone as in the first question given below.

39 Is it necessary to . . .?
¿Es necesario . . .?
es ne·the·sa·ryo

40 Is there any charge?
¿Hay que pagar algo?
ay ke pa·gar al·go

41 Ought I to/Do I have to . . .?
¿Debo . . .?
de·bo

42 Do you have . . .?
¿Tiene . . .?
tye·ne

43 What's the matter?
¿Qué pasa?
ke pa·sa

44 I've made a mistake
Me he equivocado
me e e·kee·bo·ka·do

45 I mean that . . .
Quiero decir que . . .
kye·ro de·theer ke

46 What does that mean?
¿Qué quiere decir eso?
ke kye·re de·theer e·so

47 What is this/that?
¿Qué es esto/eso?
ke es es·to/e·so

48 What time is it?
¿Qué hora es?
ke o·ra es

49 At what time?
¿A qué hora?
a ke o·ra

50 How much/many?
¿Cuánto(a)/cuántos(as)?
kwan·to(a)/kwan·tos(as)

51 How often?
¿Cuántas veces?
kwan·tas be·thes

52 Where is/are?
¿Dónde está/están?
don·de es·ta/es·tan

53 Here is/are
Aquí está/están
a·kee es·ta/es·tan

54 There is/are
Hay
ay

55 How do you say . . . in Spanish?
¿Cómo se dice . . . en español?
ko·mo se dee·the . . . en es·pan·yol

56 How long — will that take?
¿Cuánto tiempo — durará?
kwan·to tyem·po — doo·ra·ra

57 I need — something for a cough
Necesito — algo para la tos
ne·the·see·to — al·go pa·ra la tos

58 I want — a cup of coffee
Querría — una taza de café
ke·ree·a — oo·na ta·tha de ka·fe

59 I want — to go to Madrid
Quiero — ir a Madrid
kye·ro — eer a ma·dreed

60 I would like — a glass of red/white wine
Quisiera — un tinto/un blanco
kee·sye·ra — oon teen·to/oon blan·ko

61 May I — use the telephone?
¿Puedo — usar el teléfono?
pwe·do — oo·sar el te·le·fo·no

62 Do you mind if I — open the window?
¿Le importa que — abra la ventana?
le eem·por·ta ke — a·bra la ben·ta·na

63 Whom should I see about this?
¿Con quien debo hablar de esto?
kon kyen de·bo a·blar de es·to

General problems and requests

64 Can you help me, please?
¿Puede ayudarme, por favor?
pwe·de a·yoo·dar·me por fa·bor

65 Could you come with me, please?
¿Podría Ud venir conmigo, por favor?
po·dree·a oos·ted be·neer kon·mee·go por fa·bor

66 We need someone who can speak English
Necesitamos alguien que hable inglés
ne·the·see·ta·mos al·gyen ke a·ble een·gles

67 We are in a hurry
Tenemos prisa
te·ne·mos pree·sa

68 Please repeat that
Por favor repita eso
por fa·bor re·pee·ta e·so

69 I wish to leave a message for Mr Smith
Quiero dejar un recado para Señor Smith
kye·ro de·khar oon re·ka·do pa·ra sen·yor Smith

70 Is there a message/letter for me?
¿Hay algún recado/alguna carta para mí?
ay al·goon re·ka·do/al·goo·na kar·ta pa·ra mee

71 Go away!
¡Váyase!
ba·ya·se

72	Can you do it for me — at once?
	¿Puede hacermelo — inmediatemente?
	pwe·de a·ther·me·lo — ee·me·dya·ta·men·te
	— by Wednesday?
	— para el miércoles?
	— *pa·ra el myer·ko·les*
73	The machine — has broken down
	La máquina — se ha estropeado
	la ma·kee·na — se a es·tro·pe·a·do
74	I have broken — the switch/the glass
	He roto — el encendedor/el vidrio
	e ro·to — el en·then·de·dor/el bee·dryo
75	I have spilled — the water/the wine
	He tirado — el agua/el vino
	e tee·ra·do — el ag·wa/el bee·no
76	I have forgotten — my glasses/my key
	Me he olvidado — las gafas/la llave
	me e ol·bee·da·do — las ga·fas/la lya·be
77	I have left my bag — in the plane/in the bus
	He dejado el bolso — en el avión/en el autobús
	e de·Aha·do el bol·so — en el a·byon/en el ow·to·boos

Travel   (T)

General

1	I am leaving — tomorrow
	Me marcho — mañana
	me mar·cho — man·ya·na
	— on Thursday
	— el jueves
	— *el khwe·bes*
2	How long will the train/flight be delayed?
	¿Que retraso tiene el tren/el vuelo?
	ke re·tra·so tye·ne el tren/el bwe·lo
3	I have missed — my train
	He perdido — el tren
	e per·dee·do — el tren
	— my flight
	— el vuelo
	— *el bwe·lo*
4	At what time is the next — train?
	¿A qué hora sale el próximo — tren?
	a ke o·ra sa·le el prok·see·mo — tren
	— flight?
	— vuelo?
	— *bwe·lo*
	— bus?
	— autobús?
	— *ow·to·boos*
5	I am a member of the American Express party traveling to Granada
	Soy un miembro del grupo American Express que va a Granada
	soy oon myem·bro del groo·po a·me·ree·kan eks·pres ke ba a gra·na·da
6	My party has left without me
	Mi grupo se ha marchado sin mí
	mee groo·po se a mar·cha·do seen mee
7	I have lost the rest of my party
	He perdido al resto del grupo
	e per·dee·do al res·to del groo·po
8	Where do I get the connection for Granada?
	¿Cómo puedo llegar a Granada?
	ko·mo pwe·do lye·gar a gra·na·da
9	Could you please — keep my seat for me?
	¿Podría — guardarme el sitio?
	po·dree·a — gwar·dar·me el see·tyo

10	Could you please —	keep an eye on my luggage for a few moments?
	¿Podría —	cuidarme el equipaje un momento?
	po·**dree**·a —	kwee·**dar**·me el e·**kee**·pa·khe oon mo·**men**·to

Arrival and departure

11	Here is —	my passport
	Aquí está —	mi pasaporte
	a·**kee** es·**ta** —	mee pa·sa·**por**·te
		my driver's license
		mi carnet de conducir
		mee kar·**net** de kon·doo·**theer**
		my insurance
		mi póliza de seguro
		mee po·**lee**·tha de se·**goo**·ro
12	I am staying —	for two weeks
	Me voy a quedar —	dos semanas
	me boy a ke·**dar** —	dos se·**ma**·nas
		at the Hotel Hispánico
		en el Hotel Hispánico
		en el o·**tel** ees·**pa**·nee·ko

13 My wife and I are on a joint passport
Mi esposa y yo tenemos un pasaporte familiar
*mee es·**po**·sa ee yo te·**ne**·mos oon pa·sa·**por**·te fa·mee·**lyar***

14 Our children are on this passport
Nuestros hijos están en este pasaporte
***nwes**·tros **ee**·khos es·**tan** en **es**·te pa·sa·**por**·te*

15 I have nothing to declare
No tengo nada que declarar
*no **ten**·go **na**·da ke de·kla·**rar***

16 I have the usual allowance of cigarettes and liquor
Llevo la cantidad permitida de tabaco y alcohol
lye**·bo la kan·tee·**dad** per·mee·**tee**·da de ta·**ba**·ko ee al·**col

17 Those are my personal belongings
Estos son mis objetos personales
***es**·tos son mees ob·**khe**·tos per·so·**na**·les*

18 I represent Universal Chemicals
Represento a Universal Chemicals
*re·pre·**sen**·to a Universal Chemicals*

19 I am looking for the representative of Alpha Engineering
Estoy buscando al representante de Alpha Engineering
*es·**toy** boos·**kan**·do al re·pre·sen·**tan**·te de Alpha Engineering*

20 He/she was due to meet me here
Tenía que esperarme aquí
*te·**nee**·a ke es·pe·**rar**·me a·**kee***

21 The people I was to meet have not turned up
La gente que venía a encontrarme no se ha presentado
*la **khen**·te ke be·**nee**·a a en·kon·**trar**·me no se a pre·sen·**ta**·do*

Luggage

22	Please take these bags —	to platform 9
	Lleve estas maletas —	al andén número 9
	lye·be **es**·tas ma·**le**·tas —	al an·**den** noo·me·ro 9
		to a taxi
		a un taxi
		a oon **tak**·see

23 My luggage has not arrived
No ha llegado mi equipaje
*no a lye·**ga**·do mee e·kee·**pa**·khe*

24 Where is the luggage from the flight from London?
¿Dónde está el equipaje del vuelo de Londres?
***don**·de es·**ta** el e·kee·**pa**·khe del **bwe**·lo de **lon**·dres*

25 Is there a baggage checkroom?
    ¿Hay consigna?
    ay kon·seeg·na

26   Are there any — porters?
       ¿Hay — maleteros?
        ay — *ma·le·te·ros*
              — luggage carts?
              — carritos para transportar el
                equipaje?
              — *ka·rree·tos pa·ra trans·por·tar el
                e·kee·pa·khe*

27 That bag is not mine
    Esa maleta no es mía
    e·sa ma·le·ta no es mee·a

28 Where is my other bag?
    ¿Dónde está mi otra maleta?
    don·de es·ta mee o·tra ma·le·ta

29 The contents of that bag are
    fragile
    El contenido de esa maleta es
    delicado
    *el kon·te·nee·do de e·sa
    ma·le·ta es de·lee·ka·do*

30 I wish to have my luggage sent
    on ahead
    Quiero mandar el equipaje por
    adelantado
    *kye·ro man·dar el
    e·kee·pa·khe por
    a·de·lan·ta·do*

31 I sent a suitcase in advance.
    Where do I pick it up?
    Facturé la maleta. ¿Dónde
    puedo recogerla?
    *fak·too·re la ma·le·ta don·de
    pwe·do re·ko·kher·la*

32 That case is specially insured
    Esa maleta tiene un seguro
    especial
    *e·sa ma·le·ta tye·ne oon
    se·goo·ro es·pe·thyal*

33 I wish to leave these bags in
    the baggage checkroom
    Quiero dejar estas maletas en
    consigna
    *kye·ro de·khar es·tas ma·le·tas
    en kon·seeg·na*

34 I shall pick them up
    tomorrow/this evening
    Las recogeré mañana/esta
    noche
    *las re·ko·khe·re man·ya·na/
    es·ta no·che*

35 How much is it per suitcase?
    ¿Cuánto cuesta cada maleta?
    *kwan·to kwes·ta ka·da
    ma·le·ta*

36 What time do you close?
    ¿A qué hora cierran?
    a ke o·ra thye·rran

Airport and flight inquiries

37   Where do I get the bus — for Barajas airport?
       ¿Dónde cojo el autobús — para el aeropuerto de Barajas?
              don·de ko·kho el
              ow·to·boos — *pa·ra el a·e·ro·pwer·to
                              de ba·ra·khas*
                           — for the center of town?
                           — para el centro de la ciudad?
                           — *pa·ra el then·tro de la
                              thyoo·dad*

38   I wish to check my
                      luggage — to Barcelona on the Iberia   flight
            Quiero registrar mi
                     equipaje — en el vuelo de Iberia a
                                 Barcelona
            kye·ro re·khees·trar mee
            e·kee·pa·khe — *en el bwe·lo de ee·be·rya
                             a bar·the·lo·na*

39 Where is the departure/arrival board?
    ¿Dónde está el tablero de información de salidas/llegadas?
    *don·de es·ta el ta·ble·ro de een·for·ma·thyon de sa·lee·das/
    lye·ga·das*

40 When will the boarding announcement for the flight be made?
    ¿A qué hora se anunciará el vuelo?
    a ke o·ra se a·noon·thya·ra el bwe·lo

41 Which gate do I go to?
    ¿A qué puerta debo ir?
    a ke pwer·ta de·bo eer

42 Is there a snack bar/duty-free shop in the departure lounge?
    ¿Hay cafetería/tienda libre de impuestos en la sala de embarque?
    *ay ka·fe·te·ree·a/tyen·da lee·bre de eem·pwes·tos en la sa·la
    de em·bar·ke*

43 Will a meal be served on the plane?
   ¿Se servirá algo de comer en el avión?
   se ser·bee·ra al·go de ko·mer en el a·byon
44 What are weather conditions like for the flight?
   ¿Cuál es el estado del tiempo previsto para el vuelo?
   kwal es el es·ta·do del tyem·po pre·bees·to pa·ra el bwe·lo
(for answers see Making conversation, p.65).

45 Can I change my seat?
   ¿Puedo cambiar mi asiento?
   pwe·do kam·byar mee a·syen·to
46   I should like to be nearer — the front/the window
         Quisiera sentarme más — adelante/cerca de la ventana
      kee·sye·ra sen·tar·me mas — *a·de·lan·te/ther·ka de
                                    la ben·ta·na*
47 I suffer from air sickness
   Me mareo en avión
   me ma·re·o en a·byon
48 I should like to speak to the airport police
   Querría hablar con la policía del aeropuerto
   ke·rree·a a·blar kon la po·lee·thee·a del a·e·ro·pwer·to
49 I am meeting somebody arriving on a flight from Rome
   Estoy esperando a alguien que viene en el vuelo de Roma
   es·toy es·pe·ran·do a al·gyen ke bye·ne en el bwe·lo de ro·ma
50 At what time do you expect the flight from Rome to arrive?
   ¿A qué hora espera que llegue el vuelo de Roma?
   a ke o·ra es·pe·ra ke lye·ge el bwe·lo de ro·ma
51 Are there private landing facilities at Malaga airport?
   ¿Se puede aterrizar con un avión privado en Málaga?
   se pwe·de a·te·rree·thar kon oon a·byon pree·ba·do en ma·la·ga

Trains

The Spanish railroad network, RENFE, has been undergoing extensive
modernization in recent years, but can still be rather variable in comfort
and efficiency. The prestige services are the TALGO (Madrid-Barcelona)
and the TER (Madrid-Cadiz). The other services are the *expreso* and
rápido.

Inquiring

The larger stations have information desks where English may be spoken,
but otherwise you may have to use the questions below at the ticket desk.
It is always best to check the details with somebody, as timetables may be
difficult to follow.

52   Where is the — ticket office/information office?
            ¿Dónde está — la taquilla/la oficina de
                            informaciones?
            don·de es·ta — *la ta·keel·ya/la o·fee·thee·na de
                            een·for·ma·thyo·nes*
                         — timetable board?
                         — el horario?
                         — *el o·ra·ryo*
53   I want to go to Malaga — tomorrow/next Wednesday
      Quiero ir a Málaga — mañana/el miércoles que viene
      kye·ro eer a ma·la·ga — *man·ya·na/el myer·ko·les
                              ke bye·ne*
54 What are the times of trains between 8 a.m. and noon?
   ¿Qué trenes hay entre las 8 y las 12 del mediodía?
   ke tre·nes ay en·tre las o·cho ee las do·the del me·dyo·dee·a
55 Which is the fastest train?
   ¿Cuál es el tren más rápido?
   kwal es el tren mas ra·pee·do
56 Could I see a timetable, please?
   ¿Puedo ver el horario, por favor?
   pwe·do ber el o·ra·ryo por fa·bor

57 **When does the next/last train to Orense leave?**
¿A qué hora sale el próximo/último tren para Orense?
a ke o·ra sa·le el prok·see·mo/ool·tee·mo tren pa·ra o·ren·se

58 **Is it necessary to change?**
¿Hay que hacer transbordo?
ay ke a·ther trans·bor·do

59 **What time does the train arrive?**
¿A qué hora llega el tren?
a ke o·ra lye·ga el tren

Tickets and reservations

If you are traveling on one of the busy main routes it is a good idea to reserve your seat in advance. An additional charge must be paid on some of the luxury trains like the TALGO or the TER. Within Spain children between three and seven pay half-fare, and younger ones travel free. Smoking is not allowed in the compartments of Spanish trains – if you want a cigarette you will have to stand in the corridor. For overnight travel you can reserve a sleeper (*coche-cama: ko·che·ka·ma*) or a couchette (*litera: lee·te·ra*), which is a simple berth with blankets in a compartment shared by several passengers.
The railroad system in Latin America is variable.

60 **A one-way ticket to Madrid, second-class**
Un billete de segunda para Madrid
oon beel·ye·te de se·goon·da pa·ra ma·dreed

61 **A round trip ticket to Madrid, first class**
Un billete de primera para Madrid, ida y vuelta
oon beel·ye·te de pree·me·ra pa·ra ma·dreed ee·da ee bwel·ta

62 **A child's round trip to Madrid**
Un billete de niño para Madrid, ida y vuelta
oon beel·ye·te de neen·yo pa·ra ma·dreed ee·da ee bwel·ta

63 **He/she is under seven**
Tiene menos de siete anos
tye·ne me·nos de sye·te an·yos

64 **I would like to book a seat on the 10:30 to Valencia**
Quiero reservar un asiento en el tren de las diez y treinta a Valencia
kye·ro re·ser·bar oon a·syen·to en el tren de las dyeth ee treyn·ta a ba·len·thya

65 **I would like to book a seat by the window**
Quiero reservar un asiento al lado de la ventanilla
kye·ro re·ser·bar oon a·syen·to al la·do de la ben·ta·neel·ya

66 **I would like a sleeper/couchette on the 22:00 to Oviedo**
Quiero un coche-cama/una litera en el tren de las veintidós horas a Oviedo
kye·ro oon ko·che·ka·ma/oo·na lee·te·ra en el tren de las beyn·tee·dos o·ras a o·bye·do

Station and journey

67 **Which platform do I go to for the Santander train?**
¿De qué andén sale el tren para Santander?
de ke an·den sa·le el tren pa·ra san·tan·der

68 **Is this the right platform for Santander?**
¿Es éste el andén para Santander?
es es·te el an·den pa·ra san·tan·der

69 **Is this the Santander train?**
¿Es éste el tren para Santander?
es es·te el tren pa·ra san·tan·der

70 **Is there a dining car/club car?**
¿Lleva vagón-restaurante/cafetería este tren?
lye·ba ba·gon·res·tow·ran·te/ka·fe·te·ree·a es·te tren

71 **When do we get to Cadiz?**
¿Cuándo llegamos a Cádiz?
kwan·do lye·ga·mos a ka·deeth

72 **Do we stop at Burgos?**
¿Paramos en Burgos?
pa·ra·mos en boor·gos

73 **Is this a through train?**
¿Es éste un tren directo?
es es·te oon tren dee·rek·to

74 Is this the fast train?
¿Es éste el expreso?
es es·te el eks·pre·so

75 Where do I have to change for Bilbao?
¿Dónde tengo que hacer transbordo para Bilbao?
don·de ten·go ke a·ther trans·bor·do pa·ra beel·ba·o

76 Is this seat taken?
¿Está ocupado este asiento?
es·ta o·koo·pa·do es·te a·syen·to

77 This is my seat
Este es mi asiento
es·te es mee a·syen·to

78 Can you help me with my bags, please?
¿Puede ayudarme con estas maletas, por favor?
pwe·de a·yoo·dar·me kon es·tas ma·le·tas por fa·bor

79 May I open/shut the window?
¿Puedo abrir/cerrar la ventana?
pwe·do a·breer/the·rrar la ben·ta·na

80 Are we in Zaragoza yet?
¿Hemos llegado ya a Zaragoza?
e·mos lye·ga·do ya a tha·ra·go·tha

81 Are we on time?
¿Llegaremos a la hora prevista?
lye·ga·re·mos a la o·ra pre·bees·ta

Buses and subway

On buses in Spain you can pay as you enter, or buy a *bonobús* (*bo·no·boos*) for ten bus rides over any distance. A single ticket on the metro in Madrid and Barcelona will take you as far as you want to go. In Latin America most transport services have a set fare.

82 Which bus goes to the Prado Museum?
¿Que autobús tomo para ir al Prado?
ke ow·to·boos to·mo pa·ra eer al pra·do

83 Does this bus go to the Teatro Real?
¿Este autobús va al Teatro Real?
es·te ow·to·boos ba al te·a·tro re·al

84 Where should I change?
¿Dónde tengo que cambiar?
don·de ten·go ke kam·byar

85 And then, what number do I take?
¿Entonces que número tengo que coger?
en·ton·thes ke noo·me·ro ten·go ke ko·kher

86 Should I get out at the next stop for the Museum of Modern Art?
¿Tengo que bajarme en la próxima parada para ir al Museo de Arte Moderno?
ten·go ke ba·khar·me en la prok·see·ma pa·ra·da pa·ra eer al moo·se·o de ar·te mo·der·no

87 I want to go the Parque del Retiro
Quiero ir al Parque del Retiro
kye·ro eer al par·ke del re·tee·ro

88 It's a flat fare, isn't it?
¿Es precio único?
es pre·thyo oo·nee·ko
A "bonobús", please
Un bonobús por favor
oon bo·no·boos por fa·bor

89 Can you let me off at the right stop?
¿Puede parar en la parada indicada?
pwe·de pa·rar en la pa·ra·da een·dee·ka·da

90 How long does it take to get to the Cibeles?
¿Cuánto se tarda en llegar a la Cibeles?
kwan·to se tar·da en lye·gar a la thee·be·les

Taxis

91 Can you order me a taxi?
¿Me puede llamar un taxi?
me pwe·de lya·mar oon tak·see

92 Where can I get a taxi?
    ¿Dónde puedo coger un taxi?
    don·de **pwe·**do ko·**kher** oon tak·see

93   Take me to — this address, please
                        Lléveme a — esta dirección, por favor
                        lye·be·me a — es·ta dee·**rek·thyon** por fa·**bor**

94   How much is the taxi fare — to/from the airport?
            ¿Cuánto cuesta el taxi — hasta/desde el aeropuerto?
            kwan·to **kwes·**ta el **tak·**see — as·ta/**des·**de el a·e·**ro·pwer·**to

95 Please drive us around the
    town
    Denos una vuelta por la
    ciudad, por favor
    de·nos **oo·**na **bwel·**ta por la
    thyoo·dad por fa·**bor**

96 Would you put the luggage in
    the trunk?
    ¿Puede meter el equipaje en
    el maletero?
    pwe·de me·**ter** el e·kee·**pa·**khe
    en el ma·le·**te·**ro

97 I'm in a hurry
    Tengo prisa
    ten·go **pree·**sa

98 Please wait here for a few
    minutes
    Espere aquí un momento, por
    favor
    es·**pe·**re a·**kee** oon mo·**men·**to
    por fa·**bor**

99 Turn right/left please
    Tuerza a la derecha/
    izquierda, por favor
    twer·tha a la de·**re·cha/**
    eeth·**kyer·**da por fa·**bor**

100 Stop here, please
    Pare aquí, por favor
    pa·re a·**kee** por fa·**bor**

101 How much is that?
    ¿Cuánto es, por favor?
    kwan·to es por fa·**bor**

102 Keep the change
    Quédese con la vuelta
    ke·de·se kon la **bwel·**ta

Motoring

Although the more crowded towns can be difficult for the driver,
motoring in Spain should present no serious problems. Speed limits are
60 km/h in towns, 90 km/h on ordinary roads, and 100 km/h on
expressways (*autopistas:* ow·to·**pees·**tas) (see Conversion table, p.72).

Renting a car

103 A rental car should be ready for me
    Debería haber un coche alquilado esperándome
    de·be·**ree·**a a·**ber** oon **ko·**che al·kee·**la·**do es·pe·**ran·**do·me

104 I arranged it through the Speed-Link fly-drive service
    Lo he alquilado a través de la compañía Speed Link
    lo e al·kee·**la·**do a tra·**bes** de la kom·pan·**yee·**a Speed Link

105   I want to rent a car — for driving myself
            Quiero alquilar un coche — sin conductor
            kye·ro al·kee·**lar** oon
                        ko·che — seen kon·dook·**tor**
                              — with a chauffeur
                              — con chófer
                              — kon **cho·**fer

106   I want it for — five days
            Lo quiero para — cinco días
            lo **kye·**ro **pa·**ra — **theen·**ko **dee·**as

107   What is the charge — per day/week?
            ¿Cuánto cuesta — al día/a la semana?
            kwan·to **kwes·**ta — al **dee·**a/a la se·**ma·**na

108   Do you have a car that is — larger/cheaper?
            ¿Tiene un coche — más grande/más barato?
            tye·ne oon **ko·**che — mas **gran·**de/mas ba·**ra·**to

109 Is the mileage limited/unlimited?
    ¿Tiene kilometraje limitado/ilimitado?
    tye·ne kee·lo·me·**tra·**khe lee·mee·**ta·**do/ee·lee·mee·**ta·**do

110 **My wife/my husband will be driving as well**
Mi mujer/mi marido conducirá también
mee moo·kher/mee ma·ree·do kon·doo·thee·ra tam·byen

111 **I should like comprehensive insurance**
Querría un seguro a todo riesgo
ke·rree·a oon se·goo·ro a to·do ryes·go

112 **Must I return the car here?**
¿Tengo que devolver el coche aquí?
ten·go ke de·bol·ber el ko·che a·kee

113 **I should like to leave the car in Barcelona**
Querría dejar el coche en Barcelona
ke·rree·a de·khar el ko·che en bar·the·lo·na

114 **I should like the car delivered to my hotel**
Querría que me trajeran el coche al hotel
ke·rree·a ke me tra·khe·ran el ko·che al o·tel

115 **Please show me how to operate the controls**
Enséñeme cómo funcionan los mandos, por favor
en·sen·ye·me ko·mo foon·thyo·nan los man·dos por fa·bor

116 **Please explain the car documents**
¿Puede explicarme los documentos del coche?
pwe·de eks·plee·kar·me los do·koo·men·tos del ko·che

Parking

Many Spanish towns have adopted the system of the disk zone, or *zona
azul* (*tho·na a·thool*). Here you just leave a parking disk on your
windscreen, and this shows when you arrived and when you should leave.
You are usually allowed to park for about one and a half hours. Away
from the center of town you will find streets where parking is allowed
only on one side on certain days, for example during the first half of the
month or on odd-numbered dates. The system in Latin America varies.

117 **Where can I park?**
¿Dónde puedo aparcar?
don·de pwe·do a·par·kar

118 **Can I park here?**
¿Puedo aparcar aquí?
pwe·do a·par·kar a·kee

119 **Are you leaving?**
¿Se marcha Ud?
se mar·cha oos·ted

120 **Is there a parking lot nearby?**
¿Hay un aparcamiento cerca?
ay oon a·par·ka·myen·to ther·ka

121 **What time does the parking lot close?**
¿A qué hora cierra el aparcamiento?
a ke o·ra thye·rra el a·par·ka·myen·to

122 **How much does it cost per hour?**
¿Cuánto cuesta por hora?
kwan·to kwes·ta por o·ra

123 **How long can I leave the car here?**
¿Cuánto tiempo puedo dejar el coche aquí?
kwan·to tyem·po pwe·do de·khar el ko·che a·kee

124 **I will only be a few minutes**
Sólo tardaré unos minutos
so·lo tar·da·re oo·nos mee·noo·tos

125 **Do I need a parking disk?**
¿Hace falta disco de estacionamiento?
a·the fal·ta dees·ko de es·ta·thyo·na·myen·to

126 **Where can I get a parking disk?**
¿Dónde puedo comprar un disco de estacionamiento limitado?
don·de pwe·do kom·prar oon dees·ko de es·ta·thyo·na·myen·to lee·mee·ta·do

127 **Do I need parking lights?**
¿Hacen falta luces de aparcamiento?
a·then fal·ta loo·thes de a·par·ka·myen·to

Road conditions

Spanish expressways (*autopistas:* ow·to·pees·tas) and other major roads
meet international standards for fast, long-distance travel. In rural areas
roads may be variable in quality and are sometimes unimproved. In Latin
America roads such as the Pan-American Highway are very good, but

secondary roads may be poor. Traffic in Spain on major roads is likely to be heavy throughout the tourist season from May to September and especially heavy at weekends in July and August around big cities and resort areas.

128   **Is there a route that avoids the traffic?**
      ¿Hay una ruta para evitar el tráfico?
      ay oo·na roo·ta pa·ra e·bee·tar el **tra** *·fee·ko*

129   **Is there a shortcut/detour?**
      ¿Hay algún camino más corto/alguna desviación?
      ay al· **goon** *ka·* **mee** *·no mas* **kor** *·to/al·* **goo** *·na des·bya·* **thyon**

130   **Is the traffic heavy?**
      ¿Hay mucho tráfico?
      ay **moo** *·cho* **tra** *·fee·ko*

131   **What is causing this tie-up?**
      ¿Qué está produciendo este atasco?
      ke es· **ta** *pro·doo·* **thyen** *·do es·te a·* **tas** *·ko*

132   **When will the road be clear?**
      ¿Cuándo estará despejada la carretera?
      kwan *·do es·ta·* **ra** *des·pe·* **kha** *·da la ka·rre·* **te** *·ra*

133   **What is the speed limit?**
      ¿Cúal es el límite de velocidad?
      kwal es el **lee** *·mee·te de be·lo·thee·* **dad**

134   **Is there a toll on this highway?**
      ¿Es ésta una autopista de peaje?
      es es·ta oo·na ow·to· **pees** *·ta de pe·a·khe*

135   **Is the road to the Sierra Nevada snowed in?**
      ¿Hay nieve en la carretera de la Sierra Nevada?
      ay **nye** *·be en la ka·rre·* **te** *·ra de la* **sye** *·rra ne·* **ba** *·da*

136   **Is the pass open?**
      ¿Está abierto el puerto?
      es· **ta** *a·* **byer** *·to el* **pwer** *·to*

137   **Do I need studded tires/chains?**
      ¿Necesito ruedas con tacos/cadenas?
      ne·the· **see** *·to rwe·das kon* **ta** *·kos/ka·* **de** *·nas*

Road signs

The following are road signs commonly seen in Spain:

138   Aparcamiento permitido
      Parking allowed
139   Arcén
      Emergency parking
140   Autopista
      Expressway
141   Baches por obras
      Irregular surface due to road work
142   Calle bloqueada
      Road blocked
143   Calle sin salida
      No exit
144   Catación gratuita
      Free wine-tasting
145   Centro ciudad
      Town centre
146   Deslizamientos
      Ice on road
147   Desviación
      Detour
148   Obras
      Road work
149   Otras direcciones
      Other destinations
150   Paso a nivel
      Grade crossing
151   Peaje
      Toll point
152   Peligro
      Danger
153   Prohibido aparcar
      No parking
154   Reducir velocidad
      Slow down
155   Salida de emergencia
      Emergency exit
156   Todas direcciones
      All destinations

Fuel

Gasoline comes in two grades: *normal* (*nor·* **mal**) (2 star) and the higher-octane and more expensive *super* (**soo** *·per*) (4 star). Diesel fuel is also used. See Conversion tables (p.72) for fuel quantities and tire pressures.

157 15 liters of — 2 star
    Quince litros de — normal
    keen·the lee·tros 'de — nor·**mal**
    — 4 star
    — super
    — *soo·per*
    — diesel fuei
    — gas-oil
    — *ga·so·eel*

158 1,000 pesetas' worth, please
    Mil pesetas, por favor
    meel pe·se·tas por fa·bor

159 Fill her up, please
    Lleno, por favor
    lye·no por fa·bor

160 Check — the oil
    Revíseme — el aceite
    re·bee·se·me — el a·**thay**·te
    — the water
    — el agua
    — *el **ag**·wa*
    — the tire pressure
    — la presión de los neumáticos
    — *la pre·**syon** de los ne·oo·**ma**·tee·kos*

161 The pressure is 1·3
    La presión es 1,3
    *la pre·**syon** es **oo**·no **ko**·ma tres*

162 I want some distilled water
    Necesito agua destilada
    *ne·the·**see**·to **ag**·wa des·tee·**la**·da*

163 Could you clean the windshield?
    ¿Puede limpiarme el parabrisas?
    *pwe·de leem·**pyar**·me el pa·ra·**bree**·sas*

164 Could you put some water in the windshield washer?
    ¿Puede ponerme agua en el depósito del limpiacristales?
    *pwe·de po·**ner**·me **ag**·wa en el de·**po**·see·to del leem·pya·krees·**ta**·les*

165 Can I pay by credit card?
    ¿Puedo pagar con tarjeta de crédito?
    *pwe·do pa·**gar** kon tar·**khe**·ta de **kre**·dee·to*

166 Is there a lavatory/a telephone here?
    ¿Hay servicios/teléfono aquí?
    *ay ser·**bee**·thyos/te·**le**·fo·no a·**kee***

Breakdowns and repairs

167 There is something wrong with my car
    Mi coche no va bien
    *mee **ko**·che no ba byen*

168 I wish to telephone for emergency road service
    Quiero llamar por teléfono a un taller de reparaciones
    *kye·ro lya·**mar** por te·**le**·fo·no a oon tal·**yer** de re·pa·ra·**thyo**·nes*

169 My car — has broken down
    Mi coche — se ha averiado
    *mee **ko**·che* — se a a·be·**rya**·do
    — will not start
    — no arranca
    — *no a·**rran**·ka*

170 Can you send — a mechanic?
    ¿Puede mandarme — un mecánico?
    *pwe·de man·**dar**·me* — oon me·**ka**·nee·ko
    — a tow truck?
    — una grúa?
    — *oo·na **groo**·a*

171 Can you — take me to the nearest garage?
    ¿Puede — llevarme al garaje más próximo?
    pwe·de — lye·**bar**·me al ga·**ra**·khe mas **prok**·see·mo

172   Can you — give me a tow?
                        ¿Puede — remolcarme?
                        pwe·de — re·mol·**kar**·me
                                — give me a can of gasoline, please?
                                — darme una lata de gasolina, por
                                  favor?
                                — **dar**·me **oo**·na **la**·ta de ga·so·**lee**·na
                                  por fa·**bor**

173 Can you find the trouble?
     ¿Encuentra la avería?
     en·**kwen**·tra la a·be·**ree**·a

174 I have run out of gasoline
     Me he quedado sin gasolina
     me e ke·**da**·do seen ga·so·**lee**·na

175 This is broken
     Esto está roto
     es·to es·**ta** **ro**·to

176 It makes a funny noise
     Hace un ruido extraño
     a·the oon **rwee**·do eks·**tran**·yo

177 There is a funny smell
     Hay un olor raro
     ay oon o·**lor** **ra**·ro

178   The brakes — have something wrong with them
                        Los frenos — no funcionan bien
                        los **fre**·nos — no foon·**thyo**·nan byen
179   The windshield wipers — are not working
                        El limpiaparabrisas — no funciona
     el leem·pya·pa·ra·**bree**·sas — no foon·**thyo**·na

180 My windshield has shattered   189 Can you replace the exhaust
     El parabrisas estalló en   pipe?
        pedazos   ¿Puede ponerme un nuevo
     el pa·ra·**bree**·sas es·tal·**yo** en   tubo de escape?
        pe·**da**·thos   **pwe**·de po·**ner**·me oon **nwe**·bo
181 I have a flat tire   **too**·bo de es·**ka**·pe
     Tengo una rueda pinchada   190 Is it serious?
     ten·go **oo**·na **rwe**·da   ¿Es muy grave la avería?
        peen·**cha**·da   es mooy **gra**·be la a·be·**ree**·a
182 The battery is dead   191 How long will it take to repair
     La batería está descargada   it?
     la ba·te·**ree**·a es·**ta**   ¿Cuánto tardará en repararlo?
        des·kar·**ga**·da   **kwan**·to tar·da·**ra** en
183 The engine is overheating   re·pa·**rar**·lo
     El motor se calienta   192 Do you have the parts?
     el **mo**·tor se ka·**lyen**·ta   ¿Tiene los repuestos
184 There is a leak in the radiator   necesarios?
     El radiador pierde agua   **tye**·ne los re·**pwes**·tos
     el ra·dya·**dor** pyer·de **ag**·wa   ne·the·**sa**·ryos
185 I have blown a fuse   193 Can you repair it for the time
     Se ha fundido un fusible   being?
     se a foon·**dee**·do oon   ¿Puede arreglarlo
        foo·**see**·ble   provisionalmente?
186 There is a bad connection   **pwe**·de a·**rre**·**glar**·lo
     Hay un cable que hace mal   pro·bee·syo·**nal**·**men**·te
        contacto   194 Can I have an itemized bill for
     ay oon **ka**·ble ke **a**·the mal   my insurance company?
        kon·**tak**·to   ¿Me da una factura completa
187 I have lost the ignition key   para la compañía de
     He perdido la llave de   seguros?
        contacto   me da **oo**·na fak·**too**·ra
     e per·**dee**·do la **lya**·be de   kom·**ple**·ta **pa**·ra la
        kon·**tak**·to   kom·pan·**yee**·a de
188 I need a new fan belt   se·**goo**·ros
     Necesito una correa de
        ventilador
     ne·the·**see**·to **oo**·na ko·**rre**·a de
        ben·tee·la·**dor**

Accidents and the police

If you have dealings with the Spanish police over an accident or a driving offense, behave in a calm and reasonable manner, and they will do likewise. See also Emergencies (p.64).

195 I'm very sorry, officer
Lo siento mucho, agente
lo syen·to moo·cho a·khen·te

196 I am a foreigner
Soy extranjero
soy eks·tran·khe·ro

197 I did not see the sign
No ví la señal
no bee la sen·yal

198 I did not know about that regulation
No conocía esa norma
no ko·no·thee·a e·sa nor·ma

199 I did not understand the sign
No entendí el letrero
no en·ten·dee el le·tre·ro

200 Here is — my driver's license
Aquí está — mi permiso de conducir
a·kee es·ta — *mee per·mee·so de kon·doo·theer*
— my insurance (for Latin America)
— mi póliza de seguro
— *mee po·lee·tha de se·goo·ro*

201 How much is the fine?
¿Cuánto es la multa?
kwan·to es la mool·ta

202 I was driving at 80 km/h (see Conversion tables, p.72)
Iba a ochenta kilómetros por hora
ee·ba a o·chen·ta kee·lo·me·tros por o·ra

203 He/she was too close
El/ella estaba demasiado cerca
el/el·ya es·ta·ba de·ma·sya·do ther·ka

204 I did not see him/her
No le/la vi
no le/la bee

205 He/she was driving too fast
El/ella iba demasiado rápido
el/el·ya ee·ba de·ma·sya·do ra·pee·do

206 He/she did not stop
El/ella no paró
el/el·ya no pa·ro

207 He/she did not yield
El/ella no cedió el paso
el/el·ya no the·dyo el pa·so

208 He/she stopped very suddenly
Se paró de repente
se pa·ro de re·pen·te

209 He/she swerved
Dió un volantazo
dyo oon bo·lan·ta·tho

210 The car turned without signaling
El coche giró sin indicación
el ko·che khee·ro seen een·dee·ka·thyon

211 He/she ran into me
Se me echó encima
se me e·cho en·thee·ma

212 He/she passed on a curve
Adelantó en una curva
a·de·lan·to en oo·na koor·ba

213 His/her license plate number was ...
Su matrícula era ...
soo ma·tree·koo·la e·ra

214 The road was wet
La carretera estaba mojada
la ka·rre·te·ra es·ta·ba mo·kha·da

215 I skidded
Patiné
pa·tee·ne

216 My brakes failed
Me fallaron los frenos
me fal·ya·ron los fre·nos

217 I could not stop in time
No pude parar a tiempo
no poo·de pa·rar a tyem·po

218 I have run over a dog/cat
He atropellado un perro/gato
e a·tro·pel·ya·do oon pe·rro/ga·to

219 Do I need to report it?
¿Necesito dar parte?
ne·the·see·to dar par·te

220 What is your name and
      address?
      ¿Su nombre y dirección por
      favor?
      *soo **nom**·bre ee dee·rek·**thyon**
      por fa·**bor***

221 What is your insurance
      company?
      ¿Cuál es su compañía de
      seguros?
      *kwal es soo kom·pan·**yee**·a de
      se·**goo**·ros*

222 We should call the police
      Deberíamos llamar a la policía
      *de·be·**ree**·a·mos lya·**mar** a la
      po·lee·**thee**·a*

223 Will you please be a witness?
      ¿Podría hacer de testigo?
      *po·**dree**·a a·**ther** de tes·**tee**·go*

224 Do you admit responsibility?
      ¿Acepta responsabilidades?
      *a·**thep**·ta
      res·pon·sa·bee·lee·**da**·des*

225 Could we settle in cash now?
      ¿Lo arreglamos entre
      nosotros?
      *lo a·rre·**gla**·mos **en**·tre
      no·**so**·tros*

Finding the way   (F)

Questions

The simplest way to get directions is just to say where you want to go and
add "please", as you would with a taxi driver. For example, "Where is
the cathedral?" would be, "¿La catedral, por favor?". Here are some
other phrases that you may need.

1 I have lost my way
    Me he perdido
    *me e per·**dee**·do*

2 How do I get to this address?
    ¿Cómo se va a esta dirección?
    ko**·mo se ba a **es**·ta dee·rek·**thyon

3   Where is — the station/the cathedral?
            ¿Dónde está — la estación/la catedral?
            don**·de es·**ta** — la es·ta·**thyon**/la ka·te·**dral

4   Where are — the toilets?
            ¿Dónde están — los servicios?
            ***don**·de es·**tan** — los ser·**bee**·thyos*

5   I would like to go — to the center of town
              Quiero ir — al centro de la ciudad
            kye**·ro eer — al **then**·tro de la thyoo·**dad

6   We are looking for — the Tourist Information Office
            Buscamos — la Oficina de Información y
                      Turismo
            *boos·**ka**·mos — la o·fee·**thee**·na de
                      een·for·ma·**thyon** ee
                      too·**rees**·mo*

7   Can you tell me the way — to the castle?
    ¿Puede decirme por dónde
                   se va? — al castillo?
    *pwe·de de·**theer**·me por
            don·de se ba — al kas·**teel**·yo*

8 Can you show me on the map?
    ¿Puede indicármelo en el mapa?
    *pwe·de een·dee·**kar**·me·lo en el **ma**·pa*

9 Where is there a post office?
    ¿Dónde hay una oficina de correos?
    ***don**·de ay **oo**·na o·fee·**thee**·na de ko·**rre**·os*

10 Is there a service station near here?
    ¿Hay una estación de servicio por aquí?
    *ay **oo**·na es·ta·**thyon** de ser·**bee**·thyo por a·**kee***

11 Is this the right way to the museum?
    ¿Se va por aquí al museo?
    *se ba por a·**kee** al moo·**se**·o*

12 Is it far to the Casa de Campo?
    ¿Está lejos la Casa de Campo?
    *es·**ta** **le**·khos la **ka**·sa de **kam**·po*

13 How far is it from here to Irún?
¿Cuántos kilómetros hay desde aquí a Irún?
kwan·tos kee·**lo·me·**tros ay des·de a·**kee** a ee·**roon**

14 How long does it take to get there?
¿Cuánto se tarda en llegar?
kwan·to se **tar·**da en lye·**gar**

15 Can one walk there?
¿Se puede ir caminando?
se **pwe·**de eer ka·mee·**nan·**do

16 Is there a bus that goes there?
¿Hay un autobús hasta allá?
ay oon ow·to·**boos** as·ta al·**ya**

17 Which road do I take for Valladolid?
¿Cuál es la carretera de Valladolid?
kwal es la ka·**rre·te·**ra de bal·ya·do·**leed**

18 Do I turn here for Toledo?
¿Tuerzo aquí para Toledo?
twer·tho a·**kee** pa·ra to·**le·**do

19 Which is the best route to Santiago?
¿Cuál es el mejor itinerario para ir a Santiago?
kwal es el me·**khor** ee·tee·ne·**ra·**ryo **pa·**ra eer a san·**tya·**go

20 Which is the most scenic route?
¿Cuál es la ruta más pintoresca?
kwal es la **roo·**ta mas peen·to·**res·**ka

21 How do I get back onto the expressway?
¿Cómo puedo volver a la autopista?
ko·mo **pwe·**do bol·**ber** a la ow·to·**pees·**ta

22 Where does this road go to?
¿A dónde va esta carretera?
a **don·**de ba es·ta ka·**rre·te·**ra

23 Will we arrive this evening?
¿Llegaremos esta noche?
lye·ga·**re·**mos es·ta **no·**che

Answers

These are the key phrases of the answers you will receive. In this case the Spanish is given first, with the English below.

24	Vaya	— todo recto
	ba·ya	— **to·**do **rek·**to
	You go	— straight ahead
		— a la derecha
		— a la de·**re·**cha
		— right
		— a la izquierda
		— a la eeth·**kyer·**da
		— left
		— hasta
		— **as·**ta
		— as far as
25	Tuerce/gire	— a la derecha
	twer·the/**khee·**re	— a la de·**re·**cha
	Turn	— right
		— a la izquierda
		— a la eeth·**kyer·**da
		— left
26	Siga	— hacia
	see·ga	— **a·**thya
	Keep going straight	— towards
		— hasta
		— **as·**ta
		— until
27	Tome/coja	— la carretera de ...
	to·me/**ko·**kha	— la ka·**rre·te·**ra de
	Take	— the road for ...
		— la primera calle a la derecha
		— la pree·**me·**ra **kal·**ye a la de·**re·**cha
	Take	— the first street on the right

		— la segunda calle a la izquierda
		— *la se·goon·da kal·ye a la*
		eeth·kyer·da
		— the second road on the left
28	Cruce	— la calle
	kroo·the	— *la kal·ye*
	Cross	— the street
29	Cruce	— el paso a nivel
	kroo·the	— *el pa·so a nee·bel*
	Cross over	— the grade crossing
		— el puente
		— *el pwen·te*
		— the bridge
30	Está	— muy cerca de aquí
	es·ta	— *mooy ther·ka de a·kee*
	It's	— not far from here
		— en el cruce
		— *en el kroo·the*
		— at the intersection
		— junto al teatro
		— *khoon·to al te·a·tro*
		— next to the theatre
		— después del semáforo
		— *des·pwes del se·ma·fo·ro*
		— after the traffic lights
		— frente a la iglesia
		— *fren·te a la ee·gle·sya*
		— opposite the church
		— allí
		— *al·yee*
		— over there
		— en la esquina
		— *en la es·kee·na*
		— at the corner

Money   (M)

General

1	How much is that	— altogether?
	¿Cuánto es	— en total?
	kwan·to es	— *en to·tal*
2	How much is it	— to get in?
	¿Cuánto es	— la entrada?
	kwan·to es	— *la en·tra·da*
		— for a child?
		— para los niños?
		— *pa·ra los neen·yos*
		— per person?
		— por persona?
		— *por per·so·na*
		— per kilo?
		— por kilo?
		— *por kee·lo*

3 Is there any extra charge?
   ¿Hay algún recargo?
   ay al·goon re·kar·go

4 Is the tip/tax included?
   ¿Incluye servicio/impuestos?
   een·kloo·ye ser·bee·thyo/eem·pwes·tos

5	Is there a discount for	— a group?
	¿Hay descuento para	— grupos?
	ay des·kwen·to pa·ra	— *groo·pos*
		— students?
		— estudiantes?
		— *es·too·dyan·tes*

Is there a discount for — senior citizens?
¿Hay descuento para — ancianos?
*ay des·**kwen**·to **pa**·ra — an·**thya**·nos*

6 How much of a discount can you give me?
¿Cuánto descuento puede hacerme?
kwan·to des·**kwen**·to pwe·de a·**ther**·me

7 Can you give me a 10 per cent discount?
¿Me hace un descuento del 10 por ciento?
me a·the oon des·**kwen**·to del dyeth por **thyen**·to

8 Can you give me an estimate of the cost?
¿Puede hacerme un presupuesto?
pwe·de a·**ther**·me oon pre·soo·**pwes**·to

9 Do I have to pay a deposit?
¿Tengo que pagar un depósito?
ten·go ke pa·**gar** oon de·**po**·see·to

10 Do I pay in advance or afterwards?
¿Le pago por adelantado o después?
le **pa**·go por a·de·lan·**ta**·do o des·**pwes**

11 Can I pay in instalments?
¿Puedo pagarlo a plazos?
pwe·do pa·**gar**·lo a **pla**·thos

12 Do you accept traveler's checks?
¿Aceptan cheques de viaje?
a·**thep**·tan **che**·kes de **bya**·khe

13 I wish to pay by credit card
Querría pagar por tarjeta de crédito
ke·**rree**·a pa·**gar** por tar·**khe**·ta de **kre**·dee·to

14 May I have — an itemized bill?
¿Puede darme — una factura detallada?
pwe·de **dar**·me — **oo**·na fak·**too**·ra de·tal·**ya**·da
— a receipt?
— un recibo?
— oon re·**thee**·bo

15 You have given me the wrong change
Me ha dado mal el cambio
me a **da**·do mal el **kam**·byo

16 That's too much for me
Eso es demasiado para mí
e·so es de·ma·**sya**·do **pa**·ra mee

17 I have no money
No tengo dinero
no **ten**·go dee·**ne**·ro

18 I do not have enough money
No tengo suficiente dinero
no **ten**·go soo·fee·**thyen**·te dee·**ne**·ro

19 That's all, thank you
Gracias, eso es todo
gra·thyas **e**·so es **to**·do

20 Can you change a 1,000 peseta note — into 100-peseta notes?
¿Me puede cambiar un billete de mil pesetas — en billetes de 100?
me **pwe**·de kam·**byar** oon beel·**ye**·te de meel pe·**se**·tas
— en beel·**ye**·tes de thyen
— into 50-peseta pieces?
— en monedas de 50 pesetas
— en mo·**ne**·das de theen·**kwen**·ta pe·**se**·tas

21 Can you give me some small change?
¿Puede cambiarme en monedas?
pwe·de kam·**byar**·me en mo·**ne**·das

Banks and exchange offices

Banks are usually open from about 9:00 to about 14:00 including Saturdays. Exchange offices at airports and major railway stations may stay open at night and over the weekend. Remember that you need your passport when changing money. Traveler's checks issued by major banks are widely accepted, as are personal checks from Eurocheque banks. In Latin America banks open from 9:30 to 15:30 and are closed on Saturdays.

22   Will you change — these traveler's checks?
                  ¿Puede cambiarme — estos cheques de viaje?
           pwe·de kam·byar·me — *es·tos che·kes de bya·khe*
                          — these bills?
                          — estos billetes?
                          — *es·tos beel·ye·tes*

23 What is the exchange rate for dollars?
    ¿A cuánto está la libra/el dólar?
    a kwan·to es·ta la lee·bra/el do·lar

24 I would like to withdraw 50,000 pesetas
    Quiero sacar 50.000 pesetas
    kye·ro sa·kar theen·kwen·ta meel pe·se·tas

25 I would like to cash a check with my Eurocheque card
    Quisiera cobrar un cheque con mi tarjeta de Eurocheque
    kee·sye·ra ko·brar oon che·ke kon mee tar·khe·ta de ew·ro·che·ke

26 I would like to obtain a cash advance with my credit card
    ¿Puedo sacar dinero con mi tarjeta de crédito?
    pwe·do sa·kar dee·ne·ro kon mee tar·khe·ta de kre·dee·to

27 What is your commission?
    ¿Cuánto cobran de comisión?
    kwan·to ko·bran de ko·mee·syon

28 Can you contact my bank to arrange for a transfer?
    ¿Puede ponerse en contacto con mi banco para arreglar una transferencia?
    pwe·de po·ner·se en kon·tak·to kon mee ban·ko pa·ra a·rre·glar oo·na trans·fe·ren·thya

29 I have an account with the Bank of X in London/New York
    Tengo una cuenta con el Banco de X en Londres/Nueva York
    ten·go oo·na kwen·ta kon el ban·ko de X en lon·dres/ nwe·ba york

30 I have made an arrangement with this bank
    He acordado un arreglo con este banco
    e a·kor·da·do oon a·rre·glo kon es·te ban·ko

31 I would like to speak to the manager
    Quisiera hablar con el gerente
    kee·sye·ra a·blar kon el khe·ren·te

Accommodations (A)

Hotel reservations and inquiries

Hotels are grouped into categories of 1, 2, 3, 4 and 5 stars, and boarding houses (*pensiones* and *hostales: pen·syo·nes; hos·ta·les*) are graded 1, 2 or 3 stars. Two other types of accommodation are worth noting: the *paradores nacionales* (*pa·ra·do·res na·thyo·na·les*), often converted historical buildings, in beautiful settings, and the *albergues de carretera* (*al·ber·ges de ka·rre·te·ra*), set at strategic points on main roads. Most hotels can handle a reservation or inquiry in English, but if you don't want to take any chances, this section contains some of the things you might want to say by letter or telephone, or at the reception desk.

1 Dear Sirs/Gentlemen
    Muy Señores Míos
    mooy sen·yo·res mee·os

2 I wish to stay in Granada from ... to ...
    Deseo quedarme en Granada desde el dìa ... hasta el ...
    de·se·o ke·dar·me en gra·na·da des·de el dee·a ... as·ta el ...
                          — with my wife
                          — con mi esposa/mujer
                          — *kon mee es·po·sa/moo·kher*
                          — with my family
                          — con mi familia
                          — *kon mee fa·mee·lya*

3 I wish to stay for three nights
Quiero quedarme tres noches
kye·ro ke·dar·me tres no·ches

4 Can you provide the following accommodations
Desearía que me reservasen el siguiente alojamiento
de·se·a·ree·a ke me re·ser·ba·sen el see·gyen·te a·lo·kha·myen·to

   — a single room with toilet and shower/bath
   — una habitación individual con ducha/baño
   — *oo·na a·bee·ta·thyon een·dee·bee·dwal kon doo·cha/ban·yo*

   — a room with twin beds
   — una habitación de dos camas
   — *oo·na a·bee·ta·thyon de dos ka·mas*

   — a double room with a bed for a child
   — una habitación doble con una cama para un niño
   — *oo·na a·bee·ta·thyon do·ble kon oo·na ka·ma pa·ra oon neen·yo*

   — a suite with living room, bedroom and bathroom
   — una suite con salón, dormitorio y cuarto de baño
   — *oo·na sweet kon sa·lon dor·mee·to·ryo ee kwar·to de ban·yo*

5 I should like a room — that is quiet
Querría una habitación — tranquila
ke·rree·a oo·na a·bee·ta·thyon — *tran·kee·la*

   — with a view
   — con vista
   — *kon bees·ta*

   — on the first floor/second floor
   — en el piso principal/primer piso
   — *en el pee·so preen·thee·pal/pree·mer pee·so*

   — with a TV/radio
   — con televisión/radio
   — *kon te·le·bee·syon/ra·dyo*

6 Please send me a brochure about your hotel
Por favor envíeme informaciones sobre su hotel
por fa·bor en·bee·e·me een·for·ma·thyo·nes so·bre soo o·tel

7 Sincerely yours
Atentamente
a·ten·ta·men·te

8 How much is the room per night?
¿Cuánto es la habitación por noche?
kwan·to es la a·bee·ta·thyon por no·che

9 Is breakfast/tax included?
¿Está incluido el desayuno/los impuestos?
es·ta een·kloo·ee·do el de·sa·yoo·no/los eem·pwes·tos

10 How much is it — with breakfast?
¿Cuánto es — con desayuno?
kwan·to es — *kon de·sa·yoo·no*

   — with breakfast and evening meal?
   — con desayuno y cena?
   — *kon de·sa·yoo·no ee the·na*

   — with all meals?
   — con pensión completa
   — *kon pen·syon kom·ple·ta*

11 Do you have a swimming pool/sauna?
¿Tiene piscina/sauna?
tye·ne pees·thee·na/sow·na

12 Can you suggest another hotel that might have a vacancy?
¿Puede sugerirme otro hotel donde haya habitaciones?
pwe·de soo·khe·reer·me o·tro o·tel don·de a·ya a·bee·ta·thyo·nes

Checking in and out

13 I have reserved a room in the name of Smith
    Tengo reservada una habitación en nombre de Smith
    ten·go re·ser·**ba·**da **oo·**na a·bee·ta·**thyon** en **nom·**bre de smith
14 Can I see the room, please?
    ¿Puedo ver la habitación, por favor?
    pwe·do ber la a·bee·ta **thyon** por fa·**bor**
15 The room is too small/noisy
    La habitación es demasiado pequeña/ruidosa
    la a·bee·ta·**thyon** es de·ma·**sya·**do pe·**ken·**ya/rwee·**do·**sa
16 When will the room be ready?
    ¿Cuándo estará lista la habitación?
    kwan·do es·ta·**ra** lees·ta la a·bee·ta·**thyon**
17 Where is the bathroom/toilet?
    ¿Dónde está el cuarto de baño/el water?
    don·de es·**ta** el **kwar·**to de **ban·**yo/el **wa·**ter
18 I want to stay an extra night
    Quiero estar una noche más
    kye·ro es·**tar oo·**na **no·**che mas
19 We shall be leaving at 9 o'clock tomorrow morning
    Nos marcharemos mañana a las 9 de la mañana
    nos mar·cha·**re·**mos man·**ya·**na a las **nwe·**be de la man·**ya·**na
20 By what time do we have to vacate the room?
    ¿A qué hora tenemos que dejar la habitación?
    a ke o·ra te·**ne·**mos ke de·**khar** la a·bee·ta·**thyon**
21 I would like the bill, please
    La factura, por favor
    la fak·**too·**ra por fa·**bor**
22 Can I pay by credit card?
    ¿Puedo pagar con tarjeta de crédito?
    pwe·do pa·**gar** kon tar·**khe·**ta de kre·**dee·**to
23   Do you accept — traveler's checks?
                    ¿Aceptan — cheques de viaje?
                    a·**thep·**tan — **che·**kes de **bya·**khe
                               — American Express cards/checks?
                               — tarjetas de American
                                 Express/checks?
                               — tar·**khe·**tas de American Express/
                                 che·kes
24 Could you have my luggage brought down/sent on?
    ¿Podrían bajarme/mandarme el equipaje?
    po·**dree·**an ba·**khar·**me/man·**dar·**me el e·kee·**pa·**khe
25 Could you have any letters/messages forwarded?
    ¿Pueden enviarme las cartas/los recados?
    pwe·den en·bee·**ar·**me las **kar·**tas/los re·**ka·**dos

Services and practical needs

26   What time is — breakfast/lunch?
                    ¿A qué hora se sirve — el desayuno/el almuerzo?
                    a ke o·ra se **seer·**be — el de·sa·**yoo·**no/el al·**mwer·**tho
27 Can we have breakfast in our room, please?
    ¿Pueden servirnos el desayuno en la habitación, por favor?
    pwe·den ser·**beer·**nos el de·**say·yoo·**no en la a·bee·ta·**thyon**
    por fa·**bor**
28 Where can I park the car?
    ¿Dónde puedo dejar el coche?
    don·de **pwe·**do de·**khar** el **ko·**che
29 What time does the hotel close?
    ¿A qué hora cierra el hotel?
    a ke o·ra **thye·**rra el o·**tel**
30 Is there an elevator?
    ¿Hay ascensor?
    ay as·then·**sor**

31 Can I drink the tap water?
¿Se puede beber el agua del grifo?
se **pwe**·*de be*·**ber** *el ag*·*wa del* **gree**·*fo*

32 Please call me at 8 o'clock
Despiérteme a las ocho, por favor
des·**pyer**·*te*·*me a las o*·*cho por fa*·**bor**

33 Can I leave these for safekeeping?
¿Puedo dejar esto en la caja fuerte?
pwe·*do de*·**khar** *es*·*to en la* **ka**·*kha* **fwer**·*te*

34 Can I have my things out of the safe?
¿Pueden devolverme las cosas que dejé en la caja fuerte?
pwe·*den de*·*bol*·**ber**·*me las* **ko**·*sas ke de*·**khe** *en la* **ka**·*kha* **fwer**·*te*

35   Can I — make a telephone call from here?
           ¿Puedo — llamar por teléfono desde aquí?
           pwe·*do* — *lya*·*mar por te*·**le**·*fo*·*no des*·*de*
           a·**kee**
           — send a telex message from here?
           — mandar un télex desde aquí?
           — *man*·**dar** *oon* **te**·*leks des*·*de a*·**kee**

36 Are there any letters/messages for me?
¿Hay alguna carta/algún recado para mí?
ay al·**goo**·*na* **kar**·*ta/al*·**goon** *re*·**ka**·*do* **pa**·*ra mee*

37 I should like a private room for a conference/cocktail party
Querría una habitación privada para una conferencia/una fiesta
ke·**rree**·*a oo*·*na a*·*bee*·*ta*·**thyon** *pree*·**ba**·*da* **pa**·*ra oo*·*na*
kon·*fe*·**ren**·*thya/oo*·*na* **fyes**·*ta*

38 I am expecting a Señor Villegas
Espero al Señor Villegas
es·**pe**·*ro al sen*·**yor** *beel*·**ye**·*gas*

39 Could you call me when he arrives?
¿Pueden llamarme cuando llegue?
pwe·*den lya*·**mar**·*me* **kwan**·*do* **lye**·*ge*

40 Is the voltage 220 or 110?
¿La corriente es de 220 o de 110?
la ko·**rryen**·*te es de dos* **thyen**·*tos* **beyn**·*te o de* **thyen**·*to dyeth*

41   Can I have — my key?
           ¿Puede darme — la llave, por favor?
           pwe·*de dar*·*me* — *la* **lya**·*be por fa*·**bor**
           — some soap?
           — jabón, por favor?
           — *kha*·**bon** *por fa*·**bor**
           — some towels?
           — unas toallas, por favor?
           — *oo*·*nas to*·**al**·*yas por fa*·**bor**
           — some note paper?
           — papel de escribir, por favor?
           — *pa*·**pel** *de es*·**kree**·**beer** *por fa*·**bor**
           — an ashtray?
           — un cenicero, por favor?
           — *oon the*·**nee**·**the**·*ro por fa*·**bor**
           — another blanket?
           — otra manta, por favor?
           — *o*·*tra* **man**·*ta por fa*·**bor**
           — another pillow?
           — otra almohada, por favor?
           — *o*·*tra al*·**mo**·*a*·*da por fa*·**bor**

42 Can you replace the bolster with one/two pillows?
¿Puede cambiarme el almohadón por una/dos almohada(s)
pwe·*de kam*·**byar**·*me el al*·*mo*·*a*·**don** *por oo*·*na/dos al*·*mo*·*a*·*da(s)*

43 Where is the outlet for my electric razor?
¿Dónde hay un enchufe para la máquina de afeitar?
don·*de ay oon en*·**choo**·*fe* **pa**·*ra la* **ma**·*kee*·*na de a*·**fey**·*tar*

44 I cannot open the window
No puedo abrir la ventana
no **pwe**·*do a*·**breer** *la ben*·**ta**·*na*

45 The air conditioning/the heating is not working
El aire acondicionado/la calefacción no funciona
el **ay**·*re a*·*kon*·*dee*·*thyo*·**na**·*do/la ka*·*le*·*fak*·**thyon** *no foon*·**thyo**·*na*

46 I cannot turn the heat off
    No puedo apagar la
    calefacción
    *no pwe·do a·pa·gar la
    ka·le·fak·thyon*

47 I want to turn the heat
    up/down
    Quiero poner la calefacción
    más alta/baja
    *kye·ro po·ner la
    ka·le·fak·thyon mas
    al·ta/ba·kha*

48 The lock is broken
    La cerradura está rota
    la the·rra·doo·ra es·ta ro·ta

49 There is no hot water
    No hay agua caliente
    no ay ag·wa ka·lyen·te

50 The washbowl is dirty
    El lavabo está sucio
    el la·ba·bo es·ta soo·thyo

51 There is no plug in the
    washbasin
    No hay tapón en el lavabo
    no ay ta·pon en el la·ba·bo

52 There is no toilet paper
    No hay papel higiénico
    no ay pa·pel ee·khye·nee·ko

53 Do you have a laundry room?
    ¿Tienen lavandería?
    tye·nen la·ban·de·ree·a

54 I want to iron some clothes
    Quiero planchar unas cosas
    kye·ro plan·char oo·nas ko·sas

55 I want some clothes ironed
    Quiero que me planchen
    alguna ropa
    *kye·ro ke me plan·chen
    al·goo·na ro·pa*

56 Thank you, we enjoyed our
    stay very much
    Gracias, ha sido una estancia
    muy agradable
    *gra·thyas a see·do oo·na
    es·tan·thya mooy
    a·gra·da·ble*

Rented houses

57 We have arranged to rent a
    house through your agency
    Hemos contratado el alquiler
    de una casa por medio de su
    agencia
    *e·mos kon·tra·ta·do el
    al·kee·ler de oo·na ka·sa por
    me·dyo de soo a·khen·thya*

58 Here is our reservation
    Aquí está nuestra reserva
    a·kee es·ta nwes·tra re·ser·ba

59 We need two sets of keys
    Necesitamos dos juegos de
    llaves
    *ne·the·see·ta·mos dos
    khwe·gos de lya·bes*

60 Will you show us around?
    ¿Nos enseña la casa, por
    favor?
    *nos en·sen·ya la ka·sa por
    fa·bor*

61 Which is the key for this door?
    ¿Cuál es la llave de esta
    puerta?
    *kwal es la lya·be de es·ta
    pwer·ta*

62 Is the cost of electricity
    included in the rental?
    ¿Está incluida la electricidad
    en la renta?
    *es·ta een·kloo·ee·da la
    e·lek·tree·thee·dad en la
    ren·ta*

63 Where is the main switch for
    electricity?
    ¿Dónde está el interruptor de
    la luz?
    *don·de es·ta el een·te·rroop·tor
    de la looth*

64 Where is the main valve for
    shutting off water?
    ¿Dónde está la llave de cierre
    del agua?
    *don·de es·ta la lya·be de
    thye·rre del ag·wa*

65 Where is the water heater?
    ¿Dónde está el calentador de
    agua?
    *don·de es·ta el ka·len·ta·dor de
    ag·wa*

66 Please show me how this
    works
    Enséñeme cómo funciona
    esto, por favor
    *en·sen·ye·me ko·mo
    foon·thyo·na es·to por
    fa·bor*

67 How does the heating work?
    ¿Cómo funciona la
    calefacción?
    *ko·mo foon·thyo·na la
    ka·le·fak·thyon*

68 When does the maid come?
    ¿Cuando vendrá la muchacha
    a limpiar?
    *kwan·do ben·dra la
    moo·cha·cha a leem·pyar*

69 Is there any spare bedding?
    ¿Tiene más ropa de cama?
    tye·ne mas ro·pa de ka·ma

70 Where can I contact you if
    there are any problems?
    ¿Dónde puedo localizarle si
    hay algún problema?
    *don·de pwe·do
    lo·ka·lee·thar·le see ay
    al·goon pro·ble·ma*

71 The stove does not work
    La cocina no funciona
    la ko·thee·na no foon·thyo·na

72 Where is the trashcan?
¿Dónde está el cubo de la
basura?
*don·de es·ta el koo·bo de la
ba·soo·ra*

73 Is there a spare gas cylinder?
¿Hay una bombona de gas de
repuesto?
*ay oo·na bom·bo·na de gas de
re·pwes·to*

74 Where can we get logs for the
fire?
¿Dónde podemos encontrar
leña para el fuego?
*don·de po·de·mos en·kon·trar
len·ya pa·ra el fwe·go*

75 I can't open the windows
No puedo abrir las ventanas
*no pwe·do a·breer las
ben·ta·nas*

76 We can't get any water
No tenemos agua
no te·ne·mos ag·wa

77 The toilet won't flush
La cisterna no funciona
la thees·ter·na no foon·thyo·na

78 The pipe is blocked
La tubería está atascada
*la too·be·ree·a es·ta
a·tas·ka·da*

79 A fuse has blown
Se han fundido los plomos
se an foon·dee·do los plo·mos

80 There is a gas leak
Hay un escape de gas
ay oon es·ka·pe de gas

81 I need somebody to repair this
Necesito a alguien que arregle
esto
*ne·the·see·to a al·gyen ke
a·rre·gle es·to*

Camping

There are many officially recognized camping sites in Spain, especially
along the Mediterranean coast. Many of them have very good facilities. If
you can't find an official site, however, landowners will often allow you
to camp on their property, but it is essential to obtain permission.

82 Is there anywhere for us to
camp near here?
¿Hay algún sitio para acampar
cerca de aquí?
*ay al·goon see·tyo pa·ra
a·kam·par ther·ka de a·kee*

83 Have you got a site for our
tent?
¿Tiene un sitio para nuestra
tienda?
*tye·ne oon see·tyo pa·ra
nwes·tra tyen·da*

84 Do you mind if we camp on
your land?
¿Le importa que acampemos
en su terreno?
*le eem·por·ta ke a·kam·pe·mos
en soo te·rre·no*

85 This site is very muddy
Este sitio tiene mucho barro
*es·te see·tyo tye·ne moo·cho
ba·rro*

86 Could we have a more
sheltered site?
¿Tiene un sitio más abrigado?
*tye·ne oon see·tyo mas
a·bree·ga·do*

87 May we put our trailer here?
¿Podemos poner la caravana
aquí?
*po·de·mos po·ner la
ka·ra·ba·na a·kee*

88 Is there a shop on the site?
¿Hay alguna tienda en el
camping?
*ay al·goo·na tyen·da en el
kam·peeng*

89 Can I have a shower?
¿Puedo ducharme?
pwe·do doo·char·me

90 Where is the drinking water?
¿Dónde está el agua potable?
don·de es·ta el ag·wa po·ta·ble

91 Where are the toilets and
washroom?
¿Dónde están los servicios y
los lavabos?
*don·de es·tan los ser·bee·thyos
ee los la·ba·bos*

92 Where can we buy ice?
¿Dónde podemos comprar
hielo?
*don·de po·de·mos kom·prar
ye·lo*

93 Where can we wash our
dishes/our clothes?
¿Dónde podemos lavar los
platos/la ropa?
*don·de po·de·mos la·bar los
pla·tos/la ro·pa*

94 Is there another camp site near
here?
¿Hay algún otro camping cerca
de aquí?
*ay al·goon o·tro kam·peeng
ther·ka de a·kee*

95 Are there any washing
machines?
¿Tienen lavadoras?
tye·nen la·ba·do·ras

96 We need to buy a new gas cylinder
    Tenemos que comprar otra bombona de gas
    te·ne·mos ke kom·prar o·tra bom·bo·na de gas
97 I would like to change the position of my tent
    Me gustaría cambiar el sitio de mi tienda
    me goos·ta·ree·a kam·byar el see·tyo de mee tyen·da

Eating out (E)

Spain has much to offer lovers of good food. You can have memorable
meals all over the country in elegant city restaurants
or in roadside restaurants and even in bars. Set-price menus are
usually good value, but beware of *menús turísticos (me·noos
too·rees·tee·kos)* in places obviously catering to tourists, where the
standards are not likely to be high for customers who are only passing
through. The best recommendation is the presence of the Spanish
themselves. The Menu guide on p.32 will help you decide what to eat.
Don't miss the opportunity to sample local specialties. If you have your
family with you, see Children, p.60. Remember that in Spain it is not
customary to start one's evening meal much before ten o'clock.
  In Latin America there are many national specialities which are well
worth sampling.

General

1 Do you know — a good restaurant?
   ¿Conoce — un restaurante bueno?
   ko·no·the — *oon res·tow·ran·te bwe·no*
   — a restaurant specializing in
     Andalusian dishes?
   — un restaurante especializado en
     comida andaluza?
   — *oon res·tow·ran·te
     es·pe·thya·lee·tha·do
     en ko·mee·da an·da·loo·tha*
2 I would like to reserve a table — for two people
   Quisiera reservar una mesa — para dos
   *kee·sye·ra re·ser·bar oo·na
   me·sa* — *pa·ra dos*
   — for 10 o'clock
   — para las diez
   — *pa·ra las dyeth*
3 I have reserved a table in the name of ...
   He reservado una mesa a nombre de ...
   e re·ser·ba·do oo·na me·sa a nom·bre de
4 Do you have a quiet table — by the window/on the terrace?
   ¿Tienen una mesa tranquila — cerca de la ventana/en la terraza?
   *tye·nen oo·na me·sa
   tran·kee·la* — *ther·ka de la ben·ta·na/en la
   te·rra·tha*
5 Is it possible to have a private room?
   ¿Tiene un comedor privado?
   tye·ne oon ko·me·dor pree·ba·do
6 It is for a business lunch/dinner
   Es para una comida/cena de negocios
   es pa·ra oo·na ko·mee·da/the·na de ne·go·thyos
7 Señor Delgado is expecting me
   Me espera el Señor Delgado
   me es·pe·ra el sen·yor del·ga·do
8 The menu, please
   La carta, por favor
   la kar·ta por fa·bor

Menu guide

Spain is a country which still possesses an authentic and varied regional cuisine. In general, fish is to be preferred to meat, but the dishes vary from the roasts and rib-warming stews of the north to the cold soups and highly spiced rices of the Mediterranean. Here are some of them:

Hors d'oeuvres, vegetables and main dishes

Ajo blanco con manzana (Andalusia) Cold soup with almonds, garlic, moist breadcrumbs, olive oil and peeled grapes

Albóndigas Meatballs, usually in tomato sauce

Alioli (Catalonia) Garlic sauce with olive oil, lemon juice, garlic and parsley

Almejas a la marinera Steamed mussels/clams with white wine, parsley, olive oil and garlic

Angulas en cazuela Tiny freshwater eels with olive oil, chillis and garlic

Arroz con costra (Murcia) Rice with chicken and white sausage, topped with beaten egg and put in the oven for a crusty finish

Bacalao a la vizcaína (Basque country) Dried salted cod with olive oil, garlic, fried bread, red peppers, and parsley

Bacalao al pil pil Dried salted cod with chillis and garlic

Bonito con tomate Tuna fish with tomato sauce

Boquerones fritos Fresh anchovies, crisp-fried

Butifarra catalana (Catalonia) White sausage eaten raw or cooked

Cabrito asado Roasted kid

Calamares en su tinta Squid with a sauce using the ink bags of the squid

Calamares fritos Fried squid

Calamares rellenos Squid stuffed with its tentacles, parsley and garlic, then stewed in a wine and tomato sauce

Caldeirada gallega (Galicia) A Galician seafood and vegetable chowder

Callos a la madrileña (Madrid) Tripe stew with pig's trotters, ham, salami and chillis

Centollos Spider crab. The meat is often removed, cooked in white wine, and replaced in the shells

Chipirones a la plancha (Basque country) Grilled baby squid

Churros Golden brown fingers of a batter, fried in olive oil and eaten for breakfast

Cochinillo asado (Old Castile) Roasted suckling pig

Cocido Stew of chicken, beef and vegetables. There are many different regional variations, it is worth trying the local *cocido* wherever you are staying

Cordero a la chilindrón (Aragón) Spicy stew of lamb with red peppers, tomatoes, onions and garlic

Cordero lechal asado (Burgos) Roasted suckling lamb

Enseimadas mallorquinas (Majorca) Light, slightly sweet fancy bread, delicious for breakfast

Entremeses fríos/calientes Mixed hors d'oeuvres, both hot and cold, including fish, shellfish, cured pork and olives

Escabeche de pescado Fish marinated in olive oil, herbs and garlic, and served cold

Escudella catalana (Catalonia) Thick soup with vegetables, rice, white sausage and hard boiled eggs

Estofado de ternera/cordero Veal or lamb stew with green peppers, tomatoes, white wine and onions

Fabada asturiana (Asturias) Butter beans stewed with ham, salami, blood pudding and carrots

Fiambres Platter of assorted cold meats

Gambas a la plancha Grilled prawns

Gambas al ajillo Prawns with plenty of garlic and chillis

Gambas rebozadas Crisp-fried prawns in batter

Gazpacho (Andalusia) Traditional cold soup of Spain; there are many variations but basically it is water, tomatoes, cucumber, green peppers, soft breadcrumbs, vinegar, olive oil, garlic and seasoning

Huevos a la flamenca (Andalusia) Eggs cooked in an earthenware dish with salami, tomatoes and sometimes prawns and red peppers

Huevos revueltos con tomate Scrambled eggs with tomatoes

Jamón serrano Smoked ham; worth trying in all regions

Kokotxas (Basque Country) Strips from the throat or "cheek" of the hake, cooked in earthenware dishes with olive oil, garlic and parsley

Langosta a la catalana (Catalonia) Lobster with onions, carrots, grated cheese, chocolate, nutmeg and brandy

Langostinos a la plancha/vinagreta King prawns grilled/with vinaigrette sauce

Lenguados rellenos Sole stuffed with shrimps

Lubina al hinojo Bass with fennel

Manitas de cerdo rebozadas Pig's trotters, boiled, boned and fried in egg and breadcrumbs

Mariscada A platter of mixed grilled shellfish

Merluza a la vasca (Basque country) Hake with boiled potatoes, parsley, hard boiled eggs and asparagus tips

Mollejas de ternera Sweetbreads coated with egg and breadcrumbs, and fried in olive oil

Paella valenciana (Valencia) One of the most famous of Spanish dishes, *paella* varies from region to region but usually consists of rice, fish, shellfish, chicken, meat, vegetables, tomatoes and saffron

Pato a la sevillana (Andalusia) Duck casserole with onions, tomatoes, herbs, oranges and olives

Parrillada de mariscos Mixed grill of shellfish

Pez espada a la parrilla Swordfish grilled with lemon and olive oil and a touch of garlic

Pierna de cordero rellena Stuffed leg of lamb

Pinchos morunos Small cubes of meat grilled on a skewer

Pollo en pepitoria Chicken with almonds, egg yolk, saffron, garlic and herbs

Pote gallego (Galicia) Stew with haricot beans, potatoes, pork, cabbage and belly of pork

Rabo de toro (Andalusia) Oxtail stewed with vegetables

Rape en salsa verde Angler fish with wine and parsley sauce

Salsa romesco (Catalonia) Sauce made with olive oil, vinegar, garlic, almonds, hot peppers and tomatoes; served with fish or shellfish

Sardinas fritas/rebozadas/a la plancha Fresh sardines fried/fried in batter/grilled

Solomillo Fillet steak

Sopa de ajo Soup made with bread, garlic, paprika and olive oil

Sopa al cuarto de hora (Madrid) (Quarter of an hour soup) Soup containing clams, ham, onion, hard boiled eggs and sherry

Sopa de albondiguillas (Catalonia) Clear chicken soup with small meatballs; flavored with cinnamon, garlic and chervil

Sopa de mariscos Shellfish bisque, with saffron

Sopa de pescado Fish soup with rice and saffron

Tarta gallega (Galicia) Savory tart with peppers, tomatoes, meat, fish and salami

Ternera asada Roast veal

Ternera rellena Roasted stuffed roll of veal

Tortilla a la española A thick omelette with potatoes, onions and eggs

Trucha a la navarra (Navarre) Trout with red wine, herbs, olive oil and potatoes

Vieiras (Galicia) Scallops with lemon and parsley

Cheeses

Queso de Burgos (Burgos) Fresh curd cheese, sometimes eaten with sugar and honey

Queso de Idiazabal (Basque country) A cheese with a delicate, herby flavor

Queso de Mahón (Balearic Islands) A white and creamy cheese, getting darker with age

Queso manchego (La Mancha) Spain's best-known cheese, available either fresh or matured in olive oil, when it gains more bite and flavor

Queso Roncal (Navarre) Hard, slightly smoked, strongly flavored cheese

Requesón Curd cheese

Desserts

Arroz con leche Cinnamon flavoured rice pudding

Bizcochos borrachos Sponge cakes soaked in wine, rum or Malaga wine

Crema quemada a la catalana (Catalonia) Baked custard topped with brittle caramel

Crepes de almendra Pancakes filled with chopped almonds

Filloas (Galicia) Sweet pancakes

Flan Cream caramel custard

Helado Ice cream

Leche frita Thick slices of custard coated with egg and breadcrumbs and fried in olive oil

Melocotones al vino Peaches stewed in red wine

Membrillo Quince paste

Peras al vino Pears stewed in red wine

Polvorones sevillanos (Andalusia) Powdery sweetmeat with flour, sugar, almonds and cinnamon

Tocino de cielo Thick caramel custard made with egg yolks

Turrón de Alicante (Alicante) Nougat made with whole almonds and white of egg

Yemas de Santa Teresa (Avila) Sweetmeat made with egg yolks, cinnamon and lemon peel

Wines

Spain's national drink is the slightly fortified wine that we call sherry, after Jerez, in the south of the country, where it is made. It ranges in style from the delicate, dry *fino* to the full and sweet *oloroso* (see the following list for further sherry terms).

Other Spanish wines fall into two groups: the strong but generally rather uninteresting wines from the Mediterranean climate of the center, south and east; and those from the northern and western regions nearer to the Atlantic. The latter range from the fairly rough to fine, expensive wines such as the Reservas and Gran Reservas from bodegas such as Paternina and Torres.

Apart from the famous Rioja and Penedes, there are other regions of repute such as Alella, Las Campanas, León Priorato and Valdepeñas, but unless you see a name you recognize the best thing is to drink the local wine.

Strength is often given priority over finesse in Spain. A few barmen, if you are feeling low, will give you a *sol y sombra*, a mixture of Fundador brandy and *anís* (a little like Pernod, only sweeter). Spanish brandy (*Coñac*) can be good, though you get the quality you pay for. The more basic brandies should only be drunk in mixed drinks. The Spanish system of controlled appellation (*denominación de origen controlada*) dates from the post-war era and although much amended in recent years, may be felt to be over-optimistic, delimiting some areas of purely domestic interest.

Several Latin American countries produce their own wines, the Argentinian and Chilean ones being most renowned.

Unless otherwise stated, the wines in the following list come in both red and white.

Albariño del Palacio White wine with a pleasant bouquet, drunk young

Alella Small demarcated region near Barcelona, making pleasantly fresh and fruity wines

Alicante Demarcated region, producing strong, heavy wines

Almansa Demarcated region producing strong, heavy red wines

Aloque A variety of *Valdepeñas*, this is a light but strong red wine

Almendralejo Commercial wine center of the Extremadura. Much of its produce is distilled to make the alcohol for fortifying sherry

Amontillado In general use this means medium sherry; technically it means a wine which has been aged to become more powerful and pungent. A *fino* can develop into *amontillado*

Amoroso Type of sweet sherry, not much different from a sweet *oloroso*

Año 4° Año (or Años) means bottled during the fourth year after harvesting

Benicarló Town on the Mediterranean formerly making strong red wines

Blanco White

Bodega This means either a wineshop or a concern occupied in the making, blending and shipping of wine

Campanas, Las Small wine area near Pamplona. Clarete Campanas is a sturdy red. Mature 5° año Castillo de Tiebas is like a heavy Rioja reserva

Cañamero Village near Guadalupe making white wines that acquire a taste like sherry

Cariñena Demarcated region and supplier of strong everyday wine

Cava An establishment making sparkling wines by the champagne method; or a Spanish name for such wines

Cenicero Wine township in the *Rioja* Alta

Cepa Wine or grape variety

Chacolí A sharp "green wine" from the Basque coast, containing only 8%-9% alcohol

Champaña If you ask for this you will probably be given a Spanish sparkling wine. If you want the genuine article you had better ask specifically for French champagne

Clarete Light red wine (occasionally dark rosé)

Consejo Regulador Official organization for the defense and control of a *denominación de origen*

Cosecha Crop or vintage

Criado y embotellado por . . . Grown and bottled by . . .

Crianza The "nursery" where the wine is brought up. New or unaged wine is "*sin crianza*"

Denominación de origen Used of officially demarcated wine regions (see introduction p.34)

Dulce Sweet

Elaborado y envejecido por . . . Made and aged by . . .

Elciego Village in the *Rioja* Alavesa surrounded by vineyards

Espumoso Sparkling

Fino Term for the lightest and finest of sherries, completely dry, very pale and with great delicacy. Fino should always be drunk cool and fresh. Tío Pepe and Fina la Ina are classic examples

Flor A wine yeast peculiar to sherry and certain other wines that oxidize slowly and tastily under its influence

Fuenmayor Wine township in the *Rioja* Alta

Gaseoso A cheap sparkling wine made by pumping carbon dioxide into wine

Gran Vas Pressurized tanks for making inexpensive sparkling wines; also used to describe this type of wine

Haro The wine center of the *Rioja* Alta

Jerez de la Frontera Center of the sherry industry

Laguardia Attractive walled town in the wine-growing district of the *Rioja* Alavesa

León Northern region whose wines are light, dry and refreshing

Logroño Principal town of the *Rioja* region

Málaga Demarcated region around the city of Malaga. Its best dessert wines rival tawny port

Mancha/Manchuela Large demarcated region near *Valdepeñas*

Manzanilla Sherry, normally *fino* from Sanlúcar de Barrameda, with bracing, salty character

Méntrida Demarcated region west of Madrid, supplying everyday wine to the capital

Montánchez Village near Mérida, interesting because its red wines grow *flor* yeast like *fino* sherry

Monterrey Demarcated region near the northern border of Portugal, of which *Verín* is part

Montilla-Moriles Demarcated region near Cordoba, known for its crisp, sherry-like *fino* and *amontillado*

Navarra Demarcated region, making sturdy red wines for everyday drinking

Oloroso The most aromatic of sherries, heavier and less brilliant than *fino* when young, but maturing to greater richness and roundness. Naturally dry, but often sweetened for sale

Palo Cortado A sherry close to *oloroso* but with some of the character of an *amontillado*. Dry but rich and soft

Peñafiel Village on the Duero near Valladolid. Its best wines are fruity reds

Penedés Demarcated region including Villafranca del Penedés, San Sadurní de Noya and Sitges

Perelada In the demarcated region of Ampurdán on the Costa Brava. Best known for sparkling wines made both by the champagne and tank system

Priorato Demarcated region, an enclave in that of *Tarragona*, known for its strong reds

Reserva Good quality wine matured for long periods in cask. *Gran Reserva*, in *Rioja*, must have eight years in the barrel

Ribeiro Demarcated region on the northern border of Portugal – the heart of the "green wine" country

Rioja Upland region along the Ebro in the north of Spain which produces most of the country's best table wines. It is sub-divided into: Rioja Alavesa, north of the river Ebro, which produces fine red wines, mostly the lighter *claretes*; Rioja Alta, south of the Ebro and west of Logroño, a district making fine red and white wines and also some rosé; Rioja Baja, stretching east from Logroño, which makes coarser red wines, high in alcohol and often used for blending

Rosado Rosé

Rueda Small area west of Valladolid. Traditional producer of golden *flor*-growing sherry-like wines up to 17% of alcohol, now making fresh young whites such as that of the Marqués de Riscal

Rumasa The great Spanish conglomerate, which has absorbed many bodegas, including Williams and Humbert, Garvey, Paternina, Franco-Españolas and, in England, Augustus Barnett

Sangre de Toro Brand name for a rich-flavored red wine from Torres

Sangría Cold red wine cup, best made fresh by adding ice, citrus fruit, carbonated lemonade and brandy to red wine

Sanlúcar de Barrameda Center of the *Manzanilla* district

San Sadurní de Noya Town south of Barcelona, hollow with cellars where dozens of firms produce sparkling wine by the champagne method. Standards are high, even if the ultimate finesse is lacking

Seco Dry

Siglo Popular sack-wrapped *Rioja* brand from Bodegas A.G.E. Medium quality

Sitges Coastal resort south of Barcelona noted for sweet dessert wine made from Moscatel and Malvasia grapes

Tarragona 1. Table wines from the demarcated region; of little note. 2. Dessert wines from firms such as de Muller, comparable with good cream sherries. 3. The town makes vermouth and Chartreuse and exports cheap blended wine

Tierra del Vino Area west of Valladolid including the wine villages of La Nava and *Rueda*

Tinto Red

Toro Town, 150 miles northwest of Madrid, and its powerful red wine

Utiel-Requeña Demarcated region west of *Valencia*

Valbuena Made with the same grapes as *Vega Sicilia* but sold as 3° año or 5° año

Valdeorras Demarcated region east of Orense. Dry and refreshing wines

Valdepeñas Demarcated region near the border of Andalusia. The supplier of most of the carafe wine to Madrid. Its wines, though high in alcohol, are sometimes surprisingly light in flavor

Valencia Demarcated region producing earthy high-strength wine

Vega Sicilia One of the very best Spanish wines, full-bodied, fruity and almost impossible to find. Containing up to 16% alcohol *Valbuena* is (excellent) second quality

Vendimia Vintage

Verín Town near northern border of Portugal. Its wines are the strongest from Galicia, without a bubble, and up to 14% alcohol

Viña Vineyard. Several of the best *Rioja* reservas are named after their Viña, e.g. Tondonia and Bosconia (López), Zaco (Bilbaínas) etc

Vino Blanco White wine

Vino commún/corriente Ordinary wine

    clarete Light red wine

    dulce Sweet wine

    espumoso Sparkling wine

    generoso Apéritif or dessert wine rich in alcohol

    rancio Maderized (brown) white wine

    rosado Rosé wine

    seco Dry wine

    tinto Red wine

    verde Green wine, that is wine drunk young

Yecla Demarcated region north of Murcia. Its co-operative-made wines, once heavyweight champions, have been lightened and improved for export

Ordering wine

9 May I see the wine list, please?
   ¿Puedo ver la lista de vinos, por favor?
   pwe·do ber la lees·ta de bee·nos por fa·bor
10 Can you recommend a good local wine?
   ¿Puede recomendarme un vino local bueno?
   pwe·de re·ko·men·dar·me oon bee·no lo·kal bwe·no
11 Was this a good year?
   ¿Es este un buen año?
   es es·te oon bwen an·yo
12 A bottle/carafe of house wine
   Una botella/garrafa de vino de la casa
   oo·na bo·tel·ya/ga·rra·fa de bee·no de la ka·sa
13 Another bottle/half bottle, please
   Otra botella/media botella, por favor
   o·tra bo·tel·ya/me·dya bo·tel·ya por fa·bor
14 Would you bring another glass, please?
   ¿Puede traer otro vaso, por favor?
   pwe·de tra·er o·tro ba·so por fa·bor
15 What liqueurs do you have?
   ¿Qué licores tienen?
   ke lee·ko·res tye·nen

Ordering the meal and paying

16 Do you have a specialty of the day?
   ¿Tienen plato del día?
   tye·nen pla·to del dee·a
17 I will take today's special at 1,500 pesetas
   Tráigame el plato del día de mil quinientas pesetas
   tray·ga·me el pla·to del dee·a de meel kee·nyen·tas pe·se·tas
18 What would you recommend?
   ¿Qué nos recomienda?
   ke nos re·ko·myen·da
19 How is this dish cooked?
   ¿Cómo está hecho este plato?
   ko·mo es·ta e·cho es·te pla·to
20 Do you have a local specialty?
   ¿Tiene alguna especialidad local?
   tye·ne al·goo·na es·pe·thya·lee·dad lo·kal
21 I'll take that
   Tráigame eso
   tray·ga·me e·so
22   We will begin — with gazpacho
                Empezaremos — con gazpacho
                em·pe·tha·re·mos — kon gath·pa·cho
23 I will have steak and French fries
   Tráigame un filete con patatas fritas
   tray·ga·me oon fee·le·te kon pa·ta·tas free·tas
24   I like steak — very rare
           Me gusta el filete — muy poco pasado
      me goos·ta el fee·le·te — mooy po·ko pa·sa·do
                            — rare
                            — poco pasado
                            — *po·ko pa·sa·do*
                            — medium rare
                            — medianamente pasado
                            — *me·dya·na·men·te pa·sa·do*
                            — well done
                            — bien pasado
                            — *byen pa·sa·do*
25 Are vegetables included?
   ¿Incluye verduras?
   een·kloo·ye ber·doo·ras

26 Is this cheese very strong?
¿Es muy fuerte este queso?
*es mooy **fwer**·te **es**·te ke·so*

27 Does the fish (meat) come with anything else?
¿Sirven el pescado (la carne) con guarnición?
*seer·ben el pes·**ka**·do (la **kar**·ne) kon gwar·nee·**thyon***

28   That is for — me
Eso es para — mí
*e·so es **pa**·ra — mee*
— him/her
— él/ella
— *el/**el**·ya*

29   Some more — bread/water, please
Más — pan/agua, por favor
*mas — pan/**ag**·wa por fa·**bor***

30 Could I have some butter?
¿Me puede traer mantequilla?
*me **pwe**·de tra·er man·te·**keel**·ya*

31 What is this called?
¿Cómo se llama esto?
*ko·mo se **lya**·ma es·to*

32 This is not what I ordered
Esto no es lo que pedí
*es·to no es lo ke pe·**dee***

33 This is very salty
Esto está muy salado
*es·to es·**ta** mooy sa·**la**·do*

34 I wanted cheese
Quería queso
*ke·**ree**·a ke·so*

35 Have you forgotten the soup?
¿Se ha olvidado la sopa?
*se a ol·bee·**da**·do la **so**·pa*

36 This is cold
Esto está frío
*es·to es·**ta free**·o*

37 This is very good
Esto está muy bueno
*es·to es·**ta** mooy **bwe**·no*

38 I'll have a dessert
Voy a tomar un postre
*boy a to·**mar** oon **pos**·tre*

39 Could I have a salad instead of the cheese course?
¿Puedo tomar ensalada en vez de queso?
*pwe·do to·**mar** en·sa·**la**·da en beth de **ke**·so*

40 What is there for dessert?
¿Qué tienen de postre?
*ke **tye**·nen de **pos**·tre*

41 What cheeses do you have?
¿Qué quesos tiene?
*ke **ke**·sos **tye**·ne*

42 Nothing else, thank you — except coffee
Nada más, gracias — excepto café
*na·da mas **gra**·thyas eks·**thep**·to ka·**fe***
(for the various types of coffee and how to order them see under Cafés and bars p.39)

43 Waiter, could we have the bill, please?
Camarero, la cuenta por favor
*ka·ma·**re**·ro la **kwen**·ta por fa·**bor***

44 We are in a hurry
Tenemos prisa
*te·**ne**·mos **pree**·sa*

45 Is the tip included?
¿Incluye servicio?
*een·**kloo**·ye ser·**bee**·thyo*

46 There seems to be a mistake here
Hay un error aquí
*ay oon e·**rror** a·**kee***

47 What is this item?
¿A qué se refiere esto?
*a ke se re·**fye**·re es·to*

48 The meal was excellent
Ha sido una comida excelente
*a **see**·do **oo**·na ko·**mee**·da eks·the·**len**·te*

Phrases you will hear

49 ¿Una mesa para dos?
oo·na me·sa pa·ra dos
A table for two?

50 ¿Ha reservado mesa?
*a re·ser·**ba**·do me·sa*
Did you make a reservation?

51 ¿Ha(n) elegido ya?
*a(n) e·le·**khee**·do ya*
Are you ready to order?

52 ¿Con qué lo quiere?
*kon ke lo **kye**·re*
What would you like with it?

53 ¿Y después?
*ee des·**pwes***
And to follow?

54 ¿Qué quiere(n) beber/de postre?
    ke kye·re(n) be·ber/de pos·tre
    What would you like to drink/for dessert?

Cafés and bars

Bars and cafés are an essential part of Spanish life, places where you can
have breakfast, an aperitif, coffee after dinner, or just relax over a drink
at any time of day. Many serve snacks and meals. Most sell cigarettes and
have a public telephone (see Telephoning, p.53). Here we tell you how to
order your drinks. You normally pay for them when you leave rather
than when you are served.

Alcohol

55 A glass of red/white wine
    Un tinto/un blanco
    oon teen·to/oon blan·ko

56 A glass of beer from the keg
    Una cerveza
    oo·na ther·be·tha

57 A glass of draft beer
    Una caña
    oo·na kan·ya

58 A bottle of beer
    Un botellín
    oon bo·tel·yeen

59 A whiskey
    Un whisky
    oon wees·kee

60 A brandy
    Un coñac
    oon kon·yak

61 A martini
    Un martini
    oon mar·tee·nee

62 A sherry
    Un jerez
    oon khe·reth

63 A vermouth
    Un vermut
    oon ber·moot

Other alcoholic drinks you might like to try include *anís* (*a·nees* anise
liqueur), *sol y sombra* (*sol ee som·bra* brandy with anís) and *cuba libre*
(*koo·ba lee·bre* rum with coke).

Coffee, tea and chocolate

64 Black coffee
    Un café solo
    oon ka·fe so·lo

65 Coffee with milk
    Café con leche
    ka·fe kon le·che

66 Coffee with a dash of milk is
    un cortado (*kor·ta·do*)

67 Tea with milk/lemon
    Té con leche/limón
    te kon le·che/lee·mon

68 Herbal tea (usually
    chamomile)
    Una manzanilla
    oo·na man·za·neel·ya

69 Hot chocolate
    Un chocolate
    oon cho·ko·la·te

Soft drinks

Two of the most popular of these are *horchata de almendra/chufa*
(*hor·cha·ta de al·men·dra/choo·fa*) (a milky drink made from almonds)
and *granizado de limón* (*gra·nee·tha·do de lee·mon*) (a lemon drink with
crushed ice). Other soft drinks include:

70 Lemonade
    Limonada
    lee·mo·na·da

71 Orangeade
    Naranjada
    na·ran·kha·da

72 Fresh orange juice
    Zumo de naranja
    thoo·mo de na·ran·kha

73 Fresh lemon juice
    Zumo de limón
    thoo·mo de lee·mon

74 Mineral water
    Agua mineral
    ag·wa mee·ne·ral

75 A Coke/Pepsi
    Una Coca Cola/Pepsi Cola
    *oo·na ko·ka ko·la/pep·see
    ko·la*

76 Tonic water
    Tónica
    to·ni·ka

Snacks

A typically Spanish breakfast is *churros con chocolate* (**choo**·*rros kon cho·ko·***la***·te*) (sticks of fried batter dipped in hot thick chocolate in a cup, or simply with a cup of coffee). The delicious Spanish hors d'oeuvres called *tapas* (***ta***·*pas*) are also popular as a snack. Other snacks are:

77 A cheese sandwich
Un bocadillo de queso
*oon bo·ka·***deel***·yo de ke·so*

78 A toasted ham sandwich
Un sandwich de jamón
*oon sand·***weech*** *de kha·***mon**

79 A salami sandwich
Un sandwich de salchichón
*oon sand·***weech*** *de
sal·chee·***chon**

80 Potato chips
Patatas fritas
*pa·***ta***·tas **free**·tas*

81 A hard-boiled egg
Un huevo duro
oon we·bo doo·ro

82 Ham and eggs
Huevos con jamón
*we·bos kon kha·***mon**

N.B. A *bocadillo* usually means a section of French bread split down the middle with the ham etc inserted without butter. A *sandwich* usually means a toasted sliced bread sandwich.

Leisure (L)

Sightseeing

When you arrive in a town and require some general information about it you should inquire at the local *Oficina de Información y Turismo* (*o·fee·***thee***·na de een·for·ma·***thyon*** *ee too·***rees***·mo*) (Tourist Information Office). Here are some of the phrases you might wish to use there as well as in the street and at museums, churches and other sights.

1 Excuse me, can you tell me, please . . .
Perdone, puede decirme, por favor . . .
*per·***do***·ne pwe·de de·***theer***·me por fa·***bor**

2 What are the most important things to see here?
¿Qué es lo más importante de ver aquí?
*ke es lo mas eem·por·***tan***·te de ber a·***kee**

3 Where is — the main square?
¿Dónde está — la plaza mayor?
*don·de es·***ta*** — *la ***pla***·tha ma·***yor**

4 Do you have — a guidebook to the town/area (in English)?
¿Tiene — una guía de la ciudad/zona (en inglés)?
tye·ne — *oo·na gee·a de la thyoo·***dad***/
tho·na (en een·***gles***)*
— a map of the town?
— un mapa de la ciudad?
— *oon ***ma***·pa de la thyoo·***dad**
— an audio-guide to the museum/church?
— un audio-guía del museo/de la iglesia?
— *oon ow·dyo·gee·a del moo·se·o/
de la ee·***gle***·sya*

5 Are there any — local festivals?
¿Hay — fiestas locales?
ay — ***fyes***·tas lo·***ka***·les*

6 Is there — a guided tour of the town/castle?
¿Hay — una visita con guía de la ciudad/del castillo?
ay — *oo·na bee·***see***·ta kon gee·a de la
thyoo·***dad***/del kas·***teel***·yo*

Is there — a one-day excursion to Toledo?
¿Hay — una excursión de un día a Toledo?
ay — oo·na eks·koor·syon de oon dee·a
a to·le·do

7 When does the tour begin?
¿Cuándo empieza la visita?
kwan·do em·pye·tha la bee·see·ta

8 How long does it last?
¿Cuánto tiempo dura?
kwan·to tyem·po doo·ra

9 Where is the point of departure?
¿De dónde se sale?
de don·de se sa·le

10 Is there an English-speaking guide?
¿Hay un guía que hable inglés?
ay oon gee·a ke a·ble een·gles

11 What is this building?
¿Qué es este edificio?
ke es es·te e·dee·fee·thyo

12 Can we go in?
¿Podemos entrar?
po·de·mos en·trar

13 What time does the museum/castle open?
¿A qué hora abre el museo/castillo?
a ke o·ra a·bre el moo·se·o/kas·teel·yo

14 What is the admission charge?
¿Cuánto cuesta la entrada?
kwan·to kwes·ta la en·tra·da

15 Can one go to the top?
¿Se puede subir arriba?
se pwe·de soo·beer a·rree·ba

16 Is one allowed to take
photos — with flash/tripod?
¿Se pueden hacer fotos — con flash/trípode?
se pwe·den a·ther fo·tos — kon flash/tree·po·de

17 Where can one buy — slides?
¿Dónde se pueden comprar — diapositivas?
don·de se pwe·den
kom·prar — dee·a·po·see·tee·bas
— postcards?
— postales?
— pos·ta·les
— reproductions?
— reproducciones?
— re·pro·dook·thyo·nes

Beach, country and sports

Changing rooms as well as beach and sports items can often be rented on the main beaches, although sometimes only in private sections where you have to pay to enter. A red flag on Spanish and some Latin American beaches means that it is dangerous to go swimming. A yellow flag means that you can swim, but it is not recommended. If you see a green flag, go right ahead! Normally, notices will be put up.

18 Is it safe to swim here?
¿Se puede nadar sin peligro aquí?
se pwe·de na·dar seen pe·lee·gro a·kee

19 Is this a private beach?
¿Es privada esta playa?
es pree·ba·da es·ta pla·ya

20 Is the water warm/cold?
¿Está el agua caliente/fría?
es·ta el ag·wa ka·lyen·te/free·a

21 Can you recommend a quiet beach?
¿Puede recomendarme una playa tranquila?
pwe·de re·ko·men·dar·me oo·na pla·ya tran·kee·la

22 Where can we change?
   ¿Dónde podemos cambiarnos?
   don·de po·de·mos kam·byar·nos

23   Can I rent — a deck chair?
       ¿Puedo alquilar — una silla de playa?
       pwe·do al·kee·lar — oo·na seel·ya de pla·ya
           — a sunshade?
           — una sombrilla?
           — *oo·na som·breel·ya*
           — a sailboat?
           — un barco de vela?
           — *oon bar·ko de be·la*
           — a rowboat?
           — un barco de remos?
           — *oon bar·ko de re·mos*
           — a motorboat?
           — una motora?
           — *oo·na mo·to·ra*

24   Is it possible to go — sailing?
       ¿Se puede — navegar a vela?
       se pwe·de — na·be·gar a be·la
           — water-skiing?
           — hacer esquí acuático?
           — *a·ther es·kee a·kwa·tee·ko*
           — surfing?
           — hacer surfing?
           — *a·ther soor·feeng*
           — scuba diving?
           — hacer submarinismo?
           — *a·ther soob·ma·ree·nees·mo*
           — riding?
           — montar a caballo?
           — *mon·tar a ka·bal·yo*

25 What sports can one take part in here?
   ¿Qué deportes se pueden practicar aquí?
   ke de·por·tes se pwe·den prak·tee·kar a·kee

26 Is there a swimming pool?
   ¿Hay piscina?
   ay pees·thee·na

27   Where can I play — tennis?
      ¿Dónde puedo jugar al — tenis?
      don·de pwe·do khoo·gar al — te·nees
           — golf?
           — golf?
           — *golf*

28 Can I go fishing?
   ¿Se puede ir a pescar?
   se pwe·de eer a pes·kar

29 Can I rent the equipment?
   ¿Puedo alquilar el equipo?
   pwe·do al·kee·lar el e·kee·po

30 Do you know any interesting walks?
   ¿Conoce algún sitio para pasear que sea interesante?
   ko·no·the al·goon see·tyo pa·ra pa·se·ar ke se·a een·te·re·san·te

31   What are the conditions like
                      for — skiing?
        ¿Cómo están las
        condiciones para — esquiar?
        ko·mo es·tan las
        kon·dee·thyo·nes pa·ra — es·kee·ar
           — sailing?
           — hacer vela?
           — *a·ther be·la*

32 Are there any picnic areas near here?
   ¿Hay zonas de picnic cerca de aquí?
   ay tho·nas de peek·neek ther·ka de a·kee

33 What is the name of that bird/flower?
   ¿Cómo se llama ese pájaro/esa flor?
   ko·mo se lya·ma e·se pa·kha·ro/e·sa flor

Entertainment and Night life

34 How can we find out about local entertainment?
¿Cómo podemos enterarnos de las diversiones locales?
ko·mo po·de·mos en·te·rar·nos de las dee·ber·syo·nes lo·ka·les

35 Where can one go — to hear jazz/folk music?
¿Dónde se puede ir — a oír jazz/música folk?
don·de se pwe·de eer — a o·eer jass moo·see·ka folk

— to see real flamenco dancing?
— a ver baile flamenco auténtico?
— *a ber bay·le fla·men·ko ow·ten·tee·ko*

— to dance?
— a bailar?
— *a bay·lar*

— to see a floor show?
— a ver un cabaret?
a ber oon ka·ba·re?

36 Are there any — movies in English?
¿Hay — alguna película en inglés?
ay — *al·goo·na pe·lee·koo·la en een·gles*

— good night clubs/discos?
— algún club nocturno bueno/discoteca buena?
— *al·goon kloob nok·toor·no bwe·no/ dees·ko·te·ka bwe·na*

— good concerts?
— algún buen concierto?
— *al·goon bwen kon·thyer·to*

37 Have you any seats — for Wednesday evening?
¿Tiene entradas — para el miércoles por la noche?
tye·ne en·tra·das — *pa·ra el myer·ko·les por la no·che*

38 I should like to reserve — a box
Querría reservar — un palco
ke·rree·a re·ser·bar — *oon pal·ko*

— two seats in the balcony/orchestra
— dos entradas de anfiteatro/butaca
— *dos en·tra·das de an·fee·te·a·tro/ boo·ta·ka*

39 What is being performed?
¿Qué están poniendo?
ke es·tan po·nyen·do

40 Who is singing/playing?
¿Quién canta/toca?
kyen kan·ta/to·ka

41 How long does the performance last?
¿Cuánto dura la actuación?
kwan·to doo·ra la ak·twa·thyon

42 Where can one buy a program?
¿Dónde puedo comprar un programa?
don·de pwe·do kom·prar oon pro·gra·ma

43 Is there — an intermission?
¿Hay — intermedio?
ay — *een·ter·me·dyo*

— a snack bar/liquor bar?
— cafetería/bar?
— *ka·fe·te·ree·a/bar*

44 When does the performance/floor show begin?
¿Cuándo empieza la actuación/el espectáculo?
kwan·do em·pye·tha la ak·twa·thyon/el es·pek·ta·koo·lo

45 How much do the drinks cost?
¿Cuánto cuestan las bebidas?
kwan·to kwes·tan las be·bee·das

46 Is there a minimum/cover charge?
¿Hay un precio mínimo?
ay oon pre·thyo mee·nee·mo

Gambling

Your hotel or the local tourist information office should be able to advise you about the best casinos in your area. Without entering in detail into the international language of gambling, we include here some of the phrases you might need in a casino. You will need to recognize the phrases "Hagan juego" (*a·gan khwe·go*) (place your bets), and, "No va más" (*no ba mas*) (no more bets).

47 What is the minimum/ maximum stake?
 ¿Cuál es la mínima/máxima apuesta?
 kwal es la mee·nee·ma/ mak·see·ma a·pwes·ta

48 Where can I cash my chips?
 ¿Dónde puedo cambiar mis fichas?
 don·de pwe·do kam·byar mees fee·chas

49 Must one be a member to play here?
 ¿Hay que ser miembro para jugar aquí?
 ay ke ser myem·bro pa·ra khoo·gar a·kee

50 Am I allowed to tip the croupier?
 ¿Puedo darle una propina al croupier?
 pwe·do dar·le oo·na pro·pee·na al kroo·pyer

51 Where is the cashier's cage?
 ¿Dónde está la caja?
 don·de es·ta la ka·kha

52 Do you have a blackjack table here?
 ¿Tienen mesa de veintiuna aquí?
 tye·nen me·sa de beyn·tee·oo·na a·kee

53 I double (in backgammon)
 Doblo
 do·blo

54 May I have my passport back, please?
 ¿Puede devolverme el pasaporte, por favor?
 pwe·de de·bol·ber·me el pa·sa·por·te por fa·bor

Shopping (s)

General

1 What time do you close/open?
 ¿A qué hora cierran/abren?
 a ke o·ra thye·rran/a·bren

2 One of these, please
 Uno de estos, por favor
 oo·no de es·tos por fa·bor

3 Two of those, please
 Dos de aquellos, por favor
 dos de a·kel·yos por fa·bor

4 How much does that cost?
 ¿Cuánto cuesta eso?
 kwan·to kwes·ta e·so

5 I am willing to pay up to 30,000 pesetas
 Estoy dispuesto a gastarme hasta 30.000 pesetas
 es·toy dees·pwes·to a gas·tar·me as·ta treyn·ta meel pe·se·tas

6 I should like to buy — some presents
 Quiero comprar — unos regalos
 kye·ro kom·prar — oo·nos re·ga·los

7 Do you sell — sunglasses?
 ¿Venden — gafas de sol?
 ben·den — ga·fas de sol

8 Do you have any — pencils?
 ¿Tienen — lápices?
 tye·nen — la·pee·thes

9 I need — some suntan oil
 Necesito — aceite bronceador
 ne·the·see·to — a·they·te bron·the·a·dor

10 Do you sell duty-free goods?
¿Venden artículos libres de impuestos?
ben·den ar·**tee**·koo·los **lee**·bres de cem·**pwes**·tos

11   Where is — the shoe department?
                ¿Dónde está — la sección de zapatos?
             don·de es·**ta** — la sek·**thyon** de tha·**pa**·tos
                                — the food department?
                                — la sección de comestibles?
                                — la sek·**thyon** de ko·mes·**tee**·bles

12   Can I see — the hat in the window?
           ¿Puede enseñarme — el sombrero del escaparate?
        pwe·de en·sen·**yar**·me — el som·**bre**·ro del es·**ka**·pa·ra·te
                                — that hat over there?
                                — aquel sombrero de allí?
                                — a·**kel** som·**bre**·ro de al·**yee**

13 No, the other one
No, el otro
no el **o**·tro

14   Have you anything — cheaper?
               ¿Tiene algo — más barato?
             tye·ne **al**·go — mas ba·**ra**·to
                         — second-hand?
                         — de segunda mano?
                         — de se·**goon**·da **ma**·no

15 Can you show me how it works?
¿Me puede enseñar cómo funciona?
me **pwe**·de en·sen·yar **ko**·mo foon·**thyo**·na

16 I need a gadget for …
Necesito un chisme para …
ne·the·**see**·to oon **chees**·me **pa**·ra

17   Have you got — a larger one?
               ¿Tiene — uno más grande?
               tye·ne — **oo**·no mas **gran**·de
                       — a smaller one?
                       — uno más pequeño?
                       — **oo**·no mas pe·**ken**·yo

18 I'm just looking
Sólo estoy mirando
so·lo es·**toy** mee·**ran**·do

19   I'm looking for — a blouse
              Estoy buscando — una blusa
            es·**toy** boos·**kan**·do — **oo**·na **bloo**·sa

20 I like this one
Me gusta éste/ésta
me **goos**·ta **es**·te/**es**·ta

21 I don't like it
No me gusta
no me **goos**·ta

22   I'll take — this one
               Me llevo — éste/ésta
             me **lye**·bo — **es**·te/**es**·ta
                    — that one
                    — ése/ésa
                    — **e**·se/**e**·sa
                    — the other one
                    — el otro/la otra
                    — el **o**·tro/la **o**·tra

23 Please wrap it
Envuélvamelo por favor
en·**bwel**·ba·me·lo por fa·**bor**

24 There's no need to wrap it, thank you
No hace falta que lo envuelva
no **a**·the **fal**·ta ke lo en·**bwel**·ba

25 Can I have a plastic bag?
¿Puede darme una bolsa de plástico?
pwe·de **dar**·me **oo**·na **bol**·sa de **plas**·tee·ko

26 How much would it cost to send it to England/America?
¿Cuánto cuesta enviarlo a Inglaterra/América?
kwan·to **kwes**·ta en·bee·**ar**·lo a een·gla·**te**·rra/a·**me**·ree·ka

27 Please send it to this address
Por favor envíelo a esta dirección
*por fa·**bor** en·**bee**·e·lo a **es**·ta dee·rek·**thyon**

28 Please pack it carefully
Envuélvalo con cuidado, por favor
*en·**bwel**·ba·lo kon kwee·**da**·do por fa·**bor***

Food and drink

Spain boasts countless small family-run food shops and open-air markets
with stalls, which make for infinitely better shopping than the new
supermarkets. A word about weights. A kilo is just over two pounds. For
smaller and intermediate weights you would normally ask for x number
of grams (gramos: *gra·mos*).

The Spanish place great importance on what they eat and drink,
particularly on weekends. Be adventurous and try unfamiliar things if you
want to get the best out of your stay.

29 Where can I find — a baker/butcher?
¿Dónde hay — una panadería/carnicería?
*don·de ay — oo·na pa·na·de·ree·a/
kar·nee·the·ree·a*

30 Is there a health food shop near here?
¿Hay una herboristería cerca de aquí?
ay oo·na er·bo·rees·te·ree·a ther·ka de a·kee

31 What sort of cheese/butter do you have?
¿Qué clase de queso/mantequilla tiene?
ke kla·se de ke·so/man·te·keel·ya tye·ne

32 I would like — a kilo of grapes
Querría — un kilo de uvas
ke·rree·a — oon kee·lo de oo·bas

— half a kilo of tomatoes
— medio kilo de tomates
— *me·dyo kee·lo de to·ma·tes*

— a quarter kilo of sugar
— un cuarto de kilo de azúcar
— *oon kwar·to de kee·lo de
a·thoo·kar*

— 100 grams of ground coffee
— cien gramos de café molido
— *thyen gra·mos de ka·fe mo·lee·do*

— 5 slices of ham
— cinco lonchas de jamón
— *theen·ko lon·chas de kha·mon*

— half a dozen eggs
— media docena de huevos
— *me·dya do·the·na de we·bos*

33 A package of salt, please
Un paquete de sal, por favor
oon pa·ke·te de sal por fa·bor

34 A can of peas
Una lata de guisantes
oo·na la·ta de gee·san·tes

35 A liter of milk
Un litro de leche
oon lee·tro de le·che

36 A bottle of wine
Una botella de vino
oo·na bo·tel·ya de bee·no

37 Two pork chops
Dos chuletas de cerdo
dos choo·le·tas de ther·do

38 I would like enough for two
people
Quisiera suficiente para dos
personas
*kee·sye·ra soo·fee·thyen·te
pa·ra dos per·so·nas*

39 Shall I help myself?
¿Lo cojo yo mismo(a)?
lo ko·kho yo mees·mo(a)

Pharmacist

In Spain a pharmacist should be able to help you with the usual holiday
ailments. There will be an illuminated green cross outside and a sign
saying *Farmacia* (far·**ma**·thya). Although a pharmacist will stock some
toiletries and cosmetics, for a wider range you will have to go to a
Perfumería (per·foo·me·**ree**·a) or a *Droguería* (dro·ge·**ree**·a).

40   I want something for — a headache
       Necesito algo para — el dolor de cabeza
       ne·the·see to al·go pa·ra — *el do·lor de ka·be·tha*
                            — insect bites
                            — las picaduras de insectos
                            — *las pee·ka·doo·ras de een·sek·tos*
                            — chapped skin
                            — la piel agrietada
                            — *la pyel a·gree·e·ta·da*
                            — a cold
                            — el resfriado
                            — *el res·free·a·do*
                            — a cough
                            — la tos
                            — *la tos*
                            — hay fever
                            — la fiebre del heno
                            — *la fye·bre del e·no*
                            — a sore throat
                            — el dolor de garganta
                            — *el do·lor de gar·gan·ta*
                            — sunburn
                            — la quemadura del sol
                            — *la ke·ma·doo·ra del sol*
                            — toothache
                            — el dolor de muelas
                            — *el do·lor de mwe·las*
                            — an upset stomach
                            — un trastorno estomacal
                            — *oon tras·tor·no es·to·ma·kal*

41 How many do I take?
    ¿Cuántas tengo que tomar?
    kwan·tas ten·go ke to·mar

42 How often do I take them?
    ¿Cada cuánto tiempo tengo
    que tomarlas?
    *ka·da kwan·to tyem·po ten·go
    ke to·mar·las*

43 Are they safe for children to
    take?
    ¿Pueden tomarlo los niños?
    *pwe·den to·mar·lo los
    neen·yos*

44 Could I see a selection of
    perfume/toilet water?
    ¿Puede ensenarme una
    selección de perfumes/agua
    de colonia?
    *pwe·de en·sen·yar·me oo·na
    se·lek·thyon de per·foo·mes/
    ag·wa de ko·lo·nya*

45 I would like something with a
    floral scent
    Quiero algo con olor a flores
    kye·ro al·go kon o·lor a flo·res

46 May I smell/try it please?
    ¿Puedo olerlo/probarlo, por
    favor?
    *pwe·do o·ler·lo/pro·bar·lo por
    fa·bor*

Cameras and film

47   I need film — for this camera
       Necesito una película — para esta cámara
       ne·the·see·to oo·na
       pe·lee·koo·la — *pa·ra es·ta ka·ma·ra*
                      — for this cine-camera
                      — para este tomavistas
                      — *pa·ra es·te to·ma·bees·tas*

48   I want — 35mm black and white film
       Quiero — un carrete de 35mm en blanco y
                negro
       kye·ro — *oon ka·rre·te de treyn·ta ee
                  theen·ko mee·lee·me·tros en
                  blan·ko ee ne·gro*
               — fast/slow film
               — una película rápida/lenta
               — *oo·na pe·lee·koo·la ra·pee·da/
                  len·ta*

I want — a color-print film
Quiero — una película en color
kye·ro — *oo·na pe·**lee**·koo·la en ko·**lor***
— a color-slide film
— una película de diapositivas en color
— *oo·na pe·**lee**·koo·la de dee·a·po·see·**tee**·bas en ko·**lor***
— batteries for the flash
— pilas para el flash
— *pee·las **pa**·ra el flash*

49 **Can you develop this film, please?**
¿Puede revelar esta película, por favor?
*pwe·de re·be·**lar** es·ta pe·**lee**·koo·la por fa·**bor***

50 **I would like two prints of this one**
Querría dos copias de esta
*ke·**rree**·a dos **ko**·pyas de es·ta*

51 **When will the photographs be ready?**
¿Para cuándo estarán las fotos?
*pa·ra **kwan**·do es·ta·**ran** las **fo**·tos*

52 **I would like this print enlarged**
Querría una ampliación de esta foto
*ke·**rree**·a oo·na am·plee·a·**thyon** de es·ta **fo**·to*

53 **There is something wrong with my camera**
Mi cámara fotográfica no va bien
*mee **ka**·ma·ra fo·to·**gra**·fee·ka no ba byen*

54 **The film is jammed**
La película está atascada
*la pe·**lee**·koo·la es·**ta** a·tas·**ka**·da*

55 **I would like to buy a camera**
   with — a single-lens reflex
Quisiera comprar una cámara — reflex
*kee·**sye**·ra kom·**prar** oo·na*
   ka·ma·ra — *re·**fleks***
— built-in light meter
— con exposímetro incorporado
— *kon eks·po·**see**·me·tro een·kor·po·**ra**·do*
— instant developing
— con revelado instantáneo
— *kon re·be·**la**·do eens·tan·**ta**·neo*

56 **I need a** — flash attachment
Necesito — un aparato de flash
*ne·the·**see**·to* — *oon a·pa·**ra**·to de flash*
— close-up/wide-angle lens
— objetivo de primer plano/gran angular
— *ob·khe·**tee**·bo de pree·**mer pla**·no/ gran an·goo·**lar***
— camera case
— una funda para la máquina
— *oo·na **foon**·da **pa**·ra la **ma**·kee·na*

Clothes and shoes

---

57   **I am looking for** — a dress
Estoy buscando — un vestido
*es·**toy** boos·**kan**·do* — *oon bes·**tee**·do*
— a sweater
— un jersey
— *oon kher·sey*

58   **I would like something** — informal
Querría algo — de sport
*ke·**rree**·a **al**·go* — *de sport*
— for evening wear
— de vestir
— *de bes·**teer***

I would like something — for a cocktail party
Querría algo — para una fiesta
ke·**rree**·a al·go — **pa**·ra oo·na **fyes**·ta

59 Can you please show me
some — sun dresses?
¿Puede enseñarme algunos — vestidos de verano?
pwe·de en·sen·**yar**·me
al·**goo**·nos — bes·**tee**·dos de be·**ra**·no
— silk shirts?
— camisas de seda?
— ka·**mee**·sas de **se**·da

60 I would like to have a suit/pair of shoes custom-made
Quisiera que me hiciera un traje/unos zapatos a medida
kee·**sye**·ra ke me ee·**thye**·ra oon **tra**·khe/**oo**·nos tha·**pa**·tos
a me·**dee**·da

61 I would prefer a — dark material
Preferiría — una tela oscura
pre·fe·ree·**ree**·a — **oo**·na te·la os·**koo**·ra
— natural fiber
— fibra natural
— **fee**·bra na·too·**ral**

In Latin America clothes sizes are as in the United States. Shoe sizes are
as on the Continent.

62 I take a (continental) size 40
Uso la talla cuarenta
oo·so la **tal**·ya kwa·**ren**·ta

63 I take a (continental) shoe size 40
Calzo un cuarenta
kal·tho oon kwa·**ren**·ta

64 Can you measure me?
¿Puede medirme?
pwe·de me·**deer**·me

65 What is the material?
¿Qué tela es?
ke **te**·la es

66 Do you have this — in blue?
¿Tiene esto — en azul?
tye·ne es·to — en a·**thool**

67 I like — this one
Me gusta — éste/ésta
me **goos**·ta — **es**·te/**es**·ta
— that one there
— aquél/aquella de allí
— a·**kel**/a·**kel**·ya de al·**yee**
— the one in the window
— él del escaparate
— el del es·ka·pa·**ra**·te

68 May I see it in the daylight?
¿Puedo verlo a la luz?
pwe·do **ber**·lo a la **looth**

69 May I try it on?
¿Puedo probarlo?
pwe·do pro·**bar**·lo

70 Where are the dressing rooms?
¿Dónde están los probadores?
don·de es·**tan** los pro·ba·**do**·res

71 I would like a mirror
Un espejo, por favor
oon es·**pe**·kho por fa·**bor**

72 It is too — tight
Es demasiado — estrecho
es de·ma·**sya**·do — es·**tre**·cho
— small
— pequeño
— pe·**ken**·yo
— big
— grande
— **gran**·de

73 Can you — alter it?
¿Puede Ud — arreglarlo?
pwe·de oos·**ted** — a·rre·**glar**·lo

74	Can you — take it in?	
	¿Puede Ud — meterlo?	
	pwe·de oos ted — me·**ter**·lo?	
	— let it out?	
	— sacarlo?	
	— sa·**kar**·lo	
75	I'd like one — with a zipper	
	Quiero uno — con cremallera	
	kye·ro oo·no — kon kre·mal·**ye**·ra	
	— without a belt	
	— sin cinturón	
	— seen theen·too·**ron**	

76	I like it	81	Is this all you have?
	Me gusta		¿No tiene más que esto?
	me **goos**·ta		no **tye**·ne mas ke **es**·to
77	I don't like it	82	I'll take it
	No me gusta		Me lo llevo
	no me **goos**·ta		me lo **lye**·bo
78	I prefer the blue one	83	Is it washable?
	Prefiero el azul		¿Es lavable?
	pre·**fye**·ro el a·**thool**		es la·**ba**·ble
79	It does not suit me	84	Will it shrink?
	No me va bien		¿Encogerá?
	no me ba byen		en·ko·khe·**ra**
80	It does not fit	85	Must it be dry-cleaned?
	No me sienta bien		¿Hay que limpiarlo en seco?
	no me **syen**·ta byen		ay ke leem·**pyar**·lo en **se**·ko

Jewelers, silversmiths and watchmakers

86	Have you any — antique/modern jewelery?
	¿Tiene Ud — joyas antiguas/modernas?
	tye·ne oos ted — **kho**·yas an·**tee**·gwas/ mo·**der**·nas
87	I am a collector of silverware/brooches
	Soy coleccionista de plata/broches
	soy ko·lek·thyo·**nees**·ta de **pla**·ta/**bro**·ches
88	Could you show me a
	selection of your — rings/watches?
	¿Puede enseñarme una
	selección de — anillos/relojes?
	pwe·de en·sen·yar·me
	oo·na se·lek·thyon de — a·**neel**·yos/re·**lo**·khes
89	What precious stone is this?
	¿Qué piedra preciosa es ésta?
	ke **pye**·dra pre·**thyo**·sa es **es**·ta
90	Is this solid gold/silver?
	(most gold sold in Spain is 14 – 18 carat gold)
	¿Es esto oro/plata macizo(a)?
	es **es**·to **o**·ro/**pla**·ta ma·**thee**·tho(a)
91	Is it gold-/silver-plated?
	¿Es oro/plata chapado(a)?
	es **o**·ro/**pla**·ta cha·**pa**·do(a)
92	Can you repair — this watch/this necklace?
	¿Puede arreglarme — este reloj/collar?
	pwe·de a·rre·glar·me — **es**·te re·**lokh**/kol·**yar**

Books, newspapers, postcards and stationery

If you want a newspaper, you will get it at a newsstand, *un quiosco de periódicos* (*kee·os·ko de pe·ree·o·dee·kos*), while stationery is generally sold along with books in a *librería-papelería* (*lee·bre·ree·a pa·pe·le·ree·a*). Major foreign newspapers are available on the larger stands, sometimes a day or two late outside Madrid.

93	Do you have any — English/American newspapers?
	¿Tiene — periódicos ingleses/
	norteamericanos?
	tye·ne — *pe·ryo·dee·kos een·gle·ses/*
	nor·te·a·me·ree·ka·nos
	— postcards?
	— tarjetas postales?
	— *tar·khe·tas pos·ta·les*
94	I would like — some notepaper
	Quiero — papel de escribir
	kye·ro — *pa·pel de es·kree·beer*
	— some envelopes
	— sobres
	— *so·bres*
	— some mailing envelopes
	— sobres acolchados
	— *so·bres a·kol·cha·dos*
	— a ball-point pen
	— un bolígrafo
	— *oon bo·lee·gra·fo*
	— a pencil
	— un lápiz
	— *oon la·peeth*
95	I need — some airmail stickers/envelopes
	Necesito — etiquetas/sobres de avión
	ne·the·see·to — *e·tee·ke·tas/so·bres de a·byon*
	— some Scotch tape
	— papel celo
	— *pa·pel the·lo*
96	Do you sell — English paperbacks?
	¿Venden — libros de bolsillo en inglés?
	ben·den — *lee·bros de bol·seel·yo en een·gles*
	— street maps?
	— planos de la ciudad?
	— *pla·nos de la thyoo·dad*
97	Have you a postcard — of the Alhambra?
	¿Tiene una postal — de la Alhambra?
	tye·ne oo·na pos·tal — *de la a·lam·bra*

Tobacco shop

In Spain tobacco is sold in little shops called *estancos* (*es·tan·kos*), which have a red, yellow and red sign outside saying *Tabacalera SA*, as well as in most bars and cafés. British and American brands are available along with the stronger Spanish ones (the most common are "Ducados"). *Estancos* also sell stamps. In Latin America stamps are sold in the post offices (*correos: ko·rre·os*), at *Telecom* offices, and the drugstores.

98	A packet of ... please — with filter tip
	Un paquete de ... por favor — con filtro
	oon pa·ke·te de ... por fa·bor — *kon feel·tro*
	— without filter
	— sin filtro
	— *seen feel·tro*

99	Have you got any American/ English brands? ¿Tiene marcas inglesas/ norteamericanas? *tye·ne mar·kas een·gle·sas/ nor·te·a·me·ree·ka·nas*	102	A box of matches Una caja de cerillas/fósforos *oo·na ka·kha de the·reel·yas/fos·fo·ros*
100	A package of pipe tobacco Un paquete de tabaco de pipa *oon pa·ke·te de ta·ba·ko de pee·pa*	103	A cigar Un puro *oon poo·ro*
101	Some pipe cleaners Escobillas (para limpiar pipas) *es·ko·beel·yas (pa·ra leem·pyar pee·pas)*	104	A cigarette lighter Un encendedor *oon en·then·de·dor*
		105	A butane refill Un recambio para encendedor de gas *oon re·kam·byo pa·ra en·then·de·dor de gas*

Presents and souvenirs

106 I am looking for a present for my wife/husband
Busco un regalo para mi mujer/marido
boos·ko oon re·ga·lo pa·ra mee moo·kher/ma·ree·do

107 I would like to pay between 2,000 and 3,000 pesetas
Quisiera gastarme entre 2.000 y 3.000 pesetas
kee·sye·ra gas·tar·me en·tre dos meel ee tres meel pe·se·tas

108 Can you suggest anything?
¿Puede sugerirme algo?
pwe·de soo·khe·reer·me al·go

109 Have you anything suitable for a ten-year-old girl/boy?
¿Tiene algo apropiado para un niño/una niña de 10 años?
tye·ne al·go a·pro·pya·do pa·ra oon neen·yo/oo·na neen·ya de dyeth an·yos

110   Do you have something — made locally?
            ¿Tiene algo — hecho localmente?
            tye·ne al·go — *e·cho lo·kal·men·te*
                          — handmade?
                          — hecho a mano?
                          — *e·cho a ma·no*
                          — unusual?
                          — original?
                          — *o·ree·khee·nal*

Services and everyday needs (Sn)

Post office

A large Spanish post office (*correos: ko·rre·os*) can be rather confusing with a long row of desks, each providing a specific service. The ones you are most likely to need are those dealing with stamps (*venta de sellos*) and parcels (*paquetes*). Some *correos* open from 9:00 to 14:00, others open from 9:00 to 13:00, close for lunch and open again from 16:00 to 19:00. All are open Monday to Saturday. Allow 4 – 10 days for mail from abroad to reach Spain and 10 – 20 days for mail to Latin America.

1   How much is a letter — to Britain?
            ¿Qué franqueo lleva
              una carta — a Gran Bretaña?
            ke fran·ke·o lye·ba
              oo·na kar·ta — *a gran bre·tan·ya*
                          — to the United States?
                          — a los Estados Unidos?
                          — *a los es·ta·dos oo·nee·dos*

2 Six 40-peseta stamps, please
Seis sellos de cuarenta pesetas, por favor
seys sel·yos de kwa·ren·ta pe·se·tas por fa·bor

3 I would like six stamps for postcards/letters
Me da seis sellos par tarjetas postales/cartas
me da seys sel·yos pa·ra tar·khe·tas pos·ta·les/kar·tas
                          — to Britain
                          — a Gran Bretaña
                          — *a gran bre·tan·ya*
                          — to the United States
                          — a los Estados Unidos
                          — *a los es·ta·dos oo·nee·dos*

4   I want to send — this parcel
            Quiero enviar — este paquete
            kye·ro en·byar — *es·te pa·ke·te*
                          — a telegram
                          — un telegrama
                          — *oon te·le·gra·ma*

5 A telegram form, please
Un impreso para telegrama, por favor
oon eem·pre·so pa·ra te·le·gra·ma por fa·bor
6 When will it arrive?
¿Cuándo llegará?
kwan·do lye·ga·ra
7 I want to send this by registered mail
Quiero enviar esto por correo certificado
kye·ro en·byar es·to por ko·rre·o ther·tee·fee·ka·do
8 I am expecting a letter general delivery
Estoy esperando una carta a lista de correos
es·toy es·pe·ran·do oo·na kar·ta a lees·ta de ko·rre·os

Telephoning

The simplest but most expensive way to telephone is from your hotel, but
otherwise you will have to go to a *central telefónica* (*then·tral
te·le·fo·nee·ka*), or *Telecom* in Latin America. Tell the clerk the country
or place you want and he will direct you to a booth. You dial the number
yourself and the clerk will charge you afterwards, but he will connect you
for person-to-person and collect calls. Pay phones in the streets and in
bars require coins, and have lists of international and national dialing
codes.

Phrases you will use

9 Hello
Dígame/Diga
dee·ga·me/dee·ga
10 This is Peter Williams
Peter Williams al habla
Peter Williams al a·bla
11 Can I speak to Señor Villegas?
¿Podría hablar con el Señor Villegas?
po·dree·a a·blar kon el sen·yor beel·ye·gas
12 I would like to make a phone call to Britain/the United States
Quisiera hacer una llamada telefónica a Gran Bretaña/los
    Estados Unidos
*kee·sye·ra a·ther oo·na lya·ma·da te·le·fo·nee·ka a gran
    bre·tan·ya/los es·ta·dos oo·nee·dos*
13 The number I want is . . .
Quiero el número . . .
kye·ro el noo·me·ro
14   I wish to make — a collect call
            Quiero hacer — una llamada a cobro revertido
            kye·ro a·ther — *oo·na lya·ma·da a ko·bro
                                re·ber·tee·do*
                          — a person-to-person call
                          — una llamada de persona a persona
                          — *oo·na lya·ma·da de per·so·na a
                                per·so·na*
15 What is the dialing code for Zaragoza/Los Angeles?
¿Cuál es el prefijo para Zaragoza/Los Angeles?
kwal es el pre·fee·kho pa·ra tha·ra·go·tha/los an·khe·les
16 Would you write it down for me, please?
¿Puede escribirlo, por favor?
pwe·de es·kree·beer·lo por fa·bor
17 Can you put me through to international directory assistance?
¿Puede ponerme con información internacional?
pwe·de po·ner·me kon een·for·ma·thyon een·ter·na·thyo·nal
18 Which booth do I use?
¿Qué cabina uso?
ke ka·bee·na oo·so
19 May I use the phone, please?
¿Puedo usar el teléfono, por favor?
pwe·do oo·sar el te·le·fo·no por fa·bor

20 Do I need a token?
   ¿Hace falta ficha?
   a·the fal·ta fee·cha
21 Can I have three tokens,
   please?
   Tres fichas, por favor
   tres fee·chas por fa·bor
22 I have a bad connection
   Hay un cruce de línea
   ay oon kroo·the de lee·ne·a
23 We have been cut off
   Se ha cortado la comunicación
   *se ha kor·ta·do la
   ko·moo·nee·ka·thyon*
24 How much does it cost to
   telephone California/
   Argentina?
   ¿Cuánto cuesta llamar por
   teléfono a California/
   Argentina?
   *kwan·to kwes·ta lya·mar por
   te·le·fo·no a ka·lee·for·nya/
   ar·khen·tee·na*

25 Is there a cheap rate?
   ¿Hay una tarifa económica?
   *ay oo·na ta·ree·fa
   e·ko·no·mee·ka*
26 What is the time now in
   Ecuador?
   ¿Qué hora es ahora en el
   Ecuador?
   *ke o·ra es a·o·ra en el
   e·kwa·dor*
27 I cannot get through
   No consigo comunicar
   no kon·see·go ko·moo·nee·kar
28 Can I check this number/code?
   ¿Puedo comprobar este
   número/prefijo?
   *pwe·do kom·pro·bar es·te
   noo·me·ro/pre·fee·kho*
29 Do you have a directory for
   Toledo?
   ¿Tiene una guía telefónica de
   Toledo?
   *tye·ne oo·na gee·a
   te·le·fo·nee·ka de to·le·do*

Phrases you will hear

30 ¿Quién es?
   kyen es
   Who is speaking?
31 Estoy poniéndole con el Señor . . .
   es·toy po·nyen·do·le kon el sen·yor . . .
   I am putting you through to Señor . . .
32 No cuelgue/Un momento
   no kwel·ge/oon mo·men·to
   Hold the line
33 Estoy intentando ponerle
   es·toy een·ten·tan·do po·ner·le
   I am trying to connect you
34 Está comunicando
   es·ta ko·moo·nee·kan·do
   The line is busy
35 Pruebe más tarde, por favor
   prwe·be mas tar·de por fa·bor
   Please try later
36 Este número está estropeado
   es·te noo·me·ro es·ta es·tro·pe·a·do
   This number is out of order
37 No puedo obtener este número
   no pwe·do ob·te·ner es·te noo·me·ro
   I cannot reach this number
38 Hable, por favor
   a·ble por fa·bor
   Please go ahead

The hairdresser

39 I'd like to make an appointment
   Querría pedir hora
   ke·rree·a pe·deer o·ra
40   I want — a haircut
           Quiero — cortar
           kye·ro — kor·tar
                  — a trim
                  — cortar las puntas
                  — *kor·tar las poon·tas*
                  — a blow-dry
                  — secar con el secador a mano
                  — *se·kar kon el se·ka·dor a ma·no*

41	I want my hair	— fairly short
	Quiero el pelo	— bastante corto
	kye·ro el pe·lo	— *bas·tan·te kor·to*
		— not too short
		— no muy corto
		— *no mooy kor·to*
		— short and curly
		— corto y rizado
		— *kor·to ee ree·tha·do*
		— layered
		— en capas
		— *en ka·pas*
		— in bangs
		— con flequillo
		— *kon fle·keel·yo*
42	Take more off	— the front
	Córteme más	— por delante
	kor·te·me mas	— *por de·lan·te*
		— the back
		— por detrás
		— *por de·tras*
43	Not too much off	— the sides
	No me corte mucho	— a los lados
	no me kor·te moo·cho	— *a los la·dos*
		— the top
		— por arriba
		— *por a·rree·ba*
44	I like a part	— in the center
	Quiero la raya	— en el centro
	kye·ro la ra·ya	— *en el then·tro*
		— on the left
		— a la izquierda
		— *a la eeth·kyer·da*
		— on the right
		— a la derecha
		— *a la de·re·cha*
	I'd like	— a perm
	Querría	— una permanente
	ke·rree·a	— *oo·na per·ma·nen·te*
		— a curly perm
		— una permanente rizada
		— *oo·na per·ma·nen·te ree·tha·da*
		— a shampoo and set
		— lavar y marcar
		— *la·bar ee mar·kar*
		— my hair tinted
		— teñir el pelo
		— *ten·yeer el pe·lo*
		— my hair streaked
		— ponerme mechas
		— *po·ner·me me·chas*
45	I'd like	— a conditioner
	Querría	— un acondicionador
	ke·rree·a	— *oon a·kon·dee·thyo·na·dor*
		— hair spray
		— laca
		— *la·ka*

46 The water is too hot/cold
El agua está demasiado caliente/fría
el ag·wa es·ta de·ma·sya·do ka·lyen·te/free·a

47 The dryer is too hot/cold
El secador está demasiado caliente/frío
el se·ka·dor es·ta de·ma·sya·do ka·lyen·te/free·o

48 That's fine, thank you
Así está bien, gracias
a·see es·ta byen gra·thyas

Repairs and technical jobs

The following list tells you how to describe some of the things for which you might need the help of a specialist during your stay (cars are dealt with on p. 18, clothes on p. 57).

49 Where can I get this repaired?
¿Dónde pueden reparar esto?
don·de pwe·den re·pa·rar es·to

50 I am having trouble with my heating/plumbing
La calefacción/la cañería no funciona bien
la ka·le·fak·thyon/la kan·ye·ree·a no foon·thyo·na byen

This is —	broken
Esto está —	roto
es·to es·ta —	*ro·to*

51 This is not working
Esto no funciona
es·to no foon·thyo·na

52 This is damaged
Esto está estropeado
es·to es·ta es·tro·pe·a·do

53 This is blocked
Esto está atascado
es·to es·ta a·tas·ka·do

54 This is torn
Esto está rasgado
es·to es·ta ras·ga·do

55 There is a leak in the pipe/roof
Hay una gotera en el tubo/techo
ay oo·na go·te·ra en el too·bo/te·cho

56 There is a gas leak
Hay un escape de gas
ay oon es·ka·pe de gas

57 Would you have a look at this, please?
¿Podría mirarme esto, por favor?
po·dree·a mee·rar·me es·to por fa·bor

58	Can you repair —	my suitcase?
	¿Puede reparar —	mi maleta?
	pwe·de re·pa·rar —	*mee ma·le·ta?*
59	Can you —	reheel/resole these shoes?
	¿Puede —	poner tacón/suela a estos zapatos?
	pwe·de —	*po·ner ta·kon/swe·la a es·tos tha·pa·tos*
		— get it working again?
		— arreglarlo?
		— *a·rre·glar·lo*

60 Have you got a replacement part?
¿Tiene una pieza de repuesto?
tye·ne oo·na pye·tha de re·pwes·to

61 When will it be ready?
¿Cuándo estará listo?
kwan·do es·ta·ra lees·to

62 Can you do it quickly?
¿Puede hacerlo rápidamente?
pwe·de a·ther·lo ra·pee·da·men·te

63 I would like a duplicate of this key
Quisiera una copia de esta llave
kee·sye·ra oo·na ko·pya de es·ta lya·be

64	I have —	lost my key
	He —	perdido mi llave
	e —	*per·dee·do mee lya·be*
		— locked myself out
	Me he —	quedado fuera sin llave
	me e —	*ke·da·do fwe·ra seen lya·be*

65 Can you open the door?
¿Puede abrirme la puerta?
pwe·de a·breer·me la pwer·ta

66 The fuse for the lights has blown
   Se han fundido los plomos
   se an foon·dee·do los plo·mos

67 There is a loose connection
   Hay una conexión floja
   ay oo·na ko·nek·syon flo·kha

68 Sometimes it works, sometimes it doesn't
   A veces funciona, otras veces no
   a be·thes foon·thyo·na o·tras be·thes no

Laundry, dry cleaners and clothes-mending

A dry cleaner's is called *una tintorería* (*teen·to·re·ree·a*) or *una limpieza en seco* (*leem·pye·tha en se·ko*). Sometimes it is combined with *una lavandería* (*la·ban·de·ree·a*) (laundry), which will usually provide fairly quick service. A laundromat is *una lavandería automática* (*la·ban·de·ree·a ow·to·ma·tee·ka*).

69   Will you — clean this skirt?
                          ¿Puede — limpiar esta falda?
                          pwe·de — *leem·pyar es·ta fal·da*
                                 — press these trousers?
                                 — planchar estos pantalones?
                                 — *plan·char es·tos pan·ta·lo·nes*
                                 — wash and iron these shirts?
                                 — lavar y planchar estas camisas?
                                 — *la·bar ee plan·char es·tas ka·mee·sas*
                                 — wash these clothes?
                                 — lavar esta ropa?
                                 — *la·bar es·ta ro·pa*

70   This stain is — grease/ink
   Esta mancha es — de grasa/tinta
   es·ta man·cha es — *de gra·sa/teen·ta*

71 Can you get this stain out?
   ¿Puede quitar esta mancha?
   pwe·de kee·tar es·ta man·cha

72 This fabric is delicate
   Este tejido es delicado
   es·te te·khee·do es de·lee·ka·do

73 When will my things be ready?
   ¿Para cuándo estarán mis cosas?
   pa·ra kwan·do es·ta·ran mees ko·sas

74 I need them in a hurry
   Los necesito urgentemente
   los ne·the·see·to oor·khen·te·men·te

75 Is there a laundromat near by?
   ¿Hay una lavandería automático por aquí?
   ay oo·na la·ban·de·ree·a ow·to·ma·tee·ka por a·kee

76 Can I have my laundry done?
   ¿Puedo usar el servicio de lavandería?
   pwe·do oo·sar el ser·bee·thyo de la·ban·de·ree·a

77 Where can I get clothes repaired?
   ¿Dónde pueden arreglarme esta ropa?
   don·de pwe·den a·rre·glar·me es·ta ro·pa

78 Can you do invisible mending?
   ¿Sabe zurzir?
   sa·be thoor·theer

79   Could you — sew this button back on?
                         ¿Puede — coserme este botón?
                         pwe·de — *ko·ser·me es·te bo·ton*
                                — mend this tear?
                                — coserme este roto?
                                — *ko·ser·me es·te ro·to*
                                — replace this zipper?
                                — cambiar esta cremallera?
                                — *kam·byar es·ta kre·mal·ye·ra*
                                — turn up/let down the hem?
                                — subir/bajar el dobladillo?
                                — *soo·beer/ba·khar el do·bla·deel·yo*

Police and legal matters

80 I wish to call the police
Quiero llamar a la policía
kye·ro **lya**·mar a la po·**lee**·**thee**·a

81 Where is the police station?
¿Dónde está la comisaría de policía?
don·de es·**ta** la ko·mee·sa·**ree**·a de po·lee·**thee**·a

82 I should like to report — a theft
Quisiera denunciar — un robo
kee·**sye**·ra de·noon·**thyar** — oon **ro**·bo
— the loss of my camera
— la pérdida de mi cámara
— la **per**·dee·da de mee **ka**·ma·ra

83 Someone has broken into — my car/my room
Alguien ha entrado en — mi coche/habitación
al·gyen a en·**tra**·do en — mee **ko**·che/a·bee·ta·**thyon**

84 Someone has stolen — my wallet
Me han robado — la cartera
me an ro·**ba**·do — la kar·**te**·ra

85 My insurance company requires me to report it
Mi compañía de seguros exige que dé parte
me kom·pan·**yee**·a de se·**goo**·ros ek·**see**·khe ke de **par**·te

86 I have lost — my passport
He perdido — mi pasaporte
e per·**dee**·do — mee pa·sa·**por**·te

87 My son is lost
Mi hijo se ha perdido
mee **ee**·kho se a per·**dee**·do

88 I wish/I demand — to see a lawyer
Quiero/pido — ver a un abogado
kye·ro/**pee**·do — ber a oon a·bo·**ga**·do

89 Where is the British/American consulate?
¿Dónde está el consulado británico/norteamericano?
don·de es·**ta** el kon·soo·**la**·do bree·**ta**·nee·ko/
nor·te·a·me·ree·**ka**·no

Worship

Spain and all Latin American countries are predominantly Roman
Catholic, but other main denominations and religions are represented.

90 Where is there — a Catholic church?
¿Dónde hay — una iglesia católica?
don·de ay — **oo**·na ee·**gle**·sya ka·**to**·lee·ka
— a Protestant church?
— una capilla protestante?
— **oo**·na ka·**peel**·ya pro·tes·**tan**·te

91 What time is the service?
¿A qué hora son los oficios?
a ke **o**·ra son los o·**fee**·thyos

92 I'd like to see — a priest
Querría hablar con — un sacerdote
ke·**rree**·a a·**blar** kon — oon sa·ther·**do**·te
— a minister
— un pastor
— oon pas·**tor**

Business matters   (Bm)

Making appointments (see also Telephoning, p.53)

1 My name is George Baker — of Universal Chemicals
Me llamo George Baker — de Universal Chemicals
me **lya**·mo George Baker — de Universal Chemicals

2 Here is my card
  Esta es mi tarjeta
  es·ta es mee tar·khe·ta

3 Could I speak to your
  Managing Director/Buyer?
  ¿Puedo hablar con el
  director/comprador?
  *pwe·do a·blar kon el
  dee·rek·tor/kom·pra·dor*

4 He/she is expecting me to call
  El/ella está esperando mi
  llamada
  *el/el·ya es·ta es·pe·ran·do mee
  lya·ma·da*

5 Could you put me through to
  Señor Villegas?
  ¿Puede ponerme con el Señor
  Villegas?
  *pwe·de po·ner·me kon el
  sen·yor beel·ye·gas*

6 Is Señor Villegas in?
  ¿Está el Señor Villegas?
  es·ta el sen·yor beel·ye·gas

7 Is his assistant/secretary there?
  ¿Está su asistente/secretaria?
  *es·ta soo a·sees·ten·te/
  se·kre·ta·rya*

8 When will he/she be back?
  ¿Cuándo volverá?
  kwan·do bol·be·ra

9 I have an appointment with
  Señor González
  Tengo una cita con el Señor
  González
  *ten·go oo·na thee·ta kon el
  sen·yor gon·tha·leth*

10 I would like to make an
   appointment with Señor
   Villegas
   Quisiera hacer una cita con el
   Señor Villegas
   *kee·sye·ra a·ther oo·na thee·ta
   kon el sen·yor beel·ye·gas*

11 I am free on Thursday
   between 9:00 and 11:00
   Estoy libre el jueves de 9
   (nueve) a 11 (once)
   *es·toy lee·bre el khwe·bes de
   nwe·be a on·the*

12 Shall we say 10:00?
   ¿Entonces, quedamos a las 10
   (diez)?
   *en·ton·thes ke·da·mos a las
   dyeth*

Miscellaneous

---

13 I am on a business trip to Spain/Argentina
   Estoy en viaje de negocios en España/Argentina
   es·toy en bya·khe de ne·go·thyos en es·pan·ya/ar·khen·tee·na

14   I wish — to hire a secretary/typist
   Quiero — contratar una
               secretaria/mecanógrafa
   *kye·ro — kon·tra·tar oon·na se·kre·ta·rya/
   me·ka·no·gra·fa*
        — to hire a conference room
        — alquilar una sala de conferencias
        — *al·kee·lar oo·na sa·la de
   kon·fe·ren·thyas*

15 Where can I get photocopying done?
   ¿Dónde puedo hacer una fotocopia?
   don·de pwe·do a·ther oo·na fo·to·ko·pya

16 Can I send a telex from here?
   ¿Puedo enviar un télex desde aquí?
   pwe·do en·bee·ar oon te·lex des·de a·kee

17   My firm specializes in — agricultural equipment
   Mi compañía está
          especializada en — artículos agrícolas
   *mee kom·pan·yee·a es·ta
   es·pe·thya·lee·tha·da en — ar·tee·koo·los a·gree·ko·las*
        — illustrated books
        — libros ilustrados
        — *lee·bros ee·loos·tra·dos*

18   I wish — to carry out a market survey
   Quiero — hacer un estudio de mercados
   *kye·ro — a·ther oon es·too·dyo de
   mer·ka·dos*
        — to test the Spanish/Mexican
          market for this product
        — probar el mercado español/
          mejicano para este producto
        — *pro·bar el mer·ka·do es·pan·yol/
   me·khee·ka·no pa·ra es·te
   pro·dook·to*

19 **My firm is launching an advertising/sales campaign**
   Mi compañía está lanzando una campaña de publicidad/ventas
   *mee kom·pan·yee·a es·ta lan·than·do oo·na kam·pan·ya de
   poo·blee·thee·dad/ben·tas*

20 **Have you seen our catalog?**
   ¿Ha visto nuestro catálogo?
   a bees·to nwes·tro ka·ta·lo·go

21 **Can I send our sales representative to see you?**
   ¿Puedo enviar a nuestro representante de ventas a verle?
   pwe·do en·bee·ar a nwes·tro re·pre·sen·tan·te de ben·tas a ber·le

22 **I will send you a letter/telex with the details**
   Le mandaré una carta/un télex con los detalles
   le man·da·re oo·na kar·ta/oon te·lex kon los de·tal·yes

23   **Can I see — a sample of your product?**
                  ¿Puedo ver — una muestra de su producto?
                  *pwe·do ber — oo·na mwes·tra de soo
                              pro·dook·to*
                          — a selection of your goods?
                          — una selección de sus artículos?
                          *— oo·na se·lek·thyon de soos
                              ar·tee·koo·los*

24 **Can I have a copy of this document/brochure?**
   ¿Puede darme una copia de este documento/catálogo?
   pwe·de dar·me oo·na ko·pya de es·te do·koo·men·to/ka·ta·lo·go

25 **Can you give me an estimate of the cost?**
   ¿Puede hacerme un presupuesto?
   pwe·de a·ther·me oon pre·soo·pwes·to

26 **What percentage of the cost is made up by transportation?**
   ¿Qué porcentaje del coste es el transporte?
   ke por·then·ta·khe del kos·te es el trans·por·te

27   **What is the average cost — of a pocket calculator?**
       Cuál es el precio medio — de una calculadora de bolsillo?
       *kwal es el pre·thyo me·dyo — de oo·na kal·koo·la·do·ra de
                                  bol·seel·yo*

28 **What is the wholesale/retail price?**
   ¿Cuál es el precio al por mayor/menor?
   kwal es el pre·thyo al por ma·yor/me·nor

29 **What is the rate of inflation in Spain/Colombia?**
   ¿Cuál es el índice de inflación en España/Colombia?
   kwal es el een·dee·the de een·fla·thyon en es·pan·ya/ko·lom·bya

30 **How high are current rates of interest?**
   ¿Cuál es el interés actualmente?
   kwal es el een·te·res ak·twal·men·te

31 **How is the project being financed?**
   ¿Cómo está financiado el proyecto?
   ko·mo es·ta fee·nan·thya·do el pro·yek·to

32 **It's a pleasure to do business with you**
   Es un placer hacer negocios con Ud
   es oon pla·ther a·ther ne·go·thyos kon oos·ted

Children (c)

Traveling with children abroad presents its own special problems. We have grouped together here certain phrases that parents may need.

1   **Do you have — a special menu for children?**
                  ¿Tiene — un menú especial para niños?
                  *tye·ne — oon me·noo es·pe·thyal pa·ra
                          neen·yos*
                          — half portions for children?
                          — raciones pequeñas para niños?
                          *— ra·thyo·nes pe·ken·yas pa·ra
                              neen·yos*

2 **Can you warm this bottle for me?**
   ¿Puede calentar este biberón?
   pwe·de ka·len·tar es·te bee·be·ron

3 **Have you got a highchair?**
   ¿Tiene una silla alta?
   tye·ne oo·na seel·ya al·ta

4   Do you operate — a baby-sitting service?
               ¿Tienen — servicio para cuidar a los niños?
               tye·nen — *ser·bee·thyo pa·ra kwee·dar a los*
                           neen·yos
                        — a day nursery?
                        — guardería?
                        — *gwar·de·ree·a*

5   Is there — a wading pool?
               ¿Hay — una piscina infantil?
               ay — *oo·na pees·thee·na een·fan·teel*
                    — a playground?
                    — un parque infantil?
                    — *oon par·ke een·fan·teel*
                    — an amusement park?
                    — un parque de atracciones?
                    — *oon par·ke de a·trak·thyo·nes*

6 Do you know anyone who will
   baby-sit for us?
   ¿Conoce a alguien que pueda
   cuidar a los niños?
   ko·no·the a al·gyen ke pwe·da
   kwee·dar a los neen·yos

7 We shall be back at 11
   Volveremos a las once
   bol·be·re·mos a las on·the

8 She/he goes to bed at 8
   Se acuesta a las ocho
   se a·kwes·ta a las o·cho

9 Are there any organized
   activities for the children?
   ¿Hay actividades organizadas
   para los niños?
   ay ak·tee·bee·da·des
   or·ga·nee·tha·das pa·ra los
   neen·yos

10 My son has hurt himself
    Mi hijo se ha hecho daño
    mee ee·kho se a e·cho dan·yo

11 My daughter is ill
    Mi hija está enferma
    mee ee·kha es·ta en·fer·ma

12 Have you got a crib for our
    baby?
    ¿Tiene una cuna para el niño?
    tye·ne oo·na koo·na pa·ra el
    neen·yo

13 Can my son sleep in our
    room?
    ¿Puede dormir mi hijo en
    nuestra habitación?
    pwe·de dor·meer mee ee·kho
    en nwes·tra a·bee·ta·thyon

14 Are there any other children
    in the hotel?
    ¿Hay otros niños en el hotel?
    ay o·tros neen·yos en el o·tel

15 How old are your children?
    ¿Cuántos años tienen sus
    hijos?
    kwan·tos an·yos tye·nen soos
    ee·khos

16 My son is 9 years old
    Mi hijo tiene nueve años
    mee ee·kho tye·ne nwe·be
    an·yos

17 My daughter is 15 months old
    Mi hija tiene quince meses
    mee ee·kha tye·ne keen·the
    me·ses

18 Where can I feed my baby?
    Dónde puedo dar de comer al
    bebé?
    don·de pwe·do dar de ko·mer
    al be·be

19 I need some disposable diapers
    Necesito pañales de celulosa
    ne·the·see·to pan·ya·les de
    the·loo·lo·sa

Illness and Disability   (I)

The disabled

1   I suffer from — a weak heart/asthma
               Padezco — del corazón/asma
               pa·deth·ko — *del ko·ra·thon/as·ma*
2   Do you have — facilities for the disabled?
               ¿Tienen — facilidades para los minusválidos?
               tye·nen — *fa·thee·lee·da·des pa·ra los*
                           mee·noos·ba·lee·dos

Do you have — a toilet for the disabled?
¿Tienen — servicios para los minusválidos?
tye·nen — ser·bee·thyos pa·ra los
mee·noos·ba·lee·dos

3 Is there a reduced rate for disabled people?
¿Hay un precio especial para los minusválidos?
ay oon pre·thyo es·pe·thyal pa·ra los mee·noos·ba·lee·dos

4   I am unable to — climb stairs
No puedo — subir escaleras
no pwe·do — soo·beer es·ka·le·ras

— walk very far
— andar mucho
— *an·dar moo·cho*

5 Can you supply a wheelchair?
¿Puede proporcionarme una silla de ruedas?
pwe·de pro·por·thyo·nar·me oo·na seel·ya de rwe·das

6 Does your elevator accommodate a wheelchair?
¿Hay espacio en el ascensor para una silla de ruedas?
ay es·pa·thyo en el as·then·sor pa·ra oo·na seel·ya de rwe·das

Doctors and hospitals

If a visit to a doctor is necessary, you will have to pay on the spot, so proper accident and medical insurance is advisable. Ambulances also have to be paid for. The emergency operator will tell you the number to use when calling an ambulance.

Preliminary

7 I need a doctor
Necesito un médico
ne·the·see·to oon me·dee·ko

8 I feel ill
Me siento enfermo
me syen·to en·fer·mo

9 Can I have an appointment with the doctor?
¿Puedo pedir hora con el médico?
pwe·do pe·deer o·ra kon el me·dee·ko

10 I would like a general checkup
Quisiera un reconocimiento general
kee·sye·ra oon re·ko·no·thee·myen·to khe·ne·ral

11   I would like to see — a skin specialist
Quisiera ver — a un especialista de piel
kee·sye·ra ber — a oon es·pe·thya·lees·ta de pyel

— an eye specialist
— a un oculista
— *a oon o·koo·lees·ta*

In the event of an accident

12 There has been an accident
Ha habido un accidente
a a·bee·do oon ak·thee·den·te

13 Call an ambulance
Llame una ambulancia
lya·me oo·na am·boo·lan·thya

14 Get a doctor
Traiga a un médico
tray·ga a oon me·dee·ko

15 He/she is unconscious
Ha perdido el conocimiento
a per·dee·do el ko·no·thee·myen·to

16 He/she is in pain
Tiene dolores
tye·ne do·lo·res

17 He/she has been seriously injured
Está gravemente herido(a)
es·ta gra·be·men·te e·ree·do(a)

18 I have cut myself
Me he cortado
me e kor·ta·do

19 He/she has burned himself/herself
Se ha quemado
se a ke·ma·do

20 I have had a fall
Me he caído
me e ka·ee·do

21 He/she has been stung
Tiene una picadura
tye·ne oo·na pee·ka·doo·ra

22 He/she has been bitten
Ha sido mordido
a see·do mor·dee·do

23 I have hurt my arm/my leg
Me he hecho daño en el
brazo/la pierna
*me e·cho dan·yo en el
bra·tho/la pyer·na*

24 I have broken my arm
Me he roto el brazo
me e ro·to el bra·tho

25 He/she has dislocated his/
her shoulder
Se ha dislocado el hombro
se a dees·lo·ka·do el om·bro

26 He/she has sprained his/her
ankle
Se ha torcido el tobillo
se a tor·thee·do el to·beel·yo

27 I have pulled this muscle
Me he dado un tirón en un
músculo
*me e da·do oon tee·ron en oon
moos·koo·lo*

Symptoms, conditions and treatment

28 There is a swelling here
Tengo esto hinchado
ten·go es·to een·cha·do

29 It is inflamed here
Está inflamado aquí
es·ta een·fla·ma·do a·kee

30 I have a pain here
Me duele aquí
me dwe·le a·kee

31   I find it painful — to walk/to breathe
Me duele — al andar/al respirar
me dwe·le — *al an·dar/al res·pee·rar*
I have — a headache/a sore throat
Tengo — dolor de cabeza/irritación de
garganta
ten·go — *do·lor de ka·be·thal
ee·rree·ta·thyon de gar·gan·ta*
— a high temperature
— fiebre
— *fye·bre*

32 I can't sleep
No puedo dormir
no pwe·do dor·meer

33 I have sunstroke
Tengo insolación
ten·go een·so·la·thyon

34 My stomach is upset
Me duele el estómago
me dwe·le el es·to·ma·go

35 I feel nauseated
Siento náuseas
syen·to now·seas

36 I think I have food poisoning
Creo que tengo intoxicación
por alimentos
*kre·o ke ten·go
een·tok·see·ka·thyon por
a·lee·men·tos*

37 I have vomited
He vomitado
e bo·mee·ta·do

38 I have diarrhea
Tengo diarrea
ten·go dee·a·rre·a

39 I am constipated
Tengo estreñimiento
ten·go es·tren·yee·myen·to

40 I feel faint
Me siento débil
me syen·to de·beel

41 I am allergic to penicillin/to
cortisone
Soy alérgico a la
penicilina/cortisona
*soy a·ler·khee·ko a la
pe·nee·thee·lee·na/
kor·tee·so·na*

42 I have high blood pressure
Tengo la tensión alta
ten·go la ten·syon al·ta

43 I am a diabetic
Soy diabético
soy dee·a·be·tee·ko

44 I am taking these drugs
Estoy tomando estos
medicamentos
*es·toy to·man·do es·tos
me·dee·ka·men·tos*

45 Can you give me a prescription
for them?
¿Puede darme una receta para
ellos?
*pwe·de dar·me oo·na re·the·ta
pa·ra el·yos*

46 I am pregnant
Estoy embarazada
es·toy em·ba·ra·tha·da

47 I am on the pill
Estoy tomando la píldora
es·toy to·man·do la peel·do·ra

48 My blood group is . . .
Mi grupo sanguíneo es . . .
mee groo·po san·gee·ne·o es

49 I don't know my blood group
No sé mi grupo sanguíneo
*no se mee groo·po
san·gee·ne·o*

50 Must I stay in bed?
¿Tengo que quedarme en la
cama?
*ten·go ke ke·dar·me en la
ka·ma*

51 Will I be able to go out
tomorrow?
¿Podré salir mañana?
po·dre sa·leer man·ya·na

52 Will I have to go to the
hospital?
¿Tendré que ir al hospital?
ten·dre ke eer al os·pee·tal

53 How do I get reimbursed?
¿Cómo consigo que me
reembolsen?
*ko·mo kon·see·go ke me
re·em·bol·sen*

Dentists

54 I need to see the dentist
Necesito ir al dentista
ne·the·see·to eer al den·tees·ta

55 I have a toothache
Tengo dolor de muelas
ten·go do·lor de mwe·las

56 It's this one
Es ésta
es es·ta

57 I've broken a tooth
Me he roto un diente
me e ro·to oon dyen·te

58 The filling has come out
Se me ha quitado el empaste
se me a kee·ta·do el em·pas·te

59 Will you have to take it out?
¿Tiene que sacarlo?
tye·ne ke sa·kar·lo

60 Are you going to fill it?
¿Va a empastarlo?
ba a em·pas·tar·lo

61 That hurts
Eso me duele
e·so me dwe·le

62 Please give me an anesthetic
Por favor póngame un
anestésico
*por fa·bor pon·ga·me oon
a·nes·te·see·ko*

63 My gums hurt
Me duelen las encías
me dwe·len las en·thee·as

64 My dentures are broken
Se me ha roto la dentadura
postiza
*se me a ro·to la den·ta·doo·ra
pos·tee·tha*

65 Can you repair them?
¿Puede repararlos?
pwe·de re·pa·rar·los

Emergencies and accidents (Ea)

We hope you will not need the following phrases, but it is better to know
them, as they could make a difference in a critical situation.

1 Help!
¡Socorro!
so·ko·rro

2   Stop! — thief!
¡Pare — al ladrón!
pa·re — al la·dron

3 There has been an accident
Ha habido un accidente
a a·bee·do oon ak·thee·den·te

4 A fire has broken out
Ha empezado un incendio
a em·pe·tha·do oon een·then·dyo

5   I have been — robbed/attacked
Me han — robado/atacado
me an — ro·ba·do/a·ta·ka·do

6 Where is the nearest telephone/hospital?
¿Dónde está el teléfono/hospital mas próximo?
don·de es·ta el te·le·fo·no/os·pee·tal mas prok·see·mo

7   Call — a doctor
Llame — a un médico
lya·me — a oon me·dee·ko

Call	— an ambulance
Llame	— una ambulancia
lya·me	— *oo·na am·boo·lan·thya*
	— the police
	— a la policía
	— *a la po·lee·thee·a*
	— the fire department
	— a los bomberos
	— *a los bom·be·ros*

8 This is an emergency
Esto es una emergencia
es·to es oo·na e·mer·khen·thya

9 It is urgent
Es urgente
es oor·khen·te

10 Please hurry
Dése prisa, por favor
de·se pree·sa por fa·bor

11 My address is . . .
Mi dirección es . . .
mee dee·rek·thyon es

Making conversation (Mc)

Topics

The weather

1	Is it going	— to be a nice day?
	¿Va a	— hacer bueno?
	ba a	— *a·ther bwe·no*
		— to rain?
		— llover?
		— *lyo·ber*

2 It's a lovely day
Hace un buen día
a·the oon bwen dee·a

3 It's hot/cold
Hace calor/frío
a·the ka·lor/free·o

4 It's raining
Llueve
lyoo·e·be

5 It's windy
Hace aire
a·the ay·re

6 It's snowing
Está nevando
es·ta ne·ban·do

7 It's foggy
Hay niebla
ay nye·bla

8 What is the temperature?
¿Qué temperatura hace?
ke tem·pe·ra·too·ra a·the

9 Is the water warm?
¿Está caliente el agua?
es·ta ka·lyen·te el ag·wa

10 When is high tide?
¿Cuándo está la marea alta?
kwan·do es·ta la ma·re·a al·ta

11 It's a clear night
Es una noche clara
es oo·na no·che kla·ra

National and regional characteristics

This is an endlessly fruitful source of material for conversation. Here are some of the points that might be raised.

12 Which part of Spain do you come from?
¿De qué parte de España es Ud?
de ke par·te de es·pan·ya es oos·ted

13 The country has a high/low cost of living
El país tiene coste de vida alto/bajo
el pa·ees tye·ne kos·te de bee·da al·to/ba·kho

14 The people are friendly/reserved
La gente es simpática/reservada
la khen·te es seem·pa·tee·ka/re·ser·ba·da

15 In Spain etiquette is stricter/less strict than in Britain/America
En España la etiqueta es más/menos estricta que en Gran
   Bretaña/los Estados Unidos
en es·pan·ya la e·tee·ke·ta es mas/me·nos es·trik·ta ke
en gran bre·tan·ya/los es·ta·dos oo·nee·dos

16 **What sports are popular in Spain?**
¿Qué deportes son populares en España?
ke de·por·tes son po·poo·la·res en es·pan·ya

17 **Where did you spend your vacation last year?**
¿Dónde pasó sus vacaciones el año pasado?
don·de pa·so soos ba·ka·thyo·nes el a·nyo pa·sa·do

18 **Did you like it there?**
¿Le gustó allí?
le goos·to al·yee

19 **What region do you come from?**
¿De qué región es Ud?
de ke re·khyon es oos·ted

20 **What is the climate like in the Basque region?**
¿Cómo es el clima en el país vasco?
ko·mo es el klee·ma en el pa·ees bas·ko

21 **What are the people like?**
¿Cómo es la gente?
ko·mo es la khen·te

22 **Do they have their own language?**
¿Hablan un idioma diferente?
a·blan oon ee·dyo·ma dee·fe·ren·te

23 **Is the region prosperous?**
¿Es una región rica?
es oo·na re·khyon ree·ka

24 **Do you know the country around Burgos?**
¿Conoce la zona alrededor de Burgos?
ko·no·the la tho·na al·re·de·dor de boor·gos

25 **The wine/food in Old Castile is wonderful**
El vino/la comida en Castilla (la Vieja) es maravilloso(a)
*el bee·no/la ko·mee·da en kas·teel·ya (la bye·kha) es
ma·ra·beel·yo·so(a)*

26 **Where is its commercial/administrative center?**
¿Dónde es su centro comercial/administrativo?
don·de es soo then·tro ko·mer·thyal/ad·mee·nees·tra·tee·bo

27 **Santiago de Compostela is a beautiful town**
Santiago de Compostela es una ciudad muy bonita
san·tya·go de kom·pos·te·la es oo·na thyoo·dad mooy bo·nee·ta

28 **Have you ever been to Granada?**
¿Ha estado alguna vez en Granada?
a es·ta·do al·goo·na beth en gra·na·da

Breaking the ice

Here are a few stock questions and answers that tend to be exchanged by people who meet casually (see also Greetings and exchanges, p.6).

29 **Do you mind if — I sit here?**
¿Le molesta si — me siento aquí?
le mo·les·ta see — me syen·to a·kee
— **I smoke?**
— fumo?
— *foo·mo*

30 **Can I — offer you a cigarette?**
¿Quiere — un cigarrillo?
kye·re — oon thee·ga·reel·yo
— **buy you a drink?**
— tomar una copa?
— *to·mar oo·na ko·pa*

31 **May I introduce myself?**
¿Puedo presentarme yo mismo?
pwe·do pre·sen·tar·me yo mees·mo

32 **Are you Spanish/Chilean/Mexican?**
¿Es Ud español(a)/chileno(a)/mejicano(a)?
es oos·ted es·pan·yol(·yo·la)/chee·le·no(a)/me·khee·ka·no(a)

33 **I am American/English**
Soy americano(a)/inglés(esa)
soy a·me·ree·ka·no(a)/een·gles(·gle·sa)

34 I live in New York/London
Vivo en Nueva York/Londres
bee·bo en nwe·ba york/lon·dres

35 Is this your first visit to Madrid/Mexico City?
¿Es esta su primera visita a Madrid/Ciudad de México?
es es·ta soo pree·me·ra bee·see·ta a ma·dreed/thyoo·dad de me·khee·ko

36 Have you been here long?
¿Ha estado aquí mucho tiempo?
a es·ta·do a·kee moo·cho tyem·po

37 I have been here two days
He estado aquí dos días
e es·ta·do a·kee dos dee·as

38 Are you staying long?
¿Se va a quedar mucho tiempo?
se ba a ke·dar moo·cho tyem·po

39 I am staying for two weeks
Voy a quedarme quince días
boy a ke·dar·me keen·the dee·as

40 Where are you staying?
¿Dónde está viviendo?
don·de es·ta bee·byen·do

41 I am staying at the Hotel Hispánico
Estoy en el Hotel Hispánico
es·toy en el o·tel ees·pa·nee·ko

42 What is your job?
¿En qué trabaja Ud?
en ke tra·ba·kha oos·ted

43   I am — a businessman
       Soy — un hombre de negocios
       soy — *oon om·bre de ne·go·thyos*
       — a student
       — estudiante
       — *es·too·dyan·te*

44 Have you visited England/America?
¿Ha estado en Inglaterra/América?
a es·ta·do en een·gla·te·rra/a·me·ree·ka

45   What do you think of — the country?
       ¿Que piensa del — país?
       ke pyen·sa del — *pa·ees*
       — the people?
       — de la gente?
       — *de la khen·te*
       — the food?
       — de la comida?
       — *de la ko·mee·da*

46 Are you married?
¿Está casado(a)?
es·ta ka·sa·do(a)

47 Do you have any children?
¿Tiene hijos?
tye·ne ee·khos

48   Would you like — to go out with me this evening?
       ¿Le gustaría — salir conmigo esta noche?
       le goos·ta·ree·a — *sa·leer kon·mee·go es·ta no·che*
       — to have dinner/lunch with me?
       — cenar/comer conmigo?
       — *the·nar/ko·mer kon·mee·go*
       — to go to the movies/theater with me?
       — ir al cine/teatro conmigo?
       — *eer al thee·ne/te·a·tro kon·mee·go*
       to show me something of your city?
       — enseñarme algo de su ciudad?
       — *en·sen·yar·me al·go de soo thyoo·dad*

Reference (R)

The alphabet

The Spanish alphabet is the standard Roman one, but *ch*, *ll*, and *ñ* are treated as separate letters. In the following table the names of the letters are given phonetically and each letter forms the initial letter of the word on the right. This is a standard system for clarification, which might be used, for example, when a word is spelled out over the telephone.

A	for	Antonio		N	for	Navarra
a		*an·ton·yo*		*e·ne*		*na·ba·rra*
B		Barcelona		Ñ		Noño
be		*bar·the·lo·na*		*en·ye*		*nyo·nyo*
C		Carmen		O		Oviedo
the		*kar·men*		*o*		*o·bye·do*
CH		Chocolate		P		Paris
che		*cho·ko·la·te*		*pe*		*pa·rees*
D		Dolores		Q		Querido
de		*do·lor·es*		*koo*		*kay·ree·do*
E		Enrique		R		Ramón
e		*en·ree·ke*		*e·re*		*ra·mon*
F		Francia		S		Sábado
e·fe		*franth·ya*		*e·se*		*sa·ba·do*
G		Gerona		T		Tarragona
khe		*khe·ro·na*		*te*		*ta·rra·go·na*
H		Historia		U		Ulises
a·che		*ee·stor·ya*		*oo*		*oo·lee·ses*
I		Inés		V		Valencia
ee		*ee·nes*		*oo·be*		*ba·len·thya*
J		José		W		Washington
kho·ta		*kho·se*		*oo·be·do·ble*		*wo·sheeng·ton*
K		Kilo		X		Xiquena
ka		*kee·lo*		*e·kees*		*khee·ke·na*
L		Lorenzo		Y		Yegua
e·le		*lo·ren·tho*		*ee gree·e·ga*		*yeg·wa*
LL		Llobregat		Z		Zaragoza
el·ye		*lyo·bre·gat*		*the·ta*		*tha·ra·go·tha*
M		Madrid				
e·me		*ma·dreed*				

Numbers

Cardinal numbers

0 cero	10 diez	19 diecinueve
the·ro	*dyeth*	*dye·thee·nwe·be*
1 uno	11 once	20 veinte
oo·no	*on·the*	*beyn·te*
2 dos	12 doce	21 veintiuno
dos	*do·the*	*beyn·tee·oo·no*
3 tres	13 trece	22 veintidós
tres	*tre·the*	*beyn·tee·dos*
4 cuatro	14 catorce	23 veintitrés
kwa·tro	*ka·tor·the*	*beyn·tee·tres*
5 cinco	15 quince	30 treinta
theen·ko	*keen·the*	*treyn·ta*
6 seis	16 dieciséis	31 treinta y uno
seys	*dye·thee·seys*	*treyn·ta·ee·oo·no*
7 siete	17 diecisiete	32 treinta y dos
sye·te	*dye·thee·sye·e*	*treyn·ta·ee·dos*
8 ocho	18 dieciocho	40 cuarenta
o·cho	*dye·thee·o·cho*	*kwa·ren·ta*
9 nueve		
nwe·be		

50 cincuenta	100 cien	500 quinientos
theen·kwen·ta	*thyen*	*kee·nyen·tos*
60 sesenta	110 ciento diez	1,000 mil
se·sen·ta	*thyen·to dyeth*	*meel*
70 setenta	200 doscientos	2,000 dos mil
se·ten·ta	*dos·thyen·tos*	*dos meel*
80 ochenta	300 trescientos	1,000,000 un millón
o·chen·ta	*tres·thyen·tos*	*oon meel·yon*
90 noventa	400 cuatrocientos	
no·ben·ta	*kwa·tro·thyen·tos*	

Ordinal numbers

1st	9th	17th
primero	noveno	decimoséptimo
pree·me·ro	*no·be·no*	*de·thee·mo·sep·tee·mo*
2nd	10th	18th
segundo	décimo	decimoctavo
se·goon·do	*de·thee·mo*	*de·thee·mo·ok·ta·bo*
3rd	11th	19th
tercero	decimoprimero	decimonoveno
ter·the·ro	*de·thee·mo·pree·me·ro*	*de·thee·mo·no·be·no*
4th	12th	20th
cuarto	decimosegundo	vigésimo
kwar·to	*de·thee·mo·se·goon·do*	*bee·khe·see·mo*
5th	13th	N.B. Ordinals are not
quinto	decimotercero	used above twenty,
keen·to	*de·thee·mo·ter·the·ro*	and are optional after
6th	14th	ten, when cardinals
sexto	decimocuarto	are used instead. But
seks·to	*de·thee·mo·kwar·to*	note the following:
7th	15th	100th
séptimo	decimoquinto	centésimo
sep·tee·mo	*de·thee·mo·keen·to*	*then·te·see·mo*
8th	16th	1,000th
octavo	decimosexto	milésimo
ok·ta·bo	*de·thee·mo·seks·to*	*mee·le·see·mo*

Other numerical terms

a half	10 percent	five times
un medio	el diez por ciento	cinco veces
oon me·dyo	*el dyeth por thyen·to*	*theen·ko be·thes*
a quarter	a dozen	the last (one)
un cuarto	una docena	el último
oon kwar·to	*oo·na do·the·na*	*el ool·tee·mo*
a third	half a dozen	
un tercio	media docena	
oon ter·thyo	*me·dya do·the·na*	

Time

In reply to the question "¿qué hora es?" (*ke o·ra es:* what time is it?) you will hear "Son" (it is) followed by the number, unless it is one o'clock when the reply would be "es la una" (*es la oo·na*). If the time is on the hour, say 10, the answer will be "las diez" (*las dyeth*: ten hours). To indicate a.m. you add "de la mañana" (*de la man·ya·na*: in the morning), and for p.m., "de la tarde" (*de la tar·de*: in the afternoon) or "de la noche" (*de la no·che*: of the night). The only exceptions are noon "mediodía" (*me·dyo·dee·a*) and midnight "medianoche" (*me·dya·no·che*). Times in between the hours follow a pattern similar to the English one. Here are some examples.

1 9 o'clock a.m./p.m.
las nueve de la mañana/de la tarde
las nwe·be de la man·ya·na/de la tar·de

2 9:05
las nueve y cinco
las nwe·be ee theen·ko

3 9:15
las nueve y cuarto
las nwe·be ee kwar·to
4 9:30
las nueve y media
las nwe·be ee me·dya

5 9:40
las diez menos veinte
las dyeth me·nos beyn·te
6 9:45
las diez menos cuarto
las dyeth me·nos kwar·to

The same sequence using the 24-hour clock and assuming it is p.m., would be:

7 9:00 p.m.
las veintiuna horas
las beyn·tee·oo·na o·ras
8 9:05 p.m.
las veintiuna horas y cinco minutos
las beyn·tee·oo·na o·ras ee theen·ko mee·noo·tos
9 9:15 p.m.
las veintiuna horas y quince minutos
las beyn·tee·oo·na o·ras ee keen·the mee·noo·tos
10 9:30 p.m.
las veintiuna horas y treinta minutos
las byen·tee·oo·na o·ras ee treyn·ta mee·noo·tos
11 9:40 p.m.
las veintiuna horas y cuarenta minutos
las beyn·tee·oo·na o·ras ee kwa·ren·ta mee·noo·tos

Here are some other useful phrases connected with time:

tonight	after three o'clock	two hours ago
esta noche	después de las tres	hace dos horas
es·ta no·che	*des·pwes de las tres*	*a·the dos o·ras*
at night	nearly five o'clock	soon
por la noche	casi las cinco	pronto
por la no·che	*ka·see las theen·ko*	*pron·to*
in the morning	at about one o'clock	early
por la mañana	hacia la una	temprano
por la man·ya·na	*a·thya la oo·na*	*tem·pra·no*
this afternoon	in an hour's time	late
esta tarde	dentro de una hora	tarde
es·ta tar·de	*den·tro de oo·na o·ra*	*tar·de*

The calendar

Sunday	yesterday	January
domingo	ayer	enero
do·meen·go	*a·yer*	*e·ne·ro*
Monday	today	February
lunes	hoy	febrero
loo·nes	*oy*	*fe·bre·ro*
Tuesday	tomorrow	March
martes	mañana	marzo
mar·tes	*man·ya·na*	*mar·tho*
Wednesday	spring	April
miércoles	primavera	abril
myer·ko·les	*pree·ma·be·ra*	*a·breel*
Thursday	summer	May
jueves	verano	mayo
khwe·bes	*be·ra·no*	*ma·yo*
Friday	autumn (fall)	June
viernes	otoño	junio
byer·nes	*o·ton·yo*	*khoo·nyo*
Saturday	winter	July
sábado	invierno	julio
sa·ba·do	*een·byer·no*	*khoo·lyo*
on Friday	in spring	August
el viernes	en la primavera	agosto
el byer·nes	*en la pree·ma·be·ra*	*a·gos·to*
next Tuesday	in summer	September
el martes próximo	en el verano	septiembre
el mar·tes prok·see·mo	*en el be·ra·no*	*sep·tyem·bre*

October	in June	next week
octubre	en junio	la semana próxima
ok·too·bre	*en **khoo**·nyo*	*la se·**ma**·na*
November	July 6	*prok·see·ma*
noviembre	el seis de julio	last month
*no·**byem**·bre*	*el seys de **khoo**·lyo*	el mes pasado
December		*el mes pa·**sa**·do*
diciembre		
*dee·**thyem**·bre*		

Public holidays

Latin American countries each have their own Day of Independence and their national saint's day which are public holidays.

New Year's Day	January 1
Epiphany	January 6
St Joseph's Day	March 19
Maundy Thursday	
Good Friday	
Corpus Christi	
St James' Day (Spain)	July 25
Assumption	August 15
Hispanidad	October 12
All Saints' Day	November 1
Immaculate Conception	December 8
Christmas Day	December 25

Abbreviations

c/	calle (street)
Cía	compañía (company)
c.s.f.	coste, seguro y flete (cif)
dcha.	derecha (right hand)
E.E.U.U.	Estados Unidos (U.S.A.)
IVA	Impuesto sobra Valor Añadido (VAT)
izq.	izquierda (left hand)
R.A.C.E.	Real Automóvil Club de España (Spanish Automobile Club)
R.E.N.F.E.	Red Nacional de Ferrocarriles Españoles (Spanish Railroads)
R.N.E.	Radio Nacional de España (Spanish Radio)
S.A.	Sociedad Anónima (limited company)
Sr.	Señor (Mr.)
Sra.	Señora (Mrs.)
Srs.	Señores (Messrs.)
Srta.	Señorita (Miss)
T.V.E.	Televisión Española (Spanish Television)
Ud.	Usted (polite form of you)

Signs and notices (see also Road signs, p.17)

Abierto	Caja	Empuje
Open	Pay here	Push
Acceso a los andenes	Caliente	Entrada libre
This way to the trains	Hot	Entrance free
Alto/stop	Cerrado	Espere por favor
Stop	Closed	Please wait
Ascensor	Completo	Frío
Elevator	Full	Cold
Atención	Coto	Fumadores
Be careful	Game preserve	Smokers
Autoservicio	Degustación	Informaciones
Self service	Sampling (of wine, oysters, etc)	Information
Caballeros		Libre
Gentlemen		Vacant

Llamar	Privado	Reservado
Ring	**Private**	**Reserved**
No fumadores	Prohibido bañarse	Salida
Nonsmokers	**No swimming**	**Exit**
No funciona	Prohibido fumar	Salida de emergencia
Out of order	**No smoking**	**Emergency exit**
No tocar	Prohibida la entrada	Se alquila
Do not touch	**No entry**	**For rent**
Ocupado	Prohibido pisar la	Señoras
Occupied	hierba	**Ladies**
Oficina de	**Keep off the grass**	Servicio incluido
Información y	Razón:	**Tip included**
Turismo	**Apply to:**	Servicio no incluido
Tourist Information	Rebajas	**Tip not included**
Office	**Sale**	Se vende
Peligro	Recién pintado	**For sale**
Danger	**Wet paint**	Tirar
Policía		**Pull**
Police		

Conversion tables

In the tables for weight and length, the central figure may be read as
either a metric or a traditional measurement. So to convert from pounds
to kilos you look at the figure on the right, and for kilos to pounds you
want the figure on the left.

feet		meters	inches		cm	lbs		kg
3.3	1	0.3	0.39	1	2.54	2.2	1	0.45
6.6	2	0.61	0.79	2	5.08	4.4	2	0.91
9.9	3	0.91	1.18	3	7.62	6.6	3	1.4
13.1	4	1.22	1.57	4	10.6	8.8	4	1.8
16.4	5	1.52	1.97	5	12.7	11	5	2.2
19.7	6	1.83	2.36	6	15.2	13.2	6	2.7
23	7	2.13	2.76	7	17.8	15.4	7	3.2
26.2	8	2.44	3.15	8	20.3	17.6	8	3.6
29.5	9	2.74	3.54	9	22.9	19.8	9	4.1
32.9	10	3.05	3.9	10	25.4	22	10	4.5
			4.3	11	27.9			
			4.7	12	30.1			

°C	0	5	10	15	17	20	22	24	26	28	30	35	37	38	40	50	100
°F	32	41	50	59	63	68	72	75	79	82	86	95	98.4	100	104	122	212
Km	10	20	30	40	50	60	70	80	90	100				110	120		
Miles	6.2	12.4	18.6	24.9	31	37.3	43.5	49.7	56	62				68.3	74.6		

Tire pressures

lb/sq in	15	18	20	22	24	26	28	30	33	35
kg/sq cm	1.1	1.3	1.4	1.5	1.7	1.8	2	2.1	2.3	2.5

Fuel

UK gallons	1.1	2.2	3.3	4.4	5.5	6.6	7.7	8.8
liters	5	10	15	20	25	30	35	40
US gallons	1.3	2.6	3.9	5.2	6.5	7.8	9.1	10.4

Basic Spanish Grammar

NOUNS AND ARTICLES

Gender

One of the greatest differences between English and Spanish is that all Spanish nouns are either masculine, taking the masculine definite article (*el coche*, the car), or feminine, taking the feminine definite article (*la casa*, the house). Similarly, the indefinite article has masculine and feminine forms (*un coche*, a car; *una casa*, a house).

The gender of a noun can often be determined by the ending of the word. Typical masculine endings are *-o*, *-or* (*el cuchillo*, the knife; *el conductor*, the driver). Exceptions include *la radio*, the radio; *la mano*, the hand. Nouns ending in *-a*, *-ión*, *-dad*, *-tud*, *-umbre* are generally feminine (*la playa*, the beach, *la estación*, the station; *la edad*, the age). Exceptions include *el clima*, the climate; *el programa*, the program.

Some nouns have the same form for both genders, merely taking the appropriate article (*el artista*, *la artista*, the artist). Other nouns are invariable and of fixed gender (*la persona* and *la víctima* are feminine even when referring to males).

It is essential to chose the correct article, making it agree with its noun in number (singular or plural) and gender (masculine or feminine).

    Definite article: masculine singular – *el* / feminine singular – *la*
                      masculine plural – *los* / feminine plural – *las*
    Indefinite article: masculine singular – *un* / feminine singular – *una*
                        masculine plural – *unos* / feminine plural – *unas*

Hence: *el niño, los niños; un niño, unos niños:*   the boy, the boys; a   boy, some boys

    la niña, las niñas; una niña, unas niñas: the girl, the girls etc.

For groups of mixed gender the masculine plural article is used. *Los niños* can be boys, or boys and girls.

A special category of feminine nouns, those starting with stressed *a-* or *ha-*, adopt the masculine singular definite article, but the adjective will still be feminine:

    el agua fría   cold water
    el habla española   the Spanish language

Number

The plural of most nouns is formed by adding *-s* (*los hombres*, men), *-es* if the noun ends in a consonant (*las mujeres*, women), or a stressed vowel (*los rubíes*, rubies). Nouns ending in *-z* in the singular change to *-ces* in the plural (*la luz*, light, *las luces*).

Use of articles *el*, *la*

The definite article is often needed in Spanish where it is omitted in English, e.g. with nouns used in a general sense:

    la nicotina es mala para la salud   smoking is bad for the health
    la paciencia es una virtud   patience is a virtue

The definite article is used before titles, except in direct address:

    el Señor López es simpático   Mr López is friendly
    but *buenos días, Señor López*   good morning, Mr López

It is also used with the names of certain countries, e.g. *el Canadá, la China, el Japón, el Brasil, el Perú*.

It is used before parts of the body and clothing where English would use the possessive adjective:

    me he roto la pierna   I've broken my leg
    se lavaron las manos   they washed their hands
    me pongo el abrigo   I put on my coat

A + el, de + el

These contract to *al*, *del*:

    va al colegio   he goes to the school
    viene del campo   he comes from the country

This does not apply to *a + la* or *de + la* or the plural forms, which remain as separate words.

Lo

Spanish has a neuter gender; *lo* is often used before the masculine singular adjective to express abstract or general ideas:

    lo interesante es que...   the interesting thing is that...

Un, una

Spanish omits these before a noun indicating occupation, rank:

    mi hermano es camarero   my brother is a waiter

The article is used however if the noun is accompanied by an adjective:

    mi esposo es un médico importante   my husband is an important doctor

After negatives, *un, una* is often omitted:

    no tengo coche   I haven't a car

Unos, unas is similar to some, any. It is often omitted, particularly after a negative:

   no tiene primos   he hasn't any cousins
   ¿quiere Ud patatas?   would you like some potatoes?
   necesito libros   I need some books

ADJECTIVES AND THEIR AGREEMENT

Adjectives agree with their noun in number and gender. If the masculine of the adjective ends in -*o*, the feminine ends in -*a* (*hermoso, hermosa*, beautiful). Adjectives with a masculine ending in -*án, -ón, -or*, and adjectives of nationality ending in a consonant, form the feminine by adding -*a* (*hablador, habladora*, talkative; *inglés, inglesa*, English). Other adjectives have the same form for both genders:

   un libro útil, a useful book; *una mesa útil*, a useful table

Adjectives form their plural in the same way as nouns:

   la corbata azul   the blue tie   *las corbatas azules*
   el paquete pequeño   the small package   *los paquetes pequeños*

An adjective agreeing with two or more nouns of mixed gender, singular or plural, will be in the masculine:

   un tenedor y una cuchara sucios   a dirty fork and spoon
   en el día y a la hora indicados   at the time and day indicated

Position of adjectives

Adjectives generally follow the noun in Spanish, especially if descriptive, and if their meaning can only be literal:

   un libro reciente   a recent book
   una butaca cómoda   a comfortable armchair

Adjectives precede the noun if used in a figurative sense or for stylistic reasons:

   la blanca nieve   white snow

Adjectives which limit, rather than describe, always precede the noun: *mucho*, many; *poco*, few; *demasiado*, too much/many; *tanto*, so much/many; *primero*, first; *último*, last.

   muchas señoras   many ladies
   tantos periódicos   so many newspapers

Some common adjectives vary in meaning depending on their position, adopting the more literal meaning when following:

   una pobre mujer   a poor (wretched) woman
   una mujer pobre   a poor (needy) woman

Others that vary in this way are *grande, cierto, varios*.

Some adjectives, when preceding the noun, take a special short form in the masculine singular – *malo* (bad), *bueno* (good), *uno* (a), *primero* (first), *ninguno* (not any), *grande* (great):

   un gran hombre   a great man
   un buen día   one fine day
   el primer buen libro   the first good book

Possessive adjectives (his, her, your etc)

Unlike English, these agree in number and gender with the thing possessed:
nosotros tenemos nuestras propias ideas we have our own ideas *nuestras* agrees with *ideas* (feminine), not *nosotros*.

	singular	plural
my	*mi*	*mis*
your	*tu*	*tus*
his, her, its, your (polite singular)	*su*	*sus*
our	*nuestro, nuestra*	*nuestros, nuestras*
your	*vuestro, vuestra*	*vuestros, vuestras*
their, your (polite plural)	*su*	*sus*

Although *su(s)* has so many meanings, ambiguity seldom arises. If the meaning is not absolutely clear, *su(s)* can be replaced by the definite article and *de él/ella/Ud, ellos/ellas/Uds* added after the noun:

   su maleta   his/her/your/their case
   la maleta de Ud   your case
   la maleta de él/ella   his/her case

Demonstrative adjectives (this, that, these, those)

These have separate forms for masculine, feminine, singular, plural:

este chico	this boy	*estos chicos*	these boys
ese chico	that boy	*esos chicos*	those boys
aquel chico	that boy	*aquellos chicos*	those boys
esta chica	this girl	*estas chicas*	these girls
esa chica	that girl	*esas chicas*	those girls
aquella chica	that girl	*aquellas chicas*	those girls

The main difficulty is the distinction between the three words. *Este* means this (near the speaker); *ese* means that (near the person spoken to) and *aquel* means that (distant from both).

Comparative and superlative of the adjective (-*er*, -*est*)

Más + adjective forms the comparative: *más inteligente*, more intelligent.
El/la/los/las más + adjective forms the superlative: *el más alto*, the tallest, *la*

más alta montaña, the highest mountain.
Some adjectives have special forms. These have a regular plural, but do not
change their ending for the feminine:

bueno	mejor	el/la mejor
malo	peor	el/la peor
grande	mayor	el/la mayor
pequeño	menor	el/la menor

The absolute superlative conveys the quality possessed to a very high degree.
The suffix *-ísimo, a* is added to the root of the adjective:
  una niña bellísima a very beautiful girl
  un coche grandísimo an enormous car
Equality is expressed by *tan ... como*:
  este libro es tan difícil como el otro this book is as difficult as the other one.

ADVERBS

These are formed by adding *-mente* to the feminine of the adjective; *lentamente*,
slowly; *rápidamente*, fast. Placing *más* before the adverb forms the
comparative; *más fácilmente*, more easily. Placing *lo más* before it forms the
superlative:
  vengo lo más rápidamente posible I am coming as quickly as possible
Adverbs that are related to adjectives with irregular comparatives and
superlatives also have irregularity in *their* comparatives and superlatives.

bueno	good	bien	well	mejor	better	lo mejor	best
malo	bad	mal	badly	peor	worse	lo peor	worst

PRONOUNS

Pronoun Chart

	Subject	Reflexive	Indirect Object	Direct Object	Prepositional
I	yo	me	me	me	para mí, conmigo
you	tú	te	te	te	para ti, contigo
he	él	se	le (se)	le, lo	para él, consigo
she	ella	se	le (se)	le, la	para ella, consigo
it	(ello)	se	le (se)	lo, la	para ello, consigo
you	Ud	se	le (se)	le	para Ud, consigo
we	nosotros/as	nos	nos	nos	para nosotros/as
you	vosotros/as	os	os	os	para vosotros/as
they	ellos	se	les (se)	les, los	para ellos, consigo
they	ellas	se	les (se)	les, las	para ellas, consigo
you	Uds	se	les (se)	les	para Uds, consigo

Subject pronouns are not usually used except for emphasis or to avoid
confusion when the verb ending does not make the subject clear:
  voy I go   *él lo compra* he is buying it (not she, you)
Ud, Uds, however, meaning you (polite singular and plural), are often used on
their first occurrence in a sentence, then dropped. *Tú* and *vosotros* (familiar
singular and plural) are increasingly used nowadays, and always when talking to
relatives, close friends, children, and between young people.
Reflexive pronouns are used when the subject and object of the verb are the
same. They usually precede the verb, but are joined to the end of the verb if
the verb is an *infinitive, positive command*, or *-ing* form, and a written accent
may then be required to retain the stress:
  me lavo, te lavas, se lava I wash myself, you wash yourself, he/she washes
  himself/herself
  and   *quiero bañarme* I want to have a bath
  estoy bañándome I am having a bath
In Spanish a number of verbs are found in the reflexive form only, although in
English they are not reflexive; e.g. *se queja* he complains. *Se* + verb in the
third person singular is often used to express one, people, etc:
  se dice que... people say that, it is said that...
  no se va allí people don't go there
Direct and indirect object pronouns: like reflexive pronouns, these precede the
verb unless the verb is an *infinitive, positive command*, or *-ing* form:
  voy a comprarlo I am going to buy it   *cómprelo* buy it
When a direct and indirect object pronoun occur with the same verb the
indirect object pronoun usually precedes the direct:
  me lo da he gives it to me   *nos los dan* they give them to us
However, if *le* or *les* and *lo, la, los, las* occur in combination, *le* or *les* must
change to *se*:
  se lo da he gives it to him, her, you
Prepositional form: this is used when me, you, etc, are preceded by a
preposition:
  es para mí it is for me   *está delante de ti* it is in front of you
Mí, ti cannot be used when with *con*; **conmigo, contigo** are used for with me, with
you. **Consigo** is the reflexive form for with him/her/you/them.

Demonstrative pronouns (this one, those, etc)
These resemble the demonstrative adjectives, but bear a written accent on the stressed syllable:

Singular:	*éste*	(masculine)	– *ésta*	(feminine)
	ése	,,	– *ésa*	,,
	aquél	,,	– *aquélla*	,,
Plural:	*éstos*	,,	– *éstas*	,,
	ésos	,,	– *ésas*	,,
	aquéllos	,,	– *aquéllas*	,,

There is a special neuter form for each, *esto, eso, aquello*:
 eso es importante that is important

Possessive pronouns (mine, his, yours etc)
Like the possessive adjectives these must reflect the number and gender of the object possessed, not the possessor.

	Masculine Singular Noun	Feminine Singular Noun	Masculine Plural Noun	Feminine Plural Noun
mine	*el mío*	*la mía*	*los míos*	*las mías*
yours (familiar, singular)	*el tuyo*	*la tuya*	*los tuyos*	*las tuyas*
his, hers, its, yours (polite)	*el suyo*	*la suya*	*los suyos*	*las suyas*
ours	*el nuestro*	*la nuestra*	*los nuestros*	*las nuestras*
yours (familiar, plural)	*el vuestro*	*la vuestra*	*los vuestros*	*las vuestras*
theirs	*el suyo*	*la suya*	*los suyos*	*las suyas*
yours (polite, plural)	*el suyo*	*la suya*	*los suyos*	*las suyas*

 ¿de quién son estos guantes? whose are these gloves?
 son los míos, no son los tuyos they are mine, they are not yours

PREPOSITIONS
These are entered in the dictionary with examples where necessary. The main confusion will be when translating the English *for*, choosing between *por* and *para*. Basically *para* expresses purpose, *por* expresses cause, reason, origin, exchange or rate:
 un libro para el niño a book for the boy
 por mi parte for my part
It is important to remember that Spanish differs from English in the preposition required by many verbs, and each must be learnt. Some verbs requiring a preposition in English may not do so in Spanish, and vice versa:
 escuchar la radio to listen *to* the radio
 entrar en *la cocina* to enter the kitchen
The preposition *a* is placed before the direct object of a verb when the object is a specified person:
 veo a Enrique I can see Henry **but** *veo la casa* I can see the house

VERBS
Spanish verbs seem very confusing at first. Various endings must be added to the stem for different tenses. The tenses are used rather differently from English and there are many irregular and semi-irregular forms. There are also two verbs meaning *to be*. *Ser* expresses essence, basic qualities, and is used for occupation: *es español* he is Spanish, *es alto* he is tall, *es ingeniero* he is an engineer.
 Estar expresses state, location: *está enfermo* he is ill, *¿dónde está el hospital?* where is the hospital?
 Contrast: *¿cómo es su madre?* what is your mother like?
   ¿cómo está su madre? how is your mother?

Regular Verbs
The regular verb tables show the patterns for regular verbs, i.e. those not entered in this dictionary with an asterisk. For irregular and semi-irregular verbs, see p.78.
 Only five tenses are listed in the verb tables, these being adequate for basic communication. Verbs are listed by their infinitive, and grouped according to their endings: *-ar, -er, -ir*.

The Tenses
Different tenses are formed by adding specific endings to a specific stem (see table).
The Present: *llamo* = I call, I am calling, I do call.
The Future: *llamaré* = I shall call, I shall be calling. In fact, Spaniards often use the present for actions that will take place in the future:
 me voy mañana I shall go (away) tomorrow
The Past: you need to know the Imperfect, Simple Past, and Perfect.
 The Imperfect: *llamaba* = I was calling, I used to call, and sometimes I called. It is used for repeated actions:
 iba al bar todos los días I used to go to the bar every day
 It is also used for continuous or background actions:

llovía cuando salí   it was raining when I went out

Simple Past: *llamé* = I called, I did call. It is used for completed actions in the past. Contrast:

canté allí el año pasado   I sang there last year

and the imperfect

cantaba esta canción mucho   I used to sing this song a lot

The Perfect: *he llamado* = I have called, I called. You may need this for actions recently carried out at a time not yet considered as entirely past.

It is formed from the present of *haber* and the *past participle* of the verb in question. Unlike an adjective the past participle does not agree. It is formed by adding *-ado* to the stem of *-ar* verbs, and *-ido* to the stem of *-er* and *-ir* verbs. Many verbs have an irregular past participle.

In the negative, *no* is placed before the whole verb:

no he comido   I have not eaten

The Progressive Tenses: Just as *to be* + *-ing* makes the progressive or continuous tenses in English, so *estar* + *gerund* is used in Spanish. The gerund is formed by adding *-ando* to the stem of *-ar* verbs, and *-iendo* to the stem of *-er* and *-ir* verbs:

estoy hablando/comiendo/saliendo   I am talking/eating/going out

The Subjunctive Mood

Without knowing the subjunctive, basic communication is possible but confusion may arise, such as:

dice que viene   he says he is coming

dice que venga   he tells you to come

The use of the subjunctive can be summarized as:

Commands in the *Ud, Uds* form. The pronoun follows, or may be omitted.

venga Ud mañana   come tomorrow

lean las instrucciones   read the instructions

Clauses dependent on verbs of doubt, denial, hope, fear, etc., require the subjunctive in the dependent verb:

dudo que lo haga   I doubt whether he will do it

no creo que vengan   I do not think they will come

The Present Subjunctive is formed from the first person singular of the simple present. In *-ar* verbs the *-o* of the first person is replaced by *-e, -es, -e, -emos, -éis, -en*. In *-er* and *-ir* verbs the *-o* is replaced by *-a, -as, -a, -amos, -áis, -an*. A verb irregular in its simple present is also irregular in its present subjunctive: *decir – digo, diga*.

The Negative: the simple negative needs *no* before the verb. Most other negative words (*nunca, jamás, nada, nadie, ningún*) need *no* before the verb unless they precede it:

no lo compra   he does not buy it

no lo compra nunca, or *nunca lo compra*   he never buys it

Unlike English, you can combine several negative words:

no lo compra nunca nadie   nobody ever buys it

Questions: The question form is often indicated only by tone of voice. As word order is flexible this is no guide. When questions are written in Spanish they need an inverted question mark to warn you that a question follows:

está aquí   he is here   *¿está aquí?*   is he here?

Me gusta construction: I like is expressed by *me gusta*, literally it pleases me:

me gusta la casa   I like the house

le gustan las vacaciones   he likes the holidays

Regular Verbs

The table below shows how to conjugate the basic tenses of regular verbs with infinitives ending in *-ar, -er, -ir*.

INFINITIVE	hablar	comer	vivir
PRESENT	hablo	como	vivo
	hablas	comes	vives
	habla	come	vive
	hablamos	comemos	vivimos
	habláis	coméis	vivís
	hablan	comen	viven
FUTURE	hablaré	comeré	viviré
	hablarás	comerás	vivirás
	hablará	comerá	vivirá
	hablaremos	comeremos	viviremos
	hablaréis	comeréis	viviréis
	hablarán	comerán	vivirán
IMPERFECT	hablaba	comía	vivía
	hablabas	comías	vivías
	hablaba	comía	vivía
	hablábamos	comíamos	vivíamos
	hablabais	comíais	vivíais
	hablaban	comían	vivían

PERFECT	**he** hablado	**he** comido	**he** vivido
	has hablado	**has** comido	**has** vivido
	ha hablado	**ha** comido	**ha** vivido
	hemos hablado	**hemos** comido	**hemos** vivido
	habéis hablado	**habéis** comido	**habéis** vivido
	han hablado	**han** comido	**han** vivido
SIMPLE PAST	hablé	comí	viví
	hablaste	comiste	viviste
	habló	comió	vivió
	hablamos	comimos	vivimos
	hablasteis	comisteis	vivisteis
	hablaron	comieron	vivieron
PAST PARTICIPLE	hablado	comido	vivido
GERUND	hablando	comiendo	viviendo

Semi-irregular Verbs

group affected	letter affected	changes to	environment	examples
-car verbs	c	qu	before e	sacar – saqué
-zar verbs	z	c	before e	cazar – cacé
-guar verbs	u	ü	before e	averiguar – averigüé
-gar verbs	g	gu	before e	pagar – pagué
-ger -gir } verbs	g	j	before a, o	proteger – protejo dirigir – dirijo
-quir verbs	qu	c	before a, o	delinquir – delinco
-guir verbs	gu	g	before a, o	distinguir – distingo
-uir verbs	ui	y	before a, e, o	huir – huyo
-acer				nacer – nazca
-ecer -ocer } verbs	c	zc	before a, o	agradecer – agradezco conocer – conozco
-ucir				lucir – luzca
-cer -cir } verbs	c	z	before a, o	vencer – venzo zurcir – zurzo
root vowel e	e	ie	when stressed e.g. simple present 1st, 2nd, 3rd singular, 3rd plural	defender – defiende fregar – friegan
root vowel o	o	ue	when stressed e.g. simple present 1st, 2nd, 3rd singular, 3rd plural	volver – vuelve colgar – cuelgan

Irregular Verbs and Semi-irregular

These are marked in the dictionary with an asterisk. To check the irregularity first look for your verb in the irregular verb list. If you cannot find your verb look again for a verb in the same list with a similar ending, e.g. for *convenir*, see *venir*; for *contener*, see *tener*.

The irregular forms shown below are: 1) **Simple Present**, all persons 2) **Future**, first person singular only 3) **Imperfect**, first person singular only 4) **Simple Past**, all persons 5) **Past Participle** 6) **Gerund**

abrir	5) abierto
andar	4) anduve, anduviste, anduvo, anduvimos, anduvisteis, anduvieron
caber	1) quepo, cabes, cabe, cabemos, cabéis, caben 2) cabré 4) cupe, cupiste, cupo, cupimos, cupisteis, cupieron
caer	1) caigo, caes, cae, caemos, caéis, caen 4) caí, caíste, cayó, caímos, caísteis, cayeron 6) cayendo
conducir	1) conduzco, conduces, conduce, conducimos, conducís, conducen 4) conduje, condujiste, condujo, condujimos, condujisteis, condujeron
corregir	1) corrijo, corriges, corrige, corregimos, corregís, corrigen 4) corregí, corregiste, corrigió, corregimos, corregisteis, corrigieron 6) corrigiendo
cubrir	5) cubierto
dar	1) doy, das, da, damos, dais, dan 4) di, diste, dio, dimos, disteis, dieron
decir	1) digo, dices, dice, decimos, decís, dicen 2) diré 4) dije, dijiste, dijo, dijimos, dijisteis, dijeron 5) dicho 6) diciendo
deducir	see conducir
derretir	see pedir

disolver 5) *disuelto*, and see chart of semi-irregular verbs
dormir 1) *duermo, duermes, duerme, dormimos, dormís, duermen* 4) *dormí, dormiste, durmió, dormimos, dormisteis, durmieron* 6) *durmiendo*
elegir see *corregir*
escribir 5) *escrito*
estar 1) *estoy, estás, está, estamos, estáis, están* 4) *estuve, estuviste, estuvo, estuvimos, estuvisteis, estuvieron*
freír see *reír*, but 5) *frito*
gemir see *pedir*
haber 1) *he, has, ha, hemos, habéis, han* 2) *habré* 4) *hube, hubiste, hubo, hubimos, hubisteis, hubieron*
hacer 1) *hago, haces, hace, hacemos, hacéis, hacen* 2) *haré* 4) *hice, hiciste, hizo, hicimos, hicisteis, hicieron* 5) *hecho*
herir see *sentir*
hervir see *sentir*
imprimir 5) *impreso*
invertir see *sentir*
ir 1) *voy, vas, va, vamos, vais, van* 3) *iba* 4) *fui, fuiste, fue, fuimos, fuisteis, fueron* 6) *yendo*
jugar 1) *juego, juegas, juega, jugamos, jugáis, juegan* 4) *jugué, jugaste, jugó, jugamos, jugasteis, jugaron*
leer 4) *leí, leíste, leyó, leímos, leísteis, leyeron* 6) *leyendo*
medir see *pedir*
morir see *dormir*, but 5) *muerto*
oír 1) *oigo, oyes, oye, oímos, oís, oyen* 4) *oí, oíste, oyó, oímos, oísteis, oyeron* 6) *oyendo*
oler 1) *huelo, hueles, huele, olemos, oléis, huelen*
pedir 1) *pido, pides, pide, pedimos, pedís, piden* 4) *pedí, pediste, pidió, pedimos, pedisteis, pidieron* 6) *pidiendo*
poder 1) *puedo, puedes, puede, podemos, podéis, pueden* 2) *podré* 4) *pude, pudiste, pudo, pudimos, pudisteis, pudieron* 6) *pudiendo*
poner 1) *pongo, pones, pone, ponemos, ponéis, ponen* 2) *pondré* 4) *puse, pusiste, puso, pusimos, pusisteis, pusieron* 5) *puesto*
preferir see *sentir*
producir see *conducir*
pudrir 5) *podrido*
querer 1) *quiero, quieres, quiere, queremos, queréis, quieren* 2) *querré* 4) *quise, quisiste, quiso, quisimos, quisisteis, quisieron*
reducir see *conducir*
referir see *sentir*
reír 1) *río, ríes, ríe, reímos, reís, ríen* 4) *reí, reíste, rio, reímos, reísteis, rieron* 6) *riendo*
rendir see *pedir*
repetir see *pedir*
romper 5) *roto*
saber 1) *sé, sabes, sabe, sabemos, sabéis, saben* 2) *sabré* 4) *supe, supiste, supo, supimos, supisteis, supieron*
salir 1) *salgo, sales, sale, salimos, salís, salen* 2) *saldré*
satisfacer see *hacer*
seguir 1) *sigo, sigues, sigue, seguimos, seguís, siguen* 4) *seguí, seguiste, siguió, seguimos, seguisteis, siguieron* 6) *siguiendo*
sentir 1) *siento, sientes, siente, sentimos, sentís, sienten* 4) *sentí, sentiste, sintió, sentimos, sentisteis, sintieron* 6) *sintiendo*
ser 1) *soy, eres, es, somos, sois, son* 3) *era* 4) *fui, fuiste, fue, fuimos, fuisteis, fueron* 6) *siendo*
servir see *pedir*
sugerir see *sentir*
tener 1) *tengo, tienes, tiene, tenemos, tenéis, tienen* 2) *tendré* 4) *tuve, tuviste, tuvo, tuvimos, tuvisteis, tuvieron*
traer 1) *traigo, traes, trae, traemos, traéis, traen* 4) *traje, trajiste, trajo, trajimos, trajisteis, trajeron* 6) *trayendo*
valer 1) *valgo, vales, vale, valemos, valéis, valen* 2) *valdré*
venir 1) *vengo, vienes, viene, venimos, venís, vienen* 2) *vendré* 4) *vine, viniste, vino, vinimos, vinisteis, vinieron*
ver 1) *veo, ves, ve, vemos, veis, ven* 3) *veía* 5) *visto*
vestir see *pedir*
volver 5) *vuelto*, and see chart of semi-irregular verbs

SPANISH–ENGLISH DICTIONARY

a *a prep* to; a la estación *a la es·ta· thyon* to the station; a las 4 *a las 4* at 4 o'clock; tirar algo a alguien *tee·rar al·go a al·gyen* to throw something at someone; al año *al an·yo* per annum; de lunes a viernes *de loo·nes a byer·nes* Monday through Friday; a 30 kilómetros *a 30 kee·lo·me·tros* 30 kilometres away; a la izquierda/derecha *a la eeth·kyer·da/de·re·cha* on the left/right

abadejo *a·ba·de·kho m* haddock

abadía *a·ba·dee·a f* abbey

abajo *a·ba·kho adv* below; downstairs; hacia abajo *a·thya a·ba·kho* downward(s); río abajo *ree·o a·ba·kho* downstream; de abajo *de a·ba·kho* bottom; cuesta abajo *kwes·ta a·ba· kho* downhill; venir* abajo *be·neer a· ba·kho* to come down

abandonar *a·ban·do·nar vt* give up; quit (*leave*)

abanico *a·ba·nee·ko m* fan

abarcar* *a·bar·kar vt* include

abarrotería *a·ba·rro·te·ree·a f* grocery shop

abdomen *ab·do·men m* abdomen

abedul *a·be·dool m* birch

abeja *a·be·kha f* bee

abertura *a·ber·too·ra f* gap; opening

abeto *a·be·to m* fir (*tree*)

abierto(a) *a·byer·to(a) adj* open; on (*water supply*)

abogado *a·bo·ga·do m* counselor; lawyer; attorney

abolir *a·bo·leer vt* abolish

abolladura *a·bol·ya·doo·ra f* dent

abonado(a) *a·bo·na·do(a) m/f* subscriber

abonar *a·bo·nar vt* credit

abonarse a *a·bo·nar·se a vr* subscribe to

abono *a·bo·no m* subscription; fertilizer

abordar *a·bor·dar vt* tackle (*problem*)

aborto *a·bor·to m* miscarriage

abrazar* *a·bra·thar vt* embrace

abrazo *a·bra·tho m* embrace, hug; un fuerte abrazo *oon fwer·te a·bra·tho* with best wishes (*on letter*)

abrebotellas *a·bre·bo·tel·yas m* bottle opener

abrelatas *a·bre·la·tas m* can-opener

abreviatura *a·bre·bya·too·ra f* abbreviation

abrigo *a·bree·go m* coat; shelter; el abrigo de visón *a·bree·go de bee·son* mink coat; el abrigo de pieles *a·bree· go de pye·les* fur coat

abril *a·breel m* April

abrir* *a·breer vt* open (*window etc*); turn on (*water*); abrir* (con llave) *a· breer kon lya·be* to unlock □ *vi* open (*store, bank*)

abrochar *a·bro·char vt* fasten

absceso *abs·the·so m* abscess

absentismo *ab·sen·tees·mo m* absenteeism

absoluto(a) *ab·so·loo·to(a) adj* absolute; en absoluto *en ab·so·loo·to* not in the least

absorbente *ab·sor·ben·te adj* absorbent

absorber *ab·sor·ber vt* absorb; absorber una firma *ab·sor·ber oo·na feer·ma* to take over a firm

abstenerse* *abs·te·ner·se vr* abstain

abstracto(a) *abs·trak·to(a) adj* abstract

absurdo(a) *ab·soor·do(a) adj* absurd

abuela *a·bwe·la f* grandmother

abuelo *a·bwe·lo m* grandfather

aburrido(a) *a·boo·rree·do(a) adj* boring; estoy aburrido(a) *es·toy a·boo· rree·do(a)* I'm bored

acá *a·ka adv* here

acabado(a) *a·ka·ba·do(a) adj* complete; finished

acabar *a·ka·bar vt* finish; complete □ *vi* end; acaba de marcharse *a·ka· ba de mar·char·se* he's just left

acabarse *a·ka·bar·se vr* come to an end; se nos ha acabado todo el dinero *se nos a a·ka·ba·do to·do el dee·ne· ro* all our money's gone

academia *a·ka·de·mya f* academy

acampar *a·kam·par vi* camp

acariciar *a·ka·ree·thyar vt* pat; stroke

accesible *ak·the·see·ble adj* accessible

acceso *ak·the·so m* access

accesorios *ak·the·so·ryos mpl* accessories

accidente *ak·thee·den·te m* accident

acción *ak·thyon f* action; common stock (*finance*)

acciones preferentes *ak·thyo·nes pre· fe·ren·tes fpl* preferred stock

accionista *ak·thyo·nees·ta m/f* stockholder

acedía *a·the·dee·a f* heartburn

aceite *a·they·te m* oil (*edible, car etc*); el aceite bronceador *a·they·te bron· the·a·dor* suntan oil; el aceite de oliva *a·they·te de o·lee·ba* olive oil; el aceite de ricino *a·they·te de ree·thee· no* castor oil

aceituna *a·they·too·na f* olive

acelerador *a·the·le·ra·dor m* accelerator

acelerar *a·the·le·rar vi* speed up; accelerate □ *vt* rev

acento *a·then·to m* accent; el acento agudo *a·then·to a·goo·do* acute accent

acentuar *a·then·too·ar vt* emphasize (*syllable etc*)

aceptación *a·thep·ta·thyon f* acceptance

aceptar *a·thep·tar vt* accept

acera *a·the·ra f* sidewalk

acercarse *a·ther·kar·se vr* approach; acercarse a un lugar *a·ther·kar·se a oon loo·gar* to approach a place

acero *a·the·ro m* steel

achicoria *a·chee·ko·rya f* chicory

acidez *a·thee·deth f* acidity

ácido *a·thee·do m* acid

acné *ak·ne m* acne

acoger* *a·ko·kher vt* welcome

acogida *a·ko·khee·da f* welcome

acompañar *a·kom·pan·yar vt* accompany (*go with*); acompañar a alguien a su casa *a·kom·pan·yar a al·gyen a soo ka·sa* to see someone home; acompañar a alguien a la puerta *a· kom·pan·yar a al·gyen a la pwer·ta* to show someone out

acondicionador de pelo *a·kon·dee· thyo·na·dor de pe·lo m* conditioner (*for hair*)

aconsejar *a·kon·se·khar vt* advise; aconsejar a alguien que haga algo *a·*

kon·se·khar a al·gyen ke a·ga al·go to advise someone to do something

acontecer *a·kon·te·ther* vi happen

acontecimiento *a·kon·te·thee·myen·to* m event

acordarse de *a·kor·dar·se de* vr remember

acortar *a·kor·tar* vt shorten

acostarse *a·kos·tar·se* vr go to bed

acostumbrado(a) *a·kos·toom·bra·do(a)* adj usual; used to

acostumbrarse a *a·kos·toom·brar·se a* vr get used to

acre *a·kre* adj sour (sharp)

acreedor(a) *a·kre·e·dor(·ra)* m/f creditor

acrílico(a) *a·kree·lee·ko(a)* adj acrylic

actitud *ak·tee·tood* f attitude

actividad *ak·tee·bee·dad* f activity; **en actividad** *en ak·tee·bee·dad* active (volcano)

activo(a) *ak·tee·bo(a)* adj active; energetic □ m **el activo** *ak·tee·bo* assets (financial)

acto *ak·to* m action (act); act (of play)

actor *ak·tor* m actor

actriz *ak·treeth* f —**ces** actress

actual *ak·twal* adj present

actuar *ak·too·ar* vi act

acuario *a·kwa·ryo* m aquarium

acuerdo *a·kwer·do* m agreement; **el acuerdo global** *a·kwer·do glo·bal* package deal; **estar* de acuerdo con alguien** *es·tar de a·kwer·do kon al·gyen* to agree with somebody; **ponerse* de acuerdo en** *po·ner·se de a·kwer·do en* to come to an agreement

acumularse *a·koo·moo·lar·se* vr accrue; accumulate

acusación *a·koo·sa·thyon* f charge (accusation)

acusar *a·koo·sar* vt accuse

acuse de recibo *a·koo·se de re·thee·bo* m receipt; acknowledgement; **con acuse de recibo** *kon a·koo·se de re·thee·bo* by registered mail

adaptar *a·dap·tar* vt adapt

adelantado(a) *a·de·lan·ta·do(a)* adj advanced; **por adelantado** *por a·de·lan·ta·do* in advance

adelantar *a·de·lan·tar* vt pass (car); advance (money)

adelantarse *a·de·lan·tar·se* vr gain (clock); **mi reloj se adelanta** *mee re·lokh se a·de·lan·ta* my watch is fast

adelante *a·de·lan·te* adv ahead; ¡**adelante!** *a·de·lan·te* go ahead!; **hacia adelante** *a·thya a·de·lan·te* forward(s)

adelanto *a·de·lan·to* m advance (loan)

adelgazar* *a·del·ga·thar* vi slim

además *a·de·mas* adv besides (moreover); **además de él** *a·de·mas de el* besides him

adentro *a·den·tro* adv indoors; **ir* adentro** *eer a·den·tro* to go inside

adición *a·dee·thyon* f addition

adios *a·dyos* excl goodbye

adivinar *a·dee·bee·nar* vt guess

administración *ad·mee·nees·tra·thyon* f administration; **la administración pública** *ad·mee·nees·tra·thyon poob·lee·ka* civil service

admirar *ad·mee·rar* vt admire

adolescente *a·do·les·then·te* m/f teenager

adoptar *a·dop·tar* vt adopt

adornar *a·dor·nar* vt decorate

adorno *a·dor·no* m decoration

adquirir* *ad·kee·reer* vt acquire

---

adquisición *ad·kee·see·thyon* f acquisition; takeover

aduana *a·dwa·na* f customs

aduanero *a·dwa·ne·ro* m customs officer

adulto(a) *a·dool·to(a)* adj grown-up; adult; **para adultos** *pa·ra a·dool·tos* adult

advertir* *ad·ber·teer* vt warn; **advertir* a alguien de algo** *ad·ber·teer a al·gyen de al·go* to warn someone of something

aerobús *a·e·ro·boos* m air bus

aerodeslizador *a·e·ro·des·lee·tha·dor* m hovercraft

aerodinámico(a) *a·e·ro·dee·na·mee·ko(a)* adj streamlined

aerolínea *a·e·ro·lee·ne·a* f airline

aeropuerto *a·e·ro·pwer·to* m airport

aerosol *a·e·ro·sol* m aerosol

afectuoso(a) *a·fek·too·o·so(a)* adj affectionate

afeitarse *a·fey·tar·se* vr shave; **la máquina de afeitar** *ma·kee·na de a·fey·tar* shaver

aficionado(a) *a·fee·thyo·na·do(a)* m/f amateur

aficionarse a *a·fee·thyo·nar·se* a vr take up

afilado(a) *a·fee·la·do(a)* adj sharp (knife)

afiliado(a) *a·fee·lya·do(a)* adj subsidiary

afinar *a·fee·nar* vt tune (instrument)

afirmar *a·feer·mar* vt state

afligido(a) *a·flee·khee·do(a)* adj bereaved

África *a·free·ka* f Africa

África del Sur *a·free·ka del soor* f South Africa

africano(a) *a·free·ka·no(a)* adj African

afueras *a·fwe·ras* fpl outskirts; the suburbs

agarrar *a·ga·rrar* vt grab; grip

agencia *a·khen·thya* f agency; **la agencia de publicidad** *a·khen·thya de poo·blee·thee·dad* advertising agency; **la agencia de viajes** *a·khen·thya de bya·khes* travel agency

agente *a·khen·te* m agent; **el agente marítimo** *a·khen·te ma·ree·tee·mo* shipping agent; **el agente de viajes** *a·khen·te de bya·khes* travel agent

ágil *a·kheel* adj agile

agitado(a) *a·khee·ta·do(a)* adj rough (sea)

agitar *a·khee·tar* vt shake

agitarse *a·khee·tar·se* vr flap

agosto *a·gos·to* m August

agotado(a) *a·go·ta·do(a)* adj sold out; out of stock; exhausted; out of print

agraciado(a) *a·gra·thya·do(a)* adj graceful

agradable *a·gra·da·ble* adj pleasant

agradecer* *a·gra·de·ther* vt thank; **agradecer* a alguien** *a·gra·de·ther a al·gyen* to thank someone

agradecido(a) *a·gra·de·thee·do(a)* adj grateful

agrandar *a·gran·dar* vt enlarge

agresivo(a) *a·gre·see·bo(a)* adj aggressive

agrícola *a·gree·ko·la* adj agricultural

agricultor *a·gree·kool·tor* m farmer

agricultura *a·gree·kool·too·ra* f agriculture

agrietarse *a·gree·e·tar·se* vr crack; **el vaso se agrietó** *el ba·so se a·gree·e·to* the glass cracked

agua *ag·wa* f water; **el agua destilada** *ag·wa des·tee·la·da* distilled water; **el**

agua mineral *ag·wa mee·ne·ral* mineral water; el agua del grifo *ag·wa del gree·fo* tap water; el agua potable *ag·wa po·ta·ble* drinking water; el agua de Seltz *ag·wa de selts* soda water; sin agua *seen ag·wa* neat (*liquor*); el agua de tocador *ag·wa de to·ka·dor* toilet water

aguacate *a·gwa·ka·te* m avocado

aguacero *a·gwa·the·ro* m (rain) shower

aguanieve *a·gwa·nye·be* f sleet

aguantar *a·gwan·tar* vt stand (*bear*)

agudo(a) *a·goo·do(a)* adj sharp, pointed

águila *a·gee·la* f eagle

aguja *a·goo·kha* f needle; la aguja de hacer punto *a·goo·kha de a·ther poon·to* knitting needle

agujero *a·goo·khe·ro* m hole

ahí *a·ee* adv there

ahogarse *a·o·gar·se* vr drown

ahora *a·o·ra* adv now; por ahora *por a·o·ra* for the time being

ahorrar *a·o·rrar* vt save (*money*)

ahorros *a·o·rros* mpl savings

ahumado(a) *a·oo·ma·do(a)* adj smoked (*salmon etc*)

aire *ay·re* m air; manner (*attitude*); al aire libre *al ay·re lee·bre* open-air

aire acondicionado *ay·re a·kon·dee·thyo·na·do* m air-conditioning

airear *ay·re·ar* vt air (*clothes*)

aislado(a) *ays·la·do(a)* adj isolated

aislador *ays·la·dor* m insulator

ajedrez *a·khe·dreth* m chess

ají *a·khee* m chilli

ajo *a·kho* m garlic

ajustado(a) *a·khoos·ta·do(a)* adj tight (*clothes*)

ajustar *a·khoos·tar* vt adjust

ala *a·la* f □ el ala *a·la* wing

Alá *a·la* m Allah

a la carta *a la kar·ta* adv à la carte

alambre *a·lam·bre* m wire; el alambre de espino *a·lam·bre de es·pee·no* barbed wire

alargar* *a·lar·gar* vt stretch out

alarma *a·lar·ma* f alarm (*signal, apparatus*); la alarma de incendios *a·lar·ma de een·then·dyos* fire alarm

albaricoque *al·ba·ree·ko·ke* m apricot

albergue *al·ber·ge* m hostel; el albergue de juventud *al·ber·ge de khoo·ben·tood* youth hostel

albornoz *al·bor·noth* m robe

álbum *al·boom* m album

alcachofa *al·ka·cho·fa* f artichoke

alcalde *al·kal·de* m mayor

alcance *al·kan·the* m range (*of missile*); dentro del alcance de *den·tro del al·kan·the de* within the scope of; fuera de alcance *fwe·ra de al·kan·the* out of reach

alcanzar* *al·kan·thar* vt reach

alcoba *al·ko·ba* f alcove

alcohol *al·kol* m alcohol; el alcohol desnaturalizado *al·kol des·na·too·ra·lee·tha·do* methylated spirits

alcohólico(a) *al·ko·lee·ko(a)* adj alcoholic (*drink*); no alcohólico(a) *no al·ko·lee·ko(a)* soft □ m/f alcoholic

aldea *al·de·a* f village

aleación *a·le·a·thyon* f alloy

alegrarse *a·le·grar·se* vr be glad

alegre *a·le·gre* adj happy

alegría *a·le·gree·a* f joy

alejado(a) *a·le·kha·do(a)* adj away from

alemán(mana) *a·le·man(ma·na)* adj German; es alemán *es a·le·man* he's German; es alemana *a·le·ma·na*

she's German □ m el alemán *a·le·man* German

Alemania *a·le·ma·nya* f Germany; Alemania Occidental *a·le·ma·nya ok·thee·den·tal* West Germany; Alemania Oriental *a·le·ma·nya o·ryen·tal* East Germany

alergia *a·ler·khya* f allergy

alérgico(a) a *a·ler·khee·ko(a) a* adj allergic to

aletas *a·le·tas* fpl flippers (*for swimming*)

alfabeto *al·fa·be·to* m alphabet

alfarería *al·fa·re·ree·a* f pottery (*workshop*)

alfiler *al·fee·ler* m pin

alfombra *al·fom·bra* f rug; carpet

algas *al·gas* fpl seaweed

algo *al·go* pron something; ¿algo más? *al·go mas* anything else?; algo más grande *al·go mas gran·de* something bigger

algodón *al·go·don* m cotton; el algodón hidrófilo *al·go·don ee·dro·fee·lo* absorbent cotton; cotton batting

alguien *al·gyen* pron somebody, someone

algún, alguno(a) *al·goon, al·goo·no(a)* adj some, any; algunas manzanas *al·goo·nas man·tha·nas* some apples; algunos libros *al·goo·nos lee·bros* a few books; alguna vez *al·goo·na beth* ever; ¿hay alguno entre Uds que sabe cantar? *a·y al·goo·no en·tre oos·te·des ke sa·be can·tar* can any of you sing?

alianza *a·lee·an·tha* f alliance

alicates *a·lee·ka·tes* mpl pliers

alimentación *a·lee·men·ta·thyon* f food

alimentar *a·lee·men·tar* vt feed

alimento *a·lee·men·to* m food

aliviar *a·lee·byar* vt ease

alivio *a·lee·byo* m relief (*from pain, anxiety*)

allá *al·ya* adv there (*distant*); más allá de *mas al·ya* de beyond; más allá del muro *mas al·ya del moo·ro* beyond the wall; se fue para allá *se fwe pa·ra al·ya* he went there

allí *al·yee* adv there; allí están *al·yee es·tan* there they are

alma *al·ma* f soul

almacén *al·ma·then* m warehouse; store (*big shop, warehouse*); los grandes almacenes *gran·des al·ma·the·nes* department store

almacenar *al·ma·the·nar* vt store

almeja *al·me·kha* f clam; mussel

almendra *al·men·dra* f almond

almíbar *al·mee·bar* m syrup

almidón *al·mee·don* m starch

almohada *al·mo·a·da* f pillow

almohadón *al·mo·a·don* m bolster

almuerzo *al·mwer·tho* m lunch

alojamiento *a·lo·kha·myen·to* m accommodations

alojar *a·lo·khar* vt accommodate

Alpes *al·pes* mpl Alps

alpinismo *al·pee·nees·mo* m mountaineering; hacer* alpinismo *a·ther al·pee·nees·mo* to go mountaineering

alpino(a) *al·pee·no(a)* adj alpine

alquilar *al·kee·lar* vt rent (*house, car etc*); hire; charter (*plane, bus*); se alquila *se al·kee·la* for rent (*house etc*)

alquiler *al·kee·ler* m rent; rental

alrededor de *al·re·de·dor de* prep around; mirar alrededor *mee·rar al·re·de·dor* to look around; viajar alrededor del mundo *bya·khar al·re·de·dor del moon·do* to go around the world; **alrededor de $10** *al·re·de·dor de $10* around $10

alrededores *al·re·de·do·res* mpl surroundings

altar *al·tar* m altar

altavoz *al·ta·both* f speaker (*electrical*)

alternador *al·ter·na·dor* m alternator (*in car*)

alto(a) *al·to(a)* adj high (*voice, building*) □ adv high; **más alto** *mas al·to* higher; **en alta voz** *en al·ta both* loudly; **la alta fidelidad** *al·ta fee·de·lee·dad* hi-fi; **lo alto** *al·to* top (*of ladder*)

altoparlante *al·to·par·lan·te* m loudspeaker

altura *al·too·ra* f altitude; height (*of object*); **de 6 metros de altura** *de 6 me·tros de al·too·ra* 6 meters high

alubias *a·loo·byas* fpl kidney beans

alumbrado *a·loom·bra·do* m lighting

aluminio *a·loo·mee·nyo* m aluminum

alumno(a) *a·loom·no(a)* m/f pupil

alusión *a·loo·syon* f reference

alza *al·tha* f advance (*in business*); **en alza** *en al·tha* buoyant (*market*)

alzar *al·thar* vt lift

ama de casa *a·ma de ka·sa* f housewife

amable *a·ma·ble* adj pleasant (*person*); kind; **poco amable** *po·ko a·ma·ble* unkind

amaestrar *a·ma·es·trar* vt train (*dog*)

amanecer *a·ma·ne·ther* m dawn □ vi dawn

amargo(a) *a·mar·go(a)* adj bitter

amarillo(a) *a·ma·reel·yo(a)* adj yellow

amarrar *a·ma·rrar* vt tie (*string, ribbon*); moor

amatista *a·ma·tees·ta* f amethyst

ámbar *am·bar* m amber

ambición *am·bee·thyon* f ambition

ambicioso(a) *am·bee·thyo·so(a)* adj ambitious

ambiente *am·byen·te* m atmosphere

ambos(as) *am·bos(as)* adj both; **en ambos lados** *en am·bos la·dos* on either side

ambulancia *am·boo·lan·thya* f ambulance

amenaza *a·me·na·tha* f threat

amenazar *a·me·na·thar* vt threaten

América *a·me·ree·ka* f America

América del Sur *a·me·ree·ka del soor* f South America

americano(a) *a·me·ree·ka·no(a)* adj American; **es americano** *es a·me·ree·ka·no* he's American; **es americana** *es a·me·ree·ka·na* she's American

amianto *a·myan·to* m asbestos

amigdalitis *a·meeg·da·lee·tees* f tonsillitis

amigo(a) *a·mee·go(a)* m/f friend; **el/la amigo(a) por correspondencia** *a·mee·go(a) por ko·rres·pon·den·thya* pen pal

amistoso(a) *a·mees·to·so(a)* adj friendly

amontonar *a·mon·to·nar* vt pile up

amor *a·mor* m love

amortiguador *a·mor·tee·gwa·dor* m shock absorber

amortiguar *a·mor·tee·gwar* vt absorb (*shock*)

amperio *am·pe·ryo* m amp

ampliar *am·plee·ar* vt enlarge

amplificador *am·plee·fee·ka·dor* m amplifier

ampolla *am·pol·ya* f blister

amueblar *a·mwe·blar* vt furnish (*room etc*)

añadir *an·ya·deer* vt add (*comment*)

análisis *a·na·lee·sees* m analysis

analista-programador *a·na·lees·ta·pro·gra·ma·dorm* systems analyst

analizar *a·na·lee·thar* vt analyze

ananás *a·na·nas* f pineapple

ancas de rana *an·kas de ra·na* fpl frogs legs

ancho(a) *an·cho(a)* adj broad; wide; loose (*clothing*); **4 cm. de ancho** *4 cm de an·cho* 4 cm. wide

anchoa *an·cho·a* f anchovy

anchura *an·choo·ra* f width

ancla *an·kla* m anchor

andar *an·dar* vt/i walk

andén *an·den* m platform (*in station*)

andinismo *an·dee·nees·mo* m mountaineering

anémico(a) *a·ne·mee·ko(a)* adj anemic

anestésico *a·nes·te·see·ko* m anesthetic

anexo *a·nek·so* m extension (*building*)

anfiteatro *an·fee·te·a·tro* m circle (*in theater*)

anfitriona *am·fee·tryo·na* f hostess

ángel *an·khel* m angel

angora *an·go·ra* f angora

anguillas *an·geel·yas* fpl eels

anillo *a·neel·yo* m ring; **el anillo de compromiso** *a·neel·yo de kom·pro·mee·so* engagement ring; **el anillo de boda** *a·neel·yo de bo·da* wedding ring

animado(a) *a·nee·ma·do(a)* adj lively

animal *a·nee·mal* m animal; **el animal doméstico** *a·nee·mal do·mes·tee·ko* pet

aniversario *a·nee·ber·sa·ryo* m anniversary

año *an·yo* m year; **el año nuevo** *an·yo nwe·bo* New Year's Day; **el año económico** *an·yo e·ko·no·mee·ko* fiscal year; **¿cuántos años tiene?** *kwan·tos an·yos tye·ne* how old are you?

anoche *a·no·che* adv last night

anochecer *a·no·che·ther* m dusk

anorak *a·no·rak* m parka; anorak

anotar *a·no·tar* vt write down

Antártico *an·tar·tee·ko* m Antarctic

ante *an·te* m suede

antelación *an·te·la·thyon* f forward planning

antena *an·te·na* f aerial; antenna

anteojos *an·te·o·khos* mpl glasses; **los anteojos de sol** *an·te·o·khos de sol* sunglasses

antepasado(a) *an·te·pa·sa·do(a)* m/f ancestor

antepecho *an·te·pe·cho* m rail (*on bridge, balcony*)

anteproyecto *an·te·pro·yek·to* m blueprint

anterior *an·te·ryor* adj previous; earlier; **el día anterior** *el dee·a an·te·ryor* on the previous day

antes *an·tes* adv once (*formerly*); before; **nos conocemos de antes** *nos ko·no·the·mos de an·tes* we've met before; **antes de** *an·tes de* before (*in time*); **antes del mediodía** *an·tes del me·dyo·dee·a* before noon; **antes de acostarme** *an·tes de a·kos·tar·me* before I go to bed

antibiótico *an·tee·byo·tee·ko* m antibiotic

anticipar *an·tee·thee·par* vt look forward to

anticonceptivo *an·tee·kon·thep·tee·bo* m contraceptive

anticongelante *an·tee·kon·khe·lan·te* m antifreeze

anticuado(a) *an·tee·kwa·do(a)* adj out of date

anticuario *an·tee·kwa·ryo m* antique dealer

antieconómico(a) *an·tee·e·ko·no·mee·ko(a) adj* uneconomic

antigüedad *an·tee·gwe·dad f* antique

antiguo(a) *an·tee·gwo(a) adj* old; former

antihistamínico *an·tee·ees·ta·mee·nee·ko m* antihistamine

antiséptico *an·tee·sep·tee·ko m* antiseptic

anual *a·nwal adj* annual; yearly

anualmente *a·nwal·men·te adv* yearly

anudar *a·noo·dar vt* knot

anular *a·noo·lar vt* cancel

anunciar *a·noon·thyar vt* advertise (*product*); announce

anuncio *a·noon·thyo m* advertisement; commercial (*ad*); notice (*poster*); **poner* un anuncio para encontrar una secretaria** *po·ner oon a·noon·thyo pa·ra en·kon·trar oo·na se·kre·ta·rya* to advertise for a secretary

anzuelo *an·thwe·lo m* hook

apagado(a) *a·pa·ga·do(a) adj* off (*light*); **la luz está apagada** *la looth es·ta a·pa·ga·da* the light is out

apagar* *a·pa·gar vt* switch off; turn off (*light*)

apagarse* *a·pa·gar·se vr* fade; go out

aparador *a·pa·ra·dor m* sideboard

aparato *a·pa·ra·to m* appliance; el aparato para sordos *a·pa·ra·to pa·ra sor·dos* hearing aid

aparcamiento *a·par·ka·myen·to m* parking lot; **el aparcamiento doble** *a·par·ka·myen·to do·ble* double-parking

aparcar* *a·par·kar vt/i* park; **¿se puede aparcar aquí?** *se pwe·de a·par·kar a·kee* can I park here?

aparecer* *a·pa·re·ther vi* appear

aparejo *a·pa·re·kho m* tackle (*gear*)

apariencia *a·pa·ryen·thya f* appearance

apartado *a·par·ta·do m* box number; **apartado (de correos)** *a·par·ta·do (de ko·rre·os)* P.O. Box

aparte *a·par·te adv* apart (*separately*); **gastos de envío aparte** *gas·tos de en·bee·o a·par·te* postage extra

apasionante *a·pa·syo·nan·te adj* exciting

apellido *a·pel·yee·do m* surname; **el apellido de soltera** *a·pel·yee·do de sol·te·ra* maiden name

apenas *a·pe·nas adv* scarcely

apendicitis *a·pen·dee·thee·tees f* appendicitis

aperitivo *a·pe·ree·tee·bo m* aperitif

apetecer* *a·pe·te·ther vt* feel like, want; **me apetece una cerveza** *me a·pe·te·the oo·na ther·be·tha* I feel like a beer

apetito *a·pe·tee·to m* appetite

apio *a·pyo m* celery; **el apio nabo** *a·pyo na·bo* celeriac

aplastar *a·plas·tar vt* squash; crush

aplaudir *a·plow·deer vt* cheer □ *vi* clap

aplauso *a·plow·so m* applause

aplazar* *a·pla·thar vt* postpone

apoplejía *a·po·ple·khee·a f* stroke (*illness*)

apostar* *a·pos·tar vi* bet; **apostar* a** *a·pos·tar a* to back (*bet on*)

apoyar *a·po·yar vt* support; back

apoyo *a·po·yo m* support (*moral, financial*); backing

apreciar *a·pre·thyar vt* appreciate

aprender *a·pren·der vt* learn

aprendiz *a·pren·deeth m* trainee; apprentice; **el aprendiz de conductor** *a·*

pren·deeth de kon·dook·tor student driver

apresar *a·pre·sar vt* capture

apresurarse *a·pre·soo·rar·se vr* hurry

apretado(a) *a·pre·ta·do(a) adj* tight

apretar* *a·pre·tar vt* press; squeeze (*hand*); push (*button*)

aprobación *a·pro·ba·thyon f* approval

aprobar* *a·pro·bar vt* pass (*exam*); adopt (*proposal*); approve of; welcome (*event, proposal*); **no aprobar*** *no a·pro·bar* to fail (*exam*)

apropiado(a) *a·pro·pya·do(a) adj* proper (*appropriate*); suitable (*fitting*)

aprovechar *a·pro·be·char vt* take advantage of

aproximadamente *a·prok·see·ma·da·men·te adv* roughly (*approximately*); **aproximadamente $10** *a·pro·ksee·ma·da·men·te $10* about $10

aproximado(a) *a·prok·see·ma·do(a)adj* approximate; **un presupuesto aproximado** *oon pre·soo·pwes·to a·prok·see·ma·do* a rough estimate

apuesta *a·pwes·ta f* bet

apuñalar *a·poon·ya·lar vt* stab

apuntar *a·poon·tar vt* point; aim; record (*write down*); **apuntar un fusil a alguien** *a·poon·tar oon foo·seel a al·gyen* to aim a gun at someone

apurarse *a·poo·rar·se vr* hurry; **¡apúrate!** *a·poo·ra·te* hurry up!

aquel *a·kel adj* that (*masculine: remote*) □ *pron* aquél *a·kel* that one

aquella *a·kel·ya adj* that (*feminine: remote*) □ *pron* aquélla *a·kel·ya* that one

aquellas *a·kel·yas adj* those □ *pron* aquéllas *a·kel·yas* those ones

aquello *a·kel·yo pron* that (*remote*); **deme aquello** *de·me a·kel·yo* give me that

aquellos *a·kel·yos adj* those □ *pron* aquéllos *a·kel·yos* those ones

aquí *a·kee adv* here; por aquí, por favor *por a·kee por fa·bor* this way please; **¡aquí está!** *a·kee es·ta* here he/she is!; **he aquí mi hermana** *e a·kee mee er·ma·na* here's my sister; **aquí viene** *a·kee bye·ne* here he/she comes; **venga aquí** *ben·ga a·kee* come over here; **está aquí de vacaciones** *es·ta a·kee de ba·ka·thyo·nes* he's/she's over here on holiday

árabe *a·ra·be m/f* Arab □ *adj* Arabic □ *m* el árabe *a·ra·be* Arabic

arado *a·ra·do m* plow

araña *a·ran·ya f* spider

arañar *a·ran·yar vt* scratch

arancel *a·ran·thel m* tariff (*tax*)

arándano *a·ran·da·no m* cranberry

árbitro *ar·bee·tro m* referee (*sports*); umpire

árbol *ar·bol m* tree; **el árbol de levas** *ar·bol de le·bas* camshaft; **el árbol de Navidad** *ar·bol de na·bee·dad* Christmas tree

arbusto *ar·boos·to m* bush; shrub

arcada *ar·ka·da f* arcade

arcén *ar·then m* verge; berm

arcilla *ar·theel·ya f* clay

arco *ar·ko m* arch

arco iris *ar·ko ee·rees m* rainbow

arder* *ar·der vi* blaze (*fire*); **arder* vivamente** *ar·der bee·ba·men·te* to glow; **la casa está ardiendo** *la ka·sa es·ta ar·dyen·do* the house is on fire

ardilla *ar·deel·ya f* squirrel

área *a·re·a f* area

arena *a·re·na* f sand; **de arena** *de a·re·na* sandy (beach)

arenque *a·ren·ke* m herring

Argel *ar·khel* m Algiers

Argelia *ar·khe·lya* f Algeria

argelino(a) *ar·khe·lee·no(a)* adj Algerian

Argentina *ar·khen·tee·na* f Argentina

argentino(a) *ar·khen·tee·no(a)* adj Argentine

argot *ar·got* m slang

argumento *ar·goo·men·to* m plot (in play)

aritmética *a·reet·me·tee·ka* f arithmetic

arma *ar·ma* f weapon; **el arma de fuego** *ar·ma de fwe·go* firearm

armar *ar·mar* vt assemble; pitch (tent)

armario *ar·ma·ryo* m cupboard; wardrobe (furniture)

armas *ar·mas* fpl arms; coat of arms

armiño *ar·meen·yo* m ermine (fur)

aro *a·ro* m hoop

arpa *ar·pa* f harp

arquitecto *ar·kee·tek·to* m architect

arquitectura *ar·kee·tek·too·ra* f architecture

arrancar *a·rran·kar* vt switch on (engine); **arrancar algo** *a·rran·kar al·go* to pull something off

arranque *a·rran·ke* m starter (in car)

arrastrar *a·rras·trar* vt drag

arrastrarse *a·rras·trar·se* vr crawl

arrebatar *a·rre·ba·tar* vt snatch

arreglar *a·rre·glar* vt arrange; tune (engine); settle (argument); fix, **tenemos que arreglarnos sin leche** *te·ne·mos ke a·rre·glar·nos seen le·che* wc will have to go without milk

arreglo *a·rre·glo* m arrangement; agreement; **llegar a un arreglo amistoso** *lye·gar a oon a·rre·glo a·mees·to·so* to settle out of court

arrendamiento *a·rren·da·myen·to* m lease

arriba *a·rree·ba* adv upstairs; **allí arriba** *al·yee a·rree·ba* up there; **hacia arriba** *a·thya a·rree·ba* upward(s); **de arriba** *de a·rree·ba* overhead; **la casa está situada más arriba del valle** *la ka·sa es·ta see·twa·da mas a·rree·ba del bal·ye* the house is above the valley; **arriba se ven... a·rree·ba se ben** above, you can see...

arriesgar *a·rryes·gar* vt risk

arrinconar *a·rreen·ko·nar* vt shelve (project)

arrodillarse *a·rro·deel·yar·se* vr kneel down

arrojar *a·rro·khar* vt throw (down)

arroyo *a·rro·yo* m stream

arroz *a·rroth* m rice

arruga *a·rroo·ga* f wrinkle

arrugado(a) *a·rroo·ga·do(a)* adj creased

arruinar *a·rrwee·nar* vt ruin; wreck (plans)

arte *ar·te* m art; craft

arteria *ar·te·rya* f artery

artesanía *ar·te·sa·nee·a* f craftsmanship

artesano *ar·te·sa·no* m craftsman

Ártico *ar·tee·ko* m Arctic

articulación *ar·tee·koo·la·thyon* f joint (of body)

artículo *ar·tee·koo·lo* m article; **los artículos de tocador** *ar·tee·koo·los de to·ka·dor* toiletries

artificial *ar·tee·fee·thyal* adj artificial; man-made

artista *ar·tees·ta* m/f artist

artritis *ar·tree·tees* f arthritis

arzobispo *ar·tho·bees·po* m archbishop

as *as* m ace (cards)

asa *a·sa* f handle (of cup)

asado *a·sa·do* m roast meat

asador *a·sa·dor* m spit (for roasting)

asalariado *a·sa·la·rya·do* m wage earner

asaltar *a·sal·tar* vt mug; assault

asalto *a·sal·to* m raid; assault; round (in boxing)

asar *a·sar* vt roast; **asar a la parrilla** *a·sar a la pa·rreel·ya* to broil

ascender *as·then·der* vi amount to; **asciende a 10,000 pesetas** *as·thyen·de a 10,000 pe·se·tas* it amounts to 10,000 pesetas

ascenso *as·then·so* m promotion (of person)

ascensor *as·then·sor* m elevator

asegurado(a) *a·se·goo·ra·do(a)* adj insured

asegurador *a·se·goo·ra·dor* m underwriter

asegurar *a·se·goo·rar* vt insure; underwrite (insurance)

asegurarse contra *a·se·goo·rar·se kon·tra* vr insure against something

aseos *a·se·os* mpl washroom; powder room

asesinar *a·se·see·nar* vt murder

asesinato *a·se·see·na·to* m murder

asesino *a·se·see·no* m murderer

asesor *a·se·sor* m consultant; advisor

así *a·see* adv thus (in this way); **así que nos marchamos** *a·see ke nos mar·cha·mos* and so we left

Asia *a·sya* f Asia

asiático(a) *a·sya·tee·ko(a)* adj Asian

asiento *a·syen·to* m seat; **tome Ud asiento** *to·me oos·ted a·syen·to* have a seat

asignar *a·seeg·nar* vt allocate

asignatura *a·seeg·na·too·ra* f subject (for study)

asilo *a·see·lo* m home (institution)

asimismo *a·see·mees·mo* adv likewise

asir *a·seer* vt grasp (seize)

asistente(a) social *a·sees·ten·te(a) so·thyal* m/f social worker

asistir a *a·sees·teer a* vi be present at (meeting etc)

asma *as·ma* f asthma

asociación *a·so·thya·thyon* f association

áspero(a) *as·pe·ro(a)* adj rough (surface)

asperón *as·pe·ron* m grit

aspirador *as·pee·ra·dor* m vacuum cleaner

aspirina *as·pee·ree·na* f aspirin

astilla *as·teel·ya* f chip (electronics); splinter (wood)

astillero *as·teel·ye·ro* m shipyard

asunto *a·soon·to* m subject (topic); item; affair (matter); **los asuntos** *a·soon·tos* affairs

asustar *a·soos·tar* vt frighten

atacar *a·ta·kar* vt attack

atajo *a·ta·kho* m shortcut

ataque *a·ta·ke* m attack; raid (military); fit (seizure); **el ataque cardíaco** *a·ta·ke kar·dee·a·ko* heart attack

atar *a·tar* vt tie; bind; **atar un perro a un poste** *a·tar oon pe·rro a oon pos·te* to tie a dog to a post

atascarse *a·tas·kar·se* vr jam (machine)

ataúd *a·ta·ood* m coffin

Atenas *a·te·nas* f Athens

aterrado(a) *a·te·rra·do(a)* adj in a panic

aterrarse *a·te·rrar·se* vr panic

aterrizaje *a·te·rree·tha·khe* m landing

(of plane); **el aterrizaje de urgencia** *a·te·rree·tha·khe de oor·khen·thya* crash landing; **el aterrizaje forzoso** *a·te·rree·tha·khe for·tho·so* emergency landing

aterrizar *a·te·rree·thar* vi land (plane)

atestado(a) *a·tes·ta·do(a)* adj crowded

ático *a·tee·ko* m penthouse

Atlántico *at·lan·tee·ko* m Atlantic Ocean

atlas *at·las* m atlas

atleta *at·le·ta* m/f athlete

atomizador *a·to·mee·tha·dor* m spray (container)

atomizar *a·to·mee·thar* vt spray (liquid)

atraer *a·tra·er* vt attract

atrás *a·tras* adv behind; **hacia atrás** *a·thya a·tras* backwards; **mirar hacia atrás** *mee·rar a·thya a·tras* to look behind; **de atrás** *de a·tras* rear (seat); **hacia atrás** *a·thya a·tras* backward (glance)

atrasado(a) *a·tra·sa·do(a)* adj backward (child); **estar* atrasado(a)** *es·tar a·tra·sa·do(a)* to be behind schedule; **estar* atrasado con un pago** *es·tar a·tra·sa·do con oon pa·go* to be in arrears with a payment

atrasar *a·tra·sar* vt hold up (delay); **mi reloj se atrasa** *mee re·lokh se a·tra·sa* my watch is slow

atrasos *a·tra·sos* mpl backlog of work; arrears

atravesar *a·tra·be·sar* vt pierce; cross; **atravesar* la Mancha a nado** *a·tra·be·sar la Man·cha a na·do* to swim the Channel

atreverse *a·tre·ber·se* a vr dare to

atropellar *a·tro·pel·yar* vt to run down or over (car etc)

atún *a·toon* m tuna fish

aturdir *a·toor·deer* vt stun

audaz *ow·dath* adj bold

audiovisual *ow·dyo·bee·soo·al* adj audio-visual

aumentar *ow·men·tar* vt increase; boost (sales); turn up (volume); **aumentar en valor** *ow·men·tar en ba·lor* to appreciate (in value)

aumento *ow·men·to* m rise (in prices, wages); growth (in amount etc); increase

aún *a·oon* adv even

aun así *a·oon a·see* adv even so

aunque *own·ke* conj although; **aunque Ud pueda pensar...** *own·ke oos·ted pwe·da pen·sar* though you may think...

auricular *ow·ree·koo·lar* m receiver (phone)

auriculares *ow·ree·koo·la·res* mpl headphones

ausente *ow·sen·te* adj absent

Australia *ows·tra·lya* f Australia

australiano(a) *ows·tra·lya·no(a)* adj Australian; **es australiano** *es ows·tra·lya·no* he's Australian; **es australiana** *es ows·tra·lya·na* she's Australian

Austria *ows·trya* f Austria

austriaco(a) *ows·trya·ko(a)* adj Austrian

auténtico(a) *ow·ten·tee·ko(a)* adj real (genuine)

autobús *ow·to·boos* m bus

autocar *ow·to·kar* m coach (bus)

automáticamente *ow·to·ma·tee·ka·men·te* adv automatically

automático(a) *ow·to·ma·tee·ko(a)* adj automatic; **el coche/carro automático** *ko·che/ka·rro ow·to·ma·tee·ko* automatic (car)

automatización *ow·to·ma·tee·tha·thyon* f automation

automovilista *ow·to·mo·bee·lees·ta* m/f motorist

autopista *ow·to·pees·ta* f expressway; freeway; **la autopista de peaje** *ow·to·pees·ta de pe·a·khe* turnpike

autor(a) *ow·tor(·ra)* m/f author

autoservicio *ow·to·ser·bee·thyo* adj self-service

autostop *ow·to·stop* m ride; **hacer* autostop** *a·ther ow·to·stop* to hitch-hike

autostopista *ow·to·sto·pees·ta* m/f hitchhiker

avalancha *a·ba·lan·cha* f avalanche

avanzar *a·ban·thar* vi advance

aves de corral *a·bes de ko·rral* fpl poultry

avena *a·be·na* f oats

avenida *a·be·nee·da* f avenue

aventura *a·ben·too·ra* f adventure

avergonzarse *a·ber·gon·thar·se* vr be ashamed

avería *a·be·ree·a* f breakdown (of car); **la avería del motor** *a·be·ree·a del mo·tor* engine trouble

averiarse *a·be·ryar·se* vr break down (car)

aviación *a·bya·thyon* f aviation; air force

avión *a·byon* m aircraft, airplane; **en avión** *en a·byon* by air; **el avión a reacción** *a·byon a re·ak·thyon* jet (plane); **gustarle ir en avión** *goos·tar·le eer en a·byon* to like flying

avisar *a·bee·sar* vt inform

aviso *a·bee·so* m advice; warning

ayer *a·yer* adv yesterday

ayuda *a·yoo·da* f help; **la ayuda de cámara** *a·yoo·da de ka·ma·ra* valet (in hotel)

ayudar *a·yoo·dar* vt help; **¿puede ayudarme?** *pwe·de a·yoo·dar·me* can you help me?

ayuntamiento *a·yoon·ta·myen·to* m city hall; town hall

azafata *a·tha·fa·ta* f flight attendant

azafrán *a·tha·fran* m crocus; (cooking) saffron

azar *a·thar* m chance; **hecho al azar** *e·cho al a·thar* random

azúcar *a·thoo·kar* m sugar

azucarero *a·thoo·ka·re·ro* m sugar bowl

azucena *a·thoo·the·na* f lily

azul *a·thool* adj blue; **azul marino** *a·thool ma·ree·no* navy blue

B

baca *ba·ka* f roof rack

bacalao *ba·ka·la·o* m cod

bacará *ba·ka·ra* m baccarat

backgammon *bak·ga·mon* m backgammon

bacon *bey·kon* m bacon

badminton *bad·meen·ton* m badminton

bahía *ba·ee·a* f bay (on coast)

bailador(a) *bay·la·dor(·do·ra)* m/f dancer

bailar *bay·lar* vi dance

baile *bay·le* m dance; ball; **el baile folklórico** *bay·le fol·klo·ree·ko* folk dance

bajamar *ba·kha·mar* f low tide

bajar *ba·khar* vt/i go down □ vi fall (prices etc) □ vt turn down (heat, volume); **bajar a tierra** *ba·khar a tye·*

rra to land (*from ship*); **bajaba la calle** *ba·kha·ba la kal·ye* he came down the street

bajo(a) *ba·kho(a) adj* low; short (*person*); soft (*not loud*); **más bajo(a)** *mas ba·kho(a)* lower

bala *ba·la f* bullet

balance *ba·lan·the m* balance sheet; **hacer* balance** *a·ther ba·lan·the* to balance

balancear *ba·lan·the·ar vt/i* swing

balancearse *ba·lan·the·ar·se vr* swing

balanza *ba·lan·tha f* scales (*for weighing*); **la balanza de pagos** *ba·lan·tha de pa·gos* balance of payments; **la balanza comercial** *ba·lan·tha ko·mer·thyal* balance of trade

balcón *bal·kon m* balcony

balde *bal·de m* bucket

baldosa *bal·do·sa f* tile (*on floor, wall*)

ballena *bal·ye·na f* whale

ballet *ba·le m* ballet

balneario *bal·ne·a·ryo m* spa

balón *ba·lon m* ball

baloncesto *ba·lon·thes·to m* basketball

balonvólea *ba·lon·bo·le·a m* volleyball

bambú *ham·boo m* bamboo

bañarse *ban·yar·se vr* go swimming

banca *ban·ka f* banking

bancarrota *ban·ka·rro·ta f* bankruptcy

banco *ban·ko m* bank (*finance*); bench (*seat*); work table; **el banco de arena** *ban·ko de a·re·na* sandbank

banda *ban·da f* gang; band (*musical*); **la banda sonora** *ban·da so·no·ra* sound track

bandeja *ban·de·kha f* tray

bandera *ban·de·ra f* banner; flag

baño *ban·yo m* bath

banquero *ban·ke·ro m* banker

banquete *ban·ke·te m* banquet

baptista *bap·tees·ta adj* Baptist

bar *bar m* pub; bar

baraja *ba·ra·kha f* deck (*of cards*)

barajar *ba·ra·khar vt* shuffle (*cards*)

barandilla *ba·ran·deel·ya f* rail (*on stairs*)

barato(a) *ba·ra·to(a) adj* cheap; inexpensive

barba *bar·ba f* beard

barbacoa *bar·ba·ko·a f* barbecue

barbero *bar·be·ro m* barber

barbilla *bar·beel·ya f* chin

barca *bar·ka f* ferry (*small*)

barcaza *bar·ka·tha f* barge

barco *bar·ko m* ship; boat; **el barco de recreo** *bar·ko de re·kre·o* pleasure boat

barman *bar·man m* bartender

barniz *bar·neeth m* varnish

barquillo *bar·keel·yo m* cornet (*of ice cream*); wafer

barra *ba·rra f* bar; counter; **la barra de labios** *ba·rra de la·byos* lipstick; **la barra de chocolate** *ba·rra de cho·ko·la·te* bar of chocolate

barreño *ba·rren·yo m* bowl (*for washing*)

barrer *ba·rrer vt* sweep (*floor*)

barrera *ba·rre·ra f* barrier (*fence*)

barricada *ba·rree·ka·da f* road block; barricade

barril *ba·rreel m* barrel (*for beer*)

barrio *ba·rryo m* suburb; **el barrio chino** *ba·rryo chee·no* red light district

barro *ba·rro m* mud; **lleno(a) de barro** *lye·no(a) de ba·rro* muddy (*clothes*)

basar *ba·sar vt* base

base *ba·se f* base; basis

básico(a) *ba·see·ko(a) adj* basic

basketball *bas·ket·bol m* basketball

bastante *bas·tan·te adv* quite (*fairly*); **bastante grande** *bas·tan·te gran·de* big enough □ *adj* enough; plenty; **bastante leche** *bas·tan·te le·che* plenty of milk; **bastantes** *bas·tan·tes* quite a few

basto(a) *bas·to(a) adj* coarse (*texture, material*)

bastón *bas·ton m* walking stick

basura *ba·soo·ra f* garbage; rubbish

basurero *ba·soo·re·ro m* garbage dump; garbage man

bata *ba·ta f* dressing gown; housecoat

batalla *ba·tal·ya f* battle

batería *ba·te·ree·a f* battery (*in car*)

batido *ba·tee·do m* batter (*for frying*); **el batido de leche** *ba·tee·do de le·che* milkshake

batidor *ba·tee·dor m* whisk

batidora *ba·tee·do·ra f* mixer

batir *ba·teer vt* whip (*cream, eggs*); break (*record*)

baúl *ba·ool m* trunk (*for clothes etc*)

bautismo *bow·tees·mo m* baptism

baya *ba·ya f* berry

bayeta *ba·ye·ta f* dishcloth

baza *ba·tha f* trick (*in cards*)

bazar *ba·thar m* bazaar

beber *be·ber vt* drink

bebida *be·bee·da f* drink; **las bebidas alcohólicas** *be·bee·das al·ko·lee·kas* liquor

beca *be·ka f* grant (*to student*)

becerro *be·the·rro m* calf

beige *beys adj* beige; fawn

béisbol *beys·bol m* baseball

belleza *bel·ye·tha f* beauty

bellota *bel·yo·ta f* acorn

bemol *be·mol m* flat (*music*)

bendecir* *ben·de·theer vt* bless

beneficiar *be·ne·fee·thyar vt* benefit

beneficiario *be·ne·fee·thya·ryo m* payee

beneficio *be·ne·fee·thyo m* profit

berberecho *ber·be·re·cho m* cockle

berenjena *be·ren·khe·na f* eggplant; aubergine

berro *be·rro m* watercress

besar *be·sar vt* kiss

besarse *be·sar·se vr* kiss (each other)

beso *be·so m* kiss

betún *be·toon m* polish (*for shoes*)

biberón *bee·be·ron m* bottle (*baby's*)

Biblia *bee·blya f* Bible

biblioteca *bee·blyo·te·ka f* library

bicho *bee·cho m* bug (*insect*)

bicicleta *bee·thee·kle·ta f* bicycle; **ir* en bicicleta** *eer en bee·thee·kle·ta* to cycle; to go cycling

bien *byen adv* well; está bien *es·ta byen* that's all right; **muy bien** *mooy byen* (that's) fine; **lo hizo bien** *lo ee·tho byen* he did it well; **estar* bien** *es·tar byen* to be well; **le hará bien** *le a·ra byen* it'll do you good

bienes *bye·nes mpl* goods, **los bienes de equipo** *bye·nes de e·kee·po* capital goods; **los bienes raíces** *bye·nes ra·ee·thes* real estate; **los bienes de consumo** *bye·nes de kon·soo·mo* consumer goods

bienvenida *byen·be·nee·da f* welcome

bienvenido(a) *byen·be·nee·do(a) adj* welcome

biftec *beef·tek m* steak

bifurcación *bee·foor·ka·thyon f* fork (*in road*)

bigote *bee·go·te m* moustache

bigudí *bee·goo·dee m* curler (*for hair*)

bikini *bee·kee·nee m* bikini

bilingüe *bee·leen·gwe adj* bilingual

billar *beel·yar m* billiards; snooker

billete *beel·ye·te m* ticket; **el billete de banco** *beel·ye·te de ban·ko* bill; **el billete de ida** *beel·ye·te de ee·da* one-way ticket; **el billete de ida y vuelta** *beel·ye·te de ee·da ee bwel·ta* round trip (ticket); **un billete de segunda clase** *oon beel·ye·te de se·goon·da kla·se* a second class ticket; **el billete de abono** *beel·ye·te de a·bo·no* season ticket

biología *bee·o·lo·khee·a f* biology

¡bis! *bees* encore!

bizcocho *beeth·ko·cho m* spongecake

blanco(a) *blan·ko(a) adj* white; **en blanco** *en blan·ko* blank; **por favor dejar en blanco** *por fa·bor de·khar en blan·ko* please leave blank □ *m* **el blanco** *blan·ko* target

blando(a) *blan·do(a) adj* soft

blasfemar *blas·fe·mar vi* swear (curse)

bloc *blok m* pad (notepaper)

bloque *blo·ke m* block (of stone); **el bloque de pisos** *blo·ke de pee·sos* apartment block; **el bloque de oficinas** *blo·ke de o·fee·thee·nas* office block

blusa *bloo·sa f* blouse; smock

boca *bo·ka f* mouth

bocadillo *bo·ka·deel·yo m* sandwich; **un bocadillo de jamón** *oon bo·ka·deel·yo de kha·mon* a ham sandwich

bocado *bo·ka·do m* bite (of food)

boceto *bo·the·to m* sketch (drawing)

bocina *bo·thee·na f* horn (of car); **tocar° la bocina** *to·kar la bo·thee·na* to hoot (horn)

boda *bo·da f* marriage (wedding)

bodega *bo·de·ga f* wine cellar

bofetada *bo·fe·ta·da f* slap

boicotear *boy·ko·te·ar vt* boycott

boina *boee·na f* beret

bola *bo·la f* ball; **la bola de nieve** *bo·la de nye·be* snowball

boletín *bo·le·teen m* bulletin; **el boletín meteorológico** *bo·le·teen me·te·o·ro·lo·khee·ko* weather forecast

bolígrafo *bo·lee·gra·fo m* ballpoint pen

bollo *bol·yo m* roll (bread)

bolsa *bol·sa f* bag; carryall; stock exchange; **la bolsa de red** *bol·sa de red* string bag; **la bolsa de agua caliente** *bol·sa de a·gwa ka·lyen·te* hot-water bottle; **la bolsa de plástico** *bol·sa de plas·tee·ko* plastic bag; **la bolsa de la compra** *bol·sa de la kom·pra* shopping bag; **la bolsa de té** *bol·sa de te* tea bag

bolsillo *bol·seel·yo m* pocket

bolsita *bol·see·ta f* sachet

bolso *bol·so m* bag (handbag); purse

bomba *bom·ba f* bomb; pump; **la bomba de la gasolina** *bom·ba de la ga·so·lee·na* fuel pump; **sacar° con una bomba** *sa·kar kon oo·na bom·ba* to pump out

bombero *bom·be·ro m* fireman; **el cuerpo de bomberos** *kwer·po de bom·be·ros* fire department; **el coche de bomberos** *ko·che de bom·be·ros* fire engine

bombilla *bom·beel·ya f* light bulb; **la bombilla de flash** *bom·beel·ya de flash* flashbulb

boniato *bo·nya·to m* sweet potato

bonito(a) *bo·nee·to(a) adj* lovely; nice (dress, picture); pretty (dress); cute □ *m* **el bonito** *bo·nee·to* tuna fish

boom *boom m* boom (economic)

boquerón *bo·ke·ron m* whitebait

bordado(a) *bor·da·do(a) adj* embroidered □ *m* **el bordado** *bor·da·do* embroidery

borde *bor·de m* border (edge)

bordillo *bor·deel·yo m* curb

bordo *bor·do m* side (of ship); **ir°a bordo** *eer a bor·do* to go aboard; **a bordo del barco** *a bor·do del bar·ko* aboard the ship

borracho(a) *bo·rra·cho(a) adj* drunk

borrador *bo·rra·dor m* draft (rough outline); eraser

borrar *bo·rrar vt* rub out; erase

borrascoso(a) *bo·rras·ko·so(a) adj* gusty (wind)

borrón *bo·rron m* blot

bosque *bos·ke m* forest; wood

bostezar° *bos·te·thar vi* yawn

bota *bo·ta f* boot; **la bota de esquí** *bo·ta de es·kee* ski boot; **la bota de goma** *bo·ta de go·ma* wellington boot

botar *bo·tar vt* throw away; launch (ship)

bote *bo·te m* dinghy; **el bote salvavidas** *bo·te sal·ba·bee·das* lifeboat (on ship)

botella *bo·tel·ya f* bottle

botellero *bo·tel·ye·ro m* rack (for wine)

botiquín *bo·tee·keen m* first-aid kit

botón *bo·ton m* button; knob (on radio etc); **el botón de presión** *bo·ton de pre·syon* snap fastener; **el botón de camisa** *bo·ton de ka·mee·sa* stud (for collar)

botones *bo·to·nes m* bellboy; pageboy

botulismo *bo·too·lees·mo m* food poisoning

boutique *boo·teek f* boutique

boxeo *bok·se·o m* boxing

boya *bo·ya f* buoy

bragas *bra·gas fpl* pants (women's)

brazada *bra·tha·da f* stroke (swimming)

brazo *bra·tho m* arm (of person)

brea *bre·a f* tar

brécol *bre·kol m* broccoli

breve *bre·be adj* brief

brida *bree·da f* bridle

bridge *bridge m* bridge (game)

brillante *breel·yan·te adj* shiny

brillar *breel·yar vi* shine; blaze (lights); **el sol está brillando** *el sol es·ta breel·yan·do* the sun is out

brindar *breen·dar vi* propose a toast; **brindar por alguien** *breen·dar por al·gyen* to propose a toast to someone

brisa *bree·sa f* breeze

británico(a) *bree·ta·nee·ko(a) adj* British; **es británico** *es bree·ta·nee·ko* he's British; **es británica** *es bree·ta·nee·ka* she's British

brocha *bro·cha f* brush; **la brocha de afeitar** *bro·cha de a·fey·tar* shaving brush

broche *bro·che m* brooch

broma *bro·ma f* joke

bronce *bron·the m* bronze

bronceado(a) *bron·the·a·do(a) adj* sun-tanned □ *m* **el bronceado** *bron·the·a·do* tan (on skin)

broncearse *bron·the·ar·se vr* tan (in sun)

bronquitis *bron·kee·tees f* bronchitis

broqueta *bro·ke·ta f* skewer

brote *bro·te m* bud

bruja *broo·kha f* witch

brújula *broo·khoo·la f* compass

brumoso(a) *broo·mo·so(a) adj* foggy

brusco(a) *broos·ko(a) adj* abrupt (person)

Bruselas *broo·se·las fpl* Brussels

callejuela

bruto(a) *broo·to(a) adj* gross (*before deductions*)

bucear *boo·the·ar vi* dive

bueno(a) *bwe·no(a) adj* good; fine (*weather*); right; **las espinacas son buenas para la salud** *las es·pee·na·kas son bwe·nas pa·ra la sa·lood* spinach is good for you; **¡buenos días!** *bwe·nos dee·as* good morning!; **¡buenas tardes!** *bwe·nas tar·des* good afternoon!; good evening!; **¡buenas noches!** *bwe·nas no·ches* good night!

bufanda *boo·fan·da f* scarf

bujía *boo·khee·a f* spark plug

bulbo *bool·bo m* bulb

bulla *bool·ya f* noise (*loud*)

bulto *bool·to m* lump (*on skin*)

buñuelo *boo·nywe·lo m* fritter; waffle; doughnut

buque *boo·ke m* ship

burbuja *boor·boo·kha f* bubble

burro *boo·rro m* donkey

buscar* *boos·kar vt* search for; look for; look up (*word*); **iré a buscarle a la estación** *ee·re a boos·kar·le a la es·ta·thyon* I'll meet you at the station (*go to get*); **ir* a buscar** *eer a boos·kar* to fetch

busto *boos·to m* bust

butaca *boo·ta·ka f* stalls (*in theater*)

buzón *boo·thon m* letter box; mailbox

C

caballa *ka·bal·ya f* mackerel

caballero *ka·bal·ye·ro m* gentleman

caballo *ka·bal·yo m* horse; **montar a caballo** *mon·tar a ka·bal·yo* to go horseback riding; to go riding; **el caballo de carreras** *ka·bal·yo de ka·rre·ras* racehorse

cabaña *ka·ban·ya f* hut (*shed*)

cabaret *ka·ba·ret m* cabaret; night club

cabello *ka·bel·yo m* hair

caber* *ka·ber vi* fit; **no cabe** *no ka·be* it won't go in

cabestrillo *ka·bes·treel·yo m* sling (*for arm*)

cabeza *ka·be·tha f* head

cabida *ka·bee·da f* □ **el piso tiene cabida para 3 personas** *el pee·so tye·ne ka·bee·da pa·ra 3 per·so·nas* the apartment sleeps three

cabina *ka·bee·na f* cabin; **la cabina telefónica** *ka·bee·na te·le·fo·nee·ka* telephone booth

cable *ka·ble m* wire (*electrical*); lead; cable; **los cables para cargar la batería** *ka·bles pa·ra kar·gar la ba·te·ree·a* jumper cables; **el cable de toma de tierra** *ka·ble de to·ma de tye·rra* ground

cabo *ka·bo m* end

cabra *ka·bra f* goat

cabrito *ka·bree·to m* kid (*leather*)

cacahuete *ka·ka·we·te m* groundnut; peanut

cacao *ka·ka·o m* cocoa

cachemira *ka·che·mee·ra f* cashmere

cacto *kak·to m* cactus

cada *ka·da adj* every; each; **cada semana** *ka·da se·ma·na* weekly; **cada seis días** *ka·da seys dee·as* every 6th day; **cada uno(a)** *ka·da oo·no(a)* each; **cada uno de ellos** *ka·da oo·no de el·yos* each of them; **cada vez más** *ka·da beth mas* more and more

cadáver *ka·da·ber m* body (*corpse*)

cadena *ka·de·na f* chain; **la cadena de montaje** *ka·de·na de mon·ta·khe* assembly line

cadera *ka·de·ra f* hip

cadi *ka·dee m* caddie

caducado(a) *ka·doo·ka·do(a) adj* out-of-date (*passport, ticket*)

caer* *ka·er vi* drop (*fall*); **dejar caer** *de·khar ka·er* drop (*let fall*)

caerse* *ka·er·se vr* fall down; fall over

café *ka·fe m* café; coffee; **el café solo** *ka·fe so·lo* black coffee; **el café con leche** *ka·fe kon le·che* coffee with milk; **el café exprés** *ka·fe eks·pres* espresso (*coffee*)

cafetera *ka·fe·te·ra f* coffeepot; **la cafetera de filtro** *ka·fe·te·ra de feel·tro* percolator

cafetería *ka·fe·te·ree·a f* snack bar; cafetería

caída *ka·ee·da f* fall

caja *ka·kha f* box; case (*of wine*); cashdesk; **la caja de cerillas** *ka·kha de the·reel·yas* matchbox; **la caja fuerte** *ka·kha fwer·te* strongbox; **la caja de cartón** *ka·kha de kar·ton* box (*cardboard*); **la caja de ahorros** *ka·kha de a·o·rros* savings bank; **la caja de jubilaciones** *ka·kha de khoo·bee·la·thyo·nes* pension fund; **la caja de cambios** *ka·kha de kam·byos* gearbox

cajero(a) *ka·khe·ro(a) m/f* teller; cashier

cajón *ka·khon m* drawer; crate; **el cajón de embalaje** *ka·khon de em·ba·la·khe* packing case

calabacín *ka·la·ba·theen m* marrow (*vegetable*)

calabacines *ka·la·ba·thee·nes mpl* courgettes; zucchini

calabaza *ka·la·ba·tha f* squash (*gourd*); pumpkin

calabozo *ka·la·bo·tho m* dungeon

calambre *ka·lam·bre m* cramp

calavera *ka·la·be·ra f* skull

calcetín *kal·the·teen m* sock

calcio *kal·thyo m* calcium

calculadora *kal·koo·la·do·ra f* calculator

calcular *kal·koo·lar vt* calculate

cálculo *kal·koo·lo m* sum (*problem*)

caldo *kal·do m* stock (*for soup etc*)

calefacción *ka·le·fak·thyon f* heating; **la calefacción central** *ka·le·fak·thyon then·tral* central heating

calendario *ka·len·da·ryo m* calendar

calentador *ka·len·ta·dor m* heater; **el calentador de agua** *ka·len·ta·dor de ag·wa* water heater

calentar *ka·len·tar vt* heat

calidad *ka·lee·dad f* quality; **los artículos de calidad** *ar·tee·koo·los de ka·lee·dad* quality goods

cálido(a) *ka·lee·do(a) adj* warm

calientaplatos *ka·lyen·ta·pla·tos m* hotplate

caliente *ka·lyen·te adj* hot

calificado(a) *ka·lee·fee·ka·do(a) adj* qualified

calificarse* para *ka·lee·fee·kar·se pa·ra vr* qualify for (*in sports*)

calladamente *kal·ya·da·men·te adv* quietly (*speak*)

calle *kal·ye f* street; **la calle sin salida** *kal·ye seen sa·lee·da* cul-de-sac; **la calle secundaria** *kal·ye se·koon·da·rya* side-street; **la calle de dirección única** *kal·ye de dee·rek·thyon oo·nee·ka* one-way street; **la calle mayor** *kal·ye ma·yor* main street

callejón sin salida *kal·ye·khon seen sa·lee·da m* dead end; blind alley

callejuela *kal·ye·khwe·la f* alley

callo   90

callo *kal·yo* m corn (*on foot*)
callos *kal·yos* mpl tripe
calmado(a) *kal·ma·do(a)* adj calm (*sea, day, person*)
calmante *kal·man·te* m painkiller; sedative
calor *ka·lor* m heat; hace calor hoy *a·the ka·lor oy* it's warm today; tengo calor *ten·go ka·lor* I'm warm
caloría *ka·lo·ree·a* f calorie
calvo(a) *kal·bo(a)* adj bald
calzada *kal·tha·da* f roadway
calzoncillos *kal·thon·theel·yos* mpl underpants
cama *ka·ma* f bed; la cama de campaña *ka·ma de kam·pan·ya* camp-bed; las camas gemelas *ka·mas khe·me·las* twin beds; una cama de matrimonio *oo·na ka·ma de ma·tree·mo·nyo* double bed; una cama individual *oo·na ka·ma een·dee·bee·dwal* a single bed; en la cama *en la ka·ma* in bed; la cama de campaña *ka·ma de kam·pan·ya* cot
cámara *ka·ma·ra* f camera (*TV*); la cámara cinematográfica *ka·ma·ra thee·ne·ma·to·gra·fee·ka* movie camera; la cámara de comercio *ka·ma·ra de ko·mer·thyo* Chamber of Commerce; la cámara acorazada *ka·ma·ra a·ko·ra·tha·da* strongroom
camarera *ka·ma·re·ra* f barmaid; waitress
camarero *ka·ma·re·ro* m steward; barman; waiter; flight attendant
camarón *ka·ma·ron* m shrimp
camarote *ka·ma·ro·te* m cabin (*in ship*)
cambiar *kam·byar* vt exchange; cambiar algo por otra cosa *kam·byar al·go por o·tra ko·sa* to exchange something for something □ vi change; cambiar de marcha *kam·byar de mar·cha* to shift gear; sin cambiar *seen kam·byar* unchanged
cambiarse *kam·byar·se* vr change; cambiarse de casa *kam·byar·se de ka·sa* to move out; cambiarse de ropa *kam·byar·se de ro·pa* to change one's clothes
cambio *kam·byo* m change; gear (*of car*); exchange (*between currencies*); change (*money*); en cambio *en kam·byo* instead; un cambio en el tiempo *oon kam·byo en el tyem·po* a change in the weather; el cambio sincronizado de velocidades *kam·byo seen·kro·nee·tha·do de be·lo·thee·da·des* synchromesh
camello *ka·mel·yo* m camel
camilla *ka·meel·ya* f stretcher
camino *ka·mee·no* m path; track (*pathway*); lane (*in country*); camino de *ka·mee·no de* on the way; el camino equivocado *el ka·mee·no e·kee·bo·ka·do* the wrong road; ponerse* en camino *po·ner·se en ka·mee·no* to set off; ¿cuál es el camino para Londres? *kwal es el ka·mee·no pa·ra lon·dres* which is the way to London?; preguntar el camino de París *pre·goon·tar el ka·mee·no de pa·rees* to ask the way to Paris
camión *ka·myon* m truck (*vehicle*); el camión cisterna *ka·myon thees·ter·na* tanker (*truck*); el camión de mudanzas *ka·myon de moo·dan·thas* moving van
camionero *ka·myo·ne·ro* m truck driver
camioneta *ka·myo·ne·ta* f van
camisa *ka·mee·sa* f shirt

camiseta *ka·mee·se·ta* f tee shirt; undershirt
camisón *ka·mee·son* m nightgown
camote *ka·mo·te* m sweet potato
campaña *kam·pan·ya* f campaign; la campaña de publicidad *kam·pan·ya de poo·blee·thee·dad* publicity campaign; la campaña de prensa *kam·pan·ya de pren·sa* press campaign
campana *kam·pa·na* f bell (*church etc*)
campeón *kam·pe·on* m champion
campesino *kam·pe·see·no* m peasant
camping *kam·peeng* m camping; camp(ing) site; hacer* camping *a·ther kam·peeng* to go camping
campo *kam·po* m field (*on farm, for football etc*); countryside; el campo de golf *kam·po de golf* golf course; en el campo *en el kam·po* in the country; el campo de deportes *kam·po de de·por·tes* playing field
caña *kan·ya* f cane; la caña de pesca *kan·ya de pes·ka* rod (*fishing*)
Canadá *ka·na·da* m Canada
canadiense *ka·na·dyen·se* adj Canadian; es canadiense *es ka·na·dyen·se* he's Canadian; (ella) es canadiense *(el·ya) es ka·na·dyen·se* she's Canadian
canal *ka·nal* m canal; el Canal de la Mancha *ka·nal de la man·cha* the Channel
canalete *ka·na·le·te* m paddle (*oar*)
canalón *ka·na·lon* m gutter (*on building*)
canasta *ka·nas·ta* f canasta (*card game*); basket
cancelar *kan·the·lar* vt cancel; cancelar un cheque *kan·the·lar oon che·ke* to stop a check; cancelar una deuda *kan·the·lar oo·na de·oo·da* to write off a debt
cáncer *kan·ther* m cancer
cancha *kan·cha* f field (*for football etc*); la cancha de tenis *kan·cha de te·nees* tennis court
canciller *kan·theel·yer* m chancellor (*in Germany, Austria*)
canción *kan·thyon* f song; la canción folklórica *kan·thyon fol·klo·ree·ka* folk song
candado *kan·da·do* m padlock
candidato(a) *kan·dee·da·to(a)* m/f candidate (*for election*)
canela *ka·ne·la* f cinnamon
cangrejo *kan·gre·kho* m crab; el cangrejo de río *kan·gre·kho de ree·o* crawfish, crayfish (*freshwater*)
cangura *kan·goo·ra* f baby-sitter
canoa *ka·no·a* f canoe
cañón *ka·nyon* m cannon
cansado(a) *kan·sa·do(a)* adj tired; estoy cansado de eso *es·toy kan·sa·do de e·so* I'm tired of it
cansarse *kan·sar·se* vr to get tired
cantante *kan·tan·te* m/f singer
cantar *kan·tar* vt/i sing
cantera *kan·te·ra* f quarry
cantidad *kan·tee·dad* f quantity; una gran cantidad de X *oo·na gran kan·tee·dad de X* a large amount of X
cantina *kan·tee·na* f canteen
caoba *ka·o·ba* f mahogany
capa *ka·pa* f cloak; layer; coat of paint
capacitado(a) *ka·pa·thee·ta·do(a)* adj qualified
capataz *ka·pa·tath* m foreman
capaz *ka·path* adj capable; capaz de *ka·path de* capable of
capilla *ka·peel·ya* f chapel
capital *ka·pee·tal* f capital (*city*) □ m el

capital *ka·pee·tal* capital (*finance*); el capital de explotación *ka·pee·tal de eks·plo·ta·thyon* working capital

capitalismo *ka·pee·ta·lees·mo m* capitalism

capitalista *ka·pee·ta·lees·ta m/f* capitalist

capitán *ka·pee·tan m* captain; el capitán de puerto *ka·pee·tan de pwer·to* harbor master

capítulo *ka·pee·too·lo m* chapter

capó *ka·po m* hood (*of car*)

cápsula *kap·soo·la f* capsule (*of medicine*)

capucha *ka·poo·cha f* hood

cara *ka·ra f* face

caracol *ka·ra·kol m* snail

carácter *ka·rak·ter m* character

característica *ka·rak·te·rees·tee·ka f* quality (*characteristic*)

caramba *ka·ram·ba excl* well!

caramelo *ka·ra·me·lo m* toffee; caramel; sweet (*candy*); el caramelo de menta *ka·ra·me·lo de men·ta* peppermint (*confectionery*)

caramillo *ka·ra·meel·yo m* pipe (*musical*)

caravana *ka·ra·ba·na f* trailer (*home on wheels*)

carbón *kar·bon m* coal

carbono *kar·bo·no m* carbon

carburador *kar·boo·ra·dor m* carburetor

carburante *kar·boo·ran·te m* fuel

cárcel *kar·thel f* prison; en la cárcel *en la kar·thel* in jail

cardenal *kar·de·nal m* bruise; cardinal (*of church*)

carecer de *ka·re·ther de vi* lack

carga *kar·ga f* cargo; load

cargar *kar·gar vt* load; cargar $50 a la cuenta de alguien *kar·gar $50 a la kwen·ta de al·gyen* to debit $50 to someone's account

cariño *ka·reen·yo m* affection

cariñoso(a) *ka·reen·yo·so(a) adj* affectionate

carnaval *kar·na·bal m* carnival

carne *kar·ne f* meat; flesh; la carne de vaca *kar·ne de ba·ka* beef; la carne de cerdo *kar·ne de ther·do* pork; la carne en lata *kar·ne en la·ta* corned beef; la carne picada *kar·ne pee·ka·da* ground beef; la carne de venado *kar·ne de be·na·do* venison

carnero *kar·ne·ro m* mutton; sheep

carnet de identidad *kar·net de ee·den·tee·dad m* identity card

carnicería *kar·nee·the·ree·a f* butcher's (*shop*)

carnicero *kar·nee·the·ro m* butcher

caro(a) *ka·ro(a) adj* expensive

carpa *kar·pa f* tent

carpintero *kar·peen·te·ro m* carpenter

carrera *ka·rre·ra f* career; race (*sport*); run (*in stocking*); las carreras de caballos *ka·rre·ras de ka·bal·yos* horseracing

carrete *ka·rre·te m* film (*for camera*)

carretera *ka·rre·te·ra f* road; highway; la carretera de doble calzada *ka·rre·te·ra de do·ble kal·tha·da* divided highway; la carretera de circumvalación *ka·rre·te·ra de theer·koom·ba·la·thyon* beltway

carretilla *ka·rre·teel·ya f* cart; luggage cart; wheelbarrow

carril *ka·rreel m* lane (*of road*); el carril de la izquierda *el ka·rreel de la eeth·kyer·da* the outside lane (*in road*)

carrito *ka·rree·to m* cart (*for purchases*)

carro *ka·rro m* car

carta *kar·ta f* card (*playing card*); letter (*message*); la carta aérea *kar·ta a·e·re·a* air letter; la carta certificada *kar·ta ther·tee·fee·ka·da* registered letter; la carta urgente *kar·ta oor·khen·te* express letter; la carta verde *kar·ta ber·de* green card; la carta explicatoria *kar·ta eks·plee·ka·to·rya* covering letter; la carta de figura *kar·ta de fee·goo·ra* face card; la carta de navegación *kar·ta de na·be·ga·thyon* chart (*map*); jugar* a las cartas *khoo·gar a las kar·tas* to play cards

cartel *kar·tel m* cartel; poster

cárter *kar·ter m* oil pan (*in car*)

cartera *kar·te·ra f* wallet; pocketbook; portfolio; briefcase

cartero *kar·te·ro m* mailman

cartón *kar·ton m* cardboard; carton (*of yogurt etc*)

cartucho *kar·too·cho m* cartridge

casa *ka·sa f* home; house; household; la casa de campo *ka·sa de kam·po* farmhouse; la casa independiente *ka·sa een·de·pen·dyen·te* detached house; en casa *en ka·sa* at home; ir* a casa *eer a ka·sa* to go home; casa de *ka·sa de care of*, c/o; la casa de huéspedes *ka·sa de wes·pe·des* guesthouse; la Casa Blanca *ka·sa blan·ka* White House; pagado(a) por la casa *pa·ga·do(a) por la ka·sa* on the house; la casa solariega *ka·sa so·la·rye·ga* mansion; la casa de maternidad *ka·sa de ma·ter·nee·dad* maternity hospital

casado(a) *ka·sa·do(a) adj* married

casar *ka·sar vt* marry

casarse *ka·sar·se vr* marry; se casaron ayer *se ka·sa·ron a·yer* they were married yesterday

cascada *kas·ka·da f* waterfall

cáscara *kas·ka·ra f* peel; shell (*of egg*)

casco *kas·ko m* helmet; el casco protector *kas·ko pro·tek·tor* crash helmet

casero(a) *ka·se·ro(a) adj* plain (*simple: cooking etc*)

caseta *ka·se·ta f* cubicle

casi *ka·see adv* nearly; almost; casi no pude hacerlo *ka·see no poo·de ath·er·lo* I just managed it

casilla *ka·seel·ya f* locker; post-office box

casino *ka·see·no m* casino

caso *ka·so m* case (*instance*); en caso de *en ka·so de* in case of; en último caso *en ool·tee·mo ka·so* in the last resort; que viene al caso *ke bye·ne al ka·so* relevant to; no hacer* caso de *no a·ther ka·so de* to ignore

caspa *kas·pa f* dandruff

cassette *ka·set f* cassette; cartridge (*of tape*); la cassette video *ka·set bee·de·o* videocassette

castaña *kas·tan·ya f* chestnut

castaño(a) *kas·tan·yo(a) adj* brown; **castaño rojizo** *kas·tan·yo ro·khee·tho adj* maroon

castañuelas *kas·tan·we·las fpl* castanets

castigar* *kas·tee·gar vt* punish

castigo *kas·tee·go m* punishment

castillo *kas·teel·yo m* castle

casualidad *ka·swa·lee·dad f* chance; por casualidad *por ka·swa·lee·dad* by accident

catálogo *ka·ta·lo·go m* catalog

catarro *ka·ta·rro m* catarrh

catedral *ka·te·dral f* cathedral

catedrático(a) *ka·te·dra·tee·ko(a) m/f* professor

categoría *ka·te·go·ree·a f* category

católico(a) *ka·to·lee·ko(a) adj* Roman Catholic

catorce *ka·tor·the num* fourteen

caucho *kow·cho m* rubber

causa *kow·sa f* cause; reason; **a causa de** *a kow·sa* because of

causar *kow·sar vt* cause; **causar buena impresión** *kow·sar bwe·na eem·pre·syon* to impress (*win approval*)

cavar *ka·bar vt* dig

caviar *ka·byar m* caviar(e)

caza *ka·tha f* game (*hunting*)

cazador *ka·tha·dor m* hunter

cazar *ka·thar vt* hunt

cazo *ka·tho m* saucepan

cazuela *ka·thwe·la f* casserole; pan

cebada *the·ba·da f* barley

cebador *the·ba·dor m* choke

cebo *the·bo m* bait

cebolla *the·bol·ya f* onion

cebolleta *the·bol·ye·ta f* spring onion

cebollino *the·bol·yee·no m* chives

cebra *the·bra f* zebra

ceder *the·der vt/i* give in; **ceder el paso** *the·der el pa·so* to yield (*to traffic*)

cedro *the·dro m* cedar

C.E.E. *the·e·e f* E.E.C.

ceja *the·kha f* eyebrow

celda *thel·da f* cell (*in prison*)

celebrar *the·le·brar vt* celebrate

celofán *the·lo·fan m* cellophane

celoso(a) *the·lo·so(a) adj* jealous (*of person*)

Celsius *thel·syoos adj* Celsius

cementerio *the·men·te·ryo m* cemetery; graveyard

cemento *the·men·to m* cement

cena *the·na f* dinner; supper

cenicero *the·nee·the·ro m* ashtray

ceniza *the·nee·tha f* ash

centavo *then·ta·bo m* cent

centellear *then·tel·ye·ar vi* sparkle

centenario *then·te·na·ryo m* centenary

centeno *then·te·no m* rye

centésimo(a) *then·te·see·mo(a) adj* hundredth

centígrado *then·tee·gra·do adj* centigrade

centilitro *then·tee·lee·tro m* centiliter

centímetro *then·tee·me·tro m* centimeter

céntimo *then·tee·mo m* cent

centinela *then·tee·ne·la m* guard (*sentry*)

central *then·tral adj* central; **la central telefónica** *then·tral te·le·fo·nee·ka* telephone exchange

centralita *then·tra·lee·ta f* switchboard

centro *then·tro m* center; **al centro (de la ciudad)** *al then·tro (de la thyoo·dad)* downtown; **el centro de Chicago** *then·tro de chee·ka·go* downtown Chicago; **ir* al centro de la ciudad** *eer al then·tro de la thyoo·dad* to go downtown; **el centro para jóvenes** *then·tro pa·ra kho·be·nes* youth club; **el centro de la ciudad** *then·tro de la thyoo·dad* center of the city; **en el centro mismo** *en el then·tro mees·mo* right in the middle; **el centro comercial** *then·tro ko·mer·thyal* shopping center

cepillar *the·peel·yar vt* brush

cepillo *the·peel·yo m* brush; **el cepillo (de carpintero)** *the·peel·yo (de kar·peen·te·ro)* plane (*tool*); **el cepillo de dientes** *the·peel·yo de dyen·tes* tooth-brush; **el cepillo de uñas** *the·peel·yo de oon·yas* nailbrush; **el cepillo para el pelo** *the·peel·yo pa·ra el pe·lo* hair-brush

cera *the·ra f* polish; wax

cerámica *the·ra·mee·ka f* pottery

cerca *ther·ka f* fence □ *adv* near; **cerca de** *ther·ka de* close to; **muy cerca** *mooy ther·ka* close by; **cerca de la casa** *ther·ka de la ka·sa* near (to) the house; **cerca de Navidades** *ther·ka de na·bee·da·des* near (to) Christmas

cercano(a) *ther·ka·no(a) adj* close (*near*)

Cerdeña *ther·den·ya f* Sardinia

cerdo *ther·do m* pig

cereal *the·re·al m* cereal (*breakfast*)

cereales *the·re·a·les mpl* grain (*cereal crops*)

cerebro *the·re·bro m* brain

ceremonia *the·re·mo·nya f* ceremony

cereza *the·re·tha f* cherry

cerezo *the·re·tho m* cherry (*tree*)

cerilla *the·reel·ya f* match

cero *the·ro m* nil; zero

cerrado(a) *the·rra·do(a) adj* off (*water supply*); sharp (*bend*); **estar* cerrado(a)** *es·tar ther·rra·do(a)* to be shut (*door*)

cerradura *the·rra·doo·ra f* lock

cerrar* *the·rrar vt* close; block (*road*); shut; **cerrar con llave** *the·rrar kon lya·be* to lock; **cerrar* de golpe** *the·rrar de gol·pe* to bang (*door*)

cerrarse* *the·rrar·se vr* shut (*door, window*); **se cerró la puerta** *se the·rro la pwer·ta* the door closed

cerrojo *the·rro·kho m* bolt; **echar el cerrojo** *e·char el the·rro·kho* to bolt (*door, gate*)

certificado *ther·tee·fee·ka·do m* certificate; **el certificado de defunción** *ther·tee·fee·ka·do de de·foon·thyon* death certificate

certificar* *ther·tee·fee·kar vt* register

cervecería *ther·be·the·ree·a f* brewery

cerveza *ther·be·tha f* beer; lager; **la cerveza de barril** *ther·be·tha de ba·rreel* draft beer

césped *thes·ped m* lawn (*grass*)

cesta *thes·ta f* hamper; basket

chal *chal m* wrap (*shawl*)

chalé *cha·le m* bungalow

chaleco *cha·le·ko m* vest; **el chaleco salvavidas** *cha·le·ko sal·ba·bee·das* life preserver (*jacket*)

chalet *cha·let m* chalet

chalote *cha·lo·te m* scallion

champán *cham·pan m* champagne

champiñón *cham·peen·yon m* mushroom

champú *cham·poo m* shampoo

chancho *chan·cho m* pig

chándal *chan·dal m* track suit

chanquetes *chan·ke·tes mpl* whitebait

chapa ondulada *cha·pa on·doo·la·da f* corrugated iron

chaparrón *cha·pa·rron m* shower (*rain*)

chapeado(a) *cha·pe·a·do(a) adj* plated

chapotear *cha·po·te·ar vi* paddle; splash

chapoteo *cha·po·te·o m* splash

chaqueta *cha·ke·ta f* jacket; **la chaqueta de sport** *cha·ke·ta de es·port* sport coat, sport jacket; blazer; **la chaqueta de punto** *cha·ke·ta de poon·to* cardigan

charca *char·ka f* pond

charco *char·ko m* pool; puddle

charol *cha·rol m* patent leather

chasis *cha·sees m* chassis

chasquido *chas·kee·do* m crack (*noise*)

checoslovaco(a) *che·kos·lo·ba·ko(a)* adj Czech(oslovakian)

Checoslovaquia *che·ko·slo·ba·kya f* Czechoslovakia

cheque *che·ke* m check (*banking*); **el cheque en blanco** *el che·ke en blan·ko* blank check; **el cheque de viaje** *el che·ke de bya·khe* traveler's check

chicle *chee·kle* m chewing gum

chico(a) *chee·ko(a)* adj small □ **el** m **el chico** *chee·ko* boy □ f **la chica** *chee·ka* girl

chichón *chee·chon* m bump (*lump*)

Chile *chee·le* m Chile

chile *chee·le* m chili

chileno(a) *chee·le·no(a)* adj Chilean; **es chileno** *es chee·le·no* he's Chilean; **es chilena** *es chee·le·na* she's Chilean

chimenea *chee·me·ne·a f* fireplace; chimney

China *chee·na f* China

chinche *cheen·che* m thumbtack

chincheta *cheen·che·ta f* drawing pin; tack (*nail*)

chino(a) *chee·no(a)* adj Chinese □ m **el chino** *chee·no* Chinese (*language*)

Chipre *chee·pre* m Cyprus

chirivía *chee·ree·bee·a f* parsnip

chispa *chees·pa f* spark

chistera *chees·te·ra f* top hat

chistoso(a) *chees·to·so(a)* adj funny

chocar* *cho·kar* vi collide □ vt/i hit

choclo *chok·lo* m corn-on-the-cob

chocolate *cho·ko·la·te* m chocolate; **el chocolate sin leche** *cho·ko·la·te seen le·che* plain chocolate; **el chocolate con leche** *cho·ko·la·te kon le·che* milk chocolate

chofer *cho·fer* m driver (*of car*)

chófer *cho·fer* m chauffeur

chopo *cho·po* m poplar

choque *cho·ke* m crash (*collision*); bump (*knock*); **tener* un choque con el coche** *te·ner oon cho·ke kon el ko·che* to crash one's car

chueco(a) *chwe·ko(a)* adj crooked

chuleta *choo·le·ta f* T-bone steak; cutlet; **la chuleta de cerdo** *choo·le·ta de ther·do* pork chop

chupa-chups *choo·pa·choops* m lollipop

chupar *choo·par* vt suck

chupete *choo·pe·te* m pacifier; lollipop

chupón *choo·pon* m pacifier

cicatriz *thee·ka·treeth f* scar

ciclismo *thee·klees·mo* m cycling

ciclista *thee·klees·ta* m/f cyclist

ciclomotor *theek·lo·mo·tor* m moped

ciego(a) *thye·go(a)* adj blind

cielo *thye·lo* m sky

cien *thyen* num hundred; **ciento uno(a)** *thyen·to oo·no(a)* a hundred and one; **cien personas** *thyen per·so·nas* a hundred people; **cientos de libros** *thyen·tos de lee·bros* hundreds of books

ciencia *thyen·thya f* science

ciencia-ficción *thyen·thya feek·thyon f* science fiction

científico(a) *thyen·tee·fee·ko(a)* adj scientific □ m/f scientist

cierre *thye·rre* m fastener

cierto(a) *thyer·to(a)* adj definite; certain; **cierta gente** *thyer·ta khen·te* some people

cifra *thee·fra f* figure (*number*); **la cifra redonda** *thee·fra re·don·da* round figure/number

cigarillo *thee·ga·reel·yo* m cigarette

cigarro *thee·ga·rro* m cigar

cilindro *thee·leen·dro* m cylinder

cima *thee·ma f* top (*of mountain*)

cinc *theenk* m zinc

cinco *theen·ko* num five

cincuenta *theen·kwen·ta* num fifty

cine *thee·ne* m cinema

cinta *theen·ta f* ribbon; tape; **la cinta magnética de video** *theen·ta mag·ne·tee·ka de bee·de·o* videotape; **la cinta magnética** *theen·ta mag·ne·tee·ka* magnetic tape

cintura *theen·too·ra f* waist

cinturón *theen·too·ron* m belt (*for waist*); **el cinturón salvavidas** *theen·too·ron sal·ba·bee·das* life preserver; **el cinturón de seguridad** *theen·too·ron de se·goo·ree·dad* safety belt

circo *theer·ko* m circus

circuito *theer·kwee·to* m circuit

circulación *theer·koo·la·thyon f* traffic (*flow*)

circular *theer·koo·lar* vi flow (*traffic*)

círculo *theer·koo·lo* m circle

circunstancia *theer·koons·tan·thya* circumstance; **las circunstancias fuera de nuestro control** *las theer·koons·tan·thyas fwe·ra de nwes·tro kon·trol* circumstances beyond our control

ciruela *thee·rwe·la f* plum

ciruela pasa *thee·rwe·la pa·sa f* prune

cirugía *thee·roo·khee·a f* surgery (*operation*); **la cirugía estética** *thee·roo·khee·a es·te·tee·ka* plastic surgery

cirujano *thee·roo·kha·no* m surgeon

cisne *thees·ne* m swan

cita *thee·ta f* appointment; date; quotation

citación *thee·ta·thyon f* summons

citar *thee·tar* vt quote (*passage*)

ciudad *thyoo·dad f* city; town; **ir* a la ciudad** *eer a la thyoo·dad* to go to town

ciudadano *thyoo·da·da·no* m citizen

civilización *thee·bee·lee·tha·thyon f* civilization

clarete *kla·re·te* m claret

claro(a) *kla·ro(a)* adj light (*bright, pale*); plain (*clear*); **claro que sí** *kla·ro ke see* yes of course

clase *kla·se f* class; lesson; **de clase superior** *de kla·se soo·pe·ryor* high-class; **de la clase media** *de la kla·se me·dya* middle-class

clásico(a) *kla·see·ko(a)* adj classical (*music, art*)

cláusula *klow·soo·la f* clause (*in contract*)

clavar *kla·bar* vt nail

clavel *kla·bel* m carnation

clavija *kla·bee·kha f* peg

clavo *kla·bo* m nail (*metal*); stud; **el clavo (de especia)** *kla·bo (de es·pe·thya)* clove

cliente *klee·en·te* m/f customer; client

clima *klee·ma* m climate

climatizado(a) *klee·ma·tee·tha·do(a)* adj air-conditioned

clínica *klee·nee·ka f* clinic; **la clínica de reposo** *klee·nee·ka de re·po·so* nursing home

clip *kleep* m paperclip

club *kloob* m club; **el club de golf** *kloob de golf* golf club

cobarde *ko·bar·de* m/f coward

cobertizo *ko·ber·tee·tho* m shed

cobertor *ko·ber·tor* m cover (*blanket*)

cobrador *ko·bra·dor* m conductor (*on bus*)

cobrar *ko·brar* vt charge (*money*); cash (*check*); **cobrar por algo** *ko·brar por* al·go to make a charge for something

cobre ko·bre m copper

cobro ko·bro m payment

cocer* ko·ther vt cook; **cocido(a) a fuego lento** ko·thee·do(a) a fwe·go len·to braised; **la carne está cociendo** kar·ne es·ta ko·thyen·do the meat is cooking; **cocer* al vapor** ko·ther al ba·por to steam (food)

coche ko·che m car; **el coche de alquiler** ko·che de al·kee·ler rental car; **el coche deportivo** ko·che de·por·tee·bo sport(s) car

coche-cama ko·che-ka·ma m wagon-lit; sleeping car

cochecito de niño ko·che·thee·to de neen·yo m baby buggy, baby carriage; pram

coche-comedor ko·che·ko·me·dor m club car

coche patrulla ko·che pa·trool·ya m police car

cocido(a) ko·thee·do(a) adj cooked; **insuficientemente cocido(a)** een·soo·fee·thyen·te·men·te ko·thee·do(a) undercooked

cocina ko·thee·na f kitchen; cuisine; stove; **la cocina de gas** ko·thee·na de gas gas stove

cocinar ko·thee·nar vt cook; **cocinar en el horno** ko·thee·nar en el or·no to bake

cocinero(a) ko·thee·ne·ro(a) m/f cook

coco ko·ko m coconut

cocodrilo ko·ko·dree·lo m crocodile

coctel kok·tel m cocktail; **el coctel de gambas** kok·tel de gam·bas shrimp cocktail

codeína ko·de·ee·na f codeine

código de la circulación ko·dee·go de la theer·koo·la·thyon m Highway Code

código postal ko·dee·go pos·tal m zip comercial code

codo ko·do m elbow

codorniz ko·dor·neeth f quail

coger* ko·kher vt catch; get; pick (flower); **cogimos el tren** ko·khee·mos el tren we took the train; **coger* una carretera** ko·kher oon·a ka·rre·te·ra to get onto a road

cohete ko·e·te m rocket

coincidencia ko·een·thee·den·thya f coincidence

coincidir ko·een·thee·deer vi coincide

cojear ko·khe·ar vi limp

cojín ko·kheen m cushion

cojinetes ko·khee·ne·tes mpl bearings (in car)

cojo(a) ko·kho(a) m/f cripple

col kol m cabbage; **los coles de Bruselas** ko·les de broo·se·las sprouts

cola ko·la f glue; tail; train (on dress); line (people waiting); **hacer* cola a·ther** ko·la to stand in line

colaborar ko·la·bo·rar vi collaborate

colador ko·la·dor m colander; sieve; strainer; **pasar por el colador** pa·sar por el ko·la·dor to sift (sieve); **el colador de té** ko·la·dor de te tea strainer

colar ko·lar vt sieve; strain (tea etc)

colchón kol·chon m mattress; **el colchón neumático** kol·chon ne·oo·ma·tee·ko air bed

colección ko·lek·thyon f collection

coleccionar ko·lek·thyo·nar vt collect (stamps etc)

colectar ko·lek·tar vt collect (donations)

colega ko·le·ga m/f colleague

colegio ko·le·khyo m college; high school; **el colegio de segunda enseñanza** ko·le·khyo de se·goon·da en·sen·yan·tha secondary school; **el colegio privado** ko·le·khyo pree·ba·do private school

cólera ko·le·ra f anger

colesterol ko·les·te·rol m cholesterol

colgar* kol·gar vt hang; hang up (phone); **¡no cuelgue!** no kwel·ge hang on! (on phone)

cólico ko·lee·ko m colic

coliflor ko·lee·flor f cauliflower

colina ko·lee·na f hill

colinabo ko·lee·na·bo m kohlrabi

collar kol·yar m necklace

colonia ko·lo·nya f eau-de-Cologne

color ko·lor m color; **de color** de ko·lor colored; **color naranja** ko·lor na·ran·kha orange

colorado(a) ko·lo·ra·do(a) adj colored

columna ko·loom·na f column; **la columna de dirección** ko·loom·na de dee·rek·thyon steering column

columpio ko·loom·pyo m seesaw; swing

coma ko·ma m comma □ f **la coma de decimales** ko·ma de the·ma·les decimal point; **3 coma 4** 3 ko·ma 4 3 point 4

comadreo ko·ma·dre·o m gossip (chatter)

comadrona ko·ma·dro·na f midwife

combinación kom·bee·na·thyon f combination; team; **la combinación** kom·bee·na·thyon slip (underskirt)

combustible kom·boos·tee·ble m fuel

comedia ko·me·dya f comedy

comedor ko·me·dor m dining room

comentario ko·men·ta·ryo m comment

comenzar* ko·men·thar vt begin

comer ko·mer vt eat

comercial ko·mer·thyal adj commercial

comercializado(a) ko·mer·thya·lee·tha·do(a) adj commercialized (resort)

comerciante ko·mer·thyan·te m merchant; trader

comerciar ko·mer·thyar vi do business; **comerciar en algo** ko·mer·thyar en al·go to deal in something

comercio ko·mer·thyo m trade; commerce; business (firm)

comestibles ko·mes·tee·bles mpl groceries

cometa ko·me·ta f kite

cometer* ko·me·ter vt commit (crime)

cómico ko·mee·ko m comedian

comida ko·mee·da f meal; food; dinner

comienzo ko·myen·tho m start (beginning)

comisaría ko·mee·sa·ree·a f police station

comisión ko·mee·syon f commission

comité ko·mee·te m committee

como ko·mo adv how □ prep like; **¿cómo? ko·mo** what? (please repeat); **¿cómo está?** ko·mo es·ta how are you?; **¿cómo salió?** ko·mo sa·lyo how did it go?; **¿cómo se llama?** ko·mo se lya·ma what is your/its name?; **¿cómo se dice "dog" en español?** ko·mo se dee·the dog en es·pan·yol what's the Spanish for "dog"?; **¿cómo es?** ko·mo es what's it like?; **como si** ko·mo see as if, as though; **como está enfermo** ko·mo es·ta en·fer·mo since he's ill

cómoda ko·mo·da f bureau

comodidades ko·mo·dee·da·des fpl amenities

comodín *ko·mo·deen m* joker (*cards*)

cómodo(a) *ko·mo·do(a) adj* comfortable

compañía *kom·pan·yee·a f* firm; la compañía naviera *kom·pan·yee·a na·bye·ra* shipping company

comparar *kom·pa·rar vt* compare

compartimiento *kom·par·tee·myen·to m* compartment (*on train*)

compartir *kom·par·teer vt* share (*money, room*)

compás *kom·pas m* compass

compasión *kom·pa·syon f* sympathy

compatriota *kom·pa·tree·o·ta m/f* fellow countryman

competencia *kom·pe·ten·thya f* competition

competente *kom·pe·ten·te adj* competent

competidor(a) *kom·pe·tee·dor(·ra) adj* competing

completamente *kom·ple·ta·men·te adv* completely

completo(a) *kom·ple·to(a) adj* inclusive (*costs*); full up (*bus, hotel etc*)

complicado(a) *kom·plee·ka·do(a) adj* complicated; complex; elaborate

comportamiento *kom·por·ta·myen·tom* behavior

comportarse *kom·por·tar·se vr* act (*behave*)

compositor *kom·po·see·tor m* composer

compota *kom·po·ta f* preserve(s)

compra *kom·pra f* purchase; la compra a plazos *kom·pra a pla·thos* instalment plan; ir* de compras *eer de kom·pras* to go shopping

comprador *kom·pra·dor m* buyer

comprar *kom·prar vt* purchase; buy; comprar la parte de *kom·prar la par·te de* to buy out (*partner etc*)

compras *kom·pras fpl* shopping

comprender *kom·pren·der vt* understand; comprendemos que... *kom·pren·de·mos ke* we understand that...

comprensión *kom·pren·syon f* understanding

comprensivo(a) *kom·pren·see·bo(a) adj* comprehensive

comprobación en el acto *kom·pro·ba·thyon en el ak·to f* spot check

compromiso *kom·pro·mee·so m* engagement (*betrothal*); undertaking; appointment

comunicar* *ko·moo·nee·kar vi* communicate; estar* comunicando *es·tar ko·moo·nee·kan·do* to be busy (*on telephone*)

comunista *ko·moo·nees·ta m/f* Communist □ *adj* Communist

con *kon prep* with

coñac *kon·yak m* cognac; brandy

concesionario *kon·the·syo·na·ryo m* agent

concha *kon·cha f* shell

conciencia *kon·thyen·thya f* conscience

concienzudo(a) *kon·thyen·thoo·do(a) adj* thorough (*work*)

concierto *kon·thyer·to m* concert; el concierto pop *kon·thyer·to pop* pop concert

concurrido(a) *kon·koo·rree·do(a) adj* busy (*place*)

concursante *kon·koor·san·te m/f* contestant

concurso *kon·koor·so m* contest; competition; quiz

condado *kon·da·do m* county

condenar *kon·de·nar vt* condemn

condición *kon·dee·thyon f* condition; proviso; a condición que... *a kon·dee·thyon ke* on condition that...; las condiciones *kon·dee·thyo·nes* terms (*of contract*)

condimento *kon·dee·men·to m* seasoning

condimentos *kon·dee·men·tos mpl* condiments

conducción *kon·duk·thyon f* driving; piping

conducir* *kon·doo·theer vt* steer (*car*); drive (*car etc*); ¿sabe Ud conducir/ manejar? *sa·be oos·ted kon·doo·theer/ma·ne·khar* do you drive?

conductor(a) *kon·dook·tor(·ra) m/f* driver (*of car*)

conejo *ko·ne·kho m* rabbit

confección *kon·fek·thyon f* workmanship; de confección de *kon·fek·thyon* ready-to-wear

conferencia *kon·fe·ren·thya f* talk (*lecture*); conference; la conferencia a cobro revertido *kon·fe·ren·thya a ko·bro re·her·tee·do* collect call; una conferencia de persona a persona *oo·na kon·fe·ren·thya de per·so·na a per·so·na* person-to-person call

confesar* *kon·fe·sar vt* confess

confesarse* *kon·fe·sar·se vr* confess; confesarse (culpable) de algo *kon·fe·sar·se (kool·pa·ble) de al·go* to confess to something

confesión *kon·fe·syon f* confession

confianza *kon·fee·an·tha f* confidence (*trust*); la confianza en *kon·fee·an·tha en* confidence in; en confianza *en kon·fee·an·tha* in confidence; de confianza de *kon·fee·an·tha* reliable (*person*)

confiar en *kon·fee·ar en vi* trust (*person*)

confidencial *kon·fee·den·thyal adj* private (*confidential*)

confirmar *kon·feer·mar vt* confirm (*reservation etc*)

confitería *kon·fee·te·ree·a f* confectionery

confitura *kon·fee·too·ra f* jam

conflicto *kon·fleek·to m* conflict; los conflictos en este país *los kon·fleek·tos en es·te pa·ees* the troubles in this country

confort *kon·fort m* comfort (*ease*)

confundir *kon·foon·deer vt* mix up; confuse; confundir una cosa con otra *kon·foon·deer oo·na ko·sa kon o·tra* to confuse one thing with another

confusión *kon·foo·syon f* muddle

congelación de salarios *kon·khe·la·thyon de sa·la·ryos f* wage freeze

congelado(a) *kon·khe·la·do(a) adj* frozen (*food*)

congelador *kon·khe·la·dor m* freezer; deepfreeze

congelar *kon·khe·lar vt* freeze (*food*)

conjunto *kon·khoon·to m* the whole; ensemble (*clothes*)

conocedor *ko·no·the·dor m* connoisseur

conocer* *ko·no·ther vt* know (*person*); meet (*make acquaintance of*); conocer* bien algo *ko·no·ther byen al·go* to be familiar with something

conocido(a) *ko·no·thee·do(a) m/f* acquaintance

conocimiento *ko·no·thee·myen·to m* knowledge

consciente *kons·thyen·te adj* conscious

consecuencia *kon·se·kwen·thya f* consequence (*result*)

conseguir* *kon·se·geer vt* win (*contract*); **conseguir*** hacer algo *kon·se·geer a·ther al·go* to manage to do something; consiguió hacerlo *kon·si·gyo a·ther·lo* he succeeded in doing it; **conseguir*** comunicar *kon·se·geer ko·moo·nee·kar* to get through (*on phone*)

consejo *kon·se·kho m* advice; **el consejo de administración** *kon·se·kho de ad·mee·nees·tra·thyon* management (*managers*); **el consejo municipal** *kon·se·kho moo·nee·thee·pal* council (*of town*)

consentir* *kon·sen·teer vt* allow; spoil (*child*)

conserje *kon·ser·khe m* porter (*door-keeper*); janitor

conservación *kon·ser·ba·thyon f* maintenance (*of building*)

conservador(a) *kon·ser·ba·dor(·ra) adj* conservative

conservar *kon·ser·bar vt* lay down (*wine*); **conservar algo en buen orden** *kon·ser·bar al·go en bwen or·den* to keep something tidy/in good condition; **la leche no se conserva bien** *la le·che no se kon·ser·ba byen* milk doesn't keep very well

conservatorio *kon·ser·ba·to·ryo m* academy of music

considerar *kon·see·de·rar vt* consider

consigna *kon·seeg·na f* baggage checkroom

consistir en *kon·sees·teer en vi* consist of

consomé *kon·so·me m* consommé

constante *kons·tan·te adj* steady (*pace*)

construcción *kons·trook·thyon f* building

construir* *kons·troo·eer vt* build (*house*); construct

cónsul *kon·sool m* consul

consulado *kon·soo·la·do m* consulate

consultar *kon·sool·tar vt* consult; refer to; **quiero consultar a un médico** *kye·ro kon·sool·tar a oon me·dee·ko* I want to see a doctor

consultorio *kon·sool·to·ryo m* consulting room; doctor's office

consumidor *kon·soo·mee·dor m* consumer

contabilidad *kon·ta·bee·lee·dad f* accountancy

contable *kon·ta·ble m* accountant; **el contable diplomado** *kon·ta·ble dee·plo·ma·do* certified public accountant

contacto *kon·tak·to m* contact; **en contacto con** *en kon·tak·to con* in touch with; **ponerse* en contacto con** *po·ner·se en kon·tak·to* kon to contact

al contado *al con·ta·do adv* cash down

contador *kon·ta·dor m* meter

contagiarse de *kon·ta·khyar·se de vr* catch (*illness*)

contagioso(a) *kon·ta·khyo·so(a) adj* contagious

contaminación *kon·ta·mee·na·thyon f* pollution

contar* *kon·tar vt* tell (*story*); count (*objects, people*); **contar*** con *kon·tar kon* rely on (*person*); **contar* algo a alguien** *kon·tar al·go a al·gyen* to tell someone something; **cuente con 10 minutos para llegar** *kwen·te kon 10 mee·noo·tos pa·ra lye·gar* allow 10 minutes to get there; **contar* hasta 10** *kon·tar as·ta 10* to count up to 10

contemporáneo(a) *kon·tem·po·ra·ne·o(a) adj* contemporary (*modern*)

contenedor *kon·te·ne·dor m* container (*for shipping etc*)

contener* *kon·te·ner vt* contain

contenido *kon·te·nee·do m* contents

contento(a) *kon·ten·to(a) adj* pleased; content(ed)

contestar *kon·tes·tar vt/i* to answer; **contestar el teléfono** *kon·tes·tar el te·le·fo·no* to answer the phone; **le contestó punto por punto** *le kon·tes·to poon·to por poon·to* he answered him point by point

continental *kon·tee·nen·tal adj* continental

continente *kon·tee·nen·te m* mainland; continent; **el continente europeo** *kon·tee·nen·te e·oo·ro·pe·o* the Continent

continuamente *kon·teen·wa·men·te adv* continuously

continuar *kon·tee·nwar vt/i* continue (*road etc*); **continuar haciendo** *kon·tee·nwar a·thyen·do* to continue to do

continuo(a) *kon·tee·nwo(a) adj* continual; continuous

contra *kon·tra prep* against

contrabando *kon·tra·ban·do m* contraband

contrario *kon·tra·ryo m* opposite; **al contrario** *al kon·tra·ryo* on the contrary

contratación *kon·tra·ta·thyon f* recruitment

contratar *kon·tra·tar vt* recruit (*personnel*)

contratista *kon·tra·tees·ta m* contractor

contrato *kon·tra·to m* contract

contraventana *kon·tra·ben·ta·na f* shutter (*on window*)

contribución *kon·tree·boo·thyon f* tax; **la Delegación de Contribuciones** *de·le·ga·thyon de kon·tree·boo·thyo·nes* Internal Revenue

contribuir* *kon·tree·boo·eer vt/i* contribute; pay (*in tax*)

control remoto *kon·trol re·mo·to m* remote control

conurbación *ko·noor·ba·thyon f* conurbation

convalecencia *kon·ba·le·then·thya f* convalescence

convencer* *kon·ben·ther vt* convince

conveniente *kon·ben·yen·te adj* suitable

convenir* *kon·be·neer vi* be suitable/convenient; **¿le conviene el jueves?** *le kon·bye·ne el khwe·bes* does Thursday suit you?

convento *kon·ben·to m* convent

conversación *kon·ber·sa·thyon f* conversation

convidar *kon·bee·dar vt* invite

cooperar *ko·o·pe·rar vi* cooperate

cooperativa *ko·o·pe·ra·tee·ba f* cooperative

copa *ko·pa f* cup (*trophy*); **la copa de vino** *ko·pa de bee·no* wineglass

Copenhague *ko·pen·kha·ge m* Copenhagen

copia *ko·pya f* copy (*imitation*); print (*photographic*); printout; **la copia al carbón** *ko·pya al kar·bon* carbon copy

copiar *ko·pyar vt* copy

copo *ko·po m* flake (*of snow*)

copropiedad *ko·pro·pye·dad f* joint ownership

coquetear *ko·ke·te·ar vi* flirt

coraje *ko·ra·khe m* courage

coral *ko·ral m* coral
corazón *ko·ra·thon m* heart
corazones *ko·ra·tho·nes mpl* hearts (*cards*)
corbata *kor·ba·ta f* tie; necktie
Córcega *kor·the·ga f* Corsica
corchete *kor·che·te m* hook and eye
corcho *kor·cho m* cork; float (*for fishing*)
cordero *kor·de·ro m* lamb; mutton
cordial *kor·dyal adj* cordial
cordillera *cor·deel·ye·ra f* range (*of mountains*)
cordón *kor·don m* shoelace
coro *ko·ro m* choir
corona *ko·ro·na f* crown
coronación *ko·ro·na·thyon f* coronation
corral *ko·rral m* farmyard
correa *ko·rre·a f* leash; strap; **la correa del ventilador** *ko·rre·a del ben·tee·la·dor* fanbelt
correctamente *ko·rrek·ta·men·te adv* properly
correcto(a) *ko·rrek·to(a) adj* proper (*correct*); right
corredor *ko·rre·dor m* agent; **el corredor de bolsa** *ko·rre·dor de bol·sa* stockbroker; **el corredor de fincas** *co·rre·dor de feen·kas* realtor
corregir* *ko·rre·kheer vt* correct
correo *ko·rre·o m* mail; **por correo** *por ko·rre·o* by post; **mandar por correo** *man·dar por ko·rre·o* to mail; **el correo certificado** *ko·rre·o ther·tee·fee·ka·do* certified mail; **por correo aéreo** *por ko·rre·o a·e·re·o* by air mail; **comprar algo por correo** *kom·prar al·go por ko·rre·o* to buy something by mail order
correos *ko·rre·os m* post office; **tengo que ir a correos** *ten·go ke eer a co·rre·os* I must go to the post office
correr* *ko·rrer vi* run; flow; **correr* detrás de alguien** *ko·rrer de·tras de al·gyen* to run after someone
correspondencia *ko·rres·pon·den·thya f* correspondence (*mail*)
corrida de toros *ko·rree·da de to·ros f* bullfight
corriente *ko·rryen·te adj* ordinary; common (*ordinary, frequent*) □ *f* **la corriente** *ko·rryen·te* draft (*wind*); power (*electricity*); current (*of water, air*)
corrimiento de tierras *ko·rree·myen·to de tye·rras m* landslide
corroer *ko·rro·er vt* corrode
corrupción *ko·rroop·thyon f* corruption
cortacésped *kor·ta·thes·ped m* lawn mower
cortado(a) *kor·ta·do(a) adj* spoiled (*milk*); sour
cortar *kor·tar vt* cut; mow; to turn off (*water, electricity*); **cortar algo por la mitad** *kor·tar al·go por la mee·tad* to cut something in half
cortarse *kor·tar·se vr* cut oneself; **cortarse el pelo** *kor·tar·se el pe·lo* to have a haircut
corte *kor·te m* cut (*wound*), **el corte de pelo** *kor·te de pe·lo* haircut
cortés *kor·tes adj* polite
corteza *kor·te·tha f* bark (*of tree*)
cortina *kor·tee·na f* drape; curtain
corto(a) *kor·to(a) adj* short
cosa *ko·sa f* thing; **las cosas** *ko·sas* stuff (*things*); **¿dónde están sus cosas?** *don·de es·tan soos ko·sas* where are your things?

cosecha *ko·se·cha f* crop; harvest (*of grain*); vintage
cosechar *ko·se·char vt* harvest
coser *ko·ser vt/i* sew
cosméticos *kos·me·tee·kos mpl* cosmetics
cosmopolita *kos·mo·po·lee·ta adj* cosmopolitan
costa *kos·ta f* coast
Costa Azul *kos·ta a·thool f* Riviera
costar* *kos·tar vt* cost; **cuesta mucho esfuerzo** *kwes·ta moo·cho es·fwer·tho* it takes a lot of effort
coste *kos·te m* cost
costilla *kos·teel·ya f* rib
costo de la vida *kos·to de la bee·da m* cost of living
costra *kos·tra f* scab
costumbre *kos·toom·bre f* custom; habit
costura *kos·too·ra f* seam
cotillear *ko·teel·ye·ar vi* gossip
cotización *ko·tee·tha·thyon f* quotation (*price*)
cotizar* *ko·tee·thar vt* quote (*price*)
craker *kra·ker m* cracker (*crisp wafer*)
crear *kre·ar vt* create
crecer* *kre·ther vi* grow
crecimiento *kre·thee·myen·to m* growth
crédito *kre·dee·to m* credit; **a crédito** *a kre·dee·to* on credit; **dar* crédito a alguien** *dar kre·dee·to a al·gyen* to give somebody credit
creencia *kre·en·thya f* belief
creer* *kre·er vt* believe; **creo que sí** *kre·o ke see* I think so; **creer* en** *kre·er en* to believe in
crema *kre·ma adj* cream; **la crema de manos** *kre·ma de ma·nos* hand cream; **la crema (de belleza)** *kre·ma (de bel·ye·tha)* face cream; **la crema de afeitar** *kre·ma a·fey·tar* shaving cream; **la crema batida** *kre·ma ba·tee·da* mousse; **la crema de menta** *kre·ma de men·ta* crème de menthe; **la crema dental** *kre·ma den·tal* toothpaste
cremallera *kre·mal·ye·ra f* zipper
cremoso(a) *kre·mo·so(a) adj* creamy (*texture*)
Creta *kre·ta f* Crete
criar *kree·ar vt* rear; raise (*family*)
crimen *kree·men m* crime
criminal *kree·mee·nal adj* criminal
crisantemo *kree·san·te·mo m* chrysanthemum
crisis *kree·sees f* crisis; **la crisis nerviosa** *kree·sees ner·byo·sa* nervous breakdown
cristal *krees·tal m* pane; crystal
cristalería *krees·ta·le·ree·a f* glass (*glassware*)
cristiano(a) *krees·tya·no(a) m/f* Christian
criticar* *kree·tee·kar vt* criticize
croissant *krwa·san m* croissant
crol *krol m* crawl (*swimming*)
cromo *kro·mo m* chrome
cronómetro *kro·no·me·tro m* stopwatch
croqueta *kro·ke·ta f* croquette
cruce *kroo·the m* intersection (*of roads*); interchange (*on roads*); crossroads; **el cruce en T** *kroo·the en te* T-junction (*on road*)
cruce giratorio *kroo·the khee·ra·to·ryo m* traffic circle
crucero *kroo·the·ro m* cruise; **hacer* un crucero** *a·ther oon kroo·the·ro* to go on a cruise

crudo(a) *kroo·do(a) adj* crude (*oil etc*); raw (*uncooked*)

cruel *kroo·el adj* cruel; unkind (*remark*)

crupier *kroo·pyer m* croupier

cruz *krooth f* cross

cruzar *kroo·thar vt* cross (*road, sea*); **cruzar* la calle** *kroo·thar la kal·ye* to walk across the road; **cruzamos Francia en coche** *kroo·tha·mos fran·thya en ko·che* we drove across France

cuaderno *kwa·der·no m* exercise book

cuadrado(a) *kwa·dra·do(a) adj* square; **un metro cuadrado** *oon me·tro kwa·dra·do* a square meter □ *m* **el cuadrado** *kwa·dra·do* square

cuadro *kwa·dro m* picture; painting; **a cuadros** *a kwa·dros* check(er)ed (*patterned*); **los cuadros medios** *kwa·dros me·dyos* middle management

cuál *kwal pron* which one; **¿cuál de Uds?** *kwal de oos·te·des* which one of you?; **no sé cuál llevar** *no se kwal lye·bar* I don't know which to take; **después de lo cuál** *des·pwes de lo kwal* after which

cualquier *kwal·kyer adj* whichever; **deme cualquier libro** *de·me kwal·kyer lee·bro* give me any book

cualquiera *kwal·kye·ra pron* anybody at all; whichever; **cualquiera de Uds** *kwal·kye·ra de oos·te·des* either of you; **¿cuál? — cualquiera** *kwal·kwal·kye·ra* which one? — either

cuando *kwan·do conj* when; **llegó cuando nosotros salíamos** *lye·go kwan·do no·so·tros sa·lee·a·mos* he arrived as we left □ *adv/conj* **cuándo** *kwan·do* when (*in questions*)

cuanto(a) *kwan·to(a) adj* all that; as much as *adj* **cuánto(a)** *kwan·to(a)* how long/much (*in questions*); **¿cuánto tiempo?** *kwan·to tyem·po* how long?; **¿cuánto?** *kwan·to* how much?; **¿cuántos(as)?** *kwan·tos(as)* how many?; **¿cuánta gente?** *kwan·ta khen·te* how many people?; **en cuanto a esto** *en kwan·to a es·to* as for this; **¿cuánto hay de aquí a...?** *kwan·to ay de a·kee* how far is it to...?

cuarenta *kwa·ren·ta num* forty

cuarentena *kwa·ren·te·na f* quarantine

cuartel *kwar·tel m* barracks

cuarto(a) *kwar·to(a) adj* fourth □ *m* room; quarter; joint (*of meat*); **un cuarto de hora** *oon kwar·to de o·ra* a quarter of an hour; **las 4 menos cuarto** *las 4 me·nos kwar·to* (a) quarter to 4; **las 4 y cuarto** *las 4 ee kwar·to* (a) quarter past 4; **el cuarto de baño** *kwar·to de ban·yo* bathroom; **el cuarto de estar** *kwar·to de es·tar* living room

cuarzo *kwar·tho m* quartz

cuatro *kwa·tro num* four

Cuba *koo·ba f* Cuba

cubano(a) *koo·ba·no(a) adj* Cuban

cubertería *koo·ber·te·ree·a f* cutlery

cubierta *koo·byer·ta f* cover (*of book*); deck (*of ship*)

cubierto *koo·byer·to m* place setting; **el precio del cubierto** *pre·thyo del koo·byer·to* cover charge

cubo *koo·bo m* bucket; pail; **el cubo de la basura** *koo·bo de la ba·soo·ra* garbage can; **el cubo de flash** *koo·bo de flash* flashcube

cubrir *koo·breer vt* cover

cuchara *koo·cha·ra f* spoon; table-

spoon; **la cuchara de postre** *koo·cha·ra de pos·tre* dessertspoon

cucharada *koo·cha·ra·da f* spoonful

cucharadita *koo·cha·ra·dee·ta f* teaspoon (*measure*)

cucharilla *koo·cha·reel·ya f* teaspoon

cucharón *koo·cha·ron m* ladle

cuchichear *koo·chee·che·ar vi* whisper

cuchillo *koo·cheel·yo m* knife

cucurucho *koo·koo·roo·cho m* cone (*for ice cream*)

cuello *kwel·yo m* neck; collar; **el cuello alto** *kwel·yo al·to* polo neck; **el cuello de pico** *kwel·yo de pee·ko* V-neck

cuenco *kwen·ko m* basin (*dish*)

cuenta *kwen·ta f* bill; bead; account (*at bank, shop*); **tener* en cuenta el futuro** *te·ner en kwen·ta el foo·too·ro* to think ahead; **la cuenta de gastos** *kwen·ta de gas·tos* expense account; **la cuenta bancaria** *kwen·ta ban·ka·rya* bank account; **darse* cuenta de** *dar·se kwen·ta de* to realize; **que trabaja por su propia cuenta** *ke tra·ba·kha por soo pro·pya kwen·ta* self-employed; **pagar* la cuenta** *pa·gar la kwen·ta* to check out; **sin tener* en cuenta** *seen te·ner en kwen·ta* regardless of; **la cuenta corriente** *kwen·ta ko·rryen·te* checking account

cuentakilómetros *kwen·ta·kee·lo·me·tros m* odometer

cuento *kwen·to m* story

cuerda *kwer·da f* string; rope; cord (*twine*); **dar* cuerda a un reloj** *dar kwer·da a oon re·lokh* to wind up a clock

cuerno *kwer·no m* horn (*of animal*)

cuero *kwe·ro m* hide; leather

cuero cabelludo *kwe·ro ka·bel·yoo·do m* scalp

cuerpo *kwer·po m* body

cuesta *kwes·ta f* slope (*sloping ground*); hill (*slope*); **cuesta arriba** *kwes·ta a·rree·ba* uphill; **ir* cuesta arriba** *eer kwes·ta a·rree·ba* to go uphill

cuestión *kwes·tyon f* issue (*matter*); question (*subject discussed*); **es cuestión de** *es kwes·tyon de* it's a question of

cuestionario *kwes·tyo·na·ryo m* questionnaire

cueva *kwe·ba f* cave

cuidado *kwee·da·do m* care (*carefulness*); **¡cuidado!** *kwee·da·do* look out!; **¡tenga cuidado!** *ten·ga kwee·da·do* be careful!; **cuidado con el escalón** *kwee·da·do kon el es·ka·lon* mind the step

cuidadoso(a) *kwee·da·do·so(a) adj* careful (*cautious*)

cuidar *kwee·dar vt* look after; **cuidar niños** *kwee·dar neen·yos* to baby-sit; **cuidar de** *kwee·dar de* to take care of; to look after

culebra *koo·le·bra f* snake

culpa *kool·pa f* fault (*blame*); **tener* la culpa** *te·ner la kool·pa* to be to blame; **¿quién tiene la culpa?** *kyen tye·ne la kool·pa* whose fault it is?; **yo no tengo la culpa** *yo no ten·go la kool·pa* it's not my fault

culpabilidad *kool·pa·bee·lee·dad f* guilt

culpable *kool·pa·ble adj* guilty

culpar *kool·par vt* blame

cultivar *kool·tee·bar vt* cultivate; grow (*plants*)

cultura *kool·too·ra f* culture; **la cultura general** *kool·too·ra khe·ne·ral* general knowledge

cumbre *koom·bre* f summit
cumpleaños *koom·ple·an·yos* m birthday
cumplido *koom·plee·do* m compliment
cumplir *koom·pleer* vt to carry out
cuna *koo·na* f cradle; crib (baby's)
cuñada *koo·nya·da* f sister-in-law
cuñado *koon·ya·do* m brother-in-law
cuneta *koo·ne·ta* f gutter (in street)
cuota *kwo·ta* f subscription (to club); quota (of goods)
cupé *koo·pe* m coupé (car)
cupón *koo·pon* m trading stamp; coupon
cura *koo·ra* m vicar
curar *koo·rar* vt cure
curarse *koo·rar·se* vi heal (wound)
curioso(a) *koo·ryo·so(a)* adj funny (strange); quaint; curious (inquisitive)
curry *koo·rre* m curry
curso *koor·so* m course (lessons); el curso por correspondencia *koor·so por ko·rres·pon·den·thya* correspondence course; hacer* un curso para ser profesor *a·ther oon koor·so pa·ra ser pro·fe·sor* to train as a teacher; el curso acelerado *koor·so a·the·le·ra·do* crash course
curva *koor·ba* f bend; curve; la curva muy cerrada *koor·ba mooy the·rra·da* hairpin curve; tomar una curva *to·mar oo·na koor·ba* to corner; la curva sin visibilidad *koor·ba seen bee·see·bee·lee·dad* blind corner
cuscurro *koos·koo·rro* m crouton
cutis *koo·tees* m complexion
cuyo(a) *koo·yo(a)* adj whose; el hombre, cuyo hijo *el om·bre koo·yo ee·kho* the man, whose son

D

dados *da·dos* mpl dice
damas *da·mas* fpl checkers
dañar *dan·yar* vt damage
dañarse *dan·yar·se* vr to hurt oneself
danés(nesa) *da·nes(·ne·sa)* adj Danish
dañino(a) *dan·yee·no(a)* adj harmful
daño *dan·yo* m damage; los daños y perjuicios *dan·yos ee per·khwee·thyos* damages
dañoso(a) *dan·yo·so(a)* adj harmful
dar* *dar* vt give; le daremos $10 *le da·re·mos $10* we will allow $10; no dar* en *no dar en* to miss (target); dele el botón *de·le al bo·ton* press the button; el reloj dio las tres *el re·lokh dyo las tres* the clock struck three; dar* una patada a *dar oo·na pa·ta·da* a to kick (person); dar* un puntapié a *dar oon poon·ta·pye a* to kick (ball); dar* una fiesta *dar oo·na fyes·ta* to give a party; dar* algo a alguien *dar al·go a al·gyen* to give someone something; démelo *de·me·lo* give it to me
dardo *dar·do* m dart (to throw); el juego de dardos *khwe·go de dar·dos* game of darts
dátil *da·teel* m date (fruit)
datos *da·tos* mpl data; el banco de datos *ban·ko de da·tos* data bank, data base; el archivo de datos *ar·chee·bo de da·tos* data file; el proceso de datos *pro·the·so de da·tos* data processing
de *de* prep of; from; 1,000 pesetas de gasolina *1,000 pe·se·tas de ga·so·lee·na* 1,000 pesetas worth of gas; una carta de María *oo·na kar·ta de ma·*

ree·a a letter from Mary; la llave de mi cuarto *la lya·be de mee kwar·to* the key to my room; 3 de ellos *3 de el·yos* 3 of them; el 14 de junio *el 14 de khoo·nyo* 14th of June; de día *de dee·a* by day; de piedra *de pye·dra* made of stone; de Londres *de lon·dres* from London
debajo *de·ba·kho* prep under; underneath; mirar debajo *mee·rar de·ba·kho* to look below; pararse debajo *pa·rar·se de·ba·kho* to stand below; poner* la maleta debajo de la silla *po·ner la ma·le·ta de·ba·kho de la seel·ya* to put one's case below the chair; mi cuarto está debajo del suyo *mee kwar·to es·ta de·ba·kho del soo·yo* my room is below his; debajo de la mesa *de·ba·kho de la me·sa* under the table
debate *de·ba·te* m debate
deber* *de·ber* vt owe (money); debemos comprarlo *de·be·mos kom·prar·lo* we should buy it; debería hacerlo *de·be·ree·a a·ther·lo* I ought to do it; debe ganar *de·be ga·nar* he ought to win; me debe $5 *me de·be $5* he owes me $5; ¿cuándo debe llegar el tren? *kwan·do de·be lye·gar el tren* when is the train due? □ m el deber *de·ber* duty (obligation)
deberes *de·be·res* mpl homework
débil *de·beel* adj weak (person); faint (sound etc)
decenio *de·the·nyo* m decade
decente *de·then·te* adj decent
decidido(a) *de·thee·dee·do(a)* adj determined; estar* decidido a hacer algo *es·tar de·thee·dee·do a a·ther al·go* to be determined to do something
decidir *de·thee·deer* vt/i decide (between alternatives); decidir hacer algo *de·thee·deer a·ther al·go* to decide to do something
decidirse *de·thee·deer·se* vr to make up one's mind
decimal *de·thee·mal* m decimal
décimo(a) *de·thee·mo(a)* adj tenth
decimosexto(a) *de·thee·mo·seks·to(a)* adj sixteenth
decimotercero(a) *de·thee·mo·ter·the·ro(a)* adj thirteenth
decir* *de·theer* vt say; tell (fact, news); dicen que... *dee·then ke* they say that...; decirle* a alguien que haga algo *de·theer·le a al·gyen ke a·ga al·go* to tell someone to do something; se dice que es ingeniero *se dee·the ke es een·khe·nye·ro* he's supposed to be an engineer
decisión *de·thee·syon* f decision
declaración *de·kla·ra·thyon* f statement
declarar *de·kla·rar* vt declare; nada que declarar *na·da ke de·kla·rar* nothing to declare
decorar *de·ko·rar* vt decorate (adorn)
dedo *de·do* m finger; el dedo del pie *de·do del pye* toe
deducir* *de·doo·theer* vt gather (suppose)
defecto *de·fek·to* m defect
defectuoso(a) *de·fek·too·o·so(a)* adj faulty; defective
defender* *de·fen·der* vt defend
defensa *de·fen·sa* f defense □ m el defensa *de·fen·sa* back (in sports)
déficit *de·fee·theet* m deficit; shortfall
deflación *de·fla·thyon* f deflation
deformado(a) *de·for·ma·do(a)* adj deformed

defraudar *de·frow·dar* vt cheat; deceive

dejar *de·khar* vt let (*allow*); **déjeme entrar** *de·khe·me en·trar* let me in; **dejar de fumar** *de·khar de foo·mar* to give up smoking; **dejar de hacer algo** *de·khar de a·ther al·go* to stop doing something; **déjemelo a mí** *de·khe·me·lo a mee* leave it to me; **deje su abrigo aquí** *de·khe soo a·bree·go a·kee* leave your coat here; **dejar un recado** *de·khar oon re·ka·do* to leave a message; **dejar caer** *de·khar ka·er* to drop; **dejar KO** *de·khar ka·o* to knock out

delante de *de·lan·te de* prep in front of; **sentarse delante** *sen·tar·se de·lan·te* to sit in front

delantero *de·lan·te·ro* m forward (*football*) □ adj **delantero(a)** *de·lan·te·ro (·ra)* front

delegación *de·le·ga·thyon* f delegation; local office

delegar *de·le·gar* vt delegate

delgado(a) *del·ga·do(a)* adj slim; thin

delicado(a) *de·lee·ka·do(a)* adj dainty; delicate (*not robust*)

delicioso(a) *de·lee·thyo·so(a)* adj delicious

delineante *de·lee·ne·an·te* m draftsman

demanda *de·man·da* f demand; lawsuit (*for goods*)

demandar *de·man·dar* vt sue

demás *de·mas* adj rest; **todos(as) los/las demás** *to·dos(as) los/las de·mas* all the rest

demasiado *de·ma·sya·do* adv too much; **es demasiado grande** *es de·ma·sya·do gran·de* he's too big; □ adj **demasiado(a)** *de·ma·sya·do(a)* too much

demorar *de·mo·rar* vt delay (*hold up*)

demostración *de·mos·tra·thyon* f demonstration

demostrar* *de·mos·trar* vt show

denso(a) *den·so(a)* adj dense (*fog etc*); **poco denso(a)** *po·ko den·so(a)* thin (*liquid*)

dentadura postiza *den·ta·doo·ra pos·tee·tha* f dentures

dentista *den·tees·ta* m/f dentist

dentro de *den·tro de* prep inside; **estar dentro** *es·tar den·tro* to be inside; **volverá dentro de 2 días** *bol·be·ra den·tro de 2 dee·as* he'll be back in 2 days

departamento *de·par·ta·men·to* m compartment

depender de *de·pen·der de* vi depend on; **depende** *de·pen·de* it depends; **el departamento depende de él** *el de·par·ta·men·to de·pen·de de el* he's responsible for the department

dependiente(a) *de·pen·dyen·te(a)* m/f clerk (*in store*); sales assistant

deporte *de·por·te* m sport(s)

depositar *de·po·see·tar* vt deposit (*money*); lay down

depósito *de·po·see·to* m deposit; **depósito de gasolina** *de·po·see·to de ga·so·lee·na* gasoline tank

depresión económica *de·pre·syon e·ko·no·mee·ka* f slump

deprimido(a) *de·pree·mee·do(a)* adj depressed

derecha *de·re·cha* f right (*right-hand side*); **a la derecha** *a la de·re·cha* on the right; to the right

derecho(a) *de·re·cho(a)* adj straight; right (*not left*) □ adv **derecho** *de·re·cho* straight (*shoot, write etc*); □ m

el derecho *el de·re·cho* the right side (*of cloth etc*); right (*entitlement*); **los derechos de autor** *de·re·chos de ow·tor* copyright; **el derecho de paso** *de·re·cho de pa·so* right of way (*on road*); **ir derecho a casa** *eer de·re·cho a ka·sa* to go straight home; **los derechos de aduana** *de·re·chos de a·dwa·na* customs duty; **libre de derechos de aduana** *lee·bre de de·re·chos de a·dwa·na* duty-free (*goods*)

derramar *de·rra·mar* vt spill

derramarse *de·rra·mar·se* vr spill

derretir* *de·rre·teer* vt melt

derretirse* *de·rre·teer·se* vr melt; thaw (*ice*)

derribar *de·rree·bar* vt knock over

derroche *de·rro·che* m waste

derrota *de·rro·ta* f defeat

derrotar *de·rro·tar* vt defeat; beat

desabrochar *des·a·bro·char* vt unfasten

desacuerdo *des·a·kwer·do* m disagreement

desafilado(a) *des·a·fee·la·do(a)* adj blunt (*knife*)

desagradable *des·a·gra·da·ble* adj unpleasant

desagradar *des·a·gra·dar* vt displease

desaguadero *des·ag·wa·de·ro* m drain

desaliñado(a) *des·a·leen·ya·do(a)* adj untidy (*hair*)

desanimado(a) *des·a·nee·ma·do(a)* adj discouraged

desaparecer* *des·a·pa·re·ther* vi disappear

desaparecido(a) *des·a·pa·re·thee·do(a)* adj missing (*person*)

desaprobar* *des·a·pro·bar* vt disapprove of

desarmado(a) *des·ar·ma·do(a)* adj unarmed (*person*)

desarrollar *des·a·rrol·yar* vt develop (*photo*); expand (*business*)

desarrollarse *des·a·rrol·yar·se* vr expand; develop

desarrollo *des·a·rrol·yo* m development

desastre *de·sas·tre* m disaster

desatar *des·a·tar* vt untie (*parcel*)

desatascar *des·a·tas·kar* vt clear (*pipe*)

desayuno *de·sa·yoo·no* m breakfast

descafeinado(a) *des·ka·fey·na·do(a)* adj decaffeinated

descalificar* *des·ka·lee·fee·kar* vt disqualify

descalzo(a) *des·kal·tho(a)* adj barefoot

descansar *des·kan·sar* vi rest

descansillo *des·kan·seel·yo* m landing (*on stairs*)

descanso *des·kan·so* m rest; half-time

descapotable *des·ka·po·ta·ble* m convertible (*car*)

descarado(a) *des·ka·ra·do(a)* adj cheeky

descarga *des·kar·ga* f shock (*electric*)

descargado(a) *des·kar·ga·do(a)* adj flat (*battery*)

descargar* *des·kar·gar* vt unload

descaro *des·ka·ro* m cheek (*impudence*)

descolorarse *des·ko·lo·rar·se* vr fade

desconcertado(a) *des·kon·ther·ta·do(a)* adj embarrassed

descondensador *des·kon·den·sa·dor* m defroster

desconectar *des·ko·nek·tar* vt switch off (*engine*)

descongelar *des·kon·khe·lar* vt defrost; thaw (*food*); de-ice

descongelarse *des·kon·khe·lar·se* vr thaw (*frozen food*)

desconocido(a) *des·ko·no·thee·do(a)* adj unknown; strange

describir* *des·kree·beer* vt describe

descripción *des·kreep·thyon* f description

descubierto(a) *des·koo·byer·to(a)* adj bare

descubrir* *des·koo·breer* vt discover; find out

descuento *des·kwen·to* m discount; con descuento *kon des·kwen·to* at a discount; un descuento del 3% *oon des·kwen·to del 3 por thyen·to* 3% off

desde *des·de* prep since; desde ayer *des·de a·yer* since yesterday; desde que él... *des·de ke el* ever since he...

desdichado(a) *des·dee·cha·do(a)* adj unhappy

desear *de·se·ar* vt want; desire

desembarcadero *des·em·bar·ka·de·ro* m quay

desembarcar* *des·em·bar·kar* vt/i land

desenchufado(a) *des·en·choo·fa·do(a)* adj off; disconnected

deseo *de·se·o* m desire; wish

desesperado(a) *des·es·pe·ra·do(a)* adj desperate

desfile *des·fee·le* m parade

desgarrar *des·ga·rrar* vt tear; rip

desgarrarse *des·ga·rrar·se* vr rip

desgarrón *des·ga·rron* m tear

desgastar *des·gas·tar* vt wear out

desgaste *des·gas·te* m wear and tear

desgracia *des·gra·thya* f distress

desgraciadamente *des·gra·thya·da·men·te* adv unfortunately

desgraciado(a) *des·gra·thya·do(a)* adj unlucky; unfortunate (event)

deshacer* *des·a·ther* vt unpack (case); undo; destroy

deshacerse* *des·a·ther·se* vr break to pieces; come undone; vanish

desierto *de·syer·to* m desert

desilusionado(a) *des·ee·loo·syo·na·do(a)* adj disappointed

desinfectante *des·een·fek·tan·te* m disinfectant

desinfectar *des·een·fek·tar* vt disinfect

desinflado(a) *des·een·fla·do(a)* adj flat (deflated)

desleal *des·le·al* adj unfair (competition)

deslizarse *des·lee·thar·se* vr glide

deslumbrar *des·loom·brar* vt dazzle

desmayarse *des·ma·yar·se* vr faint

desmontar *des·mon·tar* vt take to pieces; throw (rider)

desnudo(a) *des·noo·do(a)* adj naked; nude

desobedecer* *des·o·be·de·ther* vt disobey

desobediente *des·o·be·dyen·te* adj disobedient

desodorante *des·o·do·ran·te* m deodorant

desorden *des·or·den* m mess; en desorden *en des·or·den* untidy (room)

desordenar *des·or·de·nar* vt make a mess of

despachar *des·pa·char* vt/i dispatch, settle

despacio *des·pa·thyo* adv slowly

despecho *des·pe·cho* m spite

despedida *des·pe·dee·da* f farewell

despedir* *des·pe·deer* vt sack (dismiss); pay off (workers); dismiss (from job); lay off (workers); despedir a alguien en la estación *des·pe·deer a al·gyen en la es·ta·thyon* to see someone off at the station

despedirse* *des·pe·deer·se* vr say goodbye

despegue *des·pe·ge* m takeoff (of plane)

despejado(a) *des·pe·kha·do(a)* adj clear; cloudless

despejar *des·pe·khar* vt clear

despensa *des·pen·sa* f larder; store room

desperdicio *des·per·dee·thyo* m rubbish

despertador *des·per·ta·dor* m alarm (clock)

despertar* *des·per·tar* vt wake

despertarse* *des·per·tar·se* vr to wake up

despistado(a) *des·pees·ta·do(a)* adj confused (muddled)

desplegar* *des·ple·gar* vt unfold

desprenderse *des·pren·der·se* vr to come off

después *des·pwes* prep after □ adv afterward(s); 4 años después *4 an·yos des·pwes* 4 years after; después de que nos fuimos *des·pwes de ke nos fwee·mos* after we had left

destacarse* *des·ta·kar·se* vr stand out

destapar *des·ta·par* vt uncover

destellar *des·tel·yar* vi flash (light)

destello *des·tel·yo* m flash

destilería *des·tee·le·ree·a* f distillery

destinatario *des·teen·na·ta·ryo* m addressee

destino *des·tee·no* m destination; con destino a *kon des·tee·no a* bound for

destornillador *des·tor·neel·ya·dor* m screwdriver

destornillar *des·tor·neel·yar* vt unscrew

destruir* *des·trweer* vt destroy

desvalorización *des·ba·lor·ee·tha·thyon* f devaluation

desván *des·ban* m attic; loft

desventaja *des·ben·ta·kha* f disadvantage; handicap

desvestirse* *des·bes·teer·se* vr undress

desviar *des·byar* vt reroute; divert

desviarse *des·bee·ar·se* vr bend (road); swerve

desvío *des·bee·o* m detour; hacer* un desvío *a·ther oon des·bee·o* to make a detour

detallado(a) *de·tal·ya·do(a)* adj itemized (bill etc); detailed

detalle *de·tal·ye* m detail; un buen detalle *oon bwen de·tal·ye* a kind gesture; en detalle *en de·tal·ye* in detail

detallista *de·tal·yees·ta* m/f retailer

detective *de·tek·tee·be* m detective

detener* *de·te·ner* vt arrest

detenerse* *de·te·ner·se* vr pause

detergente *de·ter·khen·te* m detergent

deteriorado(a) *de·te·ryo·ra·do(a)* adj shopworn

detrás de *de·tras de* prep behind

deuda *de·oo·da* f debt; estar* en deuda *es·tar en de·oo·da* to be in debt; la deuda incobrable *la de·oo·da een·ko·bra·ble* a bad debt

devaluación *de·ba·lwa·thyon* f devaluation

devaluar *de·ba·lwar* vt devalue (currency)

devolver* *de·bol·ber* vt give back; put back (replace); devolver* algo *de·bol·ber al·go* to take something back (return); devolver* el dinero a *de·bol·ber el dee·ne·ro a* to repay (person)

día *dee·a* m day; todo el día *to·do el dee·a* all day; el día de semana *dee·a de se·ma·na* weekday; poner* al día *po·ner al dee·a* to update; cada día ka·da dee·a every day; **día por día** dee·a por dee·a a day by day; **el día anterior** el dee·a an·te·ryor the day before; **el día siguiente** el dee·a see·gyen·te the next day; **el día de mercado** dee·a de mer·ka·do market-day; **día de trabajo** dee·a de tra·ba·kho working day; **¿qué día es hoy?** ke dee·a es oy what's the date today?

diabetes dee·a·be·tes f diabetes

diabético(a) dee·a·be·tee·ko(a) m/f diabetic

diagnóstico dee·ag·nos·tee·ko m diagnosis

diagonal dee·a·go·nal adj diagonal

diagrama dee·a·gra·ma m diagram

dialecto dee·a·lek·to m dialect

diamante dee·a·man·te m diamond

diamantes dee·a·man·tes mpl diamonds (cards)

diámetro dee·a·me·tro m diameter

diapositiva dee·a·po·see·tee·ba f slide (photo)

diario(a) dee·a·ryo(a) adj daily □ m daily (newspaper); diary

diarrea dee·a·rre·a f diarrhea

dibujar dee·boo·khar vt draw (picture)

dibujo dee·boo·kho m picture; drawing; design (pattern); **los dibujos animados** dee·boo·khos a·nee·ma·dos cartoon (animated)

diccionario deek·thyo·na·ryo m dictionary

diciembre dee·thyem·bre m December

dictar deek·tar vt dictate (letter)

diecinueve dye·thee·nwe·be num nineteen

dieciocho dye·thee·o·cho num eighteen

dieciseis dye·thee·seys num sixteen

diecisiete dye·thee·sye·te num seventeen

diente dyen·te m tooth; **el diente de ajo** dyen·te de a·kho clove of garlic; **los dientes postizos** dyen·tes pos·tee·thos false teeth

diesel dee·sel m diesel

diez dyeth num ten

diferencia dee·fe·ren·thya f difference

diferente dee·fe·ren·te adj different; **diferente de** dee·fe·ren·te de different from

difícil dee·fee·theel adj difficult; delicate (situation)

dificultad dee·fee·kool·tad f difficulty

digital dee·khee·tal adj digital

dilatar dee·la·tar vt expand (material)

dilatarse dee·la·tar·se vr stretch

diluido(a) dee·loo·ee·do(a) adj dilute

diluir dee·loo·eer vt dilute

dimensiones dee·men·syon·es fpl dimensions; size

dimisión dee·mee·syon f resignation

dimitir dee·mee·teer vi resign

Dinamarca dee·na·mar·ka f Denmark

dinámico(a) dee·na·mee·ko(a) adj dynamic (person)

dínamo dee·na·mo f dynamo

dinero dee·ne·ro m money; **hacer* dinero** a·ther dee·ne·ro to make money; **el dinero (contante)** dee·ne·ro (kon·tan·te) cash

dios dyos m god; **Dios** dyos God

diploma dee·plo·ma m diploma

diplomado(a) dee·plo·ma·do(a) m/f graduate

diplomático dee·plo·ma·tee·ko m diplomat

dique dee·ke m dike

dirección dee·rek·thyon f direction; management; steering (in car); address; **poner* la dirección en** po·ner

la dee·rek·thyon en to address (letter); **dirección única** dee·rek·thyon oo·nee·ka one-way (street); **la dirección particular** dee·rek·thyon par·tee·koo·lar home address

directo(a) dee·rek·to(a) adj direct; **el tren directo** tren dee·rek·to through train

director(a) dee·rek·tor(·ra) m/f conductor (of orchestra); director (of firm); principal, headmistress (of school etc); governor (of institution); president (of company); **el/la director(a) de escena** dee·rek·tor(·ra) de es·the·na producer (of play); **el director gerente** dee·rek·tor khe·ren·te managing director, M.D.; **el director de cine** dee·rek·tor de thee·ne director (of film); **el director de banco** dee·rek·tor de ban·ko bank manager

dirigir* dee·ree·kheer vt steer (boat); direct (traffic); manage (business)

disciplina dees·thee·plee·na f discipline

disc jockey deesk yo·kee m disc jockey

disco dees·ko m record; disk; **el disco de estacionamiento** dees·ko de es·ta·thyo·na·myen·to parking disk; **el disco dislocado** dees·ko dees·lo·ka·do slipped disk

discoteca dees·ko·te·ka f disco(thèque)

discreto(a) dees·kre·to(a) adj discreet

discriminación dees·kree·mee·na·thyon f discrimination (racial etc)

disculpa dees·kool·pa f excuse

disculpar dees·kool·par vt excuse

disculparse dees·kool·par·se vr apologize

discurso dees·koor·so m speech

discusión dees·koo·syon f argument (quarrel)

discutir dees·koo·teer vt discuss; argue (quarrel); **discutir algo** dees·koo·teer al·go to talk something over

diseñador dee·sen·ya·dor m designer

diseñar dee·sen·yar vt design

diseño dee·sen·yo m pattern; design (plan)

disfraz dees·frath m costume; fancy dress; disguise

disfrazado(a) dees·fra·tha·do(a) adj in disguise

disgustado(a) dees·goos·ta·do(a) adj upset

dislocar* dees·lo·kar vt dislocate

disminución dees·mee·noo·thyon f shrinkage; fall (decrease)

disminuir* dees·mee·noo·eer vt decrease

disolver* dee·sol·ber vt dissolve

disolverse* dee·sol·ber·se vr dissolve

disparar dees·pa·rar vi shoot; **disparar un fusil** dees·pa·rar oon foo·seel to fire a gun

disparo dees·pa·ro m shot

disponible dees·po·nee·ble adj available

dispositivo dees·po·see·tee·bo m gadget

dispuesto(a) dees·pwes·to(a) adj willing; **dispuesto(a) a hacer algo** dees·pwes·to(a) a a·ther al·go ready to do something

disputa dees·poo·ta f quarrel; dispute

disputar dees·poo·tar vt dispute (fact)

distancia dees·tan·thya f distance; **a corta distancia del mar** a kor·ta dees·tan·thya del mar within easy reach of the sea

distinguir* dees·teen·geer vt distinguish; **no puedo distinguir entre los dos** no pwe·do dees·teen·geer en·tre los dos I can't tell the difference between them; **distinguir* una cosa de otra cosa** *dees·teen·geer oo·na ko·sa de o·tra ko·sa* to distinguish something from something

distintivo *dees·teen·tee·bo* m badge (*of cloth*)

distraer* *dees·tra·er* vt distract

distribuidor *dees·tree·bwee·dor* m distributor; dealer; **el distribuidor automático** *dees·tree·bwee·dor ow·to·ma·tee·ko* vending machine

distrito *dees·tree·to* m district; **el distrito electoral** *dees·tree·to e·lek·to·ral* precinct (*administrative area*); **el distrito postal** *dees·tree·to pos·tal* zone (*postal*); postal district

disturbio *dees·toor·byo* m riot

diván *dee·ban* m divan

diversificar* *dee·ber·see·fee·kar* vt/i diversify

diversión *dee·ber·syon* f fun

diverso(a) *dee·ber·so(a)* adj various

divertido(a) *dee·ber·tee·do(a)* adj □ **fue muy divertido** *fwe mooy dee·ber·tee·do* it was great fun

divertirse *dee·ber·teer·se* vr enjoy oneself

dividendo *dee·bee·den·do* m dividend

dividir *dee·bee·deer* vt divide; part (*separate*); **dividir 8 por 4** *dee·bee·deer 8 por 4* to divide 8 by 4

divieso *dee·bye·so* m boil (*on skin*)

divisa *dee·bee·sa* f foreign currency

divorciado(a) *dee·bor·thya·do(a)* adj divorced

divorcio *dee·bor·thyo* m divorce

dobladillo *do·bla·deel·yo* m hem

doblar *do·blar* vt fold; bend; double

doble *do·ble* adj double; **un whisky doble** *oon wees·kee do·ble* a double whiskey; **costar el doble** *kos·tar el do·ble* to cost double

doce *do·the* num twelve

docena *do·the·na* f dozen; **4 docenas de huevos** *4 do·the·nas de we·bos* 4 dozen eggs

documentación *do·koo·men·ta·thyon* f papers (*passport etc*); **la documentación (del coche)** *do·koo·men·ta·thyon (del ko·che)* logbook (*of car*)

documento *do·koo·men·to* m document

dólar *do·lar* m dollar

doler* *do·ler* vi hurt; ache; **¡eso me duele!** *e·so me dwe·le* that hurts!

dolor *do·lor* m ache; pain; **el dolor de muelas** *do·lor de mwe·las* toothache; **tener* dolor de muelas** *te·ner do·lor de mwe·las* to have a toothache; **el dolor de cabeza** *do·lor de ka·be·tha* headache; **tener* un dolor de cabeza** *te·ner oon do·lor de ka·be·tha* to have a headache; **el dolor de oídos** *do·lor de o·ee·dos* earache; **el dolor de espalda** *do·lor de es·pal·da* backache; **el dolor de barriga** *do·lor de ba·rree·ga* stomachache; **el dolor agudo** *do·lor a·goo·do* sharp pain

doloroso(a) *do·lo·ro·so(a)* adj painful

dominar *do·mee·nar* vt control; **domina bien el francés** *do·mee·na byen el fran·thes* he speaks fluent French

domingo *do·meen·go* m Sunday; **el domingo de Pentecostés** *do·meen·go de pen·te·kos·tes* Whitsunday

don *don* m gift (*ability*)

donación *do·na·thyon* f donation (*money*)

donar *do·nar* vt donate (*funds*)

donde *don·de* conj where; **¿de dónde**

eres? *de don·de e·res* where are you from?; **¿dónde va?** *don·de ba* where are you going?; **le llevaré donde Ud quiera** *le lye·ba·re don·de oos·ted kye·ra* I'll take you anywhere you like

dorado(a) *do·ra·do(a)* adj gold-plated; golden

dormido(a) *dor·mee·do(a)* adj asleep; **estar* profundamente dormido(a)** *es·tar pro·foon·da·men·te dor·mee·do(a)* to be fast asleep

dormir* *dor·meer* vi sleep

dormitar *dor·mee·tar* vi doze

dormitorio *dor·mee·to·ryo* m bedroom; dormitory (*room*)

dorso *dor·so* m back (*reverse side*); **véase al dorso** *be·a·se al dor·so* P.T.O.

dos *dos* num two; **dos veces** *dos be·thes* twice; **las dos chicas** *las dos chee·kas* both girls

dosis *do·sees* f dosage; dose

dossier *do·syer* m record (*file*)

dotado(a) *do·ta·do(a)* adj gifted

drama *dra·ma* m drama

dramático(a) *dra·ma·tee·ko(a)* adj dramatic

drástico(a) *dras·tee·ko(a)* adj drastic

drenar *dre·nar* vt drain (*land*)

dril de algodón *dreel de al·go·don* m denim

droga *dro·ga* f drug (*narcotic*)

drogadicto(a) *dro·ga·deek·to(a)* m/f addict

ducha *doo·cha* f shower (*bath*); **tomar una ducha** *to·mar oo·na doo·cha* to have a shower

duda *doo·da* f doubt; **sin duda** *seen doo·da* no doubt

dudar *doo·dar* vt doubt; **lo dudo** *lo doo·do* I doubt it

dudoso(a) *doo·do·so(a)* adj doubtful

dulce *dool·the* adj sweet (*taste, food*) □ m candy; **dulces** *dool·thes* sweets; **el dulce de leche cuajada** *dool·the de le·che kwa·kha·da* junket

dumping *doom·peeng* m dumping (*of goods*)

duna *doo·na* f dune

duodécimo(a) *doo·o·de·thee·mo(a)* adj twelfth

duque *doo·ke* m duke

duradero(a) *doo·ra·de·ro(a)* adj durable (*fabric, article*)

duramente *doo·ra·men·te* adv roughly

durante *doo·ran·te* prep during; **durante la noche** *doo·ran·te la no·che* overnight; **andar* durante una hora** *an·dar doo·ran·te oo·na o·ra* to walk for an hour; **durante todo el año** *doo·ran·te to·do el an·yo* (all) through the year

durar *doo·rar* vt/i last; **¿cuánto tiempo dura el programa?** *kwan·to tyem·po doo·ra el pro·gra·ma* how long is the program?; **dura una hora** *doo·ra oo·na o·ra* it lasts an hour

duro(a) *doo·ro(a)* adj tough; hard; hard-boiled; stale (*bread*)

E

echado(a) *e·cha·do(a)* adj lying

echar *e·char* vt pour (*tea, milk*); throw; **echar una mirada a** *e·char oo·na mee·ra·da a* to glance at; **echo de menos a mi madre** *e·cho de me·nos a mee ma·dre* I miss my mother; **echar abajo** *e·char a·ba·kho* to knock down

echarse *e·char·se* vr lie down; **echarse a perder** *e·char·se a per·der* to go bad

eco *e·ko* m echo

economía *e·ko·no·mee·a* f economy; economics

económico(a) *e·ko·no·mee·ko(a)* adj economic; economical (use, method); **poco económico(a)** *po·ko e·ko·no·mee·ko(a)* uneconomical

economista *e·ko·no·mees·ta* m/f economist

ecuador *e·kwa·dor* m equator

eczema *ek·the·ma* m eczema

edad *e·dad* f age (of person)

edición *e·dee·thyon* f edition

edificio *e·dee·fee·thyo* m building

editor *e·dee·tor* m publisher

edredón *e·dre·don* m eiderdown; quilt; **el edredón** *e·dre·don* comforter

educación *e·doo·ka·thyon* f education

educado(a) *e·doo·ka·do(a)* adj polite; **bien educado(a)** *byen e·doo·ka·do(a)* well-behaved

educar* *e·doo·kar* vt educate

efecto *e·fek·to* m effect; **los efectos personales** *e·fek·tos per·so·na·les* belongings

eficaz *e·fee·kath* adj effective (remedy etc); **ser* eficaz** *ser e·fee·kath* to work (medicine)

eficiente *e·fee·thyen·te* adj efficient

egipcio(a) *e·kheep·thyo(a)* adj Egyptian

Egipto *e·kheep·to* m Egypt

egoísta *e·go·ees·ta* adj selfish

eje *e·khe* m axle

ejecutar *e·khe·koo·tar* vt execute

ejecutivo *e·khe·koo·tee·bo* m executive

ejemplar *e·khem·plar* m copy (of book etc); specimen

ejemplo *e·khem·plo* m example; **por ejemplo** *por e·khem·plo* for example

ejercicio *e·kher·thee·thyo* m exercise; **hacer* ejercicios en el piano** *a·ther e·kher·thee·thyos en el pya·no* to practice the piano

ejército *e·kher·thee·to* m army

él *el* pron he; him; **él mismo** *el mees·mo* himself; **es él** *es el* it's him; **déselo a él** *de·se·lo a el* give it to him

el *el* art the; **venga el viernes** *ben·ga el byer·nes* come on Friday

elástico *e·las·tee·ko* m elastic

elección *e·lek·thyon* f election; choice; **las elecciones generales** *e·lek·thyo·nes khe·ne·ra·les* general election

electricidad *e·lek·tree·thee·dad* f electricity

electricista *e·lek·tree·thees·ta* m electrician

eléctrico(a) *e·lek·tree·ko(a)* adj electric(al)

electrónica *e·lek·tro·nee·ka* f electronics

electrónico(a) *e·lek·tro·nee·ko(a)* adj electronic

elefante *e·le·fan·te* m elephant

elegante *e·le·gan·te* adj smart; stylish

elegir* *e·le·kheer* vt elect

elemento *e·le·men·to* m element

elevado(a) *e·le·ba·do(a)* adj high (price, temperature); overhead (railroad)

elevador *e·le·ba·dor* m ramp (in garage); elevator

eliminado(a) *e·lee·mee·na·do(a)* adj out (team, player)

eliminatoria *e·lee·mee·na·to·rya* f heat (sport)

ella *el·ya* pron she; her; **es ella** *es el·ya*

it's her; **ella misma** *el·ya mees·ma* herself

ellas *el·yas* pron they (feminine)

ellos *el·yos* pron they; **lo hicieron ellos mismos** *lo e·thye·ron el·yos mees·mos* they did it themselves; **¡son ellos!** *son el·yos* it's them!

embajada *em·ba·kha·da* f embassy

embajador *em·ba·kha·dor* m ambassador

embalaje *em·ba·la·khe* m packing

embalar *em·ba·lar* vt pack

embarazada *em·ba·ra·tha·da* adj pregnant; **está embarazada** *es·ta em·ba·ra·tha·da* she's expecting a baby

embarcadero *em·bar·ka·de·ro* m jetty

embarcarse* *em·bar·kar·se* vr embark; board (ship)

embargo *em·bar·go* m embargo

emboquillado(a) *em·bo·keel·ya·do(a)* adj filter-tip (cigarettes)

emborronar *em·bo·rro·nar* vt blot (ink)

embotellamiento *em·bo·tel·ya·myen·to* m bottleneck; traffic jam; tie-up

embrague *em·bra·ge* m clutch (of car)

embutidos *em·boo·tee·dos* mpl sausages

emergencia *e·mer·khen·thya* f emergency; **la salida de emergencia** *sa·lee·da de e·mer·khen·thya* emergency exit

emigrar *e·mee·grar* vi emigrate

emisión *e·mee·syon* f issue (of stocks); broadcast

emisora *e·mee·so·ra* f station (radio)

emoción *e·mo·thyon* f emotion

emotivo(a) *e·mo·tee·bo(a)* adj emotional

empalagoso(a) *em·pa·la·go·so(a)* adj too sweet (cake etc)

empalme *em·pal·me* m junction (railway); connection (train etc)

empanada *em·pa·na·da* f pie (meat)

empanadilla de salchicha *em·pa·na·deel·ya de sal·chee·cha* f sausage roll

empapelar *em·pa·pe·lar* vt paper (wall)

empaquetar *em·pak·e·tar* vt package

empaste *em·pas·te* m filling (in tooth)

emperador *em·pe·ra·dor* m emperor

empezar* *em·pe·thar* vt/i begin

empleado(a) *em·ple·a·do(a)* m/f employee

emplear *em·ple·ar* vt use; employ

empleo *em·ple·o* m employment; use

emprender *em·pren·der* vt undertake

empresa *em·pre·sa* f enterprise; project (venture); company (firm); **la empresa privada** *em·pre·sa pree·ba·da* private enterprise

empresario *em·pre·sa·ryo* m employer

empujar *em·poo·khar* vt push

en *en* prep in; into; on; **en mayo** *en ma·yo* in May; **en mi casa** *en mee ka·sa* at my house; **en absoluto** *en ab·so·loo·to* not at all; **en avión/tren/coche** *en a·byon/tren/ko·che* by air/train/car; **¿está en casa?** *es·ta en ka·sa* is he in?; **en la televisión** *en la te·le·bee·syon* on television; **en el tren** *en el tren* on the train

enaguas *e·na·gwas* fpl petticoat

enamorado(a) *e·na·mo·ra·do(a)* adj in love

enamorarse *e·na·mo·rar·se* vr fall in love

encaje *en·ka·khe* m lace

encantado(a) *en·kan·ta·do(a)* adj delighted □ excl how do you do?

encantador(a) *en·kan·ta·dor(·ra) adj* charming; glamorous

encanto *en·kan·to m* charm

encargado de *en·kar·ga·do de adj* in charge of; **el encargado de relaciones públicas** *en·kar·ga·do de re·la·thyo·nes poo·blee·kas* public relations officer

encargar* *en·kar·gar vt* order (*goods, meal*); **encargarse*** de algo *en·kar·gar·se de al·go* to deal with something; **encargarse*** de hacer *en·kar·gar·se de a·ther* to undertake to do

encendedor *en·then·de·dor m* cigarette lighter

encender* *en·then·der vt* switch on (*light*); light (*fire, cigarette*); **encender* una cerilla** *en·then·der oo·na the·reel·ya* to strike a match

encendido(a) *en·then·dee·do(a) adj* on (*light, radio*) □ *m* ignition (*car*)

encerar* *en·the·rar vt* polish (*wood*)

enchufar *en·choo·far vt* plug in

enchufe *en·choo·fe m* plug (*electric*); point (*electric outlet*); socket (*electrical*); **el enchufe múltiple** *en·choo·fe mool·tee·ple* adaptor

encía *en·thee·a f* gum (*of teeth*)

enciclopedia *en·thee·klo·pe·dee·a f* cyclopedia

encima de *en·thee·ma de prep* onto, on top of; **por encima de sus posibilidades** *por en·thee·ma de soos po·see·bee·lee·da·des* beyond his means

encogerse* *en·ko·kher·se vr* shrink; en **cogerse*** de hombros *en·ko·kher·se de om·bros* to shrug

encontrar* *en·kon·trar vt* find

encontrarse con *en·kon·trar·se kon vr* meet (*encounter*)

encorvarse *en·kor·bar·se vr* bend (*person*)

encrucijada *en·kroo·thee·kha·da f* intersection

encurtidos *en·koor·tee·dos mpl* pickles

endibia *en·dee·bya f* endive (*smooth*)

endosar *en·do·sar vt* endorse

endulzar* *en·dool·thar vt* sweeten

enemigo *e·ne·mee·go m* enemy

energía *e·ner·khee·a f* energy

enero *e·ne·ro m* January

enfadado(a) *en·fa·da·do(a) adj* angry (*person*); **estar* enfadado con alguien** *es·tar en·fa·da·do kon al·gyen* to be angry with someone

enfadarse *en·fa·dar·se vr* lose one's temper

énfasis *en·fa·sees m* emphasis; stress

enfermedad *en·fer·me·dad f* disease; sickness; illness

enfermera *en·fer·me·ra f* nurse

enfermería *en·fer·me·ree·a f* infirmary

enfermo(a) *en·fer·mo(a) adj* sick; ill

enfocar* *en·fo·kar vt* focus

enfrente de *en·fren·te de prep* opposite; **la casa de enfrente** *la ka·sa de en·fren·te* the house opposite

enfriar *en·free·ar vt* chill (*wine, food*)

engañar *en·gan·yar vt* deceive; trick

engaño *en·gan·yo m* trick (*malicious*)

engranado(a) *en·gra·na·do(a) adj* in gear

engreído(a) *en·gre·ee·do(a) adj* conceited

engrudo *en·groo·do m* paste (*glue*)

¡enhorabuena! *en·o·ra·bwe·na excl* congratulations!; **dar* la enhorabuena a alguien por algo** *dar la en·o·ra·bwe·na a al·gyen por al·go* to congratulate someone on something

enjuagar* *en·khwa·gar vt* rinse

enlace sindical *en·la·the seen·dee·kal m* shop steward

enlazar* *en·la·thar vt/i* connect; **este tren enlaza con el tren de las 16.45** *es·te tren en·la·tha kon el tren de las 16.45* this train connects with the 16:45

enmascarar *en·mas·ka·rar vt* mask

enojado(a) *en·o·kha·do(a) adj* angry

enorme *e·nor·me adj* enormous

enredar *en·re·dar vt* tangle

enrollar *en·rol·yar vt* wind

enrollar *en·rol·yar vt* roll up (*newspaper etc*)

ensalada *en·sa·la·da f* salad; **la ensalada de frutas** *en·sa·la·da de froo·tas* fruit salad

ensayar *en·sa·yar vt* test

ensayo *en·sa·yo m* essay; test; rehearsal

enseñar *en·sen·yar vt* teach; show; enseñar algo a alguien *en·sen·yar al·go a al·gyen* to teach/show someone something

enseñanza *en·sen·yan·tha f* teaching

entender *en·ten·der vt/i* understand

entero(a) *en·te·ro(a) adj* whole (*complete*)

enterrar* *en·te·rrar vt* bury (*person*)

entierro *en·tye·rro m* funeral

entonces *en·ton·thes adv* then; **entonces tiene que ser verdad** *en·ton·thes tye·ne ke ser ber·dad* then it must be true; **desde entonces** *des·de en·ton·thes* from then on

entrada *en·tra·da f* entrance (*way in*); drive (*driveway*); ticket (*for theater*); admission; entrée; **el precio de entrada** *pre·thyo de en·tra·da* admission fee

entrar *en·trar vi* go in; come in; **entrar en** *en·trar en* to enter

entre *en·tre prep* among; between

entreacto *en·tre·ak·to m* interval

entrega *en·tre·ga f* delivery (*of goods*)

entregar* *en·tre·gar vt* deliver; hand in (*goods*)

entremeses *en·tre·me·ses mpl* hors d'œuvre

entrenador *en·tre·na·dor m* coach (*instructor*)

entrenamiento *en·tre·na·myen·to m* training (*for sports*)

entrenarse *en·tre·nar·se vr* train (*athlete*)

entretanto *en·tre·tan·to adv* meanwhile

entretener* *en·tre·te·ner vt* amuse; entertain

entretenimiento *en·tre·te·nee·myen·to m* entertainment

entrevista *en·tre·bees·ta f* interview

entrometerse *en·tro·me·ter·se vr* interfere

entumecido(a) *en·too·me·thee·do(a) adj* numb

entusiasmado(a) *en·too·syas·ma·do(a) adj* excited

entusiasmo *en·too·syas·mo m* enthusiasm

entusiasta *en·too·syas·ta adj* enthusiastic

envasar *en·ba·sar vt* pack (*goods*)

envase *en·ba·se m* packing; container

envenenamiento de la sangre *en·be·ne·na·myen·to de la san·gre m* blood poisoning

enviar *en·bee·ar vt* send; enviar algo por vía terrestre *en·bee·ar al·go por bee·a te·rres·tre* to send something surface mail

envidia *en·bee·dya f* envy

envidiar *en·bee·dyar vt* envy
envidioso(a) *en·bee·dyo·so(a) adj* jealous; envious
envío *en·bee·o m* shipment; remittance
envoltura *en·bol·too·ra f* wrapping
envolver* *en·bol·ber vt* wrap; **envolver* un paquete** *en·bol·ber oon pa·ke·te* to wrap up a parcel
epidemia *e·pee·de·mya f* epidemic
epilepsia *e·pee·lep·sya f* epilepsy
época *e·po·ka f* age (*era*); **de época** *de e·po·ka* period (*furniture*)
equilibrar *e·kee·lee·brar vt* balance
equilibrio *e·kee·lee·bryo m* balance; **el equilibrio político** *e·kee·lee·bryo po·lee·tee·ko* balance of power; **perder* el equilibrio** *per·der el e·kee·lee·bryo* to lose one's balance
equipaje *e·kee·pa·khe m* luggage; baggage; **el equipaje de mano** *e·kee·pa·khe de ma·no* hand-luggage; **la reclamación de equipajes** *re·kla·ma·thyon de e·kee·pa·khes* baggage claim
equipo *e·kee·po m* team; plant; equipment
equitación *e·kee·ta·thyon f* horseback riding
equivalente *e·kee·ba·len·te adj* equivalent; **equivalente a** *e·kee·ba·len·te a* equivalent to
equivocación *e·kee·bo·ka·thyon f* mistake
equivocado(a) *e·kee·bo·ka·do(a) adj* wrong; mistaken; **eso está equivocado** *e·so es·ta e·kee·bo·ka·do* that's wrong
erótico(a) *e·ro·tee·ko(a) adj* erotic
errata *e·rra·ta f* misprint
erróneo(a) *e·rro·ne·o(a) adj* incorrect
error *e·rror m* error; mistake; **cometer un error** *ko·me·ter oon e·rror* to make a mistake; **por error** *por e·rror* in error
esa *e·sa adj* that (*feminine*) □ *pron* **ésa** *e·sa* that one
esas *e·sas adj* those (*feminine*) □ **ésas** *e·sas pron* those ones (*feminine*)
esbelto(a) *es·bel·to(a) adj* slim
esbozar* *es·bo·thar vt* sketch
escala *es·ka·la f* stopover (*air travel*); scale (*of map, thermometer, music*)
escaldar *es·kal·dar vt* scald
escalera *es·ka·le·ra f* flight of steps; stairs; ladder; **la escalera de incendios** *es·ka·le·ra de een·then·dyos* fire escape; **la escalera de tijera** *es·ka·le·ra de tee·khe·ra* stepladder
escalera mecánica *es·ka·le·ra me·ka·nee·ka f* escalator
escalfado(a) *es·kal·fa·do(a) adj* poached
escalón *es·ka·lon m* step (*stair*)
escalope *es·ka·lo·pe m* escalope
escama *es·ka·ma f* flake; scale (*of fish*); **las escamas de jabón** *es·ka·mas de kha·bon* soap-flakes
escanciador *es·kan·thya·dor m* wine waiter
Escandinavia *es·kan·dee·na·bya f* Scandinavia
escandinavo(a) *es·kan·dee·na·bo(a) adj* Scandinavian
escapar(se) *es·ka·par·se vr* escape
escaparate *es·ka·pa·ra·te m* window (*of shop*)
escape *es·ka·pe m* exhaust (*fumes*)
escarabajo *es·ka·ra·ba·kho m* beetle
escarcha *es·kar·cha f* frost
escarchado(a) *es·kar·cha·do(a) adj* glacé
escarlata *es·kar·la·ta adj* scarlet

escarola *es·ka·ro·la f* endive
escarpado(a) *es·kar·pa·do(a) adj* abrupt; steep
escasez *es·ka·seth f* shortage
escaso(a) *es·ka·so(a) adj* scarce
escena *es·the·na f* stage (*in theater*); scene
esclavo(a) *es·kla·bo(a) m/f* slave
esclusa *es·kloo·sa f* lock (*in canal*)
escoba *es·ko·ba f* broom
escocés(esa) *es·ko·thes(·the·sa) adj* Scottish; **la falda escocesa** *fal·da es·ko·the·sa* a kilt □ *m/f* **el/la escocés-s(esa)** *es·ko·thes(·the·sa)* Scot; **es escocés** *es·ko·thes* he's Scottish; **es escocesa** *es·ko·the·sa* she's Scottish
Escocia *es·ko·thya f* Scotland
escoger* *es·ko·kher vt* choose; pick
escolta *es·kol·ta f* escort
escoltar *es·kol·tar vt* escort
esconder *es·kon·der vt* hide
esconderse *es·kon·der·se vr* hide
escopeta *es·ko·pe·ta f* gun
escribir* *es·kree·beer vi* write □ *vt/i* spell (*in writing*); **escribir* en mayúsculas** *es·kree·beer en ma·yoos·koo·las* print (*write in block letters*)
escrito(a) *es·kree·to(a) adj* written; **por escrito** *por es·kree·to* in writing
escritor *es·kree·tor m* writer
escritorio *es·kree·to·ryo m* desk; study (*room*)
escritura *es·kree·too·ra f* writing
escuadra *es·kwa·dra f* fleet (*vehicles, ships*)
escuchar *es·koo·char vt/i* listen; listen to
escuela (primaria) *es·kwe·la pree·ma·rya f* grade school
escultor *es·kool·tor m* sculptor
escultura *es·kool·too·ra f* sculpture
escupir *es·koo·peer vi* spit
escurreplatos *es·koo·rre·pla·tos m* drainboard
escurrir *es·koo·rreer vt* wring (*clothes*)
ese *e·se adj* that (*masculine*) □ *pron* **ése** *e·se* that one
esencial *e·sen·thyal adj* essential (*necessary*)
esforzarse* *en es·for·thar·se en vr* make an effort to
esfuerzo *es·fwer·tho m* effort
eslavo(a) *es·la·bo(a) m/f* Slav
esmalte *es·mal·te m* enamel; **el esmalte para uñas** *es·mal·te pa·ra oon·yas* nail polish
esmeralda *es·me·ral·da f* emerald
esnob *es·nob m* snob □ *adj* snobbish
eso *e·so pron* that
esos *adj e·sos* those □ **ésos** *e·sos pron* those ones
espaciar *es·pa·thyar vt* spread (*payments*)
espacio *es·pa·thyo m* space
espada *es·pa·da f* sword
espadas *es·pa·das fpl* spades
espaguetis *es·pa·ge·tees mpl* spaghetti
espalda *es·pal·da f* back
España *es·pan·ya f* Spain
español *es·pan·yol m* Spanish □ *adj* **español(a)** *es·pan·yol(·la)* Spanish □ *m/f* **el/la español(a)** *es·pan·yo(·la)* Spaniard; **es español** *es es·pan·yol* he's Spanish; **es española** *es es·pan·yo·la* she's Spanish
esparadrapo *es·pa·ra·dra·po m* band-aid; sticking plaster
espárrago *es·pa·rra·go m* asparagus
espátula *es·pa·too·la f* spatula
especia *es·pe·thya f* spice

especial *es·pe·thyal adj* special; particular

especialista *es·pe·thya·lees·ta m* consultant (*doctor*)

especializado(a) *es·pe·thya·lee·tha·do(a) adj* skilled

especializarse *es·pe·thya·lee·thar·se vr* specialize; **especializarse en** *es·pe·thya·lee·thar·se en* to specialize in

especialmente *es·pe·thyal·men·te adv* especially; particularly

especie *es·pe·thye f* kind; **una especie de judía** *oo·na es·pe·thye de khoo·dee·a* a kind of bean

especificaciones *es·pe·thee·fee·ka·thyo·nes fpl* specifications

especificar* *es·pe·thee·fee·kar vt* specify

específico(a) *es·pe·thee·fee·ko(a) adj* specific

espécimen *es·pe·thee·men m* specimen

espectáculo *es·pek·ta·koo·lo m* entertainment; show (*in theatre*); **el mundo del espectáculo** *moon·do del es·pek·ta·koo·lo* show business; **el espectáculo de variedades** *es·pek·ta·koo·lo de ba·rye·da·des* variety show; **el espectáculo de luz y sonido** *es·pek·ta·koo·lo de looth y so·nee·do* son et lumière

espectador(a) *es·pek·ta·dor(·ra) m/f* spectator

espejo *es·pe·kho m* mirror; **el espejo retrovisor** *es·pe·kho re·tro·bee·sor* rear view mirror

Esperanto *es·pe·ran·to m* Esperanto

esperanza *es·pe·ran·tha f* hope

esperar *es·pe·rar vt* expect (*anticipate*) □ *vi* hope; wait (for); **espero que sí** *es·pe·ro ke see* I hope so; **espero que no** *es·pe·ro ke no* I hope not; **esperar a alguien** *es·pe·rar a al·gyen* to wait for someone; **hacer* esperar a alguien** *a·ther es·pe·rar a al·gyen* to keep someone waiting

espeso(a) *es·pe·so(a) adj* thick (*soup*)

espesor *es·pe·sor m* thickness

espía *es·pee·a m/f* spy

espina *es·pee·na f* bone (*of fish*)

espinaca *es·pee·na·ka f* spinach

espinazo *es·pee·na·tho m* spine (*backbone*)

espinilla *es·pee·neel·ya f* shin

espirar *es·pee·rar vi* expire

espíritu *es·pee·ree·too m* spirit (*soul*)

espolvorear *es·pol·bo·re·ar vt* sprinkle

esponja *es·pon·kha f* sponge

esposa *es·po·sa f* wife

esposas *es·po·sas fpl* handcuffs

espuma *es·poo·ma f* foam

espumoso(a) *es·poo·mo·so(a) adj* effervescent

esquí *es·kee m* skiing; ski; **el esquí acuático** *es·kee a·kwa·tee·ko* water-skiing; **hacer* esquí acuático** *a·ther es·kee a·kwa·tee·ko* to go water-skiing

esquiador(a) *es·kee·a·dor(·ra) m/f* skier

esquiar *es·kee·ar vi* ski

esquina *es·kee·na f* corner (*of streets*)

esquirol *es·kee·rol m* strikebreaker

esta *es·ta adj* this (*feminine*) □ *pron* **ésta** *es·ta* this one

estable *es·ta·ble adj* stable

establecer* *es·ta·ble·ther vt* establish

establo *es·ta·blo m* stable

estaca *es·ta·ka f* peg

estación *es·ta·thyon f* station; railroad station; service station; **la estación de**

autobuses *es·ta·thyon de ow·to·boo·ses* depot (*buses*); **la estación de servicio** *es·ta·thyon de ser·bee·thyo* gas station

estacionado(a) *es·ta·thyo·na·do(a) adj* settled (*weather*)

estacionar *es·ta·thyo·nar vt* park

estadio *es·ta·dyo m* stadium

estadista *es·ta·dees·ta m* statesman

estadística *es·ta·dees·tee·ka f* statistics; statistic

estadístico(a) *es·ta·dees·tee·ko(a) adj* statistical

estado *es·ta·do m* state (*condition*); **el Estado** *es·ta·do* the State

Estados Unidos *es·ta·dos oo·nee·dos mpl* United States (of America), US(A)

estallar *es·tal·yar vi* burst; explode

estallido *es·tal·yee·do m* bang (*of gun etc*)

estampido *es·tam·pee·do m* boom (*noise*)

estampilla *es·tam·peel·ya f* stamp (*postage*)

estancia *es·tan·thya f* stay (*period*)

estanco *es·tan·ko m* tobacconist's (*shop*)

estaño *es·tan·yo m* tin (*substance*)

estanque *es·tan·ke m* pond (*artificial*)

estanquero(a) *es·tan·ke·ro(a) m/f* tobacconist

estante *es·tan·te m* shelf

estaquilla *es·ta·keel·ya f* tent stake

estar* *es·tar vi* be (*temporary state*); **estoy** *es·toy* I am (*temporary state*)

estas *es·tas adj* these □ *pron* **éstas** *es·tas* these ones (*feminine*)

estatua *es·ta·twa f* statue

estatura *es·ta·too·ra f* height (*of person*)

este *es·te adj* this □ *pron* **éste** *es·te* this one □ *m* **el este** *es·te* east; **hacia el este** *a·thya el es·te* eastward

estera *es·te·ra f* mat

estéreo *es·te·re·o m* stereo

estereofónico(a) *es·te·re·o·fo·nee·ko(a) adj* stereo(phonic); **in stereo**

estéril *es·te·reel adj* sterile

esterilizar* *es·te·ree·lee·thar vt* sterilize

estilo *es·tee·lo m* style; **los más recientes estilos** *los mas re·thyen·tes es·tee·los* the latest fashions

estilográfica *es·tee·lo·gra·fee·ka f* fountain pen

estimado(a) *es·tee·ma·do(a) adj* □ **estimada Señora** *es·tee·ma·da sen·yo·ra* Dear Madam; **estimado Señor Smith** *es·tee·ma·do sen·yor Smith* Dear Mr. Smith

estimar *es·tee·mar vt* estimate

estipulación *es·tee·poo·la·thyon f* stipulation

estipular *es·tee·poo·lar vt* stipulate

estirar *es·tee·rar vt* stretch (*fabric etc*); spin out (*money*)

estirarse *es·tee·rar·se vr* stretch

esto *es·to pron* this; **esto es lo que quiero** *es·to es lo ke kye·ro* this is what I want

estofado *es·to·fa·do m* stew; casserole (*food*)

estola *es·to·la f* stole (*wrap*)

estómago *es·to·ma·go m* stomach

estorbar *es·tor·bar vt/i* get/be in the way (of)

estornudar *es·tor·noo·dar vi* sneeze

estornudo *es·tor·noo·do m* sneeze

estos(us) *es·tos(as) pron* these □ *pron* **éstos(as)** *es·tos(as)* these ones

estrado *es·tra·do m* platform (*in hall*)

estrangulador *es·tran·goo·la·dor m* choke (*of car*)

estrangular *es·tran·goo·lar vt* strangle

estrecho(a) *es·tre·cho(a) adj* narrow

estrella *es·trel·ya f* star

estrellarse contra *es·trel·yar·se kon·tra vr* crash into

estrenar *es·tre·nar vt* release (*book, film*)

estrenarse *es·tre·nar·se vr* open (*play*)

estreñido(a) *es·tren·yee·do(a) adj* constipated

estreñimiento *es·tren·yee·myen·to m* constipation

estreno *es·tre·no m* première

estrépito *es·tre·pee·to m* noise (*loud*)

estricto(a) *es·treek·to(a) adj* strict

estropajo *es·tro·pa·kho m* scourer

estropeado(a) *es·tro·pe·a·do(a) adj* out of order (*machine*)

estropear *es·tro·pe·ar vt* spoil (*damage*); make a mess of

estructura *es·trook·too·ra f* structure

estruendo *es·troo·en·do m* crash (*noise*)

estuche *es·too·che m* small box; case; **el estuche de manicura** *es·too·che de ma·nee·koo·ra* manicure set

estudiante *es·too·dyan·te m/f* undergraduate; student

estudiar *es·too·dyar vt/i* study

estudio *es·too·dyo m* studio; **el estudio de las posibilidades** *es·too·dyo de las po·see·bee·lee·da·des* feasibility study; **gustarle a uno los estudios** *goos·tar·le a oo·no los es·too·dyos* to enjoy one's studies

estufa *es·too·fa f* stove

estúpido(a) *es·too·pee·do(a) adj* stupid; silly

etapa *e·ta·pa f* stage (*point*); **por etapas** *por e·ta·pas* in stages

etc *et·the·te·ra abbrev* etc

ético(a) *e·tee·ko(a) adj* ethical

etiqueta *e·tee·ke·ta f* label; etiquette; ticket; tag; **poner* etiqueta a** *po·ner e·tee·ke·ta a* to label; **sin etiqueta** *seen e·tee·ke·ta* informal (*party*); **de etiqueta** *de e·tee·ke·ta* formal

étnico(a) *et·nee·ko(a) adj* ethnic

Europa *e·oo·ro·pa f* Europe

europeo(a) *e·oo·ro·pe·o(a) adj* European

evaporarse *e·ba·po·rar·se vr* evaporate

evidente *e·bee·den·te adj* obvious

evidentemente *e·bee·den·te·men·te adv* obviously

evitar *e·bee·tar vt* avoid

evolución *e·bo·loo·thyon f* evolution

exactamente *ek·sak·ta·men·te adv* exactly

exacto(a) *ek·sak·to(a) adj* accurate; exact (*detailed*); precise

exageración *ek·sa·khe·ra·thyon f* exaggeration

exagerar *ek·sa·khe·rar vt* exaggerate

examen *ek·sa·men m* examination (*exam*); **el examen de conducir** *ek·sa·men de kon·doo·theer* driving test

examinar *ek·sa·mee·nar vt* check; examine

excavadora *eks·ka·ba·do·ra f* bulldozer

excavar *eks·ka·bar vt* dig up; excavate

excedente *eks·the·den·te m* surplus

exceder *eks·the·der vt* exceed

excelente *eks·the·len·te adj* excellent

excéntrico(a) *eks·then·tree·ko(a) adj* eccentric

excepción *eks·thep·thyon f* exception

excepcional *eks·thep·thyo·nal adj* exceptional

excepto *eks·thep·to prep* except (for); except(ing)

excesivo(a) *eks·the·see·bo(a) adj* unreasonable (*demand, price*)

exceso *eks·the·so m* excess; **el exceso de velocidad** *eks·the·so de be·lo·thee·dad* speeding (*in car*); **el exceso de equipaje** *eks·the·so de e·kee·pa·khe* excess baggage

excitación *eks·thee·ta·thyon f* excitement

exclamar *eks·kla·mar vt* exclaim

excluir* *eks·kloo·eer vt* exclude

exclusividad *eks·kloo·see·bee·dad f* exclusive rights

exclusivo(a) *eks·kloo·see·bo(a) adj* exclusive

excursión *eks·koor·syon f* tour; excursion; outing; **ir* de excursión** *eer de eks·koor·syon* to go on an excursion; **la excursión a pie** *eks·koor·syon a pye* hike

excursionismo *eks·koor·syo·nees·mo m* hiking

excusa *eks·koo·sa f* excuse (*pretext*)

exigir* *ek·see·kheer vt* demand

existencia *ek·sees·ten·thya f* existence

existencias *ek·sees·ten·thyas fpl* supply (*stock*)

existir *ek·sees·teer vi* exist

éxito *ek·see·to m* success; **tener* éxito** *te·ner ek·see·to* succeed; **que tiene éxito** *ke tye·ne ek·see·to* successful (*venture*)

exótico(a) *ek·so·tee·ko(a) adj* exotic

expedición *eks·pe·dee·thyon f* expedition

expediente *eks·pe·dyen·te m* file (*dossier*)

expedir* *eks·pe·deer vt* dispatch

experiencia *eks·pe·ryen·thya f* experience; **tener* experiencia práctica** *te·ner eks·pe·ryen·thya prak·tee·ka* to have practical experience

experimentado(a) *eks·pe·ree·men·ta·do(a) adj* experienced

experimento *eks·pe·ree·men·to m* experiment

experto *eks·per·to m* expert

explicación *eks·plee·ka·thyon f* explanation

explicar* *eks·plee·kar vt* explain

explorar *eks·plo·rar vt* explore

explosión *eks·plo·syon f* blast; explosion

explotar *eks·plo·tar vt* explode

exportación *eks·por·ta·thyon f* export

exportador *eks·por·ta·dor m* exporter

exportar *eks·por·tar vt* export

exposición *eks·po·see·thyon f* presentation; show (*exhibition*); **la exposición de automóviles** *eks·po·see·thyon de ow·to·mo·bee·les* auto show

expresar *eks·pre·sar vt* express

expresión *eks·pre·syon f* expression

exprimidor *eks·pree·mee·dor m* lemon-squeezer

exprimir *eks·pree·meer vt* squeeze (*lemon*)

expuesto(a) *eks·pwes·to(a) adj* exposed; on view

extender *eks·ten·der vt* stretch; extend; spread

extensión *eks·ten·syon f* extension

exterior *eks·te·ryor m* outside □ *adj* exterior

externo(a) *eks·ter·no(a) adj* external

extintor *eks·teen·tor m* fire extinguisher

extra *eks·tra adj* extra

extraer* *eks·tra·er vt* extract

extranjero(a) *eks·tran·khe·ro(a)* adj overseas; foreign □ m/f foreigner; en el extranjero *en el eks·tran·khe·ro* overseas; abroad; ir* al extranjero *eer al eks·tran·khe·ro* to go abroad

extraño(a) *eks·tran·yo(a)* adj peculiar; odd; curious; strange

extraordinariamente *eks·tra·or·dee·na·rya·men·te* adv extraordinarily

extraordinario(a) *eks·tra·or·dee·na·ryo(a)* adj extraordinary

extravagante *eks·tra·ba·gan·te* adj extravagant

extremo *eks·tre·mo* m end (of table)

F

fábrica *fa·bree·ka* f factory; plant; la fábrica de cerveza *fa·bree·ka de ther·be·tha* brewery

fabricación *fa·bree·ka·thyon* f manufacturing; la fabricación en serie *fa·bree·ka·thyon en se·rye* mass production

fabricante *fa·bree·kan·te* m manufacturer

fabricar* *fa·bree·kar* vt manufacture; fabricar* en serie *fa·bree·kar en se·rye* to mass-produce

facciones *fak·thyo·nes* fpl features

fachada *fa·cha·da* f facade

fácil *fa·theel* adj easy

facilidades *fa·thee·lee·da·des* fpl facilities

fácilmente *fa·theel·men·te* adv easily

factor *fak·tor* m factor

factura *fak·too·ra* f invoice

facultad *fa·kool·tad* f faculty (university)

faisán *fay·san* m pheasant

faja *fa·kha* f corset; girdle

falda *fal·da* f skirt; la falda escocesa *fal·da es·ko·the·sa* kilt

fallar* *fal·yar* vi go wrong (machine); fail (brakes) □ vt trump (cards)

fallecido(a) *fal·ye·thee·do(a)* adj late; el fallecido rey *el fal·ye·thee·do rey* the late king

fallo *fal·yo* m failure (mechanical)

falsificación *fal·see·fee·ka·thyon* f forgery

falso(a) *fal·so(a)* adj false (name etc); fake

falta *fal·ta* f fault (defect); sin falta *seen fal·ta* without fail; estar* a falta de personal *es·tar a fal·ta de per·so·nal* to be short-staffed

faltar *fal·tar* vi be absent; be lacking; faltan algunas páginas *fal·tan al·goo·nas pa·khee·nas* some pages are missing; faltarle algo a alguien *fal·tar·le al·go a al·gyen* to be short of something; to need

fama *fa·ma* f reputation; fame

familia *fa·mee·lya* f family

famoso(a) *fa·mo·so(a)* adj famous

fangoso(a) *fan·go·so(a)* adj muddy (water)

fantasma *fan·tas·ma* m ghost

farmacéutico(a) *far·ma·the·oo·tee·ko(a)* m/f pharmacist; druggist

farmacia *far·ma·thya* f pharmacy; drugstore

faro *fa·ro* m headlight; lighthouse; el faro antiniebla *fa·ro an·tee·nye·bla* fog light

farol *fa·rol* m streetlamp; lamppost

farsa *far·sa* f farce

fascinante *fas·thee·nan·te* adj fascinating

fastidio *fas·tee·dyo* m bother; nuisance

fauna *fow·na* f wildlife

favor *fa·bor* m favor; hacer* un favor a alguien *a·ther oon fa·bor a al·gyen* to do someone a favor; por favor *por fa·bor* please

fe *fe* f belief; faith

febrero *fe·bre·ro* m February

fecha *fe·cha* f date; poner* fecha atrasada *po·ner fe·cha a·tra·sa·da* backdate; el meridiano de cambio de fecha *me·ree·dya·no de kam·byo de fe·cha* date line

federal *fe·de·ral* adj federal

feedback *feed·bak* m feedback

felicidad *fe·lee·thee·dad* f happiness

felicitaciones *fe·lee·thee·ta·thyo·nes* fpl congratulations

felicitar a *fe·lee·thee·tar a* vt congratulate

feliz *fe·leeth* adj glad; happy

felpudo *fel·poo·do* m doormat

femenino(a) *fe·me·nee·no(a)* adj feminine; el sexo femenino *sek·so fe·me·nee·no* the female sex

feo(a) *fe·o(a)* adj ugly

feria *fe·rya* f fair (commercial)

feroz *fe·roth* adj fierce

ferretería *fe·rre·te·ree·a* f hardware

ferretero *fe·rre·te·ro* m ironmonger

ferrocarril *fe·rro·ka·rreel* m railroad; por ferrocarril *por fe·rro·ka·rreel* by rail

ferry *fe·rry* m ferry (large)

fértil *fer·teel* adj fertile (land)

festín *fes·teen* m feast

festival *fes·tee·bal* m festival

fiambre *fee·am·bre* m cold meat

fianza *fee·an·tha* f bail (for prisoner); security (for loan); bajo fianza *ba·kho fee·an·tha* on bail

fibra *fee·bra* f fiber; la fibra de vidrio *fee·bra de bee·dryo* fiberglass

ficha *fee·cha* f chip (in gambling); token (for machine); counter (gambling)

fichero *fee·che·ro* m card index; filing cabinet

fidelidad *fee·de·lee·dad* f fidelity; de alta fidelidad *de al·ta fee·de·lee·dad* hi-fi

fiebre *fye·bre* f fever; tener* fiebre *te·ner fye·bre* to have a temperature; la fiebre del heno *fye·bre del e·no* hay fever

fieltro *fyel·tro* m felt (cloth)

fiesta *fyes·ta* f party (celebration); holiday (day); fête

figura *fee·goo·ra* f figure

fijar *fee·khar* vt fix (fasten); fijar el precio de *fee·khar el pre·thyo de* to fix the price of (goods); fijar un anuncio *fee·khar oon a·noon·thyo* to put up a notice

fila *fee·la* f row

filete *fee·le·te* m fillet (of meat, fish); el filete de lomo (de vaca) *fee·le·te de lo·mo (de ba·ka)* rump steak

filial *fee·lyal* f affiliated company

filo *fee·lo* m edge (of blade)

filtrar *feel·trar* vt filter; percolate (coffee)

filtro *feel·tro* m strainer; filter (on camera); el filtro de aceite *feel·tro de a·they·te* oil filter; el filtro de aire *feel·tro de ay·re* air filter

fin *feen* m end; el fin de semana *feen de se·ma·na* weekend; por fin *por feen* at last

final *fee·nal* adj final □ f la final *fee·nal* finals (sports) □ m el final *fee·nal* end (*of street*); **al final** *al fee·nal* eventually

finalmente *fee·nal·men·te adv* finally

financiar *fee·nan·thyar vt* finance; back (*financially*)

financiero(a) *fee·nan·thye·ro(a) adj* financial

finanzas *fee·nan·thas fpl* finance

finca *feen·ka f* farm; estate; property

fingir *feen·kheer vt/i* pretend; **fingir hacer algo** *feen·kheer a·ther al·go* to pretend to do something

finlandés(esa) *feen·lan·des(·de·sa) adj* Finnish

Finlandia *feen·lan·dya f* Finland

fino(a) *fee·no(a) adj* fine (*delicate*); thin (*material*); sheer (*stockings*)

firma *feer·ma f* signature

firmar *feer·mar vt* sign (*document*)

firme *feer·me adj* steady; firm

fiscal *fees·kal adj* fiscal

física *fee·see·ka f* physics

físico(a) *fee·see·ko(a) adj* physical

flaco(a) *fla·ko(a) adj* thin

flamenco(a) *fla·men·ko(a) adj* Flemish

flash *flash m* flash (*on camera*)

flatulencia *fla·too·len·thya f* wind (*in stomach*)

flauta *flow·ta f* flute

flecha *fle·cha f* arrow

flequillo *fle·keel·yo m* fringe (*hair*); bangs

flete *fle·te m* freight (*goods*); **el flete por avión** *fle·te por a·byon* air freight

flexible *flek·see·ble adj* flexible

flojo(a) *flo·kho(a) adj* slack (*loose*); weak (*tea*); mild (*taste*); dull (*business*)

flor *flor f* flower; blossom; bloom

florecer *flo·re·ther vi* bloom

florero *flo·re·ro m* vase

florista *flo·rees·ta m/f* florist

flota *flo·ta f* fleet

flotador *flo·ta·dor m* float (*for swimming*)

flotar *flo·tar vi* float

fluir *floo·eer vi* flow

flúor *floo·or m* fluoride

foco *fo·ko m* floodlight; spotlight

folleto *fol·ye·to m* brochure

fondo *fon·do m* bottom; background; back (*of hall, room*)

fondos *fon·dos mpl* funds

fontanero *fon·ta·ne·ro m* plumber

footing *foo·teeng m* jogging; **hacer el footing** *a·ther el foo·teeng* to go jogging

forastero *fo·ras·te·ro m* stranger

forma *for·ma f* form; shape; **de todas formas** *de to·das for·mas* all the same; **en forma** *en for·ma* fit (*strong, healthy*); **en buena forma** *en bwe·na for·ma* in good form

formación *for·ma·thyon f* training (*for job*)

formal *for·mal adj* proper (*respectable*)

formulario *for·moo·la·ryo m* form (*document*)

forro *fo·rro m* lining; **sin forro** *seen fo·rro* unlined (*clothes*)

fortalecer *for·ta·le·ther vt* strengthen

fortaleza *for·ta·le·tha f* fortress

fortuito(a) *for·twee·to(a) adj* accidental

fortuna *for·too·na f* fortune (*wealth*)

fósforo *fos·fo·ro m* match

foto *fo·to f* picture; photo

fotocopia *fo·to·ko·pya f* Xerox; photocopy

fotocopiar *fo·to·ko·pyar vt* Xerox; photocopy

fotografía *fo·to·gra·fee·a f* photography; photograph

fotografiar *fo·to·gra·fyar vt* photograph

fotógrafo *fo·to·gra·fo m* photographer

fotómetro *fo·to·me·tro m* light meter

frac *frak m* tailcoat

fracasado(a) *fra·ka·sa·do(a) m/f* failure (*person*)

fracasar *fra·ka·sar vi* fail

fracaso *fra·ka·so m* failure

fractura *frak·too·ra f* fracture (*of arm etc*)

frágil *fra·kheel adj* fragile; **frágil** *fra·kheel* handle with care

frambuesa *fram·bwe·sa f* raspberry

francés(esa) *fran·thes(·the·sa) adj* French; **es francés** *es fran·thes* he's French; **es francesa** *es fran·the·sa* she's French

francés *fran·thes m* French

Francia *fran·thya f* France

franja *fran·kha f* fringe (*edging*)

franquear *fran·ke·ar vt* cross; clear

franqueo *fran·ke·o m* postage

frasco *fras·ko m* flask

frase *fra·se f* phrase; sentence

frazada *fra·tha·da f* blanket

frecuente *fre·kwen·te adj* frequent; **poco frecuente** *po·ko fre·kwen·te* occasional

frecuentemente *fre·kwen·te·men·te adv* often

fregadero *fre·ga·de·ro m* sink (*basin*)

fregar *fre·gar vt* mop; **fregar los platos** *fre·gar los pla·tos* to do the dishes

fregona *fre·go·na f* mop

freír *fre·eer vt* fry

frenar *fre·nar vi* put on the brakes; brake

freno *fre·no m* brake; **el líquido de frenos** *lee·kee·do de fre·nos* brake fluid; **el freno de pie** *fre·no de pye* footbrake; **el freno de mano** *fre·no de ma·no* hand-brake; **los frenos de disco** *fre·nos de dees·ko* disc brakes

frente *fren·te f* forehead; **en frente** *en fren·te* opposite; **frente a** *fren·te a* facing; **de frente** *de fren·te* head-on

fresa *fre·sa f* strawberry

fresco(a) *fres·ko(a) adj* fresh; crisp; cool; wet (*paint*); sweet (*smell*)

fresno *fres·no m* ash (*tree*)

frigorífico *free·go·ree·fee·ko m* refrigerator

frijoles *free·kho·les mpl* beans

frío(a) *free·o(a) adj* cold; **tengo frío** *ten·go free·o* I'm cold

frito(a) *free·to(a) adj* fried; **un huevo frito** *oon we·bo free·to* a fried egg

frontera *fron·te·ra f* border; frontier

frotar *fro·tar vt* rub

fruncido(a) *froon·thee·do(a) adj* gathered

fruta *froo·ta f* fruit

fuego *fwe·go m* fire; **el fuego artificial** *fwe·go ar·tee·fee·thyal* fireworks; **¿tiene fuego?** *tye·ne fwe·go* have you got a light?

fuente *fwen·te f* fountain; source; spring (*of water*)

fuera *fwe·ra adv* outdoors; out (*not at home*); **estar fuera** *es·tar fwe·ra* to be outside; **pasa una semana fuera** *pa·sa oo·na se·ma·na fwe·ra* he's away for a week □ *prep* **fuera de** *fwe·ra de prep* out of (*outside*); **fuera de casa** *fwe·ra de ka·sa* away from home; **fuera de borda** *fwe·ra de bor·da* outboard; **fuera de mi alcance**

fwe·ra de mee al·kan·the beyond my reach

fuerte *fwer·te adj* strong (*person*); loud (*noise*); rich (*food*); solid

fuerza *fwer·tha f* force (*violence*); strength; **las fuerzas aéreas** *fwer·thas a·e·re·as* air force

fuga *foo·ga f* leak (*gas*)

fugarse* *foo·gar·se vr* get away (*escape*)

fumador(a) *foo·ma·dor(·ra) m/f* smoker (*person*)

fumar *foo·mar vt/i* smoke; **¿fuma Ud?** *foo·ma oos·ted* do you smoke?

funcionar *foon·thyo·nar vi* run (*machine, engine*); work (*clock, mechanism*); **estar* funcionando bien** *es·tar foon·thyo·nan·do byen* to be in working order; **hacer* funcionar** *a·ther foon·thyo·nar* to operate (*machine*); to flush (*the toilet*); **este coche funciona con gasoil** *es·te ko·che foon·thyo·na kon gas·oyl* this car runs on diesel

funcionario *foon·thyo·na·ryo m* civil servant

funda de almohada *foon·da de al·mo·a·da f* pillowcase, pillowslip

fundamentalmente *foon·du·men·tal·men·te adv* basically

fundar *foon·dar vt* establish (*business*)

furgón de equipajes *foor·gon de e·kee·pa·khes m* baggage car

furioso(a) *foo·ryo·so(a) adj* mad (*angry*)

fusible *foo·see·ble m* fuse

fusil *foo·seel m* rifle

fusión *foo·syon f* amalgamation; merger

fútbol *foot·bol m* soccer; football (*game*)

G

gafas *ga·fas fpl* glasses; goggles; eyeglasses; **las gafas de sol** *ga·fas de sol* sunglasses; **las gafas ahumadas** *ga·fas a·oo·ma·das* shades (*sunglasses*)

gaita *gay·ta f* (bag)pipes

gala *ga·la f* gala

galería *ga·le·ree·a f* gallery

galés(esa) *ga·les(·le·sa) adj* Welsh □ *m* **el galés** *ga·les* Welsh

Gales *ga·les m* Wales

galleta *gal·ye·ta f* biscuit; cookie

gallina *gal·yee·na f* hen; **la gallina de Guinea** *gal·yee·na de gee·ne·a* guinea fowl

gallo *gal·yo m* cock(erel)

galón *ga·lon m* gallon

galopar *ga·lo·par vi* gallop

galope *ga·lo·pe m* gallop; **ir* al galope** *eer al ga·lo·pe* to go at a gallop

gama *ga·ma f* range

gamba *gam·ba f* prawn

ganado *ga·na·do m* cattle

ganador(a) *ga·na·dor(·ra) m/f* winner

ganancia *ga·nan·thya f* return (*profit*)

ganar *ga·nar vi* win □ *vt* earn; gain (*obtain*); take (*win: prize*); **ganar $25 por hora** *ga·nar $25 por o·ra* to earn $25 per hour

gancho *gan·cho m* hook

ganga *gan·ga f* bargain (*cheap buy*)

gángster *gang·ster m* gangster

ganso *gan·so m* goose

garaje *ga·ra·khe m* garage

garantía *ga·ran·tee·a f* guarantee; warrant(y)

garantizar* *ga·ran·tee·thar vt* guaran-

tee; **garantizar** *ga·ran·tee·thar* underwrite (*finance*)

garganta *gar·gan·ta f* throat

gárgaras *gar·ga·ras fpl* gargling; **hacer* gárgaras** *a·ther gar·ga·ras* to gargle

garrafa *ga·rra·fa f* carafe; decanter

gas *gas m* gas; **el gas butano** *gas boo·ta·no* butane

gasa *ga·sa f* gauze

gaseoso(a) *ga·se·o·so(a) adj* fizzy

gasfitero *gas·fee·te·ro m* plumber

gasoil *gas·oyl m* diesel fuel

gasolina *ga·so·lee·na f* gasoline

gasolinera *ga·so·lee·ne·ra f* gasoline station

gastado(a) *gas·ta·do(a) adj* worn; worn-out (*object*)

gastar *gas·tar vt* waste (*money*); spend

gastarse *gas·tar·se vr* wear out (*fabric*)

gasto *gas·to m* expense (*cost*); **los gastos comerciales** *gas·tos ko·mer·thya·les* business expenses; **los gastos generales** *gas·tos khe·ne·ra·les* overhead; **los gastos** *gas·tos* expenditure; **los gastos corrientes** *gas·tos ko·rryen·tes* running costs

gastrónomo *gas·tro·no·mo m* gourmet

gato *ga·to m* cat, jack (*for car*)

gelatina *khe·la·tee·na f* jelly

gemelo *khe·me·lo m* cuff link

gemelos(as) *khe·me·los(as) m/f* twins

gemido *khe·mee·do m* groan; moan

gemir* *khe·meer vi* groan; moan

generación *khe·ne·ra·thyon f* generation

generador *khe·ne·ra·dor m* generator

general *khe·ne·ral adj* general □ *m* general (*soldier*); **en general** *en khe·ne·ral* in general

generalmente *khe·ne·ral·men·te adv* generally

género *khe·ne·ro m* gender

generoso(a) *khe·ne·ro·so(a) adj* generous

gente *khen·te f* people

geografía *khe·o·gra·fee·a f* geography

geología *khe·o·lo·khee·a f* geology

geometría *khe·o·me·tree·a f* geometry

geranio *khe·ra·nyo m* geranium

gerente *khe·ren·te m* manager □ *f* **la gerente** *khe·ren·te* manageress

gesto *khes·to m* gesture

ghetto *ge·to m* ghetto

gigante *khee·gan·te m* giant

gimnasia *kheem·na·sya f* gymnastics

gimnasio *kheem·na·syo m* gym(nasium)

ginebra *khee·ne·bra f* gin (*drink*)

Ginebra *khee·ne·bra f* Geneva

girar *khee·rar vt* turn □ *vi* spin (*rotate*)

giro postal *khee·ro pos·tal m* money order; postal order

gitano(a) *khee·ta·no(a) m/f* gypsy

glándula *glan·doo·la f* gland

glaseado(a) *gla·se·a·do m* icing (*on cake*)

glicerina *glee·the·ree·na f* glycerin(e)

global *glo·bal adj* global

globo *glo·bo m* globe (*map*); balloon

glorieta *glo·rye·ta f* roundabout

gobernador *go·ber·na·dor m* governor

gobernar* *go·ber·nar vt* govern; rule

gobierno *go·byer·no m* government

gol *gol m* goal (*sport*)

golf *golf m* golf

goloso(a) *go·lo·so(a) adj* greedy

golpe *gol·pe m* blow; bang; stroke (*golf*); hit; **el golpe de estado** *gol·pe de es·ta·do* coup d'état

golpear *gol·pe·ar vt* hit; strike; beat; bump; **golpear ligeramente** *gol·pe·ar lee·khe·ra·men·te* tap

golpearse *gol·pe·ar·se vr* knock; **golpearse la cabeza** *gol·pe·ar·se la ka·be·tha* to bang one's head
goma *go·ma f* eraser; gum
gomita *go·mee·ta f* elastic band
gordo(a) *gor·do(a) adj* fat
gorra *go·rra f* cap (*hat*)
gorrión *go·rryon m* sparrow
gorro de baño *go·rro de ban·yo m* bathing cap
gota *go·ta f* drop (*of liquid*)
gotear *go·te·ar vi* leak; drip
goteo *go·te·o m* drip
goulash *goo·lash m* goulash
grabado *gra·ba·do m* print
grabar *gra·bar vt* record; tape record
gracias *gra·thyas excl* thank you; **gracias a** *gra·thyas a* thanks to
gracioso(a) *gra·thyo·so(a) adj* funny (*amusing*)
grado *gra·do m* degree; grade; **a 2 grados bajo cero** *a 2 gra·dos ba·kho the·ro* at minus 2 degrees
graduación *gra·doo·a·thyon f* □ **un whisky de graduación de 70 por 100** *oon wees·kee de gra·doo·a·thyon de 70 por 100 a* 70° proof whiskey
gradual *gra·dwal adj* gradual
gradualmente *gra·dwal·men·te adv* gradually
graduar *gra·dwar vt* test (*sight, hearing*)
graduarse *gra·dwar·se vr* graduate (*from university*)
gráfica *gra·fee·ka f* chart (*diagram, table*)
gráfico *gra·fee·ko m* graph
gramática *gra·ma·tee·ka f* grammar
gramo *gra·mo m* gram
granada *gra·na·da f* pomegranate
Gran Bretaña *gran bre·tan·ya f* Great Britain
gran(de) *gran·de adj* large; great; tall; high (*speed, number*); great; **un(a) gran atleta** *oon(·na) gran at·le·ta* a great athlete
grandioso(a) *gran·dyo·so(a) adj* ambitious (*plan*)
granel *gra·nel m* heap; **a granel** *a gra·nel* in bulk (*in large quantities*)
granero *gra·ne·ro m* barn
granizar *gra·nee·thar vi* hail (*hailstones*)
granizo *gra·nee·tho m* hail
granja *gran·kha f* farm
grano *gra·no m* spot; pimple
grapa *gra·pa f* staple
grasa *gra·sa f* fat; grease; lubricant
grasiento(a) *gra·syen·to(a) adj* greasy
gratinado(a) *gra·tee·na·do(a) adj* au gratin
gratis *gra·tees adj* free of charge
grava *gra·ba f* gravel
gravar *gra·bar vt* assess (*for taxation*)
grave *gra·be adj* serious; deep (*voice*)
Grecia *gre·thya f* Greece
gremio *gre·myo m* union (*trade union*)
griego(a) *gree·e·go(a) adj* Greek □ **el griego** *gree·e·go* Greek
grieta *grye·ta f* crack (*split*)
grifo *gree·fo m* faucet
gripe *gree·pe f* flu
gris *grees adj* drab; gray
gritar *gree·tar vi* call; scream; shout
grito *gree·to m* shout; cry
grosella *gro·sel·ya f* red currant; **la grosella espinosa** *gro·sel·ya es·pee·no·sa* gooseberry; **la grosella negra** *gro·sel·ya ne·gra* black currant

grosero(a) *gro·se·ro(a) adj* rude (*person*)
grotesco(a) *gro·tes·ko(a) adj* grotesque
grúa *groo·a f* crane (*machine*); tow truck
gruesa *grwe·sa f* gross
grueso(a) *grwe·so(a) adj* thick
grumo *groo·mo m* lump (*in sauce*)
gruñir *groon·yeer vi* grunt; growl
grupo *groo·po m* party; group; unit (*department, squad*); **el grupo sanguíneo** *groo·po san·gee·ne·o* blood group; **el grupo de música pop** *groo·po de moo·see·ka pop* pop group; **el grupo de presión** *groo·po de pre·syon* pressure group
guante *gwan·te m* glove
guantera *gwan·te·ra f* glove compartment
guapo(a) *gwa·po(a) adj* handsome (*person*); pretty (*woman, child*)
guardabarros *gwar·da·ba·rros m* mudguard
guardacostas *gwar·da·kos·tas m* coastguard
guardaespaldas *gwar·da·es·pal·das m* bodyguard (*person*)
guardar *gwar·dar vt* put away; **guardar algo hasta más tarde** *gwar·dar al·go as·ta mas tar·de* to keep something till later; **guardar algo en la nevera** *gwar·dar al·go en la ne·be·ra* to keep something in the refrigerator
guardarropa *gwar·da·rro·pa m* cloakroom
guardería *gwar·de·ree·a f* play-group; day nursery; crèche
guardia *gwar·dya f* guard (*soldiers*)
guarniciones *gwar·nee·thyo·nes fpl* harness
guerra *ge·rra f* war; **la guerra civil** *ge·rra thee·beel* civil war; **la guerra mundial** *ge·rra moon·dyal* world war
guía *gee·a m/f* courier; guide (*person*); **el guía automático** *el gee·a ow·to·ma·tee·ko* audio-guide □ **f la guía** *gee·a* directory; **la guía telefónica** *gee·a te·le·fo·nee·ka* telephone directory; **la guía turística** *gee·a too·rees·tee·ka* guidebook
guijarro *gee·kha·rro m* pebble
guiñar *geen·yar vi* wink
guinga *geen·ga f* gingham
guión *gee·on m* dash (*in writing*); hyphen
guisantes *gee·san·tes mpl* peas
guitarra *gee·ta·rra f* guitar
gusano *goo·sa·no m* worm
gustar *goos·tar vt* like; enjoy (*concert, outing*); **gustarle mucho a uno hacer algo** *goos·tar·le moo·cho a oo·no a·ther al·go* to love doing something; **me gustaría muchísimo ir** *me goos·ta·ree·a moo·chee·see·mo eer* I'd love to go; **me gustaría un helado** *me goos·ta·ree·a oon e·la·do* I'd like an ice cream; **¿le gustaría una taza de café?** *le goos·ta·ree·a oo·na ta·tha de ka·fe* would you like a cup of coffee?
gusto *goos·to m* taste; **de mal gusto** *de mal goos·to* in poor taste; **de buen gusto** *de bwen goos·to* in good taste

H

haber *a·ber m* assets
hábil *a·beel adj* skilful
habilidad *a·bee·lee·dad f* skill; ability
habitación *a·bee·ta·thyon f* room; **la habitación doble** *a·bee·ta·thyon do·ble* double room; **una habitación in-**

dividual oo·na a·bee·ta·thyon een·dee·bee·dwal a single room; **la habitación libre** a·bee·ta·thyon lee·bre vacancy (in hotel etc)

habitante a·bee·tan·te m inhabitant

habitar a·bee·tar vt inhabit

hábito a·bee·to m habit

habitual a·bee·twal adj regular (usual)

habla a·bla f speech

hablar a·blar vt/i speak □ vi talk; **no pude hablar con él/ella** no poo·de a·blar kon el/el·ya I couldn't get through to him/her (on phone); **¿habla Ud inglés?** a·bla oos·ted een·gles do you speak English?; **hablar a alguien de algo** a·blar a al·gyen de al·go to speak to someone about something

hacer* a·ther vt do; make; **hacer* una foto** a·ther oo·na fo·to to take a photo; **hacer* un examen** a·ther oon ek·sa·men to take an exam; **voy a hacerlo** boy a a·ther·lo I'm going to do it; **hacer* hacer algo** a·ther a·ther al·go to have something done; **hace 4 años** a·the 4 an·yos 4 years ago; **hace calor** a·the ka·lor it is hot; **hacer* las camas** a·ther las ka·mas to make the beds

hacerse* a·ther·se vr develop; become; **hacerse* mayor** a·ther·se ma·yor to grow up

hacha a·cha f ax

hacia a·thya prep toward(s); **mirar hacia algo** mee·rar a·thya al·go to look towards something; **su actitud hacia los demás** soo ak·tee·tood a·thya los de·mas his attitude towards others

hacienda a·thyen·da f farm; ranch; finance; **el ministro de hacienda** mee·nees·tro de a·thyen·da Finance Minister

hada a·da f fairy

hágalo usted mismo a·ga·lo oos·ted mees·mo m do-it-yourself

haliento a·lyen·to m breath

hamaca a·ma·ka f hammock

hambre am·bre m hunger; **morirse* de hambre** mo·reer·se de am·bre to starve; **tener* hambre** te·ner am·bre to be hungry; **tengo hambre** ten·go am·bre I feel hungry

hambriento(a) am·bryen·to(a) adj hungry

hamburguesa am·boor·ge·sa f hamburger

hándicap an·dee·kap m handicap (golf)

hardware ard·wer m hardware (computing)

harina a·ree·na f flour; **la harina de maíz** a·ree·na de ma·eeth cornstarch

harto(a) ar·to(a) adj full; **estoy harto de** es·toy ar·to de I'm fed up with

hasta as·ta prep until; till; **hasta ahora** as·ta a·o·ra up till now; **hasta 6** as·ta 6 up to 6; **hasta que venga** as·ta ke ben·ga until he comes; **hasta la estación** as·ta la es·ta·thyon as far as the station

hay ay v there is/there are; **no hay de qué** no ay de ke don't mention it; **¿hay más sopa?** ay mas so·pa is there any more soup?; **¿hay alguien allí?** ay al·gyen al·yee is there anyone there?

haya a·ya f beech

la Haya la a·ya f Hague (the)

hebilla e·beel·ya f buckle

hecho(a) e·cho(a) adj finished; done (meat); ripe (cheese) □ m **el hecho** e·cho fact; **hecho(a) a mano** e·cho(a) a

mano handmade; **poco hecho(a)** po·ko e·cho(a) underdone, rare (steak)

helado e·la·do m ice cream; **el helado de vainilla** e·la·do de bay·neel·ya vanilla ice cream

helar* e·lar vi freeze

helecho e·le·cho m bracken; fern

helicóptero e·lee·kop·te·ro m helicopter

hembra em·bra adj female (animal)

hemorragia e·mo·rra·khya f hemorrhage

hemorroides e·mo·rro·ee·des fpl hemorrhoids

henderse en·der·se vr split (tear)

heno e·no m hay

heredar e·re·dar vt inherit

herida e·ree·da f injury; wound

herido(a) e·ree·do(a) adj injured

herir* e·reer vt injure

hermana er·ma·na f sister

hermanastra er·ma·nas·tra f stepsister

hermanastro er·ma·nas·tro m stepbrother

hermano er·ma·no m brother

hermético(a) er·me·tee·ko(a) adj airtight

hermoso(a) er·mo·so(a) adj beautiful

hernia er·nya f hernia

herpes er·pes fpl shingles (illness)

herramienta e·rra·myen·ta f tool

hervidor er·bee·dor m kettle

hervir* er·beer vi boil; **hervir* a fuego lento** er·beer a fwe·go len·to to simmer

hidropedal ee·dro·pe·dal m pedalo

hielo ye·lo m ice; **con hielo** kon ye·lo on the rocks (with ice)

hierba yer·ba f grass; herb

hierro ye·rro m iron (metal, golf); **el hierro fundido** ye·rro foon·dee·do cast iron

hígado ee·ga·do m liver

higiénico(a) ee·khye·nee·ko(a) adj hygienic

higo ee·go m fig

hija ee·kha f daughter

hijastra ee·khas·tra f stepdaughter

hijastro ee·khas·tro m stepson

hijo ee·kho m son

hilar ee·lar vt spin (wool)

hilas ee·las fpl lint

hilo ee·lo m thread; **el hilo de algodón** ee·lo de al·go·don cotton (thread)

himno eem·no m hymn; **el himno nacional** eem·no na·thyo·nal national anthem

hincha een·cha m fan (supporter)

hinchable een·cha·ble adj inflatable

hinchado(a) een·cha·do(a) adj swollen

hincharse een·char·se vr swell (up)

hinchazón een·cha·thon f swelling (lump)

hipermercado ee·per·mer·ka·do m superstore

hipo ee·po m hiccup; **tener* hipo** te·ner ee·po to have hiccups

hipódromo ee·po·dro·mo m racecourse; race track

hipoteca hee·po·te·ka f mortgage

hipotecar ee·po·te·kar vt mortgage

histérico(a) ees·te·ree·ko(a) adj hysterical

historia ees·to·rya f story history

histórico(a) ees·to·ree·ko(a) adj historical

hockey kho·key m hockey; **el hockey sobre hielo** kho·key so·bre ye·lo ice hockey

hogar o·gar m hearth

hoguera o·ge·ra f bonfire

hoja o·kha f leaf; blade (of knife); sheet (of paper); **la hoja de afeitar** o·kha de a·fey·tar razor blade; **la hoja de pedido** o·kha de pe·dee·do order-form

hojuela o·khwe·la f pancake

hola o·la excl hullo; hello

Holanda o·lan·da f Holland

holandés(esa) o·lan·des(·de·sa) adj Dutch □ m el holandés o·lan·des Dutch

hombre om·bre m man; **el hombre de negocios** om·bre de ne·go·thyos businessman

hombro om·bro m shoulder

homogeneizado(a) o·mo·khe·ney·tha·do(a) adj homogenized

hondo(a) on·do(a) adj deep (water, hole)

hongo on·go m derby; mushroom

honorarios o·no·ra·ryos mpl fee

honrado(a) on·ra·do(a) adj honest; **poco honrado(a)** po·ko hon·ra·do(a) dishonest

hora o·ra f hour; **ha llegado a buena hora** a lye·ga·do a bwe·na o·ra you're early; **las horas de trabajo** o·ras de tra·ba·kho business hours; **por hora** por o·ra hourly; **a la hora exacta** a la o·ra ek·sak·ta punctual (train); **la hora punta** o·ra poon·ta rush hour; **la hora del almuerzo** o·ra del al·mwer·tho lunch hour; **las horas extraordinarias** o·ras eks·tra·or·dee·na·ryas overtime; **trabajar horas extraordinarias** tra·ba·khar o·ras eks·tra·or·dee·na·ryas to work overtime; **¿qué hora es?** ke o·ra es what's the time?; **horas de visita** o·ras de bee·see·ta visiting hours

horario o·ra·ryo m timetable; schedule; **el horario de salidas** o·ra·ryo de sa·lee·das departure board; **la zona horaria** tho·na o·ra·rya time zone

horizontal o·ree·thon·tal adj level; horizontal

horizonte o·ree·thon·te m horizon

hormiga or·mee·ga f ant

hormigón or·mee·gon m concrete; **de hormigón** de or·mee·gon concrete

horno or·no m oven; **el horno de micro-ondas** or·no de mee·kro·on·das microwave oven

horquilla hor·keel·ya f hairpin

horrible o·rree·ble adj horrible

hospital os·pee·tal m hospital; **el hospital psiquiátrico** os·pee·tal see·kee·a·tree·ko mental hospital

hospitalidad os·pee·ta·lee·dad f hospitality

hotel o·tel m hotel

hoy oy adv today; **hoy en día** oy en dee·a nowadays

hoyo o·yo m pit

hueco(a) we·ko(a) adj hollow □ m gap; hole

huelga wel·ga f strike (industrial); walkout; **la huelga no oficial** wel·ga no o·fee·thyal unofficial strike; **en huelga** en wel·ga on strike; **paralizado por una huelga** pa·ra·lee·tha·do por oo·na wel·ga strikebound; **declararse en huelga** de·kla·rar·se en wel·ga to strike (workers); **la huelga de celo** wel·ga de the·lo slowdown

huelguista wel·gees·ta m/f striker

huérfano(a) wer·fa·no(a) m/f orphan

huerta wer·ta f orchard

hueso we·so m bone; stone (in fruit)

huésped wes·ped m host; lodger; guest (at hotel)

huevera we·be·ra f egg cup

huevo we·bo m egg; **un huevo pasado por agua** oon we·bo pa·sa·do por ag·wa a soft-boiled egg; **el huevo de Pascua** we·bo de pas·kwa Easter egg

huir* oo·eer vi to run away

humano(a) oo·ma·no(a) adj human

humedad oo·me·dad f moisture

húmedo(a) oo·me·do(a) adj wet (climate); damp

humo oo·mo m smoke

humor oo·mor m mood; **de mal humor** de mal oo·mor in a bad temper; **de buen humor** de bwen oo·mor in a good mood; in good spirits

hundirse oon·deer·se vr sink

húngaro(a) oon·ga·ro(a) adj Hungarian

Hungría oon·gree·a f Hungary

huracán oo·ra·kan m hurricane

I

idea ee·de·a f idea; thought

ideal ee·de·al adj ideal

idéntico(a) ee·den·tee·ko(a) adj identical

identificar* ee·den·tee·fee·kar vt identify

idiota ee·dyo·ta m/f idiot

iglesia ee·gle·sya f church

ignorante eeg·no·ran·te adj ignorant

ignorar eeg·no·rar vt not to know

igual ee·gwal adj even; equal; **me da igual** me da ee·gwal I don't care

igualmente ee·gwal·men·te adv likewise

ilegal ee·le·gal adj illegal

ilegítimo(a) ee·le·khee·tee·mo(a) adj illegitimate

ileso(a) ee·le·so(a) adj unhurt

ilimitado(a) ee·lee·mee·ta·do(a) adj unlimited

iluminación ee·loo·mee·na·thyon f lighting (on road); lighting

iluminado(a) ee·loo·mee·na·do(a) adj illuminated

ilusión ee·loo·syon f (unfounded) hope; excitement; **hacer* mucha ilusión a·ther** moo·cha ee·loo·syon to look forward to

ilusionista ee·loo·syo·nees·ta m/f conjuror

ilustración ee·loos·tra·thyon f illustration

imaginación ee·ma·khee·na·thyon f imagination

imaginar ee·ma·khee·nar vt imagine

imán ee·man m magnet

imitar ee·mee·tar vt imitate

impaciente eem·pa·thyen·te adj impatient; eager; **estar* impaciente por hacer algo** es·tar eem·pa·thyen·te por a·ther al·go to be eager to do something

impar eem·par adj odd (number)

imparcial eem·par·thyal adj unbiased

impedir* eem·pe·deer vt prevent

imperdible eem·per·dee·ble m safety pin

imperfecto(a) eem·per·fek·to(a) adj imperfect

imperio eem·pe·ryo m empire

impermeable eem·per·me·a·ble adj waterproof □ m raincoat; mack(intosh)

impersonal eem·per·so·nal adj impersonal

imponer* eem·po·ner vt impose

imponible eem·po·nee·ble adj taxable

importación *eem·por·ta·thyon* f import

importador *eem·por·ta·dor* m importer

importancia *eem·por·tan·thya* f importance

importante *eem·por·tan·te* adj important

importar *eem·por·tar* vt import; no importa *no eem·por·ta* it doesn't matter; no me importa el calor *no me eem·por·ta el ka·lor* I don't mind the heat; ¿le importa si...? *le eem·por·ta see* do you mind if...?

importe *eem·por·te* m amount (*total*)

imposible *eem·po·see·ble* adj impossible; out of the question

imprenta *eem·pren·ta* f press (*printing machine*)

imprescindible *eem·pres·theen·dee·ble* adj vital (*essential*)

impresión *eem·pre·syon* f impression

impresionante *eem·pre·syo·nan·te* adj impressive

impresor *eem·pre·sor* m printer

imprevisto(a) *eem·pre·bees·to(a)* adj unexpected

imprimir* *eem·pree·meer* vt print (*book, newspaper*)

improbable *eem·pro·ba·ble* adj unlikely

impuesto *eem·pwes·to* m tax; antes de pagar impuestos *an·tes de pa·gar eem·pwes·tos* pretax (*profit*); el impuesto sobre la renta *eem·pwes·to so·bre la ren·ta* income tax; los impuestos de lujo *eem·pwes·tos de loo·kho* excise duties; el impuesto al valor agregado *eem·pwes·to al ba·lor a·gre·ga·do* value-added tax; el impuesto sobre las empresas *eem·pwes·to so·bre las em·pre·sas* corporation tax

inapropiado(a) *een·a·pro·pyn·do(a)* adj unsuitable

incapacitado(a) *een·ka·pa·thee·ta·do(a)* adj disabled

incendiar *een·then·dyar* vt set fire to

incendio *een·then·dyo* m blaze; fire (*accident*)

incentivo *een·then·tee·bo* m incentive

incidente *een·thee·den·te* m incident (*event*)

incierto(a) *een·thyer·to(a)* adj uncertain (*fact*)

incinerador *een·thee·ne·ra·dor* m incinerator

inclinar *een·klee·nar* vt tip (*tilt*)

inclinarse *een·klee·nar·se* vr lean; inclinarse contra algo *een·klee·nar·se kon·tra al·go* to lean against something

incluir* *een·kloo·eer* vt include

inclusive *een·kloo·see·be* adj inclusive

incluso *een·kloo·so* adv including; incluso un niño podría hacerlo *een·kloo·so oon neen·yo po·dree·a a·ther·lo* even a child could do it

incomible *een·ko·mee·ble* adj inedible

incómodo(a) *een·ko·mo·do(a)* adj uncomfortable

incompleto(a) *een·kom·ple·to(a)* adj incomplete

incondicional *een·kon·dee·thyo·nal* adj unconditional (*offer*)

inconsciente *een·kons·thyen·te* adj unconscious

increíble *een·kre·ee·ble* adj incredible

indecente *een·de·then·te* adj indecent

indemnización *een·dem·nee·tha·thyon* f compensation

independencia *een·de·pen·den·thya* f independence

independiente *een·de·pen·dyen·te* adj

independent; self-contained (*apartment*)

India *een·dya* f India

indicador *een·dee·ka·dor* m gauge (*device*); el indicador de dirección *een·dee·ka·dor de dee·rek·thyon* turn signal

índice *een·dee·the* m index; el índice de inflación *een·dee·the de een·fla·thyon* rate of inflation; el índice de materias *een·dee·the de ma·te·ryas* contents (*table in book*)

indigestión *een·dee·khes·tyon* f indigestion

indigesto(a) *een·dee·khes·to(a)* adj heavy; indigestible

indio(a) *een·dyo(a)* adj Indian (*India and Americas*) □ m/f Indian

indirecto(a) *een·dee·rek·to(a)* adj indirect (*route*)

individual *een·dee·bee·dwal* adj individual

individualmente *een·dee·bee·dwal·men·te* adv individually

industria *een·doos·trya* f industry; la industria ligera *een·doos·trya lee·khe·ra* light industry

industrial *een·doos·tryal* adj industrial

ineficaz *een·e·fee·kath* adj inefficient

inevitable *een·e·bee·ta·ble* adj inevitable; unavoidable

infección *een·fek·thyon* f infection

infeccioso(a) *een·fek·thyo·so(a)* adj infectious

inferior *een·fe·ryor* adj inferior; substandard

inflación *een·fla·thyon* f inflation (*economic*)

inflamable *een·fla·ma·ble* adj flammable

inflamación *een·fla·ma·thyon* f inflammation

inflar *een·flar* vt inflate

influencia *een·floo·en·thya* f influence

influir* *een·floo·eer* vt affect

información *een·for·ma·thyon* f information

informaciones *een·for·ma·thyo·nes* fpl information desk; pregunte Ud a las informaciones *pre·goon·te oos·ted a las een·for·ma·thyo·nes* ask at the information desk

informar *een·for·mar* vt/i report

informe *een·for·me* m report

ingeniero *een·khe·nye·ro* m engineer

ingenioso(a) *een·khe·nyo·so(a)* adj clever (*plan*)

Inglaterra *een·gla·te·rra* f England

inglés(esa) *een·gles(·gle·sa)* adj English □ m el inglés *een·gles* English; es inglés *es een·gles* he's English; es inglesa *es een·gle·sa* she's English; en inglés *en een·gles* in English

ingredientes *een·gre·dyen·tes* mpl ingredients

ingreso *een·gre·so* m revenue

ingresos *een·gre·sos* mpl receipts; earnings; income

iniciales *ee·nee·thya·les* fpl initials

iniciativa privada *ee·nee·thya·tee·ba pree·ba·da* f private enterprise

injusto(a) *een·khoos·to(a)* adj unfair

inmediatamente *ee·me·dya·ta·men·te* adv at once; immediately

inmediato(a) *ee·me·dya·to(a)* adj instant

inmejorable *ee·me·kho·ra·ble* adj unbeatable (*offer*)

inmigrante *ee·mee·gran·te* m immigrant

inmóvil   116

inmóvil *ee·mo·beel adj* still *(motionless)*

inmovilizar* *een·mo·bee·lee·thar vt* immobilize; tie up *(capital)*

innecesario(a) *een·ne·the·sa·ryo(a) adj* unnecessary

inocente *ee·no·then·te adj* innocent

inoculación *ee·no·koo·la·thyon f* inoculation

inofensivo(a) *ee·no·fen·see·bo(a) adj* harmless

inoportuno(a) *een·o·por·too·no(a) adj* inconvenient *(time, place)*

inoxidable *een·ok·see·da·ble adj* rustproof; stainless *(steel)*

input *een·poot m* input *(computing)*

inquietar *een·kye·tar vt* alarm

inquilino *een·kee·lee·no m* tenant

inscribirse *eens·kree·beer·se vr* check in *(at hotel)*

insecto *een·sek·to m* insect

insignia *een·seeg·nya f* badge *(of metal)*

insistir *een·sees·teer vi* insist; insistir en algo *een·sees·teer en al·go* to insist on something

insolación *een·so·la·thyon f* sunstroke

insolente *een·so·len·te adj* insolent

insólito(a) *een·so·lee·to(a) adj* unusual

insoportable *een·so·por·ta·ble adj* unbearable *(pain)*

inspección *een·spek·thyon f* inspection; survey *(of building)*

inspeccionar *eens·pek·thyo·nar vt* inspect

inspector *eens·pek·tor m* inspector *(police, of building)*

instalarse *eens·ta·lar·se vr* move in; settle in

instantáneo(a) *eens·tan·ta·ne·o(a) adj* instant *(coffee)*

instituto *eens·tee·too·to m* institute; el instituto de enseñanza pública *eens·tee·too·to de en·sen·yan·tha poo·blee·ka* public school

instrucciones *een·strook·thyo·nes fpl* directions *(to a place)*; instructions

instructor *eens·trook·tor m* instructor

instructora *eens·trook·to·ra f* instructress

instrumento *eens·troo·men·to m* instrument

insulina *een·soo·lee·na f* insulin

insultar *een·sool·tar vt* insult

insulto *een·sool·to m* insult

inteligencia *een·te·lee·khen·thya f* intelligence

inteligente *een·te·lee·khen·te adj* intelligent

intención *een·ten·thyon f* intention; tener* la intención de hacer algo *te·ner la een·ten·thyon de a·ther al·go* to intend to do something

intencionado(a) *een·ten·thyo·na·do(a) adj* deliberate

intentar *een·ten·tar vt* attempt; intentar hacer algo *een·ten·tar a·ther al·go* to try to do something

interés *een·te·res m* interest; el interés compuesto *een·te·res kom·pwes·to* compound interest

interesado(a) *een·te·re·sa·do(a) adj* interested

interesante *een·te·re·san·te adj* interesting

interesar *een·te·re·sar vt* interest; concern *(be important to)*

interesarse en *een·te·re·sar·se en vr* be interested in

interfono *een·ter·fo·no m* intercom

interior *een·te·ryor adj* interior □ *m* inside; la pared interior *la pa·red een·te·ryor* the inside wall

intermedio *een·ter·me·dyo m* intermission *(in performance)*

intermitente *een·ter·mee·ten·te m* indicator *(of car)*

internacional *een·ter·na·thyo·nal adj* international

interno(a) *een·ter·no(a) adj* internal

interpretar *een·ter·pre·tar vt* interpret

intérprete *een·ter·pre·te m* interpreter; hacer* de intérprete *a·ther de een·ter·pre·te* to interpret

interrumpir *een·te·rroom·peer vti* disturb interrupt

interruptor *een·te·rroop·tor m* switch

interurbano(a) *een·ter·oor·ba·no(a) adj* long-distance

intervalo *een·ter·ba·lo m* break *(pause)*

interventor de cuentas *een·ter·ben·tor de kwen·tas m* auditor

inundación *ee·noon·da·thyon f* flood

inundar *ee·noon·dar vt* flood

inútil *een·oo·teel adj* useless

inválido *een·ba·lee·do m* invalid

invención *een·ben·thyon f* invention

inventar *een·ben·tar vt* invent

inventario *een·ben·ta·ryo m* inventory

invernadero *een·ber·na·de·ro m* greenhouse; conservatory

inversión *een·ber·syon f* investment

inversionista *een·ber·syo·nees·ta m/f* investor

invertir* *een·ber·teer vt* invest; invertir* (dinero) en *een·ber·teer (dee·ne·ro) en* to invest in

investigación *een·bes·tee·ga·thyon f* research; la investigación de mercados *een·bes·tee·ga·thyon de mer·ka·dos* market research

invierno *een·byer·no m* winter; los deportes de invierno *de·por·tes de een·byer·no* winter sports

invisible *een·bee·see·ble adj* invisible

invitación *een·bee·ta·thyon f* invitation

invitado(a) *een·bee·ta·do(a) m/f* guest

invitar *een·bee·tar vt* invite; le invito a tomar un helado *le een·bee·to a to·mar oon e·la·do* I'll treat you to an ice cream cone

inyección *een·yek·thyon f* injection

ir* *eer vi* go; ir* en coche a la ciudad *eer en ko·che a la thyoo·dad* to drive to town; ir* a buscar a un amigo *eer a boos·kar a oon a·mee·go* to pick up a friend; nos vamos a la playa *nos ba·mos a la pla·ya* we are going to the beach; ir* primero *eer pree·me·ro* to lead *(in contest)*; esto va con su vestido *es·to ba kon soo bes·tee·do* this goes with your dress; ir* a comprar *eer a kom·prar* to go and buy

Irán *ee·ran m* Iran

Iraq *ee·rak m* Iraq

Irlanda *eer·lan·da f* Ireland

irlandés(esa) *eer·lan·des(·de·sa) adj* Irish

irritar *ee·rree·tar vt* annoy *(thing)*

irrompible *ee·rrom·pee·ble adj* unbreakable

irse* *eer·se vr* go away; leave

isla *ees·la f* island

Israel *ees·ra·el m* Israel

Italia *ee·ta·lya f* Italy

italiano(a) *ee·ta·lya·no(a) adj* Italian □ *m* el italiano *ee·ta·lya·no* Italian

izquierda *eeth·kyer·da f* left; torcer hacia la izquierda *tor·ther a·thya la eeth·kyer·da* to turn left

izquierdo(a) *eeth·kyer·do(a) adj* left; el

lado izquierdo *el la·do eeth·kyer·do* the left side

J

jabón *kha·bon* m soap; **el jabón en polvo** *kha·bon en pol·bo* soap powder; **el jabón de afeitar** *kha·bon de a·fey·tar* shaving soap

jactarse *khak·tar·se* vr boast

jadear *kha·de·ar* vi pant

jamón *kha·mon* m ham

Japón *kha·pon* m Japan

japonés(esa) *kha·po·nes(ne·sa)* adj Japanese □ m **el japonés** *kha·po·nes* Japanese

jaqueca *kha·ke·ka* f migraine

jarabe *kha·ra·be* m syrup

jardín *khar·deen* m garden; **el jardín botánico** *khar·deen bo·ta·nee·ko* botanical gardens; **jardín zoológico** *khar·deen thuʹo·lo·khee·ko* zoo

jardinero *khar·dee·ne·ro* m gardener

jarra *khaʹrra* f pitcher; jug

jaula *khowʹla* f cage

jazz *yas* m jazz

jeep *yeep* m jeep

jefe *kheʹfe* m chief; head; boss; ruler; **el jefe de personal** *kheʹfe de per·soʹnal* personnel manager; **el jefe de ventas** *kheʹfe de benʹtas* sales manager; **el jefe de compras** *kheʹfe de komʹpras* buyer (for shop, factory); **el jefe de cocina** *kheʹfe de ko·theeʹna* chef; **el jefe de investigación de mercados** *kheʹfe de een·bes·tee·ga·thyonʹ de merʹkaʹdos* marketing manager

jengibre *khen·kheeʹbre* m ginger

jerez *kheʹreth* m sherry

jersey *kherʹsey* m pullover; (fabric, garment) jersey; **el jersey de algodón** *kherʹsey de al·goʹdon* sweatshirt

jinete *khee·neʹte* m jockey, rider

jockey *yoʹkee* m jockey

jornada *khor·naʹda* f day (length of time); **de media jornada** *de meʹdya khorʹnaʹda* part-time; **de jornada completa** *de khor·naʹda komʹpleʹta* full-time

joven *khoʹben* adj young

joya *khoʹya* f jewel; **las joyas de fantasía** *khoʹyas de fan·ta·seeʹa* costume jewelry

joyería *kho·ye·reeʹa* f jewelry; jeweler's shop

joyero *kho·yeʹro* m jeweler

jubilación *khoo·bee·la·thyonʹ* f superannuation; pension; retirement

jubilado(a) *khoo·bee·laʹdo(a)* adj retired □ m pensioner; retiree

jubilarse *khoo·bee·larʹse* vr retire

judías *khoo·deeʹas* f runner beans

judío(a) *khoo·deeʹo(a)* adj Jewish □ m/f el/la judío(a) Jew; **autorizado por la ley judía** *owʹto·ree·thaʹdo por la lay khoʹdeeʹa* kosher

judo *yooʹdo* m judo

juego *khweʹgo* m game; gambling; set (collection); **el juego de cartas** *khweʹgo de karʹtas* card game; **hacer* juego con** *aʹther khweʹgo kon* to match; **estar* en juego** *esʹtar en khweʹgo* to be at stake; **un juego de tenis** *oon khweʹgo de teʹnees* a game of tennis

jueves *khweʹbes* m Thursday

juez *khweth* m judge

jugador(a) *khoo·ga·dorʹ(·ra)* m/f player (in sport) □ m jugador *khoo·ga·dorʹ* gambler; **el/la jugador(a) de golf** *khoo·ga·dorʹ(·ra) de golf* golfer

jugar* *khoo·garʹ* vt/i play; gamble; **jugar* bien al golf** *khoo·garʹ byen al golf* to be good at golf; **jugar* con** *khoo·garʹ kon* to play with; **jugar* a cara o cruz** *khoo·garʹ a kaʹra o krooth* to toss a coin

jugete *khoo·geʹte* m toy

jugo *khooʹgo* m juice

juicio *khweeʹthyo* m trial (in law)

julio *khooʹlyo* m July

jumbo *yoomʹbo* m jumbo jet

junio *khooʹnyo* m June

junta *khoonʹta* f session; **la junta directiva** *khoonʹta dee·rek·teeʹba* board (of directors); **la junta de culata** *khoonʹta de kooʹlaʹta* gasket

juntar *khoon·tarʹ* vt join; gather (assemble)

juntarse *khoon·tarʹse* vr gather (crowd)

junto *khoonʹto* adv close

jurar *khoo·rarʹ* vi swear

justicia *khoos·tee·theeʹya* f justice

justillo *khoos·teelʹyo* m jerkin

justo(a) *khoosʹto(a)* adj fair (just)

juvenil *khoo·be·neelʹ* adj junior (class, pupil)

juventud *khoo·ben·toodʹ* f youth (period)

juzgar* *khooth·garʹ* vt judge

K

karate *ka·raʹte* m karate

Kenia *keʹnya* f Kenya

keroseno *ke·ro·seʹno* m kerosene

ketchup *ket·choopʹ* m ketchup

kilo *keeʹlo* m kilo; **$3 el kilo** *$3 el keeʹlo* $3 per kilo

kilogramo *kee·lo·graʹmo* m kilogram

kilometraje *kee·lo·me·traʹkhe* m ≈ mileage

kilómetro *kee·loʹme·tro* m kilometer; **kilómetros por hora** *kee·loʹme·tros por oʹra* ≈ miles per hour

kilovatio *kee·lo·baʹtyo* m kilowatt

kirsch *keersh* m kirsch

L

la *la* art the □ pron her; it; **tómela** *toʹme·la* take it (feminine)

labio *laʹbyo* m lip

laborable *la·bo·raʹble* adj working (day)

laboratorio *la·bo·ra·toʹryo* m laboratory; **el laboratorio de lenguas** *la·bo·ra·toʹryo de lenʹgwas* language laboratory

laca *laʹka* f hair spray

lado *laʹdo* m side; **le vi al otro lado de la calle** *le bee al oʹtro laʹdo de la kalʹye* I saw him from across the road; **al lado de** *al laʹdo de* beside; **este lado arriba** *esʹte laʹdo aʹrreeʹba* this side up; **al lado de** *al laʹdo de* by (next to)

ladrar *la·drarʹ* vi bark

ladrido *la·dreeʹdo* m bark (of dog)

ladrillo *la·dreelʹyo* m brick

ladrón *la·dronʹ* m thief; burglar

lago *laʹgo* m lake

lágrima *laʹgree·ma* f tear

lamer *la·merʹ* vt lick

lámina *laʹmeeʹna* f plate (of glass, metal)

lampa *lamʹpa* f spade

lámpara *lamʹpaʹra* f lamp; **la lámpara indicadora** *lamʹpuʹra een·dee·kaʹdoʹra* pilot light (gas); **la lámpara fluorescente** *lamʹpaʹra flooʹo·resʹthenʹte* fluorescent light; **la lámpara de pie**

lámpara de pye floor lamp; **la lámpara de rayos ultravioleta** *lam·pa·ra de ra·yos ul·tra·byo·le·ta* sunlamp

lana *la·na* f wool; **de lana** *de la·na* woolen; **la lana de cordero** *la·na de kor·de·ro* lambswool

lancha *lan·cha* f launch; **la lancha motora** *lan·cha mo·to·ra* speedboat; motorboat; **la lancha de socorro** *lan·cha de so·ko·rro* lifeboat (*from shore*)

langosta *lan·gos·ta* f lobster; crawfish, crayfish (*saltwater*)

lanolina *la·no·lee·na* f lanolin

lanzar* *lan·thar* vt launch (*product*)

lápiz *la·peeth* m pencil; **el lápiz de color** *la·peeth de ko·lor* crayon

largo(a) *lar·go(a)* adj long; **a largo plazo** *a lar·go pla·tho* long-term; **6 metros de largo** *6 me·tros de lar·go* 6 meters long

laringitis *la·reen·khee·tees* f laryngitis

las *las* pron them (*feminine*) □ *art* the

lástima *las·tee·ma* f pity; **¡qué lástima!** *ke las·tee·ma* what a shame!

lata *la·ta* f can (*container*); **en lata** *en la·ta* canned

látigo *la·tee·go* m crop; whip

latín *la·teen* m Latin

latino(a) *la·tee·no(a)* adj Latin

Latinoamérica *la·tee·no·a·me·ree·ka* f Latin America

latinoamericano(a) *la·tee·no·a·me·ree·ka·no(a)* adj Latin American

latir *la·teer* vi beat (*heart*)

latón *la·ton* m brass

lavable *la·ba·ble* adj washable

lavabo *la·ba·bo* m bathroom (*lavatory*); washbasin, washbowl

lavado *la·ba·do* m washing (*clothes*)

lavadora *la·ba·do·ra* f washing machine

lavandería *la·ban·de·ree·a* f laundry (*place*); **la lavandería automática** *la·ban·de·ree·a ow·to·ma·tee·ka* laundromat

lavaparabrisas *la·ba·pa·ra·bree·sas* m windshield washer

lavaplatos *la·ba·pla·tos* m dishwasher

lavar *la·bar* vt wash; **lavar la ropa** *la·bar la ro·pa* to do the washing; **lavar y poner** *la·bar ee po·ner* drip-dry

lavarse *la·bar·se* vr to wash (oneself), to wash up

laxante *lak·san·te* m laxative

lazo *la·tho* m loop; bow (*ribbon*)

le *le* pron him; you; to him/her/it/you

leche *le·che* f milk; **la leche en polvo** *le·che en pol·bo* dried milk; **la leche condensada** *le·che kon·den·sa·da* condensed milk; **la leche evaporada** *le·che e·ba·po·ra·da* evaporated milk; **la leche malteada** *le·che mal·te·a·da* milkshake; **la leche desnatada** *le·che des·na·ta·da* skim milk

lechería *le·che·ree·a* f dairy store

lechero *le·che·ro* m milkman

lechuga *le·choo·ga* f lettuce

lectura *lek·too·ra* f reading

leer* *le·er* vt/i read; **leer* algo rápidamente** *le·er al·go ra·pee·da·men·te* to read something through quickly

legal *le·gal* adj legal

legumbres *le·goom·bres* fpl vegetables

lejano(a) *le·kha·no(a)* adj distant

Lejano Oriente *le·kha·no o·ryen·te* m the Far East

lejos *le·khos* adv far; **más lejos** *mas le·khos* further; **lo más lejos** *lo mas le·khos* furthest; **a lo lejos** *a lo le·khos* in the distance; **está lejos** *es·ta le·khos* it's a long way

lengua *len·gwa* f language; tongue

lenguado *len·gwa·do* m sole; lemon sole

lenguaje *len·gwa·khe* m language

lente *len·te* f lens (*of glasses*)

lentejas *len·te·khas* fpl lentils

lento(a) *len·to(a)* adj slow

león *le·on* m lion

leotardos *le·o·tar·dos* mpl tights

les *les* pron them; you; to them/you

letra *le·tra* f letter (*of alphabet*); **la letra bancaria** *le·tra ban·ka·rya* bank bill; **la letra de cambio** *le·tra de kam·byo* draft (*financial*); **la letra mayúscula** *le·tra ma·yoos·koo·la* capital letter

letrero *le·tre·ro* m notice (*sign*)

levadura *le·ba·doo·ra* f yeast

levantar *le·ban·tar* vt lift; raise; **levantar la sesión** *le·ban·tar la se·syon* to adjourn

levantarse *le·ban·tar·se* vr get up; rise; **todavía no se ha levantado** *to·da·bee·a no se a le·ban·ta·do* he isn't up yet (*out of bed*)

ley *ley* f law

Libia *lee·bya* f Libya

libra *lee·bra* f pound (*currency, weight*); **la libra esterlina** *lee·bra es·ter·lee·na* sterling

libre *lee·bre* adj free; vacant (*seat, toilet*); off duty; **libre de impuestos** *lee·bre de eem·pwes·tos* tax-free; **un día libre** *oon dee·a lee·bre* a day off

librería *lee·bre·ree·a* f bookstore

libro *lee·bro* m book; **el libro de frases** *lee·bro de fra·ses* phrase book; **el libro de bolsillo** *lee·bro de bol·seel·yo* paperback; **el libro de texto** *lee·bro de teks·to* textbook; **el libro mayor** *lee·bro ma·yor* ledger

licencia *lee·then·thya* f licence; degree; **la licencia de manejar** *lee·then·thya de ma·ne·khar* driver's license

licor *lee·kor* m liqueur □ *mpl* **los licores** *lee·ko·res* spirits (*alcohol*)

liebre *lye·bre* f hare

Liechtenstein *lee·e·ches·teen* m Liechtenstein

ligero(a) *lee·khe·ro(a)* adj light (*not heavy*)

lima *lee·ma* f file (*tool*); lime (*fruit*); **el zumo de lima** *thoo·mo de lee·ma* lime juice; **la lima de uñas** *lee·ma de oon·yas* nailfile; emery board

limitar *lee·mee·tar* vt restrict (*speed*)

límite *lee·mee·te* m limit; boundary; **el límite de velocidad** *lee·mee·te de be·lo·thee·dad* speed limit

limón *lee·mon* m lemon

limonada *lee·mo·na·da* f lemonade

limpiaparabrisas *leem·pya·pa·ra·bree·sas* m windshield wiper

limpiar *leem·pyar* vt clean; polish (*shoes, metal*); wipe; bathe (*wound etc*); **limpiar en seco** *leem·pyar en se·ko* to dry-clean; **hacer* limpiar en seco un traje** *a·ther leem·pyar en se·ko oon tra·khe* to have a suit cleaned

limpio(a) *leem·pyo(a)* adj clean; **jugar* limpio** *khoo·gar leem·pyo* to play fair

limusina *lee·moo·see·na* f limousine

lindo(a) *leen·do(a)* adj sweet

línea *lee·ne·a* f line; **la línea está cortada** *la lee·ne·a es·ta kor·ta·da* the line is dead (*phone*); **la línea de puntos** *lee·ne·a de poon·tos* dotted line; **la línea aérea** *lee·ne·a a·e·re·a* airline

lino *lee·no* m linen (*cloth*)

linóleo *lee·no·le·o* m linoleum

linterna *leen·ter·na* f lantern; **la linterna eléctrica** *leen·ter·na e·lek·tree·ka* flashlight

lío *lee·o* m fuss; **armar un lío** *ar·mar oon lee·o* to make a fuss

liquidación *lee·kee·da·thyon* f liquidation; **entrar en liquidación** *en·trar en lee·kee·da·thyon* to go into liquidation

liquidar *lee·kee·dar* vt settle (*bill*)

líquido(a) *lee·kee·do* adj liquid □ m liquid

liso(a) *lee·so(a)* adj plain (*not patterned*)

lista *lees·ta* f list; **la lista de precios** *lees·ta de pre·thyos* price list; **la lista de seleccionados** *lees·ta de se·lek·thyo·na·dos* short list; **la lista de direcciones** *lees·ta de dee·rek·thyon·es* mailing list; **hacer* una lista** *a·ther oo·na lees·ta* to list; **la lista de vinos** *lees·ta de bee·nos* wine list; **la lista de espera** *lees·ta de es·pe·ra* waiting list; **por lista de correos** *por lees·ta de ko·rre·os* general delivery

listo(a) *lees·to(a)* adj clever; bright; ready; **listo(a) para comer** *lees·to(a) pa·ra ko·mer* ready-cooked

litera *lee·te·ra* f bunk; berth; couchette

literas *lee·te·ras* fpl bunk beds

literatura *lee·te·ra·too·ra* f literature

litro *lee·tro* m liter

llama *lya·ma* f flame

llamada *lya·ma·da* f call (*shout*); call (*at door*); **la llamada telefónica** *lya·ma·da te·le·fo·nee·ka* telephone call; **una llamada local** *oo·na lya·ma·da lo·kal* a local call (*on phone*)

llamar *lya·mar* vt call; **llamar a la puerta** *lya·mar a la pwer·ta* to knock (*at*) the door; **llámeme a las 7 de la mañana** *lya·me·me a las 7 de la man·ya·na* call me at 7 a.m. (*in hotel etc*)

llamarse *lya·mar·se* vr be called; **me llamo Paul** *me lya·mo Paul* my name is Paul

llano(a) *lya·no(a)* adj flat; even □ m plain

llanta *lyan·ta* f tire

llave *lya·be* f key; **la llave de cierre** *lya·be de thye·rre* stopcock; **la puerta está cerrada con llave** *la pwer·ta es·ta the·rra·da kon lya·be* the door's locked; **la llave maestra** *lya·be ma·es·tra* master key; **la llave de contacto** *lya·be de kon·tak·to* ignition key; **la llave inglesa** *lya·be een·gle·sa* wrench

llavero *lya·be·ro* m key ring

llegada *lye·ga·da* f arrival

llegar *lye·gar* vi arrive; come; **llegar*** *lye·gar a* to reach (*arrive at*); **¿cómo llegamos allí?** *ko·mo lye·ga·mos al·yee* how do we get there?; **llegar a casa** *lye·gar a ka·sa* to get home; **ha llegado el tren** *a lye·ga·do el tren* the train is in

llenar *lye·nar* vt fill; fill in/out (*form*); fill up (*cup*); **¡llénelo!** *lye·ne·lo* fill it up! (*car*)

lleno(a) *lye·no(a)* adj full; **lleno de** *lye·no de* full of; **lleno(a) de agua** *lye·no(a) de ag·wa* filled with water

llevar *lye·bar* vt bring (*person*); wear (*clothes*); carry (*in hands, arms*); lead; **llevar a alguien a la estación** *lye·bar a al·gyen a la es·ta·thyon* to take someone to the station; **lleve esto a correos** *lye·be es·to a ko·rre·os* take this to the post office; **llevar a alguien a la ciudad** *lye·bar a al·gyen*

a la thyoo·dad to give someone a ride into town; **llevar a alguien al teatro** *lye·bar a al·gyen al te·a·tro* to take someone out to the theater; **llevar al mercado** *lye·bar al mer·ka·do* to market (*product*); **esta puerta lleva al jardín** *es·ta pwer·ta lye·ba al khar·deen* this door leads into the garden

llevarse *lye·bar·se* vr take (*remove, acquire*); **llevarse algo** *lye·bar·se al·go* to take something away

llorar *lyo·rar* vi cry

llover* *lyo·ber* vi rain; **llueve** *lywe·be* it's raining; **está lloviendo** *es·ta lyo·byen·do* it's raining

llovizna *lyo·beeth·na* f drizzle

lluvia *lyoo·bya* f rain

lluvioso(a) *lyoo·byo·so(a)* adj rainy; wet (*weather, day*)

lo *lo* pron it; him; that which; **haga lo que le digo** *a·ga lo ke le dee·go* do as I say

lobo *lo·bo* m wolf

local *lo·kal* m premises □ adj local

loción *lo·thyon* f lotion; **la loción contra los insectos** *lo·thyon kon·tra los een·sek·tos* insect repellent; **la loción para después del afeitado** *lo·thyon pa·ra des·pwes del a·fey·ta·do* after-shave (lotion)

loco(a) *lo·ko(a)* adj mad; crazy

locomotora *lo·ko·mo·to·ra* f engine (*of train*)

loma *lo·ma* f ridge

lomo *lo·mo* m back; loin

lona *lo·na* f canvas

Londres *lon·dres* m London

longitud *lon·khee·tood* f length

los *los* pron them (*masculine*) □ art the; **cómprelos** *kom·pre·los* buy them

lote *lo·te* m lot

lotería *lo·te·ree·a* f lottery

loza *lo·tha* f crockery

LP *e·le pe* m LP

lucha *loo·cha* f struggle; **la lucha libre** *loo·cha lee·bre* wrestling

luchar *loo·char* vi struggle

lucrativo(a) *loo·kra·tee·bo(a)* adj profitable

lugar *loo·gar* m place; **el lugar de vacaciones** *loo·gar de ba·ka·thyo·nes* resort; **en primer lugar** *en pree·mer loo·gar* in the first place

lujo *loo·kho* m luxury; **de lujo** *de loo·kho* fancy; de luxe; luxury (*car, hotel*)

lujoso(a) *loo·kho·so(a)* adj luxurious

luna *loo·na* f moon; **la luna de miel** *loo·na de myel* honeymoon; **estamos pasando la luna de miel** *es·ta·mos pa·san·do la loo·na de myel* we're on our honeymoon

lunar *loo·nar* m spot; mole

lunes *loo·nes* m Monday

Luxemburgo *look·sem·boor·go* m Luxembourg

luz *looth* f luces light; **la luz de cruce** *looth de kroo·the* dimmer; **apagar* la luz** *a·pa·gar la looth* to put out the light; **las luces de detención** *loo·thes de de·ten·thyon* stoplights; **luz deslumbrante** *looth des·loom·bran·te* glare (*of light*); **las luces de estacionamiento** *loo·thes de es·ta·thyo·na·myen·to* parking lights; **las luces laterales** *loo·thes la·te·ra·les* sidelights (*on car*); **la luz roja** *looth ro·kha* red light (*traffic light*); **luz trasera** *looth tra·se·ra* rear light; **encender* la luz** *en·then·der la looth* to put on the light; prender la luz *pren·der la looth* to put on the light

M

macarrones *ma·ka·rro·nes mpl* macaroni

machacar* *ma·cha·kar vt* mash

macho *ma·cho adj* male

madera *ma·de·ra f* wood (*material*); la madera contrachapada *ma·de·ra kon·tra·cha·pa·da* plywood; de madera *de ma·de·ra* made out of wood; wooden

madrastra *ma·dras·tra f* stepmother

madre *ma·dre f* mother

Madrid *ma·dreed m* Madrid

madrina *ma·dree·na f* godmother

maduro(a) *ma·doo·ro(a) adj* ripe (*fruit*); mature

maestro(a) *ma·es·tro(a) m/f* teacher (*primary school*)

magia *ma·khya f* magic

mágico(a) *ma·khee·ko(a) adj* magic

magnate *mag·na·te m* tycoon

magnetofón *mag·ne·to·fon m* tape recorder; el magnetofón a cassettes *mag·ne·to·fon a ka·sets* cassette-recorder

magnetoscopio *mag·ne·tos·ko·pyo m* videocassette recorder

magnífico(a) *mag·nee·fee·ko(a) adj* grand; magnificent; great (*excellent*)

magro(a) *ma·gro(a) adj* lean (*meat*)

maicena *may·the·na f* cornstarch

maíz *ma·eeth m* corn (*cereal crop*); el maíz en la mazorca *ma·eeth en la ma·thor·ka* corn-on-the-cob; el maíz tierno *ma·eeth tyer·no* sweet corn

mal *mal adv* badly (*not well*) □ *n* evil; mal de alturas *mal de al·too·ras* mountain (air) sickness; mal genio *mal khe·nyo* bad temper

mala hierba *ma·la yer·ba f* weed

maleta *ma·le·ta f* case; suitcase; trunk (*of car*); hacer* la maleta *a·ther la ma·le·ta* to pack one's suitcase

maletero *ma·le·te·ro m* trunk (*of car*)

maletín *ma·le·teen m* grip (*case*)

maleza *ma·le·tha f* rough (*golf*)

malísimo(a) *ma·lee·see·mo adj* terrible (*weather*); very bad

malo(a) *ma·lo(a) adj* bad (*not good*); mean (*unkind*); evil; rough (*weather*); nasty; sore (*painful*)

malogrado(a) *ma·lo·gra·do(a) adj* out of order (*machine*)

malta *mal·ta f* malt

Malta *mal·ta f* Malta

malva *mal·ba adj* mauve

malvado(a) *mal·ba·do(a) adj* wicked

mamá *ma·ma f* mom(my)

mañana *man·ya·na adv* tomorrow □ *f* la mañana *man·ya·na* morning

mancha *man·cha f* stain; mark; spot

manchado(a) *man·cha·do(a) adj* stained

manchar *man·char vt* stain; mark

mandar *man·dar vt* send; mandar por correo *man·dar por ko·rre·o* to mail; mandar a buscar *man·dar a boos·kar* to send someone to fetch; mandar algo por correo urgente *man·dar al·go por ko·rre·o oor·khen·te* to send something express

mandarina *man·da·ree·na f* tangerine

mandato *man·da·to m* term of office; warrant

mandíbula *man·dee·boo·la f* jaw

mandil *man·deel m* apron; jumper (*dress*)

mandos *man·dos mpl* controls

manecilla *ma·ne·theel·ya f* hand (*of clock*)

manejar *ma·ne·khar vt* steer; drive (*car etc*)

manera *ma·ne·ra f* manner; way; de otra manera *de o·tra ma·ne·ra* otherwise; de una manera diferente *de oo·na ma·ne·ra dee·fe·ren·te* (in) a different way

manga *man·ga f* sleeve

mango *man·go m* handle

manguera *man·ge·ra f* hose (*pipe*)

manicura *ma·nee·koo·ra f* manicure

manifestación *ma·nee·fes·ta·thyon f* rally (*political*); demonstration

manillar *ma·neel·yar m* handlebar(s)

mano *ma·no f* hand; dealer (*cards*); a mano *a ma·no* by hand; dar* la mano a alguien *dar la ma·no a al·gyen* to shake hands with someone; la mano de obra *ma·no de o·bra* labor force; de segunda mano *de se·goon·da ma·no* used (*car etc*)

manopla *ma·no·pla f* mitt(en); washcloth

manso(a) *man·so(a) adj* tame

manta *man·ta f* blanket; la manta eléctrica *man·ta e·lek·tree·ka* electric blanket

manteca de cerdo *man·te·ka de ther·do f* lard

mantel *man·tel m* tablecloth

mantelería *man·te·le·ree·a f* linen (*for table*)

mantener* *man·te·ner vt* support; maintain; keep (*feed and clothe*); mantener* a alguien *man·te·ner a al·gyen* to provide for someone

mantenimiento *man·te·nee·myen·to m* maintenance; upkeep

mantequilla *man·te·keel·ya f* butter

manual *ma·nwal adj* manual □ *m* el manual *ma·nwal* handbook; el manual de gramática *ma·nwal de gra·ma·tee·ka* grammar (book)

manzana *man·tha·na f* apple; a tres manzanas *a tres man·tha·nas* 3 blocks away (*streets*)

manzano *man·tha·no m* apple tree

mapa *ma·pa m* map; el mapa de carreteras *ma·pa de ka·rre·te·ras* road map

maquillaje *ma·keel·ya·khe m* make-up

maquillarse *ma·keel·yar·se vr* make (oneself) up

máquina *ma·kee·na f* machine; la máquina de coser *ma·kee·na de ko·ser* sewing machine; la máquina de monedas *ma·kee·na de mo·ne·das* slot machine; la máquina de picar carne *ma·kee·na de pee·kar kar·ne* mincer; la máquina de afeitar *ma·kee·na de a·fey·tar* razor; la máquina tragaperras *ma·kee·na tra·ga·pe·rras* one-armed bandit; la máquina de escribir *ma·kee·na de es·kree·beer* typewriter; la máquina de fotos *ma·kee·na de fo·tos* camera; la máquina grapadora *ma·kee·na gra·pa·do·ra* stapler; la máquina automática *ma·kee·na ow·to·ma·tee·ka* pinball machine

maquinaria *ma·kee·na·rya f* machinery

maquinilla de afeitar *ma·kee·neel·ya de a·fey·tar f* safety razor

mar *mar m/f* sea; ir* por mar *eer por mar* to go by sea

Mar Adriático *mar a·dree·a·tee·ko m* Adriatic (Sea)

maravilloso(a) *ma·ra·beel·yo·so(a) adj* wonderful; marvelous

marca *mar·ka* f make; brand (*of product*); tick (*mark*); mark; la marca registrada *mar·ka re·khees·tra·da* registered trademark; la marca de fábrica *mar·ka de fa·bree·ka* brand name; la marca del contraste *mar·ka del kon·tras·te* hallmark

marcar* *mar·kar* vt score (*goal*); dial (*number*); mark; hacerse* marcar el pelo *a·ther·se mar·kar el pe·lo* to have one's hair set

Mar Caribe *mar ka·ree·be* m Caribbean (Sea)

marcha *mar·cha* f march; en marcha *en mar·cha* on (*machine*)

marcha atrás *mar·cha a·tras* f reverse (*gear*); en marcha atrás *en mar·cha a·tras* in reverse (gear); dar* marcha atrás *dar mar·cha a·tras* to back (*car*)

marchar *mar·char* vi march; perform (*business*)

marcharse *mar·char·se* vr leave (*go away*)

marco *mar·ko* m frame (*of picture*); mark (*currency*)

Mar del Norte *mar del nor·te* m North Sea

marea *ma·re·a* f tide; la marea baja *ma·re·a ba·kha* low tide; la marea alta *ma·re·a al·ta* high tide; la marea está baja *la ma·re·a es·ta ba·kha* the tide is out

mareado(a) *ma·re·a·do(a)* adj dizzy; me siento mareado *me syen·to ma·re·a·do* I feel faint; estar* mareado(a) *es·tar ma·re·a·do(a)* to be seasick

mareo *ma·re·o* m seasickness; giddiness

marfil *mar·feel* m ivory

margarina *mar·ga·ree·na* f margarine

margen *mar·khen* f margin (*on page*); el margen de beneficio *mar·khen de be·ne·fee·thyo* profit margin

marido *ma·ree·do* m husband

marina *ma·ree·na* f navy

marinero *ma·ree·ne·ro* m sailor

mariposa *ma·ree·po·sa* f butterfly; la mariposa nocturna *ma·ree·po·sa nok·toor·na* moth

mariscos *ma·rees·kos* mpl shellfish; seafood

marketing *mar·ke·teeng* m marketing

mármol *mar·mol* m marble (*material*)

marrón *ma·rron* adj brown; marrón rojizo *ma·rron ro·khee·tho* tan

marroquí *ma·rro·kee* adj Moroccan

Marruecos *ma·rrwe·kos* m Morocco

martes *mar·tes* m Tuesday; el martes de carnaval *mar·tes de kar·na·bal* Shrove Tuesday

martillo *mar·teel·yo* m hammer

martini *mar·tee·nee* m martini (*Brit*); el martini con ginebra *mar·tee·nee kon khee·ne·bra* martini (*US*)

marzo *mar·tho* m March

más *mas* adj, adv more □ conj plus; más allá *mas al·ya* beyond; más despacio *mas des·pa·thyo* more slowly; pesa más de un kilo *pe·sa mas de oon kee·lo* it weighs over a kilo; más queso *mas ke·so* more cheese; quisiera un poco más *kee·sye·ra oon po·ko mas* I'd like (some) more; más peligroso que *mas pe·lee·gro·so ke* more dangerous than; más o menos *mas o me·nos* more or less; el/la más bonito(a) *el/la mas bo·nee·to(a)* the most beautiful; más de 10 *mas de 10* more than 10; a lo más *a lo mas* at the most

masa *ma·sa* f dough

masaje *ma·sa·khe* m massage; dar* masajes *dar ma·sa·khes* to massage

masajista *ma·sa·khees·ta* m masseur □ f masseuse

máscara *mas·ka·ra* f mask; la máscara facial *mas·ka·ra fa·thyal* face pack

masculino(a) *mas·koo·lee·no(a)* adj masculine

masivo(a) *ma·see·bo(a)* adj massive

masticar* *mas·tee·kar* vt chew

mástil *mas·teel* m mast; pole

matar *ma·tar* vt kill; matar a tiros *ma·tar a tee·ros* to shoot

matemáticas *ma·te·ma·tee·kas* fpl mathematics

material *ma·te·ryal* m material; equipment

materias primas *ma·te·ryas pree·mas* fpl raw material

matrimonio *ma·tree·mo·nyo* m marriage

matriz *ma·treeth* f womb; mold

máximo(a) *mak·see·mo(a)* adj maximum □ m el máximo *mak·see·mo* maximum; llevar al máximo *lye·bar al mak·see·mo* to maximize

mayo *ma·yo* m May

mayonesa *ma·yo·ne·sa* f mayonnaise

mayor *ma·yor* adj senior; elder □ m/f el/la mayor *ma·yor* eldest; al por mayor *al por ma·yor* wholesale; tiene la mayor parte *tye·ne la ma·yor par·te* he has the most

mayoría *ma·yo·ree·a* f majority; la mayoría de la gente *la ma·yo·ree·a de la khen·te* most people; elegido por una mayoría de 5 votos *e·le·khee·do por oo·na ma·yo·ree·a de 5 bo·tos* elected by a majority of 5

mayorista *ma·yo·rees·ta* m wholesaler

mayúscula *ma·yoos·koo·la* f capital letter; en mayúscula *en ma·yoos·koo·la* in capitals; A mayúscula *a ma·yoos·koo·la* capital A

mazapán *ma·tha·pan* m marzipan

mazo *ma·tho* m mallet; el mazo de cartas *ma·tho de kar·tas* pack of cards

me *me* pron me; me lo dio *me lo dyo* he gave it to me

mecánico *me·ka·nee·ko* m mechanic

mecanismo *me·ka·nees·mo* m works (*mechanism*)

mecanógrafa *me·ka·no·gra·fa* f typist

mecanografiado(a) *me·ka·no·gra·fee·a·do(a)* adj typewritten

mecanografiar *me·ka·no·gra·fee·ar* vt type (*letter*)

mecer* *me·ther* vt rock

mecha *me·cha* f fuse; wick (*of cigarette lighter*)

media *me·dya* f sock; stocking

mediador *me·dya·dor* m troubleshooter (*political*)

mediano(a) *me·dya·no(a)* adj fair (*average*); de mediana edad *de me·dya·na e·dad* middle-aged

medianoche *me·dya·no·che* f midnight; a medianoche *a me·dya·no·che* at midnight

medicina *me·dee·thee·na* f medicine; drug

medición *me·dee·thyon* f survey (*of land*)

médico(a) *me·dee·ko(a)* adj medical □ m el médico *me·dee·ko* physician

medida *me·dee·da* f measurement; measure; a la medida *a la me·dee·da* custom-made; las medidas *me·dee·das* measurements; tomar medidas para hacer algo *to·mar me·dee·das*

pa·ra a·ther al·go to take steps to do something

medio *me·dyo* adv half □ adj medio(a) *me·dyo(a)* average; half; medium □ *m* el medio *me·dyo* middle; half; una media docena *oon·a me·dya do·the·na* a half dozen; tres kilómetros y medio *tres kee·lo·me·tros ee me·dyo* three and a half kilometers; medio abierto(a) *me·dyo a·byer·to(a)* half open; la media hora *me·dya o·ra* half-hour; por medio de *por me·dyo de* by means of; en medio de la noche *en me·dyo de la no·che* in the middle of the night; a medio camino *a me·dyo ka·mee·no* halfway; media hora *me·dya o·ra* half an hour; dos y medio *dos ee me·dyo* two and a half; los medios de información *me·dyos de in·for·ma·thyon* the media; los medios visuales *me·dyos bee·swa·les* visual aids

medio ambiente *me·dyo am·byen·te m* environment

mediocre *me·dyo·kre* adj poor (*mediocre*)

mediodía *me·dyo·dee·a m* midday; noon; a mediodía *a me·dyo·dee·a* at midday

medios *me·dyos mpl* means

medir* *me·deer vt/i* measure; ¿cuánto mide? *kwan·to mee·de* how tall are you?; ¿cuánto mide el río? *kwan·to mee·de el ree·o* how long is the river?

mediterráneo(a) *me·dee·te·rra·ne·o(a)* adj Mediterranean □ m el Mediterráneo *me·dee·te·rra·ne·o* the Mediterranean (Sea)

medusa *me·doo·sa f* jellyfish

mexicano(a) *me·khee·ka·no(a)* adj Mexican

México *me·khee·ko m* Mexico

mejilla *me·kheel·ya f* cheek

mejillón *me·kheel·yon m* mussel

mejor *me·khor* adj, adv better; best; cada vez mejor *ka·da beth me·khor* better and better; lo mejor sería... *lo me·khor se·ree·a* the best thing would be...; es el mejor *es el me·khor* he's the best

mejora *me·kho·ra f* upturn; improvement

mejorado(a) *me·kho·ra·do(a)* adj improved

mejorana *me·kho·ra·na f* marjoram

mejorar *me·kho·rar vt* improve □ vi get better

mejorarse *me·kho·rar·se vr* improve; que te mejores *ke te me·kho·res* get well soon

melaza *me·la·tha f* molasses; treacle

melocotón *me·lo·ko·ton m* peach

melodía *me·lo·dee·a f* tune

melodioso(a) *me·lo·dyo·so(a)* adj sweet (*music*)

melón *me·lon m* melon

memoria *me·mo·rya f* memory; de memoria *de me·mo·rya* by heart

mencionar *men·thyo·nar vt* mention

mendigar* *men·dee·gar vi* beg

mendigo *men·dee·go m* beggar

mendrugo *men·droo·go m* crust

menear *me·ne·ar vt* wag; shake; move

menor *me·nor* adj least; la menor cantidad *la me·nor kan·tee·dad* the least amount; menor de edad *me·nor de e·dad* under age

menos *me·nos prep* minus □ adv less; menos que/de *me·nos ke/de* less than; a menos que *a me·nos ke* unless; por lo menos *por lo me·nos* at least; me-

nos de un kilómetro *me·nos de oon kee·lo·me·tro* under a kilometer; todos menos él *to·dos me·nos el* all but him; menos carne *me·nos kar·ne* less meat; niños de menos de 10 años *neen·yos de me·nos de 10 an·yos* children under 10

mensaje *men·sa·khe m* message

mensajero *men·sa·khe·ro m* messenger

mensual *men·swal adj* monthly □ m el mensual *men·swal* monthly

menta *men·ta f* mint (*herb*); peppermint

mente *men·te f* mind

mentir* *men·teer vi* lie (*tell a lie*)

mentira *men·tee·ra f* lie (*untruth*)

mentolado(a) *men·to·la·do(a)* adj mentholated

menú *me·noo m* menu; menú fijo *me·noo fee·kho* table d'hôte

menudo(a) *me·noo·do(a)* adj small; a menudo *a me·noo·do* often

mercado *mer·ka·do m* market; el mercado de divisas *mer·ka·do de dee·bee·sas* foreign exchange market; el mercado negro *mer·ka·do ne·gro* black market

Mercado Común *mer·ka·do ko·moon m* Common Market

mercancía *mer·kan·thee·a f* commodity

mercancías *mer·kan·thee·as fpl* goods

mercería *mer·the·ree·a f* notions

merecer* *me·re·ther vt* deserve

merendar* *me·ren·dar vi* picnic; have a snack

merengue *me·ren·ge m* meringue

merienda *me·ryen·da f* tea (*meal*); picnic

merluza *mer·loo·tha f* hake

mermelada *mer·me·la·da f* jam; la mermelada de naranjas *mer·me·la·da de na·ran·khas* marmalade

mes *mes m* month

mesa *me·sa f* table; poner* la mesa *po·ner la me·sa* to set the table; la mesa plegable *me·sa ple·ga·ble* folding table

mesilla *me·seel·ya f* occasional table

meta *me·ta f* goal; finishing line

metal *me·tal m* metal

meter *me·ter vt* dip; insert (*into liquid*); métELO *me·te·lo* push it in

metodista *me·to·dees·ta m/f* Methodist

método *me·to·do m* method

métrico(a) *me·tree·ko(a)* adj metric

metro *me·tro m* meter; tape measure; subway (*railway*); ir* por metro *eer por me·tro* to go on the subway

mezcla *meth·kla f* blend; mixture

mezcladora *meth·kla·do·ra f* mixer

mezclar *meth·klar vt* mix; blend

mezclarse *meth·klar·se vr* mix

mezquita *meth·kee·ta f* mosque

mi *mee adj* my

microbio *mee·kro·byo m* germ

microbús *mee·kro·boos m* minibus

microficha *mee·kro·fee·cha f* microfiche

microfilm *mee·kro·feelm m* microfilm

micrófono *mee·kro·fo·no m* microphone

microlentillas *mee·kro·len·teel·yas fpl* contact lenses

microordenador *mee·kro·or·de·na·dor m* microcomputer

microprocesador *mee·kro·pro·the·sa·dor m* microprocessor

miedo *mye·do m* fear; tener* miedo *te·ner mye·do* to be scared; tener*

miedo de algo *te·ner mye·do de al·go* to be afraid of something

miel *myel f* honey

miembro *myem·bro m* member

mientras *myen·tras conj* while; **mientras dormía** *myen·tras dor·mee·a* as he was asleep (*while*); **mientras tanto** *myen·tras tan·to* meanwhile

miércoles *myer·ko·les m* Wednesday

miga *mee·ga f* crumb

migraña *mee·gran·ya f* migraine

mil *meel num* thousand

milésimo(a) *mee·le·see·mo(a) adj* thousandth

miligramo *mee·lee·gra·mo m* milligram

mililitro *mee·lee·lee·tro m* milliliter

milímetro *mee·lee·me·tro m* millimeter

militar *mee·lee·tar adj* military

milla *meel·ya f* mile

millón *meel·yon m* million; **los mil millones** *meel meel·yo·nes* billion

millonario *meel·yo·na·ryo m* millionaire

millonésimo(a) *meel·yo·ne·see·mo(a) adj* millionth

mimbre *meem·bre m* wicker

mina *mee·na f* lead (*in pencil*); mine (*for coal etc*)

minero *mee·ne·ro m* miner

miniatura *mee·nya·too·ra f* miniature; **un ferrocarril en miniatura** *oon fe·rro·ka·rreel en mee·nya·too·ra* a model railroad

minicomputadora *mee·nee·kom·poo·ta·do·ra f* minicomputer

minifalda *mee·nee·fal·da f* miniskirt

mínimo(a) *mee·nee·mo(a) adj* minimum □ *m* **el mínimo** *mee·nee·mo* minimum; **tiene lo mínimo** *tye·ne lo mee·nee·mo* he has the least; **el mínimo de dinero** *el mee·nee·mo de dee·ne·ro* the least money

ministerio *mee·nees·te·ryo m* ministry (*government*); **el Ministerio de Hacienda** *mee·nees·te·ryo de a·thyen·da* Treasury

ministro *mee·nees·tro m* minister (*in government*); **el Ministro de Asuntos Exteriores** *mee·nees·tro de a·soon·tos eks·te·ryo·res* foreign minister

minoría *mee·no·ree·a f* minority

minuto *mee·noo·to m* minute

mío(a) *mee·o(a) adj* my □ *pron* **el/la mío(a)** *el/la mee·o(a)* mine □ *adj* **míos(as)** *mee·os(as)* my (*plural*) □ *pron* **los/las míos(as)** *los/las mee·os(as)* mine (*plural*)

miope *mee·o·pe adj* nearsighted

mirada *mee·ra·da f* look; glance

mirar *mee·rar vt* stare; look at □ *vi* look; **mirar fijamente a alguien** *mee·rar fee·kha·men·te a al·gyen* to stare at somebody

mirlo *meer·lo m* blackbird

mis *mees adj* my (*plural*)

misa *mee·sa f* mass (*church*)

mismo(a) *mees·mo(a) adj* same; **el mismo libro que** *el mees·mo lee·bro ke* the same book as; **lo mismo por favor** *lo mees·mo por fa·bor* (the) same again please; **en el mismo centro** *en el mees·mo then·tro* right in the middle; **aquí mismo** *a·kee mees·mo* just here; **yo mismo(a)** *yo mees·mo(a)* I myself

misterio *mees·te·ryo m* mystery

mitad *mee·tad f* half; **a mitad de precio** *a mee·tad de pre·thyo* half-price

mixto(a) *meeks·to(a) adj* mixed

mochila *mo·chee·la f* back pack; rucksack

moda *mo·da f* fashion; **de moda** *de mo·da* fashionable

modales *mo·da·les mpl* manners

modelo *mo·de·lo m* model □ *m/f* model (*mannequin*)

modernizar* *mo·der·nee·thar vt* modernize

moderno(a) *mo·der·no(a) adj* modern

modesto(a) *mo·des·to(a) adj* modest

módico(a) *mo·dee·ko(a) adj* reasonable (*price*)

modificación *mo·dee·fee·ka·thyon f* modification

modificar* *mo·dee·fee·kar vt* modify; alter

modista *mo·dees·ta m/f* designer (*of clothes*)

modo *mo·do m* way; manner; form; **de todos modos** *de to·dos mo·dos* anyway (*nonetheless*); **modo de empleo** *mo·do de em·ple·o* directions for use

mohair *mo·er m* mohair

moho *mo·o m* rust; mold

mojado(a) *mo·kha·do(a) adj* wet (*clothes*)

mojarse *mo·khar·se vr* get wet

mojón *mo·khon m* landmark

molécula *mo·le·koo·la f* molecule

moler* *mo·ler vt* mill; grind

molestar *mo·les·tar vt* bother; annoy; **por favor no molestar** *por fa·bor no mo·les·tar* do not disturb; **por favor no se moleste** *por fa·bor no se mo·les·te* please don't bother

molestia *mo·les·tya f* bother (*nuisance*); **tomarse la molestia por algo** *to·mar·se la mo·les·tya por al·go* to take trouble over something

molesto(a) *mo·les·to(a) adj* troublesome

molido(a) *mo·lee·do(a) adj* ground (*coffee*)

molinillo *mo·lee·neel·yo m* mill (*for coffee*)

molino *mo·lee·no m* mill; **el molino de viento** *mo·lee·no de byen·to* windmill

momento *mo·men·to m* instant; moment; while; **un momento** *oon mo·men·to* just a minute; en este momento *en es·te mo·men·to* at present

Mónaco *mo·na·ko m* Monaco

monasterio *mo·nas·te·ryo m* monastery

moneda *mo·ne·da f* currency; coin; **las monedas** *mo·ne·das* silver (*money*)

monedero *mo·ne·de·ro m* purse

monetario(a) *mo·ne·ta·ryo(a) adj* monetary

monja *mon·kha f* nun

monje *mon·khe m* monk

mono(a) *mo·no(a) adj* sweet (*cute, pretty*) □ *m* **el mono** *mo·no* monkey; ape; overalls; dungarees □ *pref* **mono-** *mo·no* mono; **en mono** *en mo·no* in mono

monocarril *mo·no·ka·rreel m* monorail

monopolio *mo·no·po·lyo m* monopoly

monstruo *mons·troo·o m* monster

montaña *mon·tan·ya f* mountain

montañismo *mon·tan·yees·mo m* mountaineering

montañoso(a) *mon·tan·yo·so(a) adj* hilly; mountainous

montar *mon·tar vt* assemble (*parts of machine*) □ *vt/i* ride; **montar a caballo** *mon·tar a ka·bal·yo* to ride a horse; **montar en bicicleta** *mon·tar en bee·thee·kle·ta* to ride a bicycle

montecillo *mon·te·theel·yo m* hump (*on road*)

montón *mon·ton m* bundle; heap; pile

montura *mon·too·ra* f frames (*of eyeglasses*)

monumento *mo·noo·men·to* m monument

moqueta *mo·ke·ta* f wall-to-wall carpet(ing)

mora *mo·ra* f mulberry

morado(a) *mo·ra·do(a)* adj purple

mordedura *mor·de·doo·ra* f bite

morder* *mor·der* vt bite

moreno(a) *mo·re·no(a)* adj dark (*hair*)

morir* *mo·reer* vi die

morriña *mo·rreen·ya* f depression; **tener* morriña** *te·ner mo·rreen·ya* to be homesick

mortal *mor·tal* adj fatal

mosca *mos·ka* f fly

moscarda *mos·kar·da* f bluebottle

Moscú *mos·koo* m Moscow

mosquitero *mos·kee·te·ro* m mosquito net

mosquito *mos·kee·to* m mosquito; gnat

mostaza *mos·ta·tha* f mustard

mostrador *mos·tra·dor* m counter (*in shop*)

mostrar* *mos·trar* vt demonstrate (*appliance etc*); show

motel *mo·tel* m motel

motocicleta *mo·to·thee·kle·ta* f motorbike

motociclista *mo·to·thee·klees·ta* m/f motorcyclist

motor *mo·tor* m engine; motor; **el motor diesel** *mo·tor dee·sel* diesel engine

mover* *mo·ber* vt move; toss (*salad*)

moverse* *mo·ber·se* vr move

movimiento *mo·bee·myen·to* m motion; movement; **el movimiento de mercancías** *mo·bee·myen·to de mer·kan·thee·as* turnover (*in goods*)

mozo *mo·tho* m porter (*for luggage*)

muchacha *moo·cha·cha* f maid

muchedumbre *moo·che·doom·bre* f crowd

mucho *moo·cho* adv a lot, much; very □ adj **mucho(a)** *moo·cho(a)* a lot of; much **me gusta mucho** *me goos·ta moo·cho* I like it very much; **mucho mejor** *moo·cho me·khor* much better; **mucho más grande** *moo·cho mas gran·de* much bigger; **mucha leche** *moo·cha le·che* much milk; **no mucho** *no moo·cho* not much; **con mucho** *kon moo·cho* far (*much*)

muchos(as) *moo·chos(·as)* pron many

mudar *moo·dar* vt/i change

mudo(a) *moo·do(a)* adj dumb

mueble *mwe·ble* m piece of furniture

muebles *mwe·bles* mpl furniture

mueca *mwe·ka* f grimace

muelle *mwel·ye* m quay; quayside; wharf; pier; dock

muerte *mwer·te* f death

muerto(a) *mwer·to(a)* adj dead (*person*); flat (*beer*)

muestra *mwes·tra* f sample (*of goods*)

mujer *moo·kher* f woman; la mujer de negocios *moo·kher de ne·go·thyos* businesswoman; **la mujer de la limpieza** *moo·kher de la leem·pye·tha* cleaner (*of house etc*)

mujer policía *moo·kher po·lee·thee·a* f policewoman

muleta *moo·le·ta* f crutch

multa *mool·ta* f fine; ticket (*parking*)

multilingüe *mool·tee·leen·gwe* adj multilingual

multinacional *mool·tee·na·thyo·nal* adj multinational

multiplicación *mool·tee·plee·ka·thyon* f multiplication

multiplicar* *mool·tee·plee·kar* vt multiply; **multiplicar 9 por 4** *mool·tee·plee·kar 9 por 4* to multiply 9 by 4

mundo *moon·do* m world

muñeca *moon·ye·ka* f wrist; doll

muñeco de nieve *moon·ye·ko de nye·be* m snowman

Munich *moo·neech* m Munich

municipal *moo·nee·thee·pal* adj municipal

municipio *moo·nee·thee·pyo* m borough

murciélago *moor·thye·la·go* m bat (*animal*)

muro *moo·ro* m wall; **el muro exterior** *el moo·ro eks·te·ryor* the outside wall

músculo *moos·koo·lo* m muscle

museo *moo·se·o* m museum; **el museo de arte** *moo·se·o de ar·te* art gallery

música *moo·see·ka* f music; **la música ligera** *moo·see·ka lee·khe·ra* light music

músico(a) *moo·see·ko(a)* m/f musician

muslo *moos·lo* m thigh; drumstick (*of chicken*); **muslo de pollo** *moos·lo de pol·yo* chicken leg

musulmán(mana) *moo·sool·man(·na)* adj Muslim □ m/f Muslim

muy *mooy* adv very

N

nabo *na·bo* m rutabaga; **el nabo sueco** *na·bo swe·ko* swede

nácar *na·kar* m mother-of-pearl

nacer* *na·ther* vi to be born

nacido(a) *na·thee·do(a)* adj born

nacimiento *na·thee·myen·to* m birth

nación *na·thyon* f nation

nacional *na·thyo·nal* adj native; national

nacionalidad *na·thyo·na·lee·dad* f nationality

nacionalizar* *na·thyo·na·lee·thar* vt nationalize

Naciones Unidas *na·thyo·nes oo·nee·das* fpl United Nations Organization

nada *na·da* pron nothing □ adv not at all; **no veo nada** *no be·o na·da* I can't see anything; **de nada** *de na·da* not at all (*don't mention it*); **no era nada más que una equivocación** *no e·ra na·da mas ke oo·na e·kee·bo·ka·thyon* it was just a mistake

nadador(a) *na·da·dor(·ra)* m/f swimmer

nadar *na·dar* vi swim

nadie *na·dye* pron no one; nobody; **no veo a nadie** *no be·o a na·dye* I can't see anybody

naipe *nay·pe* m playing card

naranja *na·ran·kha* f orange

naranjada *na·ran·kha·da* f orangeade

narciso *nar·thee·so* m daffodil

nariz *na·reeth* f nose

nata *na·ta* f cream; **la nata batida** *na·ta ba·tee·da* whipped cream; **la nata agria** *na·ta a·grya* sour cream

natación *na·ta·thyon* f swimming

natillas *na·teel·yas* fpl custard

natural *na·too·ral* adj natural; **no natural** *no na·too·ral* unnatural

naturaleza *na·too·ra·le·tha* f nature

naturalizado(a) *na·too·ra·lee·tha·do(a)* adj naturalized

naturalmente *na·too·ral·men·te* adv naturally (*of course*); certainly

naufragar *now·fra·gar* vi to be (ship-) wrecked; **hacer* naufragar** *a·ther now·fra·gar* wreck (*ship*)

náusea *now·se·a* f nausea; sickness (*nausea*)

navaja *na·ba·kha* f pocketknife; penknife

nave *na·be* f nave; la nave espacial *na·be es·pa·thyal* spacecraft

navegación *na·be·ga·thyon* f navigation

Navidad *na·bee·dad* f Christmas; el día de Navidad *dee·a de na·bee·dad* Christmas Day

nebuloso(a) *ne·boo·lo·so(a)* adj foggy

necesario(a) *ne·the·sa·ryo(a)* adj necessary

necesidad *ne·the·see·dad* f necessity

necesitar *ne·the·see·tar* vt require; want; need

negar *ne·gar* vt deny

negarse *ne·gar·se* vr refuse; negarse a hacer algo *ne·gar·se a a·ther al·go* to refuse to do something

negativa *ne·ga·tee·ba* f refusal

negativo *ne·ga·tee·bo* m negative (*of photo*)

negociable *ne·go·thya·ble* adj negotiable

negociación *ne·go·thya·thyon* f bargaining (*negotiation*)

negociaciones *ne·go·thya·thyo·nes* fpl negotiations; talks

negociar *ne·go·thyar* vt negotiate

negocio *ne·go·thyo* m deal; business; hacer un negocio *a·ther oon ne·go·thyo* to make a bargain

negocios *ne·go·thyos* mpl business (*dealings, work*); por asuntos de negocios *por a·soon·tos de ne·go·thyos* on business

negro(a) *ne·gro(a)* adj black

nervio *ner·byo* m nerve

nervioso(a) *ner·byo·so(a)* adj tense; nervous

neto *ne·to* adj net (*income, price*)

neumático *ne·oo·ma·tee·ko* m tire

neutral *ne·oo·tral* adj neutral

nevar *ne·bar* vi snow; está nevando *es·ta ne·ban·do* it's snowing

nevera *ne·be·ra* f ice box

ni *nee* conj nor; ni ... ni *nee ... nee* neither ... nor

nido *nee·do* m nest

niebla *nye·bla* f fog; mist; hay niebla *ay nye·bla* it's foggy

nieta *nye·ta* f granddaughter

nieto *nye·to* m grandson

nietos *nye·tos* mpl grandchildren

nieve *nye·be* f snow

niña *neen·ya* f girl (*child*); baby girl

ningún, ninguno(a) *neen·goon, neen·goo·no(a)* adj no; no lo veo en ningún sitio *no lo be·o en neen·goon see·tyo* I can't see it anywhere □ pron ninguno(a) *neen·goo·no(a)* none

niño *neen·yo* m boy; baby; los niños *neen·yos* children

nivel *nee·bel* m level; standard; el nivel de vida *nee·bel de bee·da* standard of living; el nivel del mar *nee·bel del mar* sea level

no *no* adv not; no (*as answer*)

no alcohólico(a) *no al·ko·lee·ko(a)* adj nonalcoholic

noche *no·che* f night; de una noche *de oo·na no·che* overnight (*a stay*); esta noche *es·ta no·che* tonight

nochebuena *no·che·bwe·na* f Christmas Eve

nochevieja *no·che·bye·kha* f New Year's Eve

no fumador *no foo·ma·dor* m nonsmoker (*person*)

nombramiento *nom·bra·myen·to* m appointment

nombrar *nom·brar* vt appoint

nombre *nom·bre* m name; el nombre de pila *nom·bre de pee·la* forename; Christian name; en nombre de *en nom·bre de* on behalf of; el nombre comercial *nom·bre ko·mer·thyal* trade name

nómina *no·mee·na* f payroll

nominal *no·mee·nal* adj nominal (*fee*)

no obstante *no obs·tan·te* adv nevertheless

noreste *no·res·te* m northeast

normal *nor·mal* adj normal; standard; regular

normalmente *nor·mal·men·te* adv normally; usually

noroeste *no·ro·es·te* m northwest

norte *nor·te* m north; del norte *del nor·te* northern; hacia el norte *a·thya el nor·te* northward

Norteamérica *nor·te·a·me·ree·ka* f North America

nosotros(as) *no·so·tros(as)* pron we; us; nosotros(as) mismos(as) *no·so·tros(as) mees·mos(as)* we ourselves; somos nosotros *so·mos no·so·tros* it's us

nota *no·ta* f note; memo(randum); mark (*in school*)

notable *no·ta·ble* adj remarkable

notar *no·tar* vt notice

notario *no·ta·ryo* m attorney

notarse *no·tar·se* vr show (*be visible*)

noticiario *no·tee·thya·ryo* m newscast

noticias *no·tee·thyas* fpl news (*on radio, TV*)

novela *no·be·la* f novel (*book*); la novela de misterio *no·be·la de mees·te·ryo* thriller

noveno(a) *no·be·no(a)* adj ninth

noventa *no·ben·ta* num ninety

novia *no·bya* f bride; girlfriend; fiancée

noviembre *no·byem·bre* m November

novio *no·byo* m bridegroom; boyfriend; fiancé

nube *noo·be* f cloud

nublado(a) *noo·bla·do(a)* adj cloudy

nuclear *noo·kle·ar* adj nuclear (*energy, war*)

nudillo *noo·deel·yo* n knuckle

nudo *noo·do* m knot; hacer un nudo *a·ther un noo·do* to tie a knot

nuera *nwe·ra* f daughter-in-law

nuestro(a), nuestros(as) *nwes·tro(a) nwes·tros(as)* adj our □ pron el/la nuestro(a) *el/la nwes·tro(a)* ours; los/las nuestros(as) *los/las nwes·tros (·as)* ours (*plural*)

nueve *nwe·be* num nine

nuevo(a) *nwe·bo(a)* adj new

nuez *nweth* f nut; walnut

nulo(a) *noo·lo(a)* adj void (*contract*); nulo y sin efecto *noo·lo ee seen e·fek·to* null and void

número *noo·me·ro* m number (*figure*); size (*of shoes*); issue (*of magazine*); act (*at circus etc*); el número de matrícula *noo·me·ro de ma·tree·koo·la* license plate; el número de teléfono *noo·me·ro de te·le·fo·no* telephone number

nunca *noon·ka* adv never; no viene nunca *no bye·ne noon·ka* he never comes

nylon *nay·lon* m nylon

o *o conj* or; **o... o... o... o...** either... or...

obedecer* *o·be·de·ther vt* obey; **obedecer* a alguien** *o·be·de·ther a al·gyen* to obey someone

obediente *o·be·dyen·te adj* obedient

obertura *o·ber·too·ra f* overture

obispo *o·bees·po m* bishop

objetivo *ob·khe·tee·bo m* objective; target (*sales etc*); lens (*of camera*); **el objetivo granangular** *ob·khe·tee·bo gra·nan·goo·lar* wide-angle lens; **el objetivo zoom** *ob·khe·tee·bo thoom* zoom lens

objeto *ob·khe·to m* goal (*aim*); object; **los objetos de valor** *ob·khe·tos de ba·lor* valuables

obligación *o·blee·ga·thyon f* obligation; duty

obligar *o·blee·gar vt* force (*compel*); **obligar* a uno a hacer algo** *o·blee·gar a oo·no a a·ther al·go* to make someone do something

oblongo(a) *o·blon·go(a) adj* oblong

obra *o·bra f* work; **la obra de teatro** *o·bra de te·a·tro* play (*theatrical*); **la obra maestra** *o·bra ma·es·tra* masterpiece; **la obra de arte** *o·bra de ar·te* work of art

obras *o·bras fpl* road repairs

obrero(a) *o·bre·ro(a) adj* working-class □ *m* **el obrero** *o·bre·ro* workman; laborer

observación *ob·ser·ba·thyon f* remark

observar *ob·ser·bar vt* watch

obsesión *ob·se·syon f* obsession

obstáculo *obs·ta·koo·lo m* obstacle

obstrucción *obs·trook·thyon f* blockage

obstruir* *obs·troo·eer vt* block (*pipe*)

obtener* *ob·te·ner vt* get; obtain

obturador *ob·too·ra·dor m* shutter (*in camera*)

ocasión *o·ka·syon f* occasion

occidental *ok·thee·den·tal adj* western

océano *o·the·a·no m* ocean

Océano Pacífico *o·the·a·no pa·thee·fee·ko m* Pacific Ocean

ochenta *o·chen·ta num* eighty; **los años ochenta** *los a·nyos o·chen·ta* eighties (*decade*)

ocho *o·cho num* eight

ocio *o·thyo m* leisure; spare time

octavo(a) *ok·ta·bo(a) adj* eighth

octubre *ok·too·bre m* October

oculista *o·koo·lees·ta m/f* oculist

ocupado(a) *o·koo·pa·do(a) adj* engaged; busy; **ocupado(a) con otra cosa** *o·koo·pa·do(a) kon o·tra ko·sa* otherwise engaged

ocuparse de *o·koo·par·se de vr* deal with

ocurrir *o·koo·rreer vi* happen

odiar *o·dyar vt* hate

odio *o·dyo m* hatred

oeste *o·es·te m* west; **hacia el oeste** *a·thya el o·es·te* west

Oeste *o·es·te m* the West

ofender *o·fen·der vt* offend

ofensivo(a) *o·fen·see·bo(a) adj* rude

oferta *o·fer·ta f* bid; offer; **hacer* una oferta por algo** *a·ther oo·na o·fer·ta por al·go* to bid for something; **la oferta y la demanda** *la o·fer·ta ee la de·man·da* supply and demand; **la oferta para adquirir una compañía** *o·fer·ta pa·ra ad·kee·reer oo·na kom·pan·yee·a* take-over bid

oficial *o·fee·thyal m* officer □ *adj* official; **no oficial** *no o·fee·thyal* unofficial

oficina *o·fee·thee·na f* office; bureau; **la oficina de turismo** *o·fee·thee·na de too·rees·mo* tourist office; **la oficina central** *o·fee·thee·na then·tral* head office

Oficina de Correos *o·fee·thee·na de ko·rre·os f* Post Office

oficinista *o·fee·thee·nees·ta m/f* office worker

oficio *o·fee·thyo m* service (*in church*); occupation (*job*)

ofrecer* *o·fre·ther vt* offer; **ofrecer* hacer algo** *o·fre·ther a·ther al·go* to offer to do something

oído *o·ee·do m* hearing; ear

oír* *o·eer vt/i* hear

ojalá *o·kha·la excl* I wish; would to God

ojo *o·kho m* eye; **el ojo morado** *o·kho mo·ra·do* black eye; **el ojo de la cerradura** *o·kho de la the·rra·doo·ra* keyhole

ola *o·la f* wave (*in sea*)

oleoconducto *o·le·o·kon·dook·to m* pipeline

oler* *o·ler vt* smell; **oler* a ajo** *o·ler a a·kho* to smell of garlic; **huele mucho** *we·le moo·cho* it has a strong smell

olla *ol·ya f* pot (*for cooking*); **la olla a presión** *ol·ya a pre·syon* pressure cooker

olmo *ol·mo m* elm

olor *o·lor m* smell; scent

olvidar *ol·bee·dar vt* forget; **he olvidado el paraguas** *e ol·bee·da·do el pa·ra·gwas* I've left my umbrella

omitir *o·mee·teer vt* miss out; leave out

once *on·the num* eleven

onda *on·da f* wave; **la onda larga** *on·da lar·ga* long wave; **las ondas ultracortas** *on·das ool·tra·kor·tas* V.H.F.; **la onda corta** *on·da kor·ta* short wave; **la onda media** *on·da me·dya* medium wave

ondulación *on·doo·la·thyon f* wave (*in hair*)

ondulado(a) *on·doo·la·do(a) adj* wavy

onza *on·tha f* ounce

opción *op·thyon f* option

OPEP *o·pep f* OPEC

ópera *o·pe·ra f* opera

operación *o·pe·ra·thyon f* operation

opinar *o·pee·nar vi* give an opinion

opinión *o·pee·nyon f* view; opinion; **cambiar de opinión** *kam·byar de o·peen·yon* to change one's mind

oporto *o·por·to m* port (*wine*)

oportunidad *o·por·too·nee·dad f* opportunity

óptico *op·tee·ko m* optician

optimista *op·tee·mees·ta adj* optimistic

opuesto(a) *o·pwes·to(a) adj* opposite; opposing

oración *o·ra·thyon f* prayer

orden *or·den f* command □ *m* **el orden** *or·den* order (*in series*); **de segundo orden** *de se·goon·do or·den* minor (*injury*); **el orden del día** *or·den del dee·a* agenda; **el orden público** *or·den poo·blee·ko* law and order

ordenado(a) *or·de·na·do(a) adj* neat; tidy (*room*)

ordenador *or·de·na·dor m* computer

oreja *o·re·kha f* ear

organigrama *or·ga·nee·gra·ma m* flow chart

organización *or·ga·nee·tha·thyon f* organization

organizador *or·ga·nee·tha·dor m* steward (*at club*)

organizar* *or·ga·nee·thar vt* organize

órgano *or·ga·no m* organ

orgullo *or·gool·yo m* pride

orgulloso(a) *or·gool·yo·so(a) adj* proud

oriental *o·ryen·tal adj* oriental; eastern

orientarse *o·ryen·tar·se vr* take one's bearings; take a decision

Oriente *o·ryen·te m* East

Oriente Medio *o·ryen·te me·dyo m* Middle East

origen *o·ree·khen m* origin

original *o·ree·khee·nal adj* original □ *m* el original *o·ree·khee·nal* original

orilla *o·reel·ya f* shore; la orilla del mar *o·reel·ya del mar* seaside

orín *o·reen m* rust

orinal de niño *o·ree·nal de neen·yo m* pot(ty)

ornamento *or·na·men·to m* ornament

oro *o·ro m* gold; en oro macizo *en o·ro ma·thee·tho* in solid gold; de oro *de o·ro* gold

orquesta *or·kes·ta f* orchestra

oscilar *os·thee·lar vi* sway

oscuro(a) *os·koo·ro(a) adj* obscure; dark; dim; está oscuro *es·ta os·koo·ro* it's dark

oso *o·so m* bear

ostra *os·tra f* oyster

otoño *o·ton·yo m* autumn; fall

otorgar* *o·tor·gar vt* grant

otro(a) *o·tro(a) adj* other □ *pron* (el/la) otro(a) *el/la o·tro(a)* the other; another one; otra vez *o·tra beth* again; otro más *o·tro mas* one more; ¡otra cerveza, por favor! *o·tra ther·be·tha por fa·bor* another beer please!; quisiera ver otra camisa *kee·sye·ra ber o·tra ka·mee·sa* I want to see another shirt; el otro día *el o·tro dee·a* the other day

ovalado(a) *o·ba·la·do(a) adj* oval

oveja *o·be·kha f* sheep

ovillo *o·beel·yo m* ball (*of string, wool*)

oxidado(a) *ok·see·da·do(a) adj* rusty

oxidarse *ok·see·dar·se vr* rust

oxígeno *ok·see·khe·no m* oxygen

P

paciencia *pa·thyen·thya f* patience

paciente *pa·thyen·te adj* patient □ *m/f* el/la paciente *pa·thyen·te* patient

padrastro *pa·dras·tro m* stepfather

padre *pa·dre m* father; los padres *pa·dres* parents

padrino *pa·dree·no m* godfather; el padrino de boda *pa·dree·no de bo·da* best man

pagadero(a) *pa·ga·de·ro(a) adj* due (*owing*); payable

pagado(a) *pa·ga·do(a) adj* paid; pagado(a) por adelantado *pa·ga·do(a) por a·de·lan·ta·do* prepaid; mal pagado(a) *mal pa·ga·do(a)* underpaid; no pagado(a) *no pa·ga·do(a)* unpaid (*debt*)

pagar* *pa·gar vt* pay for; pay

página *pa·khee·na f* page

pago *pa·go m* payment; como pago parcial *ko·mo pa·go par·thyal* as a trade-in; el pago inicial *pa·go ee·nee·thyal* down payment

país *pa·ees m* country (*land*)

paisaje *pay·sa·khe m* scenery

Países Bajos *pa·ee·ses ba·khos mpl* Netherlands

paja *pa·kha f* straw

pajarita *pa·kha·ree·ta f* bow tie

pájaro *pa·kha·ro m* bird

Pakistán *pa·kees·tan m* Pakistan

pakistaní *pa·kees·ta·nee adj* Pakistani

pala *pa·la f* shovel; spade

palabra *pa·la·bra f* word; palabra por palabra *pa·la·bra por pa·la·bra* word for word

palacio *pa·la·thyo m* palace

palanca *pa·lan·ka f* lever; la palanca del cambio de velocidades *pa·lan·ka del kam·byo de be·lo·thee·da·des* gearshift

Palestina *pa·les·tee·na f* Palestine

palestino(a) *pa·les·tee·no(a) adj* Palestinian

pálido(a) *pa·lee·do(a) adj* pale

palillos *pa·leel·yos mpl* chopsticks

palma *pal·ma f* palm (*of hand*)

palmazo *pal·ma·tho m* smack

palmera *pal·me·ra f* palm-tree

palo *pa·lo m* stick; spar; mast; pole (*wooden*); suit (*cards*); el palo de golf *pa·lo de golf* golf club

paloma *pa·lo·ma f* pigeon; dove

palomitas de maíz *pa·lo·mee·tas de ma·eeth fpl* popcorn

palta *pal·ta f* avocado

pan *pan m* bread; loaf (*of bread*); el pan de jengibre *el pan de khen·khee·bre* gingerbread; el pan de centeno *pan de then·te·no* rye bread; el pan integral *pan een·te·gral* wholewheat bread

pana *pa·na f* corduroy; cord

panadería *pa·na·de·ree·a f* bakery

panadero *pa·na·de·ro m* baker

pañal *pan·yal m* diaper

Panamá *pa·na·ma m* Panama

panameño(a) *pa·na·men·yo(a) adj* Panamanian

panecillo *pa·ne·theel·yo m* bun

pánico *pa·nee·ko m* panic

paño *pan·yo m* flannel; cloth; duster; el paño higiénico *pan·yo ee·khye·nee·ko* sanitary napkin

panqueque *pan·ke·ke m* pancake

pantalla *pan·tal·ya f* screen; lampshade

pantalones *pan·ta·lo·nes mpl* pair of trousers; trousers; los pantalones (de mujer) *pan·ta·lo·nes (de moo·kher)* slacks; los pantalones de esquí *pan·ta·lo·nes de es·kee* ski pants; los pantalones cortos *pan·ta·lo·nes kor·tos* shorts

pantalones vaqueros *pan·ta·lo·nes ba·ke·ros mpl* jeans

pantano *pan·ta·no m* swamp; bog

pantys *pan·tees mpl* panty hose

pañuelo *pan·ywe·lo m* handkerchief; el pañuelo de papel *pan·ywe·lo de pa·pel* tissue (*handkerchief*)

papa *pa·pa f* potato □ el papa *pa·pa m* pope; las papas a la inglesa *pa·pas a la een·gle·sa* chips; las papas fritas *pa·pas free·tas* french fried potatoes, french fries

papá *pa·pa m* dad(dy)

papel *pa·pel m* paper; part (*in play*); hacer el papel de Hamlet *a·ther el pa·pel de ham·let* to act Hamlet; el papel de escribir *pa·pel de es·kree·beer* stationery; el papel higiénico *pa·pel ee·khye·nee·ko* toilet paper; el papel carbón *pa·pel kar·bon* carbon paper; el papel para cartas *pa·pel pa·ra kar·tas* notepaper; el papel de estaño *pa·pel de es·tan·yo* tin foil; el papel de seda *pa·pel de se·da* tissue paper; el papel de envolver *pa·pel de*

en·bol·ber wrapping paper; **el papel pintado** *pa·pel peen·ta·do* wallpaper; **el papel celo** *pa·pel the·lo* Scotch tape

papeleo *pa·pe·le·o m* red tape

papelera *pa·pe·le·ra f* waste paper basket

papelería *pa·pe·le·ree·a f* stationer's (shop)

papeleta *pa·pe·le·ta f* slip (*of paper*)

paperas *pa·pe·ras fpl* mumps

papilla de avena *pa·peel·ya de a·be·na f* porridge

paquete *pa·ke·te m* package; pack; packet; parcel

par *par m* pair □ *f* **la par** *par* par; **un número par** *oon noo·me·ro par* an even number; **un par de** *oon par de* a couple of (*a few*); **un par de zapatos** *oon par de tha·pa·tos* a pair of shoes; **por encima de la par** *por en·thee·ma de la par* above par

para *pa·ra prep* for; **hace calor para marzo** *a·the ka·lor pa·ra mar·tho* it's warm for March; **para hacer algo** *pa·ra a·ther al·go* in order to do something; **estaremos allí para las 4** *es·ta·re·mos al·yee pa·ra las 4* we'll be there by 4 o'clock; **listo(a) para todo** *lees·to(a) pa·ra to·do* ready for anything

parabarros *pa·ra·ba·rros m* mud-flap

parabrisas *pa·ra·bree·sas m* windshield

paracaídas *pa·ra·ka·ee·das m* parachute

parachoques *pa·ra·cho·kes m* fender; bumper (*on car*)

parada *pa·ra·da f* stop; **la parada de taxis** *pa·ra·da de tak·sees* taxi stand; **la parada discrecional** *pa·ra·da dees·kre·thyo·nal* flag stop; **la parada de autobús** *pa·ra·da de ow·to·boos* bus stop

parado(a) *pa·ra·do(a) adj* unemployed; upright; standing up

parados *pa·ra·dos mpl* the unemployed

paragolpes *pa·ra·gol·pes m* fender

paraguas *pa·ra·gwas m* umbrella

paragüero *pa·rag·we·ro m* umbrella stand

paraíso *pa·ra·ee·so m* paradise; gallery (of theater)

paralelo(a) *pa·ra·le·lo(a) adj* parallel

paralizado(a) *pa·ra·lee·tha·do(a) adj* paralyzed

parar *pa·rar vt/i* stop

pararse *pa·rar·se vr* stop; stand up; stall (*car engine*); **el coche se paró** *el ko·che se pa·ro* the car pulled in

parcela *par·the·la f* plot (*of land*)

parche *par·che m* patch

parecer* *pa·re·ther vi* seem; look; **parece el ruido de un coche** *pa·re·the·el rwee·do de oon ko·che* it sounds like a car; **parece enfermo** *pa·re·the en·fer·mo* he appears to be ill; **parece que...** *pa·re·the ke* it appears that...

parecerse* *pa·re·ther·se vr* resemble; **parecerse* a** *pa·re·ther·se a* to be similar to; **se parece a su padre** *se pa·re·the a soo pa·dre* he resembles his father

parecido(a) *pa·re·thee·do(a) adj* like; similar

pared *pa·red f* wall

pareja *pa·re·kha f* pair; partner (*dancing*); couple (*persons*)

paréntesis *pa·ren·te·sees m* bracket (*in writing*)

pariente *pa·ryen·te m/f* relation; rela-

tive; **el pariente más cercano** *pa·ryen·te mas ther·ka·no* next of kin

París *pa·rees m* Paris

parlamento *par·la·men·to m* parliament

parmesano *par·me·sa·no m* Parmesan

paro *pa·ro m* unemployment

párpado *par·pa·do m* eyelid

parque *par·ke m* park; **el parque de atracciones** *par·ke de a·trak·thyo·nes* amusement park; **el parque de bomberos** *par·ke de bom·be·ros* fire station; **el parque (de niño)** *par·ke (de neen·yo)* playpen; **parque nacional** *par·ke na·thyo·nal* national park

parquímetro *par·kee·me·tro m* parking meter

parra *pa·rra f* vine

párrafo *pa·rra·fo m* paragraph

parrilla *pa·rreel·ya f* grate; grillroom; grill (*gridiron*)

parte *par·te f* part; **la parte delantera** *par·te de·lan·te·ra* front (*foremost part*); **en alguna parte** *en al·goo·na par·te* somewhere; **en ninguna parte** *en neen·goo·na par·te* nowhere; **en parte** *en par·te* partly; **en otra parte** *en o·tra par·te* somewhere else

parterre *par·te·rre m* flowerbed

participación *par·tee·thee·pa·thyon f* participation; share (*part*); **la participación en los beneficios** *par·tee·thee·pa·thyon en los be·ne·fee·thyos* profit-sharing

participar *par·tee·thee·par vi* participate

particular *par·tee·koo·lar adj* particular; private; **la clase particular** *kla·se par·tee·koo·lar* private lesson; **en particular** *en par·tee·koo·lar* in particular

partida *par·tee·da f* departure; **la partida de nacimiento** *par·tee·da de na·thee·myen·to* birth certificate

partido *par·tee·do m* party (*political*); match (*sport*); round (*of golf*)

partir *par·teer vt* split; depart; **partir en dos** *par·teer en dos* to halve (*divide in two*); **a partir de las 8** *a par·teer de las 8* from 8 o'clock

pasa *pa·sa f* raisin; currant; **la pasa de Esmirna** *pa·sa de es·meer·na* sultana

pasado(a) *pa·sa·do(a) adj* bad (*meat*); past □ *m* **el pasado** *pa·sa·do* past; **pasado(a) de moda** *pa·sa·do(a) de mo·da* old-fashioned

pasador *pa·sa·dor m* bobby pin; cuff link

pasajero(a) *pa·sa·khe·ro(a) m/f* passenger

pasamano *pa·sa·ma·no m* handrail (*on stairs*)

pasaporte *pa·sa·por·te m* passport

pasar *pa·sar vt/i* pass; spend (*time*); **hágame el favor de pasarme el azúcar** *a·ga·me el fa·bor de pa·sar·me el a·thoo·kar* please pass the sugar; **¿pasa algo?** *pa·sa al·go* what's wrong; **¿qué le pasó?** *ke le pa·so* what happened to him?; **me pasó corriendo** *me pa·so ko·rryen·do* he ran past me; **pasar de contrabando** *pa·sar de kon·tra·ban·do* to smuggle; **pasarlo bien** *pa·sar·lo byen* to have a good time; **pasar por Londres** *pa·sar por lon·dres* to go by London (*via*)

pasarela *pa·sa·re·la f* gangway (*bridge*)

pasatiempo *pa·sa·tyem·po m* hobby

Pascua *pas·kwa f* Easter

pasearse *pa·se·ar·se vr* walk; stroll (*for pleasure, exercise*)

paseo *pa·se·o* m walk; ride (*in vehicle*); walking; stroll; avenue, promenade (*by sea*); **dar* un paseo** *dar oon pa·se·o* to go for a walk/ stroll; **dar* un paseo en coche** *dar oon pa·se·o en ko·che* to go for a drive; **el paseo a caballo** *pa·se·o a ka·bal·yo* ride (*on horse*); **el paseo marítimo** *pa·se·o ma·ree·tee·mo* front (*seaside*); promenade

pasillo *pa·seel·yo* m corridor; passage; gangway; **el pasillo mecánico** *pa·seel·yo me·ka·nee·ko* moving walkway

pasión *pa·syon* f passion

pasivo *pa·see·bo* m liabilities (*on balance sheet*)

paso *pa·so* m step; pace; **llevar el mismo paso que** *lye·bar el mees·mo pa·so ke* to keep pace with; **el paso superior** *pa·so soo·pe·ryor* overpass; **el paso a nivel** *pa·so a nee·bel* grade crossing; **el paso subterráneo** *pa·so soob·te·rra·ne·o* underpass (*for pedestrians*); **el paso interior** *pa·so een·fe·ryor* underpass (*for cars*); **el paso de peatones** *pa·so de pe·a·to·nes* crosswalk

pasta *pas·ta* f pastry; pasta; **la pasta de almendra** *pas·ta de al·men·dra* almond paste; **pasta dentífricia** *pas·ta den·tee·free·thya* tooth paste

pastel *pas·tel* m cake; **el pastel de carne** *pas·tel de kar·ne* meat paste

pastelería *pas·te·le·ree·a* f pastry (*cake*)

pastelero *pus·te·le·ro* m confectioner

pasteurizado(a) *pas·te·oo·ree·tha·do(a)* adj pasteurized

pastilla *pas·teel·ya* f tablet (*medicine*); pastille; **las pastillas para la tos** *pas·teel·yas pa·ra la tos* cough drops

pastilla (de jabón) *pas·teel·ya (de kha·bon)* f bar of soap

pastor *pas·tor* m minister (*of religion*)

pata *pa·ta* f leg (*of animal*); foot; paw

patada *pa·ta·da* f kick

patata *pa·ta·ta* f potato; **las patatas fritas (a la inglesa)** *pa·ta·tas free·tas (a la een·gle·sa)* chips; **las patatas fritas** *pa·ta·tas free·tas* french fried potatoes, french fries

paté *pa·te* m pâté

patente *pa·ten·te* f patent

patillas *pa·teel·yas* fpl sideburns

patín *pa·teen* m skate (*for ice skating*); skateboard

patinar *pa·tee·nar* vi skate; skid

patinazo *pa·tee·na·tho* m skid

patio *pa·tyo* m patio; courtyard; **el patio de recreo** *pa·tyo de re·kre·o* playground

pato *pa·to* m duck

patrón *pa·tron* m pattern (*dressmaking, knitting*); landlord

patrona *pa·tro·na* f landlady

patrulla *pa·trool·ya* f patrol

pausa *pow·sa* f pause

pavo *pa·bo* m turkey

payaso *pa·ya·so* m clown

paz *path* f peace

P.D. *pe·de* abbrev P.S.

peaje *pe·a·khe* m toll (*on road etc*)

peatón *pe·a·ton* m pedestrian

pecho *pe·cho* m breast; chest (*of body*)

pechuga *pe·choo·ga* f breast (*of poultry*)

pedacito *pe·da·thee·to* m scrap (*bit*)

pedal *pe·dal* m pedal

pedazo *pe·da·tho* m bit; piece

pediatra *pe·dya·tra* m/f pediatrician

pedicuro *pe·dee·koo·ro* m podiatrist

pedido *pe·dee·do* m order (*for goods*); **hacer* un pedido a alguien** *a·ther oon pe·dee·do a al·gyen* to place an order with someone; **el pedido renovado** *pe·dee·do re·no·ba·do* repeat order

pedir* *pe·deer* vt ask (for); **pedir* prestado algo a alguien** *pe·deer pres·ta·do al·go a al·gyen* to borrow something from someone; **volver* a pedir** *bol·ber a pe·deer* to reorder

pedregoso(a) *pe·dre·go·so(a)* adj stony

pegajoso(a) *pe·ga·kho·so(a)* adj sticky

pegar* *pe·gar* vt hit; strike; **pegar* con cola** *pe·gar kon ko·la* to glue

peinado *pey·na·do* m hair-style

peinar *pey·nar* vt comb

peine *pey·ne* m comb

p.ej. *por e·khem·plo* abbrev e.g.

peladuras *pe·la·doo·ras* fpl peel

pelar *pe·lar* vt peel

pelarse *pe·lar·se* vr peel (*person*)

peldaño *pel·dan·yo* m doorstep; stair

pelea *pe·le·a* f fight

pelear *pe·le·ar* vi fight

película *pe·lee·koo·la* f movie; film; **la película de largo metraje** *pe·lee·koo·la de lar·go me·tra·khe* feature film; **la película de miedo** *pe·lee·koo·la de mye·do* horror movie; **la película del Oeste** *pe·lee·koo·la del o·es·te* western (*movie*); **la película de suspense** *pe·lee·koo·la de soos·pen·se* thriller (*movie*)

peligro *pe·lee·gro* m danger; **fuera de peligro** *fwe·ra de pe·lee·gro* safe (*out of danger*); **un buque en peligro** *oon boo·ke en pe·lee·gro* a ship in distress

peligroso(a) *pe·lee·gro·so(a)* adj dangerous; **no peligroso(a)** *no pe·lee·gro·so(a)* safe (*not dangerous*)

pelirrojo(a) *pe·lec·rro·kho(a)* adj redhaired

pellizcar* *pel·yeeth·kar* vt pinch

pelo *pe·lo* m hair

pelota *pe·lo·ta* f ball; **la pelota de golf** *pe·lo·ta de golf* golf ball

peluca *pe·loo·ka* f wig

peluquero(a) *pe·loo·ke·ro* m/f hairdresser

pena *pe·na* f grief; **¡qué pena!** *ke pe·na* what a pity!

pendiente *pen·dyen·te* m earring □ f la **pendiente** *pen·dyen·te* slope (*angle*)

pene *pe·ne* m penis

penetrar *pe·ne·trar* vt penetrate

penicilina *pe·nee·thee·lee·na* f penicillin

pensar* *pen·sar* vi think; **pienso que...** *pyen·so ke* I feel that...; **pensar* algo bien** *pen·sar al·go byen* to think something over; **pensar* en algo** *pen·sar en al·go* to think of something; **pensar* en alguien** *pen·sar en al·gyen* to think about someone; **pensar* hacer** *pen·sar a·ther* to mean to do

pensión *pen·syon* f lodgings; boarding house; pension (*from State*)

Pentecostés *pen·te·kos·tes* m Whitsun

peor *pe·or* adj, adv worse; **hacer* algo peor** *a·ther al·go pe·or* to do something worse; **el peor** *el pe·or* the worst; **lo hizo peor que todos** *lo ee·tho pe·or ke to·dos* he did it worst of all

pepinillo *pe·pee·neel·yo* m gherkin

pepino *pe·pee·no* m cucumber

pequeño(a) *pe·ken·yo(a)* adj little; small; slight

pera *pe·ra* f pear

percha *per·cha f* coat hanger; peg (*for coat*)

perchero *per·che·ro m* hat stand

perder *per·der vt* miss (*train*); lose; **perder el tiempo** *per·der el tyem·po* to waste one's time

perderse *per·der·se vr* lose one's way

pérdida *per·dee·da f* loss

perdiz *per·deeth f* partridge

perdón *per·don m* pardon □ *excl* ¡perdón! *per·don* pardon!

perdonar *per·do·nar vt* forgive; ¡perdone Ud! *per·do·ne oos·ted* pardon me!, (I beg your) pardon!

peregrinación *pe·re·gree·na·thyon f* pilgrimage

peregrino(a) *pe·re·gree·no(a) m/f* pilgrim

perejil *pe·re·kheel m* parsley

perezoso(a) *pe·re·tho·so(a) adj* lazy

perfecto(a) *per·fek·to(a) adj* perfect

perfume *per·foo·me m* scent; perfume

pericote *pe·ree·ko·te m* mouse

perímetro torácico *pe·ree·me·tro to·ra·thee·ko m* bust measurements

periódico *pe·ree·o·dee·ko m* newspaper; el periódico de la tarde *pe·ree·o·dee·ko de la tar·de* evening paper

periodismo *pe·ryo·dees·mo m* journalism

periodista *pe·ryo·dees·ta m/f* journalist; reporter

período *pe·ree·o·do m* period (*time*; *menstruation*)

perla *per·la f* pearl

permanecer *per·ma·ne·ther vi* remain; survive (*custom*); **permanecer en casa** *per·ma·ne·ther en ka·sa* to stay at home

permanente *per·ma·nen·te adj* permanent □ *f* la permanente *per·ma·nen·te* perm

permanentemente *per·ma·nen·te·men·te adv* permanently

permiso *per·mee·so m* permission; pass; permit; leave (*holiday*); el permiso de salida *per·mee·so de sa·lee·da* exit permit; el permiso de conducir *per·mee·so de kon·doo·theer* driver's license; de permiso *de per·mee·so* on leave; permiso de pesca *per·mee·so de pes·ka* fishing license; permiso de trabajo *per·mee·so de tra·ba·kho* work permit

permitir *per·mee·teer vt* permit (*something*); **permitir a alguien que haga algo** *per·mee·teer a al·gyen ke a·ga al·go* to permit someone to do something

permitirse *per·mee·teer·se vr* afford; **permitirse un coche nuevo** *per·mee·teer·se oon ko·che nwe·bo* to afford a new car

pero *pe·ro conj* but

perro *pe·rro m* dog; el perro caliente *pe·rro ka·lyen·te* hot dog; el perro para ciegos *pe·rro pa·ra thye·gos* guidedog

persa *per·sa adj* Persian

perseguir *per·se·geer vt* chase

persiana *per·sya·na f* window shade

persona *per·so·na f* person; en persona *en per·so·na* in person; otra persona *o·tra per·so·na* someone else

personaje *per·so·na·khe m* personality; el personaje importante *per·so·na·khe eem·por·tan·te* V.I.P.

personal *per·so·nal adj* personal □ *m* el personal *per·so·nal* staff; personnel

personalidad *per·so·na·lee·dad f* personality

personalmente *per·so·nal·men·te adv* personally

perspectiva *pers·pek·tee·ba f* outlook; prospect; scene (*sight*)

perspicaz *pers·pee·kath adj* shrewd

persuadir *per·swa·deer vt* persuade; **persuadir a alguien a hacer algo** *per·swa·deer a al·gyen a a·ther al·go* to persuade someone to do something

pertenecer a *per·te·ne·ther a vi* belong to; **pertenecer a un club** *per·te·ne·ther a oon kloob* to belong to a club

pertinente *per·tee·nen·te adj* relevant

Perú *pe·roo m* Peru

peruano(a) *pe·rwa·no(a) adj* Peruvian

pesadilla *pe·sa·deel·ya f* nightmare

pesado(a) *pe·sa·do(a) adj* heavy; boring; **demasiado pesado(a)** *de·ma·sya·do pe·sa·do(a)* overweight; es muy pesado *es mooy pe·sa·do* he's a nuisance

pesar *pe·sar vt* weigh; **a pesar de** *a pe·sar de* in spite of; pesa 4 kilos *pe·sa 4 kee·los* it weighs 4 kilos

pesca *pes·ka f* fishing; catch

pescadería *pes·ka·de·ree·a f* fish shop

pescadero *pes·ka·de·ro m* fishmonger

pescadilla *pes·ka·deel·ya f* whiting

pescado *pes·ka·do m* fish (*as food*)

pescador *pes·ka·dor m* angler; fisherman

pescar *pes·kar vt/i* fish; **ir a pescar** *eer a pes·kar* to go fishing

peseta *pe·se·ta f* peseta

pesimista *pe·see·mees·ta adj* pessimistic

pésimo(a) *pe·see·mo(a) adj* awful

peso *pe·so m* peso; weight (*mass*); **peso neto** *pe·so ne·to* net weight

pestaña *pes·tan·ya f* eyelash

pestañear *pes·tan·ye·ar vi* blink

petaca *pe·ta·ka f* cigarette case

petardo *pe·tar·do m* cracker

petición *pe·tee·thyon f* request

petróleo *pe·tro·le·o m* oil (*petroleum*)

petrolero *pe·tro·le·ro m* oil tanker; tanker (*ship*)

pez *peth m, pl* peces *pe·thes* fish; el pez de colores *peth de ko·lo·res* goldfish

piano *pee·a·no m* piano; el piano de cola *pee·a·no de ko·la* grand piano

picadura *pee·ka·doo·ra f* bite (*by insect*); sting

picante *pee·kan·te adj* peppery; hot; spicy

picaporte *pee·ka·por·te m* latch

picar *pee·kar vi* itch; knock (*engine*) □ *vt* mince; sting; pierce; punch (*ticket etc*); chop (*food*)

pico *pee·ko m* pickax; peak (*of mountain*)

picor *pee·kor m* itch

picos *pee·kos mpl* spades (*cards*)

picotear *pee·ko·te·ar vt* peck

pie *pye m* foot (*of person*; *measurement*); bottom (*of page, list*); **estar de pie** *es·tar de pye* to stand; **ponerse de pie** *po·ner·se de pye* to stand up

piedad *pye·dad f* pity

piedra *pye·dra f* stone; flint (*in lighter*); la piedra preciosa *pye·dra pre·thyo·sa* gem

piel *pyel f* fur; skin; la piel de cerdo *pyel de ther·do* pigskin; la piel de carnero *pyel de kar·ne·ro* sheepskin

pierna *pyer·na f* leg; pierna de cordero *pyer·na de kor·de·ro* leg of lamb

pieza *pye·tha f* component; part (*of machine*)

pijama *pee·kha·ma m* pajamas

pila *pee·la f* battery (*for radio etc*)

pilar *pee·lar* m pillar

píldora *peel·do·ra* f pill; la píldora anticonceptiva *peel·do·ra an·tee·kon·thep·tee·ba* pill (*contraceptive*); tomar la píldora *to·mar la peel·do·ra* to be on the pill

piloto *pee·lo·to* m pilot; captain (*of plane*)

pimentero *pee·men·te·ro* m pepper pot

pimentón *pee·men·ton* m paprika

pimienta *pee·myen·ta* f pepper

pimiento *pee·myen·to* m pepper (*capsicum*); el pimiento verde/rojo *pee·myen·to ber·de/ro·kho* green/red pepper

piña *peen·ya* f pineapple

pincel *peen·thel* m brush (*for painting*)

pinchar *peen·char* vt prick; puncture

pinchazo *peen·cha·tho* m blow-out; puncture

pincho *peen·cho* m kebab

ping-pong *peeng·pong* m ping-pong

pino *pee·no* m pine

pintar *peen·tar* vt paint

pintor *peen·tor* m painter; el pintor (de brocha gorda) *peen·tor (de bro·cha gor·da)* painter (*decorator*)

pintoresco(a) *peen·to·res·ko(a)* adj picturesque

pintura *peen·too·ra* f paint; painting; pintura al óleo *peen·too·ra al o·le·o* oil painting

pinza *peen·tha* f clothespin; dart (*on clothes*)

pinzas *peen·thas* fpl tweezers

pipa *pee·pa* f pipe (*for smoking*)

piquete *pee·ke·te* m picket

piragüismo *pee·ra·gwees·mo* m canoeing

pirámide *pee·ra·mee·de* f pyramid

Pirineos *pee·ree·ne·os* mpl Pyrenees

pisar *pee·sar* vt step on; tread on; ¡no pise el césped! *no pee·se el thes·ped* get off the grass

piscina *pees·thee·na* f swimming pool; la piscina para niños *pees·thee·na pa·ra neen·yos* wading pool

piso *pee·so* m floor; story; apartment; de pisos *de pee·sos* multilevel; el primer piso *pree·mer pee·so* first floor (*Brit*), second floor (*US*)

pista *pees·ta* f track (*of animal, record, for sports*); la pista de aterrizaje *pees·ta de a·te·rree·tha·khe* runway; en pista cubierta *en pees·ta koo·byer·ta* indoor (*games*); la pista de baile *pees·ta de bay·le* dance floor; la pista de esquí *pees·ta de es·kee* ski run; la pista de hielo *pees·ta de ye·lo* rink; la pista de tenis *pees·ta de te·nees* tennis court; la pista de patinaje *pees·ta de pa·tee·na·khe* skating rink

pistolero *pees·to·le·ro* m gunman

pistón *pees·ton* m piston

pizarra *pee·tha·rra* f slate; blackboard

pizca *peeth·ka* f pinch (*of salt etc*)

pizza *peet·sa* f pizza

placa *pla·ka* f □ la placa de silicio *pla·ka de see·lee·thyo* microchip

placar *pla·kar* vi tackle (*in sports*)

placer *pla·ther* m pleasure; enjoyment

plan *plan* m scheme; plan; hacer* un plan de *a·ther oon plan de* to plan (*make a design*)

plancha *plan·cha* f iron (*for clothes*); que no necesita plancha *ke no ne·the·see·ta plan·cha* drip-dry (*shirt etc*)

planchar *plan·char* vt press; iron

planeador *pla·ne·a·dor* m glider

planear *pla·ne·ar* vt plan

planeta *pla·ne·ta* m planet

planetario *pla·ne·ta·ryo* m planetarium

planificación *pla·nee·fee·ka·thyon* f planning (*economic*)

plano(a) *pla·no(a)* adj level (*surface*) □ m plan (*drawing, design*); map (*of town*)

planta *plan·ta* f plant; sole (*of foot*)

planta baja *plan·ta ba·kha* f first floor

plantar *plan·tar* vt plant

plástico(a) *plas·tee·ko* m plastic; de plástico *de plas·tee·ko* plastic

plata *pla·ta* f silver (*metal*); money; una pulsera de plata *oo·na pool·se·ra de pla·ta* a silver bracelet

plataforma *pla·ta·for·ma* f platform; la plataforma de petróleo *pla·ta·for·ma de pe·tro·le·o* oil-rig

plátano *pla·ta·no* m banana; plane (*tree*)

platea *pla·te·a* f orchestra (*in theater*)

platero *pla·te·ro* m silversmith

platija *pla·tee·kha* f plaice

platillo *pla·teel·yo* m saucer

platino *pla·tee·no* m platinum

plato *pla·to* m plate; dish (*food*); course (*of meal*); el plato combinado *pla·to kom·bee·na·do* mixed grill

playa *pla·ya* f beach

playeras *pla·ye·ras* fpl sneakers

plaza *pla·tha* f square (*in town*); la plaza del mercado *pla·tha del mer·ka·do* marketplace; plaza de toros *pla·tha de to·ros* bull ring

plazo *pla·tho* m period; time limit; instalment; a corto plazo *a kor·to pla·tho* short term

pleamar *ple·a·mar* f high tide; la marea está a pleamar/bajamar *la ma·re·a es·ta a ple·a·mar/ba·kha·mar* the tide is in/out

plexiglás *plek·see·glas* m plexiglas

plisado(a) *plee·sa·do(a)* adj pleated

plomo *plo·mo* m lead

pluma *ploo·ma* f feather; pen

población *po·bla·thyon* f population

pobre *po·bre* adj poor

poco(a) *po·ko(a)* adj little; scanty □ m un poco *oon po·ko* a little; un poco de *oon po·ko de* a bit of; dentro de poco *den·tro de po·ko* shortly (*soon*); quedó un poco (de ello) *ke·do oon po·ko (de el·yo)* some (of it) was left; un poco más arriba del codo *oon po·ko mas a·rree·ba del ko·do* just above the elbow; por poco *por po·ko* only just; poco a poco *po·ko a po·ko* little by little

pocos(as) *po·kos(as)* adj few; hay muy pocos *ay mooy po·kos* there are very few

podar *po·dar* vt prune; trim (*hedge*)

poder* *po·der* vi be able □ m el poder *po·der* power (*authority*); no lo puedo remediar *no lo pwe·do re·me·dyar* I can't help it; ¿se puede entrar? *se pwe·de en·trar* may I come in?; puede que llueva *pwe·de ke lywe·ba* it might rain; no poder* hacer algo *no po·der a·ther al·go* to be unable to do something; ¿puede Ud con eso? *pwe·de oos·ted kon e·so* can you manage?

poderoso(a) *po·de·ro·so(a)* adj powerful (*person*)

podrido(a) *po·dree·do(a)* adj rotten

poema *po·e·ma* m poem

poesía *po·e·see·a* f poetry

polaco(a) *po·la·ko(a)* adj Polish □ m/f el/la polaco(a) *po·la·ko(a)* Pole □ m el polaco *po·la·ko* Polish

polaroid *po·la·ro·eed* adj Polaroid

policía *po·lee·thee·a* f police □ m el policía *po·lee·thee·a* officer (*police*); policeman

polietileno *po·lee·e·tee·le·no* m polyethylene

polio *po·lee·o* f polio

política *po·lee·tee·ka* f politics; policy; la política exterior *po·lee·tee·ka eks·te·ryor* foreign policy

político(a) *po·lee·tee·ko(a)* adj political □ m el político *po·lee·tee·ko* politician

póliza *po·lee·tha* f policy; la póliza de seguros *po·lee·tha de se·goo·ros* insurance policy

pollo *po·lyo* m chicken

polo *po·lo* m popsicle; pole; terminal (*electricity*)

Polonia *po·lo·nya* f Poland

Polo Norte *po·lo nor·te* m North Pole

Polo Sur *po·lo soor* m South Pole

polvo *pol·bo* m dust; powder; polvo facial *pol·bo fa·thyal* face powder; el polvo de curry *pol·bo de koo·rre* curry powder

polvoriento(a) *pol·bo·ryen·to(a)* adj dusty

polvos *pol·bos* mpl powder (*cosmetic*)

polyester *po·lyes·ter* m polyester

pomelo *po·me·lo* m grapefruit

ponche *pon·che* m punch (*drink*)

poner* *po·ner* vt put; place; switch on (*TV*); set (*alarm*); lay; poner* a media luz *po·ner a me·dya looth* to dim (*headlights*); poner* a alguien con otro *po·ner a al·gyen kon o·tro* to put someone through (*on phone*); póngame con el Sr X *pon·ga·me kon el sen·yor X* put me through to Mr X; poner* la mesa *po·ner la me·sa* to lay the table; poner* el capital *po·ner el ka·pee·tal* to put up capital; poner* a uno triste *po·ner a oo·no trees·te* to make someone sad; poner* mas fuerte *po·ner mas fwer·te* to turn up (*heat*); póngalo a mi cuenta *pon·ga·lo a mee kwen·ta* charge it to my account; ¿cuándo ponen la película? *kwan·do po·nen la pe·lee·koo·la* when is the movie on?

ponerse* *po·ner·se* vr become; place oneself; ponerse* un vestido *po·ner·se oon bes·tee·do* to put on a dress

poney *po·nee* m pony

pop *pop* adj pop (*music, art*)

popelina *po·pe·lee·na* f poplin

popular *po·poo·lar* adj popular

póquer *po·ker* m poker (*card game*)

por *por* prep for; per; via; through; about; por qué *por ke* why; 100 km por hora *100 kee·lo·me·tros por o·ra* 100 km per hour; 20 por ciento *20 por thyen·to* 20 per cent; por persona *por per·so·na* per person; por lo visto *por lo bees·to* apparently; por aquí *por a·kee* about here; this way; por la calle *por la kal·ye* along the street; por mí *por mee* for my sake; por la tarde *por la tar·de* in the evening; por todas partes *por to·das par·tes* everywhere; por el bosque *por el bos·ke* through the wood; 3 metros por 3 *3 me·tros por 3* 3 meters square; $40 por semana *$40 por se·ma·na* $40 a week

porcelana *por·the·la·na* f china; porcelain

porcentaje *por·then·ta·khe* m percentage

porción *por·thyon* f helping; portion

porque *por·ke* conj because

porrazo *po·rra·tho* m thump

portaequipajes *por·ta·e·kee·pa·khes* m luggage rack; trunk (*in car*)

portafolio *por·ta·fo·lyo* m briefcase

portarse *por·tar·se* vr behave; ¡pórtate bien! *por·ta·te byen* behave yourself!

portátil *por·ta·teel* adj portable

portavoz *por·ta·both* m spokesman

portazo *por·ta·tho* m bang (*of door*); dar* un portazo *dar oon por·ta·tho* to slam

portero *por·te·ro* m caretaker; doorman (*in hotel*); goalkeeper; el portero de noche *por·te·ro de no·che* night porter

pórtico *por·tee·ko* m porch

portilla *por·teel·ya* f porthole

portillo *por·teel·yo* m gate

Portugal *por·too·gal* m Portugal

portugués(esa) *por·too·ges(·ge·sa)* adj Portuguese □ m el portugués *por·too·ges* Portuguese

porvenir *por·be·neer* m future

posada *po·sa·da* f inn

posavasos *po·sa·ba·sos* m mat (*under a glass*)

poseer *po·se·er* vt own (*possess*)

posesión *po·se·syon* f ownership

posfechar *pos·fe·char* vt postdate

posibilidad *po·see·bee·lee·dad* f possibility; tiene buenas posibilidades de... *tye·ne bwe·nas po·see·bee·lee·da·des de* he has a good chance of...

posible *po·see·ble* adj possible; es posible que llueva *es po·see·ble ke lywe·ba* it may rain; hacer* todo lo posible *a·ther to·do lo po·see·ble* to do all one possibly can

posiblemente *po·see·ble·men·te* adv possibly

posición *po·see·thyon* f position

positiva *po·see·tee·ba* f positive

positivo(a) *po·see·tee·bo(a)* adj positive

posos *po·sos* mpl grounds; sediment (*of coffee*)

postal *pos·tal* adj postal; la (tarjeta) postal *tar·khe·ta pos·tal* postcard

poste *pos·te* m mast (*radio*); post (*pole*); el poste de tienda *pos·te de tyen·da* tent pole; el poste indicador *pos·te een·de·ka·dor* signpost

posterior *pos·te·ryor* adj back; later (*date etc*)

postor *pos·tor* m bidder

postre *pos·tre* m dessert

potencia *po·ten·thya* f power; la potencia mundial *po·ten·thya moon·dyal* world power

potente *po·ten·te* adj powerful

pozo *po·tho* m well

práctico(a) *prak·tee·ko(a)* adj convenient; practical; prácticas para las tiendas *prak·tee·ko pa·ra las tyen·das* convenient to stores; poco práctico(a) *po·ko prak·tee·ko(a)* inconvenient

Praga *pra·ga* f Prague

precedente *pre·the·den·te* f precedent

precio *pre·thyo* m price; el precio del cubierto *pre·thyo del koo·byer·to* cover charge; el precio del viaje *pre·thyo del bee·a·khe* fare (*in taxi*); el precio por unidad *pre·thyo por oo·nee·dad* unit price; el precio fijo *pre·thyo fee·kho* flat rate; el precio mínimo *pre·thyo mee·nee·mo* upset price; el precio de catálogo *pre·thyo de ka·ta·lo·go* list price; comprar algo a precio de coste *kom·prar al·go a pre·thyo de kos·te* to buy something at cost; **el precio al por menor** *pre·thyo al por me·nor* retail price; **el precio de entrada** *pre·thyo de en·tra·da* entrance fee

precioso(a) *pre·thyo·so(a) adj* precious; beautiful

precipicio *pre·thee·pee·thyo m* cliff

precipitarse *pre·thee·pee·tar·se vr* rush

precisión *pre·thee·syon f* precision

predilecto(a) *pre·dee·lek·to(a) adj* favorite

preestreno *pre·es·tre·no m* preview

preferir* *pre·fe·reer vt* prefer; **preferiría ir al cine** *pre·fe·re·ree·a eer al thee·ne* I'd rather go to the movies

prefijo *pre·fee·kho m* prefix; area code

pregunta *pre·goon·ta f* question; **hacer* una pregunta** *a·ther oo·na pre·goon·ta* to ask a question

preguntar *pre·goon·tar vt/i* ask; **preguntar la hora a alguien** *pre·goon·tar la o·ra a al·gyen* to ask someone the time; **preguntar el precio** *pre·goon·tar el pre·thyo* to ask the price

preguntarse *pre·goon·tar·se vr* wonder; **preguntarse si...** *pre·goon·tar·se see* to wonder whether...

prejuicio *pre·khwee·thyo m* prejudice

preliminar *pre·lee·mee·nar adj* preliminary

premio *pre·myo m* prize; **el Gran Premio** *gran pre·myo* Grand Prix

prenda *pren·da f* garment

prender *pren·der vt* switch on; turn on; **prender con alfiler** *pren·der kon al·fee·ler* to pin

prensa *pren·sa f* press (*newspapers, journalists*)

preocupación *pre·o·koo·pa·thyon f* worry; concern (*anxiety*)

preocupado(a) *pre·o·koo·pa·do(a) adj* worried

preparación *pre·pa·ra·thyon f* preparation

preparar *pre·pa·rar vt* prepare; fix; train; **preparar el fuego** *pre·pa·rar el fwe·go* to lay the fire; **preparar para tratamiento con ordenador** *pre·pa·rar pa·ra tra·ta·myen·to kon or·de·na·dor* to computerize (*system*)

prepararse *pre·pa·rar·se vr* to get ready; **se prepara a marcharse** *se pre·pa·ra a mar·char·se* he's preparing to leave

preparativos *pre·pa·ra·tee·bos mpl* preparations

presa *pre·sa f* dam

présbita *pres·bee·ta adj* far-sighted

presbiteriano(a) *pres·bee·te·rya·no(a) adj* Presbyterian

presentación *pre·sen·ta·thyon f* introduction; presentation

presentar *pre·sen·tar vt* present; introduce (*person*)

presentarse *pre·sen·tar·se vr* check in (*at airport*)

presente *pre·sen·te adj* present

preservativo *pre·ser·ba·tee·bo m* prophylactic (*contraceptive*)

presidente *pre·see·den·te m* president (*of country*); chairman

presión *pre·syon f* pressure; **las presiones de la vida moderna** *las pre·syo·nes de la bee·da mo·der·na* the pressures of modern life

preso *pre·so m* prisoner

préstamo *pres·ta·mo m* loan; **el préstamo bancario** *pres·ta·mo ban·ka·ryo* bank loan

prestar *pres·tar vt* lend; loan

prestigio *pres·tee·khyo m* prestige

presumido(a) *pre·soo·mee·do(a) adj* familiar (*impertinent*)

presupuesto *pre·soo·pwes·to m* estimate; budget

previsión *pre·bee·syon f* forecast

prima *pree·ma f* premium; bonus (*on salary*)

primario(a) *pree·ma·ryo(a) adj* primary

primavera *pree·ma·be·ra f* spring (*season*)

primer, primero(a) *pree·mer, pree·me·ro(a) adj* first □ *adv* primero *pree·me·ro* first; **en primera** *en pree·me·ra* in first (*gear*); **en primer lugar** *en pree·mer loo·gar* at first; in the first place; **los primeros auxilios** *pree·me·ros owk·see·lyos* first aid; **el primer ministro** *pree·mer mee·nees·tro* prime minister; **de primera** *de pree·me·ra* top (*in rank*); **de primera clase** *de pree·me·ra kla·se* first-class (*work etc*); **viajar en primera** *bee·a·khar en pree·me·ra* to travel first class

primo(a) *pree·mo(a) m/f* cousin

princesa *preen·the·sa f* princess

principal *preen·thee·pal adj* major; main □ *m* **el principal** *preen·thee·pal* dress circle

principalmente *preen·thee·pal·men·te adv* mainly

príncipe *preen·thee·pe m* prince

principiante *preen·thee·pyan·te m/f* beginner

principio *preen·thee·pyo m* principle; **al principio** *al preen·thee·pyo* originally (*at first*)

prioridad de paso *pree·o·ree·dad de pa·so f* right of way

prisa *pree·sa f* rush; haste; **tener* prisa** *te·ner pree·sa* to be in a hurry; **de prisa** *de pree·sa* fast; **darse* prisa** *dar·se pree·sa* to hurry; **¡date prisa!** *da·te pree·sa* be quick!

prismáticos *prees·ma·tee·kos mpl* field glasses; binoculars

privado(a) *pree·ba·do(a) adj* personal; private; **en privado** *en pree·ba·do* in private

probable *pro·ba·ble adj* likely; probable; **es probable que venga** *es pro·ba·ble ke ben·ga* he's likely to come

probablemente *pro·ba·ble·men·te adv* probably

probar* *pro·bar vt* try; sample (*wine*); taste; test (*product*); prove (*fact*); **probarse* un vestido** *pro·bar·se oon bes·tee·do* to try on a dress

problema *pro·ble·ma m* problem

procedimiento *pro·the·dee·myen·to m* procedure; **el procedimiento deshonesto** *pro·the·dee·myen·to des·o·nes·to* sharp practice

procesar *pro·the·sar vt* try (*in law*)

proceso *pro·the·so m* process; trial

producción *pro·dook·thyon f* production; output

producir* *pro·doo·theer vt* produce; bring in (*profit*); produce (*movie*)

productividad *pro·dook·tee·bee·dad f* productivity

producto *pro·dook·to m* product; **el producto nacional bruto** *pro·dook·to na·thyo·nal broo·to* gross national product

productor(a) *pro·dook·tor(·ra) m/f* producer

productos *pro·dook·tos mpl* produce

profesión *pro·fe·syon f* profession

profesional *pro·fe·syo·nal adj* pro-

fessional; **hacerse* profesional** *a·ther·se pro·fe·syo·nal* to turn professional
profesor(a) *pro·fe·sor(·ra) m/f* teacher (*secondary school*); **profesor(a) agregado(a)** *pro·fe·sor(·ra) a·gre·ga·do(a)* professor (*in US*); **el profesor particular** *pro·fe·sor par·tee·koo·lar* tutor
profiterole *pro·fee·te·rol m* profiterole
profundidad *pro·foon·dee·dad f* depth
profundo(a) *pro·foon·do(a) adj* deep
programa *pro·gra·ma m* program; schedule; **el programa de estudios** *pro·gra·ma de es·too·dyos* syllabus
programación *pro·gra·ma·thyon f* programming; computer programming
programador *pro·gra·ma·dor m* programmer
programar *pro·gra·mar vt* program
progresar *pro·gre·sar vi* make progress
progreso *pro·gre·so m* progress
prohibición *pro·ee·bee·thyon f* ban
prohibido(a) *pro·ee·bee·do(a) adj* prohibited; **prohibido estacionarse** *pro·ee·bee·do es·ta·thyo·nar·se* no parking (*road sign*); **prohibido el paso** *pro·ee·bee·do el pa·so* no entry; **prohibida la reventa** *pro·ee·bee·da la re·ben·ta* not for resale
prohibir *pro·ee·beer vt* ban; prohibit; forbid; **prohibir a alguien que haga algo** *pro·ee·beer a al·gyen ke a·ga al·go* to forbid someone to do something
prólogo *pro·lo·go m* introduction (*in book*)
promedio *pro·me·dyo m* average
promesa *pro·me·sa f* promise
prometer *pro·me·ter vt* promise
prometido(a) *pro·me·tee·do(a) adj* engaged (*betrothed*)
promoción *pro·mo·thyon f* promotion (*of product*)
promocionar *pro·mo·thyo·nar vt* promote
promotor *pro·mo·tor m* backer
promover* *pro·mo·ber vt* promote (*product*)
pronosticar* *pro·nos·tee·kar vt* predict
pronóstico *pro·nos·tee·ko m* forecast; prediction
pronto *pron·to adv* soon
pronunciación *pro·noon·thee·a·thyon f* pronunciation
pronunciar* *pro·noon·thyar vt* pronounce
propagarse* *pro·pa·gar·se vr* spread (*news*)
propiedad *pro·pye·dad f* property
propina *pro·pee·na f* tip (*money given*)
propio(a) *pro·pyo(a) adj* own
proponer* *pro·po·ner vt* propose (*suggest*)
proporción *pro·por·thyon f* ratio; proportion
proporcionar *pro·por·thyo·nar vt* provide; **proporcionar algo a alguien** *pro·por·thyo·nar al·go a al·gyen* to provide someone with something
proposición *pro·po·see·thyon f* proposition (*proposal*)
propósito *pro·po·see·to m* purpose; aim (*intention*); **a propósito** *a pro·po·see·to* by the way; on purpose
propietario(a) *pro·pye·ta·ryo(a) m/f* owner
propuesta *pro·pwes·ta f* proposal (*suggestion*)
prospecto *pros·pek·to m* prospectus
próspero(a) *pros·pe·ro(a) adj* prosperous; successful (*businessman*)
prostituta *pros·tee·too·ta f* call girl

protección *pro·tek·thyon f* cover (*insurance*); protection
proteger* *pro·te·kher vt* guard; protect
proteína *pro·te·ee·na f* protein
protesta *pro·tes·ta f* protest
protestante *pro·tes·tan·te adj* Protestant
protestar *pro·tes·tar vi* protest; **protestar contra una observación** *pro·tes·tar kon·tra oo·na ob·ser·ba·thyon* to object to a remark
prototipo *pro·to·tee·po m* prototype
provecho *pro·be·cho m* benefit
proveer *pro·be·er vt* supply
provincia *pro·been·thya f* province (*region*)
provinciano(a) *pro·been·thya·no(a) adj* provincial
provisional *pro·bee·syo·nal adj* temporary
próximo(a) *prok·see·mo(a) adj* next (*stop, station, week*)
proyectar *pro·yek·tar vt* show (*movie*); plan
proyecto *pro·yek·to m* project (*plan*)
proyector *pro·yek·tor m* projector
prudente *proo·den·te adj* wise (*decision*)
prueba *prwe·ba f* trial; evidence; proof; test; **a prueba** *a prwe·ba* on approval; **someter a prueba** *so·me·ter a prwe·ba* to test; **la prueba en carretera** *prwe·ba en ka·rre·te·ra* test-drive
psicología *see·ko·lo·khee·a f* psychology
psicológico(a) *see·ko·lo·khee·ko(a) adj* psychological
psicólogo(a) *see·ko·lo·go(a) m/f* psychologist
psiquiatra *see·kya·tra m/f* psychiatrist
psiquiátrico(a) *see·kya·tree·ko(a) adj* psychiatric
publicar* *poob·lee·kar vt* publish
publicidad *poo·blee·thee·dad f* publicity; advertising
público(a) *poo·blee·ko(a) adj* public □ *m* **el público** *poo·blee·ko* public; audience; **en público** *en poo·blee·ko* in public
puding *poo·deen m* pudding
pudrir* *poo·dreer vi* rot
pudrirse* *poo·dreer·se vr* go bad (*food*)
puente *pwen·te m* bridge; **el puente aéreo** *pwen·te a·e·reo* shuttle (*service*) (*airline*); **el puente de peaje** *pwen·te de pe·a·khe* toll bridge
puerro *pwe·rro m* leek
puerta *pwer·ta f* door; gate; **la puerta trasera** *pwer·ta tra·se·ra* tailgate (*of car*)
puerto *pwer·to m* pass (*in mountains*); port; harbor; **el puerto deportivo** *pwer·to de·por·tee·bo* marina
puesta *pwes·ta f* stake (*in gambling*); **la puesta del sol** *pwes·ta del sol* sunset
puesto *pwes·to m* stand; stall; position (*job*)
pulcro(a) *pool·kro(a) adj* neat (*appearance*)
pulga *pool·ga f* flea
pulgar *pool·gar m* thumb
pulmón *pool·mon m* lung
pulmonía *pool·mo·nee·a f* pneumonia
pulsera *pool·se·ra f* bracelet
puñal *poon·yal m* dagger
puñetazo *poon·ye·ta·tho m* punch (*blow*); **dar* un puñetazo a** *dar oon poon·ye·ta·tho a* to punch (*with fist*)
puño *poon·yo m* cuff (*of shirt*); fist

punta *poon·ta* f point; tip
puntada *poon·ta·da* f stitch (*sewing*)
punto *poon·to* m period (*punctuation*);
dot; point; **hacer* punto** *a·ther poon·
to* to knit; **los géneros de punto** *los
khe·ner·os de poon·to* knitwear; **el
punto de vista** *poon·to de bees·ta*
point of view; **los puntos de ventaja**
poon·tos de ben·ta·kha odds (*in betting*); **el punto de interrogación** *poon·
to de een·te·rro·ga·thyon* question
mark; **el punto muerto** *poon·to mwer·
to* neutral (*gear*); **estar* a punto de
hacer algo** *es·tar a poon·to de a·ther
al·go* to be about to do something
puntual *poon·twal* adj punctual (*person*)
punzada *poon·tha·da* f stitch (*pain*)
puré *poo·re* m purée; **el puré de patatas** *poo·re de pa·ta·tas* mashed
potatoes
puro(a) *poo·ro(a)* adj pure

Q

que *ke* conj than □ adj **qué** *ke* what,
which □ pron what; whom; **¿qué
más?** *ke mas* what else?; **el que está
en la mesa** *el ke es·ta en la me·sa* the
one on the table; **el día que...** *el dee·
a ke* the day when...; **¿qué tal?** *ke tal*
how are you getting on?; **¿qué lenguas?** *ke len·gwas* which languages?;
mejor que él *me·khor ke el* better
than him; **¿qué desea?** *ke de·se·a*
what do you want?; **¿para qué?** *pa·ra
ke* what's the point?
quebrado(a) *ke·bra·do(a)* adj bankrupt; broken
quebrar *ke·brar* vt/i break; go bankrupt
quedar *ke·dar* vi remain
quedarse *ke·dar·se* vr stay (*remain, reside*); **quedarse la noche** *ke·dar·se la
no·che* to stay the night; **quedarse
con amigos** *ke·dar·se kon a·mee·gos*
to stay with friends; **¡quédese con la
vuelta!** *ke·de·se kon la bwel·ta* keep
the change!
quehaceres *ke·a·the·res* mpl □ **los quehaceres domésticos** *ke·a·the·res do·
mes·tee·kos* housework
queja *ke·kha* f complaint
quejarse *ke·khar·se* vr grumble; **quejarse de** *ke·khar·se de* to complain
about
quemado(a) *ke·ma·do(a)* adj burned;
quemado(a) por el sol *ke·ma·do por
el sol* sunburnt (*painfully*)
quemadura *ke·ma·doo·ra* f burn; **la
quemadura del sol** *ke·ma·doo·ra del
sol* sunburn (*painful*)
quemar *ke·mar* vt burn
quemarse *ke·mar·se* vr burn (oneself);
me he quemado el brazo *me e ke·ma·
do el bra·tho* I've burned my arm
querer* *ke·rer* vt love; want (*wish for*);
quisiera un(a)... *kee·sye·ra oon(·na)*
I should like a...; **¿qué quiere Ud?** *ke
kye·re oos·ted* what would you like?;
querer* decir *ke·rer de·theer* to
mean; **querer* hacer algo** *ke·rer a·
ther al·go* to want to do something;
querer* algo muchísimo *ke·rer al·go
moo·chee·see·mo* to want something
badly
querido(a) *ke·ree·do(a)* adj dear □ m/f
darling; **la querida** *ke·ree·da* mistress
(*lover*)
queroseno *ke·ro·se·no* m kerosene
quesadilla *ke·sa·deel·ya* f cheesecake

queso *ke·so* m cheese; **el queso de nata**
ke·so de na·ta cream cheese
quiche *keesh* f quiche
quien *kyen* pron who; **¿quién?** *kyen*
who?; **¿quién es?** *kyen es* who's
that?; **¿de quién es este libro?** *de kyen
es es·te lee·bro* whose book is this?
quilate *kee·la·te* m carat
químico(a) *kee·mee·ko(a)* adj chemical, □ f **la química** *kee·mee·ka*
chemistry
quince *keen·the* num fifteen
quinto(a) *keen·to(a)* adj fifth
quiosco *kee·os·ko* m stand; **el quiosco
de periódicos** *kee·os·ko de pe·ree·o·
dee·kos* newsstand
quitar *kee·tar* vt remove, quitar el
polvo *kee·tar el pol·bo* to dust (*furniture*); **me lo quitó** *me lo kee·to* he
took it from me
quitarse *kee·tar·se* vr come out (*stain*);
take off (*clothes*)
quitasol *kee·ta·sol* m umbrella (*on
table*); parasol
quizás *kee·thas* adv perhaps

R

rábano *ra·ba·no* m radish; **rábano picante** *ra·ba·no pee·kan·te* horse
radish
rabia *ra·bya* f rabies
rabino *ra·bee·no* m rabbi
racial *ra·thyal* adj racial
racionalización *ra·thyo·na·lee·tha·
thyon* f rationalization
racionalizar* *ra·thyo·na·lee·thar* vt
rationalize
radar *ra·dar* m radar; **el control de radar** *kon·trol de ra·dar* radar trap
radiador *ra·dya·dor* m radiator
radial *ra·dyal* adj radial ply
radiar *ra·dyar* vt broadcast (*on radio*)
radio *ra·dyo* f radio; **por la radio** *por la
ra·dyo* on the radio
radiografía *ra·dyo·gra·fee·a* f X-ray
(*photo*); **hacer* una radiografía** *a·
ther oo·na ra·dyo·gra·fee·a* to X-ray
ráfaga *ra·fa·ga* f gust; squall
raíz *ra·eeth* f root
raja *ra·kha* f split (*tear*)
rallador *ral·ya·dor* m grater
rallar *ral·yar* vt grate (*food*)
rallye *ra·lee* m rally (*sporting*)
rama *ra·ma* f branch (*of tree*)
ramita *ra·mee·ta* f twig
ramo *ra·mo* m bunch (*of flowers*)
rampa *ram·pa* f ramp (*slope*)
rana *ra·na* f frog
ranchera *ran·che·ra* f station wagon;
hatchback (*car*)
rancho *ran·cho* m ranch
rango *ran·go* m rank (*status*)
ranura *ra·noo·ra* f slot
rape *ra·pe* m angler fish
rápidamente *ra·pee·da·men·te* adv
quickly
rápido(a) *ra·pee·do(a)* adj high-speed;
quick; fast (*speedy*) □ m **el rápido** *ra·
pee·do* express train
raqueta *ra·ke·ta* f racket; paddle (*table
tennis etc*); **la raqueta de tenis** *ra·ke·
ta de te·nees* tennis racket
raramente *ra·ra·men·te* adv seldom
raro(a) *ra·ro(a)* adj rare
rascacielos *ras·ka·thye·los* m skyscraper
raso *ra·so* m satin
raspar *ras·par* vt scrape
rastrillo *ras·treel·yo* m rake

rastro *ras·tro m* trace (*mark*); flea market

rata *ra·ta f* rat

ratón *ra·ton m* mouse

ravioles *ra·byo·les mpl* ravioli

raya *ra·ya f* stripe; crease; skate (*fish*); streak; part (*in hair*)

rayo *ra·yo m* beam (*of light*); ray

raza *ra·tha f* race (*people*)

razón *ra·thon f* reason; razón de *ra·thon de* apply to; a razón de *a ra·thon de* at the rate of; no tiene razón *no tye·ne ra·thon* you're wrong

razonable *ra·tho·na·ble adj* reasonable (*rational*)

reacción *re·ak·thyon f* reaction; a reacción *a re·ak·thyon* jet-propelled

reactor *re·ak·tor m* reactor

real *re·al adj* royal □ *m* el real de la feria *re·al de la fe·rya* fairground

realidad *re·a·lee·dad f* reality; truth; en realidad *en re·a·lee·dad* in fact

realizar *re·a·lee·thar vt* realize (*assets*)

realmente *re·al·men·te adv* in real terms

reanimar *re·a·nee·mar vt* revive

rebaja *re·ba·ja f* reduction (*in price*)

rebajar *re·ba·khar vt* reduce

rebajas *re·ba·khas fpl* sales (*cheap prices*)

rebaño *re·ban·yo m* flock

rebotar *re·bo·tar vi* bounce

recado *re·ka·do m* errand; message; hacer* un recado *a·ther oon re·ka·do* to run an errand

recalentarse *re·ka·len·tar·se vr* overheat (*engine*)

recargo *re·kar·go m* bank charges

recauchutado *re·kow·choo·ta·do m* retread

recepción *re·thep·thyon f* reception (*gathering, radio*); reception desk; pagar* contra recepción *pa·gar kon·tra re·thep·thyon* cash on delivery

recepcionista *re·thep·thyo·nees·ta f* receptionist (*in hotel*)

receptor de control *re·thep·tor de kon·trol m* monitor (*TV*)

recesión *re·the·syon f* recession

receta *re·the·ta f* recipe; prescription

rechazar *re·cha·thar vt* refuse; reject; ser* rechazado *ser re·cha·tha·do* to bounce (*check*)

recibir *re·thee·beer vt* receive; entertain (*give hospitality*)

recibo *re·thee·bo m* receipt

reciclaje *re·thee·kla·khe m* retraining; hacer* un reciclaje *a·ther oon re·thee·kla·khe* to retrain

reciclar *re·thee·klar vt* retrain

reciente *re·thyen·te adj* recent; más reciente *mas re·thyen·te* later (*version*)

recientemente *re·thyen·te·men·te adv* recently

recipiente *re·thee·pyen·te m* container

reclamación *re·kla·ma·thyon f* complaint

reclamar *re·kla·mar vt* claim (*lost property, baggage*) □ *vi* complain; protest

recluta *re·kloo·ta m* recruit

recogedor *re·ko·khe·dor m* dustpan

recoger *re·ko·kher vt* pick up (*object*)

recogida *re·ko·khee·da f* collection (*of mail*)

recomendar *re·ko·men·dar vt* recommend

recompensa *re·kom·pen·sa f* reward

reconocer *re·ko·no·ther vt* recognize; acknowledge (*letter*)

reconocimiento *re·ko·no·thee·myen·to* m recognition; examination (*medical*)

récord *re·kord m* record (*in sports*)

recordar *re·kor·dar vt* remind; recordar* algo a alguien *re·kor·dar al·go a al·gyen* to remind someone of something

recorrer *re·ko·rrer vt* tour; travel (*a distance*); cover (*distance*); recorrer* 10 km a pie *re·ko·rrer 10 km a pye* to walk 10 km

recortarse el pelo *re·kor·tar·se el pe·lo vr* trim (*hair*)

recreo *re·kre·o m* leisure; break

rectificación *rek·tee·fee·ka·thyon f* correction (*alteration*)

recuerdo *re·kwer·do m* souvenir; recuerdos *re·kwer·dos* regards; greetings; uno de mis recuerdos *oo·no de mees re·kwer·dos* one of my memories

recuperar *re·koo·pe·rar vt* retrieve; recover

recuperarse *re·koo·pe·rar·se vr* recover (*from illness*)

recurrir a *re·koo·rreer a vi* resort to

recursos *re·koor·sos mpl* resources

red *red f* net

redactar *re·dak·tar vt* draw up (*document*)

redada *re·da·da f* raid (*by police*)

redecilla *re·de·theel·ya f* luggage rack

redistribución *re·dees·tree·boo·thyon f* redistribution

redistribuir *re·dees·tree·boo·eer vt* redistribute

rédito *re·dee·to m* yield (*financial*)

redondo(a) *re·don·do(a) adj* round

reducción *re·dook·thyon f* reduction

reducido(a) *re·doo·thee·do(a) adj* low; limited

reducir *re·doo·theer vt* reduce; cut; reducir* a la mitad *re·doo·theer a la mee·tad* to halve (*reduce by half*)

reembolsar *re·em·bol·sar vt* refund; repay; pay back

reembolso *re·em·bol·so m* refund

reemplazar *re·em·pla·thar vt* replace (*substitute*)

reemplazo *re·em·pla·tho m* replacement

reexpedir *re·eks·pe·deer vt* redirect (*letter*)

referencia *re·fe·ren·thya f* reference

referirse a *re·fe·reer·se a vr* refer to (*allude to*); en lo que se refiere a *en lo ke se re·fye·re a* regarding; me refiero a su carta *me re·fye·ro a soo kar·ta* with reference to your letter

refinar *re·fee·nar vt* refine; sin refinar *seen re·fee·nar* raw (*unprocessed*)

refinería *re·fee·ne·ree·a f* refinery

reflector *re·flek·tor m* reflector (*on cycle, car*)

reflejar *re·fle·khar vt* reflect

reflejo *re·fle·kho m* reflection; rinse (*hair conditioner*)

refresco *re·fres·ko m* refreshment

refugiarse *re·foo·khyar·se vr* shelter (*from rain etc*)

refugio *re·foo·khyo m* shelter; island (*traffic*); median strip

regalar *re·ga·lar vt* present (*give*); give away

regaliz *re·ga·leeth m* licorice

regalo *re·ga·lo m* gift; present; el regalo de boda *re·ga·lo de bo·da* wedding present

regata *re·ga·ta f* regatta

regatear *re·ga·te·ar vi* haggle

regazo *re·ga·tho m* lap

régimen *re·khee·men m* diet (*slimming*); **estar* a régimen** *es·tar a re·khee·men* to be on a diet

región *re·khyon f* district; area; region

registro *re·khees·tro m* register

regla *re·gla f* rule (*regulation*); ruler (*for measuring*); **la regla de cálculo** *re·gla de kal·koo·lo* slide rule

reglamento *re·gla·men·to m* regulation

regordete *re·gor·de·te adj* plump

regresar *re·gre·sar vi* return (*come back*)

regreso *re·gre·so m* return

regular *re·goo·lar adj* regular

rehén *re·en m* hostage; **coger* a alguien como rehén** *ko·kher a al·gyen ko·mo re·en* to take someone hostage

reina *rey·na f* queen

Reino Unido *rey·no oo·nee·do m* United Kingdom

reír *re·eer vi* laugh; **reírse de alguien** *re·eer·se de al·gyen* to laugh at somebody

reja *re·kha f* grille

rejilla *re·kheel·ya f* rack (*for luggage*)

relación *re·la·thyon f* account; **las relaciones sexuales** *re·la·thyo·nes sek·swa·les* sexual intercourse; **las relaciones interraciales** *re·la·thyo·nes een·ter·ra·thya·les* race relations

relaciones públicas *re·la·thyo·nes poo·blee·kas fpl* public relations

relajarse *re·la·khar·se vr* relax

relámpago *re·lam·pa·go m* lightning; éclair

relativo(a) *re·la·tee·ho(a) adj* relative

religión *re·lee·khyon f* religion

religioso(a) *re·lee·khyo·so(a) adj* religious

rellenado(a) *rel·ye·na·do(a) adj* stuffed (*cushion etc*)

relleno *rel·ye·no m* dressing (*stuffing*) □ **relleno(a)** *rel·ye·no(a) adj* stuffed (*food*)

reloj *re·lokh m* clock; watch; **el reloj de caja** *el re·lokh de ka·kha* grandfather clock; **el reloj de pulsera** *re·lokh de pool·se·ra* wristwatch; **el reloj despertador** *re·lokh des·per·ta·dor* alarm clock

reluciente *re·loo·thyen·te adj* sparkling

remar *re·mar vi* row (*sport*)

remedio *re·me·dyo m* remedy

remiendo *re·myen·do m* patch (*of material*)

remitente *re·mee·ten·te m* sender

remo *re·mo m* oar; rowing (*sport*)

remojar *re·mo·khar vt* soak (*washing*)

remolacha *re·mo·la·cha f* beet

remolcador *el re·mol·ka·dor m* tug

remolcar* *re·mol·kar vt* tow (*trailer*)

remolino *re·mo·lee·no m* whirlpool

remolque *re·mol·ke m* tow rope; trailer; **a remolque** *a re·mol·ke* in tow

remover* *re·mo·ber vt* stir

rendido(a) *ren·dee·do(a) adj* worn-out (*person*)

rendimiento *ren·dee·myen·to m* performance (*of car*); yield

rendir* *ren·deer vt* yield

reñir *ren·yeer vi* quarrel

renovar* *re·no·bar vt* renew; renovate

renta *ren·ta f* income; **la renta vitalicia** *ren·ta bee·ta·lee·thya* annuity

rentabilidad *ren·ta·bee·lee·dad f* profitability

rentable *ren·ta·ble adj* profit-making; profitable

reorganización *re·or·ga·nee·tha·thyon f* reorganization

reorganizar* *re·or·ga·nee·thar vt* reorganize

reparación *re·pa·ra·thyon f* repair

reparar *re·pa·rar vt* repair; mend

repartir *re·par·teer vt* deliver (*mail*); divide (*apportion*)

reparto *re·par·to m* cast (*of play*); distribution; delivery (*of mail*)

repasar *re·pa·sar vt* revise (*school work*)

repente *re·pen·te m* start; jerk; **de repente** *de re·pen·te* suddenly

repentino(a) *re·pen·tee·no(a) adj* sudden

repetición *re·pe·tee·thyon f* repetition; encore

repetir* *re·pe·teer vt* repeat; **¿puede repetir eso?** *pwe·de re·pe·teer e·so* could you say that again?

repisa de chimenea *re·pee·sa de chee·me·ne·a f* mantelpiece

repollo *re·pol·yo m* cabbage

reportaje *re·por·ta·khe m* report (*in press*)

reposacabezas *re·po·sa·ka·be·thas m* headrest

representación *re·pre·sen·ta·thyon f* representation, performance (*of actor*); production (*of play*)

representante *re·pre·sen·tan·te m* representative

representar *re·pre·sen·tar vt* represent; produce (*play*)

república *re·poo·blee·ka f* republic

republicano(a) *re·poo·blee·ka·no(a) adj* republican

repuesto *re·pwes·to m* replacement, la pieza de repuesto *pye·tha de re·pwes·to* spare (part)

repugnancia *re·poog·nan·thya f* disgust

requesón *re·ke·son m* cottage cheese

requisito *re·kee·see·to m* requirement; qualification; **tener* los requisitos para** *te·ner los re·kee·see·tos pa·ra* to qualify for (*grant etc*)

resaca *re·sa·ka f* hangover; **tener* una resaca** *te·ner oo·na re·sa·ka* to have a hangover

resbaladizo(a) *res·ba·la·dee·tho(a) adj* slippery

resbalar *res·ba·lar vi* slip; slide

rescatar *res·ka·tar vt* rescue

rescate *res·ka·te m* rescue

reseña *re·sen·ya f* review (*of book etc*)

reserva *re·ser·ba f* reserve; store (*stock*); reservation; **la reserva en grupo** *re·ser·ba en groo·po* block reservation; **en reserva** *en re·ser·ba* in stock

reservado(a) *re·ser·ba·do(a) adj* quiet (*person*)

reservar *re·ser·bar vt* reserve

reservas *re·ser·bas fpl* reserves

resfriado *res·free·a·do m* cold (*illness*)

resfriarse *res·free·ar·se vr* catch cold

residencia *re·see·den·thya f* residence; dormitory (*of college*); hostel

residencial *re·see·den·thyal adj* residential (*area*)

resistencia *re·sees·ten·thya f* resistance; strength (*of girder, rope etc*)

resistente *re·sees·ten·te adj* strong; hard-wearing

resistir *re·sees·teer vt* resist

resolver* *re·sol·ber vt* work out; solve (*problem*)

resorte *re·sor·te m* spring (*coil*)

respaldo *res·pal·do m* back (*of chair*)

respetable *res·pe·ta·ble adj* respectable

respetar *res·pe·tar vt* respect

respeto *res·pe·to m* respect

respirar *res·pee·rar* vi breathe

responder *res·pon·der* vt/i answer; reply; be responsible; **responder a una pregunta** *res·pon·der a oo·na pre·goon·ta* to reply to a question

responsabilidad *res·pon·sa·bee·lee·dad* f responsibility

responsable *res·pon·sa·ble* adj responsible; **responsable de** *res·pon·sa·ble de* responsible for *(to blame)*

respuesta *res·pwes·ta* f answer; reply

restar *res·tar* vt deduct; subtract

restaurante *res·tow·ran·te* m restaurant

restricción *res·treek·thyon* f restriction; **la restricción económica** *res·treek·thyon e·ko·no·mee·ka* squeeze *(financial)*; **la restricción de crédito** *res·treek·thyon de kre·dee·to* credit squeeze

restringir* *res·treen·kheer* vt restrict

resultado *re·sool·ta·do* m result

resultar *re·sool·tar* vi turn out, prove to be

resumen *re·soo·men* m outline *(summary)*

retener* *re·te·ner* vt keep *(retain)*

retirar *re·tee·rar* vt withdraw *(money)*

retirarse *re·tee·rar·se* vr retire; ¡no se retire! *no se re·tee·re* hold on! *(on phone)*; **retirarse de un negocio** *re·tee·rar·se de oon ne·go·thyo* to pull out of a deal

retrasar *re·tra·sar* vt delay *(postpone)*

retrasarse *re·tra·sar·se* vr lose *(clock, watch)*; **el tren se ha retrasado** *el tren se a re·tra·sa·do* the train has been delayed

retraso *re·tra·so* m delay *(to train, plane)*; **sin retraso** *seen re·tra·so* on schedule *(train)*

retrete *re·tre·te* m lavatory

retroceder *re·tro·the·der* vi turn back

retrospectivamente *re·tros·pek·tee·ba·men·te* adv in retrospect

retumbar *re·toom·bar* vi rumble

reumatismo *re·oo·ma·tees·mo* m rheumatism

reunión *re·oo·nyon* f meeting; conference

reunirse con *re·oo·neer·se kon* vr meet *(by arrangement)*

revender *re·ben·der* vt resell

reventar *re·ben·tar* vt burst

reverencia *re·be·ren·thya* f bow; **hacer* una reverencia** *a·ther oo·na re·be·ren·thya* to bow

revés *re·bes* m reverse; **al revés** *al re·bes* upside down; **poner* algo al revés** *po·ner al·go al re·bes* to turn something upside down; **volver* algo del revés** *bol·ber al·go del re·bes* to turn something inside out

revisar *re·bee·sar* vt check *(examine)*; revise

revisión *re·bee·syon* f service *(for car)*; examination *(inspection)*; review

revisor *re·bee·sor* m conductor *(on train)*

revista *re·bees·ta* f magazine; revue; **pasar revista a** *pa·sar re·bees·ta a* to review

revolución *re·bo·loo·thyon* f revolution *(political)*; rev *(in engine)*

rey *rey* m king

rezar *re·thar* vi pray

ribera *ree·be·ra* f bank *(of river, lake)*

rico(a) *ree·ko(a)* adj rich; wealthy

ridículo(a) *ree·dee·koo·lo(a)* adj ridiculous

rienda *ryen·da* f rein

riesgo *ryes·go* m risk

rígido(a) *ree·khee·do(a)* adj stiff

rimel *ree·mel* m eyeliner; mascara

Rin *reen* m Rhine

riñón *reen·yon* m kidney

río *ree·o* m river

riqueza *ree·ke·tha* f wealth

risa *ree·sa* f laugh; laughter

risotto *ree·so·to* m risotto

ritmo *reet·mo* m rhythm

rival *ree·bal* m rival

rizado(a) *ree·tha·do(a)* adj curly

rizo *ree·tho* m curl

robar *ro·bar* vt steal; rob; **robar algo a alguien** *ro·bar al·go a al·gyen* to steal something from someone

roble *ro·ble* m oak

robo *ro·bo* m robbery

robot *ro·bot* m robot

roca *ro·ka* f rock

roce *ro·the* m graze

rociada *ro·thya·da* f spray *(of liquid)*

rociar *ro·thyar* vt sprinkle

rodaballo *ro·da·bal·yo* m turbot

rodaja *ro·da·kha* f slice; **cortar en rodajas** *kor·tar en ro·da·khas* to slice

rodar* *ro·dar* vt break in *(car)* □ vi roll *(on wheels)*

rodear *ro·de·ar* vt surround; **rodear un campo** *ro·de·ar oon kam·po* to go round a field

rodilla *ro·deel·ya* f knee; **estar* de rodillas** *es·tar de ro·deel·yas* to kneel

rodillo *ro·deel·yo* m rolling pin

rojo(a) *ro·kho(a)* adj red; **rojo de cólera** *ro·kho de ko·le·ra* red with anger

rollo *rol·yo* m roll

Roma *ro·ma* f Rome

romano(a) *ro·ma·no(a)* adj Roman

romántico(a) *ro·man·tee·ko(a)* adj romantic

rompecabezas *rom·pe·ka·be·thas* m puzzle; jigsaw *(puzzle)*

romper* *rom·per* vt smash; break

romperse* *rom·per·se* vr snap; break; **romperse* el brazo** *rom·per·se el bra·tho* to break one's arm

ron *ron* m rum

roncar* *ron·kar* vi snore

ropa *ro·pa* f clothes; **la ropa de deporte** *ro·pa de de·por·te* sportswear; **la ropa interior** *ro·pa een·te·ryor* underwear; **la ropa sucia** *ro·pa soo·thya* laundry *(clothes)*; **la ropa para caballeros** *ro·pa pa·ra ka·bal·ye·ros* haberdashery; **la ropa de caballero** *ro·pa de ka·bal·ye·ro* menswear; **la ropa de cama** *ro·pa de ka·ma* bedding; **la ropa de sport** *ro·pa de sport* casual clothes, casual wear; **la ropa blanca** *ro·pa blan·ka* linen *(for beds)*

ropero *ro·pe·ro* m closet

rosa *ro·sa* f rose □ adj pink

rosado *ro·sa·do* m rosé

roto(a) *ro·to(a)* adj ragged *(clothes)*

rotulador *ro·too·la·dor* m felt-tip pen

rozar* *ro·thar* vt scrape; graze *(skin)*

rubí *roo·bee* m ruby

rubio(a) *roo·byo(a)* adj fair; blond(e)

ruborizarse *roo·bo·ree·thar·se* vr blush

rueda *rwe·da* f wheel; **rueda trasera** *rwe·da tra·se·ra* rear wheel

rugby *roog·bee* m rugby

rugido *roo·khee·do* m roar

rugir* *roo·kheer* vi roar

ruibarbo *rooy·bar·bo* m rhubarb

ruido *rwee·do* m noise; row

ruidoso(a) *rwee·do·so(a)* adj noisy

ruina *rwee·na* f ruin; **las ruinas** *rwee·nas* ruins

ruleta *roo·le·ta* f roulette

Rumanía *roo·ma·nee·a f* Romania
rumano(a) *roo·ma·no(a) adj* Romanian □ *m* el rumano *roo·ma·no* Romanian (*language*)
rural *roo·ral adj* rural
Rusia *roo·sya f* Russia
ruso(a) *roo·so(a) adj* Russian □ *m* el ruso *roo·so* Russian (*language*)
ruta *roo·ta f* route; **la ruta turística** *roo·ta too·rees·tee·ka* scenic route
rutina *roo·tee·na f* routine; **de rutina** *de roo·tee·na* routine

S

S. A. *e·se a abbrev* Inc
sábado *sa·ba·do m* Saturday
sábana *sa·ba·na f* sheet
saber* *sa·ber vt* know (*subject, language*); **saber* hacer algo** *sa·ber a·ther al·go* to know how to do something; **sabe a pescado** *sa·be a pes·ka·do* it tastes like fish; **que yo sepa** *ke yo se·pa* as far as I know
sabio(a) *sa·byo(a) adj* wise (*person*)
sabor *sa·bor m* taste; flavor
saborear *sa·bo·re·ar vt* taste
sacacorchos *sa·ka·kor·chos m* corkscrew
sacar* *sa·kar vt* take out; **sacar* algo** *sa·kar al·go* to pull something out; **sacarse una muela** *su·kar·se oo·na mwe·la* to have a tooth taken out
sacarina *sa·ka·ree·na f* saccharin
sacerdote *sa·ther·do·te m* priest
saco *sa·ko m* sack; **el saco de dormir** *sa·ko de dor·meer* sleeping bag
sacudir *sa·koo·deer vt* shake
sagrado(a) *sa·gra·do(a) adj* holy
sal *sal f* salt; **sin sal** *seen sal* unsalted
sala *sa·la f* hall (*room*); ward (*in hospital*); auditorium; **la sala de embarque** *sa·la de em·bar·ke* departure lounge; **la sala de estar** *sa·la de es·tar* lounge (*in house*); **sala de espera** *sa·la de es·pe·ra* lounge (*at airport*); waiting room (*at station*)
salado(a) *sa·la·do(a) adj* savory; salty
salario *sa·la·ryo m* wage, wages
salchicha *sal·chee·cha f* sausage
salchichón *sal·chee·chon m* salami sausage
saldo *sal·do m* balance (*remainder owed*); **el saldo bancario** *sal·do ban·ka·ryo* bank balance; **el saldo deudor** *sal·do de·oo·dor* debit balance
salero *sa·le·ro m* salt cellar
salida *sa·lee·da f* exit; outlet (*electric*); **la salida del sol** *sa·lee·da del sol* sunrise; **los X encuentran buena salida** *los X en·kwen·tran bwe·na sa·lee·da* there is a good market for X
salir* *sa·leer vi* go outside; come out; go out; rise (*sun*); **salió corriendo de la casa** *sa·lyo ko·rryen·do de la ka·sa* he ran out of the house; **los trenes salen cada hora** *los tre·nes sa·len ka·da o·ra* the trains run every hour; **salir* sin ganar ni perder** *sa·leer seen ga·nar nee per·der* to break even
saliva *sa·lee·ba f* saliva
salmón *sal·mon m* salmon
salón *sa·lon m* lounge (*in hotel*); **el salón de belleza** *sa·lon de bel·ye·tha* beauty parlor; **el salón de té** *sa·lon de te* tearoom; **el salón de demostraciones** *sa·lon de·mos·tra·thyo·nes* showroom
salpicar* *sal·pee·kar vt* splash
salsa *sal·sa f* gravy; sauce; dressing (*salad*); **la salsa tártara** *sal·sa tar·ta·*

ra tartar sauce; **la salsa de soja** *sal·sa de so·kha* soy sauce
saltar *sal·tar vt/i* jump □ *vi* blow (*fuse*); **saltar por encima de una pared** *sal·tar por en·thee·ma de oo·na pa·red* to jump (over) a wall; **saltar con un pie** *sal·tar kon oon pye* to hop
salteado(a) *sal·te·a·do(a) adj* sauté
salto *sal·to m* jump
salud *sa·lood f* health; **¡salud!** *sa·lood* cheers!
saludable *sa·loo·da·ble adj* healthy
saludar *sa·loo·dar vt* greet; **le saluda atentamente** *le sa·loo·da a·ten·ta·men·te* yours sincerely
saludo *sa·loo·do m* greeting
salvaje *sal·ba·khe adj* wild
salvamantel *sal·ba·man·tel m* place mat
salvamanteles *sal·ba·man·te·les m* table-mat
salvar *sal·bar vt* save (*person*)
salvia *salbya f* sage (*herb*)
sanatorio *sa·na·to·ryo m* sanitarium
sanciones *san·thyo·nes fpl* sanctions
sandalia *san·da·lya f* sandal
sandía *san·dee·a f* watermelon
sangrar *san·grar vi* bleed
sangre *san·gre f* blood
sano(a) *sa·no(a) adj* healthy
santo(a) *san·to(a) m/f* saint
saque inicial *sa·ke ee·nee·thyal m* kick-off
sarampión *sa·ram·pyon m* measles
sarcástico(a) *sar·kas·tee·ko(a) adj* sarcastic
sardina *sar·dee·na f* sardine; **la sardina arenque** *sar·dee·na a·ren·ke* pilchard
sarpullido *sar·pool·yee·do m* rash
sartén *sar·ten f* fry(ing) pan; skillet
sastre *sas·tre m* tailor
satélite *sa·te·lee·te m* satellite
sátira *sa·tee·ra f* satire
satisfacer* *sa·tees·fa·ther vt* satisfy; meet (*demand*)
satisfactorio(a) *sa·tees·fak·to·ryo(a) adj* satisfactory
saturar *sa·too·rar vt* saturate (*market*)
sauna *sow·na f* sauna
sazón *sa·thon f* season; **en sazón** *en sa·thon* in season
scooter *es·koo·ter m* scooter
se *se pron* himself; herself; itself; themselves; yourself; oneself; to him/her/it; **se lavan** *se la·ban* they wash themselves; **(ella) se vistió** *(el·ya) se bees·tyo* she dressed herself
sebo *se·bo m* suet
secado a mano *se·ka·do a ma·no m* blow-dry
el secador de pelo *se·ka·dor de pe·lo m* hair-drier
secar* *se·kar vt* dry; **secar* por centrifugado** *se·kar por then·tree·foo·ga·do* to spin-dry
secarse* *se·kar·se vr* get dry
sección *sek·thyon f* department (*in store*)
seco(a) *se·ko(a) adj* dry; dried (*fruit, beans*)
secretario(a) *se·kre·ta·ryo(a) m/f* secretary; **la secretaria particular** *se·kre·ta·rya par·tee·koo·lar* personal assistant
secreto(a) *se·kre·to(a) adj* secret □ *m* el secreto *se·kre·to* secret
sector *sek·tor m* sector; **el sector privado** *sek·tor pree·ba·do* private sector; **el sector público** *sek·tor poo·blee·ko* public sector

secuestrador se·kwes·tra·dor m hijacker

secuestrar se·kwes·trar vt kidnap; hijack

secuestro aéreo se·kwes·tro a·e·re·o m hijack

secundario(a) se·koon·da·ryo(a) adj secondary; subordinate; minor

sed sed f thirst; **tener* sed** te·ner sed to be thirsty

seda se·da f silk; **un vestido de seda** oon bes·tee·do de se·da a silk dress

sedán se·dan m sedan (car)

sediento(a) se·dyen·to(a) adj thirsty

sedimentarse se·dee·men·tar·se vr settle (wine)

seguido(a) se·gee·do(a) adj continuous; **en seguida** en se·gee·da straight away; **todo seguido** to·do se·gee·do straight on

seguir* se·geer vt/i continue □ vt follow; **seguir* a alguien/algo** se·geer a al·gyen/al·go to come after someone/something; **hacer* seguir** a·ther se·geer to forward (letter)

según se·goon prep according to; **según mi opinión** se·goon mee o·pee·nyon in my opinion

segundo(a) se·goon·do(a) adj second □ m **el segundo** se·goon·do second (time); **de segunda clase** de se·goon·da kla·se second-class; **de segunda mano** de se·goon·da ma·no secondhand (car etc)

seguramente se·goo·ra·men·te adv surely

seguridad se·goo·ree·dad f security; reliability; safety; **la seguridad social** se·goo·ree·dad so·thyal social security

seguro(a) se·goo·ro(a) adj sure; reliable (car) □ m **el seguro** se·goo·ro insurance; **seguro(a) de sí mismo(a)** se·goo·ro(a) de see mees·mo(a) confident; **el seguro de vida** se·goo·ro de bee·da life insurance; **el seguro contra tercera persona** se·goo·ro kon·tra ter·the·ra per·so·na third party insurance; **el seguro contra todo riesgo** se·goo·ro kon·tra to·do ryes·go comprehensive insurance; **el seguro social** se·goo·so·thyal social security; **la compañía de seguros** kom·pan·yee·a de se·goo·ros insurance company

seis seys num six

selección se·lek·thyon f selection

sellar sel·yar vt stamp (visa)

sello sel·yo m stamp (rubber); stamp (postage); **poner* un sello** po·ner oon sel·yo to stamp (letter)

semáforo se·ma·fo·ro m traffic lights; **saltarse un semáforo en rojo** sal·tar·se oon se·ma·fo·ro en ro·kho to go through a red light

semana se·ma·na f week; **la semana pasada** la se·ma·na pa·sa·da last week

semanal se·ma·nal adj weekly

semanario se·ma·na·ryo m weekly (periodical)

Semana Santa se·ma·na san·ta f Holy Week

semejante se·me·khan·te adj alike

semicualificado(a) se·mee·kwa·lee·fee·ka·do(a) adj semiskilled

semifinal se·mee·fee·nal f semifinal

semilla se·meel·ya f seed; **la semilla de soja** se·meel·ya de so·kha soy bean

seña sen·ya f sign; **las señas** se personnel department dress

senado se·na·do m senate (political)

senador se·na·dor m senator

señal sen·yal f sign; signal; **la señal de comunicando** sen·yal de ko·moo·nee·kan·do busy signal; **hacer* señales con la mano** a·ther sen·ya·les kon la ma·no to wave; **la señal de tráfico** sen·yal de tra·fee·ko road sign; **la señal de socorro** sen·yal de so·ko·rro Mayday

señalar sen·ya·lar vt point out; signal; **señalar algo** sen·ya·lar al·go to point something out (show)

sencillo(a) sen·theel·yo(a) adj simple

sendero sen·de·ro m footpath

seno se·no m breast

señor sen·yor m gentleman; **Señor** sen·yor Mr; sir

señora sen·yo·rra f lady; **Señora** sen·yo·ra Mrs; Ms; madam

señorita sen·yo·ree·ta f Miss

sensato(a) sen·sa·to(a) adj sensible

sensibilidad sen·see·bee·lee·dad f sensitivity

sentado(a) sen·ta·do(a) adj sitting

sentar* sen·tar vt/i sit; **me sienta*** me syen·ta it fits (me); **los huevos me sientan mal** los we·bos me syen·tan mal eggs disagree with me; **ese sombrero le sienta bien** e·se som·bre·ro le syen·ta byen that hat suits you

sentarse* sen·tar·se vr sit down; **siéntese por favor** syen·te·se por fa·bor please take a seat

sentido sen·tee·do m sense; **el sentido común** sen·tee·do ko·moon sense (common sense); **el sentido del humor** sen·tee·do del oo·mor sense of humor; **tener* sentido** te·ner sen·tee·do to make sense

sentimiento sen·tee·myen·to m feeling

sentir* sen·teer vt feel; **lo siento** lo syen·to (I'm) sorry; **me siento mejor** me syen·to me·khor I feel better

separado(a) se·pa·ra·do(a) adj separate; **por separado** por se·pa·ra·do under separate cover

se(p)tiembre se(p)·tyem·bre m September

séptimo(a) sep·tee·mo(a) adj seventh

sequía se·kee·a f drought

ser* ser vi be; **es médico** es me·dee·ko he is a doctor; **es azul** es a·thool it's blue; **son las 4** son las 4 it's 4 o'clock; **¿qué es eso?** ke es e·so what is that?; **¿cuánto es?** kwan·to es how much is it?; **es decir...** es de·theer that is (to say)...; **son 5 kilómetros** son 5 kee·lo·me·tros it's 5 kilometers; **eso es** e·so es yes, that's right

sereno(a) se·re·no(a) adj calm

serie se·rye f round (of talks)

seriedad se·rye·dad f seriousness; reliability (of person)

serio(a) se·ryo(a) adj serious; trustworthy

servicio ser·bee·thyo m service; service charge; **el servicio de autobuses** ser·bee·thyo de ow·to·boo·ses bus service; **el área de servicios** a·re·a de ser·bee·thyos service area; **el servicio de habitaciones** ser·bee·thyo de ha·bee·ta·thyo·nes room service; **de servicio** de ser·bee·thyo on duty (doctor); **la rama de servicios** ra·ma de ser·bee·thyos service industry; **los servicios sociales** ser·bee·thyos so·thya·les social services; **el servicio de personal** ser·bee·thyo de per·so·nal personnel department

servicios ser·bee·thyos mpl public conveniences; restroom; comfort station

servilleta *ser·beel·ye·ta f* serviette; napkin *(for table)*

servir* *ser·beer vt* serve; **no sirve para nada** *no se·er be pa·ra na·da* it's no use; **servir* algo fresco** *ser·beer al·go fres·ko* to serve something chilled; **sírvase** *seer·ba·se* help yourself

sesenta *se·sen·ta num* sixty

sesión *se·syon f* performance *(of play)*

sesos *se·sos mpl* brains *(as food)*

seta *se·ta f* mushroom

setenta *se·ten·ta num* seventy

seto *se·to m* hedge

severo(a) *se·be·ro(a) adj* harsh *(severe)*

sexo *sek·so m* sex

sexto(a) *seks·to(a) adj* sixth

sexy *sek·see adj* sexy

shock *shok m* shock *(medical)*

sí *see adv* yes; **espero que sí** *es·pe·ro ke see* I hope so; **un día sí, otro no** *oon dee·a see o·tro no* every other day

si *see conj* whether; if

Sicilia *see·thee·lya f* Sicily

sidra *see·dra f* cider

siempre *syem·pre adv* always; **siempre que** *syem·pre ke* provided, providing; **siempre que venga** *syem·pre ke ben·ga* provided (that) he comes

sierra *sye·rra f* saw; mountain range

siesta *syes·ta f* siesta; nap

siete *sye·te num* seven

siglo *see·glo m* century

significado *seeg·nee·fee·ka·do m* meaning

significar* *seeg·nee·fee·kar vt* mean; stand for

signo *seeg·no m* sign *(mark)*

siguiente *see·gyen·te adj* following

sílaba *see·la·ba f* syllable

silbar *seel·bar vi* whistle

silbato *seel·ba·to m* whistle *(object)*

silbido *seel·bee·do m* whistle *(sound)*

silenciador *see·len·thya·dor m* muffler *(on car)*

silencio *see·len·thyo m* silence; **¡silencio!** *see·len·thyo* be quiet!

silenciosamente *see·len·thyo·sa·men·te adv* quietly

silencioso(a) *see·len·thyo·so(a) adj* silent

silla *seel·ya f* chair; **la silla tijera** *seel·ya tee·khe·ra* deckchair; **la silla plegable** *seel·ya ple·ga·ble* folding chair; **la silla alta para niño** *seel·ya al·ta pa·ra neen·yo* highchair; **la silla de montar** *seel·ya de mon·tar* saddle; **la silla de ruedas** *seel·ya de rwe·das* wheelchair

sillita de ruedas *seel·yee·ta de rwe·das f* stroller

sillón *seel·yon m* chair; armchair

silvestre *seel·bes·tre adj* wild *(flower)*

símbolo *seem·bo·lo m* symbol

simétrico(a) *see·me·tree·ko(a) adj* symmetrical

simpático(a) *seem·pa·tee·ko(a) adj* nice *(person)*

simposio *seem·po·syo m* symposium

sin *seen prep* without; **sin contar...** *seen kon·tar...* exclusive of ; **nos hemos quedado sin leche** *nos e·mos ke·da·do seen le·che* we've run out of milk; **sin blanca** *seen blan·ka* broke *(penniless)*

sinagoga *see·na·go·ga f* synagogue

sincero(a) *seen·the·ro(a) adj* sincere

sindicato *seen·dee·ka·to m* labor union; syndicate; trade union

sin embargo *seen em·bar·go conj* however; still *(nevertheless)*; **sin embargo está contento** *seen em·bar·go es·ta kon·ten·to* he's happy, though

sinfonía *seen·fo·nee·a f* symphony

sino *see·no conj* but; no este, sino ese *no es·te see·no e·se* not this, but that

sintético(a) *seen·te·tee·ko(a) adj* synthetic

síntoma *seen·to·ma m* symptom

sirena *see·re·na f* siren

sirsaca *seer·sa·ka f* seersucker

sistema *sees·te·ma m* process *(method)*; system; **el sistema de refrigeración** *sees·te·ma de re·free·khe·ra·thyon* cooling system

sistemático(a) *sees·te·ma·tee·ko(a) adj* systematic

sitio *see·tyo m* room *(space)*; place; spot; situation; position; **por todos sitios** *por to·dos see·tyos* all over the place; **en su sitio** *en soo see·tyo* in place; **fuera de su sitio** *fwe·ra de soo see·tyo* out of place

situación *see·twa·thyon f* situation; **en situación desventajosa** *en see·twa·a·thyon des·ben·ta·kho·sa* at a disadvantage

situar *see·too·ar vt* place *(put)*

slogan *es·lo·gan m* slogan

smoking *es·mo·keeng m* tuxedo; dinner jacket

sobornar *so·bor·nar vt* bribe

soborno *so·bor·no m* bribe

sobrar *so·brar vi* remain *(be left over)*

sobre *so·bre prep* on; upon; **hablar sobre algo** *a·blar so·bre al·go* to talk about something; **sobre la mesa** *so·bre la me·sa* on the table □ *m* el sobre *so·bre* envelope

sobrecarga *so·bre·kar·ga f* surcharge

sobredosis *so·bre·do·sees f* overdose

sobreexpuesto(a) *so·bre·eks·pwes·to(a) adj* overexposed *(photo)*

sobremarcha *so·bre·mar·cha f* overdrive

sobresalto *so·bre·sal·to m* shock *(fright)*

sobrevivir *so·bre·bee·beer vi* survive

sobrina *so·bree·na f* niece

sobrino *so·bree·no m* nephew

social *so·thyal adj* social

socialismo *so·thya·lees·mo m* socialism

socialista *so·thya·lees·ta adj* socialist □ *m/f* socialist

sociedad *so·thye·dad f* society; **la sociedad de préstamo imobiliario** *so·thye·dad de pres·ta·mo ee·mo·bee·lee·a·ryo* savings and loan association; **la sociedad anónima** *so·thye·dad a·no·nee·ma* corporation *(firm)*; incorporated company; joint-stock company

socio *so·thyo m* associate; partner *(in business)*; **hacerse* socio de** *a·ther·se so·thyo de* to join *(club)*

¡socorro! *so·ko·rro excl* help!

soda *so·da f* soda

sofá *so·fa m* couch; sofa

sofisticado(a) *so·fees·tee·ka·do(a) adj* sophisticated

sofocante *so·fo·kan·te adj* close; stuffy

soga *so·ga f* rope

sol *sol m* sun; sunshine; **tomar el sol** *to·mar el sol* to sunbathe

solapa *so·la·pa f* flap

solar *so·lar adj* solar □ *m* el solar *so·lar* site *(of building)*

soldado *sol·da·do m* soldier

soldar *sol·dar vt* weld

soleado(a) *so·le·a·do(a) adj* sunny

soler *so·ler vi* be used to; **solíamos ir** *so·lee·a·mos eer* we used to go

solicitar *so·lee·thee·tar vt* apply for

solicitud *so·lee·thee·tood f* application *(for job)*

sólido(a) *so·lee·do(a)* *adj* solid; strong; fast (*dye*)

sólo *so·lo* *adv* only; no sólo *no se·lo* not only; sólo hay 4 *so·lo ay 4* there are only 4

solo(a) *so·lo(a)* *adj* alone; lonely (*person*)

solo(a) *so·lo(a)* *adj* alone; lonely; straight (*drink*); lo hizo solo *lo ee·tho so·lo* he did it on his own

solomillo *so·lo·meel·yo* *m* sirloin

soltar* *sol·tar* *vt* let go; untie (*animal*)

soltero(a) *sol·te·ro(a)* *adj* single (*not married*) □ *m/f* el/la soltero(a) *sol·te·ro(a)* bachelor; spinster

solución *so·loo·thyon* *f* solution

sombra *som·bra* *f* shade; shadow

sombreador *som·bre·a·dor* *m* eye shadow

sombrero *som·bre·ro* *m* hat; sun hat

sombrilla *som·breel·ya* *f* sunshade (*over table*)

someter *so·me·ter* *vt* submit (*proposal*)

somnífero *som·nee·fe·ro* *m* sleeping pill

sonar* *so·nar* *vt/i* ring; sonarse* la nariz *so·nar·se la na·reeth* to blow one's nose

sonido *so·nee·do* *m* sound

soñar* *son·yar* *vi* dream

sonreír* *son·re·eer* *vi* smile; grin

sonrisa *son·ree·sa* *f* smile; grin

sopa *so·pa* *f* soup; la sopa milanesa *so·pa mee·la·ne·sa* minestrone (soup); la sopa de tortuga *so·pa de tor·too·ga* turtle soup

soplar *so·plar* *vi* blow (*wind*)

soportar *so·por·tar* *vt* bear; hold (*support*)

sorbete *sor·be·te* *m* sherbet

sordo(a) *sor·do(a)* *adj* deaf

sorprender *sor·pren·der* *vt* surprise

sorprendido(a) *sor·pren·dee·do(a)* *adj* surprised; sorprendido(a) por *sor·pren·dee·do(a) por* surprised at

sorpresa *sor·pre·sa* *f* surprise

sorteo *sor·te·o* *m* raffle

S.O.S. *e·se·o·e·se* *m* SOS

sótano *so·ta·no* *m* basement; cellar

soviético(a) *so·bye·tee·ko(a)* *adj* Soviet

squash *skwosh* *m* squash (*sport*)

S.R.C. *e·se·e·rre·the* *abbrev* R.S.V.P.

standard *es·tan·dar* *adj* standard (*model*)

stock *es·tok* *m* stock (*in shop*)

strip-tease *streep·tees* *m* striptease; la artista de strip-tease *ar·tees·ta de streep·tees* stripper

su *soo* *adj* his; her; their; its; your (*polite form*); su padre *soo pa·dre* his etc father; su madre *soo ma·dre* his etc mother

suave *swa·be* *adj* mild; gentle; smooth

subasta *soo·bas·ta* *f* auction

subcampeón *soob·kam·pe·on* *m* runner up

subcomisión *soob·ko·mee·syon* *f* sub-committee

subcontratista *soob·kon·tra·tees·ta* *m/f* subcontractor

subcontrato *soob·kon·tra·to* *m* subcontract

subdesarrollado(a) *soob·de·sa·rrol·ya·do(a)* *adj* underdeveloped (*country*)

subdirector *soob·dee·rek·tor* *m* deputy (*second-in-command*)

súbdito *soob·dee·to* *m* subject (*person*)

subestimar *soo·bes·tee·mar* *vt* undervalue

subexpuesto(a) *soo·beks·pwes·to(a)* *adj* underexposed

subida *soo·bee·da* *f* climb; ascent

subir *soo·beer* *vi* rise (*go up*); increase; board (*train, bus*) □ *vt* raise (*price*); climb (*tree, wall*); subir una colina *soo·beer oo·na ko·lee·na* to go up a hill

submarino *soob·ma·ree·no* *m* submarine

subordinado(a) *soo·bor·dee·na·do(a)* *m/f* subordinate

subrayar *soob·ra·yar* *vt* emphasize; underline

subsistencia *soob·sees·ten·thya* *f* keep

subterráneo(a) *soob·te·rra·ne·o(a)* *adj* underground

subtítulo *soob·tee·too·lo* *m* subtitle (*of movie*)

subtotal *soob·to·tal* *m* subtotal

suburbano(a) *soob·oor·ba·no(a)* *adj* suburban

subvención *soob·ben·thyon* *f* grant (*to institution*); subsidy

subvencionar *soob·ben·thyo·nar* *vt* subsidize

suceder* *soo·the·der* *vi* occur (*happen*)

suciedad *soo·thye·dad* *f* dirt

sucio(a) *soo·thyo(a)* *adj* dirty

sucursal *soo·koor·sal* *f* branch (*of store, bank etc*) □ *m* el sucursal *soo·koor·sal* subsidiary (*company*)

sudafricano(a) *sood·a·free·ka·no(a)* *adj* South African

sudamericano(a) *soo·da·me·ree·ka·no(a)* *adj* South American

sudar *soo·dar* *vi* sweat

sudeste *soo·des·te* *m* southeast

sudoeste *sood·o·es·te* *m* southwest

sudor *soo·dor* *m* sweat

Suecia *swe·thya* *f* Sweden

sueco(a) *swe·ko(a)* *adj* Swedish □ *m/f* el/la sueco(a) *swe·ko(a)* Swede

suegra *swe·gra* *f* mother-in-law

suegro *swe·gro* *m* father-in-law

suela *swe·la* *f* sole (*of shoe*)

sueldo *swel·do* *m* salary; pay; el sueldo neto *swel·do ne·to* take-home pay

suelo *swe·lo* *m* soil; ground; floor

suelto(a) *swel·to(a)* *adj* loose; bulk (*unpackaged*) □ *m* suelto *swel·to* change

sueñecito *swen·ye·thee·to* *m* nap (*sleep*)

sueño *swen·yo* *m* sleep; dream

suerte *swer·te* *f* luck; ¡buena suerte! *bwe·na swer·te* good luck!; mala suerte *ma·la swer·te* bad luck; tener* suerte *te·ner swer·te* to be lucky

suéter *swe·ter* *m* sweater

suficiente *soo·fee·thyen·te* *adj* enough; no tengo suficiente dinero *no ten·go soo·fee·thyen·te dee·ne·ro* I can't afford it; ¿será suficiente? *se·ra soo·fee·thyen·te* will it do? (*be enough*)

suflé *soo·fle* *m* soufflé

sufrir *soo·freer* *vt/i* suffer; sufrir un colapso *soo·freer oon ko·lap·so* to collapse (*person*)

sugerencia *soo·khe·ren·thya* *f* suggestion

sugerir* *soo·khe·reer* *vt* suggest

suicidio *soo·ee·thee·dyo* *m* suicide

Suiza *swee·tha* *f* Switzerland

suizo(a) *swee·tho(a)* *adj* Swiss

sujetador *soo·khe·ta·dor* *m* bra

sujetar *soo·khe·tar* *vt* hold in place

sujeto(a) a *soo·khe·to(a) a* *adj* subject to

suma *soo·ma* *f* sum (*total amount*)

sumamente *soo·ma·men·te* *adv* extremely

sumar *soo·mar* *vt* add (up) (*numbers*)

sumario *soo·ma·ryo m* summary

suministrar *soo·mee·nees·trar vt* supply (*goods*)

superficie *soo·per·fee·thye f* surface; top; **la superficie alquitranada** *soo·per·fee·thye al·kee·tra·na·da* tarmac

superior *soo·pe·ryor adj* superior (*quality*); upper; senior (*in rank*) □ *m* **el superior** *soo·pe·ryor* superior

supermercado *soo·per·mer·ka·do m* supermarket

superpetrolero *soo·per·pe·tro·le·ro m* supertanker

superstición *soo·pers·tee·thyon f* superstition

supervisar *soo·per·bee·sar vt* supervise

supervisor(a) *soo·per·bee·sor(·ra) m/f* supervisor

suplente *soo·plen·te adj* acting □ *m* substitute

suponer* *soo·po·ner vt* suppose; assume; figure; **supongo que vendrá** *soo·pon·go ke ben·dra* I expect he'll come; **supongo que sí** *soo·pon·go ke see* I expect so

supositorio *soo·po·see·to·ryo m* suppository

supuesto(a) *soo·pwes·to(a) adj* supposed; **por supuesto** *por soo·pwes·to* of course

sur *soor m* south; **del sur** *del soor* southern; **al sur** *al soor* southward

surf *soorf m* surfing; **el surf a vela** *soorf a be·la* windsurfing

surtido(a) *soor·tee·do(a) adj* assorted □ *m* **el surtido** *soor·tee·do* range (*variety*); choice

surtidor de gasolina *soor·tee·dor de ga·so·lee·na f* gasoline station

sus *soos adj* (*plural*) his; her; their; its; your (*polite form*); **sus hermanos/hermanas** *soos er·ma·nos/er·ma·nas* his *etc* brothers/sisters

suspender *soos·pen·der vt* suspend (*worker*)

suspensión *soos·pen·syon f* suspension (*on car*); adjournment

suspirar *soos·pee·rar vi* sigh

sustancia *soos·tan·thya f* stuff; substance

sustituir* *soos·tee·too·eer vt* substitute; **sustituir* algo por otra cosa** *soos·tee·too·eer al·go por o·tra ko·sa* to substitute something for something else

sutil *soo·teel adj* subtle

suyo(a) *soo·yo(a) adj* his; her; its; one's; their; your □ *pron* **el/la suyo(a)** *el/la soo·yo(a)* his; hers; theirs; yours

---

T

tabaco *ta·ba·ko m* tobacco

tabique *ta·bee·ke m* partition (*wall*); **sin tabiques** *seen ta·bee·kes* open-plan

tabla *ta·bla f* board; plank; table (*list*); **la tabla de surf** *ta·bla de soorf* surf board

tablero *ta·ble·ro m* dash(board); instrument panel

tablilla *ta·bleel·ya f* splint

tablón *ta·blon m* board; **el tablón de anuncios** *ta·blon de a·noon·thyos* bulletin board

taburete *ta·boo·re·te m* stool

tacaño(a) *ta·kan·yo(a) adj* mean (*miserly*)

tachar *ta·char vt* cross out

taco *ta·ko m* heel; swearword

tacón *ta·kon m* heel (*of shoe*); **los taco-**

---

nes finos *ta·ko·nes fee·nos* stiletto heels; **de tacón alto** *de ta·kon al·to* high-heeled

táctica *tak·tee·ka f* tactics

tacto *tak·to m* feel

tal *tal adj* such; **con tal que** *kon tal ke* as long as (*provided that*); **tal libro** *tal lee·bro* such a book

taladrar *ta·la·drar vt* drill (*hole*)

taladro *ta·la·dro m* drill (*tool*)

talco *tal·ko m* talc(um powder)

talento *ta·len·to m* talent

talla *tal·ya f* size (*of clothes*); **de talla grande** *de tal·ya gran·de* outsize (*clothes*)

tallarines *tal·ya·ree·nes mpl* noodles

taller *tal·yer m* workshop

tallo *tal·yo m* stem

talón *ta·lon m* heel; stub (*of check*); **el talón de equipajes** *ta·lon de e·kee·pa·khes* baggage check

talonario *ta·lo·na·ryo m* checkbook

tambalearse *tam·ba·le·ar·se vr* sway (*person*)

también *tam·byen adv* as well; also; too; **yo también** *yo tam·byen* so do I

tambor *tam·bor m* drum

tampoco *tam·po·ko adv* neither; nor; **no estuve allí ni él tampoco** *no es·too·be al·yee nee el tam·po·ko* I wasn't there and neither was he

tan *tan adv* so; **tan grande como** *tan gran·de ko·mo* as big as; **tan contento que...** *tan kon·ten·to ke* so pleased that...

tango *tan·go m* tango

tanque *tan·ke m* tank

tantear *tan·te·o m* score

tanto(a) *tan·to(a) adj* so much; such a lot of; **tanto(a) como** *tan·to(a) ko·mo* as much/many as; **tantos(as)** *tan·tos(as)* so many

tapa *ta·pa f* lid; top; appetizer

tapar *ta·par vt* plug

tapete *ta·pe·te m* rug

tapón *ta·pon m* stopper; plug (*for basin etc*); top (*of bottle*); **los tapones para los oídos** *ta·po·nes pa·ra los o·ee·dos* earplugs

taquigrafía *ta·kee·gra·fee·a f* shorthand

taquilla *ta·keel·ya f* box office; ticket office

taquimecanógrafa *ta·kee·me·ka·no·gra·fa f* shorthand typist; stenographer

tardar *tar·dar vi* be a long time

tarde *tar·de adv* late; late in the day □ *f* **la tarde** *tar·de* evening; afternoon; **de la tarde** *de la tar·de* p.m.; **más tarde** *mas tar·de* later (*to come etc*)

tardío(a) *tar·dee·o(a) adj* late (*not on time*)

tarea *ta·re·a f* job; task

tarifa *ta·ree·fa f* scale of charges; tariff; rate; **la tarifa de cambio** *ta·ree·fa de kam·byo* exchange rate

tarjeta *tar·khe·ta f* card; **la tarjeta de Navidad** *tar·khe·ta de na·bee·dad* Christmas card; **la tarjeta de crédito** *tar·khe·ta de kre·dee·to* credit card; **la tarjeta de embarque** *tar·khe·ta de em·bar·ke* boarding pass; **tarjeta verde** *tar·khe·ta ber·de* green card; **la tarjeta de felicitación** *tar·khe·ta de fe·lee·thee·ta·thyon* greeting card

tarro *ta·rro m* jar; pot

tarta *tar·ta f* pie; tart

tartán *tar·tan m* tartan

tarteleta *tar·te·le·ta f* flan

tasa *ta·sa f* rate; valuation

taxi *tak·see* m cab; taxi; **ir* en taxi** *eer en tak·see* to go by taxi

taxista *tak·sees·ta* m driver (*of taxi, bus*)

taza *ta·tha* f cup; **la taza de té** *ta·tha de te* teacup; **la taza de café** *ta·tha de ka·fe* coffee cup

tazón *ta·thon* m mug; bowl (*for food*)

té *te* m tea; **el té de menta** *te de men·ta* mint tea

te *te* pron you; yourself (*familiar form*)

teatro *te·a·tro* m theater; **ir* al teatro** *eer al te·a·tro* to go to the theater

tebeo *te·be·o* m comic

techo *te·cho* m ceiling; roof (*of car*); **el techo descapotable** *te·cho des·ka·po·ta·ble* sunroof

tecla *tek·la* f key (*of piano, typewriter*)

técnica *tek·nee·ka* f technique

técnico(a) *tek·nee·ko(a)* adj technical □ m/f **el/la técnico(a)** *tek·nee·ko(a)* technician

tecnología *tek·no·lo·khee·a* f technology

tecnológico(a) *tek·no·lo·khee·ko(a)* adj technological

tee *tee* m tee (*in golf*)

teja *te·kha* f tile (*on roof*)

tejado *te·kha·do* m roof

tejer *te·kher* vt weave; **tejer* un jersey** *te·kher oon kher·sey* to knit a sweater

tejidos *te·khee·dos* mpl textiles

tela *te·la* f material; fabric; **la tela a cuadros** *te·la a kwa·dros* plaid; **la tela cruzada** *te·la kroo·tha·da* twill; **la tela impermeable** *te·la eem·per·me·a·ble* groundcloth

tele *te·le* f TV

telecomunicaciones *te·le·ko·moo·nee·ka·thyo·nes* fpl telecommunications

telefonazo *te·le·fo·na·tho* m phone-call

telefonear *te·le·fo·ne·ar* vt call; phone; **está telefoneando** *es·ta te·le·fo·ne·an·do* he's on the phone

telefonista *te·le·fo·nees·ta* m/f switchboard operator; telephone operator

teléfono *te·le·fo·no* m phone; telephone; **estar* hablando por teléfono** *es·tar a·blan·do por te·le·fo·no* to be on the telephone; **por teléfono** *por te·le·fo·no* by telephone; **llamar por teléfono** *lya·mar por te·le·fo·no* to telephone

telegrafiar *te·le·gra·fyar* vt telegraph

telegrama *te·le·gra·ma* m wire; telegram

telémetro *te·le·me·tro* m range finder (*on camera*)

teleobjetivo *te·le·ob·khe·tee·bo* m telephoto lens

telescopio *te·les·ko·pyo* m telescope

telesilla *te·le·seel·ya* f ski lift; chairlift

televisar *te·le·bee·sar* vt televize

televisión *te·le·bee·syon* f television; **la televisión de circuito cerrado** *te·le·bee·syon de theer·kwee·to the·rra·do* closed circuit television; **la televisión en color** *te·le·bee·syon en ko·lor* color TV; **en la televisión** *en la te·le·bee·syon* on television

televisor *te·le·bee·sor* m television (*set*)

télex *te·leks* m telex; **por télex** *por te·leks* by telex; **enviar un télex** *en·byar oon te·leks* to telex

temblar* *tem·blar* vi shake; shiver

temer *te·mer* vt dread; **me temo que no** *me te·mo ke no* I'm afraid not

temperatura *tem·pe·ra·too·ra* f temperature; **tomar la temperatura a alguien** *to·mar la tem·pe·ra·too·ra a al·gyen* to take someone's temperature

tempestad *tem·pes·tad* f storm

tempestuoso(a) *tem·pes·too·o·so(a)* adj stormy

templo *tem·plo* m temple (*building*)

temporada *tem·po·ra·da* f season; **la temporada de veraneo** *la tem·po·ra·da de be·ra·ne·o* the vacation season; **fuera de temporada** *fwe·ra de tem·po·ra·da* off-season

temprano(a) *tem·pra·no(a)* adj early; **el tren que sale temprano** *tren ke sa·le tem·pra·no* the early train; **levantarse temprano** *le·ban·tar·se tem·pra·no* to get up early; **vino demasiado temprano** *bee·no de·ma·sya·do tem·pra·no* he came too soon; **más temprano** *mas tem·pra·no* earlier

tenaz *te·nath* adj stubborn

tendedero *ten·de·de·ro* m clotheshorse

tendencia *ten·den·thya* f trend; **tener* tendencia a hacer algo** *te·ner ten·den·thya a a·ther al·go* to tend to do something

tendero *ten·de·ro* m grocer □ m/f **tendero(a)** *ten·de·ro(a)* assistant (*in shop*)

tenedor *te·ne·dor* m fork

tener* *te·ner* vt have; hold; have gotten (*possess*); stock (*have in shop*); **no tenemos pan** *no te·ne·mos pan* we haven't any bread; **¿tiene pan?** *tye·ne pan* have you any bread?; **téngale quieto** *ten·ga·le kye·to* to hold him still; **tengo que irme** *ten·go ke eer·me* I must go; **Ud tiene que venir** *oos·ted tye·ne ke be·neer* you must come; **tiene más de 40 años** *tye·ne mas de 40 an·yos* he's past forty; **tengo hambre** *ten·go am·bre* I am hungry; **no tienes que venir** *no tye·nes ke be·neer* you needn't come; **no tener gasolina** *no te·ner ga·so·lee·na* to be out of gasoline; **eso no tiene nada que ver con Ud** *e·so no tye·ne na·da ke ber kon oos·ted* that doesn't concern you; **tener* cuidado** *te·ner kwee·da·do* to be careful; **tener* éxito** *te·ner ek·see·to* to succeed

teñir *ten·yeer* vt dye

tenis *te·nees* m tennis; **el tenis sobre hierba** *te·nees so·bre yer·ba* lawn tennis

tenis de mesa *te·nees de me·sa* m table tennis

tensión *ten·syon* f stress (*tension*); blood pressure

tenso(a) *ten·so(a)* adj tense (*muscles*)

tentar *ten·tar* vt tempt

tentativa *ten·ta·tee·ba* f attempt

tentempié *ten·tem·pye* m snack

teoría *te·o·ree·a* f theory

tercer, tercero(a) *ter·ther, ter·the·ro(a)* adj third

tercera *ter·the·ra* f third (*gear*)

Tercer Mundo *ter·ther moon·do* m Third World

terciopelo *ter·thyo·pe·lo* m velvet

terminal *ter·mee·nal* f terminal (*air terminal*) □ m **el terminal** *ter·mee·nal* terminal (*computer*)

terminar *ter·mee·nar* vt/i end; finish

término *ter·mee·no* m term (*word*); end

termo *ter·mo* m Thermos

termómetro *ter·mo·me·tro* m thermometer

ternera *ter·ne·ra* f veal

terraplén *te·rra·plen* m embankment

terraza *te·rra·tha* f terrace (*of café*)

terremoto *te·rre·mo·to* m earthquake

terreno *te·rre·no* m land; piece of land

terrible *te·rree·ble* adj terrible

territorio *te·rree·to·ryo* m territory

terrón *te·rron* m lump of sugar

terrorismo *te·rro·rees·mo* m terrorism

terrorista *te·rro·rees·ta* m/f terrorist

terylene *te·ree·le·ne* m dacron; terylene

tesoro *te·so·ro* m treasure

test *test* m test

testamento *tes·ta·men·to* m will (testament)

testigo *tes·tee·go* m witness; firmar como testigo *feer·mar ko·mo tes·tee·go* to witness (signature)

testimonio *tes·tee·mo·nyo* m evidence (of witness)

tetera *te·te·ra* f teapot

tetilla *te·teel·ya* f nipple; teat (for bottle)

texto *teks·to* m text

textura *teks·too·ra* f texture

tez *teth* f complexion

tía *tee·a* f aunt(ie)

tibio(a) *tee·byo(a)* adj warm

tiburón *tee·boo·ron* m shark

tiempo *tyem·po* m time, weather; justo a tiempo *khoos·to a tyem·po* just in time; a tiempo *a tyem·po* on time; poco tiempo *po·ko tyem·po* a short time; mucho tiempo *moo·cho tyem·po* a long time; en tiempos pasados *en tyem·pos pa·sa·dos* in times past

tienda *tyen·da* f store; shop; ir de tiendas *eer de tyen·das* to go round the shops; la tienda de jardinería *tyen·da de khar·dee·ne·ree·a* garden center; la tienda de campaña *tyen·da de kam·pan·ya* tent; la tienda de jugetes *tyen·da de khoo·ge·tes* toyshop

tierno(a) *tyer·no(a)* adj tender (meat, vegetables)

tierra *tye·rra* f earth; land (opposed to sea); land (soil); a tierra a *tye·rra* ashore; las tierras *tye·rras* land (property)

tiesto *tyes·to* m pot (for plant)

tigre *tee·gre* m tiger

tijeras *tee·khe·ras* fpl scissors; pair of scissors

timbre *teem·bre* m doorbell; bell

tímido(a) *tee·mee·do(a)* adj shy

timón *tee·mon* m steering wheel; rudder

tinta *teen·ta* f ink

tinte *teen·te* m dye

tintineo *teen·tee·ne·o* m jingle (advertising)

tintorería *teen·to·re·ree·a* f dry-cleaner's

tío *tee·o* m uncle

tiovivo *tee·o·bee·bo* m merry-go-round

típico(a) *tee·pee·ko(a)* adj typical

tipo *tee·po* m sort; type; fellow; el tipo de cambio *tee·po de kam·byo* rate of exchange; tener buen tipo *te·ner bwen tee·po* to have a nice figure

tira *tee·ra* f strip (stripe, length); la tira humorística *tee·ra oo·mo·rees·tee·ka* cartoon

tirador *tee·ra·dor* m knob (on door); handle; el tirador de puerta *tee·ra·dor de pwer·ta* door handle, doorknob

tirante *tee·ran·te* adj tight (rope)

tirantes *tee·ran·tes* mpl suspenders; sin tirantes *seen tee·ran·tes* strapless

tirar *tee·rar* vt throw; throw away □ vt/i pull; para tirar *pa·ra tee·rar* disposable

titular *tee·too·lar* m headline

título *tee·too·lo* m degree (university); title

tiza *tee·tha* f chalk

toalla *to·al·ya* f towel

tobillo *to·beel·yo* m ankle

tobogán *to·bo·gan* m slide (chute)

tocadiscos *to·ka·dees·kos* m record player; el tocadiscos automático *to·ka·dees·kos ow·to·ma·tee·ko* jukebox

tocador *to·ka·dor* m dressing table

tocar *to·kar* vt touch; ring the (door)bell; feel; handle; le toca a Ud *le to·ka a oos·ted* it's your turn; tocar el violín *to·kar el byo·leen* to play the violin; tocar el claxon *to·kar el klak·son* to sound one's horn

todavía *to·da·bee·a* adv yet; still; todavía no *to·da·bee·a no* not yet

todo *to·do* pron everything; all □ adj todo(a) *to·do(a)* all; todas las mesas *to·das las me·sas* all the tables; todo el pan *to·do el pan* all the bread, todo lo que Ud necesita *to·do lo ke oos·ted ne·the·see·ta* all you need; (durante) todo el día *(doo·ran·te) to·do el dee·a* all day long; todo el mundo *to·do el moon·do* everybody, everyone

toga *to·ga* f gown (academic)

toldo *tol·do* m awning

tomar *to·mar* vt take; ¿toma Ud azúcar? *to·ma oos·ted a·thoo·kar* do you take sugar?; ¿quiere tomar algo? *kye·re to·mar al·go* would you like a drink?; tomar una decisión *to·mar oo·na de·thee·syon* to take a decision; tomar el aire *to·mar el ay·re* to take off (plane)

tomate *to·ma·te* m tomato

tomillo *to·meel·yo* m thyme

tomo *to·mo* m volume (book)

tonelada *to·ne·la·da* f ton; tonne

tónica *to·nee·ka* f tonic water

tónico *to·nee·ko* m tonic (medicine)

tono *to·no* m tone; el tono de marcar *to·no de mar·kar* dial tone

tonterías *ton·te·ree·as* fpl nonsense; decir tonterías *de·theer ton·te·ree·as* to talk nonsense

tonto(a) *ton·to(a)* adj dumb (stupid)

topinambur *to·pee·nam·boor* m Jerusalem artichoke

topógrafo *to·po·gra·fo* m inspector (of land)

torbellino *tor·bel·yee·no* m whirlwind

torcedura *tor·the·doo·ra* f sprain

torcer *tor·ther* vt twist; bend □ vi turn (person, car)

torcerse *tor·ther·se* vr strain (muscle); torcerse el tobillo *tor·ther·se el to·beel·yo* to sprain one's ankle

torcido(a) *tor·thee·do(a)* adj crooked

tormenta *tor·men·ta* f thunderstorm; la tormenta de nieve *tor·men·ta de nye·be* blizzard

tornillo *tor·neel·yo* m screw

toro *to·ro* m bull

torpe *tor·pe* adj clumsy (person)

torre *to·rre* f tower; la torre de pisos *to·rre de pee·sos* apartment house; la torre de control *to·rre de con·trol* control tower

torta *tor·ta* f gateau; dar una torta *dar oo·na tor·ta* to smack

tortícolis *tor·tee·ko·lees* f stiff neck

tortilla *tor·teel·ya* f omelet

tos *tos* f cough; la tos ferina *la tos fe·ree·na* whooping cough

toser *to·ser* vi cough

tostada *tos·ta·da* f toast

tostador *tos·ta·dor* m toaster

total *to·tal* adj total □ m el total *to·tal* total; sum total

totalmente *to·tal·men·te* adv quite (*absolutely*)

trabajador *tra·ba·kha·dor* m worker

trabajar *tra·ba·khar* vi work

trabajo *tra·ba·kho* m work; job (*employment*); un trabajo bien hecho *oon tra·ba·kho byen e·cho* a good piece of work; el trabajo a destajo *tra·ba·kho a des·ta·kho* piecework; ir* al trabajo *eer al tra·ba·kho* to go to work

tracción delantera *trak·thyon de·lan·te·ra* f front-wheel drive; tracción trasera *trak·thyon tra·se·ra* rear-wheel drive

tractor *trak·tor* m tractor

tradición *tra·dee·thyon* f tradition

traducción *tra·dook·thyon* f translation

traducir* *tra·doo·theer* vt translate

traer* *tra·er* vt get (*fetch*); bring

tráfico *tra·fee·ko* m traffic (*cars*)

tragar* *tra·gar* vt/i swallow

traje *tra·khe* m suit; outfit (*clothes*); el traje de playa *tra·khe de pla·ya* sun dress; traje de calle *tra·khe de kal·ye* dress: informal; el traje de noche *tra·khe de no·che* evening dress (*woman's*); el traje de etiqueta *tra·khe de e·tee·ke·ta* evening dress (*man's*); el traje largo *tra·khe lar·go* gown (*dress*); el traje de baño *tra·khe de ban·yo* swimsuit; bathing suit; el traje de novia *tra·khe de no·bya* wedding dress

traje-pantalón *tra·khe-pan·ta·lon* m pant(s) suit

trampa *tram·pa* f trap; hacer* trampas *a·ther tram·pas* to cheat

trampolín *tram·po·leen* m divingboard

tranquilidad *tran·kee·lee·dad* f peace (*calm*)

tranquilizante *tran·kee·lee·than·te* m tranquilizer

tranquilo(a) *tran·kee·lo(a)* adj quiet; calm; peaceful

transacción *tran·sa·thyon* f transaction

transatlántico(a) *trans·at·lan·tee·ko(a)* adj transatlantic □ m el transatlántico *tran·sat·lan·tee·ko* liner (*ship*)

transbordador *trans·bor·da·dor* m carferry

transbordo *trans·bor·do* m transfer; hacer* transbordo en Marsella *a·ther trans·bor·do en Mar·sel·ya* to change trains at Marseilles

transferir* *trans·fe·reer* vt transfer

transformación *trans·for·ma·thyon* f change (*transformation*)

transistor *tran·sees·tor* m transistor

tránsito *tran·see·to* m traffic; en tránsito *en tran·see·to* in transit

transmisión *trans·mee·syon* f transmission (*of car*)

transmisor *trans·mee·sor* m transmitter

transmitir *trans·mee·teer* vt broadcast (*on television*)

transparente *trans·pa·ren·te* adj transparent; clear

transpirar *trans·pee·rar* vi perspire

transportar *trans·por·tar* vt transport; ship (*goods*)

transporte *trans·por·te* m transport

tranvía *tran·bee·a* m tram(car)

trapo *tra·po* m rag; el trapo de cocina *tra·po de ko·thee·na* dishtowel

trasero(a) *tra·se·ro(a)* adj rear (*wheel*) □ m el trasero *tra·se·ro* bottom (*of person*)

tratamiento *tra·ta·myen·to* m treatment; course of treatment

tratar *tra·tar* vt treat; process; tratar con una empresa *tra·tar kon oo·na em·pre·sa* to deal with a firm; tratar un tema *tra·tar oon te·ma* to deal with a subject

travesero *tra·be·se·ro* m bolster

travesía *tra·be·see·a* f crossing (*voyage*)

travieso(a) *tra·bye·so(a)* adj bad; naughty

treboles *tre·bo·les* mpl clubs (*in cards*)

trece *tre·the* num thirteen

treinta *treyn·ta* num thirty

tren *tren* m train; el tren de mercancías *tren de mer·kan·thee·as* freight train; en tren *en tren* by train

trenza *tren·tha* f plait (*of hair etc*)

tres *tres* num three

triángulo *tree·an·goo·lo* m triangle

tribu *tree·boo* f tribe

tribunal *tree·boo·nal* m court (*law*)

trigésimo(a) *tree·khe·see·mo(a)* adj thirtieth

trigo *tree·go* m wheat

trimestre *tree·mes·tre* m term (*of school etc*)

trinchar *treen·char* vt carve (*meat*)

trineo *tree·ne·o* m sleigh; sled(ge)

trípode *tree·po·de* m tripod

tripulación *tree·poo·la·thyon* f crew (*of ship, plane*)

triste *trees·te* adj sad; miserable; dull (*day, weather*)

triunfo *tree·oom·fo* m triumph; trump (*cards*)

trivial *tree·byal* adj trivial

trompeta *trom·pe·ta* f trumpet

tronada *tro·na·da* f thunderstorm

tronco *tron·ko* m trunk (*of tree*); log (*of wood*)

tropa *tro·pa* f troop

tropezar* *tro·pe·thar* vi slip; trip (*stumble*)

tropical *tro·pee·kal* adj tropical

trópicos *tro·pee·kos* mpl tropics

trotar *tro·tar* vi trot (*horse*)

trozo *tro·tho* m cut (*of meat*)

trucha *troo·cha* f trout

truco *troo·ko* m trick

trucos *troo·kos* mpl pool (*game*)

trueno *trwe·no* m thunder

trufa *troo·fa* f truffle (*fungus*)

trust *troost* m trust (*company*)

tu *too* adj your (*familiar form*)

tú *too* pron you (*familiar form*); tú mismo(a) *too mees·mo(a)* you yourself

tubo *too·bo* m pipe; tube; el tubo de respiración *too·bo de res·pee·ra·thyon* snorkel; el tubo de escape *too·bo de es·ka·pe* exhaust (*pipe*); el tubo de desagüe *too·bo de des·a·gwe* drainpipe

tulipán *too·lee·pan* m tulip

tumba *toom·ba* f grave

tumbona *toom·bo·na* f deckchair

tumor *too·mor* m growth (*anatomical*)

tunecino(a) *too·ne·thee·no(a)* adj Tunisian

túnel *too·nel* m tunnel

Túnez *too·neth* m Tunisia

túnica *too·nee·ka* f tunic (*of uniform*)

turco(a) *toor·ko(a)* adj Turkish

turismo *too·rees·mo* m tourism; sightseeing; tourist trade

turista *too·rees·ta* m/f tourist; la clase turista *kla·se too·rees·ta* tourist class

turno *toor·no* m shift (*of workmen*); por turno *por toor·no* in turn

turquesa *toor·ke·sa* adj turquoise
Turquía *toor·kee·a* f Turkey
turrón *too·rron* m nougat
tus *toos* adj your (*familiar form: plural*)
tutor *too·tor* m guardian
tuyo(a) *too·yo(a)* pron yours (*familiar form*)

U

úlcera *ool·the·ra* f ulcer
últimamente *ool·tee·ma·men·te* adv lately
ultimátum *ool·tee·ma·toom* m ultimatum
último(a) *ool·tee·mo(a)* adj last; las últimas noticias *las ool·tee·mas no·tee·thyas* the latest news; en último lugar *en ool·tee·mo loo·gar* last; el último de todos *ool·tee·mo de to·dos* the very last
de ultramar *de ool·tra·mar* adj overseas
ultramarinos *ool·tra·ma·ree·nos* m grocery shop
un(a) *oon(·na)* art a; an; un día *oon dee·a* one day
uña *oon·ya* f nail (*human*)
unánime *oo·na·nee·me* adj unanimous; estuvimos unánimes *es·too·bee·mos oo·na·nee·mes* we were unanimous
undécimo(a) *oon·de·thee·mo(a)* adj eleventh
Unesco *oo·nes·ko* f UNESCO
ungüento *oon·gwen·to* m ointment
único(a) *oo·nee·ko(a)* adj unique; single (*not double*); la única mujer allí *la oo·nee·ka moo·kher al·yee* the only woman there; un hijo único *oon ee·kho oo·nee·ko* an only child
unidad *oo·nee·dad* f unit (*of measurement; of machinery*)
uniforme *oo·nee·for·me* m uniform
unilateral *oo·nee·la·te·ral* adj unilateral
unión *oo·nyon* f union
Unión Soviética *oo·nyon so·bye·tee·ka* f Soviet Union
unir *oo·neer* vt connect (*join*); unite
unirse *oo·neer·se* vr merge
unisexual *oo·nee·seks·wal* adj unisex
universal *oo·nee·ber·sal* adj universal
universidad *oo·nee·ber·see·dad* f university
universo *oo·nee·ber·so* m universe
uno(a) *oo·no(·na)* num one □ pron oneself; uno debería... *oo·no de·be·ree·a* one should...; el uno al otro *el oo·no al o·tro* one another
untar *oon·tar* vt spread (*butter*)
urbanización *oor·ba·nee·tha·thyon* f development (*housing*)
urbano(a) *oor·ba·no(a)* adj urban
urgente *oor·khen·te* adj urgent
urgentemente *oor·khen·te·men·te* adv urgently
urogallo *oo·ro·gal·yo* m grouse (*bird*)
U.R.S.S. *oo·ee·rre·ee·se·ee·se* f U.S.S.R.
usar *oo·sar* vt use
uso *oo·so* m use; custom; en uso *en oo·so* in use
Usted (Ud) *oos·ted* pron you (*polite form*); Usted mismo(a) *oos·ted mees·mo(a)* you yourself (*polite form*); Ustedes (Uds) *oos·te·des* you (*plural form*); Ustedes mismos *oos·te·des mees·mos* you yourselves
útil *oo·teel* adj useful
utilizar *oo·tee·lee·thar* vt use
uva *oo·ba* f grape

V

vaca *ba·ka* f cow
vacaciones *ba·ka·thyo·nes* fpl vacation; holiday (*period*); de vacaciones *de ba·ka·thyo·nes* on vacation; on holiday
vacante *ba·kan·te* f vacancy (*job*)
vaciado *ba·thya·do* m plaster cast (*for limb*)
vaciar *ba·thyar* vt drain (*sump, pool*); empty
vacilar *ba·thee·lar* vi hesitate; vacilar en hacer algo *ba·thee·lar en a·ther al·go* to hesitate to do something
vacío(a) *ba·thee·o(a)* adj empty
vacunación *ba·koo·na·thyon* f vaccination
vado *ba·do* m ford
vagabundo *ba·ga·boon·do* m tramp
vagar *ba·gar* vi wander
vago(a) *ba·go(a)* adj vague
vagón *ba·gon* m coach (*of train*); car; el vagón de fumadores *ba·gon de foo·ma·do·res* smoker (*compartment*)
vagón-restaurante *ba·gon·res·tow·ran·te* m club car
vainilla *bay·neel·ya* f vanilla
vajilla *ba·kheel·ya* f crockery; la vajilla de plata *ba·kheel·ya de pla·ta* silver (*ware*)
vale *ba·le* m token; voucher
valer *ba·ler* vt be worth; vale la pena *ba·le la pe·na* it's worth it; más vale que nos vayamos *mas ba·le ke nos ba·ya·mos* we may as well go; vale *ba·le* it's OK
valet *ba·let* m jack (*cards*)
válido(a) *ba·lee·do(a)* adj valid
valiente *ba·lyen·te* adj brave
valioso(a) *ba·lyo·so(a)* adj worthwhile (*activity*); valuable
valle *bal·ye* m valley
valor *ba·lor* m value; el valor de primera clase *ba·lor de pree·me·ra kla·se* blue chip (*stock*); el valor en el mercado *ba·lor en el mer·ka·do* market value
valorar *ba·lo·rar* vt value
valores *ba·lo·res* mpl stocks (*financial*)
vals *bals* m waltz
válvula *bal·boo·la* f valve
vámonos *ba·mo·nos* v let's go
vándalo *ban·da·lo* m vandal
vanidoso(a) *ba·nee·do·so(a)* adj vain
en vano *en ba·no* adv in vain
vapor *ba·por* m steam; steamer (*ship*)
vaquero *ba·ke·ro* m cowboy
variable *ba·rya·ble* adj variable □ f variable
variación *ba·rya·thyon* f variation
variar *ba·ryar* vt/i vary
varicela *ba·ree·the·la* f chicken pox
variedad *ba·rye·dad* f variety
varilla graduada *ba·reel·ya gra·dwa·da* f dipstick
varios(as) *ba·ryos(as)* adj several; varias ciudades *ba·ryas thyoo·da·des* several towns; varios de nosotros *ba·ryos de no·so·tros* several of us
Varsovia *bar·so·bya* f Warsaw
vaselina *ba·se·lee·na* f vaseline; petroleum jelly
vaso *ba·so* m glass (*tumbler*)
Vaticano *ba·tee·ka·no* m Vatican
vatio *ba·tyo* m watt
vecindad *be·theen·dad* f neighborhood; las tiendas de la vecindad *las tyen·das de la be·theen·dad* the local shops

vecino(a) be·thee·no(a) m/f neighbor

vegetariano(a) be·khe·ta·rya·no(a) adj vegetarian

vehículo be·ee·koo·lo m vehicle

veinte beyn·te num twenty

veintiuna beyn·tee·oo·na f twenty one; blackjack

vejiga be·khee·ga f bladder

vela be·la f candle; sail; el deporte de la vela de·por·te de la be·la yachting; hacer* vela a·ther be·la to go yachting; sail

velero be·le·ro m sailboat

vello bel·yo m down (fluff)

velo be·lo m veil

velocidad be·lo·thee·dad f speed; segunda/tercera velocidad se·goon·da/ter·the·ra be·lo·thee·dad 2nd/3rd gear; cuarta/primera velocidad kwar·ta/pree·me·ra be·lo·thee·dad high/low gear

velocímetro be·lo·thee·me·tro m speedometer

veloz be·loth adj fast

vena be·na f vein

venado be·na·do m deer

venal be·nal adj corrupt

venda ben·da f bandage

vendaval ben·da·bal m gale

vendedor ben·de·dor m vendor; el vendedor ambulante ben·de·dor am·boo·lan·te door-to-door salesman; el vendedor de periódicos ben·de·dor de pe·ree·o·dee·kos newsdealer

vender ben·der vt sell; vender algo al por menor ben·der al·go al por me·nor to sell something retail

vendimia ben·dee·mya f harvest (of grapes); hacer* la vendimia a·ther la ben·dee·mya to harvest (grapes)

Venecia be·ne·thya f Venice

veneno be·ne·no m poison

venenoso(a) be·ne·no·so(a) adj poisonous

venezolano(a) be·ne·tho·la·no(a) adj Venezuelan

Venezuela be·ne·thwe·la f Venezuela

venir* be·neer vi come; ella vendría si... el·ya ben·dree·a see she would come if...; ¿vendremos mañana? ben·dre·mos man·ya·na shall we come tomorrow?; venga a casa con nosotros ben·ga a ka·sa kon no·so·tros come back to our place; venir* de Londres be·neer de lon·dres to come from London

venta ben·ta f sale; la venta al por menor ben·ta al por me·nor retail; la venta al por mayor ben·ta al por ma·yor wholesale

ventaja ben·ta·kha f advantage

ventana ben·ta·na f window (in house)

ventanilla ben·ta·neel·ya f window (in car, train)

ventilador ben·tee·la·dor m fan (electric, of car etc); ventilator

ventilar ben·tee·lar vt air (room)

ventisquero ben·tees·ke·ro m snowdrift

ver* ber vt/i see; watch; ver* un partido ber oon par·tee·do to watch a match

veranda be·ran·da f veranda

veraneante be·ra·ne·an·te m/f vacationer

verano be·ra·no m summer

verbal ber·bal adj verbal

verdad ber·dad f truth; de verdad de ber·dad true; lo conoce, ¿verdad? le ko·no·the ber·dad you know him, don't you?; no vino, ¿verdad? no bee·no ber·dad he didn't come, did

he?; de verdad de ber·dad really; es un problema de verdad es oon pro·ble·ma de ber·dad it's a real problem

verdadero(a) ber·da·de·ro(a) adj real

verde ber·de adj green; unripe

verdulería ber·doo·ras fpl vegetables

vereda be·re·da f pavement; sidewalk

veredicto be·re·deek·to m verdict

vergüenza ber·gwen·tha f shame

verificar* be·ree·fee·kar vt check (train time etc); audit

verja ber·kha f railings

vermut ber·moot m vermouth

verruga ber·roo·ga f wart

versión ber·syon f version

vertical ber·tee·kal adj vertical

vestíbulo bes·tee·boo·lo m hall; lobby

vestido bes·tee·do m dress; el vestido nacional bes·tee·do na·thyo·nal national dress; el vestido de premamá bes·tee·do de pre·ma·ma maternity dress

vestir* bes·teer vt dress (child)

vestirse bes·teer·se vr dress oneself

veta be·ta f grain (in wood)

vetar be·tar vt veto

veterinario be·te·ree·na·ryo m vet(erinary surgeon)

veto be·to m veto

vez beth f, pl veces be·thes time; una vez más oo·na beth mas once more; en vez de en beth de instead of; otra vez o·tra beth again; alguna vez al·goo·na beth ever; dos veces al día dos be·thes al dee·a twice a day; de vez en cuando de beth en kwan·do now and then, now and again; from time to time; la primera vez la pree·me·ra beth the first time; ¿cuántas veces? kwan·tas be·thes how many times?; a veces a be·thes sometimes; una vez oo·na beth once

vía bee·a f track; rails; la vía de agua bee·a de a·gwa leak (water); la vía de acceso bee·a de ak·the·so entrance ramp; exit ramp

viabilidad bya·bee·lee·dad f feasibility

viaducto bya·dook·to m viaduct

viajante bee·a·khan·te m salesman (rep)

viajar bya·khar m travel □ vi viajar bya·khar travel; viajar en primera clase bya·khar en pree·me·ra kla·se to travel first class; viajar directamente a Venecia bya·khar dee·rek·ta·men·te a be·ne·thya to travel to Venice direct; viajar en avión bee·a·khar en a·byon to fly

viaje bee·a·khe m journey; trip; el viaje de ida y vuelta bee·a·khe de ee·da ee bwel·ta round trip; el viaje de negocios bee·a·khe de ne·go·thyos business trip; el viaje aéreo bee·a·khe a·e·re·o air travel; el viaje organizado bee·a·khe or·ga·nee·tha·do package holiday

viajero bya·khe·ro m traveler

víbora bee·bo·ra f adder (snake)

vicepresidente bee·the·pre·see·den·te m vice chairman; vice president

viceversa bee·the·ber·sa adv vice versa

víctima beek·tee·ma f victim (of accident etc)

victoria beek·to·rya f victory

vida bee·da f life; ganarse la vida ga·nar·se la bee·da to earn one's living; para toda la vida pa·ra to·da la bee·da for life

video bee·de·o m video

vidriera bee·drye·ra f stained glass window

vidrio bee·dryo m glass

vieira byey·ra f scallop

viejo(a) bye·kho(a) adj old

Viena bye·na f Vienna

viento byen·to m wind; hace mucho viento a·the moo·cho byen·to it's very windy

viernes byer·nes m Friday; viernes santo byer·nes san·to Good Friday

viga bee·ga f beam (of wood)

vigilante bee·khee·lan·te m lifeguard

vigilar bee·khee·lar vt guard

villancico beel·yan·thee·ko m carol

viña been·ya f vineyard

vinagre bee·na·gre m vinegar

vinagreta bee·na·gre·ta f salad dressing; vinaigrette (sauce)

vinilo bee·nee·lo m vinyl

vino bee·no m wine; el vino de Mosela bee·no de mo·se·la moselle (wine); el vino de calidad bee·no de ka·lee·dad a vintage wine; el vino del Rin bee·no del reen Rhine (wine)

violencia byo·len·thya f violence

violento(a) byo·len·to(a) adj rough (not gentle)

violín byo·leen m violin

violoncelo hyo·lon·the·lo m cello

viraje bee·ra·khe m turn; swerve; el viraje en U bee·ra·khe en oo U-turn (in car)

virar bee·rar vi tack (sailing)

viruela bee·rwe·la f smallpox

visa bee·sa f visa, visé

visado bee·sa·do m visa, visé; el visado de tránsito bee·sa·do de tran·see·to transit visa

visera bee·se·ra f sun visor (in car); peak (of cap)

visible bee·see·ble adj visible

visita bee·see·ta f visit; visitor; la visita con guía bee·see·ta kon gee·a guided tour

visitar bee·see·tar vt visit

visón bee·son m mink

vista bees·ta f view; eyesight

vitamina bee·ta·mee·na f vitamin

vitrina bee·tree·na f shop window

viuda byoo·da f widow

viudo byoo·do m widower

vivacidad bee·ba·thee·dad f life (liveliness)

vivienda bee·byen·da f housing

vivir bee·beer vi live

vivo(a) bee·bo(a) adj live; alive; bright

vocabulario bo·ka·boo·la·ryo m vocabulary

vodka bod·ka f vodka

volante bo·lan·te m steering wheel

volar* bo·lar vi fly □ m el volar bo·lar flying

volcán bol·kan m volcano

voleibol bo·ley·bol m volleyball

volován bo·lo·ban m vol-au-vent

voltaje vol·ta·khe m voltage

volumen bo·loo·men m volume (sound, capacity); el volumen de ventas bo·loo·men de ben·tas volume of sales

volver* bol·ber vi to come back; to go back; return □ vt to turn something over; volver* en sí bol·ber en see to come around; revive; volver* algo bol·ber al·go to turn something round; volver* a poner bol·ber a po·ner to replace (put back)

volverse bol·ber·se vr turn round

vomitar bo·mee·tar vi vomit; be sick

votación bo·ta·thyon f ballot

votar bo·tar vi vote

voto bo·to m vote

voz both f voice; en voz alta en both al·ta aloud

vuelo bwe·lo m flight; el vuelo charter bwe·lo char·ter charter flight; vuelo nocturno bwe·lo nok·toor·no night flight; el vuelo regular bwe·lo re·goo·lar scheduled flight; el vuelo sin motor bwe·lo seen mo·tor gliding (sport)

vuelta bwel·ta f turn; return (going/coming back); round (in competition); lap (of track); dar* vueltas dar bwel·tas to twist (road); dar* vueltas a algo dar bwel·tas a al·go to turn something round; no me devolvió toda la vuelta no me de·bol·byo to·da la bwel·ta he gave me short change

vuestro(a) bwes·tro(a) adj your □ pron el/la vuestro(a) el/la bwes·tro(a) yours

W

wáter ba·ter m lavatory; toilet

whisky wees·kee m whiskey; el whisky americano wees·kee a·me·ree·ka·no bourbon; el whisky escocés wees·kee es·ko·thes Scotch (liquor); un whisky con sifón oon wees·kee kon see·fon a whiskey and soda; el whisky de centeno wees·kee de then·te·no rye (whiskey)

Y

y ee conj and

ya ya adv already

yate ya·te m yacht; el yate de motor ya·te de mo·tor cabin cruiser

yerno yer·no m son-in-law

yeso ye·so m plaster (for wall); el yeso blanco ye·so blan·ko plaster of Paris

yo yo pron I; soy yo soy yo it's me

yodo yo·do m iodine

yoga yo·ga m yoga

yogur yo·goor m yogurt; el yogur natural yo·goor na·too·ral plain yogurt

Yugoslavia yoo·gos·la·bya f Yugoslavia

yugoslavo(a) yoo·gos·la·bo(a) adj Yugoslav(ian)

Z

zambullirse tham·bool·yeer·se vr dive

zanahoria tha·na·o·rya f carrot

zancudo than·koo·do m mosquito

zanja than·kha f ditch

zapata tha·pa·ta f shoe (of brake)

zapatería tha·pa·te·ree·a f shoeshop

zapatilla tha·pa·teel·ya f slipper; la zapatilla de tenis tha·pa·teel·ya de te·nees tennis shoe

zapato tha·pa·to m shoe

zarzamora thar·tha·mo·ra f blackberry

zona tho·na f zone; la zona reservada para peatones tho·na re·ser·ba·da pa·ra pe·a·to·nes pedestrian precinct

zoo tho m zoo

zorro tho·rro m fox

zumbar thoom·bar vi roar (engine)

zumbido thoom·bee·do m roar (of engine)

zumo thoo·mo m juice; el zumo de naranja thoo·mo de na·ran·kha orange juice; el zumo de limón thoo·mo de lee·mon lemon juice

zurcir* thoor·theer vt darn

zurdo(a) thoor·do(a) adj left-handed

ENGLISH–SPANISH DICTIONARY

a *art* un(a) *oon(·a)*; **twice a day** dos veces al día *dos be·thes al dee·a*; **$40 a week** $40 por semana *$40 por se·ma·na*

abbey *n* la abadía *a·ba·dee·a*

abbreviation *n* la abreviatura *a·bre·bya·too·ra*

abdomen *n* el abdomen *ab·do·men*

ability *n* la habilidad *a·bee·lee·dad*

able *adj* □ **to be able to do something** poder* hacer algo *po·der a·ther al·go*

aboard *adv* □ **to go aboard** ir* a bordo *eer a bor·do* □ *prep* **aboard the ship** a bordo del barco *a bor·do del bar·ko*

abolish *vt* abolir *a·bo·leer*

about *prep* □ **about $10** aproximadamente $10 *a·pro·ksee·ma·da·men·te $10*; **to talk about something** hablar sobre algo *a·blar so·bre al·go* □ *adv* **things lying about** cosas tiradas por todas partes *ko·sas tee·ra·das por to·das par·tes*; **to look about** mirar alrededor *mee·rar al·re·de·dor*; **to be about to do something** estar* a punto de hacer algo *es·tar a poon·to de a·ther al·go*

above *prep* □ **the house is above the valley** la casa está situada más arriba del valle *la ka·sa es·ta see·twa·da mas a·rree·ba del bal·ye* □ *adv* **above, you can see...** arriba se ven... *a·rree·ba se ben*

abroad *adv* en el extranjero *en el eks·tran·khe·ro*; **to go abroad** ir* al extranjero *eer al eks·tran·khe·ro*

abrupt *adj* (person) brusco(a) *broos·ko(a)*; (slope) escarpado(a) *es·kar·pa·do(a)*

abscess *n* el absceso *abs·the·so*

absent *adj* ausente *ow·sen·te*

absenteeism *n* el absentismo *ab·sen·tees·mo*

absolute *adj* absoluto(a) *ab·so·loo·to(a)*

absorb *vt* (fluid) absorber *ab·sor·ber*; (shock) amortiguar *a·mor·tee·gwar*

absorbent *adj* absorbente *ab·sor·ben·te*

absorbent cotton *n* el algodón hidrófilo *al·go·don ee·dro·fee·lo*

abstain *vi* (in voting) abstenerse* *abs·te·ner·se*

abstract *adj* abstracto(a) *abs·trak·to(a)*

absurd *adj* absurdo(a) *ab·soor·do(a)*

academy *n* □ **academy of music** el conservatorio *kon·ser·ba·to·ryo*; **military academy** la academia militar *a·ka·de·mya mee·lee·tar*

accelerate *vi* acelerar *a·the·le·rar*

accelerator *n* el acelerador *a·the·le·ra·dor*

accent *n* el acento *a·then·to*

accept *vt* aceptar *a·thep·tar*

acceptance *n* la aceptación *a·thep·ta·thyon*

access *n* el acceso *ak·the·so*

accessible *adj* accesible *ak·the·see·ble*

accessories *pl* los accesorios *ak·the·so·ryos*

accident *n* el accidente *ak·thee·den·te*; **by accident** por casualidad *por ka·swa·lee·dad* I12, Ea3

accidental *adj* fortuito(a) *for·twee·to(a)*

accommodations *n* el alojamiento *a·lo·kha·myen·to* A4f

accompany *vt* (go with) acompañar *a·kom·pan·yar*

according to *prep* según *se·goon*

account *n* (at bank, shop) la cuenta *kwen·ta* M29

accountancy *n* la contabilidad *kon·ta·bee·lee·dad*

accountant *n* el contable *kon·ta·ble*

accrue *vi* acumularse *a·koo·moo·lar·se*

accumulate *vi* acumularse *a·koo·moo·lar·se*

accurate *adj* exacto(a) *eks·ak·to(a)*

accuse *vt* acusar *a·koo·sar*

ace *n* (cards) el as *as*

ache *n* el dolor *do·lor* □ *vi* doler* *do·ler*

acid *n* el ácido *a·thee·do*

acknowledge *vt* (letter) reconocer* *re·ko·no·ther*

acne *n* el acné *ak·ne*

acorn *n* la bellota *bel·yo·ta*

acquaintance *n* el/la conocido(a) *ko·no·thee·do(a)*

acquire *vt* adquirir* *ad·kee·reer*

acquisition *n* la adquisición *ad·kee·see·thyon*

acre *n* el acre *a·kre*

across *prep* □ **to walk across the road** cruzar* la calle *kroo·thar la kal·ye*; **I saw him from across the road** le vi al otro lado de la calle *le bee al o·tro la·do de la kal·ye*; **we drove across France** cruzamos Francia en coche *kroo·tha·mos fran·thya en ko·che*

acrylic *adj* acrílico(a) *a·kree·lee·ko(a)*

act *n* (of play) el acto *ak·to*; (at circus etc) el número *noo·me·ro* □ *vi* (behave) comportarse *kom·por·tar·se* □ *vt* **to act Hamlet** hacer* el papel de Hamlet *a·ther el pa·pel de ham·let*; **to act as X** actuar como X *ak·too·ar ko·mo X*

acting *adj* suplente *soo·plen·te*

action *n* (movement) la acción *ak·thyon*; (act) el acto *ak·to*

active *adj* (energetic) activo(a) *ak·tee·bo(a)*; (volcano) en actividad *en ak·tee·bee·dad*

activity *n* la actividad *ak·tee·bee·dad*

actor *n* el actor *ak·tor*

actress *n* la actriz *ak·treeth*

actually *adv* en realidad *en re·a·lee·dad*

acute accent *n* el acento agudo *a·then·to a·goo·do*

adapt *vt* adaptar *a·dap·tar*

adapter, adaptor *n* (electrical) el enchufe múltiple *en·choo·fe mool·tee·ple*

add *vt* (comment) añadir *an·ya·deer*; **add (up)** (numbers) sumar *soo·mar*

adder *n* (snake) la víbora *bee·bo·ra*

addict *n* el/la drogadicto(a) *dro·ga·deek·to(a)*

addition *n* la adición *a·dee·thyon*

address *n* la dirección *dee·rek·thyon* □ *vt* (letter) poner* la dirección en *po·ner la dee·rek·thyon en* T93, F2, S27

adhesive tape *n* (for wound) el esparadrapo *es·pa·ra·dra·po*

adjourn *vi* levantar la sesión *le·ban·tar la se·syon*

adjournment n la suspensión *soos·pen· syon*

adjust vt ajustar *a·khoos·tar*

administration n la administración *ad· mee·nees·tra·thyon*

admire vt admirar *ad·mee·rar*

admission n la entrada *en·tra·da* L14

admission fee n el precio de entrada *pre·thyo de en·tra·da*

adopt vt (child) adoptar *a·dop·tar;* (proposal) aprobar* *a·pro·bar*

Adriatic (Sea) n el Mar Adriático mar *a·dree·a·tee·ko*

adult n el adulto *a·dool·to* □ adj para adultos *pa·ra a·dool·tos*

advance vt (money) adelantar *a·de· lan·tar* □ vi avanzar *a·ban·thar* □ n (loan) el adelanto *a·de·lan·to;* in advance por adelantado *por a·de·lan· ta·do* M10

advantage n la ventaja *ben·ta·kha*

adventure n la aventura *a·ben·too·ra*

advertise vt (product) anunciar *a· noon·thyar* □ vi to advertise for a secretary poner* un anuncio para encontrar una secretaria *po·ner oon a·noon·thyo pa·ra en·kon·trar oo·na se·kre·ta·rya*

advertisement n el anuncio *a·noon· thyo*

advertising n la publicidad *poo·blee· thee·dad* Bm19

advertising agency n la agencia de publicidad *a·khen·thya de poo·blee· thee·dad*

advice n el consejo *kon·se·kho*

advise vt aconsejar *a·kon·se·khar;* to advise someone to do something aconsejar a alguien que haga algo *a· kon·se·khar a al·gyen ke a·ga al·go*

aerial n la antena *an·te·na*

aerosol n el aerosol *a·e·ro·sol*

affair n (matter) el asunto *a·soon·to;* affairs los asuntos *a·soon·tos*

affect vt influir* *een·floo·eer*

affection n el cariño *ka·reen·yo*

affectionate adj afectuoso(a) *a·fek·too· o·so(a)*

affiliated company n la filial *fee·lyal*

afford vt □ I can't afford it no tengo suficiente dinero *no ten·go soo·fee· thyen·te dee·ne·ro;* to be able to afford a new car poder* permitirse un coche nuevo *po·der per·mee·teer·se oon ko·che nwe·bo*

afraid adj □ to be afraid of something tener* miedo de algo *te·ner mye·do de al·go;* I'm afraid not me temo que no *me te·mo ke no;* I'm afraid I can't do it me temo que no puedo hacerlo *me te·mo ke no pwe·do a·ther·lo*

Africa n África (f) *a·free·ka*

African adj africano(a) *a·free·ka·no(a)*

after prep, adv después *des·pwes;* to come after someone/something seguir* a alguien/algo *se·geer a al·gyen/ al·go;* 4 years after 4 años después *4 an·yos des·pwes* □ conj after después de *des·pwes de;* after we had left después de que nos fuimos *des·pwes de ke nos fwee·mos*

afternoon n la tarde *tar·de*

aftershave (lotion) n la loción para después del afeitado *lo·thyon pa·ra des·pwes del a·fey·ta·do*

afterward(s) adv después *des·pwes*

again adv otra vez *o·tra beth*

against prep contra *kon·tra*

age n (of person) la edad *e·dad;* (era) la época *e·po·ka;* under age menor de edad *me·nor de e·dad*

agency n (office) la agencia *a·khen· thya*

agenda n el orden del día *or·den del dee·a*

agent n el agente *a·khen·te;* the Renault agent el concesionario de Renault *kon·the·syo·na·ryo de Re·nol*

aggressive adj agresivo(a) *a·gre·see· bo(a)*

agile adj ágil *a·kheel*

ago adv □ 4 years ago hace 4 años *a·the 4 an·yos*

agony n el dolor agudo *do·lor a·goo·do*

agree vt/i □ to agree with somebody estar* de acuerdo con alguien *es·tar de a·kwer·do kon al·gyen;* to agree on (price) ponerse* de acuerdo en *po·ner·se de a·kwer·do en;* onions don't agree with me las cebollas no me sientan bien *las the·bol·yas no me syen·tan byen*

agreement n el acuerdo *a·kwer·do*

agricultural adj agrícola *a·gree·ko·la*

agriculture n la agricultura *a·gree· kool·too·ra*

ahead adv □ to see something ahead ver* algo adelante *ber al·go a·de·lan· te;* to plan ahead hacer* proyectos con antelación *a·ther pro·yek·tos kon an·te·la·thyon;* to think ahead tener* en cuenta el futuro *te·ner en kwen·ta el foo·too·ro* □ prep ahead of the others más adelantado que los demás *mas a·de·lan·ta·do ke los de· mas*

aim vt apuntar *a·poon·tar;* to aim a gun at someone apuntar un fusil a alguien *a·poon·tar oon foo·seel a al· gyen* □ n (intention) el propósito *pro·po·see·to*

air n el aire *ay·re;* by air en avión *en a·byon* □ vt air (room) ventilar *ben· tee·lar;* (clothes) airear *ay·re·ar*

air bed n el colchón neumático *kol· chon ne·oo·ma·tee·ko*

air bus n el aerobús *a·e·ro·boos*

air-conditioned adj climatizado(a) *klee·ma·tee·tha·do(a)*

air conditioning n el aire acondicionado *ay·re a·kon·dee·thyo·na·do* A45

aircraft n el avión *a·byon*

air filter n el filtro de aire *feel·tro de ay·re*

air force n las fuerzas aéreas *fwer·thas a·e·re·as*

air freight n el flete por avión *fle·te por a·byon*

air letter n la carta aérea *kar·ta a·e·re·a*

airline n la línea aérea *lee·ne·a a·e·re·a*

air mail n □ by air mail por correo aéreo *por ko·rre·o a·e·re·o*

air mattress n el colchón neumático *kol·chon ne·oo·ma·tee·ko*

airplane n el avión *a·byon*

airport n el aeropuerto *a·e·ro·pwer·to* T37

airtight adj hermético(a) *er·me·tee· ko(a)*

air travel n el viaje aéreo *bee·a·khe a·e·re·o*

à la carte adv a la carta *a la kar·ta*

alarm n (signal, apparatus) la alarma *a·lar·ma* □ vt inquietar *een·kye·tar*

alarm (clock) n el despertador *des·per· ta·dor*

album n el álbum *al·boom*

alcohol n el alcohol *al·kol*

alcoholic adj (drink) alcohólico(a)

al·ko·lee·ko(a) □ n el/la alcohóli-co(a) **al·ko·lee·ko(a)**

alcove n el hueco **we·ko**

Algeria n Argelia (f) **ar·khe·lya**

Algerian adj argelino(a) **ar·khe·lee·no(a)**

Algiers n Argel (m) **ar·khel**

alike adj semejante **se·me·khan·te**

alive adj vivo(a) **bee·bo(a)**

all adj (with singular noun) todo(a) **to·do(a)**; (with plural noun) todos(as) **to·dos(as)**; all day todo el día **to·do el dee·a**; all the tables todas las mesas **to·das las me·sas**; all the bread todo el pan **to·do el pan**; all passengers todos los pasajeros **to·dos los pa·sa·khe·ros** □ pron all (singular) todo **to·do**; (plural) todos(as) **to·dos(as)**; all you need todo lo que Ud necesita **to·do lo ke oos·ted ne·the·see·ta**; all of them know that… todos ellos saben que… **to·dos el·yos sa·ben ke**

Allah n Alá (m) **a·la**

allergic to adj alérgico(a) a **a·ler·khee·ko(a) a**

allergy n la alergia **a·ler·khya**

alley n la callejuela **kal·ye·khwe·la**

alliance n la alianza **a·lee·an·tha**

allocate vt asignar **a·seeg·nar**

allow vt □ to allow someone to go dejar que se vaya alguien **de·khar ke se ba·ya al·gyen**; we will allow $10 le daremos $10 **le da·re·mos $10**; allow 10 minutes to get there cuente con 10 minutos para llegar **kwen·te kon 10 mee·noo·tos pa·ra lye·gar**

allowance n (state payment) la pensión **pen·syon**

alloy n la aleación **a·le·a·thyon**

all right adv (yes) muy bien **mooy byen**; he's all right (safe, fit) está bien **es·ta byen**; he did it all right (satisfactorily) lo ha hecho bien **lo a e·cho byen**

almond n la almendra **al·men·dra**

almond paste n la pasta de almendra **pas·ta de al·men·dra**

almost adv casi **ka·si**

alone adj solo(a) **so·lo(a)**

along prep □ along the street por la calle **por la kal·ye**

aloud adv (read) en voz alta **en both al·ta**

alphabet n el alfabeto **al·fa·be·to**

alpine adj alpino(a) **al·pee·no(a)**

Alps pl los Alpes **al·pes**

already adv ya **ya**

also adv también **tam·byen**

altar n el altar **al·tar**

alter vt modificar* **mo·dee·fee·kar**

alternator n (in car) el alternador **al·ter·na·dor**

although conj aunque **own·ke**

altitude n la altura **al·too·ra**

always adv siempre **syem·pre**

am vi □ I am (permanent state) soy **soy**; I am (temporary state) estoy **es·toy**

a.m. adv de la mañana **de la man·ya·na**

amalgamation n la fusión **foo·syon**

amateur n el/la aficionado(a) **a·fee·thyo·na·do(a)**

ambassador n el embajador **em·ba·kha·dor**

amber n (traffic light) el ámbar **am·bar**

ambition n (aim) la ambición **am·bee·thyon**

ambitious adj (person) ambicioso(a) **am·bee·thyo·so(a)**; (plan) grandioso(a) **gran·dyo·so(a)**

ambulance n la ambulancia **am·boo·lan·thya** I13

amenities pl las comodidades **ko·mo·dee·da·des**

America n América (f) **a·me·ree·ka**

American adj americano(a) **a·me·ree·ka·no(a)**; he's American es americano es **a·me·ree·ka·no**; she's American es americana es **a·me·ree·ka·na** Sn89

amethyst n la amatista **a·ma·tees·ta**

among prep entre **en·tre**

amount n (total) el importe **eem·por·te**; a large amount of X una gran cantidad de X **oo·na gran kan·tee·dad de X**; a small amount of X un poco de X **oon po·ko de X** □ vi it amounts to 10,000 pesetas asciende a 10,000 pesetas **as·thyen·de a 10,000 pe·se·tas**

amp n el amperio **am·pe·ryo**

amplifier n el amplificador **am·plee·fee·ka·dor**

amuse vt entretener* **en·tre·te·ner**

amusement park n el parque de atracciones **par·ke de a·trak·thyo·nes**

an art un(a) **oon(·na)**

analysis n el análisis **a·na·lee·sees**

analyze vt analizar* **a·na·lee·thar**

ancestor n el/la antepasado(a) **an·te·pa·sa·do(a)**

anchor n el ancla (f) **an·kla**

anchovy n la anchoa **an·cho·a**

and conj y, e **ee, e**; better and better cada vez mejor **ka·da beth me·khor**; to go and buy ir* a comprar **eer a kom·prar**

anemic adj anémico(a) **a·ne·mee·ko(a)**

anesthetic n el anestésico **a·nes·te·see·ko** I62

angel n el ángel **an·khel**

anger n la cólera **ko·le·ra**

angler n el pescador **pes·ka·dor**

angling n la pesca **pes·ka**

angora n (fabric) la angora **an·go·ra**

angry adj (person) enfadado(a) **en·fa·da·do(a)**; to be angry with someone estar* enfadado con alguien **es·tar en·fa·da·do kon al·gyen**

animal n el animal **a·nee·mal**

ankle n el tobillo **to·beel·yo**

anniversary n el aniversario **a·nee·ber·sa·ryo**

announce vt anunciar **a·noon·thyar**

annoy vt (person) molestar **mo·les·tar**; (thing) irritar **ee·rree·tar**

annual adj anual **a·noo·al**

annuity n la renta vitalicia **ren·ta bee·ta·lee·thya**

anorak n el anorak **a·no·rak**

another adj □ another beer please! otra cerveza, por favor **o·tra ther·be·tha por fa·bor**; I want to see another shirt quisiera ver otra camisa **kee·sye·ra ber o·tra ka·mee·sa**

answer n la respuesta **res·pwes·ta** □ vi responder **res·pon·der** □ vt to answer a question contestar una pregunta **kon·tes·tar oo·na pre·goon·ta**; to answer the phone contestar el teléfono **kon·tes·tar el te·le·fo·no**

ant n la hormiga **or·mee·ga**

Antarctic n el Antártico **an·tar·tee·ko**

antenna n la antena **an·te·na**

antibiotic n el antibiótico **an·tee·byo·tee·ko**

antifreeze n el anticongelante **an·tee·kon·khe·lan·te**

antihistamine n el antihistamínico **an·tee·ees·ta·mee·nee·ko**

antique n la antigüedad **an·tee·gwe·dad** S86

antique dealer n el anticuario *an·tee·kwa·ryo*

antiseptic n el antiséptico *an·tee·sep·tee·ko*

any adj □ give me any book deme cualquier libro *de·me kwal·kyer lee·bro*; we haven't any bread no tenemos pan *no te·ne·mos pan*; have you any bread? ¿tiene pan? *tye·ne pan*; is there any more soup? ¿hay más sopa? *ay mas so·pa* □ pron we haven't any no tenemos ninguno *no te·ne·mos neen·goo·no*; can any of you sing? ¿hay alguno entre Uds que sabe cantar? *ay al·goo·no en·tre oos·te·des ke sa·be can·tar*

anybody, anyone pron □ can you see anybody? ¿ve a alguien? *be a al·gyen*; I can't see anybody no veo a nadie *no be·o a na·dye*; anybody at all cualquiera *kwal·kye·ra*

anything pron □ can you see anything? ¿ve algo? *be al·go*; I can't see anything no veo nada *no be·o na·da*; anything at all cualquier cosa *kwal·kyer ko·sa*

anyway adv (nonetheless) de todos modos *de to·dos mo·dos*

anywhere adv □ I'll take you anywhere you like le llevaré donde Ud quiera *le lye·ha·re don·de oos·ted kye·ra*, I can't see it anywhere no lo veo en ningún sitio *no lo be·o en neen·goon see·tyo*

apart adv (separately) aparte *a·par·te*

apartment n el piso *pee·so*; apartment house la torre de pisos *to·rre de pee·sos*

ape n el mono *mo·no*

aperitif n el aperitivo *a·pe·ree·tee·bo*

apologize vi disculparse *dees·kool·par·se*

apparently adv por lo visto *por lo bees·to*

appear vi aparecer* *a·pa·re·ther*; he appears to be ill parece enfermo *pa·re·the en·fer·mo*; it appears that... parece que... *pa·re·the ke*

appendicitis n la apendicitis *a·pen·dee·thee·tees*

appetite n el apetito *a·pe·tee·to*

appetizer n la tapa *ta·pa*

applause n el aplauso *a·plow·so*

apple n la manzana *man·tha·na*

apple tree n el manzano *man·tha·no*

appliance n el aparato *a·pa·ra·to*

application n (for job) la solicitud *so·lee·thee·tool*

apply vi □ to apply for a job solicitar un trabajo *so·lee·thee·tar oon tra·ba·kho*

appoint vt nombrar *nom·brar*

appointment n (rendezvous) la cita *thee·ta*; (to job) el nombramiento *nom·bra·myen·to* Sn39, Bm9

appreciate vt apreciar *a·pre·thyar* □ vi (in value) aumentar en valor *ow·men·tar en ba·lor*

apprentice n el aprendiz *a·pren·deeth*

approach vi acercarse *a·ther·kar·se* □ vt to approach a place acercarse a un lugar *a·ther·kar·se a oon loo·gar*

approval n la aprobación *a·pro·ba·thyon*; on approval a prueba *a prwe·ba*

approve of vt aprobar* *a·pro·bar*

approximate adj aproximado(a) *a·pro·ksee·ma·do(a)*

apricot n el albaricoque *al·ba·ree·ko·ke*

April n abril (m) *a·breel*

apron n el mandil *man·deel*

aquarium n el acuario *a·kwa·ryo*

Arab n el árabe *a·ra·be*

Arabic adj árabe *a·ra·be* □ n el árabe *a·ra·be*

arcade n la arcada *ar·ka·da*

arch n el arco *ar·ko*

architect n el arquitecto *ar·kee·tek·to*

architecture n la arquitectura *ar·kee·tek·too·ra*

Arctic n el Ártico *ar·tee·ko*

are vi □ we are (nostros(as)) somos *(no·so·tros(as)) so·mos*; (temporary state) (nostros(as)) estamos *(no·so·tros(as)) es·ta·mos*; you are (Ud) es *(oos·ted) es*; (temporary state) (Ud) está *(oos·ted) es·ta*; they are (ellos(as)) son *(el·yos(as)) son*; (temporary state) (ellos(as)) están *(el·yos(as)) es·tan*

area n (of surface) el área (f) *a·re·a*; (region) la región *re·khyon*

Argentina n Argentina (f) *ar·khen·tee·na*

Argentine adj argentino(a) *ar·khen·tee·no(a)*

argue vi (quarrel) discutir *dees·koo·teer*

argument n (quarrel) la discusión *dees·koo·syon*

arithmetic n la aritmética *a·reet·me·tee·ka*

arm n (of person) el brazo *bra·tho* I23

armchair n el sillón *seel·yon*

arms pl las armas *ar·mas*

army n el ejército *e·kher·thee·to*

around adv □ to look around mirar alrededor *mee·rar al·re·de·dor*; things lying around cosas esparcidas por todos sitios *ko·sas es·par·thee·das por to·dos see·tyos* □ prep to go around the world viajar alrededor del mundo *bya·khar al·re·de·dor del moon·do*; the scarf around her neck la bufanda alrededor del cuello *la boo·fan·da al·re·de·dor del kwel·yo*; around $10 alrededor de $10 *al·re·de·dor de $10*

arrange vt arreglar *a·rre·glar*

arrears pl los atrasos *a·tra·sos*; to be in arrears with a payment estar* atrasado con un pago *es·tar a·tra·sa·do con oon pa·go*

arrest vt detener* *de·te·ner*

arrival n la llegada *lye·ga·da*

arrive vi llegar* *lye·gar*

arrow n la flecha *fle·cha*

art n el arte *ar·te*

artery n la arteria *ar·te·rya*

art gallery n el museo de arte *mu·se·o de ar·te*; (commercial) la galería *ga·le·ree·a*

arthritis n la artritis *ar·tree·tees*

artichoke n la alcachofa *al·ka·cho·fa*; Jerusalem artichoke el topinambur *to·pee·nam·boor*

article n el artículo *ar·tee·koo·lo*

artificial adj artificial *ar·tee·fee·thyal*

artist n el/la artista *ar·tees·ta*

as conj □ as he was asleep (because) como estaba dormido *ko·mo es·ta·ba dor·mee·do*; (while) mientras dormía *myen·tras dor·mee·a*; he arrived as we left llegó cuando nosotros salíamos *lye·go kwan·do no·so·tros sa·lee·a·mos*; do as I say haga lo que le digo *a·ga lo ke le dee·go*; as big as tan grande como *tan gran·de ko·mo*; as for this en cuanto a esto *en kwan·to a es·to*; as if, as though como si *ko·mo* see; **as well** (*too*) también *tam·byen*; **as much/many as** tan- to(a)/tantos(as) como *tan·to(a)/tan· tos(as) ko·mo*

asbestos *n* el amianto *a·myan·to*

ash *n* (*tree*) el fresno *fres·no*; (*cinders*) la ceniza *the·nee·tha*

ashamed *adj* □ **to be ashamed** aver- gonzarse* *a·ber·gon·thar·se*

ashcan *n* el cubo de la basura *koo·bo de la ba·soo·ra* A72

ashore *adv* a tierra *a tye·rra*

ashtray *n* el cenicero *the·nee·the·ro* A41

Asia *n* Asia (*f*) *a·sya*

Asian *adj* asiático(a) *a·sya·tee·ko(a)*

ask *vt/i* preguntar *pre·goon·tar*; **to ask a question** hacer* una pregunta *a·ther oo·na pre·goon·ta*; **to ask someone the time** preguntar la hora a alguien *pre·goon·tar la o·ra a al· gyen*; **to ask for something** pedir* algo *pe·deer al·go*; **to ask the price** preguntar el precio *pre·goon·tar el pre·thyo*

asleep *adj* dormido(a) *dor·mee·do(a)*

asparagus *n* el espárrago *es·pa·rra·go*

aspirin *n* la aspirina *as·pee·ree·na*

assemble *vt* (*parts of machine*) montar *mon·tar*

assembly line *n* la cadena de montaje *ka·de·na de mon·ta·khe*

asset *n* (*financial*) el activo *ak·tee·bo*

assistant *n* (*in shop*) el/la tendero(a) *ten·de·ro(a)* Bm7

associate *n* el socio *so·thyo*

association *n* la asociación *a·so·thya· thyon*

assorted *adj* surtido(a) *soor·tee·do(a)*

assume *vt* (*suppose*) suponer* *soo·po· ner*

asthma *n* el asma (*f*) *as·ma*

at *prep* □ **at 4 o'clock** a las 4 *a las 4*; **at my house** en mi casa *en mee ka·sa*; **at school** en el colegio *en el ko·le·khyo*; **to throw something at someone** tirar algo a alguien *tee·rar al·go a al·gyen*; **not at all** en absoluto *en ab·so·loo·to*; **at once** inmediatamente *ee·me·dya· ta·men·te*

Athens *n* Atenas (*f*) *a·te·nas*

athlete *n* el/la atleta *at·le·ta*

Atlantic Ocean *n* el Atlántico *at·lan· tee·ko*

atlas *n* el atlas *at·las*

attach *vt* sujetar *soo·khe·tar*

attack *vt* atacar* *a·ta·kar* □ *n* el ataque *a·ta·ke*

attempt *vt* intentar *een·ten·tar* □ *n* la tentativa *ten·ta·tee·ba*

attend *vt* (*meeting etc*) asistir a *a·sees· teer a*

attic *n* el desván *des·ban*

attitude *n* la actitud *ak·tee·tood*

attorney *n* el abogado *a·bo·ga·do*

aubergine *n* la berenjena *be·ren·khe· na*

auction *n* la subasta *soo·bas·ta*

audience *n* (*in theater*) el público *poo· blee·ko*

audio-guide *n* el guía automático *gee·a ow·to·ma·tee·ko* L4

audio-visual *adj* audiovisual *ow·dyo· bee·soo·al*

audit *vt* verificar* *be·ree·fee·kar*

auditor *n* el interventor de cuentas *een·ter·ben·tor de kwen·tas*

auditorium *n* la sala *sa·la*

au gratin *adj* gratinado(a) *gra·tee·na· do(a)*

August *n* agosto (*m*) *a·gos·to*

aunt(ie) *n* la tía *tee·a*

Australia *n* Australia (*f*) *ows·tra·lya*

Australian *adj* australiano(a) *ows·tra· lya·no(a)*; **he's Australian** es austra- liano *es ows·tra·lya·no*; **she's Aus- tralian** es australiana *es ows·tra· lya·na*

Austria *n* Austria (*f*) *ows·trya*

Austrian *adj* austriaco(a) *ows·trya· ko(a)*

author *n* el/la autor(a) *ow·to(·ra)*

automatic *adj* automático(a) *ow·to·ma· tee·ko(a)* □ *n* (*car*) el coche/carro au- tomático *ko·che/ka·rro ow·to·ma·tee· ko*

automatically *adv* automáticamente *ow·to·ma·tee·ka·men·te*

automation *n* la automatización *ow·to· ma·tee·tha·thyon*

auto(mobile) *n* el coche *ko·che*, el ca- rro (Am) *ka·rro* T103F

auto show *n* la exposición de automó- viles *eks·po·see·thyon de ow·to·mo· bee·les*

autumn *n* el otoño *o·ton·yo*

available *adj* disponible *dees·po·nee· ble*

avalanche *n* la avalancha *a·ba·lan·cha*

avenue *n* la avenida *a·be·nee·da*

average *adj* medio(a) *me·dyo(a)* □ *n* el promedio *pro·me·dyo*

aviation *n* la aviación *a·bya·thyon*

avocado *n* el aguacate *a·gwa·ka·te*, la palta (Am) *pal·ta*

avoid *vt* evitar *e·bee·tar*

away *adv* □ **away from home** fuera de casa *fwe·ra de ka·sa*; **he's away for a week** pasa una semana fuera *pa·sa oo·na se·ma·na fwe·ra*; **30 kilometers away** a 30 kilómetros *a 30 kee·lo·me· tros*

awful *adj* pésimo(a) *pe·see·mo(a)*

ax *n* el hacha (*f*) *a·cha*

axle *n* el eje *e·khe*

B

baby *n* el niño *neen·yo*; la niña *neen· ya* C18

baby buggy, baby carriage *n* el coche- cito de niño *ko·che·thee·to de neen·yo*

baby food *n* los alimentos infantiles *a·lee·men·tos een·fan·tee·les*

baby-sit *vt* cuidar niños *kwee·dar neen· yos* C4

baby-sitter *n* la cangura *kan·goo·ra*

baccarat *n* el bacará *ba·ka·ra*

bachelor *n* el soltero *sol·te·ro*

back *n* (*of person*) la espalda *es·pal· da*; (*of animal*) el lomo *lo·mo*; (*of chair*) el respaldo *res·pal·do*; (*reverse side*) el dorso *dor·so*; (*of hall, room*) el fondo *fon·do*; (*in sports*) el de- fensa *de·fen·sa* □ *adv* (*backwards*) hacia atrás *a·thya a·tras*; **come back** volver* *bol·ber*; **to go back** volver* *bol·ber* □ *vt* **back** (*support*) apoyar *a·po·yar*; (*financially*) financiar *fee· nan·thyar*; (*bet on*) apostar* a *a·pos· tar a*; **to back** (*car*) dar* marcha atrás *dar mar·cha a·tras*

backache *n* el dolor de espalda *do·lor de es·pal·da*

backdate *vt* (*letter*) poner* fecha atra- sada *po·ner fe·cha a·tra·sa·da*

backer *n* el promotor *pro·mo·tor*

backgammon *n* el backgammon *bak· ga·mon*

background *n* el fondo *fon·do*

backing *n* el apoyo *a·po·yo*

backlash n la reacción re·ak·thyon

backlog n □ backlog of work los atrasos a·tra·sos

back pack n la mochila mo·chee·la

backward adj (glance) hacia atrás a·thya a·tras; (child) atrasado(a) a·tra·sa·do(a)

backwards adv hacia atrás a·thya a·tras

bacon n el bacon bey·kon

bad adj (not good) malo(a) ma·lo(a); (naughty) travieso(a) tra·bye·so(a); to go bad (food) pudrirse* poo·dreer·se; a bad debt la deuda incobrable la de·oo·da een·ko·bra·ble

badge n (of metal) la insignia een·seeg·nya; (of cloth) el distintivo dees·teen·tee·bo

badly adv (not well) mal mal; to want something badly querer* algo muchísimo ke·rer al·go moo·chee·see·mo

badminton n el badminton bad·meen·ton

bag n (of paper) la bolsa bol·sa; (handbag) el bolso bol·so, bags (luggage) el equipaje e·kee·pa·khe B76, T22f, 78, $25

baggage n el equipaje e·kee·pa·khe

baggage car n el furgón de equipajes foor·gon de e·kee·pa·khes

baggage check n el talón de equipajes ta·lon de e·kee·pa·khes

baggage checkroom n la consigna kon·seeg·na T25, 33

baggage claim n la reclamación de equipajes re·kla·ma·thyon de e·kee·pa·khes

baggage room n la consigna kon·seeg·na

bail n (for prisoner) la fianza fee·an·tha; on bail bajo fianza ba·kho fee·an·tha

bait n (in fishing) el cebo the·bo

bake vt cocinar en el horno ko·thee·nar en el or·no

baker n el panadero pa·na·de·ro S29

bakery n la panadería pa·na·de·ree·a

balance n el equilibrio e·kee·lee·bryo; (remainder owed) el saldo sal·do; balance of power el equilibrio político e·kee·lee·bryo po·lee·tee·ko; balance of payments la balanza de pagos ba·lan·tha de pa·gos; balance of trade la balanza comercial ba·lan·tha ko·mer·thyal; to lose one's balance perder* el equilibrio per·der el e·kee·lee·bryo □ vt balance equilibrar e·kee·lee·brar; (accounts) hacer* balance a·ther ba·lan·the □ vi hacer* balance a·ther ba·lan·the

balance sheet n el balance ba·lan·the

balcony n el balcón bal·kon

bald adj calvo(a) kal·bo(a)

ball n la pelota pe·lo·ta; (inflated) el balón ba·lon; (of string, wool) el ovillo o·beel·yo; (dance) el baile bay·le

ballet n el ballet ba·le

balloon n el globo glo·bo

ballot n la votación bo·ta·thyon

bamboo n el bambú bam·boo

ban vt prohibir pro·ee·beer □ n la prohibición pro·ee·bee·thyon

banana n el plátano pla·ta·no

band n (musical) la banda ban·da

bandage n la venda ben·da

bandaid n el esparadrapo es·pa·ra·dra·po

bang n (of gun etc) el estallido es·tal·yee·do; (of door) el portazo por·ta·tho; (blow) el golpe gol·pe □ vt (door) cerrar* de golpe ther·rar de gol·pe; to bang one's head golpearse

la cabeza gol·pe·ar·se la ka·be·tha □ vi bang (gun etc) disparar dees·pa·rar

bangs pl el flequillo fle·keel·yo

bank n (of river, lake) la ribera ree·be·ra; (finance) el banco ban·ko □ vt (money) depositar en el banco de·po·see·tar en el ban·ko □ vi to bank with Smiths tener* una cuenta con Smiths te·ner oo·na kwen·ta kon Smiths M28f

bank account n la cuenta bancaria kwen·ta ban·ka·rya M29

bank balance n el saldo bancario sal·do ban·ka·ryo

bank bill n la letra bancaria le·tra ban·ka·rya

bankbook n la libreta de depósitos lee·bre·ta de de·po·see·tos

bank charges pl el recargo re·kar·go

banker n el banquero ban·ke·ro

bank loan n el préstamo bancario pres·ta·mo ban·ka·ryo

bank manager n el director de banco dee·rek·tor de ban·ko

bank note n el billete de banco beel·ye·te de ban·ko

bankrupt adj quebrado(a) ke·bra·do(a); to go bankrupt quebrar* ke·brar

bankruptcy n la bancarrota ban·ka·rro·ta

banner n la bandera ban·de·ra

banquet n el banquete ban·ke·te

baptism n el bautismo ba·oo·tees·mo

Baptist adj baptista bap·tees·ta

bar n (metal) la barra ba·rra; (counter) la barra ba·rra; (drinking establishment) el bar bar; bar of soap la pastilla (de jabón) pas·teel·ya (de kha·bon); bar of chocolate la barra de chocolate ba·rra de cho·ko·la·te L43

barbecue n la barbacoa bar·ba·ko·a

barbed wire n el alambre de espino a·lam·bre de es·pee·no

barber n el barbero bar·be·ro

bare adj (person, head) descubierto(a) des·koo·byer·to(a); to go barefoot ir* descalzo(a) eer des·kal·tho(a)

bargain n (cheap buy) la ganga gan·ga; to make a bargain hacer* un negocio a·ther oon ne·go·thyo

bargaining n (negotiation) la negociación ne·go·thya·thyon

barge n la barcaza bar·ka·tha

bark n (of tree) la corteza kor·te·tha; (of dog) el ladrido la·dree·do □ vi ladrar la·drar

barmaid n la camarera ka·ma·re·ra

barman n el camarero ka·ma·re·ro

barn n el granero gra·ne·ro

barracks pl el cuartel kwar·tel

barrel n (for beer) el barril ba·rreel

barrier n (fence) la barrera ba·rre·ra

bartender n el barman bar·man

base n la base ba·se □ vt basar ba·sar

baseball n el béisbol beys·bol

basement n el sótano so·ta·no

basic adj básico(a) ba·see·ko(a)

basically adv fundamentalmente foon·da·men·tal·men·te

basin n (dish) el cuenco kwen·ko; (for washing) el lavabo la·ba·bo A50

basis n la base ba·se

basket n la cesta thes·ta

basketball n el baloncesto ba·lon·thes·to, el basketball (Am) bas·ket·bol

bat n (animal) el murciélago moor·thye·la·go

bath n el baño ban·yo; (tub) la tina tee·na A4

bathe vi bañarse *ban·yar·se* □ vt (*wound* etc) limpiar *leem·pyar*

bathing cap n el gorro de baño *go·rro de ban·yo*

bathing suit n el traje de baño *tra·khe de ban·yo*

bathroom n el cuarto de baño *kwar·to de ban·yo*; (*lavatory*) el lavabo *la·ba·bo* A4, 17

batter n (*for frying*) el batido de rebozar *ba·tee·do de re·bo·thar*

battery n (*for radio* etc) la pila *pee·la*; (*in car*) la batería *ba·te·ree·a* T182

battle n la batalla *ba·tal·ya*

bay n (*on coast*) la bahía *ba·ee·a*

bazaar n el bazar *ba·thar*

be vi ser* *ser*; (*temporary state*) estar* *es·tar*; I am (yo) soy (*yo*) *soy*; (*temporary state*) (yo) estoy (*yo*) *es·toy*; you are Ud es *oos·ted es*; (*temporary state*) Ud está *oos·ted es·ta*; he is (él) es (*el*) *es*; (*temporary state*) (él) está (*el*) *es·ta*; we are (nosotros(as)) somos (*no·so·tros(as)*) *so·mos*; (*temporary state*) (nosotros(as)) estamos (*no·so·tros(as)*) *es·ta·mos*; they are (ellos(as)) son (*el·yos(as)*) *son*; (*temporary state*) (ellos(as)) están (*el·yos(as)*) *es·tan*; how are you? ¿cómo está Ud? *ko·mo es·ta oos·ted*; I am hungry tengo hambre *ten·go am·bre*; what is that? ¿qué es eso? *ke es e·so*; how much is it? ¿cuánto es? *kwan·to es*; it is hot hace calor *a·the ka·lor*; we are going to the beach nos vamos a la playa *nos ba·mos a la pla·ya*; we have been to Paris hemos estado en París *e·mos es·ta·do en pa·rees*; he is a doctor es médico *es me·dee·ko*

beach n la playa *pla·ya* L19

bead n la cuenta *kwen·ta*

beam n (*of wood*) la viga *bee·ga*; (*of light*) el rayo *ra·yo*

beans pl las alubias *a·loo·byas*, los frijoles (Am) *free·kho·les*

bear n el oso *o·so* □ vt soportar *so·por·tar*

beard n la barba *bar·ba*

bearings pl (*in car*) los cojinetes *ko·khee·ne·tes*; to take one's bearings orientarse *o·ryen·tar·se*

beat vt (*hit*) golpear *gol·pe·ar*; (*defeat*) derrotar *de·rro·tar* □ vi (*heart*) latir *la·teer*

beautiful adj hermoso(a) *er·mo·so(a)*

beauty n la belleza *bel·ye·tha*

because conj porque *por·ke*; because of a causa de *a kow·sa de*

become vi hacerse* *a·ther·se*

bed n la cama *ka·ma*; in bed en la cama *en la ka·ma*; to go to bed acostarse* *a·kos·tar·se* A4, I50

bedclothes pl la ropa de cama *ro·pa de ka·ma*

bedding n la ropa de cama *ro·pa de ka·ma* A69

bedroom n el dormitorio *dor·mee·to·ryo*

bee n la abeja *a·be·kha*

beech n la haya *a·ya*

beef n la carne de vaca *kar·ne de ba·ka*

beer n la cerveza *ther·be·tha* E56

beet n la remolacha *re·mo·la·cha*

beetle n el escarabajo *es·ka·ra·ba·kho*

before prep (*in time*) antes de *an·tes de*; before noon antes del mediodía *an·tes del me·dyo·dee·a*; before the king (*in space*) delante del rey *de·lan·te del rey* □ adv before antes *an·tes*; we've met before nos conocemos de antes *nos ko·no·the·mos de an·tes*

□ conj before antes de que *an·tes de ke*; before I go to bed antes de acostarme *an·tes de a·kos·tar·me*

beg vi mendigar* *men·dee·gar*

beggar n el mendigo *men·dee·go*

begin vt/i empezar* *em·pe·thar*

beginner n el/la principiante *preen·thee·pyan·te*

behalf n □ on behalf of en nombre de *en nom·bre de*

behave vi portarse *por·tar·se*; behave yourself! ¡pórtate bien! *por·ta·te byen*

behavior n el comportamiento *kom·por·ta·myen·to*

behind adv atrás *a·tras*; to look behind mirar hacia atrás *mee·rar a·thya a·tras*; to stand behind pararse detrás *pa·rar·se de·tras* □ prep behind the wall detrás de la pared *de·tras de la pa·red*; to be behind schedule estar* atrasado(a) *es·tar a·tra·sa·do(a)*

beige adj beige *beys*

belief n (*faith*) la fe *fe*; (*tenet*) la creencia *kre·en·thya*

believe vt/i creer* *kre·er*; to believe in creer* en *kre·er en*

bell n (*church* etc) la campana *kam·pa·na*; (*on door*) el timbre *teem·bre*

bellboy n el botones *bo·to·nes*

belong vi □ to belong to someone pertenecer* a alguien *per·te·ne·ther a al·gyen*; to belong to a club pertenecer* a un club *per·te·ne·ther a oon kloob*

belongings pl los efectos personales *e·fek·tos per·so·na·les*

below adv abajo *a·ba·kho*; to look below mirar debajo *mee·rar de·ba·kho*; to stand below pararse debajo *pa·rar·se de·ba·kho* □ prep to put one's case below the chair poner* la maleta debajo de la silla *po·ner la ma·le·ta de·ba·kho de la seel·ya*; my room is below his mi cuarto está debajo del suyo *mee kwar·to es·ta de·ba·kho del soo·yo*

belt n (*for waist*) el cinturón *theen·too·ron* S75

beltway n la carretera de circunvalación *ka·rre·te·ra de theer·koom·ba·la·thyon*

bench n el banco *ban·ko*

bend n la curva *koor·ba* □ vt doblar *do·blar* □ vi (*person*) encorvarse *en·kor·bar·se*; (*road*) desviarse *des·bee·ar·se*

beneath = below

benefit n el provecho *pro·be·cho*; it's of no benefit (to us) no nos beneficia *no nos be·ne·fee·thya*

berm n el arcén *ar·then*

berry n la baya *ba·ya*

berth n la litera *lee·te·ra*

beside prep al lado de *al la·do de*

besides adv (*moreover*) además *a·de·mas* □ prep besides him además de él *a·de·mas de el*

best adj mejor *me·khor* □ n he's the best es el mejor *es el me·khor* □ adv he can do it best él lo hace mejor *el lo a·the me·khor*

best man n el padrino de boda *pa·dree·no de bo·da*

bet vt/i apostar* *a·pos·tar* □ n la apuesta *a·pwes·ta*

better adj mejor *me·khor* □ adv he sings better than you canta mejor que Ud *kan·ta me·khor ke oos·ted*; to get better (*from illness*) mejorar *me·kho·rar*; they are better off than us (*richer*) son más ricos que nosotros *son mas ree·kos ke no·so·tros*

between *prep* entre *en·tre*
beyond *prep* más allá de *mas al·ya de*; beyond the wall más allá del muro *mas al·ya del moo·ro*; beyond my reach fuera de mi alcance *fwe·ra de mee al·kan·the*; beyond his means por encima de sus posibilidades *por en·thee·ma de soos po·see·bee·lee·da·des*
Bible *n* la Biblia *bee·blya*
bicycle *n* la bicicleta *bee·thee·kle·ta*
bid *vt* (amount) hacer* una oferta *a·ther oo·na o·fer·ta* □ *vi* to bid for something hacer* una oferta por algo *a·ther oo·na o·fer·ta por al·go* □ *n* bid la oferta *o·fer·ta*
bidder *n* el postor *pos·tor*
big *adj* gran, grande *gran gran·de*
bikini *n* el bikini *bee·kee·nee*
bilingual *adj* bilingüe *bee·leen·gwe*
bill *n* (account) la cuenta *kwen·ta*; (bank note) el billete de banco *beel·ye·te de ban·ko* T194, M14, 22, A21, E43
billiards *n* el billar *beel·yar*
billion *n* los mil millones *meel meel·yo·nes*
bin *n* (for refuse) el cubo de la basura *koo·bo de la ba·soo·ra*
bind *vt* (tie) atar *a·tar*
binoculars *pl* los prismáticos *prees·ma·tee·kos*
biology *n* la biología *bee·o·lo·khee·a*
birch *n* (tree) el abedul *a·be·dool*
bird *n* el pájaro *pa·kha·ro*
birth *n* el nacimiento *na·thee·myen·to*
birth certificate *n* la partida de nacimiento *par·tee·da de na·thee·myen·to*
birthday *n* el cumpleaños *koom·ple·an·yos*
biscuit *n* la galleta *gal·ye·ta*
bishop *n* el obispo *o·bees·po*
bit *n* (piece) el pedazo *pe·da·tho*; a bit of un poco de *oon po·ko de*
bite *vt* morder* *mor·der* □ *n* la mordedura *mor·de·doo·ra*; (by insect) la picadura *pee·ka·doo·ra*; (of food) el bocado *bo·ka·do*
bitter *adj* amargo(a) *a·mar·go(a)*
black *adj* negro(a) *ne·gro(a)*; a black coffee un café solo *oon ka·fe so·lo*
blackberry *n* la zarzamora *thar·tha·mo·ra*
blackbird *n* el mirlo *meer·lo*
black currant *n* la grosella negra *gro·sel·ya ne·gra*
black eye *n* el ojo morado *o·kho mo·ra·do*
blackjack *n* la veintiuna *beyn·tee·oo·na* L52
black market *n* el mercado negro *mer·ka·do ne·gro*
bladder *n* la vejiga *be·khee·ga*
blade *n* (of knife) la hoja *o·kha*
blame *vt* (reproach) culpar *kool·par*; to be to blame tener* la culpa *te·ner la kool·pa*
blank *adj* en blanco *en blan·ko*; blank check el cheque en blanco *el che·ke en blan·ko*; please leave blank por favor dejar en blanco *por fa·bor de·khar en blan·ko*
blanket *n* la manta *man·ta*, la frazada (Am) *fra·tha·da* A41
blast *n* (explosion) la explosión *eks·plo·syon*
blaze *n* (fire) el incendio *een·then·dyo* □ *vi* arder* *ar·der*; (lights) brillar *breel·yar*
blazer *n* la chaqueta de sport *cha·ke·ta de sport*

bleed *vi* sangrar *san·grar*
blend *vt* mezclar *meth·klar* □ *n* la mezcla *meth·kla*
bless *vt* bendecir* *ben·de·theer*
blind *adj* (person) ciego(a) *thye·go(a)* □ *n* (at window) el toldo *tol·do*
blind alley *n* el callejón sin salida *kal·ye·khon seen sa·lee·da*
blind corner *n* la curva sin visibilidad *koor·ba seen bee·see·bee·lee·dath*
blink *vi* pestañear *pes·tan·ye·ar*
blister *n* (on skin) la ampolla *am·pol·ya*
blizzard *n* la tormenta de nieve *tor·men·ta de nye·be*
block *n* (of stone) el bloque *blo·ke*; 3 blocks away (streets) a tres manzanas/cuadras (Am) *a tres man·tha·nas/kwa·dras*; apartment block el bloque de pisos *blo·ke de pee·sos* □ *vt* block (road) cerrar* *the·rrar*; (pipe) obstruir* *obs·troo·eer*; block letters las mayúsculas *ma·yoos·koo·las*; block booking la reserva en grupo *re·ser·ba en groo·po*
blockage *n* la obstrucción *obs·trook·thyon*
blond(e) *adj* rubio(a) *roo·byo(a)*
blood *n* la sangre *san·gre*
blood group *n* el grupo sanguíneo *groo·po san·gee·ne·o* 148, 49
blood poisoning *n* el envenenamiento de la sangre *en·be·ne·na·myen·to de la san·gre*
blood pressure *n* la tensión *ten·syon* I42
bloom *n* (flower) la flor *flor* □ *vi* florecer* *flo·re·ther*
blossom *n* la flor *flor*
blot *n* el borrón *bo·rron* □ *vt* (ink) emborronar *em·bo·rro·nar*
blouse *n* la blusa *bloo·sa* S19
blow *n* (knock) el golpe *gol·pe* □ *vi* (wind) soplar *so·plar*; (fuse) saltar *sal·tar* □ *vt* to blow one's nose sonarse* la nariz *so·nar·se la na·reeth*
blow-dry *n* el secado a mano *se·ka·do a ma·no*
blow-out *n* el pinchazo *peen·cha·tho*
blue *adj* azul *a·thool*
bluebottle *n* la moscarda *mos·kar·da*
blue chips *pl* el valor de primera clase *ba·lor de pree·me·ra kla·se*
blueprint *n* el anteproyecto *an·te·pro·yek·to*
blunt *adj* (knife) desafilado(a) *des·a·fee·la·do(a)*
blush *vi* ruborizarse *roo·bo·ree·thar·se*
board *n* (of wood) la tabla *ta·bla*; (for notices) el tablón de anuncios *tab·lon de a·noon·thyos*; (of directors) la junta directiva *khoon·ta dee·rek·tee·ba*; on board (ship, plane) a bordo *a bor·do* □ *vt* board (train, bus) subir *soo·beer*; (ship) embarcarse* *em·bar·kar·se*
boarding house *n* la casa de huéspedes *ka·sa de wes·pe·des*
boarding pass *n* la tarjeta de embarque *tar·khe·ta de em·bar·ke*
boast *vi* jactarse *khak·tar·se*
boat *n* el barco *bar·ko* L23
bobby pin *n* el pasador *pa·sa·dor*
body *n* el cuerpo *kwer·po*; (corpse) el cadáver *ka·da·ber*
bodyguard *n* (person) el guardaespaldas *gwar·da·es·pal·das*
bog *n* el pantano *pan·ta·no*
boil *vt/i* hervir* *er·beer* □ *n* (on skin) el divieso *dee·bye·so*
bold *adj* audaz *ow·dath*

bolster n el travesero tra·be·se·ro A42

bolt n el cerrojo the·rro·kho □ vt (door, gate) echar el cerrojo e·char el the·rro·kho

bomb n la bomba bom·ba

bone n el hueso we·so; (of fish) la espina es·pee·na

bonfire n la hoguera o·ge·ra

bonus n (on salary) la prima pree·ma

book n el libro lee·bro □ vt (seat) reservar re·ser·bar T64, 65

boom n (noise) el estampido es·tam·pee·do; (economic) el boom boom □ vi business is booming los negocios están en alza ne·go·thyos es·tan en al·tha

boost vt (sales) aumentar ow·men·tar

boot n la bota bo·ta

booth n (telephone) la cabina ka·bee·na

border n (edge) el borde bor·de; (of country) la frontera fron·te·ra

bored adj □ I'm bored estoy aburrido(a) es·toy a·boo·rree·do(a)

boring adj aburrido(a) a·boo·rree·do(a)

born adj nacido(a) na·thee·do(a); to be born nacer* na·ther

borough n el municipio moo·nee·thee·pyo

borrow vt pedir* prestado pe·deer pres·ta·do; to borrow something from someone pedir* prestado algo a alguien pe·deer pres·ta·do al·go a al·gyen

boss n el jefe khe·fe

botanical gardens pl el jardín botánico khar·deen bo·ta·nee·ko

both adj ambos(as) am·bos(as); both girls las dos chicas las dos chee·kas

bother vt (annoy) molestar mo·les·tar □ vi please don't bother por favor no se moleste por fa·bor no se mo·les·te □ n bother (nuisance) la molestia mo·les·tya; (effort) el fastidio fas·tee·dyo

bottle n la botella bo·tel·ya; (baby's) el biberón bee·be·ron E12, C2

bottleneck n el embotellamiento em·bo·tel·ya·myen·to

bottle opener n el abrebotellas a·bre·bo·tel·yas

bottom n el fondo fon·do; (of page, list) el pie pye; (of person) el trasero tra·se·ro □ adj de abajo de a·ba·kho

bounce vi (ball) rebotar re·bo·tar; (check) ser* rechazado ser re·cha·tha·do

bound adj □ bound for (ship) con destino a kon des·tee·no a □ n out of bounds prohibido(a) pro·ee·bee·do(a)

boundary n el límite lee·mee·te

bourbon n el whisky americano wees·kee a·me·ree·ka·no

boutique n la boutique boo·teek

bow[1] vi hacer* una reverencia a·ther oo·na re·be·ren·thya □ n la reverencia re·be·ren·thya

bow[2] n (ribbon) el lazo la·tho

bowl n (for food) el tazón ta·thon; (for washing) el barreño ba·rren·yo

bow tie n la pajarita pa·kha·ree·ta

box n la caja ka·kha; (cardboard) la caja de cartón ka·kha de kar·ton

boxing n el boxeo bok·se·o

box number n el apartado a·par·ta·do, la casilla (Am) ka·seel·ya

box office n la taquilla ta·keel·ya

boy n el niño neen·yo S109

boycott vt boicotear boy·ko·te·ar

boyfriend n el novio no·byo

bra n el sujetador soo·khe·ta·dor

bracelet n la pulsera pool·se·ra

bracken n el helecho e·le·cho

bracket n (in writing) el paréntesis pa·ren·te·sees

brain n el cerebro the·re·bro; **brains** (as food) los sesos se·sos

braised adj cocido(a) a fuego lento ko·thee·do(a) a fwe·go len·to

brake n el freno fre·no □ vi frenar fre·nar T178, 216

brake fluid n el líquido de frenos lee·kee·do de fre·nos

branch n (of tree) la rama ra·ma; (of store, bank etc) la sucursal soo·koor·sal

brand n (of product) la marca mar·ka S99

brand name n la marca de fábrica mar·ka de fa·bree·ka

brandy n el coñac kon·yak

brass n el latón la·ton

brave adj valiente ba·lyen·te

bread n el pan pan E29

break n (pause) el intervalo een·ter·ba·lo □ vt romper* rom·per; (record) batir ba·teer; to break in (car) rodar* ro·dar; to break one's arm romperse* el brazo rom·per·se el bra·tho □ vi break romperse* rom·per·se; to break down averiarse a·be·ryar·se B73, T169

breakdown n (of car) la avería a·be·ree·a

break even vi salir* sin ganar ni perder sa·leer seen ga·nar nee per·der

breakfast n el desayuno de·sa·yoo·no A9, 26

breast n el seno se·no; (chest) el pecho pe·cho; (of poultry) la pechuga pe·choo·ga

breath n el haliento a·lyen·to

breathe vi respirar res·pee·rar

breeze n la brisa bree·sa

brewery n la fábrica de cerveza fa·bree·ka de ther·be·tha

bribe vt sobornar so·bor·nar

brick n el ladrillo la·dreel·yo

bride n la novia no·bya

bridegroom n el novio no·byo

bridge n el puente pwen·te; (game) el bridge bridge

bridle n la brida bree·da

brief adj breve bre·be

briefcase n la cartera kar·te·ra, el portafolio (Am) por·ta·fo·lyo

briefs pl los calzoncillos kal·thon·theel·yos

bright adj vivo(a) bee·bo(a); (clever) listo(a) lees·to(a)

bring vt (thing) traer* tra·er; (person) llevar lye·bar; to bring in (profit) producir* pro·doo·theer

Britain n Gran Bretaña (f) gran bre·tan·ya

British adj británico(a) bree·ta·nee·ko(a); he's British es británico es bree·ta·nee·ko; she's British es británica es bree·ta·nee·ka

broad adj ancho(a) an·cho(a)

broadcast vt (on radio) radiar ra·dyar; (on television) transmitir trans·mee·teer □ n la emisión e·mee·syon

broccoli n el brécol bre·kol

brochure n el folleto fol·ye·to A6, Bm24

broil vt asar a la parrilla a·sar a la pa·rreel·ya

broke adj (penniless) sin blanca seen blan·ka

broker n el corredor de bolsa ko·rre· dor de bol·sa
bronchitis n la bronquitis bron·kee·tees
bronze n el bronce bron·the
brooch n el broche bro·che S87
broom n la escoba es·ko·ba
brother n el hermano er·ma·no
brother-in-law n el cuñado koon·ya·do
brown adj marrón ma·rron; (hair) castaño(a) kas·tan·yo(a)
bruise n el cardenal kar·de·nal
brush n (for cleaning) el cepillo the·peel·yo; (for painting) el pincel peen·thel; (for hair) el cepillo the·peel·yo □ vt cepillar the·peel·yar
Brussels n Bruselas (fpl) broo·se·las
Brussels sprouts pl las coles de Bruselas ko·les de broo·se·las
bubble n la burbuja boor·boo·kha
bucket n el cubo koo·bo
buckle n la hebilla e·beel·ya
bud n el brote bro·te
budget n el presupuesto pre·soo·pwes·to
bug n (insect) el bicho bee·cho
build vt (house) construir* kons·troo·eer
building n el edificio e·dee·fee·thyo L11
bulb n □ in bulb n el bulbo bool·bo; (light) la bombilla bom·beel·ya
bulk n □ in bulk (in large quantities) a granel a gra·nel; bulk (unpackaged) suelto(a) swel·to(a); bulk buying la compra en grandes cantidades kom·pra en gran·des kan·tee·da·des
bull n el toro to·ro
bulldozer n la excavadora eks·ka·ba·do·ra
bullet n la bala ba·la
bulletin n el boletín bo·le·teen
bulletin board n el tablón de anuncios ta·blon a·noon·thyos
bullfight n la corrida de toros ko·rree·da de to·ros
bump n (knock) el choque cho·ke; (lump) el chichón chee·chon □ vt golpear gol·pe·ar
bumper n (on car) el parachoques pa·ra·cho·kes
bun n el panecillo pa·ne·theel·yo
bunch n (of flowers) el ramo ra·mo
bundle n el montón mon·ton
bungalow n el chalé cha·le
bunk n la litera lee·te·ra; bunk beds las literas lee·te·ras
buoy n la boya bo·ya
buoyant adj (market) en alza en al·tha
bureau n (office) la oficina o·fee·thee·na
burglar n el ladrón la·dron
burn vt quemar ke·mar; I've burned my arm me he quemado el brazo me e ke·ma·do el bra·tho
burst vt estallar es·tal·yar □ vt reventar* re·ben·tar
bury vt (person) enterrar* en·te·rrar
bus n el autobús ow·to·boos T82f, F16
bush n el arbusto ar·boos·to
business n (dealings, work) los negocios ne·go·thyos; (firm) el comercio ko·mer·thyo; on business por asuntos de negocios por a·soon·tos de ne·go·thyos; to do business with someone comerciar con alguien ko·mer·thyar kon al·gyen E6, Bm13, 32
business expenses pl los gastos comerciales gas·tos ko·mer·thya·les
business hours pl las horas de trabajo o·ras de tra·ba·kho

businessman n el hombre de negocios om·bre de ne·go·thyos Mc43
business trip n el viaje de negocios bee·a·khe de ne·go·thyos
businesswoman n la mujer de negocios moo·kher de ne·go·thyos
bus service n el servicio de autobuses ser·bee·thyo de ow·to·boo·ses
bus stop n la parada de autobús pa·ra·da de ow·to·boos
bust n el busto boos·to
busy adj ocupado(a) o·koo·pa·do(a); (place) concurrido(a) kon·koo·rree·do(a) Sn34
busy signal n la señal de comunicando sen·yal de ko·moo·nee·kan·do
but conj pero pe·ro; not this, but that no este, sino ese no es·te see·no e·se □ prep all but him todos menos él to·dos me·nos el
butane n el gas butano gas boo·ta·no S105
butcher n el carnicero kar·nee·the·ro; butcher's (shop) la carnicería kar·nee·the·ree·a S29
butter n la mantequilla man·te·keel·ya E30, S31
butterfly n la mariposa ma·ree·po·sa
button n el botón bo·ton Sn79
buy vt comprar kom·prar; to buy out (partner etc) comprar la parte de com·prar la par·te de S6
buyer n (customer) el comprador kom·pra·dor; (for shop, factory) el jefe de compras khe·fe de kom·pras Bm3
by prep (next to) al lado de al la·do de; to go by London (via) pasar por Londres pa·sar por lon·dres; by air/train/car en avión/tren/coche en a·byon/tren/ko·che; we'll be there by 4 o'clock estaremos allí para las 4 es·ta·re·mos al·yee pa·ra las 4 □ adv a plane flew by pasó un avión pa·so oon a·byon
bypass n la carretera de circunvalación ka·rre·te·ra de theer·koon·ba·la·thyon

C

cab n el taxi tak·see
cabaret n el cabaret ka·ba·ret
cabbage n el repollo re·pol·yo
cabin n (in ship) el camarote ka·ma·ro·te
cabin cruiser n el yate de motor ya·te de mo·tor
cable n el cable ka·ble
cactus n el cacto kak·to
caddie n el cadi ka·dee
café n el café ka·fe
cafeteria n la cafetería ka·fe·te·ree·a
cage n la jaula khow·la
cake n el pastel pas·tel
calcium n el calcio kal·thyo
calculate vt calcular kal·koo·lar
calculator n la calculadora kal·koo·la·do·ra
calendar n el calendario ka·len·da·ryo
calf n el becerro be·the·rro
call n (shout) el grito gree·to; (on phone) la llamada lya·ma·da □ vi (shout) gritar gree·tar; (summon) llamar lya·mar; (telephone) telefonear te·le·fo·ne·ar; call me at 7 a.m. (in hotel etc) llámeme a las 7 de la mañana lya·me·me a las 7 de la man·ya·na; to be called llamarse lya·mar·se Sn12
call girl n la prostituta pros·tee·too·ta
calm adj (sea, day) calmado(a) kal·ma·

do(a); (person) tranquilo(a) *tran·kee·lo(a)*

calorie n la caloría *ka·lo·ree·a*

camel n el camello *ka·mel·yo*

camera n la máquina de fotos *ma·kee·na de fo·tos*; (TV) la cámara *ka·ma·ra* S47f

camp vi acampar *a·kam·par* A82, 84, 94

campaign n la campaña *kam·pan·ya*

camp-bed n la cama de campaña *ka·ma de kam·pan·ya*

camping n el camping *kam·peeng*; to go camping hacer* camping *a·ther kam·peeng*

camp(ing) site n el camping *kam·peeng*

camshaft n el árbol de levas *ar·bol de le·bas*

can¹ n (container) la lata *la·ta* T172, S34

can² vi poder* *po·der*; I can puedo *pwe·do*; you can Ud puede *oos·ted pwe·de*; he/she can (él/ella) puede *(el/el·ya) pwe·de*; we can (nosotros) podemos *(no·so·tros) po·de·mos*

Canada n Canadá (m) *ca·na·da*

Canadian adj canadiense *ka·na·dyen·se*; he's Canadian es canadiense *es ka·na·dyen·se*; she's Canadian (ella) es canadiense *(el·ya) es ka·na·dyen·se*

canal n el canal *ka·nal*

canasta n la canasta *ka·nas·ta*

cancel vt anular *a·noo·lar*

cancer n el cáncer *kan·ther*

candidate n (for election) el/la candidato(a) *kan·dee·da·to(a)*

candle n la vela *be·la*

candy n el dulce *dool·the*

cane n (walking stick) el bastón *bas·ton*

canned adj en lata *en la·ta*

cannon n el cañón *kan·yon*

canoe n la canoa *ka·no·a*

canoeing n □ to go canoeing hacer* piragüismo *a·ther el pee·ra·gwees·mo*

can-opener n el abrelatas *a·bre·la·tas*

canteen n la cantina *kan·tee·na*

canvas n la lona *lo·na*

cap n (hat) la gorra *go·rra*

capable adj capaz *ka·path*; capable of capaz de *ka·path de*

cape n la capa *ka·pa*

capital n (city) la capital *ka·pee·tal*; (finance) el capital *ka·pee·tal*; in capitals en mayúsculas *en ma·yoos·koo·la*; capital A A mayúscula *a ma·yoos·koo·la*

capital goods pl los bienes de equipo *bye·nes de e·kee·po*

capitalism n el capitalismo *ka·pee·ta·lees·mo*

capitalist n el/la capitalista *ka·pee·ta·lees·ta*

capital letter n la letra mayúscula *le·tra ma·yoos·koo·la*

capsule n (of medicine) la cápsula *kap·soo·la*

captain n (of ship) el capitán *ka·pee·tan*; (of plane) el piloto *pee·lo·to*

capture vt apresar *a·pre·sar*

car n el coche *ko·che*, el carro (Am) *ka·rro*; (of train) el vagón *ba·gon* T103f, A28

carafe n la garrafa *ga·rra·fa* E12

caramel n el caramelo *ka·ra·me·lo*

carat n el quilate *kee·la·te*

carbon n el carbono *kar·bo·no*

carbon copy n la copia al carbón *ko·pya al kar·bon*

carbon paper n el papel carbón *pa·pel kar·bon* ;

carburetor n el carburador *kar·boo·ra·dor*

card n (post) la tarjeta postal *tar·khe·ta pos·tal*; (playing card) la carta *kar·ta*; to play cards jugar* a las cartas *khoo·gar a las kar·tas* Bm2, M25, S93

cardboard n el cartón *kar·ton*

card game n el juego de cartas *khwe·go de kar·tas*

cardigan n la chaqueta de punto *cha·ke·ta de poon·to*

card index n el fichero *fee·che·ro*

care n (carefulness) el cuidado *kwee·da·do* □ vi I don't care me da igual *me da ee·gwal*; to take care of (children etc) cuidar de *kwee·dar de*

career n la carrera *ka·rre·ra*

careful adj (cautious) cuidadoso(a) *kwee·da·do·so(a)*; be careful! ¡tenga cuidado! *ten·ga kwee·da·do*

care of, c/o prep casa de *ka·sa de*

caretaker n el portero *por·te·ro*

car-ferry n el transbordador *trans·bor·da·dor*

cargo n la carga *kar·ga*

Caribbean (Sea) n el Mar Caribe *mar ka·ree·be*

carnation n el clavel *kla·bel*

carnival n el carnaval *kar·na·bal*

carol n el villancico *beel·yan·thee·ko*

carpenter n el carpintero *kar·peen·te·ro*

carpet n la alfombra *al·fom·bra*

carport n el cobertizo para guardar el coche *ko·ber·tee·tho pa·ra gwar·dar el ko·che*

carrot n la zanahoria *tha·na·o·rya*

carry vt (in hands, arms) levar *lye·bar*; (transport) transportar *trans·por·tar*; to carry out an order cumplir una orden *koom·pleer oo·na or·den*

carryall n la bolsa *bol·sa*

carryout adj (food) para llevarse *pa·ra lye·bar·se*

cart n (for shopping) el carrito *ka·rree·to*

cartel n el cartel *kar·tel*

carton n (box) la caja de cartón *ka·kha de kar·ton*; (of yogurt etc) el cartón *kar·ton*

cartoon n la tira humorística *tee·ra oo·mo·rees·tee·ka*; (animated) los dibujos animados *dee·boo·khos a·nee·ma·dos*

cartridge n (for camera, gun etc) el cartucho *kar·too·cho*; (of tape) la cassette *ka·set*

carve vt (meat) trinchar *treen·char*

case n la maleta *ma·le·ta*; (of wine) la caja *ka·kha*; (instance) el caso *ka·so*; just in case en caso de que *en ka·so de ke*; in case of en caso de en *ka·so de*; in any case de todos modos *de to·dos mo·dos*

cash vt (check) cobrar *ko·brar* □ n el dinero (contante) *dee·ne·ro (kon·tan·te)*; to pay cash for something pagar* algo al contado *pa·gar al·go al con·ta·do*; cash on delivery pagar* contra recepción *pa·gar kon·tra re·thep·thyon* M25, L48

cashdesk n la caja *ka·kha*

cash flow n el cash flow *kash flo*

cashier n el/la cajero(a) *ka·khe·ro(a)*

cashmere n la cachemira *ka·che·mee·ra*

casino n el casino *ka·see·no*

casserole n (food) el estofado es·to·fa·do; (dish) la cazuela ka·thwe·la

cassette n la cassette ka·set

cassette-recorder n el magnetofón a cassettes mag·ne·to·fon a ka·sets

cast n (of play) el reparto re·par·to

castanets pl las castañuelas kas·tan·we·las

cast iron n el hierro fundido ye·rro foon·dee·do

castle n el castillo kas·teel·yo F7

castor oil n el aceite de ricino a·they·te de ree·thee·no

casual clothes, casual wear n la ropa de sport ro·pa de sport

cat n el gato ga·to

catalog n el catálogo ka·ta·lo·go Bm20

catch vt coger* ko·kher; (illness) contagiarse de kon·ta·khyar·se de; to catch cold resfriarse res·free·ar·se

cathedral n la catedral ka·te·dral F3

catholic adj católico(a) ka·to·lee·ko(a)

cattle n el ganado ga·na·do

cauliflower n la coliflor ko·lee·flor

cause n la causa kow·sa □ vt causar kow·sar

cave n la cueva kwe·ba

caviar(e) n el caviar ka·byar

cedar n el cedro the·dro

ceiling n el techo te·cho

celebrate vt/i celebrar the·le·brar

celeriac n el apio nabo a·pyo na·bo

celery n el apio a·pyo

cell n (in prison) la celda thel·da

cellar n el sótano so·ta·no

cello n el violoncelo byo·lon·the·lo

cellophane n el celofán the·lo·fan

Celsius adj Celsius thel·syoos

cement n el cemento the·men·to

cemetery n el cementerio the·men·te·ryo

cent n el céntimo then·tee·mo

centenary n el centenario then·te·na·ryo

center n el centro then·tro F5

centigrade adj centígrado then·tee·gra·do

centiliter n el centilitro then·tee·lee·tro

centimeter n el centímetro then·tee·me·tro

central adj central then·tral

central heating n la calefacción central ka·le·fak·thyon then·tral A45

century n el siglo see·glo

cereal n (breakfast) el cereal the·re·al

ceremony n la ceremonia the·re·mo·nya

certain adj cierto(a) thyer·to(a)

certainly adv naturalmente na·too·ral·men·te

certificate n el certificado ther·tee·fee·ka·do

certified mail n el correo certificado ko·rre·o ther·tee·fee·ka·do

certified public accountant n el contable diplomado kon·ta·ble dee·plo·ma·do

chain n la cadena ka·de·na

chain store n la tienda con sucursales tyen·da kon soo·koor·sa·les

chair n la silla seel·ya; (armchair) el sillón seel·yon

chair-lift n la telesilla te·le·seel·ya

chairman n el presidente pre·see·den·te

chalet n el chalet cha·let

chalk n la tiza tee·tha

Chamber of Commerce n la cámara de comercio ka·ma·ra de ko·mer·thyo

champagne n el champán cham·pan

champion n el campeón kam·pe·on

chance n □ by chance por casualidad por ka·swa·lee·dad; he has a good chance of... tiene buenas posibilidades de... tye·ne bwe·nas po·see·bee·lee·da·des de

chancellor n (in Germany, Austria) el canciller kan·theel·yer

change vt/i cambiar kam·byar; to change one's clothes cambiarse de ropa kam·byar·se de ro·pa; (residence) mudar de casa; to change trains at Marseilles hacer* transbordo en Marsella a·ther trans·bor·do en Mar·sel·ya □ n change (transformation) la transformación trans·for·ma·thyon; (money) el cambio kam·byo; a change in the weather un cambio en el tiempo oon kam·byo en el tyem·po T102, M15, 21, 22

Channel n el Canal de la Mancha ka·nal de la man·cha

chapel n la capilla ka·peel·ya

chapter n el capítulo ka·pee·too·lo

character n el carácter ka·rak·ter

charge n (accusation) la acusación a·koo·sa·thyon; to make a charge for something cobrar por algo ko·brar por al·go; free of charge gratis gra·tees; to be in charge of estar* encargado de es·tar en·kar·ga·do de □ vt charge (money) cobrar ko·brar; charge it to my account póngalo a mi cuenta pon·ga·lo a mee kwen·ta M3

charm n el encanto en·kan·to

charming adj encantador(a) en·kan·ta·do(·ra)

chart n (map) la carta de navegación kar·ta de na·be·ga·thyon; (diagram, table) la gráfica gra·fee·ka

charter vt (plane, bus) alquilar al·kee·lar

charter flight n el vuelo charter bwe·lo char·ter

chase vt perseguir* per·se·geer

chassis n el chasis cha·sees

chauffeur n el chófer cho·fer, el chofer (Am) cho·fer

cheap adj barato(a) ba·ra·to(a) S14

cheat vi hacer* trampas a·ther tram·pas

check n (banking) el cheque che·ke; (bill) la cuenta kwen·ta □ vt (examine) revisar re·bee·sar; (passport, ticket) examinar ek·sa·mee·nar; (train time etc) verificar* ve·ree·fee·kar; to check in (at hotel) inscribirse eens·kree·beer·se; check in (at airport) presentarse pre·sen·tar·se; to check out pagar* la cuenta pa·gar la kwen·ta M25

checkbook n el talonario ta·lo·na·ryo

check(er)ed adj (patterned) a cuadros a kwa·dros

checkers pl las damas da·mas

checking account n la cuenta corriente kwen·ta ko·rryen·te

checkout n (in store) la caja ka·kha

checkroom n la consigna kon·seeg·na

cheek n la mejilla me·kheel·ya; (impudence) el descaro des·ka·ro

cheeky adj descarado(a) des·ka·ra·do(a)

cheer vt aplaudir a·plow·deer; cheers! ¡salud! sa·looth

cheese n el queso ke·so E26, S31

cheesecake n la quesadilla ke·sa·deel·ya

chef n el jefe de cocina khe·fe de ko·thee·na

chemical adj químico(a) kee·mee·ko(a)

chemist n (pharmacist) el farmacéutico

far·ma·the·oo·tee·ko; chemist's shop la farmacia *far·ma·thya*

chemistry *n* la química *kee·mee·ka*

cherry *n* la cereza *the·re·tha*; (tree) el cerezo *the·re·tho*

chess *n* el ajedrez *a·khe·dreth*

chest *n* (of body) el pecho *pe·cho*

chestnut *n* la castaña *kas·tan·ya*

chew *vt* masticar* *mas·tee·kar*

chewing gum *n* el chicle *chee·kle*

chicken *n* el pollo *pol·yo*

chicken pox *n* la varicela *ba·ree·the·la*

chicory *n* la achicoria *a·chee·ko·rya*

chief *n* (boss) el jefe *khe·fe*

child *n* el/la niño(a) *neen·yo(a)* A4, S43, C1, 14f

Chile *n* Chile (m) *chee·le*

Chilean *adj* chileno(a) *chee·le·no(a)*; he's Chilean es chileno *es chee·le·no*; she's Chilean es chilena *es chee·le·na*

chili *n* el chile *chee·le*

chill *vt* (wine, food) enfriar *en·free·ar*; to serve something chilled servir* algo fresco *ser·beer al·go fres·ko*

chimney *n* la chimenea *chee·me·ne·a*

chin *n* la barbilla *bar·beel·ya*

china *n* la porcelana *por·the·la·na*

China *n* China (f) *chee·na*

Chinese *adj* chino(a) *chee·no(a)* □ *n* (language) el chino *chee·no*

chip *n* (electronics) la astilla *as·teel·ya*; (in gambling) la ficha *fee·cha*

chips *pl* las patatas a la inglesa *pa·ta·tas a la een·gle·sa*, las papas a la inglesa (Am) *pa·pas a la een·gle·sa*

chives *pl* el cebollino *the·bol·yee·no*

chocolate *n* el chocolate *cho·ko·la·te*

choice *n* la elección *e·lek·thyon*; (range) el surtido *soor·tee·do*

choir *n* el coro *ko·ro*

choke *n* (of car) el estrangulador *es·tran·goo·la·dor*

cholesterol *n* el colesterol *ko·les·te·rol*

choose *vt* escoger* *es·ko·kher*

chop *vt* (food) picar* *pee·kar* □ *n* pork chop la chuleta de cerdo *choo·le·ta de ther·do*

chopsticks *pl* los palillos *pa·leel·yos*

Christian *n* el/la cristiano(a) *krees·tya·no(a)*

Christian name *n* el nombre de pila *nom·bre de pee·la*

Christmas *n* Navidad (f) *na·bee·dad*

Christmas card *n* la tarjeta de Navidad *tar·khe·ta de na·bee·dad*

Christmas Day *n* el día de Navidad *dee·a de na·bee·dad*

Christmas Eve *n* la nochebuena *no·che·bwe·na*

Christmas tree *n* el árbol de Navidad *ar·bol de na·bee·dad*

chrome *n* el cromo *kro·mo*

chrysanthemum *n* el crisantemo *kree·san·te·mo*

church *n* la iglesia *ee·gle·sya* L4, Sn90

churchyard *n* el cementerio *the·men·te·ryo*

cider *n* la sidra *see·dra*

cigar *n* el cigarro *thee·ga·rro*

cigarette *n* el cigarillo *thee·ga·reel·yo* Mc30

cigarette case *n* la petaca *pe·ta·ka*

cigarette lighter *n* el encendedor *en·then·de·dor*

cinema *n* el cine *thee·ne*

cinnamon *n* la canela *ka·ne·la*

circle *n* el círculo *theer·koo·lo*; (in theater) el anfiteatro *an·fee·te·a·tro*

circuit *n* (electric) el circuito *theer·kwee·to*

circumstances *pl* las circunstancias *theer·koon·stan·thyas*

circus *n* el circo *theer·ko*

city *n* la ciudad *thyoo·dad*; city center el centro de la ciudad *then·tro de la thyoo·dad*

city hall *n* el ayuntamiento *a·yoon·ta·myen·to*

civilization *n* la civilización *thee·bee·lee·tha·thyon*

civil servant *n* el funcionario *foon·thyo·na·ryo*

civil service *n* la administración pública *ad·mee·nees·tra·thyon poob·lee·ka*

civil war *n* la guerra civil *ge·rra thee·beel*

claim *vt* (lost property, baggage) reclamar *re·kla·mar*

clam *n* la almeja *al·me·kha*

clap *vi* aplaudir *a·plow·deer*

claret *n* el clarete *kla·re·te*

clasp *n* el broche *bro·che*

class *n* la clase *kla·se*; to travel first class viajar en primera clase *bee·a·khar en pree·me·ra kla·se*; a second class ticket un billete de segunda clase *oon beel·ye·te de se·goon·da kla·se*

classical *adj* (music, art) clásico(a) *kla·see·ko(a)*

clause *n* (in contract) la cláusula *klow·soo·la*

clay *n* la arcilla *ar·theel·ya*

clean *adj* limpio(a) *leem·pyo(a)* □ *vt* limpiar *leem·pyar*; to have a suit cleaned hacer* limpiar en seco un traje *a·ther leem·pyar en se·ko oon tra·khe* Sn69

cleaner *n* (of house etc) la mujer de la limpieza *moo·kher de la leem·pye·tha*

cleaner's *n* la tintorería *teen·to·re·ree·a*

clear *adj* (transparent) transparente *trans·pa·ren·te*; (distinct) claro(a) *kla·ro(a)*; (not blocked) despejado(a) *des·pe·kha·do(a)* □ *vt* (road) despejar *des·pe·khar*; (pipe) desatascar* *des·a·tas·kar*

clerk *n* (in office) el/la oficinista *o·fee·thee·nees·ta*; (in store) el/la dependiente(a) *de·pen·dyen·te(a)*

clever *adj* (person) listo(a) *lees·to(a)*; (plan) ingenioso(a) *een·khe·nyo·so(a)*

client *n* el/la cliente *klee·en·te*

cliff *n* el precipicio *pre·thee·pee·thyo*

climate *n* el clima *klee·ma*

climb *vt* (tree, wall) subir *soo·beer*; to climb over something franquear algo *frang·ke·ar al·go*

clinic *n* la clínica *klee·nee·ka*

clip *n* el clip *kleep*

cloak *n* la capa *ka·pa*

cloakroom *n* el guardarropa *gwar·da·rro·pa*

clock *n* el reloj *re·lokh*

close[1] *adj* (near) cercano(a) *ther·ka·no(a)*; (stuffy) sofocante *so·fo·kan·te*; close to cerca de *ther·ka de*; close by muy cerca *mooy ther·ka* T203

close[2] *vt* cerrar* *the·rrar* □ *vi* the door closed se cerró la puerta *se the·rro la pwer·ta*; when do the shops close? ¿a qué hora cierran las tiendas? *a ke o·ra thye·rran las tyen·das* A29

closed circuit television *n* la televisión de circuito cerrado *te·le·bee·syon de theer·kwee·to the·rra·do*

closet *n* el ropero *ro·pe·ro*

cloth *n* (cleaning) el paño *pan·yo*

clothes *pl* la ropa *ro·pa* A55, Sn69, 77

clotheshorse *n* el tendedero *ten·de·de·ro*

clothesline *n* la cuerda para tender la ropa *kwer·da pa·ra ten·der la ro·pa*

clothespin *n* la pinza *peen·tha*

cloud *n* la nube *noo·be*

cloudy *adj* nublado(a) *noo·bla·do(a)*

clove *n* el clavo (de especia) *kla·bo (de es·pe·thya)*; **clove of garlic** el diente de ajo *dyen·te de a·kho*

clown *n* el payaso *pa·ya·so*

club *n* (*society*) el club *kloob*; **clubs** (*in cards*) los tréboles *tre·bo·les*

club car *n* el vagón-restaurante *ba·gon·res·tow·ran·te* T70

clumsy *adj* (*person*) torpe *tor·pe*

clutch *n* (*of car*) el embrague *em·bra·ge*

coach *n* (*of train*) el vagón *ba·gon*; (*bus*) el autocar *ow·to·kar*; (*instructor*) el entrenador *en·tre·na·dor*

coal *n* el carbón *kar·bon*

coarse *adj* (*texture, material*) basto(a) *bas·to(a)*

coast *n* la costa *kos·ta*

coastguard *n* el guardacostas *gwar·da·kos·tas*

coat *n* el abrigo *a·bree·go*

coat hanger *n* la percha *per·cha*

cock(erel) *n* el gallo *gal·yo*

cockle *n* el berberecho *ber·be·re·cho*

cocktail *n* (*drink*) el coctel *kok·tel*; **shrimp cocktail** el coctel de gambas *kok·tel de gam·bas*

cocoa *n* el cacao *ka·ka·o*

coconut *n* el coco *ko·ko*

cod *n* el bacalao *ba·ka·la·o*

codeine *n* la codeína *ko·de·ee·na*

coffee *n* el café *ka·fe*; **black coffee** el café solo *ka·fe so·lo*; **coffee with milk** el café con leche *ka·fe kon le·che* B58, E64

coffee break *n* el descanso para tomar café *des·kan·so pa·ra to·mar ka·fe*

coffee cup *n* la taza de café *ta·tha de ka·fe*

coffeepot *n* la cafetera *ka·fe·te·ra*

coffee table *n* la mesita para el café *me·see·ta pa·ra el ka·fe*

coffin *n* el ataúd *a·ta·ood*

cognac *n* el coñac *kon·yak*

coin *n* la moneda *mo·ne·da*

coincide *vi* coincidir *ko·een·thee·deer*

coincidence *n* la coincidencia *ko·een·thee·den·thya*

colander *n* el colador *ko·la·dor*

cold *adj* frío(a) *free·o(a)*; **cold meat** el fiambre *fee·am·bre*; **I'm cold** tengo frío *ten·go free·o* □ *n* **cold** (*illness*) el resfriado *res·free·a·do* E36, S40

coleslaw *n* la ensalada de col *en·sa·la·da de kol*

colic *n* el cólico *ko·lee·ko*

collaborate *vi* colaborar *ko·la·bo·rar*

collapse *vi* (*person*) sufrir un colapso *soo·freer oon ko·lap·so*

collar *n* el cuello *kwel·yo*

colleague *n* el/la colega *ko·le·ga*

collect *vt* (*stamps etc*) coleccionar *ko·lek·thyo·nar*; (*donations*) colectar *ko·lek·tar*

collect call *n* la conferencia a cobro revertido *kon·fe·ren·thya a ko·bro re·ber·tee·do* Sn14

collection *n* (*of mail*) la recogida *re·ko·khee·da*

college *n* el colegio *ko·le·khyo*

collide *vi* chocar* *cho·kar*

collision *n* el choque *cho·ke*

cologne *n* la colonia *ko·lo·nya*

color *n* el color *ko·lor*; **color TV** la te-

levisión en color *te·le·bee·syon en ko·lor*

colored *adj* colorado(a) *ko·lo·ra·do(a)*, de color *de ko·lor*

comb *n* el peine *pey·ne* □ *vt* peinar *pey·nar*

come *vi* (*arrive*) llegar* *lye·gar*; **to come from London** venir* de Londres *be·neer de lon·dres*; **to come in** entrar *en·trar*; **to come off** desprenderse *des·pren·der·se*; **to come out** (*person, sun*) salir* *sa·leer*; (*stain*) quitarse *kee·tar·se*; **to come around** (*recover*) volver* en sí *bol·ber en see*

comedian *n* el cómico *ko·mee·ko*

comedy *n* la comedia *ko·me·dya*

comfort *n* (*ease*) el confort *kon·fort*

comfortable *adj* cómodo(a) *ko·mo·do(a)*

comforter *n* el edredón *e·dre·don*

comfort station *n* los servicios *ser·bee·thyos*

comic *n* el tebeo *te·be·o*

comma *n* la coma *ko·ma*

command *n* la orden *or·den*

comment *n* el comentario *ko·men·ta·ryo*

commerce *n* el comercio *ko·mer·thyo*

commercial *adj* comercial *ko·mer·thyal* □ *n* (*ad*) el anuncio *a·noon·thyo*

commercialized *adj* (*resort*) comercializado(a) *ko·mer·thya·lee·tha·do(a)*

commission *n* (*sum received*) la comisión *ko·mee·syon*

commit *vt* (*crime*) cometer *ko·me·ter*

committee *n* el comité *ko·mee·te*

commodity *n* la mercancía *mer·kan·thee·a*

common *adj* (*ordinary, frequent*) corriente *ko·rryen·te*

common stock *n* la acción *ak·thyon*

Common Market *n* el Mercado Común *mer·ka·do ko·moon*

communicate *vi* □ **to communicate with someone** comunicar* con alguien *ko·moo·nee·kar kon al·gyen*

Communist *n* el/la comunista *ko·moo·nees·ta* □ *adj* comunista *ko·moo·nees·ta*

commutation ticket *n* el billete de abono *beel·ye·te de a·bo·no*

commuter *n* el viajero con billete de abono *bya·khe·ro kon beel·ye·te de a·bo·no*

company *n* (*firm*) la empresa *em·pre·sa*

compare *vt* □ **to compare something with something** comparar algo con algo *kom·pa·rar al·go kon al·go*

compartment *n* (*on train*) el compartimiento *kom·par·tee·myen·to*

compass *n* el compás *kom·pas*

compensation *n* la indemnización *een·dem·nee·tha·thyon*

competent *adj* competente *kom·pe·ten·te*

competition *n* la competencia *kom·pe·ten·thya*

competitor *n* el competidor *kom·pe·tee·dor*

complain *vi* quejarse *ke·khar·se*; **to complain about** quejarse de *ke·khar·se de*

complaint *n* (*dissatisfaction*) la reclamación *re·kla·ma·thyon*

complete *adj* acabado(a) *a·ka·ba·do(a)* □ *vt* acabar *a·ka·bar*

completely *adv* completamente *kom·ple·ta·men·te*

complex *adj* complicado(a) *kom·plee·ka·do(a)*

complexion n el cutis koo·tees

complicated adj complicado(a) kom·plee·ka·do(a)

compliment n el cumplido koom·plee·do

component n (for car etc) la pieza pye·tha

composer n el compositor kom·po·see·tor

compound interest n el interés compuesto een·te·res kom·pwes·to

comprehensive insurance n el seguro contra todo riesgo se·goo·ro kon·tra to·do ryes·go T111

computer n el ordenador or·de·na·dor

computerize vt (system) preparar para tratamiento con ordenador pre·pa·rar pa·ra tra·ta·myen·to kon or·de·na·dor

computer programming n la programación pro·gra·ma·thyon

conceited adj engreído(a) en·gre·ee·do(a)

concern n (anxiety) la preocupación pre·o·koo·pa·thyon □ vt (be important to) interesar een·te·re·sar; that doesn't concern you eso no tiene nada que ver con Ud e·so no tye·ne na·da ke ber kon oos·ted

concert n el concierto kon·thyer·to L36

concrete n el hormigón or·mee·gon □ adj de hormigón de or·mee·gon

condemn vt condenar kon·de·nar

condensed milk n la leche condensada le·che kon·den·sa·da

condiments pl los condimentos kon·dee·men·tos

condition n la condición kon·dee·thyon; on condition that... a condición que... a kon·dee·thyon ke

conditioner n (for hair) el acondicionador de pelo a·kon·dee·thyo·na·dor de pe·lo Sn45

conductor n (on bus) el cobrador ko·bra·dor; (of orchestra) el director dee·rek·tor; (on train) el revisor re·bee·sor

cone n (for ice cream) el cucurucho koo·koo·roo·cho

confectioner n el pastelero pas·te·le·ro

confectionery n la confitería kon·fee·te·ree·a

conference n (meeting) la reunión re·oo·nyon; conferencia kon·fe·ren·thya

confess vt confesar* kon·fe·sar □ vi confesarse* kon·fe·sar·se; to confess to something confesarse (culpable) de algo kon·fe·sar·se (kool·pa·ble) de al·go

confession n la confesión kon·fe·syon

confidence n (trust) la confianza kon·fee·an·tha; confidence in la confianza en kon·fee·an·tha en; in confidence en confianza en kon·fee·an·tha

confident adj seguro(a) de sí mismo(a) se·goo·ro(a) de see mees·mo(a)

confidential adj confidencial kon·fee·den·thyal

confirm vt (reservation etc) confirmar kon·feer·mar

confuse vt confundir kon·foon·deer; to confuse one thing with another confundir una cosa con otra kon·foon·deer oo·na ko·sa kon o·tra

confused adj (muddled) despistado(a) des·pees·ta·do(a)

congratulate vt felicitar a fe·lee·thee·tar a; to congratulate someone on something dar* la enhorabuena a alguien por algo dar la en·o·ra·bwe·na a al·gyen por al·go

congratulations pl las felicitaciones fe·lee·thee·ta·thyo·nes; congratulations! ¡enhorabuena! en·o·ra·bwe·na

conjuror n el/la ilusionista ee·loo·syo·nees·ta

connect vt (join) unir oo·neer; this train connects with the 16:45 este tren enlaza con el tren de las 16.45 es·te tren en·la·tha kon el tren de las 16.45

connection n (train etc) el empalme em·pal·me T8, Sn22

connoisseur n el conocedor ko·no·the·dor

conscience n la conciencia kon·thyen·thya

conscious adj consciente kons·thyen·te

consequence n (result) la consecuencia kon·se·kwen·thya

conservative adj conservador(a) kon·ser·ba·dor(·ra)

conservatory n (greenhouse) el invernadero een·ber·na·de·ro

consider vt considerar kon·see·de·rar

consist of vt consistir en kon·sees·teer en

consommé n el consomé kon·so·me

constipated adj estreñido(a) es·tren·yee·do(a)

construct vt construir* kon·stroo·eer

consul n el cónsul kon·sool

consulate n el consulado kon·soo·la·do Sn89

consult vt consultar kon·sool·tar

consultant n (doctor) el especialista es·pe·thya·lees·ta; (other specialist) el asesor a·se·sor

consulting room n el consultorio kon·sool·to·ryo

consumer n el consumidor kon·soo·mee·dor

consumer goods pl los bienes de consumo los bye·nes de kon·soo·mo

contact vt ponerse* en contacto con po·ner·se en kon·tak·to kon

contact lenses pl las microlentillas mee·kro·len·teel·yas

contagious adj contagioso(a) kon·ta·khyo·so(a)

contain vt contener* kon·te·ner

container n el recipiente re·thee·pyen·te; (for shipping etc) el contenedor kon·te·ne·dor

contemporary adj (modern) contemporáneo(a) kon·tem·po·ra·ne·o(a)

content(ed) adj contento(a) kon·ten·to(a)

contents pl el contenido kon·te·nee·do; (table in book) el índice de materias een·dee·the de ma·te·rjas

contest n (competition) el concurso kon·koor·so

contestant n el/la concursante kon·koor·san·te

continent n el continente kon·tee·nen·te; the Continent el continente europeo kon·tee·nen·te e·oo·ro·pe·o

continental adj continental kon·tee·nen·tal

continental breakfast n el desayuno de·sa·yoo·no

continual adj continuo(a) kon·tee·nwo(a)

continue vt seguir* se·geer □ vi (road etc) continuar kon·teen·war; to continue to do continuar haciendo kon·teen·war a·thyen·do

continuous adj continuo(a) kon·teen·wo(a)

continuously adv continuamente kon·teen·wa·men·te

contraband n el contrabando kon·tra·ban·do

contraceptive n el anticonceptivo an·tee·kon·thep·tee·bo

contract n el contrato kon·tra·to

contractor n el contratista kon·tra·tees·ta

contrary n □ on the contrary al contrario al kon·tra·ryo

contribute vi contribuir* kon·tree·boo·eer

control vt dominar do·mee·nar □ n circumstances beyond our control las circunstancias fuera de nuestro control las theer·koons·tan·thyas fwe·ra de nwes·tro kon·trol

controls pl los mandos man·dos T115

control tower n la torre de control to·rre de con·trol

conurbation n la conurbación ko·noor·ba·thyon

convalescence n la convalecencia kon·ba·le·then·thya

convenient adj práctico prak·tee·ko; **convenient to stores** práctico para las tiendas prak·tee·ko pa·ra las tyen·das

convent n el convento kon·ben·to

conversation n la conversación kon·ber·sa·thyon

convertible n (car) el descapotable des·ka·po·ta·ble

convince vt convencer* kon·ben·ther

cook vt cocinar ko·thee·nar □ vi the meat is cooking la carne está cociendo la kar·ne es·ta ko·thyen·do □ n cook cl/la cocinero(a) ko·thee·ne·ro(a)

cooker n la cocina ko·thee·na

cookie n la galleta gal·ye·ta

cooking n la cocina ko·thee·na

cool adj fresco(a) fres·ko(a)

cooling system n el sistema de refrigeración sees·te·ma de re·free·khe·ra·thyon

co-operate vi cooperar ko·o·pe·rar

co-operative n la cooperativa ko·o·pe·ra·tee·ba

Copenhagen n Copenhague (m) ko·pen·ha·ge

copper n (metal) el cobre ko·bre

copy n (of book etc) el ejemplar e·khem·plar; (imitation) la copia ko·pya □ vt copiar ko·pyar Bm24

copyright n los derechos de autor de·re·chos de ow·tor

coral n el coral ko·ral

cord n (twine) la cuerda kwer·da; (fabric) la pana pa·na

cordial n el cordial kor·dyal

corduroy n la pana pa·na

cork n el corcho kor·cho

corkscrew n el sacacorchos sa·ka·kor·chos

corn n (cereal crop) el maíz ma·eeth; (on foot) el callo kal·yo

corned beef n la carne en lata kar·ne en la·ta

corner n (of streets) la esquina es·kee·na; (bend in road) la curva koor·ba □ vi tomar una curva to·mar oo·na koor·ba

cornet n (of ice cream) el barquillo bar·keel·yo

cornflakes pl los copos de maíz ko·pos de ma·eeth

corn-on-the-cob n el maíz en la mazorca ma·eeth en la ma·thor·ka, el choclo (Am) chok·lo

cornstarch n la harina de maíz a·ree·na de ma·eeth, la maicena (Am) may·the·na

coronation n la coronación ko·ro·na·thyon

corporation n (firm) la sociedad anónima so·thye·dad a·no·nee·ma; (of town) el ayuntamiento a·yoon·ta·myen·to

corporation tax n el impuesto sobre las empresas eem·pwes·to so·bre las em·pre·sas

correct adj (accurate) exacto(a) ek·sak·to(a); (proper) correcto(a) ko·rrek·to(a) □ vt corregir* ko·rre·kheer

correction n (alteration) la rectificación rek·tee·fee·ka·thyon

correspondence n (mail) la correspondencia ko·rres·pon·den·thya

correspondence course n el curso por correspondencia koor·so por ko·rres·pon·den·thya

corridor n el pasillo pa·seel·yo

corrode vt corroer ko·rro·er

corrugated iron n la chapa ondulada cha·pa on·doo·la·da

corrugated paper n el cartón ondulado kar·ton on·doo·la·do

corrupt adj venal be·nal

corruption n la corrupción ko·rroop·thyon

corset n la faja fa·kha

Corsica n Córcega (f) kor·the·ga

cosmetics pl los cosméticos kos·me·tee·kos

cosmetic surgery n la cirugía estética thee·roor·khee·a es·te·tee·ka

cosmopolitan adj cosmopolita kos·mo·po·lee·ta

cost n el coste kos·te; **to buy something at cost** comprar algo a precio de coste kom·prar al·go a pre·thyo de kos·te □ vt cost costar* kos·tar S4, Bm25f

cost of living n el costo de la vida kos·to de la bee·da

costume n (theatrical) el disfraz dees·frath

costume jewelry n las joyas de fantasía kho·yas de fan·ta·see·a

cot n la cama de campaña ka·ma de kam·pan·ya

cottage n la casita de campo ka·see·ta de kam·po

cottage cheese n el requesón re·ke·son

cotton n (fabric) el algodón al·go·don; (thread) el hilo de algodón ee·lo de al·go·don

cotton batting n el algodón hidrófilo al·go·don ee·dro·fee·lo

couch n el sofá so·fa

couchette n la litera lee·te·ra T66

cough n la tos tos □ vi toser to·ser B57, S40

cough drops pl las pastillas para la tos pas·teel·yas pa·ra la tos

cough medicine n el jarabe para la tos kha·ra·be pa·ra la tos

could vi □ we could do it podríamos hacerlo po·dree·a·mos a·ther·lo; **could I have...** podría tomar... po·dree·a to·mar

council n (of town) el consejo municipal kon·the·kho moo·nee·thee·pal

counselor n el abogado a·bo·ga·do

count n (objects, people) contar* kon·tar □ vi to count up to 10 contar* hasta 10 kon·tar as·ta 10

counter n (in shop) el mostrador mos·tra·dor; (gambling) la ficha fee·cha

counterfoil n el talón ta·lon

country n (land) el país pa·ees; (not town) el campo kam·po; in the country en el campo en el kam·po Mc13

countryside *n* el campo *kam·po*

county *n* el condado *kon·da·do*

coup d'état *n* el golpe de estado *gol·pe de es·ta·do*

coupé *n* (*car*) el cupé *koo·pe*

couple *n* (*persons*) la pareja *pa·re·kha*; a couple of (*a few*) un par de *oon par de*

coupon *n* el cupón *koo·pon*

courage *n* el coraje *ko·ra·khe*

courgettes *pl* los calabacines *ka·la·ba·thee·nes*

courier *n* el/la guía *gee·a*

course *n* (*lessons*) el curso *koor·so*; (*of meal*) el plato *pla·to*; (*for golf*) el campo *kam·po*; course of treatment el tratamiento *tra·ta·myen·to*

court *n* (*law*) el tribunal *tree·boo·nal*; (*tennis etc*) la cancha *kan·cha*

courtyard *n* el patio *pa·tyo*

cousin *n* el/la primo(a) *pree·mo(a)*

cover *n* (*of book*) la cubierta *koo·byer·ta*; (*blanket*) el cobertor *ko·ber·tor*; (*insurance*) la protección *pro·tek·thyon*; under separate cover por separado *por se·pa·ra·do* □ *vt* cover cubrir* *koo·breer*; (*distance*) recorrer *re·ko·rrer*

cover charge *n* el precio del cubierto *pre·thyo del koo·byer·to*

covering letter *n* la carta explicatoria *kar·ta eks·plee·ka·to·rya*

cow *n* la vaca *ba·ka*

coward *n* el/la cobarde *ko·bar·de*

cowboy *n* el vaquero *ba·ke·ro*

crab *n* el cangrejo *kan·gre·kho*

crack *n* (*split*) la grieta *grye·ta*; (*noise*) el chasquido *chas·kee·do* □ *vt* to crack a glass agrietar un vaso *a·gree·e·tar oon ba·so* □ *vi* the glass cracked el vaso se agrietó *el ba·so se a·gree·e·to*

cracker *n* (*crisp wafer*) el craker *kra·ker*; (*paper toy*) el petardo *pe·tar·do*

cradle *n* la cuna *koo·na*

craft *n* el arte *ar·te*

craftsman *n* el artesano *ar·te·sa·no*

cramp *n* el calambre *ka·lam·bre*

cranberry *n* el arándano *a·ran·da·no*

crane *n* (*machine*) la grúa *groo·a*

crash *n* (*noise*) el estruendo *es·troo·en·do*; (*collision*) el choque *cho·ke* □ *vt* to crash one's car tener* un choque con el coche *te·ner oon cho·ke kon el ko·che* □ *vi* to crash into something estrellarse contra algo *es·trel·yar·se kon·tra al·go*

crash course *n* el curso acelerado *koor·so a·the·le·ra·do*

crash helmet *n* el casco protector *kas·ko pro·tek·tor*

crash-landing *n* el aterrizaje de urgencia *a·te·rree·tha·khe de oor·khen·thya*

crate *n* el cajón *ka·khon*

crawfish, crayfish *n* (*freshwater*) el cangrejo de río *kan·gre·kho de ree·o*; (*saltwater*) la langosta *lan·gos·ta*

crawl *vi* arrastrarse *a·rras·trar·se* □ *n* (*swimming*) el crol *krol*

crayon *n* el lápiz de color *la·peeth de ko·lor*

crazy *adj* loco(a) *lo·ko(a)*

cream *n* la nata *na·ta*; (*cosmetic*) la crema *kre·ma* □ *adj* crema *kre·ma*

cream cheese *n* el queso de nata *ke·so de na·ta*

creamy *adj* (*texture*) cremoso(a) *kre·mo·so(a)*

crease *n* la raya *ra·ya*

creased *adj* arrugado(a) *a·rroo·ga·do(a)*

create *vt* crear *kre·ar*

crèche *n* la guardería *gwar·de·ree·a*

credit *n* el crédito *kre·dee·to*; on credit a crédito *a kre·dee·to*; to give somebody credit dar* crédito a alguien *dar kre·dee·to a al·gyen* □ *vt* to credit 10,000 pesetas to someone's account abonar 10,000 pesetas a cuenta de alguien *a·bo·nar 10,000 pe·se·tas a kwen·ta de al·gyen*

credit card *n* la tarjeta de crédito *tar·khe·ta de kre·dee·to* T165, M13

creditor *n* el/la acreedor(a) *a·kre·e·dor(·ra)*

credit squeeze *n* la restricción de crédito *res·treek·thyon de kre·dee·to*

crème de menthe *n* la crema de menta *kre·ma de men·ta*

Crete *n* Creta (*f*) *kre·ta*

crew *n* (*of ship, plane*) la tripulación *tree·poo·la·thyon*

crib *n* (*baby's*) la cuna *koo·na*

cricket *n* (*sport*) el críquet *kree·ket*

criminal *adj* criminal *kree·mee·nal*

cripple *n* el/la cojo(a) *ko·kho(a)*

crisis *n* la crisis *kree·sees*

crisp *adj* fresco(a) *fres·ko(a)*

criticize *vt* criticar* *kree·tee·kar*

crockery *n* la loza *lo·tha*

crocodile *n* el cocodrilo *ko·ko·dree·lo*

crocus *n* el azafrán *a·tha·fran*

croissant *n* el croissant *krwa·san*

crooked *adj* torcido(a) *tor·thee·do(a)*, chueco(a) (*Am*) *chwe·ko(a)*

crop *n* (*harvest*) la cosecha *ko·se·cha*; (*whip*) el látigo *la·tee·go*

croquet *n* el croquet *kro·ket*

croquette *n* la croqueta *kro·ke·ta*

cross *n* la cruz *krooth* □ *vt* (*road, sea*) cruzar* *kroo·thar*; to cross out tachar *ta·char*

crossing *n* (*voyage*) la travesía *tra·be·see·a*

crossroads *n* el cruce *kroo·the*

crosswalk *n* el paso de peatones *pa·so de pe·a·to·nes*

croupier *n* el crupier *kroo·pyer*

crouton *n* el cuscurro *koos·koo·rro*

crowd *n* la muchedumbre *moo·che·doom·bre*

crowded *adj* atestado(a) *a·tes·ta·do(a)*

crown *n* la corona *ko·ro·na*

crude *adj* (*oil etc*) crudo(a) *kroo·do(a)*

cruel *adj* cruel *kroo·el*

cruise *n* el crucero *kroo·the·ro*; to go on a cruise hacer* un crucero *a·ther oon kroo·the·ro*

crumb *n* la miga *mee·ga*

crush *vt* aplastar *a·plas·tar*

crust *n* el mendrugo *men·droo·go*

crutch *n* la muleta *moo·le·ta*

cry *vi* llorar *lyo·rar* □ *n* el grito *gree·to*

crystal *n* (*glass*) el cristal *krees·tal*

Cuba *n* Cuba (*f*) *koo·ba*

Cuban *adj* cubano(a) *koo·ba·no(a)*

cube *n* el terrón *te·rron*

cubicle *n* la caseta *ka·se·ta*

cucumber *n* el pepino *pe·pee·no*

cuddle *vt* abrazar* *a·bra·thar*

cuff *n* (*of shirt*) el puño *poo·nyo*

cuff link *n* el gemelo *khe·me·lo*

cuisine *n* la cocina *ko·thee·na*

cul-de-sac *n* la calle sin salida *kal·ye seen sa·lee·da*

cultivate *vt* cultivar *kool·tee·bar*

culture *n* la cultura *kool·too·ra*

cup *n* la taza *ta·tha*; (*trophy*) la copa *ko·pa*

cupboard *n* el armario *ar·ma·ryo*

curb *n* el bordillo *bor·deel·yo*

cure *vt* curar *koo·rar*

curious *adj* (*inquisitive*) curioso(a) *koo·ryo·so(a)*; (*strange*) extraño(a) *eks·tran·yo(a)*

curl *n* el rizo *ree·tho*

curler *n* (*for hair*) el bigudí *bee·goo·dee*

curly *adj* rizado(a) *ree·tha·do(a)*

currant *n* la pasa *pa·sa*

currency *n* la moneda *mo·ne·da*; **foreign currency** la divisa *dee·bee·sa*

current *n* (*of water, air*) la corriente *ko·rryen·te*

curry *n* el curry *koo·rre*

curry powder *n* el polvo de curry *pol·bo de koo·rre*

curtain *n* la cortina *kor·tee·na*

curve *n* la curva *koor·ba* T212

cushion *n* el cojín *ko·kheen*

custard *n* las natillas *na·teel·yas*

custom *n* la costumbre *kos·toom·bre*

customer *n* el/la cliente *klee·en·te*

custom-made *adj* a la medida *a la me·dee·da* S60

customs *n* la aduana *a·dwa·na*

customs duty *n* los derechos de aduana *de·re·chos de a·dwa·na*

customs officer *n* el aduanero *a·dwa·ne·ro*

cut *vt* cortar *kor·tar*; (*reduce*) reducir* *re·doo·theer*; (*dilute*) diluir *dee·loo·eer*; **to cut oneself** cortarse *kor·tar·se* □ *n* (*wound*) el corte *kor·te*; (*of meat*) el trozo *tro·tho* Sn40

cute *adj* (*pretty*) bonito(a) *bo·nee·to(a)*

cutlery *n* la cubertería *koo·ber·te·ree·a*

cutlet *n* la chuleta *choo·le·ta*

cut-rate *adj* a precio reducido *a pre·thyo re·doo·thee·do*

cycle *vi* ir* en bicicleta *eer en bee·thee·kle·ta*

cycling *n* el ciclismo *thee·klees·mo*; **to go cycling** ir* en bicicleta *eer en bee·thee·kle·ta*

cyclist *n* el/la ciclista *thee·klees·ta*

cylinder *n* el cilindro *thee·leen·dro*

Cyprus *n* Chipre (*m*) *chee·pre*

Czechoslovakia *n* Checoslovaquia (*f*) *che·ko·slo·ba·kya*

Czech(oslovakian) *adj* checoslovaco(a) *che·kos·lo·ba·ko(a)*

D

dacron *n* el terylene *te·ree·le·ne*

dad(dy) *n* el papá *pa·pa*

daffodil *n* el narciso *nar·thee·so*

dagger *n* el puñal *poon·yal*

daily *adj* diario(a) *dee·a·ryo(a)* □ *n* (*newspaper*) el diario *dee·a·ryo*

dainty *adj* delicado(a) *de·lee·ka·do(a)*

dairy store *n* la lechería *le·che·ree·a*

dam *n* la presa *pre·sa*

damage *n* el daño *dan·yo*; **damages** los daños y perjuicios *dan·yos ee per·khwee·thyos* □ *vt* **damage** dañar *dan·yar* Sn52

damp *adj* húmedo(a) *oo·me·do(a)*

dance *vi* bailar *bay·lar* □ *n* el baile *bay·le* (*ball*); la danza *dan·tha* L35

dandruff *n* la caspa *kas·pa*

danger *n* el peligro *pe·lee·gro*

dangerous *adj* peligroso(a) *pe·lee·gro·so(a)*

Danish *adj* danés(nesa) *da·nes(·ne·sa)*

dare *vi* □ **to dare to do something** atreverse a hacer algo *a·tre·ber·se a a·ther al·go*

dark *adj* oscuro(a) *os·koo·ro(a)*; (*hair*) moreno(a) *mo·re·no(a)*; **it's dark** está oscuro *es·ta os·koo·ro*

darling *n* la querido(a) *ke·ree·do(a)*

darn *vt* zurcir* *thoor·theer*

dart *n* (*to throw*) el dardo *dar·do*; (*on clothes*) la pinza *peen·tha*; **game of darts** el juego de dardos *khwe·go de dar·dos*

dash *n* (*in writing*) el guión *gee·on*

dash(board) *n* el tablero de instrumentos *ta·ble·ro de eens·troo·men·tos*

data *pl* los datos *da·tos*

data bank, data base *n* el banco de datos *ban·ko de da·tos*

data file *n* el archivo de datos *ar·chee·bo de da·tos*

data processing *n* el proceso de datos *pro·the·so de da·tos*

date *n* (*day*) la fecha *fe·cha*; (*appointment*) la cita *thee·ta*; (*fruit*) el dátil *da·teel*; **what's the date today?** ¿qué día es hoy? *ke dee·a es oy*; **out of date** anticuado(a) *an·tee·kwa·do(a)*

date line *n* el meridiano de cambio de fecha *me·ree·dya·no de kam·byo de fe·cha*

daughter *n* la hija *ee·kha* C11

daughter-in-law *n* la nuera *nwe·ra*

dawn *n* el amanecer *a·ma·ne·ther*

day *n* el día *dee·a*; (*length of time*) la jornada *khor·na·da*; **every day** cada día *ka·da dee·a*; **day by day** día por día *dee·a por dee·a*; **the day before** el día anterior el *dee·a an·te·ryor*; **the next or following day** el día siguiente *el dee·a see·gyen·te* T106

day nursery *n* la guardería *gwar·de·ree·a* C5

dazzle *vt* deslumbrar *des·loom·brar*

dead *adj* (*person*) muerto(a) *mwer·to(a)*; (*battery*) descargado(a) *des·kar·ga·do(a)*; **the line is dead** (*phone*) la línea está cortada *la lee·ne·a es·ta kor·ta·da*

dead end *n* el callejón sin salida *kal·ye·khon seen sa·lee·da*

deaf *adj* sordo(a) *sor·do(a)*

deal *n* el negocio *ne·go·thyo* □ *vi* **to deal with a firm** tratar con una empresa *tra·tar kon oo·na em·pre·sa*; **to deal with a subject** tratar un tema *tra·tar oon te·ma*; **to deal in something** comerciar en algo *ko·mer·thyar en al·go*

dealer *n* el distribuidor *dees·tree·bwee·dor*; (*cards*) la mano *ma·no*

dear *adj* querido(a) *ke·ree·do(a)*; (*expensive*) caro(a) *ka·ro(a)*; **Dear Sir** estimado Señor *es·tee·ma·do sen·yor*; **Dear Madam** estimada Señora *es·tee·ma·da sen·yo·ra*; **Dear Mr. Smith** estimado Señor Smith *es·tee·ma·do sen·yor Smith*

death *n* la muerte *mwer·te*

death certificate *n* el certificado de defunción *ther·tee·fee·ka·do de de·foon·thyon*

debate *n* el debate *de·ba·te*

debit *n* el saldo deudor *sal·do de·oo·dor* □ *vt* **to debit $50 to someone's account** cargar $50 a la cuenta de alguien *kar·gar $50 a la kwen·ta de al·gyen*

debt *n* la deuda *de·oo·da*; **to be in debt** estar* en deuda *es·tar en de·oo·da*

decade *n* el decenio *de·the·nyo*

decaffeinated *adj* descafeinado(a) *des·ka·fey·na·do(a)*

decanter n la garrafa *ga·rra·fa*
deceive vt engañar *en·gan·yar*
December n diciembre (m) *dee·thyem·bre*
decent adj decente *de·then·te*
decide vi (between alternatives) decidir *de·thee·deer*; **to decide to do something** decidir hacer algo *de·thee·deer a·ther al·go*
decimal n el decimal *de·thee·mal*
decimal point n la coma de decimales *ko·ma de thee·ma·les*
decision n la decisión *de·thee·syon*
deck n (of ship) la cubierta *koo·byer·ta*; (of cards) la baraja *ba·ra·kha*
deck chair n la tumbona *toom·bo·na* L23
declare vt declarar *de·kla·rar*; **nothing to declare** nada que declarar *na·da ke de·kla·rar*
decorate vt (adorn) decorar *de·ko·rar*, (paint) pintar *peen·tar*
decorations pl los adornos *a·dor·nos*
decrease vt disminuir* *dees·mee·noo·eer*
deduct vt restar *res·tar*
deep adj (water, hole) hondo(a) *on·do(a)*; (voice) grave *gra·be*
deepfreeze n el congelador *kon·khe·la·dor*
deer n el venado *be·na·do*
defeat vt derrotar *de·rro·tar* □ n la derrota *de·rro·ta*
defect n el defecto *de·fek·to*
defective adj defectuoso(a) *de·fek·too·o·so(a)*
defend vt defender* *de·fen·der*
defense n la defensa *de·fen·sa*
deficit n el déficit *de·fee·theet*
definite adj (distinct) claro(a) *kla·ro(a)*; (certain) cierto(a) *thyer·to(a)*
definitely adv sin ninguna duda *seen neen·goo·na doo·da*; **he's definitely ill** sin duda está enfermo *seen doo·da es·ta en·fer·mo*
deflation n la deflación *de·fla·thyon*
deformed adj deformado(a) *de·for·ma·do(a)*
defrost vt descongelar *des·kon·khe·lar*
defroster n el descondensador *des·kon·den·sa·dor*
degree n el grado *gra·do*; (university) el título *tee·too·lo*
de-ice vt descongelar *des·kon·khe·lar*
delay vt (hold up) demorar *de·mo·rar*, (postpone) retrasar *re·tra·sar*; **the train has been delayed** el tren se ha retrasado *el tren se a re·tra·sa·do* □ n delay (of train, plane) el retraso *re·tra·so*
delegate vt delegar* *de·le·gar*
delegation n la delegación *de·le·ga·thyon*
deliberate adj intencionado(a) *een·ten·thyo·na·do(a)*
deliberately adv a propósito *a pro·po·see·to*
delicate adj (not robust) delicado(a) *de·lee·ka·do(a)*; (situation) difícil *dee·fee·theel*
delicatessen n la tienda que vende manjares exquisitos *tyen·da ke ben·de man·kha·res eks·kee·see·tos*
delicious adj delicioso(a) *de·lee·thyo·so(a)*
delighted adj encantado(a) *en·kan·ta·do(a)*
deliver vt (mail) repartir *re·par·teer*; (goods) entregar* *en·tre·gar*
delivery n (of mail) el reparto *re·par·to*; (of goods) la entrega *en·tre·ga*

de luxe adj de lujo *de loo·kho*
demand vt exigir* *ek·see·kheer* □ n (for goods) la demanda *de·man·da*
demonstrate vt (appliance etc) mostrar* *mos·trar*
demonstration n la demostración *de·mos·tra·thyon*; (political) la manifestación *ma·nee·fes·ta·thyon*
denim n el dril de algodón *dreel de al·go·don*
Denmark n Dinamarca (f) *dee·na·mar·ka*
dense adj (fog etc) denso(a) *den·so(a)*
dent n la abolladura *a·bol·ya·doo·ra*
dentist n el/la dentista *den·tees·ta* I54
dentures pl la dentadura postiza *den·ta·doo·ra pos·tee·tha* I64
deny vt negar* *ne·gar*
deodorant n el desodorante *des·o·do·ran·te*
department n (in store) la sección *sek·thyon* S11
department store n los grandes almacenes *gran·des al·ma·the·nes*
departure board n el horario de salidas *o·ra·ryo de sa·lee·das* T39
departure lounge n la sala de embarque *sa·la de em·bar·ke*
depend vi □ **it depends** depende *de·pen·de*; **to depend on** depender de *de·pen·der de*
deposit n el depósito *de·po·see·to* □ vt (money) depositar *de·po·see·tar* M9
depot n la estación de autobuses *es·ta·thyon de ow·to·boo·ses*
depressed adj (person) deprimido(a) *de·pree·mee·do(a)*
depth n la profundidad *pro·foon·dee·dad*
deputy n (second-in-command) el subdirector *soob·dee·rek·tor*
derby n el hongo *on·go*
describe vt describir* *des·kree·beer*
description n la descripción *des·kreep·thyon*
desert n el desierto *de·syer·to*
deserve vt merecer* *me·re·ther*
design n (plan) el diseño *dee·sen·yo*; (pattern) el dibujo *dee·boo·kho* □ vt diseñar *dee·sen·yar*
designer n el diseñador *dee·sen·ya·dor*; (of clothes) el/la modista *mo·dees·ta*
desire n el deseo *de·se·o*
desk n (in office) el escritorio *es·kree·to·ryo*; (reception) la recepción *re·thep·thyon*
desperate adj desesperado(a) *de·ses·pe·ra·do(a)*
despite prep a pesar de *a pe·sar de*
dessert n el postre *pos·tre*
dessertspoon n la cuchara de postre *koo·cha·ra de pos·tre*
destination n el destino *des·tee·no*
destroy vt destruir* *des·trweer*
detached house n la casa independiente *ka·sa een·de·pen·dyen·te*
detail n el detalle *de·tal·ye*; **in detail** en detalle *en de·tal·ye* Bm22
detailed adj detallado(a) *de·tal·ya·do(a)*
detective n el detective *de·tek·tee·be*
detergent n el detergente *de·ter·khen·te*
determined adj decidido(a) *de·thee·dee·do(a)*; **to be determined to do something** estar* decidido a hacer algo *es·tar de·thee·dee·do a a·ther al·go*
detour n el desvío *des·bee·o*; **to make a detour** hacer* un desvío *a·ther oon des·bee·o* T129

devaluation n la devaluación *de·ba·lwa·thyon*

devalue vt (*currency*) devaluar *de·ba·lwar*

develop vi hacerse* *a·ther·se* □ vt (*photo*) desarrollar *des·a·rrol·yar*

developing country n el país en desarrollo *pa·ees en des·a·rrol·yo*

development n (*housing*) la urbanización *oor·ba·nee·tha·thyon*

diabetes n la diabetes *dee·a·be·tes*

diabetic n el/la diabético(a) *dee·a·be·tee·ko(a)*

diagnosis n el diagnóstico *dee·ag·nos·tee·ko*

diagonal adj diagonal *dee·a·go·nal*

diagram n el diagrama *dee·a·gra·ma*

dial vt (*number*) marcar* *mar·kar*

dialect n el dialecto *dee·a·lek·to*

dial tone n el tono de marcar *to·no de mar·kar*

diameter n el diámetro *dee·a·me·tro*

diamond n el diamante *dee·a·man·te*; **diamonds** (*cards*) los diamantes *dee·a·man·tes*

diaper n el pañal *pan·yal* C19

diarrhea n la diarrea *dee·a·rre·a*

diary n el diario *dee·a·ryo*

dice n los dados *da·dos*

dictate vt (*letter*) dictar *deek·tar*

dictionary n el diccionario *deek·thyo·na·ryo*

die vi morir* *mo·reer*

diesel n el diesel *dee·sel*

diesel engine n el motor diesel *mo·tor dee·sel*

diesel fuel n el gasoil *gas·oyl*

diet n (*slimming*) el régimen *re·khee·men*; **to be on a diet** estar* a régimen *es·tar a re·khee·men*

difference n la diferencia *dee·fe·ren·thya*

different adj diferente *dee·fe·ren·te*; **different from** diferente de *dee·fe·ren·te de*

difficult adj difícil *dee·fee·theel*

difficulty n la dificultad *dee·fee·kool·tad*

dig vt (*ground*) cavar *ka·bar*; **to dig up** excavar *eks·ka·bar*

digital adj digital *dee·khee·tal*

dike n el dique *dee·ke*

dilute vt diluido(a) *dee·loo·ee·do(a)*

dim adj (*light*) oscuro(a) □ vt poner* a media luz *po·ner a me·dya looth*

dimensions pl las dimensiones *dee·men·syon·es*

dimmer n la luz de cruce *looth de kroo·the*

diner n el restaurante barato *res·tow·ran·te ba·ra·to*

dinghy n el bote *bo·te*

dining car n el coche-comedor *ko·che·ko·me·dor*

dining room n el comedor *ko·me·dor*

dinner n la comida *ko·mee·da* E6

dinner jacket n el smoking *es·mo·keen*

dinner party n la cena *the·na*

dip vt (*into liquid*) meter *me·ter*

diploma n el diploma *dee·plo·ma*

diplomat n el diplomático *dee·plo·ma·tee·ko*

dipstick n la varilla graduada *ba·reel·ya gra·dwa·da*

direct adj directo(a) *dee·rek·to(a)* □ adv **to fly to Venice direct** viajar directamente a Venecia *bya·khar dee·rek·ta·men·te a be·ne·thya* □ vt **direct** (*traffic*) dirigir* *dee·ree·kheer*

direction n la dirección *dee·rek·thyon*; **directions** (*to a place*) las instruccio-

nes *een·strook·thyo·nes*; **directions for use** modo de empleo *mo·do de em·ple·o*

director n (*of firm*) el director *dee·rek·tor*; (*of film*) el director de cine *dee·rek·tor de thee·ne* Bm3

directory n la guía *gee·a*; (*telephone*) la guía telefónica *gee·a te·le·fo·nee·ka* Sn29

dirt n la suciedad *soo·thye·dad*

dirty adj sucio(a) *soo·thyo(a)* A50

disabled adj incapacitado(a) *een·ka·pa·thee·ta·do(a)* C19

disadvantage n la desventaja *des·ben·ta·kha*; **at a disadvantage** en situación desventajosa *en see·too·a·thyon des·ben·ta·kho·sa*

disagree vi □ **to disagree with somebody** no estar* de acuerdo con alguien *no es·tar de a·kwer·do kon al·gyen*; **eggs disagree with me** los huevos me sientan mal *los we·bos me syen·tan mal*

disagreement n el desacuerdo *des·a·kwer·do*

disappear vi desaparecer* *des·a·pa·re·ther*

disappointed adj desilusionado(a) *des·ee·loo·syo·na·do(a)*

disapprove vi □ **to disapprove of something** desaprobar* algo *des·a·pro·bar al·go*

disaster n el desastre *de·sas·tre*

disc brakes pl los frenos de disco *fre·nos de dees·ko*

discipline n la disciplina *dees·thee·plee·na*

disc jockey n el disc jockey *deesk yo·kee*

disco(thèque) n la discoteca *dees·ko·te·ka*

discount n el descuento *des·kwen·to*; **at a discount** con descuento *kon des·kwen·to* M5f

discouraged adj desanimado(a) *des·a·nee·ma·do(a)*

discover vt descubrir* *des·koo·breer*

discreet adj discreto(a) *dees·kre·to(a)*

discrimination n (*racial etc*) la discriminación *dees·kree·mee·na·thyon*

discuss vt discutir *dees·koo·teer*

disease n la enfermedad *en·fer·me·dad*

disguise n el disfraz *dees·frath*; **in disguise** disfrazado(a) *dees·fra·tha·do(a)*

disgust n la repugnancia *re·poog·nan·thya*

disgusted adj disgustado(a) *dees·goos·ta·do(a)*

dish n la fuente *fwen·te*; (*food*) el plato *pla·to* E19

dishcloth n la bayeta *ba·ye·ta*

dishonest adj poco honrado(a) *po·ko hon·ra·do(a)*

dishtowel n el trapo de cocina *tra·po de ko·thee·na*

dish up vt servir* *ser·beer*

dishwasher n el lavaplatos *la·ba·pla·tos*

disinfect vt desinfectar *des·een·fek·tar*

disinfectant n el desinfectante *des·een·fek·tan·te*

disk n el disco *dees·ko*; **slipped disk** el disco dislocado *dees·ko dees·lo·ka·do*

dislocate vt dislocar* *dees·lo·kar*

dismiss vt (*from job*) despedir* *des·pe·deer*

disobedient adj desobediente *des·o·be·dyen·te*

disobey vt desobedecer* *des·o·be·de·ther*

dispatch vt expedir* *eks·pe·deer*
disposable adj para tirar *pa·ra tee·rar* C19
dispute vt (fact) disputar *dees·poo·tar* □ n la disputa *dees·poo·ta*; (industrial) el conflicto *kon·fleek·to*
disqualify vt descalificar* *des·ka·lee·fee·kar*
dissolve vt disolver* *dee·sol·ber* □ vi disolverse* *dee·sol·ber·se*
distance n la distancia *dees·tan·thya*; in the distance a lo lejos *a lo le·khos*
distant adj lejano(a) *le·kha·no(a)*
distilled water n el agua destilada *ag·wa des·tee·la·da*
distillery n la destilería *des·tee·le·ree·a*
distinct adj (clear) claro(a) *kla·ro(a)*
distinguish vt distinguir* *dees·teen·geer*; to distinguish something from something distinguir* una cosa de otra cosa *dees·teen·geer oo·na ko·sa de o·tra ko·sa*
distract vt distraer* *dees·tra·er*
distress n la desgracia *des·gra·thya*; a ship in distress un buque en peligro *oon boo·ke en pe·lee·gro*
distributor n el distribuidor *dees·tree·bwee·dor*
district n (of town) el distrito *dees·tree·to*; (in country) la región *re·khyon*
disturb vt (interrupt) interrumpir* *een·terr·oom·peer*; do not disturb por favor no molestar *por fa·bor no mo·les·tar*
ditch n la zanja *than·kha*
divan n el diván *dee·ban*
dive vi zambullirse *tham·bool·yeer·se* □ n el salto (al agua) *sal·to (al ag·wa)*
diversify vt/i diversificar* *dee·ber·see·fee·kar*
divert vt (stream) desviar *des·bee·ar*
divide vt (separate) dividir *dee·bee·deer*; (apportion) repartir *re·par·teer*; to divide 8 by 4 dividir 8 por 4 *dee·bee·deer 8 por 4*
divided highway n la carretera de doble calzada *ka·rre·te·ra de do·ble kal·tha·da*
dividend n el dividendo *dee·bee·den·do*
divingboard n el trampolín *tram·po·leen*
divorce n el divorcio *dee·bor·thyo*
divorced adj divorciado(a) *dee·bor·thya·do(a)*
dizzy adj (person) mareado(a) *ma·re·a·do(a)*
do vt/i hacer* *a·ther*; will it do? (be enough) ¿será suficiente? *se·ra soo·fee·thyen·te*; (be suitable) ¿conviene? *kon·bye·ne*; you know him, don't you? le conoce, ¿verdad? *le ko·no·the ber·dad*; he didn't come, did he? no vino, ¿verdad? *no bee·no ber·dad*
dock n el muelle *mwel·ye*
doctor n el médico *me·dee·ko*; it's Doctor Smith es Doctor(a) Smith *es dok·tor(·ra) Smith* I7f
doctor's office n el consultorio *kon·sool·to·ryo*
document n el documento *do·koo·men·to* Bm24
dog n el perro *pe·rro*
do-it-yourself n hágalo usted mismo *a·ga·lo oos·ted mees·mo*
doll n la muñeca *moon·ye·ka*
dollar n el dólar *do·lar*
dollar bill n el billete de un dólar *beel·ye·te de oon do·lar*
donate vt (funds) donar *do·nar*

donation n (money) la donación *do·na·thyon*
done adj (meat) hecho(a) *e·cho(a)*; (vegetables) cocido(a) *ko·thee·do(a)*
donkey n el burro *boo·rro*
door n la puerta *pwer·ta* A61
doorbell n el timbre *teem·bre*
door handle, doorknob n el tirador de puerta *tee·ra·dor de pwer·ta* A61
doorman n (in hotel) el portero *por·te·ro*
doormat n el felpudo *fel·poo·do*
doorstep n el peldaño *pel·dan·yo*
door-to-door salesman n el vendedor ambulante *ben·de·dor am·boo·lan·te*
dormitory n (room) el dormitorio *dor·mee·to·ryo*; (of college) la residencia *re·see·den·thya*
dosage n la dosis *do·sees*
dose n la dosis *do·sees*
dot n el punto *poon·to*
dotted line n la línea de puntos *lee·ne·a de poon·tos*
double vt doblar *do·blar* □ adv to cost double costar el doble *kos·tar el do·ble* □ adj double doble *do·ble*; a double whiskey un whisky doble *oon wees·kee do·ble*
double bed n una cama de matrimonio *oo·na ka·ma de ma·tree·mo·nyo* A4
double-parking n el aparcamiento doble *a·par·ka·myen·to do·ble*
double room n la habitación doble *a·bee·ta·thyon do·ble* A4
doubt n la duda *doo·da*; no doubt sin duda *seen doo·da*; without (a) doubt sin duda *seen doo·da* □ vt doubt to dudar *doo·dar*; I doubt it lo dudo *lo doo·do*
doubtful adj dudoso(a) *doo·do·so(a)*
dough n la masa *ma·sa*
doughnut n el buñuelo *boon·ywe·lo*
dove n la paloma *pa·lo·ma*
down n (fluff) el vello *bel·yo* □ adv to come down venir* *be·neer a·ba·kho*; (down) he came down the street bajaba la calle *ba·kha·ba la kal·ye*
downhill adv cuesta abajo *kwes·ta a·ba·kho*
down payment n el pago inicial *pa·go ee·nee·thyal*
downstairs adv abajo *a·ba·kho*
downstream adv río abajo *ree·o a·ba·kho*
downtown adv al centro (de la ciudad) *al then·tro (de la thyoo·dad)* □ adj downtown Chicago el centro de Chicago *then·tro de chee·ka·go*; to go downtown ir al centro de la ciudad *eer al then·tro de la thyoo·dad*
downward(s) adv hacia abajo *a·thya a·ba·kho*
doze vi dormitar *dor·mee·tar*
dozen n la docena *do·the·na*; 4 dozen eggs 4 docenas de huevos *4 do·the·nas de we·bos*
drab adj gris *grees*
draft n (wind) la corriente *ko·rryen·te*; (financial) la letra de cambio *le·tra de kam·byo*; (rough outline) el borrador *bo·rra·dor*
draft beer n la cerveza de barril *ther·be·tha de ba·rreel*
draftsman n el delineante *de·lee·ne·an·te*
drag vt arrastrar *a·rras·trar*
drain n el desaguadero *des·ag·wa·de·ro* □ vt (land) drenar *dre·nar*; (vegetables) secar *se·kar*; (sump, pool) vaciar *ba·thyar*

drainboard *n* el escurreplatos *es·koo·rre·pla·tos.*

drainpipe *n* el tubo de desagüe *too·bo de des·a·gwe*

drama *n* (*art*) el drama *dra·ma*

dramatic *adj* dramático(a) *dra·ma·tee·ko(a)*

drape *n* la cortina *kor·tee·na*

drastic *adj* drástico(a) *dras·tee·ko(a)*

draw *vt* (*picture*) dibujar *dee·boo·khar*; to draw out (*money*) estirar *es·tee·rar*; to draw up (*document*) redactar *re·dak·tar*

drawer *n* el cajón *ka·khon*

drawing *n* el dibujo *dee·boo·kho*

drawing pin *n* la chincheta *cheen·che·ta*

dread *vt* temer *te·mer*

dream *n* el sueño *swen·yo* □ *vi* soñar* *son·yar*

dress *n* el vestido *bes·tee·do* □ *vt* (*child*) vestir* *bes·teer* □ *vi* (*oneself*) vestirse* *bes·teer·se* S57

dress circle *n* el principal *preen·thee·pal*

dressing *n* (*salad*) la salsa *sal·sa*; (*stuffing*) el relleno *rel·ye·no*

dressing gown *n* la bata *ba·ta*

dressing table *n* el tocador *to·ka·dor*

dried *adj* (*fruit, beans*) seco(a) *se·ko(a)*; dried milk la leche en polvo *le·che en pol·bo*

drift *vi* (*boat*) ir* a la deriva *eer a la de·ree·ba*

drill *n* (*tool*) el taladro *ta·la·dro* □ *vt* (*hole*) taladrar *ta·la·drar*

drink *vt* beber *be·ber* □ *n* la bebida *be·bee·da*; have a drink! ¿quiere tomar algo? *kye·re to·mar al·go* L45

drinking water *n* el agua potable *ag·wa po·ta·ble* A90

drip *vi* el goteo *go·te·o* □ *vi* gotear *go·te·ar*

drip-dry *vt* lavar y poner *la·bar ee po·ner* □ *adj* (*shirt etc*) que no necesita plancha *ke no che·see·ta plan·cha*

drive *vt/i* (*car etc*) conducir* *kon·doo·theer*, manejar (*Am*) *ma·ne·khar*; do you drive? ¿sabe Ud conducir/manejar? *sa·be oos·ted kon·doo·theer/ma·ne·khar*; to drive to town ir* en coche a la ciudad *eer en ko·che a la thyoo·dad* □ *n* drive (*journey*) el viaje *bya·khe*; (*driveway*) la entrada *en·tra·da*; to go for a drive dar* un paseo en coche *dar oon pa·se·o en ko·che*; left-hand drive la conducción a la izquierda *kon·duk·thyon a la eeth·kyer·da*; front-wheel drive la tracción delantera *trak·thyon de·lan·te·ra* T110, 205

driver *n* (*of car*) el/la conductor(a) *kon·dook·tor(·ra)*, el chofer (*Am*) *cho·fer*; (*of taxi, bus*) el taxista *tak·sees·ta*

driver's license *n* el permiso de conducir *per·mee·so de kon·doo·theer*, la licencia de manejar (*Am*) *lee·then·thya de ma·ne·khar* T11

drizzle *n* la llovizna *lyo·beeth·na*

drop *n* (*of liquid*) la gota *go·ta* □ *vt* (*let fall*) dejar caer *de·khar ka·er* □ *vi* (*fall*) caer* *ka·er*

drought *n* la sequía *se·kee·a*

drown *vi* ahogarse *a·o·gar·se*

drug *n* (*medicine*) la medicina *me·dee·thee·na*; (*narcotic*) la droga *dro·ga* I46

druggist *n* el/la farmacéutico(a) *far·ma·the·oo·tee·ko(a)*

drugstore *n* la farmacia *far·ma·thya*

drum *n* el tambor *tam·bor*

drumstick *n* (*of chicken*) el muslo *moos·lo*

drunk *adj* borracho(a) *bo·rra·cho(a)*

dry *adj* seco(a) *se·ko(a)* □ *vt* secar* *se·kar*

dry-clean *vt* limpiar en seco *leem·pyar en se·ko*

dry-cleaner's *n* la tintorería *teen·to·re·ree·a*

duck *n* el pato *pa·to*

due *adj* (*owing*) pagadero(a) *pa·ga·de·ro(a)*; when is the train due? ¿cuándo debe llegar el tren? *kwan·do de·be lye·gar el tren*

duke *n* el duque *doo·ke*

dull *adj* (*day, weather*) triste *trees·te*; (*boring*) aburrido(a) *a·boo·rree·do(a)*

dumb *adj* mudo(a) *moo·do(a)*; (*stupid*) tonto(a) *ton·to(a)*

dump *n* (*for rubbish*) el basurero *ba·soo·re·ro*

dumping *n* (*of goods*) el dumping *doom·peeng*

dumpling *n* la masa hervida *ma·sa her·bee·da*

dune *n* la duna *doo·na*

dungarees *pl* el mono *mo·no*

dungeon *n* el calabozo *ka·la·bo·tho*

durable *adj* (*fabric, article*) duradero(a) *doo·ra·de·ro(a)*

during *prep* durante *doo·ran·te*

dusk *n* el anochecer *a·no·che·ther*

dust *n* el polvo *pol·bo* □ *vt* (*furniture*) quitar el polvo *kee·tar el pol·bo*

dustpan *n* el recogedor *re·ko·khe·dor*

dusty *adj* polvoriento(a) *pol·bo·ryen·to(a)*

Dutch *adj* holandés(esa) *o·lan·des(·de·sa*); he's Dutch es holandés *es o·lan·des*; she's Dutch es holandesa *es o·lan·de·sa* □ *n* Dutch el holandés *o·lan·des*

duty *n* (*obligation*) el deber *de·ber*; (*function*) la obligación *o·blee·ga·thyon*; (*tax*) los derechos de aduana *de·re·chos de a·dwa·na*; on duty (*doctor*) de servicio de *ser·bee·thyo*; off duty libre *lee·bre*

duty-free *adj* (*goods*) libre de impuestos *lee·bre de eem·pwes·tos* T42, S10

dye *n* el tinte *teen·te* □ *vt* teñir *ten·yeer*

dynamic *adj* (*person*) dinámico(a) *dee·na·mee·ko(a)*

dynamo *n* la dínamo *dee·na·mo*

E

each *adj* cada *ka·da* □ *pron* cada uno(a) *ka·da oo·no(a)*; each of them cada uno de ellos *ka·da oo·no de el·yos*

eager *adj* impaciente *eem·pa·thyen·te*; to be eager to do something estar* impaciente por hacer algo *es·tar eem·pa·thyen·te por a·ther al·go*

eagle *n* el águila (*f*) *a·gee·la*

ear *n* la oreja *o·re·kha*

earache *n* el dolor de oídos *do·lor de o·ee·dos*; to have an earache tener* un dolor de oídos *te·ner oon do·lor de o·ee·dos*

earlier *adj* anterior *an·te·ryor* □ *adv* más temprano *mas tem·pra·no*

early *adj* temprano(a) *tem·pra·no(a)*; you're early ha llegado a buena hora *a lye·ga·do a bwe·na o·ra*; the early train el tren que sale temprano *tren ke sa·le tem·pra·no*; to get up early levantarse temprano *le·ban·tar·se tem·pra·no*

earn *vt* ganar *ga·nar*

earnings *pl* los ingresos *een·gre·sos*

earplugs *pl* los tapones para los oídos *ta·po·nes pa·ra los o·ee·dos*

earring *n* el pendiente *pen·dyen·te*

earth *n* la tierra *tye·rra*

earthquake *n* el terremoto *te·rre·mo·to*

ease *vt* (*pain*) aliviar *a·lee·byar*

easily *adv* fácilmente *fa·theel·men·te*

east *n* el este *es·te*; **the East** el Oriente *o·ryen·te* □ *adv* **east** hacia el este *a·thya el es·te*

Easter *n* la Pascua *pas·kwa*; **at Easter** en Semana Santa *en se·ma·na san·ta*

Easter egg *n* el huevo de Pascua *we·bo de pas·kwa*

eastern *adj* oriental *o·ryen·tal*

East Germany *n* Alemania Oriental (*f*) *a·le·ma·nya o·ryen·tal*

easy *adj* fácil *fa·theel*

eat *vt* comer *ko·mer*

eau-de-Cologne *n* la colonia *ko·lo·nya*

eccentric *adj* excéntrico(a) *eks·then·tree·ko(a)*

echo *n* el eco *e·ko*

éclair *n* el relámpago *re·lam·pa·go*

economic *adj* económico(a) *e·ko·no·mee·ko(a)*

economical *adj* (*use, method*) económico(a) *e·ko·no·mee·ko(a)*

economics *n* la economía *e·ko·no·mee·a*

economist *n* el/la economista *e·ko·no·mees·ta*

economy *n* (*of country*) la economía *e·ko·no·mee·a*

eczema *n* el eczema *ek·the·ma*

edge *n* el borde *bor·de*; (*of blade*) el filo *fee·lo*

edition *n* la edición *e·dee·thyon*

educate *vt* educar* *e·doo·kar*

education *n* la educación *e·doo·ka·thyon*

E.E.C. *n* la C.E.E. *the·e·e*

eels *pl* las anguilas *an·geel·yas*

effect *n* el efecto *e·fek·to*; **to take effect** surtir efecto *soor·teer e·fek·to*

effective *adj* (*remedy etc*) eficaz *e·fee·kath*

efficient *adj* eficiente *e·fee·thyen·te*

effort *n* el esfuerzo *es·fwer·tho*

e.g. *abbrev* p.ej. *por e·khem·plo*

egg *n* el huevo *we·bo* S32

egg cup *n* la huevera *we·be·ra*

eggplant *n* la berenjena *be·ren·khe·na*

Egypt *n* Egipto (*m*) *e·kheep·to*

Egyptian *adj* egipcio(a) *e·kheep·thyo(a)*

eiderdown *n* el edredón *e·dre·don*

eight *num* ocho *o·cho*

eighteen *num* dieciocho *dye·thee·o·cho*

eighth *adj* octavo(a) *ok·ta·bo(a)*

eighties *pl* (*decade*) los años ochenta *los a·nyos o·chen·ta*

eighty *num* ochenta *o·chen·ta*

either *pron* □ **either of you** cualquiera de Uds *kwal·kye·ra de os·te·des*; **which one?** - **either** ¿cuál? - cualquiera *kwal · kwal·kye·ra* □ *adj* on **either side** en ambos lados en *am·bos la·dos* □ *conj* **either ... or ... o ... o ... o ... o ...**

elaborate *adj* complicado(a) *kom·plee·ka·do(a)*

elastic *n* el elástico *e·las·tee·ko*

elastic band *n* la gomita *go·mee·ta*

elbow *n* el codo *ko·do*

elder *adj* mayor *ma·yor*

eldest *adj* el/la mayor *ma·yor*

elect *vt* elegir* *e·le·kheer*

election *n* la elección *e·lek·thyon*

electric(al) *adj* eléctrico(a) *e·lek·tree·ko(a)*

electric blanket *n* la manta eléctrica *man·ta e·lek·tree·ka*

electrician *n* el electricista *e·lek·tree·thees·ta*

electricity *n* la electricidad *e·lek·tree·thee·dad* A62, 63

electronic *adj* electrónico(a) *e·lek·tro·nee·ko(a)*

electronics *n* la electrónica *e·lek·tro·nee·ka*

elegant *adj* elegante *e·le·gan·te*

element *n* el elemento *e·le·men·to*

elephant *n* el elefante *e·le·fan·te*

elevator *n* el ascensor *as·then·sor*, el elevador (Am) *e·le·ba·dor* A30

eleven *num* once *on·the*

eleventh *adj* undécimo(a) *oon·de·thee·mo(a)*

elm *n* el olmo *ol·mo*

else *adj* □ **somewhere else** en otra parte *en o·tra par·te*; **someone else** otra persona *o·tra per·so·na*

embankment *n* el terraplén *te·rra·plen*

embargo *n* el embargo *em·bar·go*

embark *vi* embarcarse* *em·bar·kar·se*

embarrassed *adj* desconcertado(a) *des·kon·ther·ta·do(a)*

embassy *n* la embajada *em·ba·kha·da*

embrace *vt* abrazar* *a·bra·thar*

embroidered *adj* bordado(a) *bor·da·do(a)*

embroidery *n* el bordado *bor·da·do*

emerald *n* la esmeralda *es·me·ral·da*

emergency *n* la emergencia *e·mer·khen·thya* Ea8

emergency exit *n* la salida de emergencia *sa·lee·da de e·mer·khen·thya*

emergency landing *n* el aterrizaje forzoso *a·te·rree·tha·khe for·tho·so*

emery board *n* la lima de uñas *lee·ma de oon·yas*

emigrate *vi* emigrar *e·mee·grar*

emotion *n* la emoción *e·mo·thyon*

emotional *adj* (*person*) emotivo(a) *e·mo·tee·bo(a)*

emperor *n* el emperador *em·pe·ra·dor*

emphasis *n* el énfasis *en·fa·sees*; **emphasis on something** el énfasis sobre algo *el en·fa·sees so·bre al·go*

emphasize *vt* subrayar *soob·ra·yar*; (*syllable etc*) acentuar *a·then·too·ar*

empire *n* el imperio *eem·pe·ryo*

employ *vt* (*worker*) emplear *em·ple·ar*

employee *n* el/la empleado(a) *em·ple·a·do(a)*

employer *n* el empresario *em·pre·sa·ryo*

employment *n* el empleo *em·ple·o*

empty *adj* vacío(a) *ba·thee·o(a)* □ *vt* vaciar *ba·thee·ar*

enamel *n* el esmalte *es·mal·te*

enclosure *n* (*in letter*) la carta adjunta *kar·ta ad·khoon·ta*

encore *n* la repetición *re·pe·tee·thyon*; **encore!** ¡bis! *bees*

encyclop(a)edia *n* la enciclopedia *en·thee·klo·pe·dee·a*

end *n* el fin *feen*; (*of street*) el final *fee·nal*; (*of table*) el extremo *eks·tre·mo* □ *vt* terminar *ter·mee·nar* □ *vi* acabar *a·ka·bar*

endive *n* (*smooth*) la endibia *en·dee·bya*; (*curly*) la escarola *es·ka·ro·la*

endorse *vt* (*document*) endosar *en·do·sar*

enemy *n* el enemigo *e·ne·mee·go*

energetic *adj* activo(a) *ak·tee·bo(a)*

energy n la energía e·ner·khee·a
engaged adj (betrothed) prometido(a) pro·me·tee·do(a); (busy) ocupado(a) o·koo·pa·do(a)
engagement n (betrothal) el compromiso kom·pro·mee·so
engagement ring n el anillo de compromiso a·neel·yo de kom·pro·mee·so
engine n (motor) el motor mo·tor; (of train) la locomotora lo·ko·mo·to·ra T183
engineer n el ingeniero een·khe·nye·ro
England n Inglaterra (f) een·gla·te·rra
English adj inglés(esa) een·gles(·gle·sa); he's English es inglés es een·gles; she's English es inglesa es een·gle·sa □ n English el inglés een·gles; in English en inglés en een·gles
enjoy vt (concert, outing) gustar goos·tar; to enjoy oneself divertirse dee·ber·teer·se
enjoyment n el placer pla·ther
enlarge vt agrandar a·gran·dar
enormous adj enorme e·nor·me
enough pron suficiente soo·fee·thyen·te; have you enough? ¿tiene Ud suficiente? tye·ne oos·ted soo·fee·thyen·te □ adj enough time suficiente tiempo soo·fee·thyen·te tyem·po; enough books suficientes libros soo·fee·thyen·tes lee·bros □ adv big enough bastante grande bas·tan·te gran·de S38
ensemble n (clothes) el conjunto kon·khoon·to
enter vt (room) entrar en en·trar en □ vi entrar en·trar
enterprise n la empresa em·pre·sa; private enterprise la empresa privada em·pre·sa pree·ba·da
entertain vt (amuse) entretener* en·tre·te·ner; (give hospitality) recibir re·thee·beer
entertainment n (show) el espectáculo es·pek·ta·koo·lo
enthusiasm n el entusiasmo en·too·syas·mo
enthusiastic adj entusiasta en·too·syas·ta
entrance n (way in) la entrada en·tra·da
entrance fee n el precio de entrada pre·thyo de en·tra·da
entrée n la entrada en·tra·da
entry n (way in) la entrada en·tra·da
envelope n el sobre so·bre S94
envious adj envidioso(a) en·bee·dyo·so(a)
environment n el medio ambiente me·dyo am·byen·te
envy vt envidiar en·bee·dyar □ n la envidia en·bee·dya
epidemic n la epidemia e·pee·de·mya
epilepsy n la epilepsia e·pee·lep·sya
equal adj igual ee·gwal
equator n el ecuador e·kwa·dor
equipment n el equipo e·kee·po L29
equivalent adj equivalente e·kee·ba·len·te; equivalent to equivalente a e·kee·ba·len·te a
erase vt borrar bo·rrar
eraser n el borrador bo·rra·dor
ermine n (fur) el armiño ar·meen·yo
erotic adj erótico(a) e·ro·tee·ko(a)
errand n el recado re·ka·do; to do or run an errand hacer* un recado a·ther oon re·ka·do
error n el error e·rror; in error por error por e·rror

escalator n la escalera mecánica es·ka·le·ra me·ka·nee·ka
escalope n el escalope es·ka·lo·pe
escape vi escapar(se) es·ka·par·se
escort vt escoltar es·kol·tar □ n la escolta es·kol·ta
especially adv especialmente es·pe·thyal·men·te
Esperanto n el Esperanto es·pe·ran·to
espresso (coffee) n el café exprés ca·fe eks·pres
essay n el ensayo en·sa·yo
essential adj (necessary) esencial e·sen·thyal
establish vt establecer* es·ta·ble·ther; (business) fundar foon·dar
estate n (property) la finca feen·ka
estimate vt estimar es·tee·mar □ n el presupuesto pre·soo·pwes·to M8, Bm25
etc abbrev etc et·the·te·ra
ethical adj ético(a) e·tee·ko(a)
ethnic adj étnico(a) et·nee·ko(a)
etiquette n la etiqueta e·tee·ke·ta
Europe n Europa (f) e·oo·ro·pa
European adj europeo(a) e·oo·ro·pe·o(a)
evaporate vi evaporarse e·ba·po·rar·se
evaporated milk n la leche evaporada le·che e·ba·po·ra·da
even adj (level) llano(n) lya·no(a); (equally matched) igual ee·gwal; an even number un número par oon noo·me·ro par □ adv even faster aún más rápido a·oon mas ra·pee·do; even a child could do it incluso un niño podría hacerlo een·kloo·so oon neen·yo po·dree·a a·ther·lo; even so aun así a·oon a·see
evening n la tarde tar·de; in the evening por la tarde Mc48
evening dress n (woman's) el traje de noche tra·khe de no·che; (man's) el traje de etiqueta tra·khe de e·tee·ke·ta
evening paper n el periódico de la tarde pe·ree·o·dee·ko de la tar·de
event n el acontecimiento a·kon·te·thee·myen·to
eventually adv al final al fee·nal
ever adv alguna vez al·goo·na beth; have you ever been to London? ¿ha estado alguna vez en Londres? a es·ta·do al·goo·na beth en lon·dres; ever since he... desde que él... des·de ke el; he's been there ever since desde aquel momento ha permanecido allí des·de a·kel mo·men·to a per·ma·ne·thee·do al·yee
every adj cada ka·da; every other day un día sí, otro no oon dee·a see o·tro no; every 6th day cada seis días ka·da seys dee·as
everybody, everyone pron todo el mundo to·do el moon·do
everything pron todo to·do
everywhere adv por todas partes por to·das par·tes
evidence n (proof) la prueba prwe·ba; (of witness) el testimonio tes·tee·mo·nyo
evil adj malo(a) ma·lo(a)
evolution n la evolución e·bo·loo·thyon
ex- pref ex- eks
exact adj exacto(a) ek·sak·to(a); preciso(a) pre·thee·so(a)
exactly adv exactamente ek·sak·ta·men·te
exaggerate vt/i exagerar ek·sa·khe·rar

exaggeration n la exageración *ek·sa·
khe·ra·thyon*
examination n (*exam*) el examen *ek·
sa·men*; (*inspection*) la revisión *re·
bee·syon*; (*medical*) el reconocimiento *re·ko·no·thee·myen·to*
examine vt (*inspect*) examinar *ek·sa·
mee·nar*
example n el ejemplo *e·khem·plo*; for
example por ejemplo *por e·khem·plo*
exceed vt exceder *eks·the·der*
excellent adj excelente *eks·the·len·te*
except (for), **except(ing)** prep excepto
eks·thep·to
exception n la excepción *eks·thep·
thyon*
exceptional adj excepcional *eks·thep·
thyo·nal*
excess n el exceso *eks·the·so*
excess baggage n el exceso de equipaje
eks·the·so de e·kee·pa·khe
exchange vt cambiar *kam·byar*; to exchange something for something
cambiar algo por otra cosa *kam·byar
al·go por o·tra ko·sa* □ n exchange
(*between currencies*) el cambio *kam·
byo*; (*telephone*) la central telefónica
then·tral te·le·fo·nee·ka
exchange rate n la tarifa de cambio *ta·
ree·fa de kam·byo* M23
excise duties pl los impuestos de lujo
eem·pwes·tos de loo·kho
excited adj entusiasmado(a) *en·too·
syas·ma·do(a)*
excitement n la excitación *eks·thee·ta·
thyon*
exciting adj apasionante *a·pa·syo·
nan·te*
exclaim vi exclamar *eks·kla·mar*
exclude vt excluir* *eks·kloo·eer*
exclusive adj exclusivo(a) *eks·kloo·see·
bo(a)*; exclusive rights la exclusividad *eks·kloo·see·bee·dad*; exclusive
of ... sin contar ... *seen kon·tar ...*
excursion n la excursión *eks·koor·
syon*; to go on an excursion ir* de excursión *eer de eks·koor·syon*
excuse vt disculpar *dees·kool·par*; excuse me perdón *per·don* □ n excuse
(*pretext*) la excusa *eks·koo·sa*
execute vt (*kill*) ejecutar *e·khe·koo·tar*
executive n el ejecutivo *e·khe·koo·
tee·bo*
exercise n el ejercicio *e·kher·thee·thyo*
exercise book n el cuaderno *kwa·
der·no*
exhaust n (*fumes*) el escape *es·ka·pe*;
(*pipe*) el tubo de escape *too·bo de
es·ka·pe*
exhausted adj agotado(a) *a·go·ta·
do(a)*
exhibition n la exposición *eks·po·see·
thyon*
exist vi existir *ek·sees·teer*
existence n la existencia *ek·sees·ten·
thya*
exit n la salida *sa·lee·da*
exit permit n el permiso de salida *per·
mee·so de sa·lee·da*
exotic adj exótico(a) *ek·so·tee·ko(a)*
expand vt (*material*) dilatar *dee·la·tar*;
(*business*) desarrollar *des·a·rrol·yar*
□ vi (*material*) dilatarse *dee·la·tar·se*;
(*business*) desarrollarse *des·a·rrol·
yar·se*
expect vt (*anticipate*) esperar *es·pe·rar*;
I expect he'll come supongo que ven-
drá *soo·pon·go ke ben·dra*; I expect
so supongo que sí *soo·pon·go ke see*;
she's expecting a baby está embarazada *es·ta em·ba·ra·tha·da*

expedition n la expedición *eks·pe·dee·
thyon*
expenditure n los gastos *gas·tos*
expense n (*cost*) el gasto *gas·to*; expenses los gastos *gas·tos*
expense account n la cuenta de gastos
kwen·ta de gas·tos
expensive adj caro(a) *ka·ro(a)*
experience n la experiencia *eks·pe·
ryen·thya*
experienced adj experimentado(a) *eks·
pe·ree·men·ta·do(a)*
experiment n el experimento *eks·pe·
ree·men·to*
expert n el experto *eks·per·to*
expire vi espirar *es·pee·rar*
explain vt explicar* *eks·plee·kar*
explanation n la explicación *eks·plee·
ka·thyon*
explode vi explotar *eks·plo·tar*
explore vt explorar *eks·plo·rar*
explosion n la explosión *eks·plo·syon*
export n la exportación *eks·por·ta·
thyon* □ vt exportar *eks·por·tar*
exporter n el exportador *eks·por·ta·
dor*
express vt expresar *eks·pre·sar* □ adv
to send something express mandar
algo por correo urgente *man·dar al·
go por ko·rre·o oor·khen·te*
expression n la expresión *eks·pre·syon*
express letter n la carta urgente *kar·ta
oor·khen·te*
express train n el rápido *ra·pee·do*
expressway n la autopista *ow·to·
pees·ta* F21
extension n (*building*) el anexo *a·nek·
so*; (*phone*) la extensión *eks·ten·syon*
exterior adj exterior *eks·te·ryor*
external adj externo(a) *eks·ter·no(a)*
extra adj extra *eks·tra*; postage extra
gastos de envío aparte *gas·tos de en·
bee·o a·par·te* □ adv extra extraordinariamente *eks·tra·or·dee·na·rya·
men·te* M3, A18
extraordinary adj extraordinario(a)
eks·tra·or·dee·na·ryo(a)
extravagant adj extravagante *eks·tra·
ba·gan·te*
extremely adv sumamente *soo·ma·
men·te*
eye n el ojo *o·kho*
eyebrow n la ceja *the·kha*
eyeglasses pl las gafas *ga·fas*, los anteojos (Am) *an·te·o·khos*
eyelash n la pestaña *pes·tan·ya*
eyelid n el párpado *par·pa·do*
eyeliner n el rímel *ree·mel*
eye shadow n el sombreador *som·bre·
a·dor*
eyesight n la vista *bees·ta*

F

fabric n la tela *te·la* Sn72
face n la cara *ka·ra*
face card n la carta de figura *kar·ta de
fee·goo·ra*
face cloth n la manopla *ma·no·pla*
face cream n la crema (de belleza) *kre·
ma (de bel·ye·tha)*
facilities pl las facilidades *fa·thee·lee·
da·des*
facing prep frente a *fren·te a*
fact n el hecho *e·cho*; in fact en realidad *en re·a·lee·dad*
factor n el factor *fak·tor*
factory n la fábrica *fa·bree·ka*
faculty n (*university*) la facultad *fa·
kool·tad*

fade vi apagarse* *a·pa·gar·se*; (color) descolorarse *des·ko·lo·rar·se*

Fahrenheit adj Fahrenheit *fa·ren·hayt*

fail vi fracasar *fra·ka·sar*; (brakes) fallar *fal·yar* □ vt (exam) no aprobar *no a·pro·bar* □ n without fail sin falta *seen fal·ta*

failure n el fracaso *fra·ka·so*; (person) el/la fracasado(a) *fra·ka·sa·do(a)*; (mechanical) el fallo *fal·yo*

faint vi desmayarse *des·ma·yar·se* □ adj (sound etc) débil *de·beel*; I feel faint me siento mareado *me syen·to ma·re·a·do*

fair adj (just) justo(a) *khoos·to(a)*; (hair) rubio(a) *roo·byo(a)*; (average) mediano(a) *me·dya·no(a)* □ adv to play fair jugar* limpio *khoo·gar leem·pyo* □ n fair (commercial) la feria *fe·rya*

fairground n el real de la feria *re·al de la fe·rya*

fairly adv (rather) bastante *bas·tan·te*

fairy n el hada (f) *a·da*

faith n la fe *fe*

faithfully adv □ yours faithfully le saluda atentamente *le sa·loo·da a·ten·ta·men·te*

fake adj falso(a) *fal·so(a)*

fall vi (person) caerse* *ka·er·se*; (prices etc) bajar *ba·khar*; to fall down caerse* *ka·er·se*; to fall in love enamorarse *e·na·mo·rar·se* □ n fall la caída *ka·ee·da*; (decrease) la disminución *dees·mee·noo·thyon*; (season) el otoño *o·ton·yo*

false adj (name etc) falso(a) *fal·so(a)*; false teeth los dientes postizos *dyen·tes pos·tee·thos*

familiar adj (impertinent) presumido(a) *pre·soo·mee·do(a)*; to be familiar with something conocer* bien algo *ko·no·ther byen al·go*

family n la familia *fa·mee·lya* A2

famous adj famoso(a) *fa·mo·so(a)*

fan n (folding) el abanico *a·ba·nee·ko*; (electric, of car etc) el ventilador *ben·tee·la·dor*; (supporter) el hincha *een·cha*

fanbelt n la correa del ventilador *ko·rre·a del ben·tee·la·dor*

fancy adj de lujo *de loo·kho*

fancy dress n el disfraz *dees·frath*

far adv lejos *le·khos*; (much) con mucho *kon moo·cho*; how far is it to…? ¿cuánto hay de aquí a…? *kwan·to ay de a·kee a*; as far as the station hasta la estación *as·ta la es·ta·thyon*; as far as I know que yo sepa *ke yo se·pa*; the Far East el Lejano Oriente *le·kha·no o·ryen·te*

farce n la farsa *far·sa*

fare n el precio del billete *pre·thyo del beel·ye·te*; (in taxi) el precio del viaje *pre·thyo del bee·a·khe*

farm n la finca *feen·ka*

farmer n el agricultor *a·gree·kool·tor*

farmhouse n la casa de campo *ka·sa de kam·po*

farmyard n el corral *ko·rral*

far-sighted adj présbita *pres·bee·ta*

farther adv más lejos *mas le·khos*

farthest adv lo más lejos *lo mas le·khos*

fascinating adj fascinante *fas·thee·nan·te*

fashion n la moda *mo·da*; the latest fashions los más recientes estilos *los mas re·thyen·tes es·tee·los*

fashionable adj de moda *de mo·da*

fast adj (speedy) rápido(a) *a ra·pee·do(a)*; (dye) sólido(a) *so·lee·do(a)*;

my watch is fast mi reloj se adelanta *mee re·lokh se a·de·lan·ta* □ adv fast de prisa *de pree·sa*; to be fast asleep estar* profundamente dormido(a) *es·tar pro·foon·da·men·te dor·mee·do(a)* T55, 205

fasten vt atar *a·tar*; fasten seat belts abrochar los cinturones *a·bro·char los theen·too·ro·nes*

fat adj (person) gordo(a) *gor·do(a)* □ n la grasa *gra·sa*

fatal adj mortal *mor·tal*

father n el padre *pa·dre*; yes, Father (priest) sí padre *see pa·dre*

father-in-law n el suegro *swe·gro*

faucet n el grifo *gree·fo* A31

fault n (defect) la falta *fal·ta*; (blame) la culpa *kool·pa*; whose fault is it? ¿quién tiene la culpa? *kyen tye·ne la kool·pa*; it's not my fault yo no tengo la culpa *yo no ten·go la kool·pa*

faulty adj defectuoso(a) *de·fek·too·o·so(a)*

favor n el favor *fa·bor*; to do someone a favor hacer* un favor a alguien *a·ther oon fa·bor a al·gyen*; I'm not in favor of that idea no estoy de acuerdo con esa idea *no es·toy de a·kwer·do kon e·sa ee·de·a*

favorite adj predilecto(a) *pre·dee·lek·to(a)*

fawn adj beige *be·ees*

fear n el miedo *mye·do*

feasibility n la viabilidad *bya·bee·lee·dad*

feasibility study n el estudio de las posibilidades *es·too·dyo de las po·see·bee·lee·da·des*

feast n el festín *fes·teen*

feather n la pluma *ploo·ma*

feature film n la película de largo metraje *pe·lee·koo·la de lar·go me·tra·khe*

features pl las facciones *fak·thyo·nes*

February n febrero (m) *fe·bre·ro*

federal adj federal *fe·de·ral*

fed up adj □ I'm fed up estoy harto de *es·toy ar·to de*

fee n los honorarios *o·no·ra·ryos*

feed vt alimentar *a·lee·men·tar* □ vi comer *ko·mer*

feedback n el feedback *feed·bak*

feel vt (touch) tocar* *to·kar*; I feel that… pienso que… *pyen·so ke* □ vi it feels soft parece blando al tacto *pa·re·the blan·do al tak·to*; I feel hungry tengo hambre *ten·go am·bre*; I feel better me siento mejor *me syen·to me·khor*; I feel like a beer me apetece una cerveza *me a·pe·te·the oo·na ther·be·tha*

feeling n la sensibilidad *sen·see·bee·lee·dad*; (emotion) el sentimiento *sen·tee·myen·to*

fellow n el tipo *tee·po*; fellow countryman el/la compatriota *kom·pa·tree·o·ta*

felt n (cloth) el fieltro *fyel·tro*

felt-tip pen n el rotulador *ro·too·la·dor*

female adj (animal) hembra *em·bra*; the female sex el sexo femenino *sek·so fe·me·nee·no*

feminine adj femenino(a) *fe·me·nee·no(a)*

fence n la cerca *ther·ka*

fender n (on car) el parachoques *pa·ra·cho·kes*

fern n el helecho *e·le·cho*

ferry n (small) la barca *bar·ka*; (large) el ferry *fe·rry*

fertile adj (land) fértil *fer·teel*

festival n el festival fes·tee·bal L5

fetch vt ir* a buscar eer a boos·kar

fête n la fiesta fyes·ta

fever n la fiebre fye·bre

few adj pocos(as) po·kos(as); **a few books** algunos libros al·goo·nos lee·bros □ pron **there are very few** hay muy pocos ay mooy po·kos; **there are quite a few** hay bastantes ay bas·tan·tes

fiancé(e) n el/la novio(a) no·byo(a)

fiber n la fibra fee·bra S61

fiberglass n la fibra de vidrio fee·bra de bee·dryo

fiction n las novelas no·be·las

field n (on farm, for football etc) el campo kam·po, (for football etc) la cancha (Am) kan·cha

field glasses pl los prismáticos prees·ma·tee·kos

fierce adj feroz fe·roth

fifteen num quince keen·the

fifth adj quinto(a) keen·to(a)

fifty num cincuenta theen·kwen·ta

fig n el higo ee·go

fight vi pelear pe·le·ar □ n la pelea pe·le·a

figure n (of human) la figura fee·goo·ra; (number) la cifra thee·fra; **to have a nice figure** tener* buen tipo te·ner bwen tee·po □ vt **figure** (suppose) suponer* soo·po·ner

file n (tool) la lima lee·ma; (dossier) el expediente eks·pe·dyen·te

filing cabinet n el fichero fee·che·ro

fill vt llenar lye·nar; **to fill in/out** (form) llenar lye·nar; **to fill up** (cup) llenar lye·nar; **fill it up!** (car) ¡llénelo! lye·ne·lo

fillet n (of meat, fish) el filete fee·le·te

filling adj (food) que llena ke lye·na □ n (in tooth) el empaste em·pas·te I58

filling station n la estación de servicio es·ta·thyon de ser·bee·thyo

film n (movie) la película pe·lee·koo·la; (for camera) el carrete ka·rre·te L36, S47f

filter n el filtro feel·tro; (on camera) el filtro* de luz feel·tro de looth

filter-tip adj (cigarettes) emboquillado(a) em·bo·keel·ya·do(a) S98

final adj final fee·nal

finally adv finalmente fee·nal·men·te

finals pl (sports) la final fee·nal

finance n las finanzas fee·nan·thas □ vt financiar fee·nan·thyar

Finance Minister n el ministro de hacienda mee·nees·tro de a·thyen·da

financial adj financiero(a) fee·nan·thye·ro(a)

find vt encontrar* en·kon·trar; **to find out** descubrir* des·koo·breer

fine adj (delicate) fino(a) fee·no(a); (weather) bueno(a) bwe·no(a); **(that's) fine** muy bien mooy byen □ n la multa mool·ta T200

finger n el dedo de·do

finish vt/i acabar a·ka·bar

Finland n Finlandia (f) feen·lan·dya

Finnish adj finlandés(esa) feen·lan·des(·de·sa)

fire n el fuego fwe·go; (accident) el incendio een·then·dyo; **the house is on fire** la casa está ardiendo la ka·sa es·ta ar·dyen·do; **to set fire to** incendiar een·then·dyar □ vt **to fire a gun** parar un fusil dees·pa·rar oon foo·seel; **to fire someone** (dismiss) despedir* a alguien des·pe·deer a al·gyen A74, Ea4

fire alarm n la alarma de incendios u·lar·ma de een·then·dyos

firearm n el arma de fuego (f) ar·ma de fwe·go

fire department n el cuerpo de bomberos kwer·po de bom·be·ros Ea7

fire engine n el coche de bomberos ko·che de bom·be·ros

fire escape n la escalera de incendios es·ka·le·ra de een·then·dyos

fire extinguisher n el extintor eks·teen·tor

fireman n el bombero bom·be·ro

fireplace n la chimenea chee·me·ne·a

fire station n el parque de bomberos par·ke de bom·be·ros

fireworks pl el fuego artificial fwe·go ar·tee·fee·thyal

firm n la compañía kom·pan·yee·a □ adj firme feer·me Bm17

first adj primero(a) pree·me·ro(a) □ adv primero pree·me·ro □ n **in first** (gear) en primera en pree·me·ra; **at first** en primer lugar en pree·mer loo·gar

first aid n los primeros auxilios pree·me·ros owk·see·lyos

first aid kit n el botiquín bo·tee·keen

first-class adj (work etc) de primera clase de pree·me·ra kla·se; **to travel first class** viajar en primera bee·a·khar en pree·me·ra

first floor n la planta baja plan·ta ba·kha A5

first name n el nombre de pila nom·bre de pee·la

fir (tree) n el abeto a·be·to

fiscal adj fiscal fees·kal

fiscal year n el año económico an·yo e·ko·no·mee·ko

fish n el pez peth; (as food) el pescado pes·ka·do E27

fishing n la pesca pes·ka; **to go fishing** ir* a pescar eer a pes·kar L28

fishing rod n la caña de pescar kan·ya de pes·kar

fishmonger n el pescadero pes·ka·de·ro

fist n el puño poon·yo

fit adj (strong, healthy) en forma en for·ma; (suitable) apropiado(a) a·pro·pya·do(a) □ vt/i **it fits (me)** me sienta me syen·ta □ n **fit** (seizure) el ataque a·ta·ke

five num cinco theen·ko

fix vt (fasten) fijar fee·khar; (arrange, mend) arreglar a·rre·glar; (prepare) preparar pre·pa·rar

fizzy adj gaseoso(a) ga·se·o·so(a)

flag n la bandera ban·de·ra

flag stop n la parada discrecional pa·ra·da dees·kre·thyo·nal

flake n la escama es·ka·ma; (of snow) el copo ko·po

flame n la llama lya·ma

flammable adj inflamable een·fla·ma·ble

flan n la tarteleta tar·te·le·ta

flannel n (facecloth) el paño pan·yo

flap n la solapa so·la·pa □ vi (sail) agitarse a·khee·tar·se

flash n el destello des·tel·yo; (on camera) el flash flash □ vi (light) destellar des·tel·yar S56

flashbulb n la bombilla de flash bom·beel·ya de flash

flashcube n el cubo de flash koo·bo de flash

flashlight n la linterna eléctrica leen·ter·na e·lek·tree·ka

flask n el frasco fras·ko

flat *adj* llano(a) *lya·no(a)*; *(deflated)* desinflado(a) *des·een·fla·do(a)*; *(battery)* descargado(a) *des·kar·ga·do(a)*; *(beer)* muerto(a) *mwer·to(a)*; B flat *(music)* el si bemol *see be·mol*; flat rate el precio fijo *pre·thyo fee·kho*

flavor *n* el sabor *sa·bor*

flea *n* la pulga *pool·ga*

flea market *n* el rastro *ras·tro*

fleet *n* la flota *flo·ta*; fleet of vehicles la escuadra *es·kwa·dra*

Flemish *adj* flamenco(a) *fla·men·ko(a)*

flesh *n* la carne *kar·ne*

flexible *adj* flexible *flek·see·ble*

flight *n* el vuelo *bwe·lo*; flight of steps la escalera *es·ka·le·ra* T2f, 38, 49

flight attendant *n* la azafata *a·tha·fa·ta*; el camarero *ka·ma·re·ro*

flint *n* *(in lighter)* la piedra *pye·dra*

flippers *pl* *(for swimming)* las aletas *a·le·tas*

flirt *vi* coquetear *ko·ke·te·ar*

float *vi* flotar *flo·tar* □ *n* *(for swimming)* el flotador *flo·ta·dor*; *(for fishing)* el corcho *kor·cho*

flock *n* el rebaño *re·ban·yo*

flood *n* la inundación *ee·noon·da·thyon*

floodlight *n* el foco *fo·ko*

floodlit *adj* iluminado(a) con focos *ee·loo·mee·na·do(a) kon fo·kos*

floor *n* el suelo *swe·lo*; 1st floor *(Brit)*, 2nd floor *(US)* el primer piso *pree·mer pee·so* A5

floor lamp *n* la lámpara de pie *lam·pa·ra de pye*

florist *n* el/la florista *flo·rees·ta*

flour *n* la harina *a·ree·na*

flow *vi* fluir* *floo·eer*; *(traffic)* circular *theer·koo·lar*

flow chart *n* el organigrama *or·ga·nee·gra·ma*

flower *n* la flor *flor* L33

flowerbed *n* el parterre *par·te·rre*

flu *n* la gripe *gree·pe*

fluent *adj* □ he speaks fluent French domina bien el francés *do·mee·na byen el fran·thes*

fluorescent light *n* la lámpara fluorescente *lam·pa·ra floo·o·res·then·te*

fluoride *n* el flúor *floo·or*

flush *vt* □ to flush the toilet hacer* funcionar *a·ther foon·thyo·nar*

flute *n* la flauta *flow·ta*

fly *n* la mosca *mos·ka* □ *vi* volar* *bo·lar*; *(passengers)* viajar en avión *bee·a·khar en a·byon*

flying *n* el volar *bo·lar*; to like flying gustarle ir en avión *goos·tar·le eer en a·byon*

flyover *n* *(road)* el paso superior *pa·so soo·pe·ree·or*

foam *n* la espuma *es·poo·ma*

focus *vt* enfocar* *en·fo·kar*

fog *n* la niebla *nye·bla*

foggy *adj* nebuloso(a) *ne·boo·lo·so(a)*; it's foggy hay niebla *ay nye·bla*

fog light *n* el faro antiniebla *fa·ro an·tee·nye·bla*

foil *n* *(for food)* el papel de plata *pa·pel de pla·ta*

fold *vt* doblar *do·blar*

folding chair *n* la silla plegable *seel·ya ple·ga·ble*

folding table *n* la mesa plegable *me·sa ple·ga·ble*

folk dance *n* el baile folklórico *bay·le fol·klo·ree·ko* L35

folk song *n* la canción folklórica *kan·thyon fol·klo·ree·ka*

follow *vt/i* seguir* *se·geer*

following *adj* siguiente *see·gyen·te*

food *n* la comida *ko·mee·da*

food poisoning *n* intoxicación por alimentos *een·tok·see·ka·thyon por a·lee·men·tos*

foot *n* *(of person)* el pie *pye*; *(of animal)* la pata *pa·ta*; *(measurement)* el pie *pye*

football *n* *(soccer)* el fútbol *foot·bol*; *(ball)* el balón *ba·lon*

footbrake *n* el freno de pie *fre·no de pye*

footpath *n* el sendero *sen·de·ro*

for *prep* por *por*, para *pa·ra*; do it for me hágalo por mí *a·ga·lo por mee*; to buy something for someone comprar algo para alguien *kom·prar al·go pa·ra al·gyen*; to sell something for 1,000 pesetas vender algo por 1,000 pesetas *ben·der al·go por 1,000 pe·se·tas*; ready for anything listo(a) para todo *lees·to(a) pa·ra to·do*; to leave for London marcharse a Londres *mar·char·se a lon·dres*; to walk for an hour andar* durante una hora *un·dar doo·ran·te oo·na o·ra*; what's the Spanish for "dog"? ¿cómo se dice "dog" en español? *ko·mo se dee·the dog en es·pan·yol*; it's warm for March hace calor para marzo *a·the ka·lor pa·ra mar·tho*

forbid *vt* prohibir *pro·ee·beer*; to forbid someone to do something prohibir a alguien que haga algo *pro·ee·beer a al·gyen ke a·ga al·go*; it is forbidden está prohibido *es·ta pro·ee·bee·do*

force *n* *(violence)* la fuerza *fwer·tha* □ *vt* *(compel)* obligar* *o·blee·gar*

ford *n* el vado *ba·do*

forecast *n* el pronóstico *pro·nos·tee·ko*; *(weather)* la previsión meteorológica *pre·bee·syon me·te·o·ro·lo·khee·ka*

forehead *n* la frente *fren·te*

foreign *adj* extranjero(a) *eks·tran·khe·ro(a)*

foreigner *n* el/la extranjero(a) *eks·tran·khe·ro(a)* T196

foreign exchange market *n* el mercado de divisas *mer·ka·do de dee·bee·sas*

foreign policy *n* la política exterior *po·lee·tee·ka eks·te·ryor*

foreman *n* el capataz *ka·pa·tath*

forename *n* el nombre de pila *nom·bre de pee·la*

forest *n* el bosque *bos·ke*

forgery *n* la falsificación *fal·see·fee·ka·thyon*

forget *vt* olvidar *ol·bee·dar*

forgive *vt* perdonar *per·do·nar*

fork *n* el tenedor *te·ne·dor*; *(in road)* la bifurcación *bee·foor·ka·thyon*

form *n* la forma *for·ma*; *(document)* el formulario *for·moo·la·ryo*; in good form en buena forma *en bwe·na for·ma*

formal *adj* de etiqueta *de e·tee·ke·ta*

fortnight *n* los quince días *keen·the dee·as*

fortune *n* *(wealth)* la fortuna *for·too·na*

forty *num* cuarenta *kwa·ren·ta*

forward *vt* *(letter)* hacer* seguir *a·ther se·geer*

forward(s) *adv* hacia adelante *a·thya a·de·lan·te*; the seat is too far forward el asiento está demasiado hacia adelante *el a·syen·to es·ta de·ma·syu·do a·thya a·de·lan·te*

fountain *n* la fuente *fwen·te*

fountain pen *n* la estilográfica *es·tee·lo·gra·fee·ka*

four *num* cuatro *kwa·tro*

fourteen *num* catorce *ka·tor·the*

fourth *adj* cuarto(a) *kwar·to(a)*

fox *n* el zorro *tho·rro*

fracture *n* (*of arm etc*) la fractura *frak·too·ra*

fragile *adj* frágil *fra·kheel*

frame *n* (*of picture*) el marco *mar·ko*; **frames** (*of eyeglasses*) la montura *mon·too·ra*

France *n* Francia (*f*) *fran·thya*

free *adj* libre *lee·bre*; (*costing nothing*) gratis *gra·tees* Bm11

freeway *n* la autopista *ow·to·pees·ta*

freeze *vi* helar* *e·lar* □ *vt* (*food*) congelar *kon·khe·lar*

freezer *n* el congelador *kon·khe·la·dor*

freight *n* (*goods*) el flete *fle·te*

freight train *n* el tren de mercancías *tren de mer·kan·thee·as*

French *adj* francés(esa) *fran·thes(·the·sa)*; he's French es francés *es fran·thes*; she's French es francesa *es fran·the·sa* □ *n* French el francés *fran·thes*

french fried potatoes, french fries *pl* las patatas fritas *pa·ta·tas free·tas*, las papas fritas (Am) *pa·pas free·tas* E23

frequent *adj* frecuente *fre·kwen·te*

fresh *adj* fresco(a) *fres·ko(a)*

Friday *n* viernes (*m*) *byer·nes*

fridge *n* el frigorífico *free·go·ree·fee·ko*

fried *adj* frito(a) *free·to(a)*; **a fried egg** un huevo frito *oon we·bo free·to*

friend *n* el/la amigo(a) *a·mee·go(a)*

friendly *adj* amistoso(a) *a·mees·to·so(a)* Mc14

frighten *vt* asustar *a·soos·tar*

fringe *n* (*hair*) el flequillo *fle·keel·yo*; (*edging*) la franja *fran·kha*

fritter *n* el buñuelo *boon·ywe·lo*

frog *n* la rana *ra·na*

frogs legs *pl* las ancas de rana *an·kas de ra·na*

from *prep* de; **from London** de Londres *de lon·dres*; **from 8 o'clock** a partir de las 8 *a par·teer de las 8*; **a letter from Mary** una carta de María *oo·na kar·ta de ma·ree·a*; **water from the faucet** el agua del grifo *ag·wa del gree·fo*

front *adj* delantero(a) *de·lan·te·ro(a)* □ *n* (*foremost part*) la parte delantera *par·te de·lan·te·ra*; (*seaside*) el paseo marítimo *pa·se·o ma·ree·tee·mo*; **to sit in front** sentarse* delante *sen·tar·se de·lan·te*

frontier *n* la frontera *fron·te·ra*

front-wheel drive *n* la tracción delantera *trak·thyon de·lan·te·ra*

frost *n* la escarcha *es·kar·cha*

frozen *adj* (*food*) congelado(a) *kon·khe·la·do(a)*

fruit *n* la fruta *froo·ta*

fruit salad *n* la ensalada de frutas *en·sa·la·da de froo·tas*

fry *vt* freír* *fre·eer*

fry(ing) pan *n* la sartén *sar·ten*

fuel *n* el carburante *kar·boo·ran·te*

fuel pump *n* la bomba de la gasolina *bom·ba de la ga·so·lee·na*

full *adj* lleno(a) *lye·no(a)*; **full of** lleno de *lye·no de*; **full up** (*bus etc*) completo(a) *com·ple·to(a)*

full stop *n* el punto *poon·to*

full-time *adj, adv* de jornada completa *de khor·na·da kom·ple·ta*

fun □ **it was great fun** fue muy divertido *fwe mooy dee·ber·tee·do*

funds *pl* los fondos *fon·dos*

funeral *n* el entierro *en·tye·rro*

funny *adj* (*amusing*) gracioso(a) *gra·thyo·so(a)*; (*strange*) curioso(a) *koo·ryo·so(a)*

fur *n* la piel *pyel*

fur coat *n* el abrigo de pieles *a·bree·go de pye·les*

furnish *vt* (*room etc*) amueblar *a·mwe·blar*

furniture *n* los muebles *mwe·bles*

further *adv* más lejos *mas le·khos*

furthest *adv* lo más lejos *lo mas le·khos*

fuse *n* el fusible *foo·see·ble* A79

fuss *n* el lío *lee·o*; **to make a fuss** armar un lío *ar·mar oon lee·o*

future *n* el porvenir *por·be·neer*

G

gadget *n* el dispositivo *dees·po·see·tee·bo* S16

gain *vt* (*obtain*) ganar *ga·nar* □ *vi* (*clock*) adelantar *a·de·lan·tar*

gala *n* la gala *ga·la*

gale *n* el vendaval *ben·da·bal*

gallery *n* la galería *ga·le·ree·a*; (*in theater*) el paraíso *pa·ra·ee·so*

gallon *n* el galón *ga·lon*

gallop *vi* galopar *ga·lo·par* □ *n* el galope *ga·lo·pe*; **to go at a gallop** ir* al galope *eer al ga·lo·pe*

gamble *vi* jugar* *khoo·gar*

gambler *n* el jugador *khoo·ga·dor*

gambling *n* el juego *khwe·go*

game *n* el juego *khwe·go*; (*hunting*) la caza *ka·tha*; **a game of tennis** un juego de tenis *oon khwe·go de te·nees*

gang *n* la banda *ban·da*

gangster *n* el gángster *gang·ster*

gangway *n* (*passage*) el pasillo *pa·seel·yo*; (*bridge*) la pasarela *pa·sa·re·la*

gap *n* el hueco *we·ko*

garage *n* el garaje *ga·ra·khe* T171

garbage *n* la basura *ba·soo·ra*

garbage can *n* el cubo de la basura *koo·bo de la ba·soo·ra*

garden *n* el jardín *khar·deen*

garden center *n* la tienda de jardinería *tyen·da de khar·dee·ne·ree·a*

gardener *n* el jardinero *khar·dee·ne·ro*

gargle *vi* hacer* gárgaras *a·ther gar·ga·ras*

garlic *n* el ajo *a·kho*

garlic sausage *n* el salchichón de ajo *sal·chee·chon de a·kho*

garment *n* la prenda *pren·da*

gas *n* el gas *gas*; **gas stove** la cocina de gas *ko·thee·na de gas*

gasket *n* la junta de culata *khoon·ta de koo·la·ta*

gas(oline) *n* la gasolina *ga·so·lee·na* T157, 172, 174

gas station *n* la estación de servicio *es·ta·thyon de ser·bee·thyo*

gate *n* (*of garden*) el portillo *por·teel·yo*; (*of building*) la puerta *pwer·ta*

gateau *n* la torta *tor·ta*

gather *vt* (*assemble*) juntar *khoon·tar* □ *vi* (*crowd*) juntarse *khoon·tar·se*; (*suppose*) deducir* *de·doo·theer*

gathered *adj* fruncido(a) *froon·thee·do(a)*

gauge *n* (*device*) el indicador *een·dee·ka·dor*

gauze *n* la gasa *ga·sa*

gay *adj* (*merry*) alegre *a·le·gre*

gear *n* (*equipment*) el equipo *e·kee·po*;

(*of car*) el cambio *kam·byo*; **in gear** engranado(a) *en·gra·na·do(a)*; **2nd/3rd gear** segunda/tercera velocidad *se·goon·da/ter·the·ra be·lo·thee·dad*; **high/low gear** cuarta/primera velocidad *kwar·ta/pree·me·ra be·lo·thee·dad*

gearbox *n* la caja de cambios *ka·kha de cam·byos*

gearshift *n* la palanca del cambio de velocidades *pa·lan·ka del kam·byo de be·lo·thee·da·des*

gem *n* la piedra preciosa *pye·dra pre·thyo·sa*

gender *n* el género *khe·ne·ro*

general *adj* general *khe·ne·ral* □ *n* (*soldier*) el general *khe·ne·ral*; **in general** en general *en khe·ne·ral*

general delivery *adv* por lista de correos *por lees·ta de ko·rre·os* Sn8

general election *n* las elecciones generales *e·lek·thyo·nes khe·ne·ra·les*

general knowledge *n* la cultura general *kool·too·ra khe·ne·ral*

generally *adv* generalmente *khe·ne·ral·men·te*

general practitioner, G.P. *n* el médico de medicina general *me·dee·ko de me·dee·thee·na khe·ne·ral*

generation *n* la generación *khe·ne·ra·thyon*

generator *n* (*electrical*) el generador *khe·ne·ra·dor*

generous *adj* generoso(a) *khe·ne·ro·so(a)*

Geneva *n* Ginebra (*f*) *khee·ne·bra*

gentle *adj* suave *swa·be*

gentleman *n* el caballero *ka·bal·ye·ro*

genuine *adj* auténtico(a) *ow·ten·tee·ko(a)*

geography *n* la geografía *khe·o·gra·fee·a*

geology *n* la geología *khe·o·lo·khee·a*

geometry *n* la geometría *khe·o·me·tree·a*

geranium *n* el geranio *khe·ra·nyo*

germ *n* el microbio *mee·kro·byo*

German *adj* alemán(mana) *a·le·man (·ma·na)*; he's German es alemán *es a·le·man*; she's German es alemana *es a·le·ma·na* □ *n* German el alemán *a·le·man*

Germany *n* Alemania (*f*) *a·le·ma·nya*

gesture *n* el gesto *khes·to*; **a kind gesture** un buen detalle *oon bwen de·tal·ye*

get *vt* (*obtain*) obtener* *ob·te·ner*; (*fetch*) traer* *tra·er*; (*receive*) recibir *re·thee·beer*; (*prepare*: food) preparar *pre·pa·rar*; (*catch*: illness) coger* *ko·kher*; **to have got(ten)** (*possess*) tener* *te·ner*; **to get tired** cansarse *kan·sar·se*; **to get ready** prepararse *pre·pa·rar·se*; **how do we get there?** ¿cómo llegamos allí? *ko·mo lye·ga·mos al·yee*; **to get home** llegar* a casa *lye·gar a ka·sa*; **get off the grass** ¡no pise el césped! *no pee·se el thes·ped*; **to get one's hair cut** cortarse el pelo *kor·tar·se el pe·lo*; **to get away** (*escape*) fugarse* *foo·gar·se*; **how are you getting on?** ¿qué tal? *ke tal*; **to get onto a road** coger* una carretera *ko·kher oon·a ka·rre·te·ra*; **to get through** (*on phone*) conseguir* comunicar *kon·se·geer ko·moo·nee·kar*; **to get up** levantarse *le·ban·tar·se*

gherkin *n* el pepinillo *pe·pee·neel·yo*

ghetto *n* el ghetto *ge·to*

ghost *n* el fantasma *fan·tas·ma*

giant *n* el gigante *khee·gan·te*

gift *n* el regalo *re·ga·lo*; (*ability*) el don *don*

gifted *adj* dotado(a) *do·ta·do(a)*

gift token *n* el vale de regalo *ba·le de re·ga·lo*

gift-wrap *vt* envolver* en papel de regalo *en·bol·ber en pa·pel de re·ga·lo*

gin *n* (*drink*) la ginebra *khee·ne·bra*

ginger *n* el jengibre *khen·khee·bre*

ginger ale *n* el ginger ale

gingerbread *n* el pan de jengibre *el pan de khen·khee·bre*

gingham *n* la guinga *geen·ga*

gipsy *n* el gitano *khee·ta·no*

girdle *n* (*corset*) la faja *fa·kha*

girl *n* (*child*) la niña *neen·ya*; (*young woman*) la chica *chee·ka* S109

girlfriend *n* la novia *no·bya*

give *vt* dar* *dar*; **to give a party** dar* una fiesta *dar oo·na fyes·ta*; **to give someone something** dar* algo a alguien *dar al·go a al·gyen*; **to give away** regalar *re·ga·lar*; **to give back** devolver* *de·bol·ber*; **to give in** (*yield*) ceder *the·der*; **to give up** (*abandon hope*) abandonar *a·ban·do·nar*; **to give up smoking** dejar de fumar *de·khar de foo·mar*; **to give way** (*traffic*) ceder el paso *the·der el pa·so*

glacé *adj* escarchado(a) *es·kar·cha·do(a)*

glad *adj* feliz *fe·leeth*; I was glad to hear... me alegré cuando supe... *me a·le·gre kwan·do soo·pe*

glamorous *adj* encantador(a) *en·kan·ta·dor(·ra)*

glance *n* la mirada *mee·ra·da* □ *vi* to glance at echar una mirada a *e·char oo·na mee·ra·da a*

gland *n* la glándula *glan·doo·la*

glare *n* (*of light*) la luz deslumbrante *looth des·loom·bran·te*

glass *n* el vidrio *bee·dryo*; (*tumbler*) el vaso *ba·so*; (*glassware*) la cristalería *krees·ta·le·ree·a* B74, E14

glasses *pl* las gafas *ga·fas*, los anteojos (Am) *an·te·o·khos* B76

glide *vi* deslizarse *des·lee·thar·se*

glider *n* el planeador *pla·ne·a·dor*

gliding *n* (*sport*) el vuelo sin motor *bwe·lo seen mo·tor*

global *adj* global *glo·bal*

globe *n* (*map*) el globo *glo·bo*

globe artichoke *n* la alcachofa *al·ka·cho·fa*

glove *n* el guante *gwan·te*

glove compartment *n* la guantera *gwan·te·ra*

glow *vi* arder vivamente *ar·der bee·ba·men·te*

glue *n* la cola *ko·la* □ *vt* pegar* con cola *pe·gar kon ko·la*

glycerin(e) *n* la glicerina *glee·the·ree·na*

gnat *n* el mosquito *mos·kee·to*

go *vi* ir* *eer*; (*leave*) irse* *eer·se*; (*clock, machine*) funcionar *foon·thyo·nar*; **to go shopping** ir* de compras *eer de kom·pras*; **to go bad** echarse a perder *e·char·se a per·der*; **how did it go?** ¿cómo salió? *ko·mo sa·lyo*; **the books go here** los libros se ponen aquí *los lee·bros se po·nen a·kee*; **it won't go in** no cabe *no ka·be*; **all our money's gone** se nos ha acabado todo el dinero *se nos a a·ka·ba·do to·do el dee·ne·ro*; **I'm going to do it** voy a hacerlo *boy a a·ther·lo*; **go ahead!** ¡adelante! *a·de·lan·te*; **to go away** irse* *eer·se*; **to go back** volver* *bol·ber*; **to go down** bajar *ba·khar*; **to go in** entrar *en·trar*; **to go out** salir* *sa·leer*; **this goes with your dress** esto va con su vestido *es·to ba kon soo bes·tee·do*; **we will have to go without milk** tenemos que arreglarnos sin leche *te·ne·mos ke a·rre·glar·nos seen le·che*

goal *n* (*sport*) el gol *gol*; (*aim*) el objeto *ob·khe·to*

goat *n* la cabra *ka·bra*

god *n* el dios *dyos*; **God** Dios (*m*) *dyos*

godfather *n* el padrino *pa·dree·no*

godmother *n* la madrina *ma·dree·na*

goggles *pl* las gafas *ga·fas*

gold *n* el oro *o·ro* □ *adj* de oro *de o·ro*; **gold-plated** dorado(a) *do·ra·do(a)* S90, 91

golden *adj* dorado(a) *do·ra·do(a)*

goldfish *n* el pez de colores *peth de ko·lo·res*

golf *n* el golf *golf* L27

golf ball *n* la pelota de golf *pe·lo·ta de golf*

golf club *n* el palo de golf *pa·lo de golf*; (*association*) el club de golf *kloob de golf*

golf course *n* el campo de golf *kam·po de golf*

golfer *n* el/la jugador(a) de golf *khoo·ga·dor(·ra) de golf*

good *adj* bueno(a) *bwe·no(a)*; (*well-behaved*) bien educado(a) *byen e·doo·ka·do(a)*; **to be good at golf** jugar* bien al golf *khoo·gar byen al golf*; **spinach is good for you** las espinacas son buenos para la salud *las es·pee·na·kas son bwe·nas pa·ra la sa·lood*; **it'll do you good** le hará bien *le a·ra byen*; **good morning!** ¡buenos días! *bwe·nos dee·as*; **good afternoon!** ¡buenas tardes! *bwe·nas tar·des*; **good evening!** ¡buenas tardes! *bwe·nas tar·des*; **good night!** ¡buenas noches! *bwe·nas no·ches*

goodbye *excl* adios *a·dyos*

Good Friday *n* viernes santo *byer·nes san·to*

goods *pl* las mercancías *mer·kan·thee·as*

goose *n* el ganso *gan·so*

gooseberry *n* la grosella espinosa *gro·sel·ya es·pee·no·sa*

gossip *vi* cotillear *ko·teel·ye·ar* □ *n* (*chatter*) el comadreo *ko·ma·dre·o*

goulash *n* el goulash *goo·lash*

gourmet *n* el gastrónomo *gas·tro·no·mo*

govern *vt* (*country*) gobernar* *go·ber·nar*

government *n* el gobierno *go·byer·no*

governor *n* (*of colony*) el gobernador *go·ber·na·dor*; (*of institution*) el director *dee·rek·tor*

gown *n* (*dress*) el traje largo *tra·khe lar·go*; (*academic*) la toga *to·ga*

grab *vt* agarrar *a·ga·rrar*

graceful *adj* agraciado(a) *a·gra·thya·do(a)*

grade *n* el grado *gra·do*

grade crossing *n* el paso a nivel *pa·so a nee·bel* F29

grade school *n* la escuela (primaria) *es·kwe·la pree·ma·rya*

gradual *adj* gradual *gra·doo·al*

gradually *adv* gradualmente *gra·dwal·men·te*

graduate *n* (*from university*) el/la diplomado(a) *dee·plo·ma·do(a)* □ *vi* graduarse *gra·dwar·se*

grain *n* (*cereal crops*) los cereales *the·re·a·les*; (*in wood*) la veta *be·ta*

gram *n* el gramo *gra·mo*

grammar *n* la gramática *gra·ma·tee·ka*; **grammar (book)** el manual de gramática *man·wal de gra·ma·tee·ka*

grand *adj* magnífico(a) *mag·nee·fee·ko(a)*

grandchild *n* el/la nieto(a) *nye·to(a)*

granddaughter *n* la nieta *nye·ta*

grandfather *n* el abuelo *a·bwe·lo*

grandfather clock *n* el reloj de caja *re·lokh de ka·kha*

grandmother *n* la abuela *a·bwe·la*

grand piano *n* el piano de cola *pee·a·no de ko·la*

Grand Prix *n* el Gran Premio *gran pre·myo*

grandson *n* el nieto *nye·to*

grant *n* (*to student*) la beca *be·ka*; (*to institution*) la subvención *soob·ben·thyon* □ *vt* (*wish*) otorgar* *o·tor·gar*

grape *n* la uva *oo·ba* S32

grapefruit *n* el pomelo *po·me·lo*

grapefruit juice *n* el jugo de pomelo *khoo·go de po·me·lo*

graph *n* el gráfico *gra·fee·ko*

grasp *vt* (*seize*) asir* *a·seer*

grass *n* la hierba *yer·ba*

grate *n* la parrilla *pa·rreel·ya* □ *vt* (*food*) rallar *ral·yar*

grateful *adj* agradecido(a) *a·gra·de·thee·do(a)*

grater *n* el rallador *ral·ya·dor*

grave *n* la tumba *toom·ba*

gravel *n* la grava *gra·ba*

graveyard *n* el cementerio *the·men·te·ryo*

gravy *n* la salsa *sal·sa*

gray *adj* gris *grees*

graze *n* el roce *ro·the* □ *vt* (*skin*) rozar* *ro·thar*

grease *n* la grasa *gra·sa*

greasy *adj* grasiento(a) *gra·syen·to(a)*

great *adj* grande *gran·de*; (*excellent*) magnífico(a) *mag·nee·fee·ko(a)*; **a great athlete** un(·a) gran atleta *oon (·a) gran at·le·ta*

Great Britain *n* Gran Bretaña (*f*) *gran bre·tan·ya*

Greece *n* Grecia (*f*) *gre·thya*

greedy *adj* goloso(a) *go·lo·so(a)*

Greek *adj* griego(a) *gree·e·go(a)* □ *n* el griego *gree·e·go*

green *adj* verde *ber·de*

green card *n* la carta verde *kar·ta ber·de*

greenhouse *n* el invernadero *een·ber·na·de·ro*

green salad *n* la ensalada *en·sa·la·da*

greet *vt* saludar *sa·loo·dar*

greeting *n* el saludo *sa·loo·do*

greeting card *n* la tarjeta de felicitación *tar·khe·ta de fe·lee·thee·ta·thyon*

grief *n* la pena *pe·na*

grill *n* (*gridiron*) la parrilla *pa·rreel·ya* □ *vt* asar a la parrilla *a·sar a la pa·rreel·ya*

grillroom *n* la parrilla *pa·rreel·ya*

grimace *n* la mueca *mwe·ka*

grin *vi* sonreír* *son·re·eer* □ *n* la sonrisa *son·ree·sa*

grind *vt* moler* *mo·ler*

grip *vt* agarrar *a·ga·rrar* □ *n* (*case*) el maletín *ma·le·teen*

grit *n* el asperón *as·pe·ron*

groan *vi* gemir* *khe·meer* □ *n* el gemido *khe·mee·do*

grocer *n* el tendero *ten·de·ro*

groceries *pl* los comestibles *ko·mes·tee·bles*

grocery shop *n* el ultramarinos *ool·tra·ma·ree·nos*, la abarrotería (Am) *a·ba·rro·te·ree·a*

gross *n* la gruesa *grwe·sa* □ *adj* (*before deductions*) bruto(a) *broo·to(a)*

gross national product, GNP *n* el producto nacional bruto *pro·dook·to na·thyo·nal broo·to*

grotesque *adj* grotesco(a) *gro·tes·ko(a)*

ground *n* el suelo *swe·lo*; (*electrical*) el cable de toma de tierra *ka·ble de to·ma de tye·rra* □ *adj* (*coffee*) molido(a) *mo·lee·do(a)*; **ground beef** la carne picada *kar·ne pee·ka·da*

groundcloth *n* la tela impermeable *te·la eem·per·me·ab·le*

ground floor *n* la planta baja *plan·ta ba·kha*

groundnut *n* el cacahuete *ka·ka·we·te*

grounds *pl* (*land*) el terreno *te·rre·no*; (*of coffee*) los posos *po·sos*

group *n* el grupo *groo·po*

grouse *n* (*bird*) el urogallo *oo·ro·gal·yo*

grow *vi* crecer* *kre·ther* □ *vt* (*plants*) cultivar *kool·tee·bar*; **to grow up** hacerse* *a·ther·se ma·yor*

growl *vi* gruñir *groon·yeer*

grown-up *adj* adulto(a) *a·dool·to(a)* □ *n* el/la adulto(a) *a·dool·to(a)*

growth *n* el crecimiento *kre·thee·myen·to*; (*in amount etc*) el aumento *ow·men·to*; (*anatomical*) el tumor *too·mor*

grumble *vi* quejarse *ke·khar·se*

grunt *vi* gruñir *groon·yeer*

guarantee *n* la garantía *ga·ran·tee·a* □ *vt* garantizar* *ga·ran·tee·thar*

guard *vt* (*prisoner*) vigilar *bee·khee·lar*; (*protect*) proteger* *pro·te·kher* □ *n* (*sentry*) el centinela *then·tee·ne·la*; (*soldiers*) la guardia *gwar·dya*

guardian *n* el tutor *too·tor*

guess *vt* adivinar *a·dee·bee·nar*

guest *n* el/la invitado(a) *een·bee·ta·do(a)*; (*at hotel*) el huésped *wes·ped*

guest-house *n* la casa de huéspedes *ka·sa de wes·pe·des*

guest-room *n* el cuarto de invitados *kwar·to de een·bee·ta·dos*

guide *n* (*person*) el/la guía *gee·a*

guidebook *n* la guía turística *gee·a too·rees·tee·ka* L4

guidedog *n* el perro para ciegos *pe·rro pa·ra thye·gos*

guided tour *n* la visita con guía *bee·see·ta kon gee·a* L6

guilt *n* la culpabilidad *kool·pa·bee·lee·dad*

guilty *adj* culpable *kool·pa·ble*

guinea fowl *n* la gallina de Guinea *gal·yee·na de gee·ne·a*

guitar *n* la guitarra *gee·ta·rra*

gum *n* (*of teeth*) la encía *en·thee·a*; (*chewing gum*) el chicle *chee·kle* 163

gun *n* la escopeta *es·ko·pe·ta*

gunman *n* el pistolero *pees·to·le·ro*

gust *n* la ráfaga *ra·fa·ga*

gusty *adj* (*wind*) borrascoso(a) *bo·rras·ko·so(a)*

gutter *n* (*in street*) la cuneta *koo·ne·ta*; (*on building*) el canalón *ka·na·lon*

gym(nasium) *n* el gimnasio *kheem·na·syo*

gymnastics *n* la gimnasia *kheem·na·sya*

gypsy *n* el/la gitano(a) *khee·ta·no(a)*

H

haberdashery *n* la ropa para caballeros *ro·pa pa·ra ka·bal·ye·ros*

habit *n* la costumbre *kos·toom·bre*

haddock *n* el abadejo *a·ba·de·kho*

Hague (the) *n* la Haya *la a·ya*

hail *n* el granizo *gra·nee·tho* □ *vi* it's hailing está granizando *es·ta gra·nee·than·do*

hair *n* el pelo *pe·lo* Sn40, 41

hairbrush *n* el cepillo para el pelo *the·peel·yo pa·ra el pe·lo*

haircut *n* (*style*) el corte de pelo *kor·te de pe·lo*; to have a haircut cortarse el pelo *kor·tar·se el pe·lo* Sn40

hairdresser *n* el/la peluquero(a) *pe·loo·ke·ro(a)*

hair-drier *n* el secador de pelo *se·ka·dor de pe·lo* Sn47

hairpin *n* la horquilla *hor·keel·ya*

hairpin curve *n* la curva muy cerrada *koor·ba mooy the·rra·da*

hair spray *n* la laca *la·ka*

hair-style *n* el peinado *pey·na·do*

half *n* la mitad *mee·tad*; half an hour media hora *me·dya o·ra*; one and a half dos y medio *dos ee me·dyo*; to cut something in half cortar algo por la mitad *kor·tar al·go por la mee·tad* □ *adj* a half dozen una media docena *oon·a me·dya do·the·na*; three and a half kilometers tres kilómetros y medio *tres kee·lo·me·tros ee me·dyo* □ *adv* half medio *me·dyo*; half open medio abierto(a) *me·dyo a·byer·to(a)*

half-fare *n* el medio billete *me·dyo beel·ye·te*

half-hour *n* la media hora *me·dya o·ra*

half-price *adj* a mitad de precio *a mee·tad de pre·thyo*

half-time *n* el descanso *des·kan·so*

halfway *adv* a medio camino *a me·dyo ka·mee·no*

hall *n* (*entrance*) el vestíbulo *bes·tee·boo·lo*; (*room*) la sala *sa·la*

hallmark *n* la marca del contraste *mar·ka del kon·tras·te*

halve *vt* (*divide in two*) partir en dos *par·teer en dos*; (*reduce by half*) reducir* a la mitad *re·doo·theer a la mee·tad*

ham *n* el jamón *kha·mon* S32

hamburger *n* la hamburguesa *am·boor·ge·sa*

hammer *n* el martillo *mar·teel·yo*

hammock *n* la hamaca *a·ma·ka*

hamper *n* le cesta *thes·ta*

hand *n* la mano *ma·no*; (*of clock*) la manecilla *ma·ne·theel·ya*; by hand a mano *a ma·no* □ *vt* to hand someone something dar* algo a alguien *dar al·go a al·gyen*

handbag *n* el bolso *bol·so*

handbook *n* el manual *ma·noo·al*

hand-brake *n* el freno de mano *fre·no de ma·no*

hand cream *n* la crema de manos *kre·ma de ma·nos*

handcuffs *pl* las esposas *es·po·sas*

handicap *n* la desventaja *des·ben·ta·kha*; (*golf*) el hándicap *an·dee·kap*

handkerchief *n* el pañuelo *pan·yoo·we·lo*

handle *n* (*of door*) el tirador *tee·ra·dor*; (*of cup*) el asa (f) *a·sa*; (*of knife, for winding*) el mango *man·go* □ *vt* (*touch*) tocar* *to·kar*; (*deal with*) encargarse de *en·kar·gar·se de*; handle with care frágil *fra·kheel*

handlebar(s) *n* el manillar *ma·neel·yar*

hand-luggage *n* el equipaje de mano *e·kee·pa·khe de ma·no*

handmade *adj* hecho(a) a mano *e·cho(a) a ma·no* S110

handrail n (on stairs) el pasamano pa·sa·ma·no

handsome adj (person) guapo(a) gwa·po(a)

hang vt colgar* kol·gar; (criminal) ahorcar* a·or·kar □ vi colgar* kol·gar; hang on! (on phone) ¡no cuelgue! no kwel·ge; to hang up (phone) colgar* kol·gar

hangover n la resaca re·sa·ka; to have a hangover tener* una resaca te·ner oo·na re·sa·ka

happen vi ocurrir o·koo·rreer; what happened to him? ¿qué le pasó? ke le pa·so

happiness n la felicidad fe·lee·thee·dad

happy adj feliz fe·leeth

harbor n el puerto pwer·to

harbor master n el capitán de puerto ka·pee·tan de pwer·to

hard adj (not soft) duro(a) doo·ro(a); (difficult) difícil dee·fee·theel □ adv (work) mucho moo·cho

hard-boiled adj duro(a) doo·ro(a)

hardware n la ferretería fe·rre·te·ree·a; (computing) el hardware ard·wer

hard-wearing adj resistente re·sees·ten·te

hare n la liebre lye·bre

harmful adj dañino(a) dan·yee·no(a)

harmless adj inofensivo(a) ee·no·fen·see·bo(a)

harness n las guarniciones gwar·nee·thyo·nes

harp n el arpa ar·pa

harsh adj (severe) severo(a) se·be·ro(a)

harvest n (of grain) la cosecha ko·se·cha; (of grapes) la vendimia ben·dee·mya □ vt (grain) cosechar ko·se·char; (grapes) hacer* la vendimia a·ther la ben·dee·mya

haste n la prisa pree·sa

hat n el sombrero som·bre·ro S12

hatchback n (car) la ranchera ran·che·ra

hate vt odiar o·dyar

hatred n el odio o·dyo

hat stand n el perchero per·che·ro

have vt tener* te·ner; (meal) tomar to·mar; to have a shower tomar una ducha to·mar oo·na doo·cha; to have a drink tomar algo to·mar al·go; she has to do it (ella) tiene que hacerlo (el·ya) tye·ne ke a·ther·lo; to have something done hacer* hacer algo a·ther a·ther al·go

hay n el heno e·no

hay fever n la fiebre del heno fye·bre del e·no S40

he pron él el; here he is! ¡aquí está! a·kee es·ta

head n la cabeza ka·be·tha; (chief) el jefe khe·fe

headache n el dolor de cabeza do·lor de ka·be·tha; to have a headache tener* un dolor de cabeza te·ner oon do·lor de ka·be·tha S40

headlight n el faro fa·ro

headline n el titular tee·too·lar

headmaster n el director dee·rek·tor

headmistress n la directora dee·rek·to·ra

head office n la oficina central o·fee·thee·na then·tral

head-on adj de frente de fren·te

headphones pl los auriculares ow·ree·koo·la·res

headrest n el reposa-cabezas re·po·sa·ka·be·thas

heal vi (wound) curarse koo·rar·se

health n la salud sa·lood

health foods pl los alimentos naturales a·lee·men·tos na·too·ra·les

health service n la seguridad social se·goo·ree·dad so·thyal

healthy adj (person) sano(a) sa·no(a)

heap n el montón mon·ton

hear vt/i oír* o·eer; I can't hear (you) no te oigo no te oy·go

hearing aid n el aparato para sordos a·pa·ra·to pa·ra sor·dos

heart n el corazón ko·ra·thon; by heart de memoria de me·mo·rya; hearts (cards) los corazones ko·ra·tho·nes I1

heart attack n el ataque cardíaco a·ta·ke kar·dee·a·ko

heartburn n la acedía a·the·dee·a

hearth n el hogar o·gar

heat n el calor ka·lor; (sport) la eliminatoria e·lee·mee·na·to·rya

heater n el calentador ka·len·ta·dor

heating n la calefacción ka·le·fak·thyon A45, 47

heavy adj pesado(a) pe·sa·do(a); (food) indigesto(a) een·dee·khes·to(a)

hedge n el seto se·to

heel n el talón ta·lon; (of shoe) el tacón ta·kon

height n (of object) la altura al·too·ra; (of person) la estatura es·ta·too·ra

helicopter n el helicóptero e·lee·kop·te·ro

hello excl hola o·la B4, 5

helmet n el casco kas·ko

help n la ayuda a·yoo·da; help! ¡socorro! so·ko·rro □ vt ayudar a·yoo·dar; can you help me? ¿puede ayudarme? pwe·de a·yoo·dar·me; help yourself sírvase seer·ba·se; I can't help it no lo puedo remediar no lo pwe·do re·me·dyar B64

helping n la porción por·thyon

hem n el dobladillo do·bla·deel·yo Sn79

hemorrhoids pl las hemorroides e·mo·rro·ee·des

hen n la gallina gal·yee·na

her pron ella el·ya; it's her es ella es el·ya; give it to her déselo a ella de·se·lo a el·ya □ adj her su soo, (plural) sus soos

herbs pl las hierbas yer·bas

here adv aquí a·kee; here's my sister he aquí mi hermana e a·kee mee er·ma·na; here she comes aquí viene a·kee bye·ne

hernia n la hernia er·nya

herring n el arenque a·ren·ke

hers pron el/la suyo(a) el/la soo·yo(a); (plural) los/las suyos(as) los/las soo·yos(as)

herself pron ella misma el·ya mees·ma; she did it herself lo hizo ella misma lo ee·tho el·ya mees·ma; she dressed herself (ella) se vistió (el·ya) se bees·tyo

hesitate vi vacilar ba·thee·lar; to hesitate to do something vacilar en hacer algo ba·thee·lar en a·ther al·go

hiccup n el hipo ee·po; to have (the) hiccups tener* hipo te·ner ee·po

hide n (leather) el cuero kwe·ro □ vt esconder es·kon·der □ vi esconderse es·kon·der·se

hi-fi adj de alta fidelidad de al·ta fee·de·lee·dad □ n la alta fidelidad al·ta fee·de·lee·dad

high adj (mountain, building) alto(a) al·to(a); (speed, number) grande gran·de; (price, temperature) eleva-

do(a) *e·le·ba·do(a)*; (pitch, voice) agudo(a) *a·goo·do(a)* □ adv alto *al·to*; 6 meters high de 6 metros de altura *de 6 me·tros de al·too·ra*
highchair n la silla alta para niño *seel·ya al·ta pa·ra neen·yo* C3
high-class adj de clase superior *de kla·se soo·pe·ryor*
higher adj más alto *mas al·to*
high-heeled adj de tacón alto *de ta·kon al·to*
high school n el colegio *ko·le·khyo*
high-speed adj rápido(a) *ra·pee·do(a)*
high tide n la marea alta *ma·re·a al·ta*
highway n la carretera *ka·rre·te·ra*
Highway Code n el código de la circulación *ko·dee·go de la theer·koo·la·thyon*
hijack vt secuestrar *se·kwes·trar*
hijacker n el secuestrador *se·kwes·tra·dor*
hike n la excursión a pie *eks·koor·syon a pye*
hiking n el excursionismo a pie *eks·koor·syo·nees·mo a pye*
hill n la colina *ko·lee·na*; (slope) la cuesta *kwes·ta*
hilly adj montañoso(a) *mon·tan·yo·so(a)*
him pron él *el*; it's him es él es *el*; give it to him déselo a él *de·se·lo a el*
himself pron él mismo *el mees·mo*; he did it himself él mismo lo hizo *el mees·mo lo ee·tho*; he dresses himself se viste él mismo *se bees·te el mees·mo*
hip n la cadera *ka·de·ra*
hire vt alquilar *al·kee·lar*; to hire something out alquilar algo *al·kee·lar al·go*
his adj su *soo*, (plural) sus *soos* □ pron el/la suyo(a) *el/la soo·yo(a)*; (plural) los/las suyos(as) *los/las soo·yos(as)*
history n la historia *ees·to·rya*
hit vt golpear *gol·pe·ar*; (with car) chocar* *cho·kar* □ n (blow) el golpe *gol·pe*
hitch vt □ to hitch a lift or a ride hacer* autostop *a·ther ow·to·stop*
hitchhike vi hacer* autostop *a·ther ow·to·stop*
hitchhiker n el/la autostopista *ow·to·sto·pees·ta*
hobby n el pasatiempo *pa·sa·tyem·po*
hockey n el hockey *kho·key*
hold vt tener* *te·ner*; (contain) contener* *kon·te·ner*; (support) soportar *so·por·tar*; hold him still téngale quieto *ten·ga·le kye·to*; hold on! (on phone) ¡no se retire! *no se re·tee·re*; to hold up (delay) atrasar *a·tra·sar*
hole n el agujero *a·goo·khe·ro*
holiday n (day) la fiesta *fyes·ta*; (period) las vacaciones *ba·ka·thyo·nes*; on holiday de vacaciones *de ba·ka·thyo·nes*
Holland n Holanda (f) *o·lan·da*
hollow adj hueco(a) *we·ko(a)*
holy adj sagrado(a) *sa·gra·do(a)*
home n la casa *ka·sa*, (Institution) el asilo *a·see·lo*; at home en casa en *ka·sa*; to go home ir* a casa *eer a ka·sa*
home address n la dirección particular *dee·rek·thyon par·tee·koo·lar*
homesick adj □ to be homesick tener* morriña *te·ner mo·rreen·ya*
homework n los deberes *de·be·res*
homogenized adj homogeneizado(a) *o·mo·khe·ney·tha·do(a)*
honest adj honrado(a) *on·ra·do(a)*
honey n la miel *myel*

honeymoon n la luna de miel *loo·na de myel*; we're on our honeymoon estamos pasando la luna de miel *es·ta·mos pa·san·do la loo·na de myel*
hood n la capucha *ka·poo·cha*; (of car) el capó *ka·po*
hook n el gancho *gan·cho*; (fishing) el anzuelo *an·thwe·lo*; hook and eye el corchete *kor·che·te*
hoop n el aro *a·ro*
hoot vi (horn) tocar* la bocina *to·kar la bo·thee·na*
hop vi saltar con un pie *sal·tar kon oon pye*
hope n la esperanza *es·pe·ran·tha* □ vi esperar *es·pe·rar*; I hope so espero que sí *es·pe·ro ke see*; I hope not espero que no *es·pe·ro ke no*
horizon n el horizonte *o·ree·thon·te*
horizontal adj horizontal *o·ree·thon·tal*
horn n (of animal) el cuerno *kwer·no*; (of car) la bocina *bo·thee·na*
horrible adj horrible *o·rree·ble*
horror movie n la película de miedo *pe·lee·koo·la de mye·do*
hors d'oeuvre n los entremeses *en·tre·me·ses*
horse n el caballo *ka·bal·yo*
horseback riding n la equitación *e·kee·ta·thyon*; to go horseback riding montar a caballo *mon·tar a ka·bal·yo*
horse-racing n las carreras de caballos *ka·rre·ras de ka·bal·yos*
hose n (pipe) la manguera *man·ge·ra* Ea6
hospital n el hospital *os·pee·tal* 152, Ea6
hospitality n la hospitalidad *os·pee·ta·lee·dad*
host n el huésped *wes·ped*
hostage n el rehén *re·en*; to take someone hostage coger* a alguien como rehén *ko·kher a al·gyen ko·mo re·en*
hostel n la residencia *re·see·den·thya*
hostess n la anfitriona *an·fee·tryo·na*
hot adj caliente *ka·lyen·te*; (spicy) picante *pee·kan·te*
hot dog n el perro caliente *pe·rro ka·lyen·te*
hotel n el hotel *o·tel* A6, 29
hotplate n el calientaplatos *ka·lyen·ta·pla·tos*
hot-water bottle n la bolsa de agua caliente *bol·sa de a·gwa ka·lyen·te*
hour n la hora *o·ra*
hourly adv por hora *por o·ra*
house n la casa *ka·sa*; on the house pagado(a) por la casa *pa·ga·do(a) por la ka·sa* A57f
housecoat n la bata *ba·ta*
household n la casa *ka·sa*
housekeeper n el ama de casa (f) *a·ma de ka·sa*
housewife n el ama de casa (f) *a·ma de ka·sa*
housework n los quehaceres domésticos *ke·a·the·res do·mes·tee·kos*
housing n la vivienda *bee·byen·da*
hovercraft n el aerodeslizador *a·e·ro·des·lee·tha·dor*
how adv como *ko·mo*; how are you? ¿cómo está? *ko·mo es·ta*; how do you do? encantado(a) *en·kan·ta·do(a)*; how long? ¿cuánto tiempo? *kwan·to tyem·po*; how long have you been here? ¿cuánto tiempo ha estado aquí? *kwan·to tyem·po a es·ta·do a·kee*; how many? ¿cuántos(as)? *kwan·tos(as)*; how much? ¿cuánto? *kwan·to*; how many people? ¿cuánta

gente? *kwan·ta khen·te*; how much milk? ¿cuánta leche? *kwan·ta le·che*

however *conj* sin embargo *seen em·bar·go*

hug *vt* abrazar* *a·bra·thar*

hullo *excl* hola *o·la*

human *adj* humano(a) *oo·ma·no(a)*

hump *n* (on road) el montecillo *mon·te·theel·yo*

hundred *num* cien *thyen*; **a hundred and one** ciento uno(a) *thyen·to oo·no(a)*; **a hundred people** cien personas *thyen per·so·nas*; **hundreds of books** cientos de libros *thyen·tos de lee·bros*

hundredth *adj* centésimo(a) *then·te·see·mo(a)*

Hungarian *adj* húngaro(a) *oon·ga·ro(a)*

Hungary *n* Hungría (f) *oon·gree·a*

hunger *n* el hambre *am·bre*

hungry *adj* hambriento(a) *am·bryen·to(a)*; **to be hungry** tener* hambre *te·ner am·bre*

hunt *vt* cazar* *ka·thar*

hurricane *n* el huracán *oo·ra·kan*

hurry *n* la prisa *darse* prisa pree·sa*, apurarse (Am) *a·poo·rar·se*; **hurry up!** ¡date prisa! *da·te pree·sa*, ¡apúrate! (Am) *a·poo·ra·te* □ *n* to be in a hurry tener* prisa *te·ner pree·sa* B67, T97, Ea10

hurt *vi* doler* *do·ler*; **that hurts!** ¡eso me duele! *e·so me dwe·le*; **to hurt oneself** dañarse *dan·yar·se*

husband *n* el marido *ma·ree·do* T107, S106

hut *n* (shed) la cabaña *ka·ban·ya*; (on mountain) el albergue *al·ber·ge*

hygienic *adj* higiénico(a) *ee·khye·nee·ko(a)*

hymn *n* el himno *eem·no*

hyphen *n* el guión *gee·on*

hysterical *adj* histérico(a) *ees·te·ree·ko(a)*

I

I *pron* yo *yo*

ice *n* el hielo *ye·lo*; **with ice** con hielo *kon ye·lo* A92

ice box *n* la nevera *ne·be·ra*

ice cream *n* el helado *e·la·do*

ice cube *n* el cubito de hielo *koo·bee·to de ye·lo*

ice hockey *n* el hockey sobre hielo *kho·key so·bre ye·lo*

icing *n* (on cake) el glaseado *gla·se·a·do*

idea *n* la idea *ee·de·a*

ideal *adj* ideal *ee·de·al*

identical *adj* idéntico(a) *ee·den·tee·ko(a)*

identify *vt* identificar* *ee·den·tee·fee·kar*

identity card *n* el carnet de identidad *kar·net de ee·den·tee·dad*

idiot *n* el/la idiota *ee·dyo·ta*

if *conj* si *see*

ignition *n* (car) el encendido *en·then·dee·do*

ignition key *n* la llave de contacto *lya·be de kon·tak·to* T187

ignorant *adj* ignorante *eeg·no·ran·te*

ignore *vt* (person) no hacer* caso de *no a·ther ka·so de*

ill *adj* enfermo(a) *en·fer·mo(a)*

illegal *adj* ilegal *ee·le·gal*

illegitimate *adj* ilegítimo(a) *ee·le·khee·tee·mo(a)*

illness *n* la enfermedad *en·fer·me·dad*

illustration *n* la ilustración *ee·loos·tra·thyon*

imagination *n* la imaginación *ee·ma·khee·na·thyon*

imagine *vt* imaginar *ee·ma·khee·nar*

imitate *vt* imitar *ee·mee·tar*

immediate *adj* primero(a) *pree·me·ro(a)*

immediately *adv* inmediatamente *ee·me·dya·ta·men·te*

immersion heater *n* el calentador de agua *ka·len·ta·dor de a·gwa*

immigrant *n* el inmigrante *ee·mee·gran·te*

impatient *adj* impaciente *eem·pa·thyen·te*

imperfect *adj* imperfecto(a) *eem·per·fek·to(a)*

impersonal *adj* impersonal *eem·per·so·nal*

import *n* la importación *eem·por·ta·thyon* □ *vt* importar *eem·por·tar*

importance *n* la importancia *eem·por·tan·thya*

important *adj* importante *eem·por·tan·te* L2

importer *n* el importador *eem·por·ta·dor*

impossible *adj* imposible *eem·po·see·ble*

impress *vt* (win approval) causar buena impresión *kow·sar bwe·na eem·pre·syon*

impression *n* la impresión *eem·pre·syon*

impressive *adj* impresionante *eem·pre·syo·nan·te*

improve *vt* mejorar *me·kho·rar* □ *vi* mejorarse *me·kho·rar·se*

improvement *n* la mejora *me·kho·ra*

in *prep* en *en*; **it's in the box** está en la caja *es·ta en la ka·kha*; **in May** en mayo *en ma·yo*; **he'll be back in 2 days** volverá dentro de 2 días *bol·be·ra den·tro de 2 dee·as*; **in town** en la ciudad *en la thyoo·dad* □ *adv* **is he in?** ¿está en casa? *es·ta en ka·sa*; **the train is in** ha llegado el tren *a lye·ga·do el tren*

incentive *n* el incentivo *een·then·tee·bo*

inch *n* la pulgada *pool·ga·da*

incident *n* (event) el incidente *een·thee·den·te*

incinerator *n* el incinerador *een·thee·ne·ra·dor*

include *vt* incluir* *een·kloo·eer*

including *prep* incluso *een·kloo·so*

inclusive *adj* (costs) completo(a) *kom·ple·to(a)*; **from 6th to 12th inclusive** del 6 hasta el 12 inclusive *del 6 as·ta el 12 een·kloo·see·be*

income *n* los ingresos *een·gre·sos*

income tax *n* el impuesto sobre la renta *eem·pwes·to so·bre la ren·ta*

incomplete *adj* incompleto(a) *een·kom·ple·to(a)*

inconvenient *adj* poco práctico(a) *po·ko prak·tee·ko(a)*; (time, place) inoportuno(a) *ino·por·too·no(a)*

incorrect *adj* erróneo(a) *e·rro·ne·o(a)*

increase *vt* aumentar *ow·men·tar* □ *vi* subir *soo·beer* □ *n* el aumento *ow·men·to*

incredible *adj* increíble *een·kre·ee·ble*

indecent *adj* indecente *een·de·then·te*

independence *n* la independencia *een·de·pen·den·thya*

independent *adj* independiente *een·de·pen·dyen·te*

index *n* el índice *een·dee·the*

indexed *adj* (interest rates etc) de

acuerdo con el coste de vida *de a·kwer·do kon el kos·te de bee·da*
India *n* la India *een·dya*
Indian *adj* (*India and Americas*) indio(a) *een·dyo(a)* □ *n* el/la indio(a) *een·dyo(a)*
indicator *n* (*of car*) el intermitente *een·ter·mee·ten·te*
indigestible *adj* indigesto(a) *een·dee·khes·to(a)*
indigestion *n* la indigestión *een·dee·khes·tyon*
indirect *adj* (*route*) indirecto(a) *een·dee·rek·to(a)*
individual *adj* individual *een·dee·bee·dwal*
individually *adv* individualmente *een·dee·bee·dwal·men·te*
indoor *adj* (*games*) en pista cubierta *en pees·ta koo·byer·ta*
indoors *adv* (*be*) en casa *en ka·sa*; (*go*) adentro *a·den·tro*
industrial *adj* industrial *een·doos·tryal*
industry *n* la industria *een·doos·trya*
inedible *adj* incomible *een·ko·mee·ble*
inefficient *adj* ineficaz *een·e·fee·kath*
inevitable *adj* inevitable *een·e·bee·ta·ble*
inexpensive *adj* barato(a) *ba·ra·to(a)*
infection *n* la infección *een·fek·thyo·n(a)*
infectious *adj* infeccioso(a) *een·fek·thyo·so(a)*
inferior *adj* inferior *een·fe·ryor*
inflammation *n* la inflamación *een·fla·ma·thyon* I29
inflatable *adj* hinchable *een·cha·ble*
inflate *vt* inflar *een·flar*
inflation *n* (*economic*) la inflación *een·fla·thyon*
influence *n* la influencia *een·floo·en·thya*
inform *vt* avisar *a·bee·sar*
informal *adj* (*party*) sin etiqueta *seen e·tee·ke·ta*; dress: informal traje de calle *tra·khe de kal·ye*
information *n* la información *een·for·ma·thyon* T52
information desk *n* las informaciones *een·for·ma·thyo·nes*; ask at the information desk pregunte Ud a las informaciones *pre·goon·te oos·ted a las een·for·ma·thyo·nes*
ingredients *pl* los ingredientes *een·gre·dyen·tes*
inhabit *vt* habitar *a·bee·tar*
inhabitant *n* el habitante *a·bee·tan·te*
inherit *vt* heredar *e·re·dar*
initials *pl* las iniciales *ee·nee·thya·les*
injection *n* la inyección *een·yek·thyon*
injure *vt* herir* *e·reer*
injured *adj* herido(a) *e·ree·do(a)* I17
injury *n* la herida *e·ree·da*
ink *n* la tinta *teen·ta*
inn *n* la posada *po·sa·da*
innocent *adj* inocente *ee·no·then·te*
inoculation *n* la inoculación *ee·no·koo·la·thyon*
input *n* (*computing*) el input *een·poot*
insect *n* el insecto *een·sek·to* S40
insect repellent *n* la loción contra los insectos *lo·thyon kon·tra los een·sek·tos*
inside *n* el interior *een·te·ryor* □ *adj* the inside wall la pared interior *la pa·red een·te·ryor* □ *prep* inside the box dentro de la caja *den·tro de la ka·kha* □ *adv* to be inside estar* dentro *estar den·tro*; to go inside ir* adentro *eer a·den·tro*; to turn something inside out volver* algo del revés *bol·ber al·go del re·bes*

insist *vi* insistir *een·sees·teer*; to insist on something insistir en algo *een·sees·teer en al·go*
insolent *adj* insolente *een·so·len·te*
inspect *vt* inspeccionar *eens·pek·thyo·nar*
inspector *n* (*of building, police*) el inspector *eens·pek·tor*
instalment *n* el plazo *pla·tho*
instalment plan *n* la compra a plazos *kom·pra a pla·thos*
instant *adj* inmediato(a) *ee·me·dya·to(a)*; instant coffee el café instantáneo *ka·fe eens·tan·ta·ne·o* □ *n* instant el momento *mo·men·to*
instead *adv* en cambio *en kam·byo*; instead of en vez de *en beth de*
institute *n* el instituto *eens·tee·too·to*
instructions *pl* las instrucciones *eens·trook·thyo·nes*; instructions for use el modo de empleo *mo·do de em·ple·o*
instructor *n* el instructor *eens·trook·tor*
instructress *n* la instructora *een·strook·to·ra*
instrument *n* el instrumento *eens·troo·men·to*
insulin *n* la insulina *een·soo·lee·na*
insult *n* el insulto *een·sool·to* □ *vt* insultar *een·sool·tar*
insurance *n* el seguro *se·goo·ro* T111
insurance company *n* la compañía de seguros *kom·pun·yee·a de se·goo·ros* T194
insurance policy *n* la póliza de seguros *po·lee·tha de se·goo·ros*
insure *vt* asegurar *a·se·goo·rar* □ *vi* to insure against something asegurarse contra algo *a·se·goo·rar·se kon·tra al·go*
insured *adj* asegurado(a) *a·se·goo·ra·do(a)*
intelligence *n* la inteligencia *een·te·lee·khen·thya*
intelligent *adj* inteligente *een·te·lee·khen·te*
intend *vt* □ to intend to do something tener* la intención de hacer algo *te·ner la een·ten·thyon de a·ther al·go*
intention *n* la intención *een·ten·thyon*
interchange *n* (*on roads*) el cruce *kroo·the*
intercom *n* el interfono *een·ter·fo·no*
interest *n* el interés *een·te·res* □ *vt* interesar *een·te·re·sar*
interested *adj* interesado(a) *een·te·re·sa·do(a)*; to be interested in interesarse en *een·te·re·sar·se en*
interesting *adj* interesante *een·te·re·san·te*
interest rate *n* la tasa de interés *ta·sa de een·te·res*
interfere *vi* entrometerse *en·tro·me·ter·se*
interior *adj* interior *een·te·ryor*
intermission *n* (*in performance*) el intermedio *een·ter·me·dyo* L43
internal *adj* interno(a) *een·ter·no(a)*
Internal Revenue *n* la Delegación de Contribuciones *de·le·ga·thyon de kon·tree·boo·thyo·nes*
international *adj* internacional *een·ter·na·thyo·nal*
interpret *vt* interpretar *een·ter·pre·tar* □ *vi* hacer* de intérprete *a·ther de een·ter·pre·te*
interpreter *n* el intérprete *een·ter·pre·te*
interrupt *vt/i* interrumpir *een·te·rroom·peer*
intersection *n* (*of roads*) el cruce *kroo·the*

interview n (*for job*) la entrevista *en·tre·bees·ta*

into prep en *en*

introduce vt (*person*) presentar *pre·sen·tar* Mc31

introduction n (*in book*) el prólogo *pro·lo·go*; (*social*) la presentación *pre·sen·ta·thyon*

invalid n el inválido *een·ba·lee·do*

invent vt inventar *een·ben·tar*

invention n la invención *een·ben·thyon*

inventory n el inventario *een·ben·ta·ryo*

invest vt invertir* *een·ber·teer* □ vi to invest in invertir* (*dinero*) en *een·ber·teer* (*dee·ne·ro*) en

investment n la inversión *een·ber·syon*

investor n el/la inversionista *een·ber·syo·nees·ta*

invisible adj invisible *een·bee·see·ble*

invitation n la invitación *een·bee·ta·thyon*

invite vt invitar *een·bee·tar*

invoice n la factura *fak·too·ra*

iodine n el yodo *yo·do*

Iran n Irán (*m*) *ee·ran*

Iraq n Iraq (*m*) *ee·rak*

Ireland n Irlanda (*f*) *eer·lan·da*

Irish adj irlandés(esa) *eer·lan·des(·de·sa*); he's Irish es irlandés *es eer·lan·des*; she's Irish es irlandesa *es eer·lan·de·sa*

iron n (*metal, golf*) el hierro *ye·rro*; (*for clothes*) la plancha *plan·cha* □ vt planchar *plan·char*

ironmonger n el ferretero *fe·rre·te·ro*

is vi □ she/he is ella/él es *el·ya/el es*; (*temporary state*) ella/él está *el·ya/el es·ta*

island n la isla *ees·la*; (*traffic*) el refugio *re·foo·khyo*

Israel n Israel (*m*) *ees·ra·el*

issue n (*matter*) la cuestión *kwes·tyon*; (*of magazine*) el número *noo·me·ro*; (*of stocks*) la emisión *e·mee·syon*

it pron □ it's blue es azul *es a·thool*; take it (*masculine*) tómelo *to·me·lo*; (*feminine*) tómela *to·me·la*; it's me soy yo *soy yo*; it's raining está lloviendo *es·ta lyo·byen·do*; it's 5 kilometers son 5 kilómetros *son 5 kee·lo·me·tros*

Italian adj italiano(a) *ee·ta·lya·no(a)* □ n el italiano *ee·ta·lya·no*

Italy n Italia (*f*) *ee·ta·lya*

itch n el picor *pee·kor* □ vi picar* *pee·kar*

item n el asunto *a·soon·to*

itemized adj (*bill etc*) detallado(a) *de·tal·ya·do(a)*

its adj su *soo*; (*plural*) sus *soos*

ivory n el marfil *mar·feel*

J

jack n (*for car*) el gato *ga·to*; (*cards*) el valet *ba·let*

jacket n la chaqueta *cha·ke·ta*

jail n la cárcel *kar·thel*; in jail en la cárcel *en la kar·thel*

jam vi (*machine*) atascarse *a·tas·kar·se* □ n la mermelada *mer·me·la·da*; (*in traffic*) el embotellamiento *em·bo·tel·ya·myen·to*

janitor n el conserje *kon·ser·khe*

January n enero (*m*) *e·ne·ro*

Japan n Japón *kha·pon*

Japanese adj japonés(esa) *kha·po·nes(ne·sa*); he's Japanese es japonés *es kha·po·nes*; she's Japanese es ja-

ponesa *kha·po·ne·sa* □ n Japanese el japonés *kha·po·nes*

jar n el tarro *ta·rro*

jaw n la mandíbula *man·dee·boo·la*

jazz n el jazz *yas* L35

jealous adj (*of things*) envidioso(a) *en·bee·dyo·so(a)*; (*of person*) celoso(a) *the·lo·so(a)*

jeans pl los pantalones vaqueros *pan·ta·lo·nes ba·ke·ros*

jeep n el jeep *yeep*

jellyfish n la medusa *me·doo·sa*

jerkin n el justillo *khoos·teel·yo*

jersey n (*fabric, sweater*) el jersey *kher·sey*

jet n (*plane*) el avión a reacción *a·byon a re·ak·thyon*

jetty n el embarcadero *em·bar·ka·de·ro*

Jew n el judío *khoo·dee·o*

jewel n la joya *kho·ya*

jeweler n el joyero *kho·ye·ro*

jewelry n las joyas *kho·yas* S86

Jewish adj judío(a) *khoo·dee·o(a)*

jigsaw (puzzle) n el rompecabezas *rom·pe·ka·be·thas*

jingle n (*advertising*) el tintineo *teen·tee·ne·o*

job n (*employment*) el trabajo *tra·ba·kho*; (*task*) la tarea *ta·re·a* Mc42

jockey n el jockey *yo·kee*

jogging n (*sport*) el footing *foo·teeng*; to go jogging hacer* el footing *a·ther el foo·teeng*

join vt juntar *khoon·tar*; (*club*) hacerse* socio de *a·ther·se so·thyo de*; do join us véngase con nosotros *ben·ga·se kon no·so·tros*

joint n (*of body*) la articulación *ar·tee·koo·la·thyon*; (*of meat*) el cuarto *kwar·to*

joint ownership n la copropiedad *ko·pro·pye·dad*

joint-stock company n la sociedad anónima *so·thye·dad a·no·nee·ma*

joke n la broma *bro·ma*

joker n (*cards*) el comodín *ko·mo·deen*

journalist n el/la periodista *pe·ryo·dees·ta*

journey n el viaje *bee·a·khe*

joy n la alegría *a·le·gree·a*

jubilee n el aniversario *a·nee·ber·sa·ryo*

judge n el juez *khweth* □ vt juzgar *khooth·gar*; I can't judge no puedo opinar *no pwe·do o·pee·nar*

judo n el judo *yoo·do*

jug n la jarra *kha·rra*

juice n el zumo *thoo·mo* E72

jukebox n el tocadiscos automático *to·ka·dees·kos ow·to·ma·tee·ko*

July n julio (*m*) *khoo·lyo*

jumbo jet n el jumbo *yoom·bo*

jump vt/i saltar *sal·tar*; to jump (over) a wall saltar por encima de una pared *sal·tar por en·thee·ma de oo·na pa·red*

jumper n (*dress*) el mandil *man·deel*

jumper cables pl los cables para cargar la batería *ka·bles pa·ra kar·gar la ba·te·ree·a*

junction n (*in road*) el cruce *kroo·the*; (*railway*) el empalme *em·pal·me*

June n junio (*m*) *khoo·nyo*

junior adj (*class, pupil*) juvenil *khoo·be·neel*

junket n el dulce de leche cuajada *dool·the de le·che kwa·kha·da*

just adv □ just here aquí mismo *a·kee mees·mo*; he's just left acaba de marcharse *a·ka·ba de mar·char·se*; it was

just a mistake no era nada más que una equivocación *no e·ra na·da mas ke oo·na e·kee·bo·ka·thyon*; **I just managed it** casi no pude hacerlo *ka·see no poo·de ath·er·lo*; **just above the elbow** un poco más arriba del codo *oon po·ko mas a·rree·ba del ko·do*; **it only just missed** por poco no dio en el blanco *por po·ko no dyo en el blan·ko*; **he arrived just now** acaba de llegar *a·ka·ba de lye·gar*

justice *n* la justicia *khoos·tee·thya*

K

karate *n* el karate *ka·ra·te*

kebab *n* el pincho *peen·cho*

keep *n* la subsistencia *soob·sees·ten·thya*; **to earn one's keep** ganarse la vida *ga·nar·se la bee·da* □ *vt* **keep** (retain) retener* *re·te·ner*; (feed and clothe) mantener* *man·te·ner*; **to keep something till later** guardar algo hasta más tarde *gwar·dar al·go as·ta mas tar·de*; **to keep something in the refrigerator** guardar algo en la nevera *gwar·dar al·go en la ne·be·ra*; **keep the change!** ¡quédese con la vuelta! *ke·de·se kon la bwel·ta*; **to keep something tidy** conservar algo en buen orden *kon·ser·bar al·go en bwen or·den*; **milk doesn't keep very well** la leche no se conserva bien *la le·che no se kon·ser·ba byen*

Kenya *n* Kenia (f) *ka·nya*

kerosene *n* el keroseno *ke·ro·se·no*

ketchup *n* el ketchup *ket·choop*

kettle *n* el hervidor *er·bee·dor*

key *n* la llave *lya·be*; (of piano, typewriter) la tecla *tek·la* B76, A41, 61

keyhole *n* el ojo de la cerradura *o·kho de la ther·ra·doo·ra*

key ring *n* el llavero *lya·be·ro*

kick *n* la patada *pa·ta·da* □ *vt* (person) dar* una patada a *dar oo·na pa·ta·da a*; (ball) dar* un puntapié a *dar oon poon·ta·pye a*

kid *n* (leather) el cabrito *ka·bree·to*

kidnap *vt* secuestrar *se·kwes·trar*

kidney *n* el riñón *reen·yon*

kidney beans *pl* las alubias *a·loo·byas*

kill *vt* matar *ma·tar*

killer *n* el asesino *a·se·see·no*

kilo *n* el kilo *kee·lo* S32

kilogram *n* el kilogramo *kee·lo·gra·mo*

kilometer *n* el kilómetro *kee·lo·me·tro*

kilowatt *n* el kilovatio *kee·lo·ba·tyo*

kilt *n* la falda escocesa *fal·da es·ko·the·sa*

kind *n* (type) la especie *es·pe·thye*; **a kind of bean** una especie de judía *oo·na es·pe·thye de khoo·dee·a* □ *adj* kind amable *a·ma·ble*

king *n* el rey *rey*

kirsch *n* el kirsch *keersh*

kiss *vt* besar *be·sar*; **to kiss (each other)** besarse *be·sar·se* □ *n* kiss el beso *be·so*

kitchen *n* la cocina *ko·thee·na*

kite *n* la cometa *ko·me·ta*

kleenex *n* el pañuelo de papel *pan·we·lo de pa·pel*

knee *n* la rodilla *ro·deel·ya*; **to sit on someone's knee** sentarse* en las rodillas de uno *sen·tar·se en las ro·deel·yas de oo·no*

kneel *vi* estar* de rodillas *es·tar de ro·deel·yas*; **to kneel down** arrodillarse *a·rro·deel·yar·se*

knife *n* el cuchillo *koo·cheel·yo*

knit *vt/i* hacer* punto *a·ther poon·to*;

to knit a sweater tejer* un jersey *te·kher oon kher·sey*

knitting needle *n* la aguja de hacer punto *a·goo·kha de a·ther poon·to*

knitwear *n* los géneros de punto *los khe·ner·os de poon·to*

knob *n* (on door) el tirador *tee·ra·dor*; (on radio etc) el botón *bo·ton*

knock *vt* golpear *gol·pe·ar*; **to knock (at) the door** llamar a la puerta *lya·mar a la pwer·ta*; **to knock down** echar abajo *e·char a·ba·kho*; **to knock out** dejar KO *de·khar ka·o* □ *vi* knock (engine) picar *pee·kar*

knot *vt* anudar *a·noo·dar* □ *n* el nudo *noo·do*; **to tie a knot** hacer* un nudo *a·ther oon noo·do*

know *vt* (person) conocer* *ko·no·ther*; (fact) saber* *sa·ber*; (subject, language) saber* *sa·ber*; **to know how to do something** saber* hacer algo *sa·ber a·ther al·go*

knowledge *n* el conocimiento *ko·no·thee·myen·to*

knuckle *n* el nudillo *noo·deel·yo*

kohlrabi *n* el colinabo *ko·lee·na·bo*

kosher *adj* autorizado por la ley judía *ow·to·ree·tha·do por la lay khoo·dee·a*

L

label *n* la etiqueta *e·tee·ke·ta* □ *vt* poner* etiqueta a *po·ner e·tee·ke·ta a*

labor *n* la mano de obra *ma·no de ob·ra*

laboratory *n* el laboratorio *la·bo·ra·to·ryo*

laborer *n* el obrero *o·bre·ro*

labor force *n* la mano de obra *ma·no de ob·ra*

labor union *n* el sindicato *seen·dee·ka·to*

lace *n* el encaje *en·ka·khe*; (of shoe) el cordón *kor·don*

ladder *n* la escalera *es·ka·le·ra*

ladle *n* el cucharón *koo·cha·ron*

lady *n* la señora *sen·yo·ra*

lager *n* la cerveza *ther·be·tha*

lake *n* el lago *la·go*

lamb *n* el cordero *kor·de·ro*

lambswool *n* la lana de cordero *la·na de kor·de·ro*

lamp *n* la lámpara *lam·pa·ra*

lamppost *n* el farol *fa·rol*

lampshade *n* la pantalla *pan·tal·ya*

land *n* (opposed to sea) la tierra *tye·rra*; (country) el campo *kam·po*; (soil) la tierra *tye·rra*; (property) las tierras *tye·rras* □ *vi* (from ship) bajar a tierra *ba·khar a tye·rra*; (plane) aterrizar *a·te·rree·thar*

landing *n* (of plane) el aterrizaje *a·te·rree·tha·khe*; (on stairs) el descansillo *des·kan·seel·yo*

landing strip *n* la pista de aterrizaje *pees·ta de a·te·rree·tha·khe*

landlady *n* la patrona *pa·tro·na*

landlord *n* el patrón *pa·tron*

landmark *n* el mojón *mo·khon*

landslide *n* el corrimiento de tierras *ko·rree·myen·to de tye·rras*

lane *n* (in country) el camino *ka·mee·no*; (in town) la callejuela *kal·ye·khwe·la*; (of road) el carril *ka·rreel*

language *n* la lengua *len·gwa*; (way one speaks) el lenguaje *len·gwa·khe*

language laboratory *n* el laboratorio de lenguas *la·bo·ra·to·ryo de len·gwas*

lanolin *n* la lanolina *la·no·lee·na*

lap n (of track) la vuelta bwel·ta; (of person) el regazo re·ga·tho

lard n la manteca de cerdo man·te·ka de ther·do

larder n la despensa des·pen·sa

large adj grande gran·de

laryngitis n la laringitis la·reen·khee·tees

last adj último(a) ool·tee·mo(a); last night anoche a·no·che; last week la semana pasada la se·ma·na pa·sa·da □ adv last en último lugar en ool·tee·mo loo·gar; at last por fin por feen □ vi last durar doo·rar

latch n el picaporte pee·ka·por·te

late adj (not on time) tardío(a) tar·dee·o(a) □ adv tarde tar·de; late in the day tarde tar·de; the latest news las últimas noticias las ool·tee·mas no·tee·thyas; the late king el fallecido rey el fal·ye·thee·do rey

lately adv últimamente ool·tee·ma·men·te

later adj (date etc) posterior pos·te·ryor; (version) más reciente mas re·thyen·te □ adv (to come etc) más tarde mas tar·de

Latin n el latín la·teen □ adj latino(a) la·tee·no(a)

Latin America n Latinoamérica (f) la·tee·no·a·me·ree·ka

Latin American adj latinoamericano(a) la·tee·no·a·me·ree·ka·no(a)

laugh vi reír* re·eer; to laugh at somebody reírse de alguien re·eer·se de al·gyen □ n la risa ree·sa

laughter n la risa ree·sa

launch n la lancha lan·cha □ vt (ship) botar bo·tar; (product) lanzar* lan·thar

laundromat n la lavandería automática la·ban·de·ree·a ow·to·ma·tee·ka Sn75

laundry n (place) la lavandería la·ban·de·ree·a; (clothes) la ropa sucia ro·pa soo·thya A53, Sn76

lavatory n el wáter ba·ter T166

law n la ley ley; law and order el orden público or·den poo·blee·ko

lawn n (grass) el césped thes·ped

lawn mower n el cortacésped kor·ta·thes·ped

lawn tennis n el tenis sobre hierba te·nees so·bre yer·ba

lawyer n el abogado a·bo·ga·do Sn88

laxative n el laxante lak·san·te

lay vt poner* po·ner; to lay the table poner* la mesa po·ner la me·sa; to lay the fire preparar el fuego pre·pa·rar el fwe·go; to lay down depositar de·po·see·tar; (wine) conservar konser·bar; to lay off (workers) despedir* des·pe·deer

layer n la capa ka·pa

lazy adj perezoso(a) pe·re·tho·so(a)

lead¹ n el llevar lye·bar □ vi lead (in contest) ir* primero eer pree·me·ro; this door leads into the garden esta puerta lleva al jardín es·ta pwer·ta lye·ba al khar·deen □ n lead (electrical) el cable ka·ble; (dog's) la correa ko·rre·a

lead² n el plomo plo·mo; lead (in pencil) la mina mee·na

leaf n la hoja o·kha

leak n (water) la vía de agua bee·a de a·gwa; (gas) la fuga foo·ga □ vi gotear go·te·ar T184, Sn56

lean adj (meat) magro(a) ma·gro(a) □ vi inclinarse een·klee·nar·se; to lean against something inclinarse

contra algo een·klee·nar·sekon·tra al·go

learn vt aprender a·pren·der

lease n el arrendamiento a·rren·da·myen·to

leash n la correa ko·rre·a

least adj □ the least money el mínimo de dinero el mee·nee·mo de dee·ne·ro; the least amount la menor cantidad la me·nor kan·tee·dad □ adv the least expensive el menos caro el me·nos ka·ro □ n he has the least tiene lo mínimo tye·ne lo mee·nee·mo; at least por lo menos por lo me·nos; not in the least en absoluto en ab·so·loo·to

leather n el cuero kwe·ro

leave n (holiday) el permiso per·mee·so; on leave de permiso de per·mee·so de □ vi irse* eer·se □ vt (room) marcharse de mar·char·se de; (club, school) dejar de ir a de·khar de eer a; I've left my umbrella he olvidado el paraguas e ol·bee·da·do el pa·ra·gwas; leave it to me déjemelo a mí de·khe·me·lo a mee; leave your coat here deje su abrigo aquí de·khe soo a·bree·go a·kee; to leave a message dejar un recado de·khar oon re·ka·do; to leave out (omit) omitir o·mee·teer

lecture n la conferencia kon·fe·ren·thya

ledger n el libro mayor lee·bro ma·yor

leek n el puerro pwe·rro

left adv □ there's some cream left queda un poco de crema ke·da oon po·ko de kre·ma; to turn left torcer hacia la izquierda tor·ther a·thya la eeth·kyer·da □ adj the left side el lado izquierdo el la·do eeth·kyer·do T99

left-handed adj zurdo(a) thoor·do(a)

leg n (of person) la pierna pyer·na; (of animal) la pata pa·ta; leg of lamb pierna de cordero pyer·na de kor·de·ro; chicken leg el muslo de pollo moos·lo de pol·yo 123

legal adj legal le·gal

leisure n el ocio o·thyo

leisure center n el centro de recreo then·tro de re·kre·o

lemon n el limón lee·mon

lemonade n la limonada lee·mo·na·da

lemon juice n el zumo de limón thoo·mo de lee·mon

lemon sole n el lenguado len·gwa·do

lemon-squeezer n el exprimidor eks·pree·mee·dor

lend vt prestar pres·tar

length n la longitud lon·khee·tood

lens n (of glasses) la lente len·te; (of camera) el objetivo ob·khe·tee·bo

lentils pl las lentejas len·te·khas

less adj □ less meat menos carne me·nos kar·ne □ adv less quickly más despacio mas des·pa·thyo □ n he has less time menos tye·ne me·nos; less than menos que me·nos ke

lesson n la clase kla·se

let vt (allow) dejar de·khar; (rent out) alquilar al·kee·lar; to let someone do something permitir a alguien que haga algo per·mee·teer a al·gyen ke a·ga al·go; let me in déjeme entrar de·khe·me en·trar; let's go vámonos ba·mo·nos; they let him go dejaron irse le de·kha·ron eer·se; to let (house etc) se alquila al·kee·la; to let someone down defraudar a alguien de·frow·dar a al·gyen

letter n (of alphabet) la letra *le·tra*; (message) la carta *kar·ta* B70, A25, 36, Sn1

letter box n el buzón *boo·thon*

lettuce n la lechuga *le·choo·ga*

level n el nivel *nee·bel* □ adj (surface) plano(a) *pla·no(a)*; (horizontal) horizontal *o·ree·thon·tal*

lever n la palanca *pa·lan·ka*

Levis pl los pantalones vaqueros *pan·ta·lo·nes ba·ke·ros*

liabilities pl (on balance sheet) el pasivo *pa·see·bo*

library n la biblioteca *bee·blyo·te·ka*

Libya n Libia (f) *lee·bya*

license n (for driving) el permiso de conducir *per·mee·so de kon·doo·theer*

license plate n el número de matrícula *noo·me·ro de ma·tree·koo·la*

lick vt lamer *la·mer*

licorice n el regaliz *re·ga·leeth*

lid n la tapa *ta·pa*

lie n (untruth) la mentira *men·tee·ra* □ vi estar echado(a) *es·tar e·cha·do(a)*; (tell a lie) mentir* *men·teer*; to lie down echarse *e·char·se*

Liechtenstein n Liechtenstein (m) *lee·e·ches·teen*

life n la vida *bee·da*; (liveliness) la vivacidad *bee·ba·thee·dad*; for life para toda la vida *pa·ra to·da la bee·da*

lifebelt n el cinturón salvavidas *theen·too·ron sal·ba·bee·das*

lifeboat n (on ship) el bote salvavidas *bo·te sal·ba·bee·das*; (from shore) la lancha de socorro *lan·cha de so·ko·rro*

lifeguard n el vigilante *bee·khee·lan·te*

life insurance n el seguro de vida *se·goo·ro de bee·da*

life jacket n el chaleco salvavidas *cha·le·ko sal·ba·bee·das*

life preserver n (belt) el cinturón salvavidas *theen·too·ron sal·ba·bee·das*; (jacket) el chaleco salvavidas *cha·le·ko sal·ba·bee·das*

lift vt levantar *le·ban·tar*

light vt (fire, cigarette) encender* *en·then·der* □ n la luz *looth*; (traffic light) el semáforo *se·ma·fo·ro*; have you got a light? ¿tiene fuego? *tye·ne fwe·go* □ adj (bright, pale) claro(a) *kla·ro(a)*; (not heavy) ligero(a) *lee·khe·ro(a)*; light music la música ligera *moo·see·ka lee·khe·ra*; as soon as it was light en el momento en que amaneció *en el mo·men·to en ke a·ma·ne·thyo*

light bulb n la bombilla *bom·beel·ya*

lighter n el encendedor *en·then·de·dor* S104

lighthouse n el faro *fa·ro*

light industry n la industria ligera *een·doos·trya lee·khe·ra*

lighting n (on road) la iluminación *ee·loo·mee·na·thyon*

light meter n el fotómetro *fo·to·me·tro*

lightning n el relámpago *re·lam·pa·go*

like prep como *ko·mo* □ vt gustar *goos·tar*; what's it like? ¿cómo es? *ko·mo es* □ vt like gustar *goos·tar*; I'd like to go me gustaría ir *me goos·ta·ree·a eer*; I'd like an ice cream me gustaría un helado *me goos·ta·ree·a oon e·la·do*; what would you like? ¿qué quiere Ud? *ke kye·re oos·ted* S20

likely adj probable *pro·ba·ble*; he's likely to come es probable que venga *es pro·ba·ble ke ben·ga*

lily n la azucena *a·thoo·the·na*

lime n (fruit) la lima *lee·ma*

lime juice n el zumo de lima *thoo·mo de lee·ma*

limit n el límite *lee·mee·te*

limousine n la limusina *lee·moo·see·na*

limp vi cojear *ko·khe·ar*

line n la línea *lee·ne·a*; (railway) el ferrocarril *fe·rro·ka·rreel*; (telephone)la línea *lee·ne·a*; the line is busy la línea está comunicando la línea está comunicando; to stand in line hacer* cola *a·ther ko·la*

linen n (cloth) el lino *lee·no*; (for beds) la ropa blanca *ro·pa blan·ka*; (for table) la mantelería *man·te·le·ree·a*

liner n (ship) el transatlántico *tran·sat·lan·tee·ko*

lining n el forro *fo·rro*

linoleum n el linóleo *lee·no·le·o*

lint n las hilas *ee·las*

lion n el león *le·on*

lip n el labio *la·byo*

lipstick n la barra de labios *ba·rra de la·byos*

liqueur n el licor *lee·kor* E15

liquid n el líquido *lee·kee·do* □ adj líquido(a) *lee·kee·do(a)*

liquid assets pl el activo líquido *ak·tee·bo lee·kee·do*

liquidation n la liquidación *lee·kee·da·thyon*; to go into liquidation entrar en liquidación *en·trar en lee·kee·da·thyon*

liquor n las bebidas alcohólicas *be·bee·das al·ko·lee·kas* L43

list n la lista *lees·ta* □ vt hacer* una lista *a·ther oo·na lees·ta*

listen vi escuchar *es·koo·char*; to listen to escuchar *es·koo·char*

list price n el precio de catálogo *pre·thyo de ka·ta·lo·go*

liter n el litro *lee·tro* T157, S35

literature n la literatura *lee·te·ra·too·ra*

little adj pequeño(a) *pe·ken·yo(a)* □ n a little un poco *oon po·ko*

live¹ adj (alive) vivo(a) *bee·bo(a)*

live² vi vivir *bee·beer*; (reside) vivir en *bee·beer en*

lively adj animado(a) *a·nee·ma·do(a)*

liver n el hígado *ee·ga·do*

living room n el cuarto de estar *kwar·to de es·tar*

load n la carga *kar·ga* □ vt cargar *kar·gar*

loaf (of bread) n el pan *pan*

loan n el préstamo *pres·ta·mo* □ vt prestar *pres·tar*

lobby n (entrance) el vestíbulo *bes·tee·boo·lo*

lobster n la langosta *lan·gos·ta*

local adj local *lo·kal*; the local shops las tiendas de la vecindad *las tyen·das de la be·theen·dad*; a local call (on phone) una llamada local *oo·na lya·ma·da lo·kal* E10

lock n (on door) la cerradura *the·rra·doo·ra*; (in canal) la esclusa *es·kloo·sa* □ vt cerrar* con llave *the·rrar kon lya·be*; the door's locked la puerta está cerrada con llave *la pwer·ta es·ta the·rra·da kon lya·be* A48

locker n la casilla *ka·seel·ya*

lodger n el huésped *wes·ped*

lodgings pl la pensión *pen·syon*

loft n el desván *des·ban*

log n (of wood) el tronco *tron·ko*

logbook n (of car) la documentación (del coche) *do·koo·men·ta·thyon (del ko·che)*

lollipop n el chupa-chups *choo·pa·choops*, el chupete (Am) *choo·pe·te*

London n Londres (m) *lon·dres*
lonely adj (person) solo(a) *so·lo(a)*
long adj largo(a) *lar·go(a)*; how long is
the river? ¿cuánto mide el río? *kwan·
to mee·de el ree·o*; 6 meters long 6
metros de largo 6 *me·tros de largo*;
how long is the program? ¿cuánto
tiempo dura el programa? *kwan·to
tyem·po doo·ra el pro·gra·ma*; 6
months long que dura 6 meses *ke
doo·ra 6 me·ses* □ adv long durante
mucho tiempo *doo·ran·te moo·cho
tyem·po*; all day long (durante) todo
el día *(doo·ran·te) to·do el dee·a*; I
shan't be long no tardaré mucho *no
tar·da·re moo·cho*; as long as
(provided that) con tal que *kon tal ke*
long-distance adj interurbano(a) *een·
ter·oor·ba·no(a)*
long drink n la bebida larga *be·bee·da
lar·ga*
long-term adj a largo plazo *a lar·go
pla·tho*
long wave n la onda larga *on·da lar·ga*
look n la mirada *mee·ra·da*; (appearance) la apariencia *a·pa·ryen·thya*
□ vi mirar *mee·rar*; (appear) parecer* *pa·re·ther*; to look at mirar *mee·
rar*; to look like parecerse a *pa·re·
ther·se a*; to look after cuidar de
kwee·dar de; to look for buscar*
boos·kar; to look forward to hacer*
mucha ilusión *a·ther moo·cha ee·loo·
syon*; look out! ¡cuidado! *kwee·da·
do*; to look up (word) buscar* *boos·
kar*
loop n el lazo *la·tho*
loose adj (knot, screw) suelto(a) *swel·
to(a)*; (clothing) ancho(a) *an·cho(a)*
lose vt perder* *per·der*; to lose one's
way perderse* *per·der·se* □ vi lose
(clock, watch) retrasarse *re·tra·sar·se*
Sn87
loss n la pérdida *per·dee·da* Sn82
lot n (at auction) el lote *lo·te*; lots of or
a lot of milk mucha leche *moo·cha le·
che*; lots of or a lot of people mucha
gente *moo·cha khen·te*; a lot better
mucho mejor *moo·cho me·khor*
lotion n la loción *lo·thyon*
lottery n la lotería *lo·te·ree·a*
loud adj (voice) alto(a) *al·to(a)*;
(noise) fuerte *fwer·te*
loudly adv en alta voz *en al·ta both*
loudspeaker n el altavoz *al·ta·both*, el
altoparlante (Am) *al·to·par·lan·te*
lounge n (in house) la sala de estar *sa·
la de es·tar*; (in hotel) el salón *sa·lon*;
(at airport) la sala de espera *sa·la de
es·pe·ra*
love vt querer* *ke·rer*; to love doing
something gustarle mucho a uno hacer algo *goos·tar·le moo·cho a oo·no
a·ther al·go*; I'd love to go me gustaría muchísimo ir *me goos·ta·ree·a
moo·chee·see·mo eer* □ n love el
amor *a·mor*; in love enamorado(a) *e·
na·mo·ra·do(a)*; love from (on letter)
un abrazo *oon a·bra·tho*
lovely adj bonito(a) *bo·nee·to(a)*; we
had a lovely time lo pasamos muy
bien *lo pa·sa·mos mwee byen*
low adj bajo(a) *ba·kho(a)*
Low Countries pl los Países Bajos *pa·
ee·ses ba·khos*
lower adj más bajo(a) *mas ba·kho(a)*
low tide n la marea baja *ma·re·a ba·
kha*
LP n el LP *e·le pe*
Ltd abbrev S. A. *e·se·a*
luck n la suerte *swer·te*; good luck!

¡buena suerte! *bwe·na swer·te*; bad
luck mala suerte *ma·la swer·te*
lucky adj □ to be lucky tener* suerte
te·ner swer·te
luggage n el equipaje *e·kee·pa·khe*
T23f, E6
luggage cart n la carretilla *ka·rre·
teel·ya* T26
luggage rack n (in train) la redecilla *re·
de·theel·ya*; (on car) el portaequipajes *por·ta·e·kee·pa·khes*
lump n (on skin) el bulto *bool·to*; (in
sauce) el grumo *groo·mo*; lump of
sugar el terrón *te·rron*
lunch n el almuerzo *al·mwer·tho* A26,
E6
lunch hour n la hora del almuerzo *o·ra
del al·mwer·tho*
lung n el pulmón *pool·mon*
Luxembourg n Luxemburgo (m) *look·
sem·boor·go*
luxurious adj lujoso(a) *loo·kho·so(a)*
luxury n el lujo *loo·kho* □ adj (car,
hotel) de lujo *de loo·kho*

M

macaroni n los macarrones (mpl) *ma·
ka·rro·nes*
machine n la máquina *ma·kee·na*
machinery n la maquinaria *ma·kee·na·
rya*
mackerel n la caballa *ka·bal·ya*
mack(intosh) n el impermeable *eem·
per·me·ab·le*
mad adj (insane) loco(a) *lo·ko(a)*; (angry) furioso(a) *foo·ryo·so(a)*
madam n señora (f) *sen·yo·ra*
Madeira n (wine) el vino de Madeira
bee·no de ma·dey·ra
made-to-measure adj a la medida *a la
me·dee·da*
Madrid n Madrid (m) *ma·dreed*
magazine n (journal) la revista *re·
bees·ta*
magic n la magia *ma·khya* □ adj mági-
co(a) *ma·khee·ko(a)*
magnet n el imán *ee·man*
magnetic tape n la cinta magnética
theen·ta mag·ne·tee·ka
magnificent adj magnífico(a) *mag·nee·
fee·ko(a)*
mahogany n la caoba *ka·o·ba*
maid n la muchacha *moo·cha·cha* A68
maiden name n el apellido de soltera
a·pel·yee·do de sol·te·ra
maid service n el servicio de señora de
la limpieza *ser·bee·thyo de sen·yo·ra
de la leem·pye·tha*
mail n el correo *ko·rre·o* □ vt mandar
por correo *man·dar por ko·rre·o*
mailbox n el buzón *boo·thon*
mailing list n la lista de direcciones
lees·ta de dee·rek·thyon·es
mailman n el cartero *kar·te·ro*
mail order n □ to buy something by
mail order comprar algo por correo
kom·prar al·go por ko·rre·o
main adj principal *preen·thee·pal* □ n
to turn the electricity/water off at the
main cortar la electricidad/el agua
kor·tar la e·lek·tree·thee·dad/el ag·wa
mainland n el continente *kon·tee·
nen·te*
mainly adv principalmente *preen·thee·
pal·men·te*
maintenance n el mantenimiento *man·
te·nee·myen·to*; (of building) la conservación *kon·ser·ba·thyon*
major adj principal *preen·thee·pal*
majority n la mayoría *ma·yo·ree·a*;

elected by a majority of 5 elegido por una mayoría de 5 votos *e·le·khee·do por oo·na ma·yo·ree·a de 5 bo·tos*

make n (*of product*) la marca *mar·ka* □ vt hacer* *a·ther;* **to make the beds** hacer* las camas *a·ther las ka·mas;* **to make someone sad** poner* a uno triste *po·ner a oo·no trees·te;* **to make someone do something** obligar a uno a hacer algo *o·blee·gar a oo·no a a·ther al·go;* **to make do with** something arreglarse con algo *a·rre·glar·se kon al·go;* **to make (oneself) up** maquillarse *ma·keel·yar·se*

make-up n el maquillaje *ma·keel·ya·khe*

male adj macho *ma·cho*

mallet n el mazo *ma·tho*

malt n la malta *mal·ta*

Malta n Malta (f) *mal·ta*

man n el hombre *om·bre*

manage vt (*business*) dirigir* *dee·ree·kheer;* **can you manage?** ¿puede Ud con eso? *pwe·de oos·ted kon e·so;* **to manage to do something** conseguir* hacer algo *kon·se·geer a·ther al·go*

management n (*of business*) la dirección *dee·rek·thyon;* (*managers*) el consejo de administración *kon·se·kho de ad·mee·nees·tra·thyon*

manager n el gerente *khe·ren·te* M31

manageress n la gerente *khe·ren·te*

managing director, M.D. n el director gerente *dee·rek·tor khe·ren·te*

manicure n la manicura *ma·nee·koo·ra*

manicure set n el estuche de manicura *es·too·che de ma·nee·koo·ra*

man-made adj artificial *ar·tee·fee·thyal*

manner n (*way*) la manera *ma·ne·ra;* (*attitude*) el aire *ay·re*

manners pl los modales *mo·da·les*

manpower n la mano de obra *ma·no de o·bra*

mansion n la casa solariega *ka·sa so·la·rye·ga*

mantelpiece n la repisa de chimenea *re·pee·sa de chee·me·ne·a*

manual adj manual *ma·nwal* □ n (*book*) el manual *ma·nwal*

manufacture vt fabricar* *fa·bree·kar*

manufacturer n el fabricante* *fa·bree·kan·te*

manufacturing n la fabricación *fa·bree·ka·thyon*

many adj muchos *moo·chos* □ adj **many books** muchos libros *moo·chos lee·bros*

map n (*of country*) el mapa *ma·pa;* (*of town*) el plano *pla·no* F8, L4, S96

marble n (*material*) el mármol *mar·mol;* (*ball*) la bola *bo·la*

March n marzo (m) *mar·tho*

march vi marchar *mar·char* □ n la marcha *mar·cha*

margarine n la margarina *mar·ga·ree·na*

margin n (*on page*) el margen *mar·khen*

marina n el puerto deportivo *pwer·to de·por·tee·bo*

marjoram n la mejorana *me·kho·ra·na*

mark n la marca *mar·ka;* (*stain*) la mancha *man·cha;* (*currency*) el marco *mar·ko;* (*in school*) la nota *no·ta* □ vt marcar* *mar·kar;* (*stain*) manchar *man·char*

market n el mercado *mer·ka·do;* **there is a good market for X** X se encuentran buena salida *los X en·kwen·tran bwe·na sa·lee·da* □ vt market (*pro-*

duct) llevar al mercado *lye·bar al mer·ka·do* Bm18f

market-day n el día de mercado *dee·a de mer·ka·do*

marketing n el marketing *mar·ke·teeng*

marketing manager n el jefe de investigación de mercados *khe·fe de een·bes·tee·ga·thyon de mer·ka·dos*

market-place n la plaza del mercado *pla·tha del mer·ka·do*

market research n la investigación de mercados *een·bes·tee·ga·thyon de mer·ka·dos*

market value n el valor en el mercado *ba·lor en el mer·ka·do*

marmalade n la mermelada de naranjas *mer·me·la·da de na·ran·khas*

maroon adj castaño (rojizo) *kas·tan·yo (ro·khee·tho)*

marriage n el matrimonio *ma·tree·mo·nyo;* (*wedding*) la boda *bo·da*

married adj casado(a) *ka·sa·do(a);* **they were married yesterday** se casaron ayer *se ka·sa·ron a·yer* Mc46

marrow n (*vegetable*) el calabacín *ka·la·ba·theen*

marry vt casar *ka·sar* □ vi casarse *ka·sar·se*

martini n (*Brit*) el martini *mar·tee·nee;* (*US*) el martini con ginebra *mar·tee·nee kon khee·ne·bra*

marvelous adj maravilloso(a) *ma·ra·bee·lyo·so(a)*

marzipan n el mazapán *ma·tha·pan*

mascara n el rímel *ree·mel*

masculine adj masculino(a) *mas·koo·lee·no(a)*

mash vt machacar* *ma·cha·kar*

mashed potatoes pl el puré de patatas *poo·re de pa·ta·tas*

mask n la máscara *mas·ka·ra* □ vt enmascarar *en·mas·ka·rar*

mass n (*church*) la misa *mee·sa;* **a mass of blossom** el cubierto de flores *el koo·byer·to de flo·res*

massage n el masaje *ma·sa·khe* □ vt dar* masajes a *dar ma·sa·khes a*

masseur n el masajista *ma·sa·khees·ta*

masseuse n la masajista *ma·sa·khees·ta*

massive adj masivo(a) *ma·see·bo(a)*

mass-produce vt fabricar* en serie *fa·bree·kar en se·rye*

mass production n la fabricación en serie *fa·bree·ka·thyon en se·rye*

mast n (*ship's*) el mástil *mas·teel;* (*radio*) el poste *pos·te*

master n el maestro *ma·es·tro*

master key n la llave maestra *lya·be ma·es·tra*

masterpiece n la obra maestra *o·bra ma·es·tra*

mat n la estera *es·te·ra;* (*place mat*) el tapete *ta·pe·te;* (*under a glass*) el posavasos *po·sa·ba·sos*

match n la cerilla *the·reel·ya;* el fósforo (Am) *fos·fo·ro;* (*sport*) el partido *par·tee·do* □ vt hacer* juego con *a·ther khwe·go kon* S102

matchbox n la caja de cerillas *ka·kha de the·reel·yas*

material n el material *ma·te·ryal;* (*fabric*) la tela *te·la* S61

maternity dress n el vestido de premamá *bes·tee·do de pre·ma·ma*

maternity hospital n la casa de maternidad *ka·sa de ma·ter·nee·dad*

mathematics n las matemáticas *ma·te·ma·tee·kas*

matter n □ **what's the matter?** ¿qué pasa? *ke pa·sa* □ vi **it doesn't matter** no importa *no eem·por·ta*

mattress *n* el colchón *kol·chon*
mature *adj* maduro(a) *ma·doo·ro(a)*
mauve *adj* malva *mal·ba*
maximize *vt* llevar al máximo *lye·bar al mak·see·mo*
maximum *n* el máximo *mak·see·mo*
  □ *adj* máximo(a) *mak·see·mo(a)*
May *n* mayo (*m*) *ma·yo*
may *vi* □ may I come in? ¿se puede entrar? *se pwe·de en·trar*; it may rain es posible que llueva *es po·see·ble ke lywe·ba*; we may as well go más vale que nos vayamos *mas ba·le ke nos ba·ya·mos*
Mayday *n* la señal de socorro *sen·yal de so·ko·rro*
mayonnaise *n* la mayonesa *ma·yo·ne·sa*
mayor *n* el alcalde *al·kal·de*
me *pron* me *me*; give it to me démelo *de·me·lo*; he gave it to me me lo dio *me lo dyo*; it's me soy yo *soy yo*
meal *n* la comida *ko·mee·da* T43, E48
mean *adj* (*miserly*) tacaño(a) *ta·kan·yo(a)*; (*unkind*) malo(a) *ma·lo(a)*
  □ *vt* (*signify*) significar* *seeg·nee·fee·kar*; to mean to do pensar* hacer *pen·sar a·ther*
meaning *n* el significado *seeg·nee·fee·ka·do*
means *pl* los medios *me·dyos*; by means of por medio de *por me·dyo de*
meanwhile *adv* mientras tanto *myen·tras tan·to*
measles *n* el sarampión *sa·ram·pyon*
measure *vt/i* medir* *me·deer*
measurements *pl* las medidas *me·dee·das*; bust measurements el perímetro torácico *pe·ree·me·tro to·ra·thee·ko*
meat *n* la carne *kar·ne*
mechanic *n* el mecánico *me·ka·nee·ko* T169
media *pl* los medios de información *me·dyos de in·for·ma·thyon*
median strip *n* el refugio *re·foo·khyo*
medical *adj* médico(a) *me·dee·ko(a)*
medicine *n* (*pills etc*) la medicina *me·dee·thee·na*
Mediterranean *adj* mediterráneo(a) *me·dee·te·rra·ne·o(a)*; the Mediterranean (Sea) el (Mar) Mediterráneo *mar me·dee·te·rra·ne·o*
medium *adj* medio(a) *me·dyo(a)*; medium wave la onda media *on·da me·dya*
meet *vt* (*encounter*) encontrarse con *en·kon·trar·se kon*; (*make acquaintance of*) conocer* *ko·no·ther*; (*by arrangement*) reunirse con *re·oo·neer·se kon*; (*demand*) satisfacer* *sa·tees·fa·ther*; I'll meet you at the station (*go to get*) iré a buscarle a la estación *ee·re a boos·kar·le a la es·ta·thyon*
meeting *n* la reunión *re·oo·nyon*
melon *n* el melón *me·lon*
melt *vi* derretirse* *de·rre·teer·se* □ *vt* derretir* *de·rre·teer*
member *n* el miembro *myem·bro* T5
memo(randum) *n* la nota *no·ta*
memory *n* la memoria *me·mo·rya*; one of my memories uno de mis recuerdos *oo·no de mees re·kwer·dos*
mend *vt* reparar *re·pa·rar*
menswear *n* la ropa de caballero *ro·pa de ka·bal·ye·ro*
mental hospital *n* el hospital psiquiátrico *os·pee·tal see·kee·a·tree·ko*
mentholated *adj* mentolado(a) *men·to·la·do(a)*

mention *vt* mencionar *men·thyo·nar*; don't mention it no hay de qué *no ay de ke*
menu *n* el menú *me·noo* E8
merchant *n* el comerciante *ko·mer·thyan·te*
merge *vi* unirse *oo·neer·se*
merger *n* la fusión *foo·syon*
meringue *n* el merengue *me·ren·ge*
merry *adj* alegre *a·le·gre*
merry-go-round *n* el tiovivo *tee·o·bee·bo*
mess *n* el desorden *des·or·den*; to make a mess desordenar *des·or·de·nar*; to make a mess of (*spoil*) estropear *es·tro·pe·ar*
message *n* el mensaje *men·sa·khe* B70, A25, 36
messenger *n* el mensajero *men·sa·khe·ro*
metal *n* el metal *me·tal*
meter *n* el contador *kon·ta·dor*; (*measure*) el metro *me·tro*
method *n* el método *me·to·do*
Methodist *n* el/la metodista *me·to·dees·ta*
methylated spirits *pl* el alcohol desnaturalizado *al·kol des·na·too·ra·lee·tha·do*
metric *adj* métrico(a) *me·tree·ko(a)*
Mexican *adj* mexicano(a) *me·khee·ka·no(a)*; he's Mexican es mexicano *es me·khee·ka·no*; she's Mexican es mexicana *es me·khee·ka·na*
Mexico *n* México (*m*) *me·khee·ko*
microchip *n* la placa de silicio *pla·ka de see·lee·thyo*
microcomputer *n* el microordenador *mee·kro·or·de·na·dor*
microfiche *n* la microficha *mee·kro·fee·cha*
microfilm *n* el microfilm *mee·kro·feelm*
microphone *n* el micrófono *mee·kro·fo·no*
microprocessor *n* el microprocesador *mee·kro·pro·the·sa·dor*
microwave oven *n* el horno de microondas *or·no de mee·kro·on·das*
midday *n* el mediodía *me·dyo·dee·a*; at midday a mediodía *a me·dyo·dee·a*
middle *n* el medio *me·dyo*; right in the middle en el centro mismo *en el then·tro mees·mo*; in the middle of the night en medio de la noche *en me·dyo de la no·che*
middle-aged *adj* de mediana edad *de me·dya·na e·dad*
middle-class *adj* de la clase media *de la kla·se me·dya*
Middle East *n* el Oriente Medio *o·ryen·te me·dyo*
middle management *pl* los cuadros medios *kwa·dros me·dyos*
midnight *n* la medianoche *me·dya·no·che*; at midnight a medianoche *a me·dya·no·che*
midwife *n* la comadrona *ko·ma·dro·na*
might *vi* □ it might rain puede que llueva *pwe·de ke lywe·ba*; we might as well go más vale que nos vayamos *mas ba·le ke nos ba·ya·mos*
migraine *n* la jaqueca *kha·ke·ka*
mild *adj* suave *swa·be*; (*taste*) flojo(a) *flo·kho(a)*
mile *n* la milla *meel·ya*
miles per hour, m.p.h. ≈ kilómetros por hora *kee·lo·me·tros por o·ra*
mileage *n* ≈ kilometraje *kee·lo·me·tra·khe* T109
military *adj* militar *mee·lee·tar*

milk *n* la leche *le·che* E65, S35

milk chocolate *n* el chocolate con leche *cho·ko·la·te kon le·che*

milkman *n* el lechero *le·che·ro*

milkshake *n* el batido de leche *ba·tee·do de le·che*, la leche malteada (Am) *le·che mal·te·a·da*

mill *n* el molino *mo·lee·no*; (*for coffee*) el molinillo *mo·lee·neel·yo* □ *vt* moler* *mo·ler*

milligram *n* el miligramo *mee·lee·gra·mo*

milliliter *n* el mililitro *mee·lee·lee·tro*

millimeter *n* el milímetro *mee·lee·me·tro*

million *num* el millón *meel·yon*

millionaire *n* el millonario *meel·yo·na·ryo*

millionth *adj* millonésimo(a) *meel·yo·ne·see·mo(a)*

mince *vt* picar *pee·kar*

mincer *n* la máquina de picar carne *ma·kee·na de pee·kar kar·ne*

mind *n* la mente *men·te*; to change one's mind cambiar de opinión *kam·byar de o·peen·yon*; to make up one's mind decidirse *de·thee·deer·se* □ *vt* I don't mind the heat no me importa el calor *no me eem·por·ta la ka·lor*; I don't mind no me importa *no me eem·por·ta*; never mind no importa *no eem·por·ta*; do you mind if ...? ¿le importa si ...? *le eem·por·ta see*; mind the step cuidado con el escalón *kwee·da·do con el es·ka·lon*

mine *pron* el mío *el mee·o*; la mía *la mee·a*; (*plural*) los míos *los mee·os*; las mías *las mee·as* □ *n* (*for coal etc*) la mina *mee·na*

miner *n* el minero *mee·ne·ro*

mineral water *n* el agua mineral (*f*) *a·gwa mee·ne·ral*

minestrone (soup) *n* la sopa milanesa *so·pa mee·la·ne·sa*

minibus *n* el microbús *mee·kro·boos*

minicomputer *n* la minicomputadora *mee·nee·kom·poo·ta·do·ra*

minimum *n* el mínimo *mee·nee·mo* □ *adj* mínimo(a) *mee·nee·mo(a)*

miniskirt *n* la minifalda *mee·nee·fal·da*

minister *n* (*in government*) el ministro *mee·nees·tro*; (*of religion*) el pastor *pas·tor*

ministry *n* (*government*) el ministerio *mee·nees·te·ryo*

mink *n* (*fur*) el visón *bee·son*

mink coat *n* el abrigo de visón *a·bree·go de bee·son*

minor *adj* (*road*) secundario(a) *se·koon·da·ryo(a)*; (*injury*) de segundo orden *de se·goon·do or·den*; minor operation una operación sin importancia *oo·na o·pe·ra·thyon seen eem·por·tan·thya*

minority *n* la minoría *mee·no·ree·a*

mint *n* (*herb*) la menta *men·ta*; (*confectionery*) el caramelo de menta *ka·ra·me·lo de men·ta*

minus *prep* menos *me·nos*; at minus 2 degrees a 2 grados bajo cero *a 2 gra·dos ba·kho the·ro*

minute *n* el minuto *mee·noo·to*; just a minute un momento *oon mo·men·to*

mirror *n* el espejo *es·pe·kho* S71

miscarriage *n* el aborto *a·bor·to*

miserable *adj* triste *trees·te*

misprint *n* la errata *e·rra·ta*

Miss *n* Señorita (*f*) *sen·yo·ree·ta*

miss *vt* (*target*) no dar* en *no dar en*; (*train*) perder* *per·der*; I miss my mother echo de menos a mi madre *e·cho de me·nos a mee ma·dre*; I miss London echo de menos Londres *e·cho de me·nos lon·dres*; to miss out omitir *o·mee·teer*

missing *adj* (*object*) que falta *ke fal·ta*; (*person*) desaparecido(a) *des·a·pa·re·thee·do(a)*; some pages are missing faltan algunas páginas *fal·tan al·goo·nas pa·khee·nas*; my wallet is missing he perdido mi cartera *e per·dee·do mee kar·te·ra*

mist *n* la niebla *nye·bla*

mistake *n* el error *e·rror*; by mistake por equivocación *por e·kee·bo·ka·thyon*; to make a mistake cometer* un error *ko·me·ter oon e·rror* E46

mistress *n* (*lover*) la querida *ke·ree·da*

mitt(en) *n* la manopla *ma·no·pla*

mix *vt* mezclar *meth·klar*; to mix up (*confuse*) confundir *kon·foon·deer* □ *vi* mix mezclarse *meth·klar·se*

mixed *adj* (*co-ed*) mixto(a) *meeks·to(a)*; mixed grill el plato combinado *pla·to kom·bee·na·do*

mixer *n* la batidora *ba·tee·do·ra*

mixture *n* la mezcla *meth·kla*

moan *n* el gemido *khe·mee·do* □ *vi* gemir* *khe·meer*

model *n* el modelo *mo·de·lo*; (*mannequin*) el/la modelo *mo·de·lo*; a model railroad un ferrocarril en miniatura *oon fe·rro·ka·rreel en mee·nya·too·ra*

modern *adj* moderno(a) *mo·der·no(a)* S86

modernize *vt* modernizar *mo·der·nee·thar*

modest *adj* modesto(a) *mo·des·to(a)*

modification *n* la modificación *mo·dee·fee·ka·thyon*

modify *vt* modificar* *mo·dee·fee·kar*

mohair *n* el mohair *mo·er*

molasses *n* la melaza *me·la·tha*

molecule *n* la molécula *mo·le·koo·la*

moment *n* el momento *mo·men·to*; at the moment en este momento *en es·te mo·men·to*

mom(my) *n* la mamá *ma·ma*

Monaco *n* Monaco (*m*) *mo·na·ko*

monastery *n* el monasterio *mo·nas·te·ryo*

Monday *n* lunes (*m*) *loo·nes*

monetary *adj* monetario(a) *mo·ne·ta·ryo(a)*

money *n* el dinero *dee·ne·ro*; to make money hacer* dinero *a·ther dee·ne·ro* M17f

money order *n* el giro postal *khee·ro pos·tal*

monitor *n* (*TV*) el receptor de control *re·thep·tor de kon·trol*

monk *n* el monje *mon·khe*

monkey *n* el mono *mo·no*

mono *adj* mono- *mo·no*; in mono en mono *en mo·no*

monopoly *n* el monopolio *mo·no·po·lyo*

monorail *n* el monocarril *mo·no·ka·rreel*

monster *n* el monstruo *mons·troo·o*

month *n* el mes *mes*

monthly *adj* mensual *men·swal* □ *n* el mensual *men·swal*

monument *n* el monumento *mo·noo·men·to*

mood *n* el humor *oo·mor*; in a good mood de buen humor *de bwen oo·mor*

moon *n* la luna *loo·na*

moor *vt* amarrar *a·ma·rrar*

mop *n* la fregona *fre·go·na* □ *vt* fregar* *fre·gar*

moped n el ciclomotor *theek·lo·mo·tor*

more adj más *mas*; more cheese más queso *mas ke·so*; more people más gente *mas khen·te* □ **pron** I'd like (some) more quisiera un poco más *kee·sye·ra oon po·ko mas* □ **adv** more dangerous than más peligroso que *mas pe·lee·gro·so ke*; more or less más o menos *mas o me·nos*

morning n la mañana *man·ya·na*

Moroccan adj marroquí *ma·rro·kee*

Morocco n Marruecos (m) *ma·rrwe·kos*

mortgage n la hipoteca *hee·po·te·ka* □ **vt** hipotecar *ee·po·te·kar*

Moscow n Moscú (m) *mos·koo*

moselle n (wine) el vino de Mosela *bee·no de mo·se·la*

mosque n la mezquita *meth·kee·ta*

mosquito n el mosquito *mos·kee·to*, el zancudo (Am) *than·koo·do*

mosquito net n el mosquitero *mos·kee·te·ro*

most adv □ the most beautiful el/la más bonito(a) *el/la mas bo·nee·to(a)* □ **adj** most people la mayoría de la gente *la ma·yo·ree·a de la khen·te*; the most cars el número más grande de coches *el noo·me·ro mas gran·de de ko·ches* □ **pron** he has the most tiene la mayor parte *tye·ne la ma·yor par·te*; at the most a lo más *a lo mas*; to make the most of aprovechar al máximo *a·pro·be·char al mak·see·mo*

motel n el motel *mo·tel*

moth n la mariposa nocturna *ma·ree·po·sa nok·toor·na*

mother n la madre *ma·dre*

mother-in-law n la suegra *swe·gra*

motion n (movement) el movimiento *mo·bee·myen·to*

motor n el motor *mo·tor*

motorbike n la motocicleta *mo·to·thee·kle·ta*

motorboat n la lancha motora *lan·cha mo·to·ra*

motorcyclist n el/la motociclista *mo·to·thee·klees·ta*

motorist n el/la automovilista *ow·to·mo·bee·lees·ta*

mount vt montar *mon·tar*

mountain n la montaña *mon·tan·ya*

mountaineering n el alpinismo *al·pee·nees·mo*, el andinismo (Am) *an·dee·nees·mô*; to go mountaineering hacer* alpinismo *a·ther al·pee·nees·mo*

mouse n el ratón *ra·ton*, el pericote (Am) *pe·ree·ko·te*

mousse n la crema batida *kre·ma ba·tee·da*

mouth n la boca *bo·ka*; (of animal) la boca *bo·ka*

move vt mover* *mo·ber* □ **vi** moverse *mo·ber·se*; (traffic) circular *theer·koo·lar*; to move in instalarse *eens·ta·lar·se*; to move out cambiarse de casa *kam·byar·se de ka·sa*

movement n el movimiento *mo·bee·myen·to*

movie n la película *pe·lee·koo·la* L36

movie camera n la cámara cinematográfica *ka·ma·ra thee·ne·ma·to·gra·fee·ka*

moving van n el camión de mudanzas *ka·myon de moo·dan·thas*

moving walkway n el pasillo mecánico *pa·seel·yo me·ka·nee·ko*

mow vt cortar *kor·tar*

mower n el cortacésped *kor·ta·thes·ped*

Mr n Señor (m) *sen·yor*

Mrs n Señora (f) *sen·yo·ra*

Ms n Señora (f) *sen·yo·ra*

much adv □ much better mucho mejor *moo·cho me·khor*; much bigger mucho más grande *moo·cho mas gran·de* □ **adj** much milk mucha leche *moo·cha le·che* □ **pron** have you got much? ¿tiene Ud mucho? *tye·ne oos·ted moo·cho*; not much no mucho *no moo·cho*

mud n el barro *ba·rro*

muddle n la confusión *kon·foo·syon*; in a muddle en desorden *en des·or·den*

muddy adj (water) fangoso(a) *fan·go·so(a)*; (clothes) lleno(a) de barro *lye·no(a) de ba·rro*

mud-flap n el parabarros *pa·ra·ba·rros*

mudguard n el guardabarros *gwar·da·ba·rros*

muffler n (on car) el silenciador *see·len·thya·dor*

mug n el tazón *ta·thon* □ **vt** asaltar *a·sal·tar*

multilevel adj de pisos *de pee·sos*

multilingual adj multilingüe *mool·tee·leen·gwe*

multinational adj multinacional *mool·tee·na·thyon·al*

multiple store n la sucursal *soo·koor·sal*

multiplication n la multiplicación *mool·tee·plee·ka·thyon*

multiply vt multiplicar* *mool·tee·plee·kar*; to multiply 9 by 4 multiplicar 9 por 4 *mool·tee·plee·kar 9 por 4*

mumps n las paperas *pa·pe·ras*

Munich n Munich (m) *moo·neech*

municipal adj municipal *moo·nee·thee·pal*

murder n el asesinato *a·se·see·na·to* □ **vt** asesinar *a·se·see·nar*

muscle n el músculo *moos·koo·lo*

museum n el museo *moo·se·o* F11, L4, I3

mushroom n el champiñón *cham·peen·yon*, el hongo (Am) *on·go*

music n la música *moo·see·ka* L34

musician n el/la músico(a) *moo·see·ko(a)*

Muslim adj musulmán(mana) *moo·sool·man(·na)* □ n el/la musulmán(mana) *moo·sool·man(·ma·na)*

mussel n el mejillón *me·kheel·yon*, la almeja (Am) *al·me·kha*

must vi □ I must go tengo que irme *ten·go ke eer·me*; you must come Ud tiene que venir *oos·ted tye·ne ke be·neer*

mustard n la mostaza *mos·ta·tha*

mutton n el cordero *kor·de·ro*, el carnero (Am) *kar·ne·ro*

my adj mi *mee*, mis *mees*; my father mi padre *mee pa·dre*; my mother mi madre *mee ma·dre*; my brothers/sisters mis hermanos/hermanas *mees er·ma·nos/er·ma·nas*

myself pron yo mismo(a) *yo mees·mo(a)*; I washed myself me lavé *me la·be*; I did it myself lo hice yo mismo *lo ee·the yo mees·mo*

mystery n el misterio *mees·te·ryo*

N

nail n (human) la uña *oon·ya*; (metal) el clavo *kla·bo* □ **vt** clavar *kla·bar*

nailbrush n el cepillo de uñas *the·peel·yo de oon·yas*

nailfile n la lima de uñas *lee·ma de oon·yas*

nail polish n el esmalte para uñas *es·mal·te pa·ra oon·yas*

naked adj desnudo(a) *des·noo·do(a)*

name n el nombre *nom·bre*; what is your name? ¿cómo se llama? *ko·mo se lya·ma*; my name is Paul me llamo Paul *me lya·mo Paul* B11

nap n (sleep) el sueñecito *swen·ye·thee·to*

napkin n (for table) la servilleta *ser·beel·ye·ta*

narrow adj estrecho(a) *es·tre·cho(a)*

nasty adj malo(a) *ma·lo(a)*

nation n la nación *na·thyon*

national adj nacional *na·thyo·nal*; national anthem el himno nacional *eem·no na·thyo·nal*; national dress el vestido nacional *bes·tee·do na·thyo·nal*

nationality n la nacionalidad *na·thyo·na·lee·dad*

nationalize vt nacionalizar* *na·thyo·na·lee·thar*

native adj nacional *na·thyo·nal*

natural adj natural *na·too·ral*

naturalized adj naturalizado(a) *na·too·ra·lee·tha·do(u)*

naturally adv (of course) naturalmente *na·too·ral·men·te*

nature n la naturaleza *na·too·ra·le·tha*; (character) el carácter *ka·rak·ter*; (type, sort) el tipo *tee·po*

naughty adj travieso(a) *tra·bye·so(a)*

nausea n la náusea *now·se·a*

nave n la nave *na·be*

navy n la marina *ma·ree·na*

navy blue adj azul marino *a·thool ma·ree·no*

near adv cerca *ther·ka* □ prep near (to) the house cerca de la casa *ther·ka de la ka·sa*; near (to) Christmas cerca de Navidades *ther·ca de na·bee·da·des*

nearby adv cerca *ther·ka*

nearly adv casi *ka·see*

nearsighted adj miope *mee·o·pe*

neat adj (appearance) pulcro(a) *pool·kro(a)*; (room) ordenado(a) *or·de·na·do(a)*; (liquor) sin agua *seen ag·wa*

necessary adj necesario(a) *ne·the·sa·ryo(a)*

neck n el cuello *kwel·yo*

necklace n el collar *kol·yar*

necktie n la corbata *kor·ba·ta*

need vt necesitar *ne·the·see·tar*; I need to go tengo que ir *teng·go ke eer*; you needn't come no tienes que venir *no tye·nes ke be·neer* S9

needle n la aguja *a·goo·kha*

negative n (of photo) el negativo *ne·ga·tee·bo*

negotiable adj negociable *ne·go·thya·ble*

negotiate vi negociar *ne·go·thyar*

negotiations pl las negociaciones *ne·go·thya·thyo·nes*

neighbor n el/la vecino(a) *be·thee·no(a)*

neighborhood n la vecindad *be·theen·dad*

neither pron ninguno(a) *neen·goo·no(a)* □ adv neither ... nor ni ... ni *nee ... nee* □ conj I wasn't there and neither was he no estuve allí ni él tampoco *no es·too·be al·yee nee el tam·po·ko*

nephew n el sobrino *so·bree·no*

nerve n el nervio *ner·byo*; (courage) el coraje *ko·ra·khe*

nervous adj (person) nervioso(a) *ner·*

**byo·so(a)*; nervous breakdown la crisis nerviosa *kree·sees ner·byo·sa*

nest n el nido *nee·do*

net n la red *red* □ adj (income, price) neto *ne·to*; net weight peso neto *pe·so ne·to*

neutral adj neutral *ne·oo·tral* □ n (gear) el punto muerto *poon·to mwer·to*

never adv nunca *noon·ka*; he never comes no viene nunca *no bye·ne noon·ka*

new adj nuevo(a) *nwe·bo(a)*

news n las nuevas *nwe·bas*; (on radio, TV) las noticias *no·tee·thyas*

newsdealer n el vendedor de periódicos *ben·de·dor de pe·ree·o·dee·kos*

newspaper n el periódico *pe·ree·o·dee·ko* S93

newsstand n el quiosco de periódicos *kee·os·ko de pe·ree·o·dee·kos*

New Year's Day n el año nuevo *an·yo nwe·bo*

New Year's Eve n la nochevieja *no·che·bye·kha*

next adj (stop, station, week) próximo(a) *prok·see·mo(a)*; next of kin el pariente más cercano *pa·ryen·te mas ther·ka·no*

nice adj (place, holiday) bonito(a) *bo·nee·to(a)*; (person) simpático(a) *seem·pa·tee·ko(a)*; (dress, picture) bonito(a) *bo·nee·to(a)*

niece n la sobrina *so·bree·na*

night n la noche *no·che* A8

night club n el cabaret *ka·ba·ret* L36

nightgown n el camisón *ka·mee·son*

nightmare n la pesadilla *pe·sa·deel·ya*

night porter n el portero de noche *por·te·ro de no·che*

night school n la escuela nocturna *es·kwe·la nok·toor·na*

nil n el cero *the·ro*

nine num nueve *nwe·be*

nineteen num diecinueve *dye·thee·nwe·be*

ninety num noventa *no·ben·ta*

ninth adj noveno(a) *no·be·no(a)*

nipple n (on bottle) la tetilla *te·teel·ya*

no adv (as answer) no *no*

nobody pron nadie *na·dye*; I can see nobody no veo a nadie *no be·o a na·dye*

noise n el ruido *rwee·do*; (loud) el estrépito *es·tre·pee·to*, la bulla (Am) *bool·ya*

noisy adj ruidoso(a) *rwee·do·so(a)*

nominal adj (fee) nominal *no·mee·nal*

non- pref no *no*

nonalcoholic adj no alcohólico(a) *no al·ko·lee·ko(a)*

none pron ninguno(a) *neen·goo·no(a)*

nonsense n las tonterías *ton·te·ree·as*

nonsmoker n (person) el no fumador *no foo·ma·dor*; (compartment) el departamento para no fumadores *de·par·ta·men·to pa·ra no foo·ma·do·res*

noodles pl los tallarines *tal·ya·ree·nes*

noon n el mediodía *me·dyo·dee·a*

no one pron nadie *na·dye*; I can see no one no veo a nadie *no be·o a na·dye*

normal adj normal *nor·mal*

normally adv (usually) normalmente *nor·mal·men·te*

north n el norte *nor·te* □ adv hacia el norte *a·thya el nor·te*

North America n Norteamérica (f) *nor·te·a·me·ree·ka*

northeast n el noreste *no·res·te*

northern adj del norte *del nor·te*

North Pole n el Polo Norte *po·lo nor·te*

North Sea n el Mar del Norte *mar del nor·te*

northwest n el noroeste *no·ro·es·te*

nose n la nariz *na·reeth*

nosebleed n la hemorragia nasal *e·mo·rra·khya na·sal*

not adv no no; **he did not** or **didn't do it** no lo hizo *no lo ee·tho*; **not at all** nada *na·da*; (don't mention it) de nada *de na·da*

note n (music) la nota *no·ta*; (letter) el recado *re·ka·do*; (banknote) el billete *beel·ye·te* M20f

notepaper n el papel para cartas *pa·pel pa·ra kar·tas* A41, S94

nothing n la nada *na·da*

notice n (poster) el anuncio *a·noon·thyo*; (sign) el letrero *le·tre·ro* □ vt notar *no·tar*

notions pl la mercería *mer·the·ree·a*

nougat n el turrón *too·rron*

nought n el cero *the·ro*

novel n (book) la novela *no·be·la*

November n noviembre (m) *no·byem·bre*

now adv ahora *a·o·ra*; **now and then, now and again** de vez en cuando *de beth en kwan·do*

nowadays adv hoy en día *oy en dee·a*

nowhere adv en ninguna parte *en neen·goo·na par·te*

nuclear adj (energy, war) nuclear *noo·kle·ar*

nude adj desnudo(a) *des·noo·do(a)*

nuisance n el fastidio *fas·tee·dyo*; **he's a nuisance** es muy pesado *es mooy pe·sa·do*

null and void adj nulo y sin efecto *noo·lo ee seen e·fek·to*

numb adj (with cold) entumecido(a) *en·too·me·thee·do(a)*

number n (figure) el número *noo·me·ro* Sn13

nun n la monja *mon·kha*

nurse n la enfermera *en·fer·me·ra* □ vt (patient) cuidar *kwee·dar*

nursery n el cuarto de los niños *kwar·to de los neen·yos*

nursing home n la clínica de reposo *klee·nee·ka de re·po·so*

nylon n el nylon *nay·lon*

O

oak n el roble *ro·ble*

oar n el remo *re·mo*

oats pl la avena *a·be·na*

obedient adj obediente *o·be·dyen·te*

obey vi obedecer* *o·be·de·ther* □ vt to obey someone obedecer a alguien *o·be·de·ther a al·gyen*

object[1] n el objeto *ob·khe·to*

object[2] vi □ to object to a remark protestar contra una observación *pro·tes·tar kon·tra oo·na ob·ser·ba·thyon*

objective n el objetivo *ob·khe·tee·bo*

obligation n la obligación *o·blee·ga·thyon*

oblong adj oblongo(a) *o·blon·go(a)*

obscure adj oscuro(a) *os·koo·ro(a)*

obsession n la obsesión *ob·se·syon*

obstacle n el obstáculo *obs·ta·koo·lo*

obtain vt obtener* *ob·te·ner*

obvious adj evidente *e·bee·den·te*

obviously adv evidentemente *e·bee·den·te·men·te*

occasion n la oportunidad *o·por·too·nee·dad*; (special event) la ocasión *o·ka·syon*

occasional adj (event) poco frecuente *po·ko fre·kwen·te*

occasionally adv de vez en cuando *de beth en kwan·do*

occupation n (job) el oficio *o·fee·thyo*

occur vi (happen) suceder* *soo·the·der*

ocean n el océano *o·the·a·no*

o'clock adv □ at 3 o'clock a las 3 *a las 3*; it's 4 o'clock son las 4 *son las 4*

October n octubre (m) *ok·too·bre*

odd adj (number) impar *eem·par*; (strange) extraño(a) *eks·tran·yo(a)*

odds pl (in betting) los puntos de ventaja *poon·tos de ben·ta·kha*

odometer n el cuentakilómetros *kwen·ta·kee·lo·me·tros*

of prep de *de*; **a friend of mine** un(a) amigo(a) mío(a) *oo·n(a) a·mee·go(a) mee·o(a)*; **3 of them** 3 de ellos *3 de el·yos*; **14th of June** el 14 de junio *el 14 de khoo·nyo*; **made of stone** de piedra *de pye·dra*

of course adv por supuesto *por soo·pwes·to*

off adj (machine) apagado(a) *a·pa·ga·do(a)*; (radio) desenchufado(a) *des·en·choo·fa·do(a)*; (water supply) cerrado(a) *the·rra·do(a)*; (light) apagado(a) *a·pa·ga·do(a)* □ adv **a day off** un día libre *oon dee·a lee·bre*; **3% off** un descuento del 3% *oon des·kwen·to del 3 por thyen·to*; **6 kilometers off** a 6 kilómetros *a 6 kee·lo·me·tros* □ prep to fall off a wall caerse* de una pared *ka·er·se de oo·na pa·red*; **off the main road** alejado(a) de la carretera *a·le·kha·do de la ka·rre·te·ra*

offend vt ofender *o·fen·der*

offer vt ofrecer* *o·fre·ther*; **to offer to do something** ofrecer* hacer algo *o·fre·ther a·ther al·go* □ n offer la oferta *o·fer·ta*

office n la oficina *o·fee·thee·na*; (doctor's) el consultorio *kon·sool·to·ryo* T52

office-block n el bloque de oficinas *blo·ke de o·fee·thee·nas*

office hours pl las horas de trabajo *o·ras de tra·ba·kho*

officer n (in army etc) el oficial *o·fee·thyal*; (police) el policía *po·lee·thee·a*

office worker n el/la oficinista *o·fee·thee·nees·ta*

official adj oficial *o·fee·thyal*

off-season adj fuera de temporada *fwe·ra de tem·po·ra·da*

offshore adj (island) a poca distancia de la costa *a po·ka dees·tan·thya de la kos·ta*; **offshore sailing** la navegación costera *na·be·ga·thyon kos·te·ra*

often adv a menudo *a me·noo·do*

oil n (edible, car etc) el aceite *a·they·te*; (petroleum) el petróleo *pe·tro·le·o* T160

oil filter n el filtro de aceite *feel·tro de a·they·te*

oil pan n (in car) el cárter *kar·ter*

oil-rig n la plataforma de petróleo *pla·ta·for·ma de pe·tro·le·o*

oil tanker n el petrolero *pe·tro·le·ro*

ointment n el ungüento *oon·gwen·to*

O.K., okay adv (agreement) de acuerdo *a·kwer·do*; it's OK vale *ba·le*

old adj viejo(a) *bye·kho(a)*; **how old are you?** ¿cuántos años tiene? *kwan·tos an·yos tye·ne*

old-fashioned adj pasado(a) de moda *pa·sa·do(a) de mo·da*

olive n la aceituna *a·they·too·na*

olive oil *n* el aceite de oliva *a·they·te de o·lee·ba*

omelet *n* la tortilla *tor·teel·ya*

on *adj* (*machine*) en marcha *en mar·cha*; (*light, radio*) encendido(a) *en·then·dee·do(a)*; (*water supply*) abierto(a) *a·byer·to(a)*; **when is the movie on?** ¿cuándo ponen la película? *kwan·do po·nen la pe·lee·koo·la* □ *prep* on sobre *so·bre*; **on the table** sobre la mesa *so·bre la me·sa*; **on the train** en el tren *en el tren*; **on the wall** en la pared *en la pa·red*; **on the left/right** a la izquierda/derecha *a la eeth·kyer·da/de·re·cha*; **come on Friday** venga el viernes *ben·ga el byer·nes*; **on television** en la televisión *en la te·le·bee·syon*

once *adv* una vez *oo·na beth*; (*formerly*) antes *an·tes*; **once more** una vez más *oo·na beth mas*

one *num* uno(a) *oo·no(a)*; **one day un día** *oon dee·a* □ *pron* which one cuál *kwal*; **the one on the table** el que está en la mesa *el ke es·ta en la me·sa*; **this one** éste(a) *es·te(a)*; **one should...** uno debería *oo·no de·be·ree·a*; **one another** el uno al otro *el oo·no al o·tro*

one-armed bandit *n* la máquina tragaperras *ma·kee·na tra·ga·pe·rras*

one-day excursion *n* el billete de ida y vuelta en un día *beel·ye·te de ee·da ee bwel·ta en oon dee·a* L88

oneself *pron* uno(a) mismo(a) *oo·no(a) mees·mo(a)*; **to dress oneself** vestirse *bes·teer·se*

one-way street *n* la calle de dirección única *kal·ye de dee·rek·thyon oo·nee·ka*

one-way ticket *n* el billete de ida *beel·ye·te de ee·da* T60

onion *n* la cebolla *the·bol·ya*

only *adv* sólo *so·lo*; **there are only 4** sólo hay 4 *so·lo ay 4* □ *adj* **the only woman there** la única mujer allí *la oo·nee·ka moo·kher al·yee*; **an only child** un hijo único *oon ee·kho oo·nee·ko*; **not only** no sólo *no so·lo*

onto *prep* encima de *en·thee·ma de*

OPEC *n* la OPEP *o·pep*

open *adj* abierto(a) *a·byer·to(a)* □ *vt* (*window etc*) abrir* *a·breer* □ *vi* (*store, bank*) abrir* *a·breer*; (*play*) estrenarse *es·tre·nar·se* B62, L13

open-air *adj* al aire libre *al ay·re lee·bre*

open-plan *adj* sin tabiques *seen ta·bee·kes*

opera *n* la ópera *o·pe·ra*

operate *vt* (*machine*) hacer* funcionar *a·ther foon·thyo·nar*

operation *n* la operación *o·pe·ra·thyon*

operator *n* él/la telefonista *te·le·fo·nees·ta*

opinion *n* la opinión *o·pee·nyon*; **in my opinion** según mi opinión *se·goon mee o·pee·nyon*

opportunity *n* la oportunidad *o·por·too·nee·dad*

opposite *adv* en frente *en fren·te*; **the house opposite** la casa de enfrente *la ka·sa de en·fren·te*; **the opposite sex** el sexo opuesto *el sek·so o·pwes·to* □ *n* **opposite** el contrario *kon·tra·ryo* □ *prep* enfrente de *en·fren·te de*

optician *n* el óptico *op·tee·ko*

optimistic *adj* optimista *op·tee·mees·ta*

option *n* la opción *op·thyon*

or *conj* o *o*

orange *n* la naranja *na·ran·kha* □ *adj* color naranja *ko·lor na·ran·kha*

orangeade *n* la naranjada *na·ran·kha·da*

orange juice *n* el zumo de naranja *thoo·mo de na·ran·kha*

orchard *n* la huerta *wer·ta*

orchestra *n* la orquesta *or·kes·ta*; (*in theater*) la platea *pla·te·a*

order *n* (*in series*) el orden *or·den*; (*command*) la orden *or·den*; (*for goods*) el pedido *pe·dee·do*; **out of order** (*machine*) estropeado(a) *es·tro·pe·a·do(a)*, malogrado(a) (Am) *ma·lo·gra·do(a)*; **in order to do something** para hacer algo *pa·ra a·ther al·go* □ *vt* order (*goods, meal*) encargar* *en·kar·gar*

order-form *n* la hoja de pedido *o·kha de pe·dee·do*

ordinary *adj* corriente *ko·rryen·te*

organ *n* (*instrument*) el órgano *or·ga·no*

organization *n* la organización *or·ga·nee·tha·thyon*

organize *vt* organizar* *or·ga·nee·thar*

oriental *adj* oriental *o·ryen·tal*

origin *n* el origen *o·ree·khen*

original *adj* original *o·ree·khee·nal* □ *n* el original *o·ree·khee·nal*

originally *adv* (*at first*) al principio *al preen·thee·pyo*

ornament *n* el ornamento *or·na·men·to*

orphan *n* el/la huérfano(a) *wer·fa·no(a)*

other *adj* otro(a) *o·tro(a)*; **the other day** el otro día *el o·tro dee·a* □ *pron* **the other** el/la otro(a) *el/la o·tro(a)* S13

otherwise *adv* de otra manera *de o·tra ma·ne·ra*; **otherwise engaged** ocupado(a) con otra cosa *o·koo·pa·do(a) kon o·tra ko·sa*

ought *vi* **I ought to do it** debería hacerlo *de·be·ree·a a·ther·lo*; **he ought to win** debe ganar *de·be ga·nar*; **that ought to do that** debe bastar *e·so de·be bas·tar*

ounce *n* la onza *on·tha*

our *adj* nuestro(a), nuestros(as) *nwes·tro(a) nwes·tros(as)*; **our father** nuestro padre *nwes·tro pa·dre*; **our mother** nuestra madre *nwes·tra ma·dre*; **our brothers/sisters** nuestros hermanos/nuestras hermanas *nwes·tros(as) er·ma·nos(as)*

ours *pron* el/la nuestro(a) *el/la nwes·tro(a)*; (*plural*) los nuestros *los nwes·tros*, las nuestras *las nwes·tras*

ourselves *pron* nosotros(as) mismos(as) *no·so·tros(as) mees·mos(as)*; **we dressed ourselves** nos vestimos *nos bes·tee·mos*

out *adv* (*not at home*) fuera *fwe·ra*; (*team, player*) eliminado(a) *e·lee·mee·na·do(a)*; **the tide is out** la marea está baja *la ma·re·a es·ta ba·kha*; **the sun is out** el sol está brillando *el sol es·ta breel·yan·do*; **the light is out** la luz está apagada *la looth es·ta a·pa·ga·da* □ *prep* out of (*outside*) fuera de *fwe·ra de*; **to be out of gasoline** no tener gasolina *no te·ner ga·so·lee·na*; **made out of wood** de madera *de ma·de·ra*; **he ran out of the house** salió corriendo de la casa *sa·lyo ko·rryen·do de la ka·sa*

outboard *adj* fuera de borda *fwe·ra de bor·da*

outdoor *adj* al aire libre *al ay·re lee·bre*

outdoors adv fuera *fwe·ra*
outfit n (clothes) el traje *tra·khe*
outing n la excursión *eks·koor·syon*
outlet n (electric) la salida *sa·lee·da*
outline n (summary) el resumen *re·soo·men*
outlook n la perspectiva *pers·pek·tee·ba*
out-of-date adj (passport, ticket) caducado(a) *ka·doo·ka·do(a)*
output n la producción *pro·dook·thyon*
outside n el exterior *eks·te·ryor*; the outside wall el muro exterior *el moo·ro eks·te·ryor*; the outside lane (in road) el carril de la izquierda *el ka·rreel de la eeth·kyer·da* □ prep outside the house fuera de la casa *fwe·ra de la ka·sa* □ adv to be outside estar* fuera *es·tar fwe·ra*; to go outside salir* *sa·leer*
outsize adj (clothes) de talla grande *de tal·ya gran·de*
outskirts pl las afueras *a·fwe·ras*
oval adj ovalado(a) *o·ba·la·do(a)*
oven n el horno *or·no*
over adv □ to fall over caerse* *ka·er·se*; to knock over derribar *de·rree·bar*; to turn something over volver* algo *bol·ber al·go*; come over here venga aquí *ben·ga a·kee*; he's over here on holiday está aquí de vacaciones *es·ta a·kee de ba·ka·thyo·nes*; the match is over se acabó el partido *se a·ka·bo el par·tee·do* □ prep to jump over something saltar algo *sal·tar al·go*; it weighs over a kilo pesa más de un kilo *pe·sa mas de oon kee·lo*
overall n el mono *mo·no*
overalls pl el mono *mo·no*
overcoat n el abrigo *a·bree·go*
overdose n la sobredosis *so·bre·do·sees*
overdraft n el saldo deudor *sal·do dew·dor*
overdrive n la sobremarcha *so·bre·mar·cha*
overexposed adj (photo) sobreexpuesto(a) *so·bre·eks·pwes·to(a)*
overhead adj (railway) elevado(a) *e·le·ba·do(a)* □ adv de arriba *de a·rree·ba* □ n los gastos generales *gas·tos khe·ne·ra·les*
overheat vi (engine) recalentarse* *re·ka·len·tar·se*
overnight adj (a stay) de una noche de *oo·na no·che* □ adv (happen) durante la noche *doo·ran·te la no·che*
overpass n el paso superior *pa·so soo·pe·ryor*
overseas adv en el extranjero *en el eks·tran·khe·ro* □ adj (market) de ultramar *de ool·tra·mar*; (visitor) extranjero(a) *eks·tran·khe·ro(a)*
overtime n las horas extraordinarias *o·ras eks·tra·or·dee·na·ryas*; to work overtime trabajar horas extraordinarias *tra·ba·khar o·ras eks·tra·or·dee·na·ryas*
overture n la obertura *o·ber·too·ra*
overweight adj (baggage, person) demasiado pesado(a) *de·ma·sya·do pe·sa·do(a)*
owe vt (money) deber* *de·ber*; he owes me $5 me debe $5 *me de·be $5*
own adj propio(a) *pro·pyo(a)* □ n he did it on his own lo hizo solo *lo e·tho so·lo* □ vt own (possess) poseer *po·se·er*
owner n el/la propietario(a) *pro·pye·ta·ryo(a)*
ownership n la posesión *po·se·syon*
oxygen n el oxígeno *ok·see·khe·no*

oyster n la ostra *os·tra*

pace n el paso *pa·so*; to keep pace with llevar el mismo paso que *lye·bar el mees·mo pa·so ke*
Pacific Ocean n el Océano Pacífico *o·the·a·no pa·thee·fee·ko*
pacifier n el chupete *choo·pe·te*, el chupón (Am) *choo·pon*
pack vt (goods) envasar *en·ba·sar*; to pack one's suitcase hacer* la maleta *a·ther la ma·le·ta* □ n pack el paquete *pa·ke·te*; (of cards) la baraja *ba·ra·kha*
package n el paquete *pa·ke·te* S33, 100
package deal n el acuerdo global *a·kwer·do glo·bal*
package holiday n el viaje organizado *bee·a·khe or·ga·nee·tha·do*
packet n el paquete *pa·ke·te* S33
packing n (material) el embalaje *em·ba·la·khe*
packing case n el cajón de embalaje *ka·khon de em·ba·la·khe*
pad n (notepaper) el bloc *el blok*
paddle n (oar) el canalete *ka·na·le·te*; (table tennis etc) la raqueta *ra·ke·ta* □ vi chapotear *cha·po·te·ar*
padlock n el candado *kan·da·do*
page n la página *pa·khee·na* □ vt hacer* llamar *a·ther lya·mar*
pageboy n el botones *bo·to·nes*
paid adj (vacation) pagado(a) *pa·ga·do(a)*
pail n el cubo *koo·bo*
pain n el dolor *do·lor* I30, 31
painful adj doloroso(a) *do·lo·ro·so(a)*
painkiller n el calmante *kal·man·te*
paint n la pintura *peen·too·ra* □ vt pintar *peen·tar*
painter n el pintor *peen·tor*; (decorator) el pintor (de brocha gorda) *peen·tor (de bro·cha gor·da)*
painting n (picture) el cuadro *kwa·dro*
pair n el par *par*; (of people) la pareja *pa·re·kha*; pair of shoes par de zapatos *par de tha·pa·tos*; pair of scissors las tijeras *tee·khe·ras*; pair of trousers los pantalones *pan·ta·lo·nes*
pajamas pl el pijama *pee·kha·ma*
Pakistan n Pakistán (m) *pa·kees·tan*
Pakistani adj pakistaní *pa·kees·ta·nee*
palace n el palacio *pa·la·thyo*
pale adj (face) pálido(a) *pa·lee·do(a)*; (color) claro(a) *kla·ro(a)*
Palestine n Palestina (f) *pa·les·tee·na*
Palestinian adj palestino(a) *pa·les·tee·no(a)*
palm n (of hand) la palma *pal·ma*
palm-tree n la palmera *pal·me·ra*
pan n (saucepan) la cazuela *ka·thwe·la*; (frying pan) la sartén *sar·ten*
Panama n Panamá (m) *pa·na·ma*
Panamanian adj panameño(a) *pa·na·men·yo(a)*
pancake n la hojuela *o·khwe·la*, el panqueque (Am) *pan·ke·ke*
pane n el cristal *krees·tal*
panic n el pánico *pa·nee·ko*; in a panic aterrado(a) *a·te·rra·do(a)* □ vi panic aterrarse *a·te·rrar·se*
pant vi jadear *kha·de·ar*
panties pl las bragas *bra·gas*
pantomime n el espectáculo musical de Navidad *es·pek·ta·koo·lo moo·see·kal de na·bee·dad*
pants pl los pantalones *pan·ta·lo·nes*; (undergarment: men's) los calzonzi-

llos kal·thon·theel·yos; (women's) las bragas bra·gas

pant(s) suit n el traje-pantalón tra·khe·pan·ta·lon

panty hose n los pantys pan·tees

paper n el papel pa·pel; (newspaper) el periódico pe·ree·o·dee·ko; papers (passport etc) la documentación do·koo·men·ta·thyon □ vt paper (wall) empapelar em·pa·pe·lar

paperback n el libro de bolsillo lee·bro de bol·seel·yo S96

paprika n el pimentón pee·men·ton

par n (golf) el par par; (business) la par par; **above par** por encima de la par por en·thee·ma de la par

parachute n el paracaídas pa·ra·ka·ee·das

parade n el desfile des·fee·le

paragraph n el párrafo pa·rra·fo

parallel adj paralelo(a) pa·ra·le·lo(a)

paralyzed adj paralizado(a) pa·ra·lee·tha·do(a)

parasol n el quitasol kee·ta·sol

parcel n el paquete pa·ke·te Sn4

pardon excl perdón per·don; pardon me!, (I beg your) pardon! ¡perdone Ud! per·do·ne oos·ted

parents pl los padres pa·dres

Paris n Paris (m) pa·rees

Parisian adj parisino(a) pa·ree·see·no(a)

park n el parque par·ke □ vt aparcar* a·par·kar □ vi can I park here? ¿se puede aparcar aquí? se pwe·de a·par·kar a·kee T117f

parka n el anorak a·no·rak

parking disk n el disco de estacionamiento dees·ko de es·ta·thyo·na·myen·to T125

parking lights pl las luces de estacionamiento loo·thes de es·ta·thyo·na·myen·to T127

parking lot n el aparcamiento a·par·ka·myen·to T120

parking meter n el parquímetro par·kee·me·tro

parking ticket n la multa por aparcamiento indebido mool·ta por a·par·ka·myen·to een·de·bee·do

parliament n el parlamento par·la·men·to

Parmesan n el parmesano par·me·sa·no

parsley n el perejil pe·re·kheel

parsnip n la chirivía chee·ree·bee·a

part n la parte par·te; (of machine) la pieza pye·tha; (in hair) la raya ra·ya; (in play) el papel pa·pel □ vt (separate) dividir dee·bee·deer Mc12, Sn44

participate vi participar par·tee·thee·par

participation n la participación par·tee·thee·pa·thyon

particular adj particular par·tee·koo·lar; (special) especial es·pe·thyal □ n **in particular** en particular en par·tee·koo·lar

particularly adv especialmente es·pe·thyal·men·te

partition n (wall) el tabique ta·bee·ke

partly adv en parte en par·te

partner n (in business) el socio so·thyo; (dancing) la pareja pa·re·kha

partridge n la perdiz per·deeth

part-time adj de media jornada de me·dya khor·na·da

party n (celebration) la fiesta fyes·ta; (group) el grupo groo·po; (political) el partido par·tee·do T5f, S58

pass n (permit) el permiso per·mee·so;

(in mountains) el puerto pwer·to □ vt pasar pa·sar; (car) adelantar a·de·lan·tar; (exam) aprobar* a·pro·bar; **please pass the sugar** hágame el favor de pasarme el azúcar a·ga·me el fa·bor de pa·sar·me el a·thoo·kar

passage n el pasillo pa·seel·yo

passenger n el/la pasajero(a) pa·sa·khe·ro(a)

passenger seat n el asiento del pasajero a·syen·to del pa·sa·khe·ro

passion n la pasión pa·syon

passport n el pasaporte pa·sa·por·te T11f, L54, SN86

past adj pasado(a) pa·sa·do(a) □ n el pasado pa·sa·do □ adv to run past pasar corriendo pa·sar ko·rryen·do □ prep **he ran past me** me pasó corriendo me pa·so ko·rryen·do; **he's past forty** tiene más de 40 años tye·ne mas de 40 an·yos

pasta n la pasta pas·ta

paste n (glue) el engrudo en·groo·do; **meat paste** el pastel de carne pas·tel de kar·ne

pasteurized adj pasteurizado(a) pas·te·oo·ree·tha·do(a)

pastille n la pastilla pas·teel·ya

pastry n la pasta pas·ta; (cake) la pastelería pas·te·le·ree·a

pat vt acariciar a·ka·ree·thyar

patch n (of material) el remiendo re·myen·do; (for eye) el parche par·che; (spot) la mancha man·cha

pâté n el paté pa·te

patent n la patente pa·ten·te

patent leather n el charol cha·rol

path n el camino ka·mee·no

patience n la paciencia pa·thyen·thya

patient adj paciente pa·thyen·te □ n el/la paciente pa·thyen·te

patio n el patio pa·tyo

pattern n el diseño dee·sen·yo; (dressmaking, knitting) el patrón pa·tron

pause n la pausa pow·sa □ vi detenerse* de·te·ner·se

pavement n (sidewalk) la acera a·the·ra, la vereda (Am) be·re·da; (roadway) la calzada kal·tha·da

paw n la pata pa·ta

pay n el sueldo swel·do □ vt pagar* pa·gar; **to pay back** (money) reembolsar re·em·bol·sar; **to pay for** pagar* pa·gar; **to pay off** (workers) despedir* des·pe·deer

payable adj pagadero(a) pa·ga·de·ro(a)

payee n el beneficiario be·ne·fee·thya·ryo

paying guest n el huésped que paga wes·ped ke pa·ga

payment n el pago pa·go

payroll n la nómina no·mee·na

peace n la paz path; (calm) la tranquilidad tran·kee·lee·dad

peaceful adj tranquilo(a) tran·kee·lo(a)

peach n el melocotón me·lo·ko·ton

peak n (of cap) la visera bee·se·ra; (of mountain) el pico pee·ko

peak hours pl las horas punta o·ras poon·ta

peanut n el cacahuete ka·ka·we·te

pear n la pera pe·ra

pearl n la perla per·la

peas pl los guisantes gee·san·tes S34

pebble n el guijarro gee·kha·rro

peck vt picotear pee·ko·te·ar

peculiar adj (strange) extraño(a) eks·tran·yo(a)

pedal n el pedal pe·dal

pedalo n el hidropedal ee·dro·pe·dal

pedestrian *n* el peatón *pe·a·ton*
pedestrian crossing *n* el paso de peatones *pa·so de pe·a·to·nes*
pedestrian precinct *n* la zona reservada para peatones *tho·na re·ser·ba·da pa·ra pe·a·to·nes*
pediatrician *n* el/la pediatra *pe·dya·tra*
peel *vt* pelar *pe·lar* □ *vi* (*person*) pelarse *pe·lar·se* □ *n* las peladuras *pe·la·doo·ras*
peg *n* la estaca *es·ta·ka*; (*for coat*) la percha *per·cha*
pen *n* la pluma *ploo·ma* B54
pencil *n* el lápiz *la·peeth* S8
penetrate *vt* penetrar *pe·ne·trar*
penicillin *n* la penicilina *pe·nee·thee·lee·na*
penis *n* el pene *pe·ne*
penknife *n* la navaja *na·ba·kha*
pen pal *n* el/la amigo(a) por correspondencia *a·mee·go(a) por ko·rres·pon·den·thya*
pension *n* (*from State*) la pensión *pen·syon*; (*from company*) la jubilación *khoo·bee·la·thyon*
pensioner *n* el jubilado *khoo·bee·la·do*
pension fund *n* la caja de jubilaciones *ka·kha de khoo·bee·la·thyo·nes*
penthouse *n* el ático *a·tee·ko*
people *pl* la gente *khen·te* Mc14, 21
pepper *n* la pimienta *pee·myen·ta*; (*capsicum*) el pimiento *pee·myen·to*; green/red pepper el pimiento verde/rojo *pee·myen·to ber·de/ro·kho*
peppermint *n* (*confectionery*) el caramelo de menta *ka·ra·me·lo de men·ta*; (*plant*) la menta *men·ta*
pepper pot *n* el pimentero *pee·men·te·ro*
peppery *adj* picante *pee·kan·te*
per *prep* por *por*; 100 km per hour 100 km por hora *100 kee·lo·me·tros por o·ra*; to earn $25 per hour ganar $25 por hora *ga·nar $25 por o·ra*; $3 per kilo $3 al kilo *$3 el kee·lo*; per person por persona *por per·so·na*; per day al día *al dee·a*; per annum al año *al an·yo*; 20 per cent 20 por ciento *20 por thyen·to*
percentage *n* el porcentaje *por·then·ta·khe*
percolate *vt* (*coffee*) filtrar *feel·trar*
percolator *n* la cafetera de filtro *ca·fe·te·ra de feel·tro*
perfect *adj* perfecto(a) *per·fek·to(a)*
perform *vi* (*business*) marchar *mar·char*
performance *n* (*of actor*) la representación *re·pre·sen·ta·thyon*; (*of play*) la sesión *se·syon*; (*of car*) el rendimiento *ren·dee·myen·to* L41, 44
perfume *n* el perfume *per·foo·me* S44
perhaps *adv* quizás *kee·thas*; perhaps he'll come quizás venga *kee·thas ben·ga*
period *n* (*of time*) el período *pe·ree·o·do*; (*punctuation*) el punto *poon·to*; (*menstruation*) el período *pe·ree·o·do* □ *adj* (*furniture*) de época *de e·po·ka*
perm *n* la permanente *per·ma·nen·te* Sn44
permanent *adj* permanente *per·ma·nen·te*
permanently *adv* permanentemente *per·ma·nen·te·men·te*
permanent wave *n* la permanente *per·ma·nen·te*
permission *n* el permiso *per·mee·so*
permit *vt* (*something*) permitir *per·mee·teer*; to permit someone to do

something permitir a alguien que haga algo *per·mee·teer a al·gyen ke a·ga al·go* □ *n* permit el permiso *per·mee·so*
Persian *adj* persa *per·sa*
person *n* la persona *per·so·na*; in person en persona *en per·so·na*
personal *adj* personal *per·so·nal*; (*private*) privado(a) *pree·ba·do(a)*
personal assistant, P. A. *n* la secretaria particular *se·kre·ta·rya par·tee·koo·lar*
personality *n* (*character*) la personalidad *per·so·na·lee·dad*; (*celebrity*) el personaje *per·so·na·khe*
personally *adv* personalmente *per·so·nal·men·te*
personnel *n* el personal *per·so·nal*
personnel department *n* el servicio de personal *ser·bee·thyo de per·so·nal*
personnel manager *n* el jefe de personal *khe·fe de per·so·nal*
person-to-person call *n* una conferencia de persona a persona *oo·na kon·fe·ren·thya de per·so·na a per·so·na*
Peru *n* el Perú *pe·roo*
Peruvian *adj* peruano(a) *per·wa·no(a)*
peseta *n* la peseta *pe·se·ta*
peso *n* el peso *pe·so*
pessimistic *adj* pesimista *pe·see·mees·ta*
pet *n* el animal doméstico *a·nee·mal do·mes·tee·ko*
petroleum jelly *n* la vaselina *ba·se·lee·na*
petticoat *n* las enaguas *e·na·gwas*
pharmacist *n* el/la farmacéutico(a) *far·ma·thew·tee·ko(a)*
pharmacy *n* la farmacia *far·ma·thya*
pheasant *n* el faisán *fay·san*
phone *n* el teléfono *te·le·fo·no*; he's on the phone está telefoneando *es·ta te·le·fo·ne·an·do* □ *vt* phone telefonear *te·le·fo·ne·ar* Sn19
phone-call *n* el telefonazo *te·le·fo·na·tho* Sn12
photo *n* la foto *fo·to* L16, S51
photocopy *n* la fotocopia *fo·to·ko·pya* □ *vt* fotocopiar *fo·to·ko·pyar* Bm15
photograph *n* la fotografía *fo·to·gra·fee·a* □ *vt* fotografiar *fo·to·gra·fyar* S51
photographer *n* el fotógrafo *fo·to·gra·fo*
photography *n* la fotografía *fo·to·gra·fee·a*
phrase *n* la frase *fra·se*
phrase book *n* el libro de frases *lee·bro de fra·ses*
physical *adj* físico(a) *fee·see·ko(a)*
physics *n* la física *fee·see·ka*
piano *n* el piano *pee·a·no*
pick *n* (*pickaxe*) el pico *pee·ko* □ *vt* (*flower*) coger* *ko·kher*; (*choose*) escoger* *es·ko·kher*; to pick up (*object*) recoger* *re·ko·kher*; to pick up a friend ir* a buscar a un amigo *eer a boos·kar a oon a·mee·go*
pickaxe *n* el pico *pee·ko*
picket *n* el piquete *pee·ke·te*
pickles *pl* las conservas en vinagre *kon·ser·bas en bee·na·gre*
picnic *n* la merienda *me·ryen·da*; to go on a picnic ir* a merendar al campo *eer a me·ren·dar al kam·po* L32
picture *n* el cuadro *kwa·dro*; (*drawing*)

el dibujo *dee·boo·kho*; (*photo*) la foto *fo·to*; (*movie*) la película *pe·lee·koo·la*

pie *n* la tarta *tar·ta*; (*meat*) la empanada *em·pa·na·da*

piece *n* el pedazo *pe·da·tho*; **piece of furniture** el mueble *mwe·ble*; **a good piece of work** un trabajo bien hecho *oon tra·ba·kho byen e·cho*

piecework *n* el trabajo a destajo *tra·ba·kho a des·ta·kho*

pier *n* el muelle *mwel·ye*

pierce *vt* atravesar* *a·tra·be·sar*

pig *n* el cerdo *ther·do*, el chancho (Am) *chan·cho*

pigeon *n* la paloma *pa·lo·ma*

pigskin *n* la piel de cerdo *pyel de ther·do*

pile *n* el montón *mon·ton* □ *vt* to pile up amontonar *a·mon·to·nar*

pill *n* la píldora *peel·do·ra*; (*contraceptive*) la píldora anticonceptiva *peel·do·ra an·tee·kon·thep·tee·ba*; **to be on the pill** tomar la píldora *to·mar la peel·do·ra*

pillar *n* el pilar *pee·lar*

pillow *n* la almohada *al·mo·a·da* A41

pillowcase, pillowslip *n* la funda de almohada *foon·da de al·mo·a·da*

pilot *n* el piloto *pee·lo·to*

pilot light *n* (*gas*) la lámpara indicadora *lam·pa·ra een·dee·ka·do·ra*

pimple *n* el grano *gra·no*

pin *n* el alfiler *al·fee·ler*, (*safety pin*) el imperdible *eem·per·dee·ble* □ *vt* prender con alfiler *pren·der kon al·fee·ler*

pinball *n* la máquina automática *ma·kee·na ow·to·ma·tee·ka*

pinch *vt* pellizcar* *pel·yeeth·kar* □ *n* (*of salt etc*) la pizca *peeth·ka*

pine *n* el pino *pee·no*

pineapple *n* la piña *peen·ya*

ping-pong *n* el ping-pong *peeng·pong*

pink *adj* rosa *ro·sa*

pint *n* la pinta *peen·ta*; **a pint of beer** una pinta de cerveza *oo·na peen·ta de ther·be·tha*

pipe *n* (*tube*) el tubo *too·bo*; (*for smoking*) la pipa *pee·pa*; (*musical*) el caramillo *ka·ra·meel·yo*; (*bag*)pipes la gaita *gay·ta* A78, S100

pipeline *n* el oleoconducto *o·le·o·kon·dook·to*

piston *n* el pistón *pees·ton*

pit *n* el hoyo *o·yo*

pitch *vt* (*tent*) armar *ar·mar*

pitcher *n* la jarra *kha·rra*

pity *n* la piedad *pye·dad*; **what a pity!** ¡qué pena! *ke pe·na*

pizza *n* la pizza *peet·sa*

place *n* el sitio *see·tyo*; (*town*) el lugar *loo·gar*; (*seat*) el asiento *a·syen·to*; **in place** en su sitio *en soo see·tyo*; **out of place** (*object*) fuera de su sitio *fwe·ra de soo see·tyo*; **come back to our place** venga a casa con nosotros *ben·ga a ka·sa kon no·so·tros* □ *vt* place (*put*) situar *see·too·ar*; (*a bet*) poner* *po·ner*; **to place an order with someone** hacer* un pedido a alguien *a·ther oon pe·dee·do a al·gyen*

place mat *n* el salvamantel *sal·ba·man·tel*

place setting *n* el cubierto *koo·byer·to*

plaice *n* la platija *pla·tee·kha*

plaid *n* la tela a cuadros *te·la a kwa·dros*

plain *n* el llano *lya·no* □ *adj* (*clear*) claro(a) *kla·ro(a)*; (*simple: cooking etc*) casero(a) *ka·se·ro(a)*; (*not patterned*) liso(a) *lee·so(a)*; **plain chocolate** el chocolate sin leche *cho·ko·la·te seen le·che*; **plain yogurt** el yogur natural *yo·goor na·too·ral*

plait *n* (*of hair etc*) la trenza *tren·tha*

plan *n* (*scheme*) el plan *plan*; (*map*) el mapa *ma·pa*; (*drawing, project*) el plano *pla·no* □ *vt* planear *pla·ne·ar*; (*make a design*) hacer* un plan de *a·ther oon plan de*

plane *n* el avión *a·byon*; (*tree*) el plátano *pla·ta·no*; (*tool*) el cepillo (de carpintero) *the·peel·yo (de kar·peen·te·ro)*; **by plane** en avión *en a·byon* B77

planet *n* el planeta *pla·ne·ta*

planetarium *n* el planetario *pla·ne·ta·ryo*

plank *n* la tabla *ta·bla*

planning *n* (*economic*) la planificación *pla·nee·fee·ka·thyon*

plant *n* la planta *plan·ta*; (*factory*) la fábrica *fa·bree·ka*; (*equipment*) el equipo *e·kee·po* □ *vt* plantar *plan·tar*

plaster *n* (*for wall*) el yeso *ye·so*; **plaster cast** (*for limb*) el vaciado *ba·thya·do*; **plaster of Paris** el yeso blanco *ye·so blan·ko*

plastic *n* el plástico *plas·tee·ko* □ *adj* de plástico *de plas·tee·ko*; **plastic surgery** la cirugía estética *thee·roo·khee·a es·te·tee·ka*

plastic bag *n* la bolsa de plástico *bol·sa de plas·tee·ko* S25

plate *n* el plato *pla·to*; (*of glass, metal*) la lámina *la·mee·na*

plated *adj* □ **gold plated** chapeado(a) en oro *cha·pe·a·do(a) en o·ro*

platform *n* (*in station*) el andén *an·den*; (*in hall*) el estrado *es·tra·do*; (*oil-rig*) la plataforma *pla·ta·for·ma* T67f

platinum *n* el platino *pla·tee·no*

play *vt/i* jugar* *khoo·gar*; **to play football** jugar* al fútbol *khoo·gar al foot·bol*; **to play the violin** tocar* el violín *to·kar el byo·leen*; **to play with** jugar con *khoo·gar kon* □ *n* play (*theatrical*) la obra de teatro *o·bra de te·a·tro*

player *n* (*in sport*) el/la jugador(a) *khoo·ga·dor(·ra)*

playground *n* el patio de recreo *pa·tyo de re·kre·o* C9

play-group *n* la guardería *gwar·de·ree·a*

playing card *n* el naipe *nay·pe*

playing field *n* el campo de deportes *kam·po de de·por·tes*

playpen *n* el parque (de niño) *par·ke (de neen·yo)*

pleasant *adj* agradable *a·gra·da·ble*; (*person*) amable *a·ma·ble*

please *adv* por favor *por fa·bor*

pleased *adj* contento(a) *kon·ten·to(a)*

pleasure *n* el placer *pla·ther*

pleasure boat *n* el barco de recreo *bar·ko de re·kre·o*

pleated *adj* plisado(a) *plee·sa·do(a)*

plenty *n* □ **plenty of milk** bastante leche *bas·tan·te le·che*; **thank you, that's plenty** gracias, es suficiente *gra·thyas es soo·fee·thyen·te*

plexiglas *n* el plexiglás *plek·see·glas*

pliers *pl* los alicates *a·lee·ka·tes*

plimsolls *pl* las zapatillas de tenis *tha·pa·teel·yas de te·nees*

plot *n* (*of land*) la parcela *par·the·la*; (*in play*) el argumento *ar·goo·men·to*

plow n el arado a·ra·do

plug n (for basin etc) el tapón ta·pon; (electric) el enchufe en·choo·fe; (in car) la bujía boo·khee·a □ vt tapar ta·par; to plug something in enchufar algo en·choo·far al·go

plum n la ciruela thee·rwe·la

plumber n el fontanero fon·ta·ne·ro, el gasfitero (Am) gas·fee·te·ro

plump adj regordete re·gor·de·te

plus prep más mas

plywood n la madera contrachapada ma·de·ra kon·tra·cha·pa·da

p.m. adv de la tarde de la tar·de

pneumonia n la pulmonía pool·mo·nee·a

poached adj escalfado(a) es·kal·fa·do(a)

P.O. Box n el apartado (de correos) a·par·ta·do (de ko·rre·os), la casilla (Am) ka·seel·ya

pocket n el bolsillo bol·seel·yo

pocketbook n la cartera kar·te·ra

pocketknife n la navaja na·ba·kha

pocket money n el dinero para gastos pequeños dee·ne·ro pa·ra gas·tos pe·ken·yos

podiatrist n el pedicuro pe·dee·koo·ro

poem n el poema po·e·ma

poetry n la poesía po·e·see·a

point vt (gun) apuntar a·poon·tar □ vi to point at or to something señalar algo con el dedo sen·ya·lar al·go kon el de·do; to point something out (show) señalar algo sen·ya·lar al·go □ n point el punto poon·to; (tip) la punta poon·ta; (in time) el momento mo·men·to; (in space) el sitio see·tyo; (electric outlet) el enchufe en·choo·fe; decimal point la coma ko·ma; 3 point 4 3 coma 4 3 ko·ma 4; he answered him point by point le contestó punto por punto le kon·tes·to poon·to por poon·to; what's the point? ¿para qué? pa·ra ke

point of view n el punto de vista poon·to de bees·ta

poison n el veneno be·ne·no

poisonous adj venenoso(a) be·ne·no·so(a)

poker n (card game) el póquer po·ker

Poland n Polonia (f) po·lo·nya

Polaroid adj polaroid po·la·ro·eed

pole n (wooden) el palo pa·lo

Pole n el/la polaco(a) po·la·ko(a)

police n la policía po·lee·thee·a T195f, Sn80f

police car n el coche patrulla ko·che pa·trool·ya

policeman n el policía po·lee·thee·a

police station n la comisaría ko·mee·sa·ree·a

policewoman n la mujer policía moo·kher po·lee·thee·a

policy n la política po·lee·tee·ka; (insurance) la póliza po·lee·tha

polio n la polio po·lyo

polish n (for shoes) el betún be·toon; (for floor) la cera the·ra □ vt polish (shoes, metal) limpiar leem·pyar; (wood) encerar en·therar

Polish adj polaco(a) po·la·ko(a) he's Polish es polaco es po·la·ko; she's Polish es polaca es po·la·ka □ n Polish el polaco po·la·ko

polite adj educado(a) e·doo·ka·do(a)

political adj político(a) po·lee·tee·ko(a)

politician n el político po·lee·tee·ko

politics n la política po·lee·tee·ka

pollution n la contaminación kon·ta·mee·na·thyon

polo n el polo po·lo

polo neck n el cuello alto kwel·yo al·to

polyester n el polyester po·lyes·ter

polyethylene n el polietileno po·lee·e·tee·le·no

polyethylene bag n la bolsa de plástico bol·sa de plas·tee·ko

pomegranate n la granada gra·na·da

pond n (natural) la charca char·ka; (artificial) el estanque es·tan·ke

pony n el poney po·nee

pool n (of rain) el charco char·ko; (swimming) la piscina pees·thee·na; (game) los trucos troo·kos A11

poor adj pobre po·bre; (mediocre) mediocre me·dyo·kre

pop adj (music, art) pop pop

pop concert n el concierto pop kon·thyer·to pop

popcorn n las palomitas de maíz pa·lo·mee·tas de ma·eeth

pope n el papa pa·pa

pop group n el grupo de música pop groo·po de moo·see·ka pop

poplar n el chopo cho·po

poplin n la popelina po·pe·lee·na

popsicle n el polo po·lo

popular adj popular po·poo·lar; (fashionable) de moda de mo·da

population n la población po·bla·thyon

porcelain n la porcelana por·the·la·na

porch n el pórtico por·tee·ko

pork n la carne de cerdo kar·ne de ther·do S37

porridge n la papilla de avena pa·peel·ya de a·be·na

port n (for ships) el puerto pwer·to; (wine) el oporto o·por·to

portable adj portátil por·ta·teel

porter n (for luggage) el mozo mo·tho; (doorkeeper) el conserje kon·ser·khe T26

portfolio n la cartera kar·te·ra

porthole n la portilla por·teel·ya

portion n la porción por·thyon

Portugal n Portugal (m) por·too·gal

Portuguese adj portugués(esa) por·too·ges(·ge·sa); he's Portuguese es portugués es por·too·ges; she's Portuguese es portuguesa es por·too·ge·sa □ n Portuguese el portugués por·too·ges

position n (of body) la posición po·see·thyon; (place) el sitio see·tyo; (job) el puesto pwes·to

positive adj positivo(a) po·see·tee·bo(a)

possibility n la posibilidad po·see·bee·lee·dad

possible adj posible po·see·ble

possibly adv posiblemente po·see·ble·men·te; to do all one possibly can hacer° todo lo posible a·ther to·do lo po·see·ble

post n (pole) el poste pos·te; (mail) el correo ko·rre·o; by post por correo por ko·rre·o □ vt post mandar por correo man·dar por ko·rre·o Sn1f

postage n el franqueo fran·ke·o

postal adj postal pos·tal

postal district n el distrito postal dees·tree·to pos·tal

postal order n el giro postal khee·ro pos·tal

post-box n el buzón boo·thon

postcard n la (tarjeta) postal tar·khe·ta pos·tal L17, S93, Sn3

post-code n el código postal ko·dee·go pos·tal

postdate vt posfechar pos·fe·char

poster n el cartel kar·tel

postman n el cartero *kar·te·ro*

post office n correos (m) *ko·rre·os*; the Post Office la Oficina de Correos *o·fee·thee·na de ko·rre·os*; I must go to the post office tengo que ir a correos *ten·go ke eer a ko·rre·os* F9

post-office box n el apartado (de correos) *a·par·ta·do (de ko·rre·os)*, la casilla (Am) *ka·seel·ya*

postpone vt aplazar *a·pla·thar*

pot n (for cooking) la olla *ol·ya*; (for jam) el tarro *ta·rro*; (for plant) el tiesto *tyes·to*

potato n la patata *pa·ta·ta*, la papa (Am) *pa·pa*

pottery n la cerámica *the·ra·mee·ka*; (workshop) la alfarería *al·fa·re·ree·a*

pot(ty) n el orinal de niño *o·ree·nal de neen·yo*

poultry n las aves de corral *a·bes de ko·rral*

pound n (currency, weight) la libra *lee·bra*

pour vt (tea, milk) echar *echar* □ vi correr abundantemente *ko·rrer a·boon·dan·te·men·te*

powder n el polvo *pol·bo*; (cosmetic) los polvos *pol·bos*

powder room n los ascos *a·se·os*

power n (of machine) la potencia *po·ten·thya*; (authority) el poder *po·der*; (electricity) la corriente *ko·rryen·te*

powerful adj potente *po·ten·te*; (person) poderoso(a) *po·de·ro·so(a)*

P.R. n las relaciones públicas *re·la·thyo·nes poo·blee·kas*

practical adj práctico(a) *prak·tee·ko(a)*; to have practical experience tener* experiencia práctica *te·ner eks·pe·ryen·thya prak·tee·ka*

practice vt/i □ to practice running entrenarse a correr *en·tre·nar·se a co·rrer*; to practice the piano hacer* ejercicios en el piano *a·ther e·kher·thee·thyos en el pya·no*

Prague n Praga (f) *pra·ga*

pram n el cochecito de niño *ko·che·thee·to de neen·yo*

prawn n la gamba *gam·ba*

pray vi rezar *re·thar*

prayer n la oración *o·ra·thyon*

precinct n (administrative area) el distrito electoral *dees·tree·to e·lek·to·ral*

precious adj (jewel etc) precioso(a) *pre·thyo·so(a)*

precise adj exacto(a) *e·sak·to(a)*

precision n la precisión *pre·thee·syon*

predict vt pronosticar* *pro·nos·tee·kar*

prediction n el pronóstico *pro·nos·tee·ko*

prefer vt preferir* *pre·fe·reer*

preferred stock n las acciones preferentes *ak·thyo·nes pre·fe·ren·tes*

pregnant adj embarazada *em·ba·ra·tha·da* I48

prejudice n el prejuicio *pre·khwee·thyo*

preliminary adj preliminar *pre·lee·mee·nar*

première n el estreno *es·tre·no*

premises pl el local *lo·kal*

premium n la prima *pree·ma*

prepaid adj pagado(a) por adelantado *pa·ga·do(a) por a·de·lan·ta·do*

preparation n la preparación *pre·pa·ra·thyon*; preparations (for trip) los preparativos *pre·pa·ra·tee·bos*

prepare vt preparar *pre·pa·rar* □ vi he's preparing to leave se prepara a marcharse *se pre·pa·ra a mar·char·se*

Presbyterian adj presbiteriano(a) *pres·bee·te·rya·no(a)*

prescription n la receta *re·the·ta*

present adj presente *pre·sen·te*; the present king el rey actual *el rey ak·twal* □ n present (gift) el regalo *re·ga·lo*; at present en este momento *en es·te mo·men·to* □ vt present (give) regalar *re·ga·lar* S6, 106

presentation n la exposición *eks·po·see·thyon*

preserve(s) n la compota *kom·po·ta*

president n (of country) el presidente *pre·see·den·te*; (of company) el director *dee·rek·tor*

press n (newspapers, journalists) la prensa *pren·sa*; (printing machine) la imprenta *eem·pren·ta* □ vt apretar* *a·pre·tar*; (iron) planchar *plan·char*; press the button dele al botón *de·le al bo·ton*

press-campaign n la campaña de prensa *kam·pan·ya de pren·sa*

pressure n la presión *pre·syon*; the pressures of modern life las presiones de la vida moderna *las pre·syo·nes de la bee·da mo·der·na* T161

pressure cooker n la olla a presión *ol·ya a pre·syon*

pressure group n el grupo de presión *groo·po de pre·syon*

prestige n el prestigio *pres·tee·khyo*

pretax adj (profit) antes de pagar impuestos *an·tes de pa·gar eem·pwes·tos*

pretend vi fingir *feen·kheer*; to pretend to do something fingir hacer algo *feen·kheer a·ther al·go*

pretty adj (woman, child) guapo(a) *gwa·po(a)*; (dress) bonito(a) *bo·nee·to(a)*

preview n el preestreno *pre·es·tre·no*

previous adj anterior *an·te·ryor*; on the previous day el día anterior *el dee·a an·te·ryor*

price n el precio *pre·thyo* □ vt (goods) fijar el precio de *fee·khar el pre·thyo de* Bm28

price list n la lista de precios *lees·ta de pre·thyos*

price range n la gama de precios *ga·ma de pre·thyos*

prick vt pinchar *peen·char*

pride n el orgullo *or·gool·yo*

priest n el sacerdote *sa·ther·do·te* Sn93

primary adj (education) primario(a) *pree·ma·ryo(a)*

prime minister, P.M. n el primer ministro *pree·mer mee·nees·tro*

prince n el príncipe *preen·thee·pe*

princess n la princesa *preen·the·sa*

principal n (of school etc) el/la director(a) *dee·rek·tor(·ra)*

print vt (book, magazine) imprimir* *eem·pree·meer*; (write in block letters) escribir* en mayúsculas *es·kree·beer en ma·yoos·koo·las* □ n el grabado *gra·ba·do*; (photographic) la copia *ko·pya*; out of print agotado(a) *a·go·ta·do(a)* S50

printer n el impresor *eem·pre·sor*

printout n la copia *ko·pya*

prison n la cárcel *kar·thel*

prisoner n el preso *pre·so*

private adj privado(a) *pree·ba·do(a)*; (confidential) confidencial *kon·fee·den·thyal*; private lesson la clase particular *kla·se par·tee·koo·lar*; in private en privado *en pree·ba·do* A37, E5

private enterprise n la iniciativa privada *ee·nee·thya·tee·ba pree·ba·da*

private sector n el sector privado *sek· tor pree·ba·do*

prize n el premio *pre·myo*

probable adj probable *pro·ba·ble*

probably adv probablemente *pro·ba· ble·men·te*

problem n el problema *pro·ble·ma* A70

procedure n el procedimiento *pro·the· dee·myen·to*

process n el proceso *pro·the·so*; *(method)* el sistema *sees·te·ma* □ vt tratar *tra·tar*; *(application, order)* ocuparse de *o·koo·par·se de*

produce vt *(manufacture)* producir* *pro·doo·theer*; *(play)* representar *re· pre·sen·tar*; *(movie)* producir* *pro· doo·theer* □ n *(products)* los productos *pro·dook·tos*

producer n el/la productor(a) *pro· dook·tor(·a)*; *(of play)* el/la director(a) de escena *dee·rek·tor(·a) de es·the·na*; *(of movie)* el/la productor(a) *pro·dook·tor(·a)*

product n el producto *pro·dook·to* Bm18, 23

production n la producción *pro·dook· thyon*; *(of play)* la representación *re· pre·sen·ta·thyon*

productivity n la productividad *pro· dook·tee·bee·dad*

profession n la profesión *pro·fe·syon*

professional adj profesional *pro·fe·syo· nal*

professor n el/la catedrático(a) *ka·te· dra·tee·ko(a)*; *(associate)* el/la profesor(a) agregado(a) *pro·fe·sor(·ra) a· gre·ga·do(a)*

profit n el beneficio *be·ne·fee·thyo*

profitability n la rentabilidad *ren·ta· bee·lee·dad*

profitable adj rentable *ren·ta·ble*

profiterole n el profiterole *pro·fee·te· rol*

profit-making adj rentable *ren·ta·ble*

profit margin n el margen de beneficio *mar·khen de be·ne·fee·thyo*

profit-sharing n la participación en los beneficios *par·tee·thee·pa·thyon en los be·ne·fee·thyos*

program n el programa *pro·gra·ma* □ vt programar *pro·gra·mar* L42

programmer n *(person)* el programador *pro·gra·ma·dor*

programming n *(computer)* la programación *pro·gra·ma·thyon*

progress n el progreso *pro·gre·so*; to make progress progresar *pro·gre·sar*

prohibit vt prohibir *pro·ee·beer*

project n *(plan)* el proyecto *pro·yek· to*; *(venture)* la empresa *em·pre·sa* Bm31

projector n el proyector *pro·yek·tor*

promenade n *(by sea)* el paseo *pa·se·o*

promise n la promesa *pro·me·sa* □ vt prometer *pro·me·ter*

promote vt *(person)* ascender* *as·then· der*; *(product)* promover* *pro·mo·ber*

promotion n *(of person)* el ascenso *as· then·so*; *(of product)* la promoción *pro·mo·thyon*

pronounce vt pronunciar *pro·noon· thyar*

pronunciation n la pronunciación *pro· noon·thee·a·thyon*

proof n la prueba *prwe·ba*; a 70° proof whiskey un whisky de graduación de 70 por 100 *oon wees·kee de gra·doo· a·thyon de 70 por 100*

proper adj *(appropriate)* apropiado(a) *a·pro·pya·do(a)*; *(correct)* correcto(a) *ko·rrek·to(a)*; *(respectable)* formal *for·mal*

properly adv correctamente *ko·rrek·ta· men·te*

property n la propiedad *pro·pye·dad*; *(estate)* la finca *feen·ka*

prophylactic n *(contraceptive)* el preservativo *pre·ser·ba·tee·bo*

proposal n *(suggestion)* la propuesta *pro·pwes·ta*

propose vt *(suggest)* proponer* *pro·po· ner*; to propose a toast to someone brindar por alguien *breen·dar por al· gyen*

proposition n *(proposal)* la proposición *pro·po·see·thyon*

prospect n la perspectiva *pers·pek·tee· ba*

prospectus n el prospecto *pros·pek·to*

prosperous adj próspero(a) *pros·pe· ro(a)*

protect vt proteger* *pro·te·kher*

protein n la proteína *pro·te·ee·na*

protest n la protesta *pro·tes·ta* □ vi protestar *pro·tes·tar*

Protestant adj protestante *pro·tes· tan·te* Sn90

prototype n el prototipo *pro·to·tee·po*

proud adj orgulloso(a) *or·gool·yo· so(a)*

prove vt probar* *pro·bar*

provide vt proporcionar *pro·por·thyo· nar*; to provide someone with something proporcionar algo a alguien *pro·por·thyo·nar al·go a al·gyen* □ vi to provide for someone mantener* a alguien *man·te·ner a al·gyen*

provided, providing conj siempre que *syem·pre ke*; provided (that) he comes siempre que venga *syem·pre ke ben·ga*

province n *(region)* la provincia *pro· been·thya*

provincial adj provinciano(a) *pro· been·thya·no(a)*

proviso n la condición *kon·dee·thyon*

prune n la ciruela pasa *thee·rwe·la pa·sa*

P.S. abbrev P.D. *pe·de*

psychiatric adj psiquiátrico(a) *see·kya· tree·ko(a)*

psychiatrist n el/la psiquiatra *see· kya·tra*

psychological adj psicológico(a) *see· ko·lo·khee·ko(a)*

psychologist n el/la psicólogo(a) *see· ko·lo·go(a)*

psychology n la psicología *see·ko·lo· khee·a*

P.T.O. abbrev véase al dorso *be·a·se al dor·so*

pub n el bar *bar*

public adj público(a) *poo·blee·ko(a)* □ n el público *poo·blee·ko*; in public en público *en poo·blee·ko*

public conveniences pl los servicios *ser·bee·thyos*

publicity n la publicidad *poo·blee·thee· dad*

publicity campaign n la campaña de publicidad *kam·pan·ya de poo·blee· thee·dad* Bm19

public relations n las relaciones públicas *re·la·thyo·nes poo·blee·kas*

public relations officer n el encargado de relaciones públicas *en·kar·ga·do de re·la·thyo·nes poo·blee·kas*

public school n el instituto de enseñanza pública *eens·tee·too·to de en· sen·yan·tha poob·lee·ka*

public sector n el sector público *sek·tor poo·blee·ko*
publish vt publicar* *poo·blee·kar*
publisher n el editor *e·dee·tor*
pudding n el puding *poo·deen*
puddle n el charco *char·ko*
pull vt/i tirar *tee·rar*; to pull something out sacar* algo *sa·kar al·go*; to pull out of a deal retirarse de un negocio *re·tee·rar·se de oon ne·go·thyo*; the car pulled in el coche se paró *el ko·che se pa·ro*; he pulled out to pass the car se salió de la fila para adelantar el coche *se sa·lyo de la fee·la pa·ra a·de·lan·tar el ko·che*; to pull something off arrancar* algo *a·rran·kar al·go*
pullover n el jersey *kher·sey*
pump n la bomba *bom·ba* □ vt sacar* con una bomba *sa·kar kon oo·na bom·ba*
pumpkin n la calabaza *ka·la·ba·tha*
punch n (*blow*) el puñetazo *poon·ye·ta·tho*; (*drink*) el ponche *pon·che* □ vt (*with fist*) dar* un puñetazo a *dar oon poon·ye·ta·tho a*; (*ticket etc*) picar* *pee·kar*
punctual adj (*person*) puntual *poon·twal*; (*train*) a la hora exacta *a la o·ra ek·sak·ta*
puncture n el pinchazo *peen·cha·tho*
punish vt castigar* *kas·tee·gar*
punishment n el castigo *kas·tee·go*
pupil n el/la alumno(a) *a·loom·no(a)*
purchase n la compra *kom·pra* □ vt comprar *kom·prar*
pure adj puro(a) *poo·ro(a)*
purée n el puré *poo·re*
purple adj morado(a) *mo·ra·do(a)*
purpose n el propósito *pro·po·see·to*; on purpose a propósito *a pro·po·see·to*
purse n (*for money*) el monedero *mo·ne·de·ro*; (*lady's bag*) el bolso *bol·so*
push vt empujar *em·poo·khar*; (*button*) apretar* *a·pre·tar*; (*product*) promocionar *pro·mo·thyo·nar*; push it in métélo *me·te·lo*
put vt poner* *po·ner*; to put a question hacer* una pregunta *a·ther oo·na pre·goon·ta*; to put one's things away guardar las cosas *gwar·dar las ko·sas*; to put back (*replace*) devolver* *de·bol·ber*; to put down a parcel poner* un paquete en el suelo *po·ner oon pa·ke·te en el swe·lo*; to put on a dress ponerse* un vestido *po·ner·se oon bes·tee·do*; to put on the light encender* la luz *en·then·der la looth*, prender la luz (Am) *pren·der la looth*; to put on the brakes frenar *fre·nar*; to put out the light apagar* la luz *a·pa·gar la looth*; he put out his hand alargó la mano *a·lar·go la ma·no*; to put someone through (*on phone*) poner* a alguien con otro *po·ner a al·gyen kon o·tro*; to put up a notice fijar un anuncio *fee·khar oon a·noon·thyo*; to put up capital poner* el capital *po·ner el ka·pee·tal*
puzzle n el rompecabezas *rom·pe·ka·be·thas*
pyramid n la pirámide *pee·ra·mee·de*
Pyrenees pl los Pirineos *pee·ree·ne·os*

Q

quail n la codorniz *ko·dor·neeth*
quaint adj curioso(a) *koo·ryo·so(a)*
qualification n (*diploma etc*) el requi-

sito *re·kee·see·to*; (*restriction*) la reserva *re·ser·ba*
qualified adj capacitado(a) *ka·pa·thee·ta·do(a)*
qualify for vt (*grant etc*) tener* los requisitos para *te·ner los re·kee·see·tos pa·ra*; (*in sports*) calificarse* para *ka·lee·fee·kar·se pa·ra*
quality n la calidad *ka·lee·dad*; (*characteristic*) la característica *ka·rak·te·rees·tee·ka*; quality goods los artículos de calidad *ar·tee·koo·los de ka·lee·dad*
quantity n la cantidad *kan·tee·dad*
quarantine n la cuarentena *kwa·ren·te·na*
quarrel n la disputa *dees·poo·ta* □ vi reñir *ren·yeer*
quarry n la cantera *kan·te·ra*
quart n ≈ el litro *lee·tro*
quarter n el cuarto *kwar·to*; a quarter of an hour un cuarto de hora *oon kwar·to de o·ra*; (a) quarter to 4 las 4 menos cuarto *las 4 me·nos kwar·to*; (a) quarter past 4 las 4 y cuarto *las 4 ee kwar·to*
quartz n el cuarzo *kwar·tho*
quay n el muelle *mwel·ye*
quayside n el muelle *mwel·yo*
queen n la reina *rey·na*
queer adj (*strange*) extraño(a) *eks·tran·yo(a)*
question n la pregunta *pre·goon·ta*; (*subject discussed*) la cuestión *kwes·tyon*; to ask a question hacer* una pregunta *a·ther oo·na pre·goon·ta*; it's a question of es cuestión de *es kwes·tyon de*; out of the question imposible *eem·po·see·ble*
question mark n el punto de interrogación *poon·to de een·te·rro·ga·thyon*
questionnaire n el cuestionario *kwes·tyo·na·ryo*
quiche n la quiche *keesh*
quick adj rápido(a) *ra·pee·do(a)*; be quick! ¡date prisa! *da·te pree·sa*, ¡apúrate! (Am) *a·poo·ra·te*
quickly adv rápidamente *ra·pee·da·men·te*
quiet adj (*place*) tranquilo(a) *tran·kee·lo(a)*; (*person*) reservado(a) *re·ser·ba·do(a)*; (*holiday*) tranquilo(a) *tran·kee·lo(a)*; be quiet! ¡silencio! *see·len·thyo* A5
quietly adv (*speak*) calladamente *kal·ya·da·men·te*; (*walk, work*) silenciosamente *see·len·thyo·sa·men·te*
quilt n el edredón *e·dre·don*
quit vt/i (*leave*) abandonar *a·ban·do·nar*
quite adv (*fairly*) bastante *bas·tan·te*; (*absolutely*) totalmente *to·tal·men·te*; quite a few bastantes *bas·tan·tes*
quiz n el concurso *kon·koor·so*
quota n (*of goods*) la cuota *kwo·ta*
quotation n (*passage*) la cita *thee·ta*; (*price*) la cotización *ko·tee·tha·thyon*
quote vt (*passage*) citar *thee·tar*; (*price*) cotizar* *ko·tee·thar*

R

rabbi n el rabino *ra·bee·no*
rabbit n el conejo *ko·ne·kho*
rabies n la rabia *ra·bya*
race n (*passage*) la raza *ra·tha*; (*sport*) la carrera *ka·rre·ra*; the races las carreras *ka·rre·ras*
racecourse n el hipódromo *ee·po·dro·mo*

racehorse n el caballo de carreras ka·
bal·yo de ka·rre·ras

race relations pl las relaciones interraciales re·la·thyo·nes een·ter·ra·thya·
les

race track n el hipódromo ee·po·
dro·mo

racial adj racial ra·thyal

rack n (for luggage) la rejilla re·kheel·
ya; (for wine) el botellero bo·tel·ye·
ro; (for dishes) el escurreplatos es·
koo·rre·pla·tos

racket n (tennis) la raqueta ra·ke·ta

radar n el radar ra·dar

radar trap n el control de radar kon·
trol de ra·dar

radial ply adj radial ra·dyal

radiator n (of car etc) el radiador ra·
dya·dor T184

radio n la radio ra·dyo; on the radio
por la radio por la ra·dyo

radish n el rábano ra·ba·no

rag n el trapo tra·po

ragged adj (clothes) roto(a) ro·to(a)

raid n (military) el ataque a·ta·ke; (by
police) la redada re·da·da; (by crimi-
nals) el asalto a·sal·to

rail n (on stairs) la barandilla ba·ran·
deel·ya; (on bridge, balcony) el antepecho an·te·pe·cho; rails (for train)
la vía bee·a; by rail por ferrocarril
por fe·rro·ka·rreel

railings pl la verja ber·kha

railroad n el ferrocarril fe·rro·ka·rreel

railroad station n la estación es·ta·
thyon

rain n la lluvia lyoo·bya □ vi llover*
lyo·ber; it's raining llueve lywe·be

rainbow n el arco iris ar·ko ee·rees

raincoat n el impermeable eem·per·
me·a·ble

rainy adj lluvioso(a) lyoo·byo·so(a)

raise vt levantar le·ban·tar; (price) subir soo·beer; (family) criar kree·ar
□ n el aumento ow·men·to

raisin n la pasa pa·sa

rake n el rastrillo ras·treel·yo

rally n (political) la manifestación ma·
nee·fes·ta·thyon; (sporting) el rallye
ra·lee

ramp n (slope) la rampa ram·pa; (in
garage) el elevador e·le·ba·dor; entrance ramp la vía de acceso bee·a de
ak·the·so; exit ramp la vía de acceso
bee·a de ak·the·so

ranch n el rancho ran·cho

random adj hecho al azar e·cho al a·
thar; at random al azar al a·thar

range n (variety) el surtido soor·tee·
do; (of mountains) la cordillera cor·
deel·ye·ra; (of missile) el alcance al·
kan·the □ vi to range from X to Y
abarcar* desde X hasta Y a·bar·kar
des·de X as·ta Y

range finder n (on camera) el telémetro te·le·me·tro

rank n (status) el rango ran·go

rare adj raro(a) ra·ro(a); (steak) poco
hecho(a) po·ko e·cho(a)

rash n el sarpullido sar·pool·yee·do

raspberry n la frambuesa fram·bwe·sa

rat n la rata ra·ta

rate n (price) la tarifa ta·ree·fa; at the
rate of a razón de a ra·thon de; rate
of inflation el índice de inflación een·
dee·the de een·fla·thyon; rate of exchange el tipo de cambio tee·po de
kam·byo Sn25

rates pl (local tax) la contribución municipal kon·tree·boo·thyon moo·nee·
thee·pal

rather adv (quite) bastante bas·tan·te;
I'd rather go to the movies preferería
ir al cine pre·fe·re·ree·a eer al thee·ne

ratio n la proporción pro·por·thyon

rationalization n la racionalización ra·
thyo·na·lee·tha·thyon

rationalize vt racionalizar ra·thyo·na·
lee·thar

ravioli n los raviolis ra·byo·les

raw adj (uncooked) crudo(a) kroo·
do(a); (unprocessed) sin refinar seen
re·fee·nar

raw material n las materias primas ma·
te·ryas pree·mas

ray n el rayo ra·yo

razor n la máquina de afeitar ma·kee·
na de a·fey·tar A43

razor blade n la hoja de afeitar o·kha
de a·fey·tar

reach vt (arrive at) llegar* a lye·gar a;
(with hand) alcanzar* al·kan·thar;
(contact) ponerse* en contacto con
po·ner·se en kon·tak·to kon □ n out
of reach fuera de alcance fwe·ra de
al·kan·the; within easy reach of the
sea a corta distancia del mar a kor·ta
dees·tan·thya del mar

reaction n (chemical, response) la
reacción re·ak·thyon

reactor n el reactor re·ak·tor

read vt/i leer* le·er

readdress vt cambiar las señas de kam·
byar las sen·yas de

reading n la lectura lek·too·ra

ready adj listo(a) lees·to(a); ready to
do something dispuesto(a) a hacer
algo dees·pwes·to(a) a a·ther al·go
Sn61

ready-cooked adj listo(a) para comer
lee·sto(a) pa·ra ko·mer

ready-made adj (clothes) de confección
de kon·fek·thyon

ready-to-wear adj de confección de
kon·fek·thyon

real adj verdadero(a) ber·da·de·ro(a);
(genuine) auténtico(a) ow·ten·tee·
ko(a); it's a real problem es un
problema de verdad es oon pro·ble·ma
de ber·dad; in real terms realmente
re·al·men·te

real estate n los bienes raíces bye·nes
ra·ee·thes

realize vt darse* cuenta de dar·se
kwen·ta de; (assets) realizar* re·a·lee·
thar

really adv de verdad de ber·dad

realtor n el corredor de fincas co·rre·
dor de feen·kas

rear adj (seat) de atrás de a·tras;
(wheel) trasero(a) tra·se·ro(a) □ vt
(children, cattle) criar kree·ar

rear view mirror n el espejo retrovisor
es·pe·kho re·tro·bee·sor

reason n la razón ra·thon; (cause) la
causa kow·sa

reasonable adj razonable ra·tho·na·
ble; (price) módico(a) mo·dee·ko(a)

receipt n el recibo re·thee·bo; (for parcel) el acuse de recibo a·koo·se de
re·thee·bo; receipts (income) los ingresos een·gre·sos M14

receive vt recibir re·thee·beer

receiver n (phone) el auricular ow·ree·
koo·lar

recent adj reciente re·thyen·te

recently adv recientemente re·thyen·te·
men·te

reception n (gathering, in hotel etc) la
recepción re·thep·thyon

reception desk n la recepción re·thep·
thyon

receptionist n (in hotel) la recepcionista re·thep·thyo·nees·ta

recession n la recesión re·the·syon

recipe n la receta re·the·ta

recognize vt reconocer* re·ko·no·ther

recommend vt recomendar* re·ko·men·dar E10, 18

record n (register) la relación re·la·thyon; (file) el dossier do·syer; (disk) el disco dees·ko; (in sports) el récord re·kord □ adj (production, crop etc) sin precedente seen pre·the·den·te □ vt (sound) grabar gra·bar; (write down) apuntar a·poon·tar

record player n el tocadiscos to·ka·dees·kos

recover vi (from illness) recuperarse re·koo·pe·rar·se

recruit vt (personnel) contratar kon·tra·tar □ n el recluta re·kloo·ta

recruitment n la contratación kon·tra·ta·thyon

red adj rojo(a) ro·kho(a)

red currant n la grosella roja gro·sel·ya ro·kha

red-haired adj pelirrojo(a) pe·lee·rro·kho(a)

redirect vt (letter) reexpedir* re·eks·pe·deer

redistribute vt redistribuir* re·dees·tree·boo·eer

redistribution n la redistribución re·dees·tree·boo·thyon

red light n (traffic light) la luz roja looth ro·kha; **to go through a red light** saltarse un semáforo en rojo sal·tar·se oon se·ma·fo·ro en ro·kho

red light district n el barrio chino ba·rryo chee·no

red tape n el papeleo pa·pe·le·o

reduce vt reducir* re·doo·theer; (price) rebajar re·ba·khar □ vi (lose weight) adelgazar* a·del·ga·thar

reduction n la reducción re·dook·thyon; (in price) la rebaja re·ba·ja

referee n (sports) el árbitro ar·bee·tro

reference n la referencia re·fe·ren·thya; **his reference to this matter** su alusión a este asunto soo a·loo·syon a es·te a·soon·to; **with reference to your letter** me refiero a su carta me re·fye·ro a soo kar·ta

refer to vt (allude to) referirse* a re·fe·reer·se a; (consult) consultar kon·sool·tar

refine vt refinar re·fee·nar

refinery n la refinería re·fee·ne·ree·a

reflect vt reflejar re·fle·khar

reflector n (on cycle, car) el reflector re·flek·tor

refreshments pl los refrescos ré·fres·kos

refrigerator n el frigorífico free·go·ree·fee·ko

refund vt reembolsar re·em·bol·sar □ n el reembolso re·em·bol·so

refusal n la negativa ne·ga·tee·ba

refuse vt rechazar* re·cha·thar; **to refuse to do something** negarse a hacer algo ne·gar·se a a·ther al·go

regarding prep en lo que se refiere a en lo ke se re·fye·re a

regardless of prep sin tener* en cuenta seen te·ner en kwen·ta

regatta n la regata re·ga·ta

region n la región re·khyon Mc19

register n el registro re·khees·tro

registered letter n la carta certificada kar·ta ther·tee·fee·ka·da Sn7

registered mail n by registered mail con acuse de recibo kon a·koo·se de re·thee·bo Sn7

registered trademark n la marca registrada mar·ka re·khees·tra·da

regret vt sentir* sen·teer

regular adj regular re·goo·lar; (usual) habitual a·bee·twal; (ordinary) corriente ko·rryen·te; (size) normal nor·mal

regulation n (rule) el reglamento re·gla·men·to

rehearsal n el ensayo en·sa·yo

rein n la rienda ryen·da

reject vt rechazar* re·cha·thar □ n el artículo con defecto ar·tee·koo·lo kon de·fek·to

relation n el/la pariente pa·ryen·te

relative n el/la pariente pa·ryen·te □ adj relativo(a) re·la·tee·bo(a)

relax vi relajarse re·la·khar·se

release vt (prisoner) soltar* sol·tar; (book, film) estrenar es·tre·nar

relevant adj pertinente per·tee·nen·te; **relevant to** que viene al caso ke bye·ne al ka·so

reliability n (of person) la seriedad se·rye·dad; (of car) la seguridad se·goo·ree·dad

reliable adj (person) de confianza de kon·fyan·tha; (car) seguro(a) se·goo·ro(a)

relief n (from pain, anxiety) el alivio a·lee·byo

religion n la religión re·lee·khyon

religious adj (person) religioso(a) re·lee·khyo·so(a)

rely on vt (person) contar* con kon·tar kon

remain vi permanecer* per·ma·ne·ther; (be left over) sobrar so·brar

remark n la observación ob·ser·ba·thyon

remarkable adj notable no·ta·ble

remedy n el remedio re·me·dyo

remember vt acordarse* de a·kor·dar·se de

remind vt recordar* re·kor·dar; **to remind someone of something** recordar* algo a alguien re·kor·dar al·go a al·gyen

remittance n el envío en·bee·o

remote control n el control remoto kon·trol re·mo·to

remove vt quitar kee·tar; (stain) sacar* sa·kar

renew vt (subscription, passport) renovar* re·no·bar

rent n el alquiler al·kee·ler □ vt (house, car etc) alquilar al·kee·lar A57, L23

rental n el alquiler al·kee·ler A62

rental car n el coche de alquiler ko·che de al·kee·ler T103

reorder vt (goods) volver* a pedir bol·ber a pe·deer

reorganization n la reorganización re·or·ga·nee·tha·thyon

reorganize vt reorganizar re·or·ga·nee·thar

repair vt reparar re·pa·rar T191, Sn49

repay vt (sum) reembolsar re·em·bol·sar; (person) devolver* el dinero a de·bolber el dee·ne·ro a

repeat vt repetir* re·pe·teer B26

repeat order n el pedido renovado pe·dee·do re·no·ba·do

repetition n la repetición re·pe·tee·thyon

replace vt (put back) volver* a poner bol·ber a po·ner; (substitute) reemplazar re·em·pla·thar T189

replacement *n* el reemplazo *rem·pla·tho* Sn60

reply *vi* responder *res·pon·der*; **to reply to a question** responder a una pregunta *res·pon·der a oo·na pre·goon·ta* □ *n* **reply** la respuesta *res·pwes·ta*

report *vt* (*tell about*) informar *een·for·mar*; (*in press*) informar *een·for·mar* □ *n* el informe *een·for·me*; (*in press*) el reportaje *re·por·ta·khe*

reporter *n* (*press*) el/la periodista *pe·ryo·dees·ta*

represent *vt* (*symbolize*) representar *re·pre·sen·tar*; (*act as deputy for*) representar *re·pre·sen·tar*

representative *n* el representante *re·pre·sen·tan·te* T19, Bm21

republic *n* la república *re·poo·blee·ka*

republican *adj* republicano(a) *re·poo·blee·ka·no(a)*

reputation *n* la fama *fa·ma*

request *n* la petición *pe·tee·thyon*

require *vt* (*need*) necesitar *ne·the·see·tar*

requirement *n* el requisito *re·kee·see·to*

reroute *vt* desviar *des·byar*

resale *n* □ **not for resale** prohibida la reventa *pro·ee·bee·da la re·ben·ta*

rescue *vt* rescatar *res·ka·tar* □ *n* el rescate *res·ka·te*

research *n* la investigación *een·bes·tee·ga·thyon*

resell *vt* revender *re·ben·der*

resemble *vt* parecerse* *pa·re·ther·se*; **he resembles his father** se parece a su padre *se pa·re·the a soo pa·dre*

reservation *n* la reserva *re·ser·ba* A58

reserve *vt* reservar *re·ser·bar* A13, E2, L38

reserves *pl* las reservas *re·ser·bas*

residence *n* la residencia *re·see·den·thya*

residential *adj* (*area*) residencial *re·see·den·thyal*

resign *vi* dimitir *dee·mee·teer*

resignation *n* la dimisión *dee·mee·syon*

resist *vt* resistir *re·sees·teer*

resistance *n* (*to illness*) la resistencia *re·sees·ten·thya*

resort *n* el lugar de vacaciones *loo·gar de ba·ka·thyo·nes*; **in the last resort** en último caso *en ool·tee·mo ka·so* □ *vi* **to resort** to recurrir a *re·koo·rreer a*

resources *pl* los recursos *re·koor·sos*

respect *n* el respeto *res·pe·to* □ *vt* respetar *res·pe·tar*

respectable *adj* respetable *res·pe·ta·ble*

responsibility *n* la responsabilidad *res·pon·sa·bee·lee·dad*; **this is your responsibility** esto le incumbe a Ud *es·to le een·koom·be a oos·ted*

responsible *adj* responsable *res·pon·sa·ble*; **responsible for** (*to blame*) responsable de *res·pon·sa·ble de*; **he's responsible for the department** el departamento depende de él *el de·par·ta·men·to de·pen·de de el*

rest *vi* descansar *des·kan·sar* □ *n* (*repose*) el descanso *des·kan·so*; **all the rest** todos(as) los/las demás *to·dos(as) los/las de·mas*

restaurant *n* el restaurante *res·tow·ran·te* E1f

restrict *vt* restringir* *res·treen·kheer*; (*speed*) limitar *lee·mee·tar*

restriction *n* la restricción *res·treek·thyon*

restroom *n* los servicios *ser·bee·thyos*

result *n* el resultado *re·sool·ta·do*

retail *n* la venta al pormenor *ben·ta al porme·nor*; **to sell something retail** vender algo al por menor *ben·der al·go al por me·nor* □ *vt* **retail** vender al por menor *ben·der al por me·nor*

retailer *n* el/la detallista *de·tal·yees·ta*

retail price *n* el precio al por menor *pre·thyo al por me·nor* Bm28

retire *vi* jubilarse *khoo·bee·lar·se*

retired *adj* jubilado(a) *khoo·bee·la·do(a)*

retiree *n* el jubilado *khoo·bee·la·do*

retirement *n* la jubilación *khoo·bee·la·thyon*

retrain *vt* reciclar *re·thee·klar* □ *vi* hacer* un reciclaje *a·ther oon re·thee·kla·khe*

retraining *n* el reciclaje *re·thee·kla·khe*

retread *n* el recauchutado *re·kow·choo·ta·do*

retrieve *vt* (*data*) recuperar *re·koo·pe·rar*

retrospect *n* □ **in retrospect** retrospectivamente *re·tros·pek·tee·ba·men·te*

return *vi* (*come back*) regresar *re·gre·sar*; (*go back*) volver* *bol·ber* □ *vt* devolver* *de·bol·ber* □ *n* (*going/coming back*) la vuelta *bwel·ta*; (*profit*) la ganancia *ga·nan·thya*

rev *n* (*in engine*) la revolución *re·bo·loo·thyon* □ *vt* acelerar *a·the·le·rar*

revenue *n* el ingreso *een·gre·so*

reverse *n* (*gear*) la marcha atrás *mar·cha a·tras*; **in reverse** (*gear*) en marcha atrás *en mar·cha a·tras* □ *vt* **to reverse the charges** poner* una conferencia a cobro revertido *po·ner oo·na kon·fe·ren·thya a ko·bro re·ber·tee·do*

reversed charge call *n* la conferencia a cobro revertido *kon·fe·ren·thya a ko·bro re·ber·tee·do*

review *n* la revisión *re·bee·syon*; (*of book etc*) la reseña *re·sen·ya* □ *vt* pasar revista *pa·sar re·bees·ta*

revise *vt* (*estimate etc*) revisar *re·bee·sar*; (*school work*) repasar *re·pa·sar*

revive *vt* (*person*) reanimar *re·a·nee·mar* □ *vi* volver* en sí *bol·ber en see*

revolution *n* (*political*) la revolución *re·bo·loo·thyon*

revue *n* la revista *re·bees·ta*

reward *n* la recompensa *re·kom·pen·sa*

rheumatism *n* el reumatismo *re·oo·ma·tees·mo*

Rhine *n* el Rin *reen*

Rhine (**wine**) *n* el vino del Rin *bee·no del reen*

rhubarb *n* el ruibarbo *rooy·bar·bo*

rhythm *n* el ritmo *reet·mo*

rib *n* la costilla *kos·teel·ya*

ribbon *n* la cinta *theen·ta*

rice *n* el arroz *a·rroth*

rich *adj* rico(a) *ree·ko(a)*; (*food*) fuerte *fwer·te*

ride *n* (*in vehicle*) el paseo *pa·se·o*; (*on horse*) el paseo a caballo *pa·se·o a ka·bal·yo*; **to go for a ride** (*by car*) dar* un paseo en coche *dar oon pa·se·o en ko·che*; **to give someone a ride into town** llevar a alguien a la ciudad *lye·bar a al·gyen a la thyoo·dad*; **it's only a short ride** es una distancia muy corta *es oo·na dees·tan·thya mooy kor·ta* □ *vt* **to ride a horse** montar a caballo *mon·tar a ka·bal·yo*; **to ride a bicycle** montar en bicicleta *mon·tar en bee·thee·kle·ta*

ridge *n* la loma *lo·ma*

ridiculous *adj* ridículo(a) *ree·dee·koo·lo(a)*

riding n la equitación e·kee·ta·thyon; to go riding montar a caballo mon·tar a ka·bal·yo

rifle n el fusil foo·seel

right adj (correct) correcto(a) ko·rrek·to(a); (morally good) bueno(a) bwe·no(a); (not left) derecho(a) de·re·cho(a); yes, that's right eso es e·so es □ adv to turn right torcer* a la derecha tor·ther a la de·re·cha; right in the middle en el mismo centro en el mees·mo then·tro □ n right (right-hand side) la derecha de·re·cha; (entitlement) el derecho de·re·cho; on the right a la derecha a la de·re·cha; to the right a la derecha a la de·re·cha T99

right-handed adj que usa la mano derecha ke oo·sa la ma·no de·re·cha

right of way n (on road) el derecho de paso de·re·cho de pa·so

ring n (on finger) el anillo a·neel·yo; (circle) el círculo theer·koo·lo □ vt to ring the (doorbell) tocar* to·kar □ vi ring sonar* so·nar S88

rink n la pista de hielo pees·ta de ye·lo

rinse vt enjuagar* en·khwa·gar □ n (hair conditioner) el reflejo re·fle·kho

riot n el disturbio dees·toor·byo

rip vt desgarrar des·ga·rrar □ vi desgarrarse des·ga·rrar·se

ripe adj (fruit) maduro(a) ma·doo·ro(a); (cheese) hecho(a) e·cho(a)

rise vi (go up) subir soo·beer; (person) levantarse le·ban·tar·se; (sun) salir* sa·leer □ n (in prices, wages) el aumento ow·men·to

risk n el riesgo ryes·go □ vt arriesgar a·rryes·gar

risotto n el risotto ree·so·to

rival n el rival ree·bal; a rival firm una compañía competidora oo·na kom·pan·yee·a kom·pe·tee·do·ra

river n el río ree·o

Riviera n la Costa Azul kos·ta a·thool

road n la carretera ka·rre·te·ra T128f, F17f

road block n la barricada ba·rree·ka·da

road map n el mapa de carreteras ma·pa de ka·rre·te·ras

road sign n la señal de tráfico sen·yal de tra·fee·ko

road test n la prueba en carretera prwe·ba en ka·rre·te·ra

road works pl las obras o·bras

roar vi (person) rugir* roo·kheer; (lion) rugir* roo·kheer; (engine) zumbar thoom·bar □ n (of person) el rugido roo·khee·do; (of lion) el rugido roo·khee·do; (of engine) el zumbido thoom·bee·do

roast vt asar a·sar; roast meat el asado a·sa·do

rob vt robar ro·bar

robbery n el robo ro·bo

robe n (after bath) el albornoz al·bor·noth

robot n el robot ro·bot

rock n la roca ro·ka; on the rocks (with ice) con hielo kon ye·lo □ vt rock mecer* me·ther

rocket n el cohete ko·e·te

rock ('n' roll) n el rock and roll rok·an·rol

rod n (metallic) la barra ba·rra; (fishing) la caña de pesca kan·ya de pes·ka

roll n el rollo rol·yo; (bread) el bollo bol·yo □ vt (on wheels) rodar* ro·

dar; to roll up (newspaper etc) enrollar en·rol·yar □ vi roll rodar* ro·dar

roller skates pl los patines pa·tee·nes

rolling pin n el rodillo ro·deel·yo

Roman adj romano(a) ro·ma·no(a); Roman Catholic católico(a) ka·to·lee·ko(a)

Romania n Rumanía (f) roo·ma·nee·a

Romanian adj rumano(a) roo·ma·no(a) □ n (language) el rumano roo·ma·no

romantic adj romántico(a) ro·man·tee·co(a)

Rome n Roma (f) ro·ma

roof n el tejado te·kha·do; (of car) el techo te·cho

roof rack n la baca ba·ka

room n la habitación a·bee·ta·thyon; (space) el sitio see·tyo A4f

room service n el servicio de habitaciones ser·bee·thyo de ha·bee·ta·thyo·nes

root n la raíz ra·eeth

rope n la cuerda kwer·da

rose n la rosa ro·sa

rosé n el rosado ro·sa·do

rot vi pudrir* poo·dreer

rotten adj (wood etc) podrido(a) po·dree·do(a)

rough n (golf) la maleza ma·le·tha □ adj (surface) áspero(n) a·spe·ro(a); (weather) malo(a) ma·lo(a); (sea) agitado(a) a·khee·ta·do(a); (not gentle) violento(a) byo·len·to(a); a rough estimate un presupuesto aproximado oon pre·soo·pwes·to a·prok·see·ma·do

roughly adv duramente doo·ra·men·te; (approximately) aproximadamente a·prok·see·ma·da·men·te

roulette n la ruleta roo·le·ta

round adj redondo(a) re·don·do(a) □ n (circle) el círculo theer·koo·lo; (in competition) la vuelta bwel·ta; (in boxing) el asalto a·sal·to; (of golf) el partido par·tee·do; (of talks) la serie se·rye □ prep to go round a field rodear un campo ro·de·ar oon kam·po; we sat round the table nos sentamos alrededor de la mesa nos sen·ta·mos al·re·de·dor de la me·sa; to go round the shops ir* de tiendas eer de tyen·das; it's round the corner está muy cerca, doblando la esquina es·ta mooy ther·ka do·blan·do la es·kee·na □ adv to turn something round dar* vueltas a algo dar bwel·tas a al·go

round figure/number n la cifra redonda thee·fra re·don·da

round trip n el viaje de ida y vuelta bya·khe de ee·da ee bwel·ta

round trip (ticket) n el billete de ida y vuelta beel·ye·te de ee·da ee bwel·ta T61, 62

route n la ruta roo·ta T128, F19

routine n la rutina roo·tee·na □ adj de rutina de roo·tee·na

row¹ n la fila fee·la □ vi row (sport) remar re·mar

row² n (noise) el ruido rwee·do

rowing n (sport) el remo re·mo

royal adj real re·al

R.S.V.P. abbrev S.R.C. e·se e·re se

rub vt frotar fro·tar; to rub out borrar bo·rrar

rubber n (material) el caucho kow·cho

rubber band n la goma go·ma

rubbish n la basura ba·soo·ra; (nonsense) las tonterías ton·te·ree·as

ruby n el rubí roo·bee

rucksack n la mochila mo·chee·la

rudder n el timón *tee·mon*

rude adj (*person*) grosero(a) *gro·se·ro(a)*; (*remark*) ofensivo(a) *o·fen·see·bo(a)*

rug n la alfombra *al·fom·bra*

rugby n el rugby *roog·bee*

ruin n la ruina *rwee·na* □ vt arruinar *a·rrwee·nar*

ruins pl las ruinas *rwee·nas*

rule n (*regulation*) la regla *re·gla*; (*for measuring*) la regla *re·gla* □ vt gobernar* *go·ber·nar*

ruler n (*leader*) el jefe *khe·fe*; (*for measuring*) la regla *re·gla*

rum n el ron *ron*

rumble vi retumbar *re·toom·bar* □ n el retumbar *re·toom·bar*

rump steak n el filete de lomo (de vaca) *fee·le·te de lo·mo (de ba·ka)*

run n (*outing*) el paseo *pa·se·o*; (*in stocking*) la carrera *ka·rre·ra* □ vi correr* *ko·rrer*; (*machine, engine*) funcionar *foon·thyo·nar*; the trains run every hour los trenes salen cada hora *los tre·nes sa·len ka·da o·ra*; the road runs past the house el camino pasa por delante de la casa *el ka·mee·no pa·sa por de·lan·te de la ka·sa*; this car runs on diesel este coche funciona con gasoil *es·te ko·che foon·thyo·na kon gas·oyl*; to run after someone correr* detrás de alguien *ko·rrer de·tras de al·gyen*; to run away huir* *oo·eer*; to run down or over (*car etc*) atropellar *a·tro·pel·yar*; we've run out of milk nos hemos quedado sin leche *nos e·mos ke·da·do seen le·che* □ vt run (*a business, country*) dirigir* *dee·ree·kheer*

runner beans pl las judías *khoo·dee·as*

running costs pl los gastos corrientes *gas·tos ko·rryen·tes*

runway n la pista de aterrizaje *pees·ta de a·te·rree·tha·khe*

rural adj rural *roo·ral*

rush vi precipitarse *pre·thee·pee·tar·se* □ vt (*goods*) mandar urgentemente *man·dar oor·khen·te·men·te* □ n la prisa *pree·sa*; we had a rush of orders nos han inundado de pedidos *nos an ee·noon·da·do de pe·dee·dos*

rush hour n la hora punta *o·ra poon·ta*

Russia n Rusia (f) *roo·sya*

Russian adj ruso(a) *roo·so(a)*; he's Russian es ruso *es roo·so*; she's Russian es rusa *es roo·sa* □ n Russian (*language*) el ruso *roo·so*

rust n el orín *o·reen* □ vi oxidarse *ok·see·dar·se*

rustproof adj inoxidable *een·ok·see·da·ble*

rusty adj oxidado(a) *ok·see·da·do(a)*

rutabaga n el nabo *na·bo*

rye n el centeno *then·te·no*; rye (*whiskey*) el whisky de centeno *wees·kee de then·te·no*

rye bread n el pan de centeno *pan de then·te·no*

S

saccharin n la sacarina *sa·ka·ree·na*

sachet n la bolsita *bol·see·ta*

sack n el saco *sa·ko* □ vt (*dismiss*) despedir* *des·pe·deer*

sad adj triste *trees·te*

saddle n la silla de montar *seel·ya de mon·tar*

safe adj (*out of danger*) fuera de peligro *fwe·ra de pe·lee·gro*; (*not dangerous*) no peligroso(a) *no pe·lee·gro·so(a)* □ n la caja fuerte *ka·kha fwer·te* A34

safeguard n la protección *pro·tek·thyon*

safety n la seguridad *se·goo·ree·dad*

safety belt n el cinturón de seguridad *theen·too·ron de se·goo·ree·dad*

safety pin n el imperdible *eem·per·dee·ble*

sage n (*herb*) la salvia *sal·bya*

sail n la vela *be·la* □ vi hacer* vela *a·ther be·la* L23, 24

sailboat n el velero *be·le·ro*

sailor n el marinero *ma·ree·ne·ro*

saint n el/la santo(a) *san·to(a)*

sake n □ for my sake por mí *por mee*

salad n la ensalada *en·sa·la·da* E39

salad dressing n la vinagreta *bee·na·gre·ta*

salary n el sueldo *swel·do*

sale n la venta *ben·ta*; on sale or return vendido con derecho a cambiarlo *ben·dee·do kon de·re·cho a kam·byar·lo* Bm19, 21

sales pl (*cheap prices*) las rebajas *re·ba·khas*

sales assistant n el/la dependiente *de·pen·dyen·te*

salesman n (*rep*) el viajante *bee·a·khan·te*

sales manager n el jefe de ventas *khe·fe de ben·tas*

saliva n la saliva *sa·lee·ba*

salmon n el salmón *sal·mon*

saloon n (*bar*) el bar *bar*

salt n la sal *sal* S33

salt cellar n el salero *sa·le·ro*

salty adj salado(a) *sa·la·do(a)* E33

same adj mismo(a) *mees·mo(a)*; the same book as (*similar*) el mismo libro que *el mees·mo lee·bro ke* □ pron all the same de todas formas *de to·das for·mas*; (the) same again please! lo mismo por favor *lo mees·mo por fa·bor*

sample n (*of goods*) la muestra *mwes·tra* □ vt (*wine*) probar* *pro·bar* Bm23

sanctions pl las sanciones *san·thyo·nes*

sand n la arena *a·re·na*

sandal n la sandalia *san·da·lya*

sandbank n el banco de arena *ban·ko de a·re·na*

sandwich n el bocadillo *bo·ka·deel·yo*; a ham sandwich un bocadillo de jamón *oon bo·ka·deel·yo de kha·mon* E77

sandy adj (*beach*) de arena *de a·re·na*

sanitarium n el sanatorio *sa·na·to·ryo*

sanitary napkin n el paño higiénico *pan·yo ee·khye·nee·ko*

sarcastic adj sarcástico(a) *sar·kas·tee·ko(a)*

sardine n la sardina *sar·dee·na*

Sardinia n Cerdeña (f) *ther·den·ya*

satellite n el satélite *sa·te·lee·te*

satin n el raso *ra·so*

satire n (*play*) la sátira *sa·tee·ra*

satisfactory adj satisfactorio(a) *sa·tees·fak·to·ryo(a)*

satisfy vt satisfacer* *sa·tees·fa·ther*

saturate vt (*market*) saturar *sa·too·rar*

Saturday n el sábado *sa·ba·do*

sauce n la salsa *sal·sa*

saucepan n el cazo *ka·tho*

saucer n el platillo *pla·teel·yo*

sauna n la sauna *sow·na*

sausage n la salchicha *sal·chee·cha*

sausage roll n la empanadilla de salchicha *em·pa·na·deel·ya de sal·chee·cha*

sauté adj salteado(a) *sal·te·a·do(a)*

save vt (*person*) salvar *sal·bar*; (*money*) ahorrar *a·o·rrar*

savings account n la cartilla de ahorros *kar·teel·ya de a·o·rros*

savings and loan association n la sociedad de préstamo imobiliario *so·thye·dad de pres·ta·mo ee·mo·bee·lee·a·ryo*

savings bank n la caja de ahorros *ka·kha de a·o·rros*

savory adj (*not sweet*) salado(a) *sa·la·do(a)*

say vt decir* *de·theer*; could you say that again? ¿puede repetir eso? *pwe·de re·pe·teer e·so*

scab n la costra *kos·tra*

scald vt escaldar *es·kal·dar*

scale n (*of fish*) la escama *es·ka·ma*; (*of map, thermometer, music*) la escala *es·ka·la*; **scale of charges** la tarifa *ta·ree·fa*

scales pl (*for weighing*) la balanza *ba·lan·tha*

scallion n el chalote *cha·lo·te*

scallop n la vieira *byey·ra*

scalp n el cuero cabelludo *kwe·ro ka·bel·yoo·do*

scampi n las gambas *gam·bas*

Scandinavia n Escandinavia *es·kan·dee·na·bya*

Scandinavian adj escandinavo(a) *es·kan·dee·na·bo(a)*

scar n la cicatriz *thee·ka·treeth*

scarce adj escaso(a) *es·ka·so(a)*

scarcely adv apenas *a·pe·nas*

scared adj □ **to be scared** tener* miedo *te·ner mye·do*

scarf n la bufanda *boo·fan·da*

scarlet adj escarlata *es·kar·la·ta*

scene n la escena *es·the·na*; (*sight*) la perspectiva *pers·pek·tee·ba*

scenery n el paisaje *pay·sa·khe*

scenic route n la ruta turística *roo·ta too·rees·tee·ka* F20

scent n (*smell*) el olor *o·lor*; (*perfume*) el perfume *per·foo·me* S45

schedule n el programa *pro·gra·ma*; (*of trains etc*) el horario *o·ra·ryo*; **on schedule** (*train*) sin retraso *seen re·tra·so*

scheduled flight n el vuelo regular *bwe·lo re·goo·lar*

scheme n (*plan*) el plan *plan*

school n el colegio *ko·le·khyo*

science n la ciencia *thyen·thya*

science fiction n la ciencia-ficción *thyen·thya·feek·thyon*

scientific adj científico(a) *thyen·tee·fee·ko(a)*

scientist n el/la científico(a) *thyen·tee·fee·ko(a)*

scissors pl las tijeras *tee·khe·ras*

scooter n el scooter *es·koo·ter*

scope n □ **within the scope of** dentro del alcance de *den·tro del al·kan·the de*

score n el tanteo *tan·te·o* □ vt (*goal*) marcar* *mar·kar*

Scot n el/la escocés(cesa) *es·ko·thes (·the·sa)*

Scotch n (*liquor*) el whisky escocés *wees·kee es·ko·thes*

Scotch tape n el papel celo *pa·pel the·lo* S95

Scotland n Escocia (f) *es·ko·thya*

Scottish adj escocés(esa) *es·ko·thes (·the·sa)*; he's Scottish es escocés *es es·ko·thes*; she's Scottish es escocesa *es es·ko·the·sa*

scourer n el estropajo *es·tro·pa·kho*

scrap n (*bit*) el pedacito *pe·da·thee·to*

scrape vt rozar* *ro·thar*

scratch vt arañar *a·ran·yar*

scream vi gritar *gree·tar*

screen n la pantalla *pan·tal·ya*

screw n el tornillo *tor·neel·yo*

screwdriver n el destornillador *des·tor·neel·ya·dor*

sculpture n la escultura *es·kool·too·ra*

sea n el mar *mar*; **to go by sea** ir* por mar *eer por mar*

seafood n los mariscos *ma·rees·kos*

seafront n el paseo marítimo *pa·se·o ma·ree·tee·mo*

sea level n el nivel del mar *nee·bel del mar*

seam n la costura *kos·too·ra*

search vt registrar *re·khees·trar*; **to search for** buscar* *boos·kar*

seasick adj □ **to be seasick** estar* mareado(a) *es·tar ma·re·a·do(a)*

seaside n la orilla del mar *o·reel·ya del mar*

season n la temporada *tem·po·ra·da*; **the vacation season** la temporada de veraneo *la tem·po·ra·da de be·ra·ne·o*; **strawberries are in season** las fresas están en sazón *las fre·sas es·tan en sa·thon*

seasoning n el condimento *kon·dee·men·to*

season ticket n el billete de abono *beel·ye·te de a·bo·no*

seat n el asiento *a·syen·to*; **please take a seat** siéntese por favor *syen·te·se por fa·bor* T9, 45, 64, 76, L37

seat belt n el cinturón de seguridad *theen·too·ron de se·goo·ree·dad*

seaweed n las algas *al·gas*

second n (*time*) el segundo *se·goon·do* □ adj segundo(a) *se·goon·do(a)*

secondary adj (*importance*) secundario(a) *se·koon·da·ryo(a)*

secondary school n el colegio de segunda enseñanza *ko·le·khyo de se·goon·da en·sen·yan·tha*

second-class adj de segunda clase *de se·goon·da kla·se*

second floor n el primer piso *pree·mer pee·so* A5

secondhand adj (*car etc*) de segunda mano *de se·goon·da ma·no* S14

secret adj secreto(a) *se·kre·to(a)* □ n el secreto *se·kre·to*

secretary n el/la secretario(a) *se·kre·ta·ryo(a)* Bm7

secretary of state n el Ministro de Asuntos Exteriores *mee·nees·tro de a·soon·tos eks·te·ryo·res*

sector n (*economy*) el sector *sek·tor*; **private sector** el sector privado *sek·tor pree·ba·do*; **public sector** el sector público *sek·tor poob·lee·ko*

security n (*at airport*) la seguridad *se·goo·ree·dad*; (*for loan*) la fianza *fee·an·tha*

sedan n (*car*) el sedán *se·dan*

sedative n el calmante *kal·man·te*

see vt/i ver* *ber*; I want to see a doctor quiero consultar a un médico *kye·ro kon·sool·tar a oon me·dee·ko*; **to see someone off at the station** despedir* a alguien en la estación *des·pe·deer a al·gyen en la es·ta·thyon*; **to see someone home** acompañar a alguien a su casa *a·kom·pan·yar a al·gyen a soo ka·sa*; **to see to something** encargarse* de algo *en·kar·gar·se de al·go*

seed n la semilla *se·meel·ya*

seem vi parecer* *pa·re·ther*

seersucker n la sirsaca *seer·sa·ka*

seesaw n el columpio *ko·loom·pyo*

seldom adv raramente *ra·ra·men·te*

selection n la selección *se·lek·thyon* Bm23, S44, 88

self-contained adj (apartment) independiente *een·de·pen·dyen·te*

self-employed adj que trabaja por su propia cuenta *ke·tra·ba·kha por soo pro·pya kwen·ta*

selfish adj egoista *e·go·ees·ta*

self-service adj autoservicio *ow·to·ser·bee·thyo*

sell vt vender *ben·der* S7

semifinal n la semifinal *se·mee·fee·nal*

semiskilled adj semicualificado(a) *se·mee·kwa·lee·fee·ka·do(a)*

senate n (political) el senado *se·na·do*

senator n el senador *se·na·dor*

send vt enviar *en·bee·ar*

sender n el remitente *re·mee·ten·te*

senior adj (in rank) superior *soo·pe·ryor*; (in age) mayor *ma·yor*

sense n el sentido *sen·tee·do*; (common sense) el sentido común *sen·tee·do ko·moon*; sense of humor el sentido del humor *sen·tee·do del oo·mor*; to make sense tener* sentido *te·ner sen·tee·do*

sensible adj sensato(a) *sen·sa·to(a)*

sentence n la frase *fra·se*

separate adj separado(a) *se·pa·ra·do(a)*

September n se(p)tiembre (m) *se(p)·tyem·bre*

serious adj serio(a) *se·ryo(a)*

serve vt servir* *ser·beer*

service n el servicio *ser·bee·thyo*; (for car) la revisión *re·bee·syon*; (in church) el oficio *o·fee·thyo*

service area n el área de servicios *a·re·a de ser·bee·thyos*

service charge n el servicio *ser·bee·thyo* M4, E45

service industry n la rama de servicios *ra·ma de ser·bee·thyos*

service station n la estación de servicio *es·ta·thyon de ser·bee·thyo* F10

serviette n la servilleta *ser·beel·ye·ta*

set n (collection) el juego *khwe·go* □ vt (alarm) poner* *po·ner*; to set the table poner* la mesa *po·ner la me·sa*; to have one's hair set hacerse* marcar el pelo *a·ther·se mar·kar el pe·lo*; to set off or out ponerse* en camino *po·ner·se en ka·mee·no*

settle vt (argument) arreglar *a·rre·glar*, (bill) liquidar *lee·kee·dar* □ vi (wine) sedimentarse *se·dee·men·tar·se*; to settle out of court llegar a un arreglo amistoso *lye·gar a oon a·rre·glo a·mees·to·so*; to settle in instalarse *eens·ta·lar·se*

settled adj (weather) estacionado(a) *es·ta·thyo·na·do(a)*

seven num siete *sye·te*

seventeen num diecisiete *dye·thee·sye·te*

seventeenth adj diecisiete *dye·thee·sye·te*

seventh adj séptimo(a) *sep·tee·mo(a)*

seventy num setenta *se·ten·ta*

several adj varios(as) *ba·ryos(as)*; several towns varias ciudades *ba·ryas thyoo·da·des* □ pron several of us varios de nosotros *ba·ryos de no·so·tros*

sew vi coser *ko·ser*

sewing machine n la máquina de coser *ma·kee·na de ko·ser*

sex n el sexo *sek·so*

sexual intercourse n las relaciones sexuales *re·la·thyo·nes sek·swa·les*

sexy adj sexy *sek·see*

shade n la sombra *som·bra*; (for lamp) la pantalla *pan·tal·ya*

shades pl (sunglasses) las gafas ahumadas *ga·fas a·oo·ma·das*

shadow n la sombra *som·bra*

shake vt agitar *a·khee·tar*; to shake hands with someone dar* la mano a alguien *dar la ma·no a al·gyen* □ vi shake temblar* *tem·blar*

shall vi □ I shall do it lo haré *lo a·re*; shall I do it? ¿quiere que lo haga? *kye·re ke lo a·ga*; shall we come tomorrow? ¿vendremos mañana? *ben·dre·mos man·ya·na*

shallow adj poco profundo(a) *po·ko pro·foon·do(a)*

shame n la vergüenza *ber·gwen·tha*; what a shame! ¡qué lástima! ¡ke las·tee·ma*

shampoo n el champú *cham·poo* Sn45

shandygaff n la cerveza con gaseosa *ther·be·tha kon ga·se·o·sa*

shape n la forma *for·ma*

share n (part) la participación *par·tee·thee·pa·thyon*; (finance) la acción *ak·thyon* □ vt (money, room) compartir *kom·par·teer*

shark n el tiburón *tee·boo·ron*

sharp adj (knife) afilado(a) *a·fee·la·do(a)*; (bend) cerrado(a) *the·rra·do(a)*

sharp practice n el procedimiento deshonesto *pro·the·dee·myen·to des·o·nes·to*

shave vi afeitarse *a·fey·tar·se*

shaver n la máquina de afeitar *ma·kee·na de a·fey·tar*

shaving brush n la brocha de afeitar *bro·cha de a·fey·tar*

shaving cream n la crema de afeitar *kre·ma de a·fey·tar*

shaving soap n el jabón de afeitar *kha·bon de a·fey·tar*

shawl n el chal *chal*

she pron ella *el·ya*; here she is ¡aquí está (ella)! *a·kee es·ta (el·ya)*

shed n el cobertizo *ko·ber·tee·tho*

sheep n la oveja *o·be·kha*

sheepskin n la piel de carnero *pyel de kar·ne·ro*

sheer adj (stockings) fino(a) *fee·no(a)*

sheet n la sábana *sa·ba·na*; (of paper) la hoja *o·kha*

shelf n el estante *es·tan·te*

shell n (of egg) la cáscara *kas·ka·ra*; (of fish) la concha *kon·cha*

shellfish n (on menu) los mariscos *ma·rees·kos*

shelter n (for waiting under) el refugio *re·foo·khyo* □ vi (from rain etc) refugiarse *re·foo·khyar·se*

shelve vi (beach) estar* en declive *es·tar en de·klee·be* □ vt (project) arrinconar *a·rreen·ko·nar*

sherbet n el sorbete *sor·be·te*

sherry n el jerez *khe·reth*

shift n (change) el cambio *kam·byo*; (of workmen) el turno *toor·no* □ vt to shift gear cambiar de marcha *kam·byar de mar·cha*

shin n la espinilla *es·pee·neel·ya*

shine vi brillar *breel·yar*

shingles n (illness) las herpes *er·pes*

shiny adj brillante *breel·yan·te*

ship n el barco *bar·ko* □ vt (goods) transportar *trans·por·tar*

shipbuilding n la construcción naval *kons·trook·thyon na·bal*

shipment n el envío *en·bee·o*

shipping agent *n* el agente marítimo *a·khen·te ma·ree·tee·mo*
shipping company *n* la compañía naviera *kom·pan·yee·a na·bye·ra*
shipyard *n* el astillero *as·teel·ye·ro*
shirt *n* la camisa *ka·mee·sa* S59, Sn70
shiver *vi* temblar* *tem·blar*
shock *n* (*fright*) el sobresalto *so·bre·sal·to*; (*medical*) el shock *shok*; (*electric*) la descarga *des·kar·ga*
shock absorber *n* el amortiguador *a·mor·tee·gwa·dor*
shoe *n* el zapato *tha·pa·to*; (*of brake*) la zapata *tha·pa·ta* S11, 60
shoelace *n* el cordón *kor·don*
shoeshop *n* la zapatería *tha·pa·te·ree·a*
shoot *vt* (*injure*) herir* con un fusil *e·reer kon oon foo·seel*; (*kill*) matar a tiros *ma·tar a tee·ros* □ *vi* disparar *dees·pa·rar*
shop *n* la tienda *tyen·da*
shoplifting *n* el robo en tiendas *ro·bo en tyen·das*
shopping *n* las compras *kom·pras*; to go shopping ir* de compras *eer de kom·pras*
shopping bag *n* la bolsa de la compra *bol·sa de la kom·pra*
shopping center *n* el centro comercial *then·tro ko·mer·thyal*
shop steward *n* el enlace sindical *en·la·the seen·dee·kal*
shop window *n* el escaparate *es·ka·pa·ra·te*, la vitrina (Am) *bee·tree·na*
~~shopworn *adj* deteriorado(a) *deeyon·ra·do(a)*~~
shore *n* la orilla *o·reel·ya*
short *adj* corto(a) *kor·to(a)*; (*person*) bajo(a) *ba·kho(a)*; to be short of something faltarle algo a alguien *fal·tar·le al·go a al·gyen*; he gave me short change no me devolvió toda la vuelta *no me de·bol·byo to·da la bwel·ta*
shortage *n* la escasez *es·ka·seth*
shortbread *n* la mantecada *man·te·ka·da*
shortcut *n* el atajo *a·ta·kho* T129
short drink *n* la copita *ko·pee·ta*
shorten *vt* acortar *a·kor·tar*
shortfall *n* el déficit *de·fee·theet*
shorthand *n* la taquigrafía *ta·kee·gra·fee·a*
shorthand typist *n* la taquimecanógrafa *ta·kee·me·ka·no·gra·fa*
short list *n* la lista de seleccionados *lees·ta de se·lek·thyo·na·dos*
shortly *adv* (*soon*) dentro de poco *den·tro de po·ko*
shorts *pl* los pantalones cortos *pan·ta·lo·nes kor·tos*; (*underwear*) los calzoncillos *kal·thon·theel·yos*
short-staffed *adj* □ to be short-staffed estar* a falta de personal *es·tar a fal·ta de per·so·nal*
short term *adj* a corto plazo a *kor·to pla·tho*
short wave *n* la onda corta *on·da kor·ta*
shot *n* el disparo *dees·pa·ro*
should *vi* □ we should buy it debemos comprarlo *de·be·mos kom·prar·lo*; I should like a... quisiera un(a)... *kee·sye·ra oon(a)*
shoulder *n* el hombro *om·bro*
shout *n* el grito *gree·to* □ *vi* gritar *gree·tar*
shovel *n* la pala *pa·la*
show *n* (*exhibition*) la exposición *eks·po·see·thyon*; (*in theater*) el espectáculo *es·pek·ta·koo·lo* □ *vt* mostrar*

mos·trar; (*movie*) proyectar *pro·yek·tar*; to show someone out acompañar a alguien a la puerta *a·kom·pan·yar a al·gyen a la pwer·ta* □ *vi* show (*be visible*) notarse *no·tar·se* L44
show business *n* el mundo del espectáculo *moon·do del es·pek·ta·koo·lo*
shower *n* (*rain*) el chaparrón *cha·pa·rron*; (*bath*) la ducha *doo·cha* A4, 80
showroom *n* el salón de demostraciones *sa·lon de de·mos·tra·thyo·nes*
shrewd *adj* perspicaz *pers·pee·kath*
shrimp *n* el camarón *ka·ma·ron*
shrink *vi* encogerse* *en·ko·kher·se*
shrinkage *n* la disminución *dees·mee·noo·thyon*
Shrove Tuesday *n* el martes de carnaval *mar·tes de kar·na·bal*
shrub *n* el arbusto *ar·boos·to*
shrug *vi* encogerse* de hombros *en·ko·kher·se de om·bros*
shut *vt* cerrar* *the·rrar*; to be shut (*door*) estar* cerrado(a) *es·tar the·rra·do(a)* □ *vi* shut (*door, window*) cerrarse* *the·rrar·se*
shutter *n* (*on window*) la contraventana *kon·tra·ben·ta·na*; (*in camera*) el obturador *ob·too·ra·dor*
shuttle (service) *n* (*airline*) el puente aéreo *pwen·te a·e·reo*
shy *adj* tímido(a) *tee·mee·do(a)*
Sicily *n* Sicilia (*f*) *see·thee·lya*
sick *adj* (*ill*) enfermo(a) *en·fer·mo(a)*; to be sick (*vomit*) vomitar *bo·mee·tar*; to feel sick sentirse* mareado *sen·teer·se ma·re·a·do*
sickly *adj* enfermizo(a) *en·fer·mee·tho(a)*
sickness *n* (*illness*) la enfermedad *en·fer·me·dad*; (*nausea*) la náusea *now·se·a*
side *n* el lado *la·do*; the right side (*of cloth etc*) el derecho *el de·re·cho*; the wrong side el revés *re·bes*; this side up este lado arriba *es·te la·do a·rree·ba*
sideboard *n* el aparador *a·pa·ra·dor*
sidelights *pl* (*on car*) las luces laterales *loo·thes la·te·ra·les*
side-street *n* la calle secundaria *kal·ye se·koon·da·rya*
sidewalk *n* la acera *a·the·ra*, la vereda (Am) *be·re·da*
siesta *n* la siesta *syes·ta*
sieve *n* el colador *ko·la·dor* □ *vt* colar *ko·lar*
sift *vt* (*sieve*) pasar por el colador *pa·sar por el ko·la·dor*
sigh *vi* suspirar *soos·pee·rar*
sight *n* la vista *bees·ta*; to see the sights visitar los puntos de interés *bee·see·tar los poon·tos de een·te·res*
sightseeing *n* el turismo *too·rees·mo*
sign *n* (*mark*) el signo *seeg·no*; (*with hand*) la seña *sen·ya*; (*notice*) la señal *sen·yal* □ *vt* (*document*) firmar *feer·mar* T197
signal *n* la señal *sen·yal*
signature *n* la firma *feer·ma*
signpost *n* el poste indicador *pos·te een·dee·ka·dor*
silence *n* el silencio *see·len·thyo*
silent *adj* silencioso(a) *see·len·thyo·so(a)*
silk *n* la seda *se·da*; a silk dress un vestido de seda *oon bes·tee·do de se·da* S59
silly *adj* estúpido(a) *es·too·pee·do(a)*
silver *n* (*metal*) la plata *pla·ta*; (*money*) las monedas *mo·ne·das*; (*ware*) la vajilla de plata *ba·kheel·ya de pla·ta*;

a silver bracelet una pulsera de plata *oo·na pool·se·ra de pla·ta* S87, 90

similar *adj* parecido(a) *pa·re·thee·do(a)*; to be similar to parecerse* a *pa·re·ther·se a*

simmer *vi* hervir* a fuego lento *er·beer a fwe·go len·to*

simple *adj* sencillo(a) *sen·theel·yo(a)*

since *prep* desde *des·de*; since yesterday desde ayer *des·de a·yer*; I've been here since 4 o'clock he estado aquí desde las 4 *e es·ta·do a·kee des·de las 4* □ *conj* since we arrived desde que llegamos *des·de ke lye·ga·mos*; since he's ill como está enfermo *ko·mo es·ta en·fer·mo*

sincere *adj* sincero(a) *seen·the·ro(a)*

sincerely *adv* □ yours sincerely le saluda atentamente *le sa·loo·da a·ten·ta·men·te*

sing *vt/i* cantar *kan·tar*

single *adj* (not double) único(a) *oo·nee·ko(a)*; (not married) soltero(a) *sol·te·ro(a)*; a single bed una cama individual *oo·na ka·ma een·dee·bee·dwal*; a single room una habitación individual *oo·na a·bee·ta·thyon een·dee·bee·dwal*; a single ticket un billete de ida *oon beel·ye·te de ee·da*

sink *n* (basin) el fregadero *fre·ga·de·ro* □ *vi* (in water) hundirse *oon·deer·se*

sir *n* señor (m) *sen·yor*

siren *n* la sirena *see·re·na*

sirloin *n* el solomillo *so·lo·meel·yo*

sister *n* la hermana *er·ma·na*

sister-in-law *n* la cuñada *koon·ya·da*

sit *vi* sentarse *sen·tar·se*; we were sitting at the table estábamos sentados a la mesa *es·ta·ba·mos sen·ta·dos a la me·sa*; to sit down sentarse* *sen·tar·se*

site *n* (of building) el solar *so·lar*

sitting room *n* el cuarto de estar *kwar·to de es·tar*

situation *n* (place) el sitio *see·tyo*; (circumstances) la situación *see·twa·thyon*

six *num* seis *seys*

sixteen *num* dieciseis *dye·thee·seys*

sixteenth *adj* decimosexto(a) *de·thee·mo·seks·to(a)*

sixth *adj* sexto(a) *seks·to(a)*

sixty *num* sesenta *se·sen·ta*

size *n* las dimensiones *dee·men·syo·nes*; (of clothes) la talla *tal·ya*; (of shoes) el número *noo·me·ro* S62

skate *n* (for ice or on rollers) el patín *pa·teen*; (fish) la raya *ra·ya* □ *vi* patinar *pa·tee·nar*

skateboard *n* el patín *pa·teen*

skating rink *n* la pista de patinaje *pees·ta de pa·tee·na·khe*

sketch *n* (drawing) el boceto *bo·the·to* □ *vt* esbozar* *es·bo·thar*

skewer *n* la broqueta *bro·ke·ta*

ski *n* el esquí *es·kee* □ *vi* esquiar *es·kee·ar* L31

ski boot *n* la bota de esquí *bo·ta de es·kee*

skid *n* el patinazo *pa·tee·na·tho* □ *vi* patinar *pa·tee·nar*

skier *n* el/la esquiador(a) *es·kee·a·dor(·ra)*

skiing *n* el esquí *es·kee*; to go skiing esquiar *es·kee·ar*

ski lift *n* la telesilla *te·le·seel·ya*

skill *n* la habilidad *a·bee·lee·dad*

skilled *adj* (workers) especializado(a) *es·pe·thya·lee·tha·do(a)*

skillet *n* la sartén *sar·ten*

skim milk *n* la leche desnatada *le·che des·na·ta·da*

skin *n* la piel *pyel* S40

ski pants *pl* los pantalones de esquí *pan·ta·lo·nes de es·kee*

skirt *n* la falda *fal·da* Sn69

ski run *n* la pista de esquí *pees·ta de es·kee*

skull *n* la calavera *ka·la·be·ra*

sky *n* el cielo *thye·lo*

skyscraper *n* el rascacielos *ras·ka·thye·los*

slack *adj* (loose) flojo(a) *flo·kho(a)*; (loose) suelto(a) *swel·to(a)*

slacks *pl* los pantalones (de mujer) *pan·ta·lo·nes (de moo·kher)*

slam *vt* dar* un portazo *dar oon por·ta·tho*

slang *n* el argot *ar·got*

slap *vt* dar* una bofetada a *dar oo·na bo·fe·ta·da a*

slate *n* la pizarra *pee·tha·rra*

Slav *n* el/la eslavo(a) *es·la·bo(a)*

slave *n* el/la esclavo(a) *es·kla·bo(a)*

sled(ge) *n* (toboggan) el trineo *tree·ne·o*

sleep *n* el sueño *swen·yo* □ *vi* dormir* *dor·meer* □ *vt* the apartment sleeps three el piso tiene cabida para 3 personas *el pee·so tye·ne ka·bee·da pa·ra 3 per·so·nas*

sleeping bag *n* el saco de dormir *sa·ko de dor·meer*

sleeping car *n* el coche-cama *ko·che·ka·ma* T66

sleeping pill *n* el somnífero *som·nee·fe·ro*

sleet *n* la aguanieve *a·gwa·nye·be*

sleeve *n* la manga *man·ga*

sleigh *n* el trineo *tree·ne·o*

slice *n* la rodaja *ro·da·kha* □ *vt* cortar en rodajas *kor·tar en ro·da·khas* S32

slide *vi* resbalar *res·ba·lar* □ *n* (chute) el tobogán *to·bo·gan*; (photo) la diapositiva *dee·a·po·see·tee·ba*

slide rule *n* la regla de cálculo *re·gla de kal·koo·lo*

slight *adj* (small) pequeño(a) *pe·ken·yo(a)*

slim *adj* delgado(a) *del·ga·do(a)*

sling *n* (for arm) el cabestrillo *ka·bes·treel·yo*

slip *vi* (slide) resbalar *res·ba·lar*; (trip) tropezar* *tro·pe·thar* □ *n* (underskirt) la combinación *kom·bee·na·thyon*; (of paper) la papeleta *pa·pe·le·ta*

slipper *n* la zapatilla *tha·pa·teel·ya*

slippery *adj* resbaladizo(a) *res·ba·la·dee·tho(a)*

slogan *n* el slogan *es·lo·gan*

slope *n* (angle) la pendiente *pen·dyen·te*; (sloping ground) la cuesta *kwes·ta*

slot *n* la ranura *ra·noo·ra*

slot machine *n* la máquina de monedas *ma·kee·na de mo·ne·das*

slow *adj* lento(a) *len·to(a)*; my watch is slow mi reloj se atrasa *mee re·lokh se a·tra·sa* □ *vi* to slow down or up ir* más despacio *eer mas des·pa·thyo*

slowdown *n* la huelga de celo *wel·ga de the·lo*

slump *n* la depresión económica *de·pre·syon e·ko·no·mee·ka* □ *vi* bajar de pronto *ba·khar de pron·to*

smack *vt* dar* una torta *dar oo·na tor·ta* □ *n* el palmazo *pal·ma·tho*

small *adj* pequeño(a) *pe·ken·yo(a)* A15

smallpox *n* la viruela *bee·rwe·la*

smart *adj* elegante *e·le·gan·te*

smash *vt* romper* *rom·per*

smell *n* el olor *o·lor* □ *vt* oler* *o·ler*
□ *vi* **to smell of garlic** oler* a ajo *o·
ler a a·kho*

smile *n* la sonrisa *son·ree·sa* □ *vi* sonreír* *son·re·eer*

smock *n* la blusa *bloo·sa*

smoke *n* el humo *oo·mo* □ *vt/i* fumar
foo·mar; **do you smoke?** ¿fuma Ud?
foo·ma oos·ted

smoked *adj* (*salmon etc*) ahumado(a)
a·oo·ma·do(a)

smoker *n* (*person*) el/la fumador(a)
foo·ma·dor(·a); (*compartment*) el vagón de fumadores *ba·gon de foo·ma·
do·res*

smooth *adj* suave *swa·be*

smuggle *vt* pasar de contrabando *pa·
sar de kon·tra·ban·do*

snack *n* el tentempié *ten·tem·pye*

snack bar *n* la cafetería *ka·fe·te·ree·a*
L48

snail *n* el caracol *ka·ra·kol*

snake *n* la culebra *koo·le·bra*

snap *vi* (*break*) romperse* *rom·per·se*

snap fastener *n* el botón de presión
bo·ton de pre·syon

snatch *vt* arrebatar *a·rre·ba·tar*

sneakers *pl* las playeras *pla·ye·ras*

sneeze *n* el estornudo *es·tor·noo·do*
□ *vi* estornudar *es·tor·noo·dar*

snob *n* el esnob *es·nob*

snobbish *adj* esnob *es·nob*

snooker *n* el billar *beel·yar*

snore *vi* roncar* *ron·kar*

snorkel *n* el tubo de respiración *too·bo
de res·pee·ra·thyon*

snow *n* la nieve *nye·be* □ *vi* nevar* *ne·
bar*; **it's snowing** está nevando *es·ta
ne·ban·do*

snowball *n* la bola de nieve *bo·la de
nye·be*

snowdrift *n* el ventisquero *ben·tees·
ke·ro*

snowman *n* el muñeco de nieve *moon·
ye·ko de nye·be*

snuff *n* el rapé *ra·pe*

so *adv* □ **so pleased that...** tan con-
tento que... *tan kon·ten·to ke*; **I hope
so** espero que sí *es·pe·ro ke see*; **so
many** tantos(as) *tan·tos(as)*; **so much**
tanto(a) *tan·to(a)* □ *conj* **and so we
left** así que nos marchamos *a·see ke
nos mar·cha·mos*; **so do I** yo también
yo tam·byen; **so is he** él también *el
tam·byen*; **he did it so that I would go**
lo hizo para que yo fuera *lo ee·tho
pa·ra ke yo fwe·ra*

soak *vt* (*washing*) remojar *re·mo·khar*

soap *n* el jabón *kha·bon* A41

soap-flakes *pl* las escamas de jabón *es·
ka·mas de kha·bon*

soap powder *n* el jabón en polvo *kha·
bon en pol·bo*

sober *adj* (*not drunk*) sereno(a) *se·re·
no(a)*

soccer *n* el fútbol *foot·bol*

social *adj* social *so·thyal*

socialism *n* el socialismo *so·thya·
lees·mo*

socialist *n* el/la socialista *so·thya·lees·ta*
□ *adj* socialista *so·thya·lees·ta*

social security *n* la seguridad social *se·
goo·ree·dad so·thyal*

social services *pl* los servicios sociales
ser·bee·thyos so·thya·les

social worker *n* el/la asistente(a) social
a·sees·ten·te(a) so·thyal

society *n* la sociedad *so·thye·dad*

sock *n* el calcetín *kal·the·teen*, la media (Am) *me·dya*

socket *n* (*electrical*) el enchufe *en·
choo·fe*

soda *n* (*chemical*) la soda *so·da*; a
whiskey and soda un whisky con sifón *oon wees·kee kon see·fon*

soda water *n* el agua de Seltz (*f*) *ag·wa
de selts*

sofa *n* el sofá *so·fa*

soft *adj* (*not hard*) blando(a) *blan·
do(a)*; (*not loud*) bajo(a) *ba·kho(a)*;
(*drink*) no alcohólico(a) *no al·ko·lee·
ko(a)*

soft-boiled *adj* □ **a soft-boiled egg** un
huevo pasado por agua *oon we·bo
pa·sa·do por ag·wa*

software *n* el software

soil *n* el suelo *swe·lo*

solar *adj* solar *so·lar*

soldier *n* el soldado *sol·da·do*

sold out *adj* agotado(a) *a·go·ta·do(a)*

sole *n* (*of foot*) la planta *plan·ta*; (*of
shoe*) la suela *swe·la*; (*fish*) el lenguado *len·gwa·do*

solid *adj* (*not hollow, not liquid*) sóli-
do(a) *so·lee·do(a)*; (*strong*) fuerte
fwer·te; **in solid gold** en oro macizo
en o·ro ma·thee·tho

solution *n* la solución *so·loo·thyon*

solve *vt* (*problem*) resolver* *re·sol·ber*

some *adj* □ **some apples** algunas manzanas *al·goo·nas man·tha·nas*; **some
bread** pan *pan*; **some people** cierta
gente *thyer·ta khen·te* □ *pron* **some
(of it) was left** quedó un poco (de
ello) *ke·do oon po·ko (de el·yo)*;
some (of them) were..., algunos (de
ellos) fueron... *al·goo·nos (de el·yos)
fwe·ron*

somebody, someone *pron* alguien *al·
gyen*

someplace *adv* en alguna parte *en al·
goo·na par·te*

something *pron* algo *al·go*; **something
bigger** algo más grande *al·go mas
gran·de*

sometimes *adv* a veces *a be·thes*

somewhere *adv* en alguna parte *en al·
goo·na par·te*

son *n* el hijo *ee·kho* Sn87, C10

son et lumière *n* el espectáculo de luz
y sonido *es·pek·ta·koo·lo de looth y
so·nee·do*

song *n* la canción *kan·thyon*

son-in-law *n* el yerno *yer·no*

soon *adv* pronto *pron·to*; **he came too
soon** vino demasiado temprano *bee·
no de·ma·sya·do tem·pra·no* B9

sophisticated *adj* sofisticado(a) *so·fees·
tee·ka·do(a)*

sore *adj* (*painful*) malo(a) *ma·lo(a)*

sorry *adj* afligido(a) *a·flee·khee·do(a)*;
(I'm) sorry lo siento *lo syen·to*

sort *n* (*kind*) el tipo *tee·po*

SOS *n* el S.O.S *e·se·o·e·se*

soufflé *n* el suflé *soo·fle*

soul *n* el alma (*f*) *al·ma*

sound *n* el sonido *so·nee·do* □ *vt* **it
sounds like a car** parece el ruido de
un coche *pa·re·the el rwee·do de oon
ko·che* □ *vt* **to sound one's horn** tocar* el claxon *to·kar el klak·son*

sound track *n* la banda sonora *ban·da
so·no·ra*

soup *n* la sopa *so·pa*

sour *adj* (*sharp*) acre *a·kre*; (*milk*) cor-
tado(a) *kor·ta·do(a)*; **sour cream** la
nata agria *na·ta a·grya*

source *n* la fuente *fwen·te*

south *n* el sur *soor* □ *adv* al sur al sur
□ *n* **southeast** el sudeste *soo·des·te*;
southwest el sudoeste *sood·o·es·te*

South Africa n el África del Sur (f) *a·free·ka del soor*

South African adj sudafricano(a) *sood·a·free·ka·no(a)*

South America n la América del Sur *a·me·ree·ka del soor*

South American adj sudamericano(a) *soo·da·me·ree·ka·no(a)*

southern adj del sur *del soor*

South Pole n el Polo Sur *po·lo soor*

souvenir n el recuerdo *re·kwer·do*

Soviet adj soviético(a) *so·bye·tee·ko(a)*

Soviet Union n la Unión Soviética *oo·nyon so·bye·tee·ka*

soy beans pl la semilla de soja *se·meel·ya de so·kha*

soy sauce n la salsa de soja *sal·sa de so·kha*

spa n el balneario *bal·ne·a·ryo*

space n el espacio *es·pa·thyo*

spacecraft n la nave espacial *na·be es·pa·thyal*

spade n la pala *pa·la*, la lampa (Am) *lam·pa*; **spades** (cards) los picos *pee·kos*

spaghetti n los espaguetis *es·pa·ge·tees*

Spain n España (f) *es·pan·ya*

Spaniard n el/la español(a) *es·pan·yol(·la)*

Spanish adj español(a) *es·pan·yol(·a)*; he's Spanish es español *es·es·pan·yol*; she's Spanish es española *es·es·pan·yo·la* □ n Spanish el español *es·pan·yol*

spare adj □ spare wheel la rueda de repuesto *rwe·da de re·pwes·to*; spare time el ocio *o·thyo* □ n spare (part) la pieza de repuesto *pye·tha de re·pwes·to* T192

spare rib n la costilla de cerdo *kos·teel·ya de ther·do*

spark n la chispa *chees·pa*

sparkle vi centellear *then·tel·ye·ar*

sparkling adj (wine) reluciente *re·loo·thyen·te*

spark plug n la bujía *boo·khee·a*

sparrow n el gorrión *go·rryon*

spatula n la espátula *es·pa·too·la*

speak vt/i hablar *a·blar*; do you speak English? ¿habla Ud inglés? *a·bla oos·ted een·gles*; to speak to someone about something hablar a alguien de algo *a·blar a al·gyen de al·go* B24f

speaker n (electrical) la altavoz *al·ta·both*

special adj especial *es·pe·thyal* E17

specialize vi especializarse *es·pe·thya·lee·thar·se*; to specialize in especializarse en *es·pe·thya·lee·thar·se en* Bm17

specific adj específico(a) *es·pe·thee·fee·ko(a)*

specifications pl las especificaciónes *es·pe·thee·fee·ka·thyo·nes*

specify vt especificar* *es·pe·thee·fee·kar*

specimen n el ejemplar *e·khem·plar*; (medical) el espécimen *es·pe·thee·men*

speech n el habla (f) *a·bla*; (oration) el discurso *dees·koor·so*

speed n la velocidad *be·lo·thee·dad* □ vi to speed up acelerar *a·the·le·rar*

speedboat n la lancha motora *lan·cha mo·to·ra*

speeding n (in car) el exceso de velocidad *es·the·so de be·lo·thee·dad*

speed limit n el límite de velocidad *lee·mee·te de be·lo·thee·dad* T133

speedometer n el velocímetro *be·lo·thee·me·tro*

spell vt (in writing) escribir* *es·kree·beer* □ n (period) el período corto *pe·ree·o·do kor·to*

spend vt (money) gastar *gas·tar*; (time) pasar *pa·sar*

spice n la especia *es·pe·thya*

spicy adj picante *pee·kan·te*

spider n la araña *a·ran·ya*

spill vt derramar *de·rra·mar* □ vi derramarse *de·rra·mar·se* B75

spin vi (rotate) girar *khee·rar* □ vt (wool) hilar *ee·lar*

spinach n la espinaca *es·pee·na·ka*

spin-dry vt secar* por centrifugado *se·kar por then·tree·foo·ga·do*

spine n (backbone) el espinazo *es·pee·na·tho*

spirit n (soul) el espíritu *es·pee·ree·too*; **spirits** (alcohol) los licores *lee·ko·res*; in good spirits de buen humor *de bwen oo·mor*

spit vi escupir *es·koo·peer* □ n (for roasting) el asador *a·sa·dor*

spite n el despecho *des·pe·cho*; in spite of a pesar de *a pe·sar de*

splash n el chapoteo *cha·po·te·o* □ vt salpicar* *sal·pee·kar* □ vi chapotear *cha·po·te·ar*

splint n la tablilla *ta·bleel·ya*

splinter n (wood) la astilla *as·teel·ya*

split vt (tear) partir *par·teer*, (divide, share) dividir *dee·bee·deer* □ vi (tear) henderse *en·der·se* □ n la raja *ra·kha*

spoil vt (damage) estropear *es·tro·pe·ar*; (child) consentir* *kon·sen·teer*

spoiled adj (milk) cortado(a) *kor·ta·do(a)*

spokesman n el portavoz *por·ta·both*

sponge n la esponja *es·pon·kha*; (cake) el bizcocho *beeth·ko·cho*

spoon n la cuchara *koo·cha·ra*

spoonful n la cucharada *koo·cha·ra·da*

sport coat, sport jacket n la chaqueta de sport *cha·ke·ta de es·port*

sport(s) n el deporte *de·por·te* L25, Mc16

sport(s) car n el coche deportivo *ko·che de·por·tee·bo*

sportswear n la ropa de deporte *ro·pa de de·por·te*

spot n (patch) la mancha *man·cha*; (dot) el lunar *loo·nar*; (pimple) el grano *gra·no*; (locality) el sitio *see·tyo*; on the spot en el lugar *en el loo·gar*

spot check n la comprobación en el acto *kom·pro·ba·thyon en el ak·to*

spotlight n el foco *fo·ko*

sprain n la torcedura *tor·the·doo·ra* □ vt to sprain one's ankle torcerse* el tobillo *tor·ther·se el to·beel·yo*

spray n (of liquid) la rociada *ro·thya·da*; (container) el atomizador *a·to·mee·tha·dor* □ vt (liquid) atomizar* *a·to·mee·thar*

spread vt (butter) untar *oon·tar*; (news) propagarse *pro·pa·gar·se*; (payments) espaciar *es·pa·thyar*; to spread something out extender algo *eks·ten·der al·go*

spring n (season) la primavera *pree·ma·be·ra*; (coil) el resorte *re·sor·te*; (of water) la fuente *fwen·te*

spring onion n la cebolleta *the·bol·ye·ta*

sprinkle vt □ to sprinkle with water rociar con agua *ro·thyar kon ag·wa*; to sprinkle with sugar espolvorear de azúcar *es·pol·bo·re·ar de a·thoo·kar*

sprouts pl los coles de Bruselas *ko·les de broo·se·las*

spy n el/la espía es·pee·a

squall n la ráfaga ra·fa·ga

square n el cuadrado kwa·dra·do; (in town) la plaza pla·tha □ adj cuadrado(a) kwa·dra·do(a); **a square meter** un metro cuadrado oon me·tro kwa·dra·do; **3 meters square** 3 metros por 3 3 me·tros por 3 L3

squash vt (crush) aplastar a·plas·tar □ n (sport) el squash skwosh; (gourd) la calabaza ka·la·ba·tha

squeeze vt (lemon) exprimir eks·pree·meer; (hand) apretar* a·pre·tar □ n (financial) la restricción económica res·treek·thyon e·ko·no·mee·ka

squirrel n la ardilla ar·deel·ya

stab vt apuñalar a·poon·ya·lar

stable n el establo es·ta·blo □ adj estable es·ta·ble

stadium n el estadio es·ta·dyo

staff n el personal per·so·nal

stage n (in theater) la escena es·the·na; (point) la etapa e·ta·pa; **in stages** por etapas por e·ta·pas

stain n la mancha man·cha □ vt manchar man·char Sn70

stained glass window n la vidriera bee·drye·ra

stainless adj (steel) inoxidable een·ok·see·da·ble

stair n el peldano pel·dan·yo I4

staircase n la escalera es·ka·le·ra

stairs pl la escalera es·ka·le·ra

stake n (in gambling) la puesta pwes·ta; **to be at stake** estar* en juego es·tar en khwe·go

stale adj (bread) duro(a) doo·ro(a); **the room smells stale** el cuarto huele a moho el kwar·to we·le a mo·o

stall n (stand) el puesto pwes·to □ vi (car engine) pararse pa·rar·se

stalls pl (in theater) la butaca boo·ta·ka L38

stamp n (postage) el sello sel·yo, la estampilla (Am) es·tam·peel·ya; (rubber) el sello sel·yo □ vt (letter) poner* un sello po·ner oon sel·yo; (visa) sellar sel·yar Sn2

stand n (stall) el puesto pwes·to □ vi estar* de pie es·tar de pye; **to stand up** ponerse* de pie po·ner·se de pye □ vt stand (put) poner* po·ner; (bear) aguantar a·gwan·tar; **to stand for** (signify) significar* seeg·nee·fee·kar; **to stand out** destacarse* des·ta·kar·se

standard n el nivel nee·bel □ adj (size) normal nor·mal; (model) standard es·tan·dar

standard of living n el nivel de vida nee·bel de bee·da

staple n la grapa gra·pa

stapler n la máquina grapadora ma·kee·na gra·pa·do·ra

star n (in sky, movies etc) la estrella es·trel·ya

starch n el almidón al·mee·don

stare vi mirar mee·rar; **to stare at somebody** mirar fijamente a alguien mee·rar fee·kha·men·te a al·gyen

start vt/i empezar* em·pe·thar, comenzar* ko·men·thar □ n (beginning) el comienzo ko·myen·tho

starter n (in car) el arranque a·rran·ke

starve vi morirse* de hambre mo·reer·se de am·bre

state vt afirmar a·feer·mar □ n (condition) el estado es·ta·do; **the State** el Estado es·ta·do; **the States** los Estados Unidos es·ta·dos oo·nee·dos

statement n la declaración de·kla·ra·thyon

station n la estación es·ta·thyon; (radio) la emisora e·mee·so·ra F3

stationer's (shop) n la papelería pa·pe·le·ree·a

stationery n el papel de escribir pa·pel de es·kree·beer

station wagon n la ranchera ran·che·ra

statistic n la estadística es·ta·dees·tee·ka

statistical adj estadístico(a) es·ta·dees·tee·ko(a)

statistics n la estadística es·ta·dees·tee·ka

statue n la estatua es·ta·twa

stay n (period) la estancia es·tan·thya □ vi (remain, reside) quedarse ke·dar·se; **to stay the night** quedarse la noche ke·dar·se la no·che; **to stay with friends** quedarse con amigos ke·dar·se kon a·mee·gos; **to stay in** permanecer* en casa per·ma·ne·ther en ka·sa; **to stay up** (at night) no acostarse* no a·kos·tar·se A2, 56

steady adj firme feer·me; (pace) constante kons·tan·te

steak n el filete fee·le·te E23

steal vt robar ro·bar; **to steal something from someone** robar algo a alguien ro·bar al·go a al·gyen Sn84

steam n el vapor ba·por □ vt (food) cocer* al vapor ko·ther al ba·por

steamer n (ship) el vapor ba·por

steel n el acero a·the·ro

steep adj escarpado(a) es·kar·pa·do(a)

steer vt (car) conducir* kon·doo·theer, manejar (Am) ma·ne·khar; (boat) dirigir* dee·ree·kheer

steering n (in car) la dirección dee·rek·thyon

steering column n la columna de dirección ko·loom·na de dee·rek·thyon

steering wheel n el volante bo·lan·te, el timón (Am) tee·mon

stem n el tallo tal·yo

stenographer n la taquimecanógrafa ta·kee·me·ka·no·gra·fa

step n (pace) el paso pa·so; (stair) el escalón es·ka·lon; **to take steps to do something** tomar medidas para hacer algo to·mar me·dee·das pa·ra a·ther al·go

stepbrother n el hermanastro er·ma·nas·tro

stepdaughter n la hijastra ee·khas·tra

stepfather n el padrastro pa·dras·tro

stepladder n la escalera de tijera es·ka·le·ra de tee·khe·ra

stepmother n la madrastra ma·dras·tra

stepsister n la hermanastra er·ma·nas·tra

stepson n el hijastro ee·khas·tro

stereo(phonic) adj estereofónico(a) es·te·re·o·fo·nee·ko(a) □ n el estéreo es·te·re·o; **in stereo** estereofónico(a) es·te·re·o·fo·nee·ko(a)

sterile adj estéril es·te·reel

sterilize vt (disinfect) esterilizar* es·te·ree·lee·thar

sterling n la libra esterlina lee·bra es·ter·lee·nar

stew n el estofado es·to·fa·do

steward n el camarero ka·ma·re·ro; (at club) el organizador or·ga·nee·tha·dor

stick n el palo pa·lo □ vt (with glue etc) pegar* pe·gar

sticking plaster n el esparadrapo es·pa·ra·dra·po

sticky adj pegajoso(a) pe·ga·kho·so(a)

stiff adj rígido(a) *ree·khee·do(a)*; a stiff neck la tortícolis *tor·tee·ko·lees*

stiletto heels pl los tacones finos *ta·ko·nes fee·nos*

still adj (motionless) inmóvil *ee·mo·beel*; (wine etc) no espumoso(a) *no es·poo·mo·so(a)* □ adv (up to this time) todavía *to·da·bee·a*; (nevertheless) sin embargo *seen em·bar·go*

sting vt/i picar* *pee·kar* □ n la picadura *pee·ka·doo·ra*

stipulate vt estipular *es·tee·poo·lar*

stipulation n la estipulación *es·tee·poo·la·thyon*

stir vt remover* *re·mo·ber*

stitch n (sewing) la puntada *poon·ta·da*; (pain) la punzada *poon·tha·da*

stock vt (have in shop) tener* *te·ner* □ n (in shop) el stock *es·tok*; (for soup etc) el caldo *kal·do*; stocks (financial) los valores *ba·lo·res*; in stock en reserva *en re·ser·ba*; out of stock agotado(a) *a·go·ta·do(a)*

stockbroker n el corredor de bolsa *ko·rre·dor de bol·sa*

stock exchange n la bolsa *bol·sa*

stockholder n el/la accionista *ak·thyo·nees·ta*

stocking n la media *me·dya*

stole n (wrap) la estola *es·to·la*

stomach n el estómago *es·to·ma·go* S40, I34

stomach ache n el dolor de barriga *do·lor de ba·rree·ga*; I have (a) stomach ache tengo dolor de estómago *ten·go do·lor de es·to·ma·go* A40

stone n la piedra *pye·dra*; (in fruit) el hueso *we·so*

stony adj pedregoso(a) *pe·dre·go·so(a)*

stool n el taburete *ta·boo·re·te*

stop n (bus stop) la parada *pa·ra·da* □ vi pararse *pa·rar·se*; to stop doing something dejar de hacer algo *de·khar de a·ther al·go* □ vt stop parar *pa·rar*; to stop someone doing something impedir* que alguien haga algo *eem·pe·deer ke al·gyen a·ga al·go*; to stop a check cancelar un cheque *kan·the·lar oon che·ke* T206f, T86, 89

stopcock n la llave de cierre *lya·be de thye·rre*

stoplights pl las luces de detención *loo·thes de de·ten·thyon*

stopover n (air travel) la escala *es·ka·la*

stopper n el tapón *ta·pon*

stopwatch n el cronómetro *kro·no·me·tro*

store vt almacenar *al·ma·the·nar* □ n (stock) la reserva *re·ser·ba*; (shop) la tienda *tyen·da*; (big shop, warehouse) el almacén *al·ma·then*

store room n la despensa *des·pen·sa*

storm n la tempestad *tem·pes·tad*

stormy adj tempestuoso(a) *tem·pes·too·o·so(a)*

story n la historia *ees·to·rya*; (of house) el piso *pee·so*

stove n la cocina *ko·thee·na* A71

straight adj derecho(a) *de·re·cho(a)*; (drink) solo(a) *so·lo(a)* □ adv (shoot, write etc) derecho *de·re·cho*; to go straight home ir* derecho a casa *eer de·re·cho a ka·sa*; straight away en seguida *en se·gee·da* F24

strain vt (tea etc) colar *co·lar*; (muscle) torcerse* *tor·ther·se*

strainer n el colador *ko·la·dor*

strange adj (unknown) desconocido(a) *des·ko·no·thee·do(a)*; (unusual) extraño(a) *eks·tran·yo(a)*

stranger n el forastero *fo·ras·te·ro*

strangle vt estrangular *es·tran·goo·lar*

strap n la correa *ko·rre·a*

strapless adj sin tirantes *seen tee·ran·tes*

straw n la paja *pa·kha*

strawberry n la fresa *fre·sa*

streak n la raya *ra·ya*

stream n el arroyo *a·rro·yo*

streamlined adj (car) aerodinámico(a) *a·e·ro·dee·na·mee·ko*

street n la calle *kal·ye* F28

streetcar n el tranvía *tran·bee·a*

streetlamp n el farol *fa·rol*

strength n la fuerza *fwer·tha*; (of girder, rope etc) la resistencia *re·sees·ten·thya*

strengthen vt fortalecer* *for·ta·le·ther*

stress n (emphasis) el énfasis *en·fa·sees*; (tension) la tensión *ten·syon*

stretch vt (fabric etc) estirar *es·tee·rar* □ vi estirarse *es·tee·rar·se*

stretcher n la camilla *ka·meel·ya*

strict adj estricto(a) *es·treek·to(a)*

strike vt (hit) golpear *gol·pe·ar*; to strike a match encender* una cerilla *en·then·der oo·na the·reel·ya*; the clock struck three el reloj dio las tres *el re·lokh dyo las tres* □ vi strike (workers) declararse en huelga *de·kla·rar·se en wel·ga* □ n (industrial) la huelga *wel·ga*; on strike en huelga *en wel·ga*

strikebound adj paralizado por una huelga *pa·ra·lee·tha·do por oo·na wel·ga*

strikebreaker n el esquirol *es·kee·rol*

striker n el/la huelgista *wel·gees·ta*

string n la cuerda *kwer·da*

string bag n la bolsa de red *bol·sa de red*

strip n (stripe, length) la tira *tee·ra*

stripe n la raya *ra·ya*

strip lighting n el alumbrado de neón *a·loom·bra·do de ne·on*

stripper n la artista de strip-tease *ar·tees·ta de streep·tees*

striptease n el strip-tease *streep·tees*

stroke vt acariciar *a·ka·ree·thyar* □ n (swimming) la brazada *bra·tha·da*; (golf) el golpe *gol·pe*; (illness) la apoplejía *a·po·ple·khee·a*

stroll n el paseo *pa·se·o*; to go for a stroll dar* un paseo *dar oon pa·se·o*

stroller n la sillita de ruedas *seel·yee·ta de rwe·das*

strong adj (person) fuerte *fwer·te*; (structure, material) sólido(a) *so·lee·do(a)*; it has a strong smell huele mucho *we·le moo·cho*

strongbox n la caja fuerte *ka·kha fwer·te*

strongroom n la cámara acorazada *ka·ma·ra a·ko·ra·tha·da*

structure n la estructura *es·trook·too·ra*; (building) el edificio *e·dee·fee·thyo*

struggle n la lucha *loo·cha* □ vi (physically) luchar *loo·char*; to struggle to do something esforzarse* en hacer algo *es·for·thar·se en a·ther al·go*

stub n (record) el talón *ta·lon*

stubborn adj tenaz *te·nath*

stuck adj atascado(a) *a·tas·ka·do(a)*

stud n el clavo *kla·bo*; (for collar) el botón de camisa *bo·ton de ka·mee·sa*

student n el/la estudiante *es·too·dyan·te* M5

student driver n el aprendiz de conductor *a·pren·deeth de kon·dook·tor*

studio n el estudio *es·too·dyo*

study *vt/i* estudiar *es·too·dyar* □ *n* (room) el escritorio *es·kree·to·ryo*; **to enjoy one's studies** gustarle a uno los estudios *goos·tar·le a oo·no los es·too·dyos*

stuff *n* (things) las cosas *ko·sas*; (substance) la sustancia *soos·tan·thya*

stuffed *adj* (cushion etc) rellenado(a) *rel·ye·na·do(a)*; (chicken) relleno(a) *rel·ye·no(a)*

stuffing *n* (in chicken etc) el relleno *rel·ye·no*

stuffy *adj* sofocante *so·fo·kan·te*

stun *vt* aturdir *a·toor·deer*

stupid *adj* estúpido(a) *es·too·pee·do(a)*

style *n* el estilo *es·tee·lo*

stylish *adj* elegante *e·le·gan·te*

subcommittee *n* la subcomisión *soob·ko·mee·syon*

subcontract *n* el subcontrato *soob·kon·tra·to*

subcontractor *n* el/la subcontratista *soob·kon·tra·tees·ta*

subject *n* (topic) el asunto a *soon·to*, (person) el súbdito *soob·dee·to*; (in school) la asignatura *a·seeg·na·too·ra* □ *adj* **subject to** sujeto(a) a *soo·khe·to(u) a*

submarine *n* el submarino *soob·ma·ree·no*

submit *vt* (proposal) someter *so·me·ter*

subordinate *adj* secundario(a) *se·koon·da·ryo(a)* □ *n* el/la subordinado(a) *soo·bor·dee·na·do(a)*

subordinate *n* el/la ~~~~~ ~~~~ *na·do*

subscribe *vt* (periodical) abonarse a *a·bo·nar·se a*

subscription *n* (to periodical) el abono *a·bo·no*; (to club) la cuota *kwo·ta*

subsidiary *adj* afiliado(a) *a·fee·lya·do(a)* □ *n* (company) el sucursal *soo·koor·sal*

subsidize *vt* subvencionar *soob·ben·thyo·nar*

subsidy *n* la subvención *soob·ben·thyon*

substance *n* la sustancia *soos·tan·thya*

substandard *adj* inferior *een·fer·yor*

substitute *n* el suplente *soo·plen·te* □ *vt* **to substitute something for something else** sustituir* algo por otra cosa *soos·tee·too·eer al·go por o·tra ko·sa*

subtitle *n* (of movie) el subtítulo *soob·tee·too·lo*

subtle *adj* sutil *soo·teel*

subtotal *n* el subtotal *soob·to·tal*

subtract *vt* restar *res·tar*

suburb *n* el barrio *ba·rryo*; **the suburbs** las afueras *a·fwe·ras*

suburban *adj* suburbano(a) *soob·oor·ba·no(a)*

subway *n* (underground passage) el paso subterráneo *pa·so soob·te·rra·ne·o*; (railway) el metro *me·tro*

succeed *vi* tener* éxito *te·ner ek·see·to*; **he succeeded in doing it** consiguió hacerlo *kon·se·gyo a·ther·lo*

success *n* el éxito *ek·see·to*

successful *adj* (venture) que tiene éxito *ke tye·ne ek·see·to*; (businessman) próspero(a) *pros·pe·ro(a)*

such *adj* tal *tal*; **such a lot of** tanto(a) *tan·to(a)*; **such a book** tal libro *tal lee·bro*; **such books** tales libros *ta·les lee·bros*; **such kindness** tal amabilidad *tal a·ma·bee·lee·dad*

suck *vt* chupar *choo·par*

sudden *adj* repentino(a) *re·pen·tee·no(a)*

suddenly *adv* de repente *de re·pen·te* T208

sue *vt* demandar *de·man·dar*

suede *n* el ante *an·te*

suet *n* el sebo *se·bo*

suffer *vt/i* sufrir *soo·freer*

sugar *n* el azúcar *a·thoo·kar* S32

sugar bowl *n* el azucarero *a·thoo·ka·re·ro*

suggest *vt* sugerir* *soo·khe·reer*

suggestion *n* la sugerencia *soo·khe·ren·thya*

suicide *n* el suicidio *soo·ee·thee·dyo*

suit *n* el traje *tra·khe*; (cards) el palo *pa·lo* □ *vt* **that hat suits you** ese sombrero le sienta bien *e·se som·bre·ro le syen·ta byen*; **does Thursday suit you?** ¿le conviene el jueves? *le kon·bye·ne el khwe·bes* S60

suitable *adj* conveniente *kon·ben·yen·te*; (fitting) apropiado(a) *a·pro·pya·do(a)* S109

suitcase *n* la maleta *ma·le·ta* TJ1f, Sn58

sultana *n* la pasa de Esmirna *pa·sa de es·meer·na*

sum *n* (total amount) la suma *soo·ma*, (problem) el cálculo *kal·koo·lo*

summary *n* el sumario *soo·ma·ryo*

summer *n* el verano *be·ra·no*

summons *n* la citación *thee·ta·thyon*

sum total *n* el total *to·tal*

sun *n* el sol *sol*

sunbathe *vi* tomar el sol ~~~~~ ~~~~~

sunburn *n* (painful) la quemadura del sol *ke·ma·doo·ra del sol* S40

sunburned *adj* bronceado(a) *bron·the·a·do(a)* (painfully) quemado(a) por el sol *ke·ma·do por el sol*

Sunday *n* el domingo *do·meen·go*

sun dress *n* el traje de playa *tra·khe de pla·ya*

sunglasses *pl* las gafas de sol *ga·fas de sol*, los anteojos de sol (Am) *an·te·o·khos de sol* S7

sun hat *n* el sombrero *som·bre·ro*

sunlamp *n* la lámpara de rayos ultravioleta *lam·pa·ra de ra·yos ul·tra·byo·le·ta*

sunny *adj* soleado(a) *so·le·a·do(a)*

sunrise *n* la salida del sol *sa·lee·da del sol*

sunroof *n* el techo descapotable *te·cho des·ka·po·ta·ble*

sunset *n* la puesta del sol *pwes·ta del sol*

sunshade *n* (over table) la sombrilla *som·breel·ya*

sunshine *n* el sol *sol*

sunstroke *n* la insolación *een·so·la·thyon* I33

suntan *n* el bronceado *bron·the·a·do*

sun-tanned *adj* bronceado(a) *bron·the·a·do(a)*

suntan oil *n* el aceite bronceador *a·they·te bron·the·a·dor* S9

sun visor *n* (in car) la visera *bee·se·ra*

superannuation *n* la jubilación *khoo·bee·la·thyon*

superior *adj* (quality) superior *soo·pe·ryor* □ *n* el superior *soo·pe·ryor*

supermarket *n* el supermercado *soo·per·mer·ka·do*

superstition *n* la superstición *soo·pers·tee·thyon*

superstore *n* el hipermercado *ee·per·mer·ka·do*

supertanker *n* el superpetrolero *soo·per·pe·tro·le·ro*

supervise *vt* supervisar *soo·per·bee·sar*

supervisor n el/la supervisor(a) *soo·per·bee·sor(·ra)*

supper n la cena *the·na*

supply vt (*goods*) suministrar *soo·mee·nees·trar*; **to supply someone with something** proveer a alguien de algo *pro·be·er a al·gyen de al·go* □ n **supply** (*stock*) las existencias *ek·sees·ten·thyas*; **supply and demand** la oferta y la demanda *la o·fer·ta ee la de·man·da*

support vt apoyar *a·po·yar*; (*financially*) mantener* *man·te·ner* □ n (*moral, financial*) el apoyo *a·po·yo*

suppose vt suponer* *soo·po·ner*; **he's supposed to be an engineer** se dice que es ingeniero *se dee·the ke es een·khe·nye·ro*; **you're supposed to do it today** debes hacerlo hoy *de·bes a·ther·lo oy*

suppository n el supositorio *soo·po·see·to·ryo*

surcharge n la sobrecarga *so·bre·kar·ga*

sure adj (*person*) seguro(a) *se·goo·ro(a)*; (*fact*) cierto(a) *thyer·to(a)*; **it's sure to work** seguro que funcionará *se·goo·ro ke foon·thyo·na·ra*

surely adv seguramente *se·goo·ra·men·te*

surface n la superficie *soo·per·fee·thye*

surface mail n □ **to send something surface mail** enviar algo por vía terrestre *en·byar al·go por bee·a te·rres·tre*

surf board n la tabla de surf *ta·bla de soorf*

surfing n el surf *soorf*; **to go surfing** hacer* el surf *a·ther el soorf*

surgeon n el cirujano *thee·roo·kha·no*

surgery n (*operation*) la cirugía *thee·roo·khee·a*

surname n el apellido *a·pel·yee·do*

surplus n el excedente *eks·the·den·te*

surprise vt sorprender *sor·pren·der* □ n la sorpresa *sor·pre·sa*

surprised adj sorprendido(a) *sor·pren·dee·do(a)*; **surprised at** sorprendido(a) por *sor·pren·dee·do(a) por*

surround vt rodear *ro·de·ar*

surroundings pl los alrededores *al·re·de·do·res*

survey n (*of land*) la medición *me·dee·thyon*; (*of building*) la inspección *een·spek·thyon*

surveyor n (*of land*) el topógrafo *to·po·gra·fo*; (*of building*) el inspector *een·spek·tor*

survive vi sobrevivir *so·bre·bee·beer*; (*custom*) permanecer* *per·ma·ne·ther*

suspend vt (*worker*) suspender *soos·pen·der*

suspenders pl los tirantes *tee·ran·tes*

suspension n (*on car*) la suspensión *soos·pen·syon*

swallow vt/i tragar* *tra·gar*

swamp n el pantano *pan·ta·no*

swan n el cisne *thees·ne*

sway vi (*person*) tambalearse *tam·ba·le·ar·se*; (*building, bridge*) oscilar *os·thee·lar*

swear vi (*curse*) blasfemar *blas·fe·mar*; **he swears that...** jura que... *khoo·ra ke*

sweat n el sudor *soo·dor* □ vi sudar *soo·dar*

sweater n el suéter *swe·ter* S57

sweatshirt n el jersey de algodón *kher·sey de al·go·don*

Swede n el/la sueco(a) *swe·ko(a)*

swede n el nabo sueco *na·bo swe·ko*

Sweden n Suecia (f) *swe·thya*

Swedish adj sueco(a) *swe·ko(a)*

sweep vt (*floor*) barrer *ba·rrer*

sweet n (*candy*) el caramelo *ka·ra·me·lo* □ adj (*taste, food*) dulce *dool·the*; (*smell*) fresco(a) *fres·ko(a)*; (*music*) melodioso(a) *me·lo·dyo·so(a)*; (*cute, pretty*) mono(a) *mo·no(a)*

sweet corn n el maíz tierno *ma·eeth tyer·no*, el choclo (Am) *cho·klo*

sweet potato n el boniato *bo·nya·to*, el camote (Am) *ka·mo·te*

swell (up) vi (*limb etc*) hincharse *een·char·se*

swelling n (*lump*) la hinchazón *een·cha·thon* I28

swerve vi desviarse *des·byar·se*

swim vi nadar *na·dar* □ vt **to swim the Channel** atravesar* la Mancha a nado *a·tra·be·sar la Man·cha a na·do* L18

swimming n la natación *na·ta·thyon*; **to go swimming** bañarse *ban·yar·se*

swimming pool n la piscina *pees·thee·na* L26

swimming trunks pl el traje de baño *tra·khe de ban·yo*

swimsuit n el traje de baño *tra·khe de ban·yo*

swing n el columpio *ko·loom·pyo* □ vi balancearse *ba·lan·the·ar·se* □ vt balancear *ba·lan·the·ar*

Swiss adj suizo(a) *swee·tho(a)*

switch n el interruptor *een·te·rroop·tor* □ vt **to switch on** (*light*) encender* *en·then·der*, prender (Am) *pren·der*; (*engine*) arrancar* *a·rran·kar*; (*TV*) poner* *po·ner*; **to switch off** apagar* *a·pa·gar*; (*engine*) desconectar *des·ko·nek·tar* B74

switchboard n la centralita *then·tra·lee·ta*

switchboard operator n el/la telefonista *te·le·fo·nees·ta*

Switzerland n Suiza (f) *swee·tha*

swollen adj hinchado(a) *een·cha·do(a)*

sword n la espada *es·pa·da*

syllable n la sílaba *see·la·ba*

syllabus n el programa de estudios *pro·gra·ma de es·too·dyos*

symbol n el símbolo *seem·bo·lo*

symmetrical adj simétrico(a) *see·me·tree·ko(a)*

sympathetic adj comprensivo(a) *kom·pren·see·bo(a)*

sympathy n la compasión *kom·pa·syon*

symphony n la sinfonía *seen·fo·nee·a*

symposium n el simposio *seem·po·syo*

symptom n el síntoma *seen·to·ma*

synagogue n la sinagoga *see·na·go·ga*

synchromesh n el cambio sincronizado de velocidades *kam·byo seen·kro·nee·tha·do de be·lo·thee·da·des*

syndicate n el sindicato *seen·dee·ka·to*

synthetic adj sintético(a) *seen·te·tee·ko(a)*

syrup n el almíbar *al·mee·bar*; (**golden**) **syrup** la melaza refinada *me·la·tha re·fee·na·da*

system n el sistema *sees·te·ma*

systematic adj sistemático(a) *sees·te·ma·tee·ko(a)*

systems analyst n el analista-programador *a·na·lees·ta-pro·gra·ma·dor*

T

tab n la etiqueta *e·tee·ke·ta*

table n la mesa *me·sa*; (*list*) la tabla *ta·bla* E2f

tablecloth n el mantel *man·tel*

table-mat n el salvamanteles *sal·ba·man·te·les*

tablespoon n la cuchara *koo·cha·ra*; (*measure*) la cucharada *koo·cha·ra·da*

tablet n (*medicine*) la pastilla *pas·teel·ya*

table tennis n el tenis de mesa *te·nees de me·sa*

tack n (*nail*) la chincheta *cheen·che·ta* □ *vi* (*sailing*) virar *bee·rar*

tackle *vt* (*problem*) abordar *a·bor·dar*; (*in sports*) placar* *pla·kar* □ n (*gear*) el aparejo *a·pa·re·kho*

tactics *pl* la táctica *tak·tee·ka*

tag n la etiqueta *e·tee·ke·ta*

tail n la cola *ko·la*

tailcoat n el frac *frak*

tailgate n (*of car*) la puerta trasera *pwer·ta tra·se·ra*

tailor n el sastre *sas·tre*

take *vt* (*remove, acquire*) llevarse *lye·bar·se*, (*whi. prize*) ganar *ga·nar*, he took it from me me lo quitó *me lo kee·to*; to take someone to the station llevar a alguien a la estación *lye·bar a al·gyen a la es·ta·thyon*; take this to the post office lleve esto a correos *lye·be es·to a ko·rre·os*; to take a photo hacer* una foto *a·ther oo·na fo·to*; we took the train cogimos el tren *ko·khee·mos el tren*; do you take sugar? ¿toma Ud azúcar? *to·ma oos·ted a·thoo·kar*; I'm taking French at school estudio francés en el colegio *es·too·dyo fran·thes en el ko·le·khyo*; to take a decision tomar una decisión *to·mar oo·na de·thee·syon*; to take an exam hacer* un examen *a·ther oon ek·sa·men*; it takes a lot of effort cuesta mucho esfuerzo *kwes·ta moo·cho es·fwer·tho*; it takes an hour dura una hora *doo·ra oo·na o·ra*; to take something away llevarse algo *lye·bar·se al·go*; to take something back (*return*) devolver* algo *de·bol·ber al·go*; to take off (*clothes*) quitarse *kee·tar·se*; (*plane*) tomar el aire *to·mar el ay·re*; to take someone out to the theater llevar a alguien al teatro *lye·bar a al·gyen al te·a·tro*; to have a tooth taken out sacarse* una muela *sa·kar·se oo·na mwe·la*; to take over a firm absorber una firma *ab·sor·ber oo·na feer·ma*; to take up a sport aficionarse a un deporte *a·fee·thyo·nar·se a oon de·por·te*

take-away *adj* (*food*) para llevarse *pa·ra lye·bar·se*

take-home pay n el sueldo neto *swel·do ne·to*

takeoff n (*of plane*) el despegue *des·pe·ge*

takeover n la adquisición *ad·kee·see·thyon*

take-over bid n la oferta para adquirir una compañía *o·fer·ta pa·ra ad·kee·reer oo·na kom·pan·yee·a*

talc(um powder) n el talco *tal·ko*

talent n el talento *ta·len·to*

talk *vi* hablar *a·blar*; to talk to someone about something hablar a alguien de algo *a·blar a al·gyen de al·go*; to talk something over discutir algo *dees·koo·teer al·go* □ *vt* to talk nonsense decir* tonterías *de·theer ton·te·ree·as*; talk (*lecture*) la conferencia *kon·fe·ren·thya*; talks (*negotiations*) las negociaciones (*fpl*) *ne·go·thya·thyo·nes*

tall *adj* grande *gran·de*; how tall are you? ¿cuánto mides? *kwan·to mee·des*

tame *adj* (*animal*) manso(a) *man·so(a)*

tan *adj* marrón (rojizo) *ma·rron ro·khee·tho* □ n (*on skin*) el bronceado *bron·the·a·do* □ *vi* (*in sun*) broncearse *bron·the·ar·se*

tangerine n la mandarina *man·da·ree·na*

tangle *vt* enredar *en·re·dar*

tango n el tango *tan·go*

tank n el tanque *tan·ke*

tanker n (*ship*) el petrolero *pe·tro·le·ro*; (*truck*) el camión cisterna *ka·myon thees·ter·na*

tap n (*for water*) el grifo *gree·fo* □ *vt* golpear ligeramente *gol·pe·ar lee·khe·ra·men·te* A31

tape n la cinta *theen·ta*; (*magnetic*) la cinta magnética *theen·ta mag·ne·tee·ka*

tape measure n el metro *me·tro*

tape record *vt* grabar *gra·bar*

tape recorder n el magnetofón *mag·ne·to·fon*

tap-water n el agua del grifo (*f*) *a·gwa del gree·fo* A31

tar n la brea *bre·a*

target n el blanco *blan·ko*; (*sales etc*) el objetivo *ob·khe·tee·bo*

tariff n (*list of charges*) la tarifa *ta·ree·fa*; (*tax*) el arancel *a·ran·thel*

tarmac n la superficie alquitranada *soo·per·fee·thye al·kee·tra·na·da*

tart n la tarta *tar·ta*

tartan n el tartán *tar·tan*; a tartan skirt la falda escocesa *fal·da es·ko·the·sa*

tartar sauce n la salsa tártara *sal·sa tar·ta·ra*

task n la tarea *ta·re·a*

taste n el sabor *sa·bor*; in poor taste de mal gusto *de mal goos·to*; in good taste de buen gusto *de bwen goos·to* □ *vt* saborear *sa·bo·re·ar*; (*try*) probar* *pro·bar*; I can't taste the garlic no noto el sabor del ajo *no no·to el sa·bor del a·kho* □ *vi* it tastes like fish sabe a pescado *sa·be a pes·ka·do*

tax n (*on goods*) el impuesto *eem·pwes·to*, la contribución *kontree·boo·thyon*; (*on income*) el impuesto *eem·pwes·to* □ *vt* (*goods*) gravar con un impuesto *gra·bar kon oon eem·pwes·to*; (*income*) imponer* contribuciones a *eem·po·ner kon·tree·boo·thyo·nes a* A9, M4

taxable *adj* imponible *eem·po·nee·ble*

taxation n los impuestos *eem·pwes·tos*

tax-free *adj* libre de impuestos *lee·bre de eem·pwes·tos*

taxi n el taxi *tak·see*; to go by taxi ir* en taxi *eer en tak·see* T91f

taxi stand n la parada de taxis *pa·ra·da de tak·sees*

T-bone steak n la chuleta *choo·le·ta*

tea n el té *te*; (*meal*) la merienda *me·ryen·da*; mint tea el té de menta *te de men·ta* E67

tea bag n la bolsa de té *bol·sa de te*

teach *vt* enseñar *en·sen·yar*; to teach someone something enseñar algo a alguien *en·sen·yar al·go a al·gyen*

teacher n (*secondary school*) el/la profesor(a) *pro·fe·sor(ra)*; (*primary school*) el/la maestro(a) *ma·es·tro(a)*

teacup n la taza de té *ta·tha de te*

team n el equipo *e·kee·po*

teapot n la tetera *te·te·ra*

tear[1] *vt* (*rip*) desgarrar *des·ga·rrar* □ n tear el desgarrón *des·ga·rron* Sn79

tear² *n* la lágrima *la·gree·ma*; in tears llorando *lyo·ran·do*

tearoom *n* el salón de té *sa·lon de te*

teaspoon *n* la cucharilla *koo·cha·reel·ya*; (measure) la cucharadita *koo·cha·ra·dee·ta*

tea strainer *n* el colador de té *ko·la·dor de te*

teat *n* (for bottle) la tetilla *te·teel·ya*

technical *adj* técnico(a) *tek·nee·ko(a)*

technician *n* el/la técnico(a) *tek·nee·ko(a)*

technique *n* la técnica *tek·nee·ka*

technological *adj* tecnológico(a) *tek·no·lo·khee·ko(a)*

technology *n* la tecnología *tek·no·lo·khee·a*

tee *n* (in golf) el tee *tee*

teenager *n* el/la adolescente *a·do·les·then·te*

tee shirt *n* la camiseta *ka·mee·se·ta*

telecommunications *pl* las telecomunicaciones *te·le·ko·moo·nee·ka·thyo·nes*

telegram *n* el telegrama *te·le·gra·ma* Sn4

telegraph *vt* telegrafiar *te·le·gra·fyar*

telephone *n* el teléfono *te·le·fo·no*; to be on the telephone estar* hablando por teléfono *es·tar a·blan·do por te·le·fo·no*; by telephone por teléfono *por te·le·fo·no* □ *vt* telephone (person) llamar por teléfono *lya·mar por te·le·fo·no* T166, A35, Ea6, Sn9f

telephone booth *n* la cabina telefónica *ka·bee·na te·le·fo·nee·ka* Sn18

telephone call *n* la llamada telefónica *lya·ma·da te·le·fo·nee·ka* Sn12

telephone directory *n* la guía telefónica *gee·a te·le·fo·nee·ka* Sn29

telephone exchange *n* la central telefónica *then·tral te·le·fo·nee·ka*

telephone number *n* el número de teléfono *noo·me·ro de te·le·fo·no* Sn13, 28

telephone operator *n* el/la telefonista *te·le·fo·nees·ta*

telephoto lens *n* el teleobjetivo *te·le·ob·khe·tee·bo*

telescope *n* el telescopio *te·les·ko·pyo*

televise *vt* televisar *te·le·bee·sar*

television *n* la televisión *te·le·bee·syon*; (set) el televisor *te·le·bee·sor*; on television en la televisión *en la te·le·bee·syon*

telex *n* el télex *te·leks*; by telex por télex *por te·leks* □ *vt* telex enviar un télex *en·byar oon te·leks* A35, Bm16

tell *vt* (fact, news) decir* *de·theer*; (story) contar* *kon·tar*; to tell someone something contar* algo a alguien *kon·tar al·go a al·gyen*; to tell someone to do something decirle* a alguien que haga algo *de·theer·le a al·gyen ke a·ga al·go*; I can't tell the difference between them no puedo distinguir entre los dos *no pwe·do dees·teen·geer en·tre los dos*

teller *n* el/la cajero(a) *ka·khe·ro(a)*

temper *n* □ in a bad temper de mal humor *de mal oo·mor*; to lose one's temper enfadarse *en·fa·dar·se*

temperature *n* la temperatura *tem·pe·ra·too·ra*; to have a temperature (fever) tener* fiebre *te·ner fye·bre*; to take someone's temperature tomar la temperatura a alguien *to·mar la tem·pe·ra·too·ra a al·gyen* I31

temple *n* (building) el templo *tem·plo*

temporary *adj* provisional *pro·bee·syo·nal*

tempt *vt* tentar *ten·tar*

ten *num* diez *dyeth*

tenant *n* el inquilino *een·kee·lee·no*

tend *vi* □ to tend to do something tener* tendencia a hacer algo *te·ner ten·den·thya a a·ther al·go*

tender *adj* (meat, vegetables) tierno(a) *tyer·no(a)* □ *vi* to tender for something hacer* una oferta para algo *a·ther oo·na o·fer·ta pa·ra al·go*

tennis *n* el tenis *te·nees* L27

tennis court *n* la pista de tenis *pees·ta de te·nees*, la cancha de tenis (Am) *kan·cha de te·nees*

tennis racket *n* la raqueta de tenis *ra·ke·ta de te·nees*

tense *adj* (muscles) tenso(a) *ten·so(a)*; (person) nervioso(a) *ner·byo·so(a)*

tent *n* la tienda de campaña *tyen·da de kam·pan·ya*, la carpa (Am) *kar·pa* A83

tenth *adj* décimo(a) *de·thee·mo(a)*

tent pole *n* el poste de tienda *pos·te de tyen·da*

tent stake *n* la estaquilla *es·ta·keel·ya*

term *n* (of school etc) el trimestre *tree·mes·tre*; (word) el término *ter·mee·no*; during his term of office durante su mandato *doo·ran·te soo man·da·to*; terms (of contract) las condiciones *kon·dee·thyo·nes*

terminal *n* (air terminal) la terminal *ter·mee·nal*; (buses) la estación de autobuses *es·ta·thyon de ow·to·boo·ses*; (electricity) el polo *po·lo*; (computer) el terminal *ter·mee·nal*

terrace *n* (of café) la terraza *te·rra·tha*

terrible *adj* terrible *te·rree·ble*; (weather) malísimo *ma·lee·see·mo*

territory *n* el territorio *te·rree·to·ryo*

terrorism *n* el terrorismo *te·rro·rees·mo*

terrorist *n* el/la terrorista *te·rro·rees·ta*

terylene *n* el terylene *te·ree·le·ne*

test *n* (trial, check) la prueba *prwe·ba*; (medical) el análisis *a·na·lee·sees*; (in school etc) el test test; (driving test) el examen de conducir *ek·sa·men de kon·doo·theer* □ *vt* (product) probar* *pro·bar*; (sight, hearing) graduar *gra·doo·ar*; (ability) someter a prueba *so·me·ter a prwe·ba*

test-drive *n* la prueba en carretera *prwe·ba en ka·rre·te·ra*

text *n* el texto *teks·to*

textbook *n* el libro de texto *lee·bro de teks·to*

textiles *pl* los tejidos *te·khee·dos*

texture *n* la textura *teks·too·ra*

than *conj* que *ke*; better than him mejor que él *me·khor ke el*; more than 10 más de 10 *mas de 10*

thank *vt* agradecer* *a·gra·de·ther*; to thank someone agradecer* a alguien *a·gra·de·ther a al·gyen*; thank you gracias *gra·thyas*; thanks to gracias a *gra·thyas a*

that *adj* (masculine) ese *e·se*, (feminine) esa *e·sa*; (masculine: remote) aquel *a·kel*, (feminine: remote) aquella *a·kel·ya*; that one (masculine) ése *e·se*, (feminine) ésa *e·sa*; (masculine: remote) aquél *a·kel*, (feminine: remote) aquélla *a·kel·ya* □ *pron* that eso *e·so*; (remote) aquello *a·kel·yo*; give me that deme aquello/eso *de·me a·kel·yo/e·so*; that's what I want eso es lo que quiero *e·so es lo ke kye·ro*; what's that? ¿qué es eso? *ke es e·so*; who's that? ¿quién es? *kyen es*; that is (to say)... es decir... *es de·theer*;

the photo that I gave you la foto que te di *la fo·to ke te de* □ *conj* I hope that... espero que... *es·pe·ro ke*

thaw *vi* (ice) derretirse* *de·rre·teer·se*; (frozen food) descongelarse *des·kon· khe·lar·se* □ *vt* (food) descongelar *des·kon·khe·lar*

the *art* □ the boy el niño *el neen·yo*; the woman la mujer *la moo·kher*; the boys los niños *los neen·yos*; the women las mujeres *las moo·khe·res*

theater *n* el teatro *te·a·tro*; to go to the theater ir* al teatro *eer al te·a·tro*

their *adj* su *soo*, sus *soos*; their father su padre *soo pa·dre*; their mother su madre *soo ma·dre*; their brothers/ sisters sus hermanos/hermanas *soos er·ma·nos/er·ma·nas*

theirs pron el suyo *el soo·yo*, la suya *la soo·ya*; (plural) los suyos *los soo·yos*, las suyas *las soo·yas*

them *pron* los *los*, las *las*; buy them cómprelos(las) *kom·pre·los(las)*; show them the books muéstreles los libros *mwes·tre·les los lee·bros*; he spoke to them les habló *les a·blo*; it's them! ¡son ellos! *son el·yos*

themselves *pron* □ they wash them-selves se lavan *se la·ban*; they did it themselves lo hicieron ellas/ellos mis-mos(as) *lo ee·thye·ron el·yas(as) mees·mos(as)*

then *adv* entonces *en·ton·thes*; then it must be true entonces tiene que ser *verdad entonthes tyene ke ser ber-dad*; from then on desde entonces *des·de en·ton·thes*

theory *n* la teoría *te·o·ree·a*

there *adv* allí *al·yee*; (distant) allá *al·ya*; there is/there are hay *ay*; is there anyone there? ¿hay alguien allí? *ay al·gyen al·yee*; he went there se fue para allá *se fwe pa·ra al·ya*; there he/ she is! ¡ahí está *a·ee es·ta*

thermometer *n* el termómetro *ter·mo· me·tro*

Thermos *n* el termo *ter·mo*

these *adj* estos(as) *es·tos(as)*; these boys estos chicos *es·tos chee·kos*; these women estas mujeres *es·tas moo·khe·res* □ pron these estos(as) *es·tos(as)*; take these tome estos(as) *to·me es·tos(as)*; these are what I want estos(as) son los/las que quiero *es·tos(as) son los/las ke kye·ro*; what are these? ¿qué son estos(as)? *ke son es·tos(as)*

they *pron* ellos *el·yos*, ellas *el·yas*; they say that... (people in general) dicen que... *dee·then ke*; there they are allí están *al·yee es·tan*

thick *adj* grueso(a) *grwe·so(a)*; (soup) espeso(a) *es·pe·so(a)*; 3 meters thick 3 metros de espesor *3 me·tros de es·pe·sor*

thief *n* el ladrón *la·dron* Ea2

thin *adj* delgado(a) *del·ga·do(a)*; (ma-terial) fino(a) *fee·no(a)*; (liquid) poco denso(a) *po·ko den·so(a)*

thing *n* la cosa *ko·sa*; the best thing would be... lo mejor sería... *lo me· khor se·ree·a*; where are your things? ¿dónde están sus cosas? *don·de es· tan soos ko·sas*

think *vi* pensar* *pen·sar*; to think of something pensar* en algo *pen·sar en al·go*; to think about someone pen-sar* en alguien *pen·sar en al gyen*; I think so creo que sí *kre·o ke see*; to think something over pensar* algo bien *pen·sar al·go byen*

third *adj* tercero(a) *ter·the·ro(a)* □ *n* third (gear) (la) tercera *ter·the·ra*

third party insurance *n* el seguro con-tra tercera persona *se·goo·ro kon·tra ter·the·ra per·so·na*

Third World *n* el Tercer Mundo *ter· ther moon·do*

thirsty *adj* sediento(a) *se·dyen·to(a)*; to be thirsty tener* sed *te·ner sed*

thirteen *num* trece *tre·the*

thirteenth *adj* decimotercero(a) *de· thee·mo·ter·the·ro(a)*

thirtieth *adj* trigésimo(a) *tree·khe·see· mo(a)*

thirty *num* treinta *treyn·ta*

this *adj* este *es·te*; (feminine) esta *es·ta*; this boy este chico *es·te chee·ko*; this woman esta mujer *es·ta moo·kher* □ *pron* this one éste *es·te*; ésta *es·ta* (fe-minine); this *es·to*; this is what I want esto es lo que quiero *es·to es lo ke kye·ro*; what's this? ¿qué es esto? *ke es es·to*; who's this? ¿quién es? *kyen*

thorough *adj* (work) concienzudo(a) *kon·thyen·thoo·do(a)*

those *adj* esos *e·sos*; feminine esas *e· sas*, (remote) aquellos *a·kel·yos* (fe-minine) aquellas *a·kel·yas*; those boys aquellos chicos *a·kel·yos chee· kos*, those women aquellas mujeres *a·kel·yas moo·khe·res* □ pron those ésos *e·sos*; (feminine) ésas *e·sas*; give me those deme ésos *de·me e·sos*; those are what I want ésos son los que quiero *e·sos son los ke kye·ro*; what are those? ¿qué son ésos? *ke son e·sos*

though *conj*, *adv* □ though you may think... aunque Ud pueda pensar... *own·ke oos·ted pwe·da pen·sar*; he's happy, though sin embargo está con-tento *seen em·bar·go es·ta kon·ten·to*

thought *n* la idea *ee·de·a*

thousand *num* mil *meel*

thousandth *adj* milésimo(a) *mee·le·see· mo(a)*

thread *n* el hilo *ee·lo*

threat *n* la amenaza *a·me·na·tha*

threaten *vt* amenazar* *a·me·na·thar*

three *num* tres *tres*

thriller *n* (film) la película de suspense *pe·lee·koo·la de soos·pen·se*; (book) la novela de misterio *no·be·la de mees·te·ryo*

throat *n* la garganta *gar·gan·ta* S40

throttle *n* (in car) el acelerador *a·the· le·ra·dor*

through *prep* por *por*; through the wood por el bosque *por el bos·ke*; (all) through the year durante todo el año *doo·ran·te to·do el an·yo*; Mon-day through Friday de lunes a vier-nes *de loo·nes a byer·nes* □ *adv* to read something through quickly leer* algo rápidamente *le·er al·go ra·pee· da·men·te*; I couldn't get through (on phone) no pude hablar con él/ella *no poo·de a·blar kon el/el·ya*; put me through to Mr X póngame con el Sr X *pon·ga·me kon el sen·yor X*; when I'm through with my work cuando haya terminado mi trabajo *kwan·do a·ya ter·mee·na·do mee tra·ba·kho*

through train *n* el tren directo *tren dee·rek·to*

throw *vt* tirar *tee·rar*; (rider) desmon-tar *des·mon·tar*; to throw a 6 (dice) echar un 6 *e·char oon 6*; to throw away tirar *tee·rar*, botar (Am) *bo·tar*

thumb *n* el pulgar *pool·gar* □ *vt* to

thumb a ride hacer* autostop *a·ther ow·to·stop*

thumbtack n el chinche *cheen·che*

thump n (*noise*) el porrazo *po·rra·tho*

thunder n el trueno *trwe·no*

thunderstorm n la tormenta *tor·men·ta*

Thursday n jueves (*m*) *khwe·bes*

thus adv (*in this way*) así *a·see*

thyme n el tomillo *to·meel·yo*

tick n (*mark*) la marca *mar·ka* □ vt marcar* *mar·kar* □ vi (*clock*) hacer* tictac *a·ther teek·tak*

ticket n el billete *beel·ye·te*; (*for theater*) la entrada *en·tra·da*; (*label*) la etiqueta *e·tee·ke·ta*; (*parking*) la multa *mool·ta* T60f

ticket office n la taquilla *ta·keel·ya* T52

tickle vt hacer* cosquillas a *a·ther kos·keel·yas a*

tide n la marea *ma·re·a*; the tide is in/ out la marea está a pleamar/bajamar *la ma·re·a es·ta a ple·a·mar/ba·kha·mar* Mc10

tidy adj (*person*) ordenado(a) *or·de·na·do(a)*; (*room, papers*) bien arreglado(a) *byen a·rre·gla·do(a)*

tie n la corbata *kor·ba·ta* □ vt (*string, ribbon*) atar *a·tar*, amarrar (Am) *a·ma·rrar*; to tie a dog to a post atar un perro a un poste *a·tar oon pe·rro a oon pos·te*; to tie up a parcel envolver* un paquete *en·bol·ber oon pa·ke·te*; to tie up capital inmovilizar* *een·mo·bee·lee·thar*

tie-up n (*traffic*) el embotellamiento *em·bo·tel·ya·myen·to* T131

tiger n el tigre *tee·gre*

tight adj (*rope*) tirante *tee·ran·te*; (*clothes*) ajustado(a) *a·khoos·ta·do(a)*; (*schedule*) apretado(a) *a·pre·ta·do(a)*

tights pl los leotardos *le·o·tar·dos*

tile n (*on floor, wall*) la baldosa *bal·do·sa*; (*on roof*) la teja *te·kha*

till prep hasta *as·ta* □ n (*cash register*) la caja *ka·kha*

time n el tiempo *tyem·po*; what's the time? ¿qué hora es? *ke o·ra es*; the time is 5 o'clock son las 5 *son las 5*; the first time la primera vez *la pree·me·ra beth*; how many times? ¿cuántas vezes? *kwan·tas be·thes*; a short time poco tiempo *po·ko tyem·po*; a long time mucho tiempo *moo·cho tyem·po*; in times past en tiempos pasados *en tyem·pos pa·sa·dos*; to have a good time pasarlo bien *pa·sar·lo byen*; for the time being por ahora *por a·o·ra*; from time to time de vez en cuando *de beth en kwan·do*; just in time justo a tiempo *khoos·to a tyem·po*; on time a tiempo *a tyem·po* T4, L14, S1, T76

timetable n (*for trains etc*) el horario *o·ra·ryo* T52, 56

time zone n la zona horaria *tho·na o·ra·rya*

tin n (*substance*) el estaño *es·tan·yo*

tin foil n el papel de estaño *pa·pel de es·tan·yo*

tip n (*end*) la punta *poon·ta*; (*money given*) la propina *pro·pee·na* □ vt (*tilt*) inclinar *een·klee·nar*

tire n el neumático *ne·oo·ma·tee·ko*, la llanta (Am) *lyan·ta* T181, 137, 160

tired adj cansado(a) *kan·sa·do(a)*; I'm tired of it estoy cansado de eso *es·toy kan·sa·do de e·so*

tissue n (*handkerchief*) el pañuelo de papel *pan·ywe·lo de pa·pel*

tissue paper n el papel de seda *pa·pel de se·da*

title n el título *tee·too·lo*

T-junction n (*on road*) el cruce en T *kroo·the en te*

to prep a *a*; to the station a la estación *a la es·ta·thyon*; to go to London ir* a Londres *eer a lon·dres*; to Portugal a Portugal *a por·too·gal*; to school al colegio *al ko·le·khyo*; to town a la ciudad *a la thyoo·dad*; give it to me démelo *de·me·lo*; he wants to leave quiere irse *kye·re eer·se*; I forgot to do… he olvidado hacer … *e ol·bee·da·do a·ther*; the key to my room la llave de mi cuarto *la lya·be de mee kwar·to*

toast n la tostada *tos·ta·da*; to propose a toast to someone brindar por alguien *breen·dar por al·gyen*

toaster n el tostador *tos·ta·dor*

tobacco n el tabaco *ta·ba·ko* S100

tobacconist n el/la estanquero(a) *es·tan·ke·ro(a)*

tobacconist's (shop) n el estanco *es·tan·ko*

today adv hoy *oy*

toe n el dedo del pie *de·do del pye*

toffee n el caramelo *ka·ra·me·lo*

together adv juntos *khoon·tos*

toilet n el wáter *wa·ter* A4, A91, F4

toilet paper n el papel higiénico *pa·pel ee·khye·nee·ko* A52

toiletries pl los artículos de tocador *ar·tee·koo·los de to·ka·dor*

toilet water n el agua de tocador (*f*) *a·gwa de to·ka·dor*

token n (*voucher*) el vale *ba·le*; (*for machine*) la ficha *fee·cha* Sn20

toll n (*on road etc*) el peaje *pe·a·khe* T134

toll bridge n el puente de peaje *pwen·te de pe·a·khe*

tomato n el tomate *to·ma·te*

tomorrow adv mañana *man·ya·na*

ton n la tonelada *to·ne·la·da*

tone n el tono *to·no*

tongue n la lengua *len·gwa*

tonic n (*medicine*) el tónico *to·nee·ko*

tonic water n la tónica *to·nee·ka*

tonight adv esta noche *es·ta no·che*

tonne n la tonelada *to·ne·la·da*

tonsillitis n la amigdalitis *a·meeg·da·lee·tees*

too adv (*also*) también *tam·byen*; he's too big es demasiado grande *es de·ma·sya·do gran·de*; too much demasiado *de·ma·sya·do*; too many books demasiados libros *de·ma·sya·dos lee·bros*

tool n la herramienta *e·rra·myen·ta*

tooth n el diente *dyen·te* I57

toothache n el dolor de muelas *do·lor de mwe·las*; to have a toothache tener* dolor de muelas *te·ner do·lor de mwe·las* S40

toothbrush n el cepillo de dientes *the·peel·yo de dyen·tes*

toothpaste n la crema dental *kre·ma den·tal*

top n (*of mountain*) la cima *thee·ma*; (*of ladder*) lo alto *al·to*; (*of table*) la superficie *soo·per·fee·thye*; (*lid*) la tapa *ta·pa*; (*of bottle*) el tapón *ta·pon*; on top of encima de *en·thee·ma de* □ adj top de encima *de en·thee·ma*; (*in rank*) de primera de *pree·me·ra*; (*best*) mejor *me·khor* L15

top hat n la chistera *chees·te·ra*

topic n el asunto *a·soon·to*

toss vt (*salad*) mover* *mo·ber*; to toss a

coin jugar* a cara o cruz *khoo·gar a ka·ra o krooth*
total n el total *to·tal* □ *adj* total *to·tal*
touch vt tocar* *to·kar* □ n in touch with en contacto *en kon·tak·to con*
tough *adj* duro(a) *doo·ro(a)*
tour n la excursión *eks·koor·syon* □ *vt (town)* recorrer *re·ko·rrer* L6f
tourism n el turismo *too·rees·mo*
tourist n el/la turista *too·rees·ta*
tourist class n la clase turista *kla·se too·rees·ta*
tourist office n la oficina de turismo *o·fee·thee·na de too·rees·mo* F6
tourist trade n el turismo *too·rees·mo*
tow vt (trailer) remolcar* *re·mol·kar*; in tow a remolque *a re·mol·ke* T122
toward(s) prep hacia *a·thya*; to look towards something mirar hacia algo *mee·rar a·thya al·go*; to come towards someone venir* hacia alguien *be·neer a·thya al·gyen*; his attitude towards others su actitud hacia los demás *soo ak·tee·tood a·thya los de·mas*
tow-bar n (on car) la barra del remolcador *ba rra del re·mol·ka·dor*
towel n la toalla *to·al·ya* A41
tower n la torre *to·rre*
town n la ciudad *thyoo·dad*; to go to town in* a la ciudad *eer a la thyoo·dad* T95, F5, L4
town hall n el ayuntamiento *a·yoon·ta·myen·to*
tow truck n la grúa *groo·a*
toy n el juguete *khoo·ge·te*
toyshop n la tienda de juguetes *tyen·da de khoo·ge·tes*
trace n (mark) el rastro *ras·tro*
track n (of animal, record, for sports) la pista *pees·ta*; (pathway) el camino *ka·mee·no*; (for trains) la vía *bee·a*
track suit n el chándal *chan·dal*
tractor n el tractor *trak·tor*
trade n el comercio *ko·mer·thyo*
trade-in n □ as a trade-in como pago parcial *ko·mo pa·go par·thyal*
trade mark n la marca registrada *mar·ka re·khees·tra·da*
trade name n el nombre comercial *nom·bre ko·mer·thyal*
trader n el/la comerciante *ko·mer·thyan·te*
trade union n el sindicato *seen·dee·ka·to*
trading stamp n el cupón *koo·pon*
tradition n la tradición *tra·dee·thyon*
traffic n (cars) el tráfico *tra·fee·ko* T130
traffic circle n el cruce giratorio *kroo·the khee·ra·to·ryo*
traffic jam n el embotellamiento *em·bo·tel·ya·myen·to*
traffic lights pl el semáforo *se·ma·fo·ro*
trailer n (for goods) el remolque *re·mol·ke*; (home on wheels) la caravana *ka·ra·ba·na* A87
train n el tren *tren*; (on dress) la cola *ko·la*; by train en tren *en tren* □ vt train (apprentice) preparar *pre·pa·rar*; (dog) amaestrar *a·ma·es·trar* □ vi (athlete) entrenarse *en·tre·nar·se*; to train as a teacher hacer* un curso para ser profesor *a·ther oon koor·so pa·ra ser pro·fe·sor* T2f, 54f
trainee n el aprendiz *a·pren·deeth*
training n (for job) la formación *for·ma·thyon*; (for sports) el entrenamiento *en·tre·na·myen·to*
tram(car) n el tranvía *tran·bee·a*

tramp n el vagabundo *ba·ga·boon·do*
tranquilizer n el tranquilizante *tran·kee·lee·than·te*
transaction n la transacción *tran·sak·thyon*
transatlantic *adj* transatlántico(a) *trans·at·lan·tee·ko(a)*
transfer vt (money) transferir* *trans·fe·reer*
transistor n el transistor *tran·sees·tor*
transit n □ in transit en tránsito *en tran·see·to*
transit visa n el visado de tránsito *bee·sa·do de tran·see·to*
translate vt traducir* *tra·doo·theer*
translation n la traducción *tra·dook·thyon*
transmission n (of car) la transmisión *trans·mee·syon*
transmitter n el transmisor *trans·mee·sor*
transparent *adj* transparente *trans·pa·ren·te*
transport n el transporte *trans·por·te* □ vt transportar *trans·por·tar*
trap n la trampa *tram·pa*
trash n la basura *ba·soo·ra*
trash can n el cubo de la basura *koo·bo de lu bu·soo·ra* A72
travel n el viajar *bya·khar* □ vi viajar *bya·khar* □ vt (a distance) recorrer *re·ko·rrer*
travel agency n la agencia de viajes *a·khen·thya de bya·khes*
travel agent n el agente de viajes *a·khen·te de bya·khes*
traveler n el viajero *bya·khe·ro*
traveler's check n el cheque de viaje *che·ke de bya·khe* M12, 22, A23
tray n la bandeja *ban·de·kha*
treacle n la melaza *me·la·tha*
treasure n el tesoro *te·so·ro*
Treasury n el Ministerio de Hacienda *mee·nees·te·ryo de a·thyen·da*
treat vt tratar *tra·tar*; I'll treat you to an ice cream le invito a tomar un helado *le een·bee·to a to·mar oon e·la·do* □ n a little treat un placer *pla·ther*
treatment n el tratamiento *tra·ta·myen·to*
tree n el árbol *ar·bol*
trend n la tendencia *ten·den·thya*
trial n (test) la prueba *prwe·ba*; (in law) el juicio *khwee·thyo*
triangle n el triángulo *tree·an·goo·lo*
tribe n la tribu *tree·boo*
trick n (clever act) el truco *troo·ko*; (malicious) el engaño *en·gan·yo*; (in cards) la baza *ba·tha* □ vt engañar *en·gan·yar*
trifle n (dessert) el dulce de bizcocho borracho *dool·the de beeth·ko·cho bo·rra·cho*
trim vt (hedge) podar *po·dar*; (hair) recortarse el pelo *re·kor·tar·se el pe·lo*; (decorate) adornar *a·dor·nar*
trip n (journey) el viaje *bya·khe*; (excursion) la excursión *eks·koor·syon*; to go on a trip to the beach ir* de excursión a la playa *eer de eks·koor·syon a la pla·ya* □ vi trip (stumble) tropezar* *tro·pe·thar*
tripe n los callos *kal·yos*
tripod n el trípode *tree·po·de*
trivial *adj* trivial *tree·byal*
trolley n (for purchases) el carrito *ka·rree·to*; (for luggage) la carretilla *ka·rre·teel·ya*
troop n la tropa *tro·pa*
tropical *adj* tropical *tro·pee·kal*

tropics *pl* los trópicos *tro·pee·kos*

trot *vi* (*horse*) trotar *tro·tar*

trouble *n* (*problems*) los problemas *pro·ble·mas*; **the troubles in this country** los conflictos en este país *los kon·fleek·tos en es·te pa·ees*; **to take trouble over something** tomarse la molestia por algo *to·mar·se la mo·les·tya por al·go*; **stomach trouble** los problemas gástricos *pro·ble·mas gas·tree·kos*; **engine trouble** la avería del motor *a·be·ree·a del mo·tor*; **to be in trouble** estar* en un apuro *es·tar en oon a·poo·ro* Sn50

trouble-shooter *n* (*political*) el mediador *me·dya·dor*; (*technical*) el localizador de averías *lo·ka·lee·tha·dor de a·be·ree·as*

trousers *pl* los pantalones *pan·ta·lo·nes* Sn69

trouser-suit *n* el traje-pantalón *tra·khe·pan·ta·lon*

trout *n* la trucha *troo·cha*

truck *n* (*vehicle*) el camión *ka·myon*

truckstop *n* el restaurante de carretera *res·tow·ran·te de ka·rre·te·ra*

true *adj* de verdad *de ber·dad*

truffle *n* (*fungus*) la trufa *troo·fa*

truly *adv* □ **yours truly** le saluda atentamente *le sa·loo·da a·ten·ta·men·te* □ *vt* fallar *fal·yar*

trump *n* (*cards*) el triunfo *tree·oom·fo*

trumpet *n* la trompeta *trom·pe·ta*

trunk *n* (*of tree*) el tronco *tron·ko*; (*for clothes etc*) el baúl *ba·ool*; (*in car*) el portaequipajes *por·ta·e·kee·pa·khes* T96

trust *vt* (*person*) confiar en *kon·fee·ar en* □ *n* (*company*) el trust *troost*

truth *n* la verdad *ber·dad*

try *vt* probar* *pro·bar*; (*in law*) procesar *pro·the·sar*; **to try to do something** intentar hacer algo *een·ten·tar a·ther al·go*; **to try on a dress** probarse* un vestido *pro·bar·se oon bes·tee·do*

T-shirt *n* la camiseta *ka·mee·se·ta*

tube *n* el tubo *too·bo*

Tuesday *n* martes (*m*) *mar·tes*

tulip *n* el tulipán *too·lee·pan*

tuna fish *n* el atún *a·toon*

tune *n* la melodía *me·lo·dee·a* □ *vt* (*engine*) arreglar *a·rre·glar*; (*instrument*) afinar *a·fee·nar*

tunic *n* (*of uniform*) la túnica *too·nee·ka*

Tunisia *n* Túnez (*m*) *too·neth*

Tunisian *adj* tunecino(a) *too·ne·thee·no(a)*

tunnel *n* el túnel *too·nel*

turbot *n* el rodaballo *ro·da·bal·yo*

turkey *n* el pavo *pa·bo*

Turkey *n* Turquía (*f*) *toor·kee·a*

Turkish *adj* turco(a) *toor·ko(a)*

Turkish delight *n* el capricho de reina *ka·pree·cho de rey·na*

turn *n* (*bend in road*) la curva *koor·ba*; **it's your turn** le toca a Ud *le to·ka a oos·ted*; **in turn** por turno *por toor·no* □ *vi* turn (*person, car*) torcer* *tor·ther*; **he turned (around)** se volvió *se bol·byo*; **to turn back** retroceder* *re·tro·the·der*; **to turn professional** hacerse* profesional *a·ther·se pro·fe·syo·nal* □ *vt* turn girar *khee·rar*; **to turn on** (*light*) encender* *en·then·der*, prender (Am) *pren·der*; (*water*) abrir* *a·breer*; **to turn off** (*light*) apagar* *a·pa·gar*; (*water*) cortar *kor·tar*; **to turn down** (*heat, volume*) bajar *ba·khar*; **to turn up** (*heat*) poner*

más fuerte *po·ner mas fwer·te*; (*volume*) aumentar *ow·men·tar*; **to turn something over** volver* algo *bol·ber al·go*

turnover *n* (*money*) el volumen de ventas *bo·loo·men de ben·tas*; (*in goods*) el movimiento de mercancías *mo·bee·myen·to de mer·kan·thee·as*

turnpike *n* la autopista de peaje *ow·to·pees·ta de pe·a·khe*

turn signal *n* el indicador de dirección *een·dee·ka·dor de dee·rek·thyon*

turquoise *adj* turquesa *toor·ke·sa*

turtle soup *n* la sopa de tortuga *so·pa de tor·too·ga*

tutor *n* el profesor particular *pro·fe·sor par·tee·koo·lar*

tuxedo *n* el smoking *es·mo·keeng*

TV *n* la tele *te·le*

tweed *n* el tweed *tweed*

tweezers *pl* las pinzas *peen·thas*

twelfth *adj* duodécimo(a) *doo·o·de·thee·mo(a)*

twelve *num* doce *do·the*

twenty *num* veinte *beyn·te*

twice *adv* dos veces *dos be·thes*

twig *n* la ramita *ra·mee·ta*

twill *n* la tela cruzada *te·la kroo·tha·da*

twin beds *pl* las camas gemelas *ka·mas khe·me·las*

twins *pl* los/las gemelos(as) *khe·me·los(as)*

twist *vt* torcer* *tor·ther* □ *vi* (*road*) dar* vueltas *dar bwel·tas*

two *num* dos *dos*

two-piece *n* el dos piezas *dos pye·thas*

tycoon *n* el magnate *mag·na·te*

type *n* (*sort*) el tipo *tee·po* □ *vt* (*letter*) mecanografiar *me·ka·no·gra·fee·ar*

typewriter *n* la máquina de escribir *ma·kee·na de es·kree·beer*

typewritten *adj* mecanografiado(a) *me·ka·no·gra·fee·a·do(a)*

typical *adj* típico(a) *tee·pee·ko(a)*

typist *n* la mecanógrafa *me·ka·no·gra·fa* Bm14

U

ugly *adj* (*object, person*) feo(a) *fe·o(a)*

ulcer *n* la úlcera *ool·the·ra*

ultimatum *n* el ultimátum *ool·tee·ma·toom*

umbrella *n* el paraguas *pa·ra·gwas*; (*on table*) el quitasol *kee·ta·sol*

umbrella stand *n* el paragüero *pa·rag·we·ro*

umpire *n* el árbitro *ar·bee·tro*

unable *adj* □ **to be unable to do something** no poder* hacer algo *no po·der a·ther al·go*

unanimous *adj* (*decision*) unánime *oo·na·nee·me*; **we were unanimous** estuvimos unánimes *es·too·bee·mos oo·na·nee·mes*

unarmed *adj* (*person*) desarmado(a) *des·ar·ma·do(a)*

unavoidable *adj* inevitable *een·e·bee·ta·ble*

unbearable *adj* (*pain*) insoportable *een·so·por·ta·ble*

unbeatable *adj* (*offer*) inmejorable *een·me·kho·ra·ble*

unbiased *adj* imparcial *eem·par·thyal*

unbreakable *adj* irrompible *ee·rrom·pee·ble*

uncertain *adj* (*fact*) incierto(a) *een·thyer·to(a)*

unchanged *adj* sin cambiar *seen kam·byar*

uncle *n* el tío *tee·o*

uncomfortable *adj* incómodo(a) *een·ko·mo·do(a)*

unconditional *adj* (*offer*) incondicional *een·kon·dee·thyo·nal*

unconscious *adj* inconsciente *een·kons·thyen·te*

uncover *vt* destapar *des·ta·par*

under *prep* debajo *de·ba·kho*; under the table debajo de la mesa *de·ba·kho de la me·sa*; under a kilometer menos de un kilómetro *me·nos de oon kee·lo·me·tro*; under repair en reparación *en re·pa·ra·thyon*; children under 10 niños de menos de 10 años *neen·yos de me·nos de 10 an·yos*

underclothes *pl* la ropa interior *ro·pa een·te·ryor*

undercooked *adj* insuficientemente cocido(a) *een·soo·fee·thyen·te·men·te ko·thee·do(a)*

underdeveloped *adj* (*country*) subdesarrollado(a) *soob·de·sa·rrol·ya·do(a)*

underdone *adj* (*meat*) poco hecho(a) *po·ko e·cho(a)*; (*food in general*) medio asado(a) *me·dyo a·sa·do(a)*

underexposed *adj* subexpuesto(a) *soob·eks·pwes·to(a)*

undergraduate *n* el/la estudiante *es·too·dyan·te*

underground *adj* (*pipe etc*) subterráneo(a) *soob·te·rra·ne·o(a)* □ *n* underground railway el metro *me·tro*

underline *vt* subrayar *soob·ra·yar*

underneath *prep* debajo *de·ba·kho*; underneath the book debajo del libro *de·ba·kho del lee·bro*

underpaid *adj* mal pagado(a) *mal pa·ga·do(a)*

underpants *pl* los calzoncillos *kal·thon·theel·yos*

underpass *n* (*for pedestrians*) el paso subterráneo *pa·so soob·te·rra·ne·o*; (*for cars*) el paso inferior *pa·so een·fe·ryor*

undershirt *n* la camiseta *ka·mee·se·ta*

understand *vt/i* comprender *kom·pren·der*; we understand that... comprendemos que... *kom·pren·de·mos ke* B21f

understanding *n* la comprensión *kom·pren·syon*; (*agreement*) el acuerdo *a·kwer·do*

undertake *vt* emprender *em·pren·der*; to undertake to do encargarse* de hacer *en·kar·gar·se de a·ther*

undertaking *n* (*enterprise*) la empresa *em·pre·sa*; (*promise*) el compromiso *kom·pro·mee·so*

undervalue *vt* subestimar *soob·es·tee·mar*

underwear *n* la ropa interior *ro·pa een·te·ryor*

underwrite *vt* (*insurance*) asegurar *a·se·goo·rar*; (*finance*) garantizar *ga·ran·tee·thar*

underwriter *n* el asegurador *a·se·goo·ra·dor*

undo *vt* deshacer* *des·a·ther*

undress *vt* desvestir* *des·bes·teer* □ *vi* desvestirse* *des·bes·teer·se*

unearned income *n* la renta *ren·ta*

uneconomic *adj* antieconómico(a) *an·tee·e·ko·no·mee·ko(a)*

uneconomical *adj* poco económico(a) *po·ko e·ko·no·mee·ko(a)*

unemployed *adj* parado(a) *pa·ra·do(a)*; the unemployed los parados *pa·ra·dos*

unemployment *n* el paro *pa·ro*

UNESCO *n* la Unesco *oo·nes·ko*

unfair *adj* injusto(a) *een·khoos·to(a)*; (*competition*) desleal *des·le·al*

unfasten *vt* desabrochar *des·a·bro·char*

unfold *vt* desplegar* *des·ple·gar*

unfortunate *adj* (*event*) desgraciado(a) *des·gra·thya·do(a)*

unfortunately *adv* desgraciadamente *des·gra·thya·da·men·te*

unhappy *adj* desdichado(a) *des·dee·cha·do(a)*

uniform *n* el uniforme *oo·nee·for·me*

unilateral *adj* unilateral *oo·nee·la·te·ral*

union *n* la unión *oo·nyon*; (*trade union*) el gremio *gre·myo*

unique *adj* único(a) *oo·nee·ko(a)*

unisex *adj* unisexual *oo·nee·seks·wal*

unit *n* (*of machinery*) la unidad *oo·nee·dad*; (*department, squad*) el grupo *groo·po*; (*of measurement*) la unidad *oo·nee·dad*; (*furniture*) el elemento *e·le·men·to*

unite *vt* unir *oo·neer*

United Kingdom, U.K. *n* el Reino Unido *reyno oo·nee·do*

United Nations Organization, UN, UNO *n* las Naciones Unidas *na·thyo·nes oo·nee·das*

United States (of America), US(A) *n* los Estados Unidos *es·ta·dos oo·nee·dos*

unit price *n* el precio por unidad *pre·thyo por oo·nee·dad*

universal *adj* universal *oo·nee·ber·sal*

universe *n* el universo *oo·nee·ber·so*

university *n* la universidad *oo·nee·ber·see·dad*

unkind *adj* (*person*) poco amable *po·ko a·ma·ble*; (*remark*) cruel *kroo·el*

unknown *adj* desconocido(a) *des·ko·no·thee·do(a)*

unless *conj* □ unless we come a no ser que vengamos *a no ser ke ben·ga·mos*

unlikely *adj* improbable *eem·pro·ba·ble*

unlimited *adj* ilimitado(a) *ee·lee·mee·ta·do(a)*

unlined *adj* (*clothes*) sin forro *seen fo·rro*

unlisted *adj* que no está en la guía *ke no es·ta en la gee·a*

unload *vt* descargar* *des·kar·gar*

unlock *vt* abrir* (con llave) *a·breer kon lya·be*

unlucky *adj* desgraciado(a) *des·gra·thya·do(a)*

unnatural *adj* no natural *no na·too·ral*

unnecessary *adj* innecesario(a) *een·ne·the·sa·ryo(a)*

unofficial *adj* no oficial *no o·fee·thyal*; unofficial strike la huelga no oficial *wel·ga no o·fee·thyal*

unpack *vt* (*case*) deshacer* *des·a·ther*; (*clothes*) sacar* *sa·kar*

unpaid *adj* (*debt*) no pagado(a) *no pa·ga·do(a)*

unpleasant *adj* desagradable *des·a·gra·da·ble*

unprofitable *adj* poco lucrativo(a) *po·ko loo·kra·tee·bo(a)*

unreasonable *adj* (*demand, price*) excesivo(a) *eks·the·see·bo(a)*

unripe *adj* verde *ber·de*

unsalted *adj* (*butter*) sin sal *seen sal*

unscrew *vt* destornillar *des·tor·neel·yar*

unskilled labor *n* la mano de obra no calificada *ma·no de o·bra no ka·lee·fee·ka·da*

unsuitable *adj* inapropiado(a) *een·a·pro·pya·do(a)*

untidy *adj* (*room*) en desorden *en des·*

or·den; (*hair*) desaliñado(a) *des·a·
leen·ya·do(a)*

untie *vt* (*parcel*) desatar *des·a·tar*;
(*animal*) soltar* *sol·tar*

until *prep* hasta *as·ta* □ *conj* until he
comes hasta que venga *as·ta ke
ben·ga*

unusual *adj* insólito(a) *een·so·lee·to(a)*
S110

unwrap *vt* deshacer* *des·a·ther*

up *prep* □ to go up a hill subir una colina *soo·beer oo·na ko·lee·na*; up till
now hasta ahora *as·ta a·o·ra*; up to 6
hasta 6 *as·ta* 6 □ *adv* up there allí
arriba *al·yee a·rree·ba*; he isn't up yet
(*out of bed*) todavía no se ha levantado *to·da·bee·a no se a le·ban·ta·do*

update *vt* poner* al día *po·ner al dee·a*

uphill *adv* cuesta arriba *kwes·ta a·rree·
ba*; to go uphill *ir** cuesta arriba *eer
kwes·ta a·rree·ba*

upkeep *n* el mantenimiento *man·te·
nee·myen·to*

upon *prep* sobre *so·bre*

upper *adj* superior *soo·pe·ryor*; the
upper class la clase alta *kla·se al·ta*

upset price *n* el precio mínimo *pre·
thyo mee·nee·mo*

upside down *adv* al revés *al re·bes*; to
turn something upside down poner*
algo al revés *po·ner al·go al re·bes*

upstairs *adv* arriba *a·rree·ba*

upturn *n* (*in business*) la mejora *me·
kho·ra*

upward(s) *adv* hacia arriba *a·thya
a·rree·ba*

urban *adj* urbano(a) *oor·ba·no(a)*

urgent *adj* urgente *oor·khen·te*

urgently *adv* urgentemente *oor·khen·
te·men·te*

us *pron* nosotros *no·so·tros*; it's us somos nosotros *so·mos no·so·tros*

use *n* el empleo *em·ple·o*; in use en
uso *en oo·so*; it's no use no sirve para
nada *no seer·be pa·ra na·da* □ *vt* use
emplear *em·ple·ar*

used *adj* (*car etc*) de segunda mano *de
se·goon·da ma·no*; to get used to
acostumbrarse a *a·kos·toom·brar·se
a* □ *vi* we used to go solíamos ir *so·
lee·a·mos eer*

useful *adj* útil *oo·teel*

useless *adj* inútil *een·oo·teel*

U.S.S.R. *n* la U.R.S.S. *oo·e·rre·e·se·
e·se*

usual *adj* acostumbrado(a) *a·kos·
toom·bra·do(a)*

usually *adv* normalmente *nor·mal·
men·te*

U-turn *n* (*in car*) el viraje en U *bee·ra·
khe en oo*

V

vacancy *n* (*job*) la vacante *ba·kan·te*;
(*in hotel etc*) la habitación libre
a·bee·ta·thyon lee·bre; no vacancies
completo *kom·ple·to* A12

vacant *adj* (*seat, toilet*) libre *lee·bre*

vacation *n* las vacaciones *ba·ka·thyo·
nes*; on vacation de vacaciones *de
ba·ka·thyo·nes* Mc17

vacationer *n* el/la veraneante *be·ra·ne·
an·te*

vaccination *n* la vacunación *ba·koo·
na·thyon*

vacuum cleaner *n* el aspirador *as·pee·
ra·dor*

vague *adj* vago(a) *ba·go(a)*

vain *adj* vanidoso(a) *ba·nee·do·so(a)*;
in vain en vano *en ba·no*

valet *n* (*in hotel*) el ayuda de cámara
a·yoo·da de ka·ma·ra

valid *adj* válido(a) *ba·lee·do(a)*

valley *n* el valle *bal·ye*

valuable *adj* valioso(a) *ba·lyo·so(a)*

valuables *pl* los objetos de valor *ob·
khe·tos de ba·lor*

value *n* el valor *ba·lor* □ *vt* valorar *ba·
lo·rar*

value-added tax *n* el impuesto al valor
agregado *eem·pwes·to al ba·lor a·gre·
ga·do*

valve *n* la válvula *bal·boo·la*

van *n* la camioneta *ka·myo·ne·ta*

vandal *n* el vándalo *ban·da·lo*

vanilla *n* la vainilla *bay·neel·ya*; vanilla
ice cream el helado de vainilla *e·la·
do de bay·neel·ya*

variable *adj* variable *ba·rya·ble* □ *n* la
variable *ba·rya·ble*

variation *n* la variación *ba·rya·thyon*

variety *n* la variedad *ba·rye·dad*

variety show *n* el espectáculo de variedades *es·pek·ta·koo·lo de ba·rye·
da·des*

various *adj* diverso(a) *dee·ber·so(a)*

varnish *n* el barniz *bar·neeth*

vary *vi* variar *ba·ryar*

vase *n* el florero *flo·re·ro*

vaseline *n* la vaselina *ba·se·lee·na*

Vatican *n* el Vaticano *ba·tee·ka·no*

veal *n* la ternera *ter·ne·ra*

vegetables *pl* las legumbres *le·goom·
bres*, las verduras (*Am*) *ber·doo·ras*
E25

vegetarian *adj* vegetariano(a) *be·khe·
ta·rya·no(a)*

vehicle *n* el vehículo *be·ee·koo·lo*

veil *n* el velo *be·lo*

vein *n* la vena *be·na*

velvet *n* el terciopelo *ter·thyo·pe·lo*

vending machine *n* el distribuidor automático *dees·tree·bwee·dor ow·to·
ma·tee·ko*

vendor *n* el vendedor *ben·de·dor*

Venezuela *n* Venezuela (*f*) *be·ne·
thwe·la*

Venezuelan *adj* venezolano(a) *be·ne·
tho·la·no(a)*

Venice *n* Venecia (*f*) *be·ne·thya*

venison *n* la carne de venado *kar·ne de
be·na·do*

ventilator *n* el ventilador *ben·tee·la·dor*

venture *n* la empresa *em·pre·sa*

veranda *n* la veranda *be·ran·da*

verbal *adj* (*agreement*) verbal *ber·bal*

verdict *n* el veredicto *be·re·deek·to*

verge *n* el arcén *ar·then*

vermouth *n* el vermut *ber·moot*

version *n* la versión *ber·syon*

versus *prep* contra *kon·tra*

vertical *adj* vertical *ber·tee·kal*

very *adv* muy *mooy*; the very last el último de todos *ool·tee·mo de to·dos*; I
like it very much me gusta mucho *me
goos·ta moo·cho*; I haven't very much
no tengo mucho *no ten·go moo·cho*

vest *n* el chaleco *cha·le·ko*

vet(erinary surgeon) *n* el veterinario
be·te·ree·na·ryo

veto *vt* vetar *be·tar* □ *n* el veto *be·to*

V.H.F. *abbrev* las ondas ultra-cortas
on·das ool·tra·kor·tas

via *prep* por *por*

viaduct *n* el viaducto *bya·dook·to*

vicar *n* el cura *koo·ra*

vice chairman *n* el vicepresidente *bee·
the·pre·see·den·te*

vice president *n* el vicepresidente *bee·
the·pre·see·den·te*

vice versa *adv* viceversa *bee·the·ber·sa*

victim n (of accident etc) la víctima beek·tee·ma

victory n la victoria beek·to·rya

video n el vídeo bee·de·o; on video en la televisión en la te·le·bee·syon

videocassette n la cassette vídeo ka·se·te bee·de·o

videocassette recorder n el magnetoscopio mag·ne·tos·ko·pyo

videotape n la cinta magnética de vídeo theen·ta mag·ne·tee·ka de vee·de·o

Vienna n Viena (f) bye·na

view n la vista bees·ta; (opinion) la opinión o·pee·nyon A5

villa n (country house, vacation home) la casa de campo ka·sa de kam·po

village n la aldea al·de·a

vinaigrette (sauce) n la vinagreta bee·na·gre·ta

vine n la parra pa·rra

vinegar n el vinagre bee·na·gre

vineyard n la viña been·ya

vintage n la cosecha ko·se·cha; ▢ vintage wine el vino de calidad bee·no de ka·lee·dad

vinyl n el vinilo bee·nee·lo

violence n la violencia byo·len·thya

violin n el violín byo·leen

V.I.P. n el personaje importante per·so·na·khe eem·por·tan·te

visa, visé n el visado bee·sa·do, la visa (Am) bee·sa

visible adj visible bee·see·ble

visit n (to relatives hospital) ___ ▢ n la visita bee·see·ta Mc35

visitor n la visita bee·see·ta

visual aids pl los medios visuales me·dyos bee·swa·les

vital adj (essential) imprescindible eem·pres·theen·dee·ble

vitamin n la vitamina bee·ta·mee·na

V-neck n el cuello de pico kwel·yo de pee·ko

vocabulary n el vocabulario bo·ka·boo·la·ryo

vodka n la vodka bod·ka

voice n la voz both

void adj (contract) nulo(a) noo·lo(a)

vol-au-vent n el volován bo·lo·ban

volcano n el volcán bol·kan

volleyball n el balónvolea ba·lon·bo·le·a, el voleibol (Am) bo·ley·bol

voltage n el voltaje vol·ta·khe

volume n (sound, capacity) el volumen bo·loo·men; (book) el tomo to·mo; volume of sales el volumen de ventas bo·loo·men de ben·tas

vomit vi vomitar bo·mee·tar

vote n el voto bo·to ▢ vi votar bo·tar

voucher n el vale ba·le

W

wading pool n la piscina para niños pees·thee·na pa·ra neen·yos C5

wafer n el barquillo bar·keel·yo

waffle n el buñuelo boon·ywe·lo

wag vt (tail) menear me·ne·ar

wage, wages n el salario sa·la·ryo

wage earner n el asalariado a·sa·la·rya·do

wage freeze n la congelación de salarios kon·khe·la·thyon de sa·la·ryos

wagon n el carro ka·rro

wagon-lit n el coche cama ko·che ka·ma

waist n la cintura theen·too·ra

wait vi esperar es·pe·rar; to wait for someone esperar a alguien es·pe·rar a al·gyen; to keep someone waiting

hacer* esperar a alguien a·ther es·pe·rar a al·gyen

waiter n el camarero ka·ma·re·ro E43

waiting list n la lista de espera lees·ta de es·pe·ra

waiting room n (at station) la sala de espera sa·la de es·pe·ra

waitress n la camarera ka·ma·re·ra

wake vi despertar* des·per·tar ▢ vi to wake up despertarse des·per·tar·se

Wales n Gales (m) ga·les

walk vi andar* an·dar; (for pleasure, exercise) pasearse pa·se·ar·se ▢ vt to walk 10 km recorrer 10 km a pie re·ko·rrer 10 km a pye ▢ n walk el paseo pa·se·o; to go for a walk dar* un paseo dar oon pa·se·o L30

walking n el paseo pa·se·o

walking stick n el bastón bas·ton

walkout n la huelga wel·ga

wall n (inside) la pared pa·red; (outside) el muro moo·ro

wallet n la cartera kar·te·ra Sn84

wallpaper n el papel pintado pa·pel peen·ta·do

wall-to-wall carpet(ing) n la moqueta mo·ke·ta

walnut n la nuez nweth

waltz n el vals bals

wander vi vagar* ba·gar

want vt (wish for) querer* ke·rer; (need) necesitar ne·the·see·tar; to want to do something querer* hacer algo ke·rer a·ther al·go

war n la guerra ge·rra

ward n (in hospital) la sala sa·la

wardrobe n (furniture) el armario ar·ma·ryo

warehouse n el almacén al·ma·then

warm adj cálido(a) ka·lee·do(a); it's warm today hace calor hoy a·the ka·lor oy; I'm warm tengo calor ten·go ka·lor

warn vt advertir* ad·ber·teer; to warn someone of something advertir* a alguien de algo ad·ber·teer a al·gyen de al·go

warrant(y) n la garantía ga·ran·tee·a

Warsaw n Varsovia (f) bar·so·bya

wart n la verruga be·rroo·ga

was vi ▢ I was yo era yo e·ra; (temporary state) yo estaba yo es·ta·ba; he was el era el e·ra; él estaba el es·ta·ba

wash vt lavar la·bar ▢ vi to wash (oneself), to wash up lavarse la·bar·se A93

washable adj lavable la·ba·ble S83

washbasin, washbowl n el lavabo la·ba·bo A50

washcloth n la manopla ma·no·pla

washing n (clothes) el lavado la·ba·do; to do the washing lavar la ropa la·bar la ro·pa

washing machine n la lavadora la·ba·do·ra A95

washroom n los aseos a·se·os A91

waste n el derroche de·rro·che; (rubbish) la basura ba·soo·ra ▢ vt gastar gas·tar; to waste one's time perder* el tiempo per·der el tyem·po

waste paper basket n la papelera pa·pe·le·ra

watch n el reloj re·lokh ▢ vt (look at) mirar mee·rar; (TV, play) ver* ber; (spy on) observar ob·ser·bar; to watch a match ver* un partido ber oon par·tee·do S88

water n el agua (f) ag·wa A31, L20, Mc9

watercress n el berro be·rro

waterfall n la cascada *kas·ka·da*
water heater n el calentador de agua *ka·len·ta·dor de ag·wa* A65
watermelon n la sandía *san·dee·a*
waterproof adj impermeable *eem·per·me·a·ble*
water-skiing n el esquí acuático *es·kee a·kwa·tee·ko*; **to go water-skiing** hacer* esquí acuático *a·ther es·kee a·kwa·tee·ko*
watt n el vatio *ba·tyo*
wave vi hacer* señales con la mano *a·ther sen·ya·les kon la ma·no* □ n (in sea) la ola *o·la*; (in hair) la ondulación *on·doo·la·thyon*
wavy adj (hair) ondulado(a) *on·doo·la·do(a)*
wax n la cera *the·ra*
way n (manner) la manera *ma·ne·ra*; (in) **a different way** de una manera diferente *de oo·na ma·ne·ra dee·fe·ren·te*; **which is the way to London?** ¿cuál es el camino para Londres? *kwal es el ka·mee·no pa·ra lon·dres*; **to ask the way to Paris** preguntar el camino de París *pre·goon·tar el ka·mee·no de pa·rees*; **it's a long way** está lejos *es·ta le·khos*; **to be in the way** estorbar *es·tor·bar*; **on the way** camino de *ka·mee·no de*; **this way please** por aquí, por favor *por a·kee por fa·bor*; **by the way** a propósito a *a pro·po·see·to* F1f
we pron nosotros(as) *no·so·tros(as)*
weak adj (person) débil *de·beel*; (tea) flojo(a) *flo·kho(a)*
wealth n la riqueza *ree·ke·tha*
wealthy adj rico(a) *ree·ko(a)*
weapon n el arma (f) *ar·ma*
wear vt (clothes) llevar *lye·bar* □ vi (fabric) gastarse *gas·tar·se*; **to wear something out** desgastar *des·gas·tar*; **wear and tear** el desgaste *des·gas·te*
weather n el tiempo *tyem·po*
weather forecast n el boletín meteorológico *bo·le·teen me·te·o·ro·lo·khee·ko*
weave vt tejer *te·kher*
wedding n la boda *bo·da*
wedding dress n el traje de novia *tra·khe de no·bya*
wedding present n el regalo de boda *re·ga·lo de bo·da*
wedding ring n el anillo de boda *a·neel·yo de bo·da*
Wednesday n miércoles (m) *myer·ko·les*
weed n la mala hierba *ma·la yer·ba*
week n la semana *se·ma·na* T107
weekday n el día de semana *dee·a de se·ma·na*
weekend n el fin de semana *feen de se·ma·na*
weekly adj semanal *se·ma·nal* □ adv cada semana *ka·da se·ma·na* □ n (periodical) el semanario *se·ma·na·ryo*
weigh vt pesar *pe·sar*; **it weighs 4 kilos** pesa 4 kilos *pe·sa 4 kee·los*
weight n (mass) el peso *pe·so*
welcome adj bienvenido(a) *byen·be·nee·do(a)* □ n la acogida *a·ko·khee·da* □ vt (person) acoger* *a·ko·kher*; (event, proposal) aprobar* *a·pro·bar*
weld vt soldar *sol·dar*
well n (for water) el pozo *po·tho* □ adv **he did it well** lo hizo bien *lo ee·tho byen*; **to be well** estar* bien *es·tar byen*; **get well soon** que te mejores *ke*

te mejores *me·kho·res*; **well!** ¡caramba! *ka·ram·ba*
wellington boot n la bota de goma *bo·ta de go·ma*
Welsh adj galés(esa) *ga·les(·le·sa)* □ n el galés *ga·les*
were vi □ **you** you were Ud/Uds era(n) *oos·ted(·es) e·ra(n)*; (temporary state) Ud/Uds estaba(n) *oos·ted(·es) es·ta·ba(n)*; **we were** nosotros(as) éramos *no·so·tros(as) e·ra·mos*; nosotros estábamos *no·so·tros es·ta·ba·mos*; **they were** ellos/ellas eran *el·yos/el·yas e·ran*; ellos/ellas estaban *el·yos/el·yas es·ta·ban*
west n el oeste *o·es·te*; **the West** el Oeste *o·es·te* □ adv **west** hacia el oeste *a·thya el o·es·te*
western adj occidental *ok·thee·den·tal* □ n (movie) la película del Oeste *pe·lee·koo·la del o·es·te*
West Germany n Alemania Occidental (f) *a·le·ma·nya ok·thee·den·tal*
wet adj (clothes) mojado(a) *mo·kha·do(a)*; (weather, day) lluvioso(a) *lyoo·byo·so(a)*; (paint) fresco(a) *fres·ko(a)*; (climate) húmedo(a) *oo·me·do(a)*; **to get wet** mojarse *mo·khar·se*
whale n la ballena *bal·ye·na*
wharf n el muelle *mwel·ye*
what adj qué *ke*; **what book?** ¿qué libro? *ke le·bro* □ pron **what** qué *ke*; **what's happened?** ¿qué ha pasado? *ke a pa·sa·do*; **what do you want?** ¿qué desea? *ke de·se·a*; **I saw what happened** vi lo que pasó *bee lo ke pa·so*; **I saw what you did** vi lo que hizo Ud *bee lo ke ee·tho oos·ted*; **what's it called?** ¿cómo se llama? *ko·mo se lya·ma*; **what a mess!** (in room) ¡qué desorden! *ke des·or·den*; **what?** (please repeat) ¿cómo? *ko·mo*
wheat n el trigo *tree·go*
wheel n la rueda *rwe·da*; (steering wheel) el volante *bo·lan·te*, el timón (Am) *tee·mon*
wheelbarrow n la carretilla *ka·rre·teel·ya*
wheelchair n la silla de ruedas *seel·ya de rwe·das* I5
when conj cuando *kwan·do*; (in questions) cuándo *kwan·do*; **the day when we...** el día que... *dee·a ke*
where conj donde *don·de*; **where are you from?** ¿de dónde eres? *de don·de e·res*; **where are you going?** ¿dónde va? *don·de ba*
whether conj si see
which adj que *ke*; **which languages?** ¿qué lenguas? *ke len·gwas*; **which one of you?** ¿cuál de Uds? *kwal de oos·te·des* □ pron **the book**, which is long el libro, que es largo *el lee·bro ke es lar·go*; **the apple which you ate** la manzana que comió la *man·tha·na ke ko·myo*; **I don't know which to take** no sé cuál llevar *no se kwal lye·bar*; **after which** después de lo cuál *des·pwes de lo kwal*; **the chair on which** la silla sobre la que *la seel·ya so·bre la ke*
while n el momento *mo·men·to* □ conj mientras *myen·tras*
whip n el látigo *la·tee·go* □ vt (cream, eggs) batir *ba·teer*
whipped cream n la nata batida *na·ta ba·tee·da*
whirlpool n el remolino *re·mo·lee·no*
whirlwind n el torbellino *tor·bel·yee·no*
whisk n el batidor *ba·tee·dor*

whiskey *n* el whisky *wees·kee*

whisper *vi* cuchichear *koo·chee·che·ar*

whistle *n* (*sound*) el silbido *seel·bee·do*; (*object*) el silbato *seel·ba·to* □ *vi* silbar *seel·bar*

white *adj* blanco(a) *blan·ko(a)*

whitebait *n* los chanquetes *chan·ke·tes*

White House *n* la Casa Blanca *ka·sa blan·ka*

whiting *n* la pescadilla *pes·ka·deel·ya*

Whitsun *n* el Pentecostés *pen·te·kos·tes*

Whitsunday *n* el domingo de Pentecostés *do·meen·go de pen·te·kos·tes*

who *pron* quien *kyen*; (*plural*) quienes *kye·nes*; the one who el/la que *el/la ke*; who? ¿quién? *kyen*

whole *adj* (*complete*) entero(a) *en·te·ro(a)*

wholesale *n* la venta al por mayor *ben·ta al por ma·yor* □ *adj, adv* al por mayor *al por ma·yor* Bm28

wholesaler *n* el mayorista *ma·yo·rees·ta*

wholewheat bread *n* el pan integral *pan een·te·gral*

whom *pron* que *ke*; quien *kyen*; the man whom you see el hombre que ve Ud *el om·bre ke be oos·ted*; the boy with whom... el niño con quien el *neen·yo kon kyen*

whooping cough *n* la tos ferina *tos fe·ree·na*

whose *adj* □ whose book is this? ¿de quién es este libro? *de kyen es es·te lee·bro*; the man, whose son is home, bre, cuyo hijo *el om·bre koo·yo ee·kho*; I know whose it is sé de quien es *se de kyen es*

why *adv* por qué *por ke*

wick *n* (*of cigarette lighter*) la mecha *me·cha*

wicked *adj* malvado(a) *mal·ba·do(a)*

wicker *n* el mimbre *meem·bre*

wide *adj* (*broad*) ancho(a) *an·cho(a)*; (*range*) grande *gran·de*; 4 cm. wide 4 cm. de ancho *4 cm de an·cho*

wide-angle lens *n* el objetivo granangular *ob·khe·tee·bo gra·nan·goo·lar*

widow *n* la viuda *byoo·da*

widower *n* el viudo *byoo·do*

width *n* la anchura *an·choo·ra*

wife *n* la esposa *es·po·sa* T110, A2, S106

wig *n* la peluca *pe·loo·ka*

wild *adj* (*animal*) salvaje *sal·ba·khe*; (*flower*) silvestre *seel·bes·tre*; (*tribe*) salvaje *sal·ba·khe*

wildlife *n* la fauna *fow·na*

will *n* (*testament*) el testamento *tes·ta·men·to* □ *vi* he will do it lo hará *lo a·ra*

willing *adj* □ willing to do something dispuesto(a) a hacer algo *dees·pwes·to(a) a a·ther al·go*

win *vt/i* ganar *ga·nar*; (*contract*) conseguir* *kon·se·geer*

wind[1] *n* (*breeze*) el viento *byen·to*; wind (*in stomach*) la flatulencia *fla·too·len·thya*

wind[2] *vt* enrollar *en·rol·yar*; to wind a bandage round something envolver* una venda alrededor de algo *en·bol·ber oo·na ben·da al·re·de·dor de al·go*; to wind up a clock dar* cuerda a un reloj *dar kwer·da a oon re·lokh*

windmill *n* el molino de viento *mo·lee·no de byen·to*

window *n* (*in house*) la ventana *ben·ta·na*; (*in car, train*) la ventanilla *ben·*

**ta·neel·ya*; (*of shop*) el escaparate *es·ka·pa·ra·te* B62

window shade *n* la persiana *per·sya·na*

window shopping *n* el escaparate *es·ka·pa·ra·te*

windshield *n* el parabrisas *pa·ra·bree·sas* T163

windshield washer *n* el lavaparabrisas *la·ba·pa·ra·bree·sas* T164

windshield wiper *n* el limpiaparabrisas *leem·pya·pu·ru·bree·sas* T179

windsurfing *n* el surf a vela *soorf a be·la*; to go windsurfing practicar* el surf a vela *prak·tee·kar el soorf a be·la*

windy *adj* (*place*) expuesto(a) al viento *eks·pwes·to(a) al byen·to*; it's windy hace mucho viento *a·the moo·cho byen·to*

wine *n* el vino *bee·no* B60, E9f, S36

wine cellar *n* la bodega *bo·de·ga*

wineglass *n* la copa de vino *ko·pa de bee·no*

wine list *n* la lista de vinos *lees·ta de bee·nos*

wine waiter *n* el escanciador *es·kan·thya·dor*

wing *n* el ala (*f*) *a·la*

wink *vi* guiñar *geen·yar*

winner *n* el/la ganador(a) *ga·na·dor(·ra)*

winter *n* el invierno *een·byer·no*

winter sports *pl* los deportes de invierno *de·por·tes de een·byer·no*

wipe *vt* limpiar *leem·pyar*; to wipe off limpiar un trapo *leem·pyar kon oon tra·po*

wire *n* el alambre *a·lam·bre*; (*electrical*) el cable *ka·ble*; (*telegram*) el telegrama *te·le·gra·ma*

wise *adj* (*person*) sabio(a) *sa·byo(a)*; (*decision*) prudente *proo·den·te*

wish *n* el deseo *de·se·o*; with best wishes un fuerte abrazo *oon fwer·te a·bra·tho* □ *vt/i* I wish I could... ojalá pudiera... *o·kha·la poo·dye·ra*; to wish for something desear algo *de·se·ar al·go*

witch *n* la bruja *broo·kha*

with *prep* con *kon*; the man with the umbrella el hombre con el paraguas *el om·bre kon el pa·rag·was*; red with anger rojo de cólera *ro·kho de ko·le·ra*; filled with water lleno(a) de agua *lye·no de ag·wa*

withdraw *vt* (*money*) retirar *re·tee·rar*

without *prep* sin *seen*

witness *n* el testigo *tes·tee·go* □ *vt* (*signature*) firmar como testigo *feer·mar ko·mo tes·tee·go* T223

wobble *vi* (*chair etc*) ser* poco firme *ser po·ko feer·me*

wolf *n* el lobo *lo·bo*

woman *n* la mujer *moo·kher*

womb *n* la matriz *ma·treeth*

wonder *vi* □ to wonder whether... preguntarse si... *pre·goon·tar·se see*

wonderful *adj* maravilloso(a) *ma·ra·beel·yo·so(a)*

wood *n* (*material*) la madera *ma·de·ra*; (*forest*) el bosque *bos·ke*

wooden *adj* de madera *de ma·de·ra*

wool *n* la lana *la·na*

woolen *adj* de lana *de la·na*

word *n* la palabra *pa·la·bra*; word for word palabra por palabra *pa·la·bra por pa·la·bra*

work *n* el trabajo *tra·ba·kho*; (*art, literature*) la obra *o·bra*; to go to work ir* al trabajo *eer al tra·ba·kho* □ *vi* work trabajar *tra·ba·khar*; (*clock, mechanism*) funcionar *foon·thyo·nar*; (*medicine*) ser* eficaz *ser e·fee·kath*; to work out (*problem*) resolver* *re·sol·ber* Sn51

workday *n* el día laborable *dee·a la·bo·ra·ble*

worker *n* el trabajador *tra·ba·kha·dor*

work force *n* la mano de obra *ma·no de o·bra*

working capital *n* el capital de explotación *ka·pee·tal de eks·plo·ta·thyon*

working-class *adj* obrero(a) *o·bre·ro(a)*

working hours *pl* las horas de trabajo *o·ras de tra·ba·kho*

working order *n* □ to be in working order estar* funcionando bien *es·tar foon·thyo·nan·do byen*

workman *n* el obrero *o·bre·ro*

work of art *n* la obra de arte *o·bra de ar·te*

works *pl* (*mechanism*) el mecanismo *me·ka·nees·mo*

workshop *n* el taller *tal·yer*

world *n* el mundo *moon·do*

world power *n* la potencia mundial *po·ten·thya moon·dyal*

world war *n* la guerra mundial *ge·rra moon·dyal*

worm *n* el gusano *goo·sa·no*

worn *adj* gastado(a) *gas·ta·do(a)*

worn-out *adj* (*object*) gastado(a) *gas·ta·do(a)*; (*person*) rendido(a) *ren·dee·do(a)*

worried *adj* preocupado(a) *pre·o·koo·pa·do(a)*

worry *n* la preocupación *pre·o·koo·pa·thyon*

worse *adj* □ it's worse (than the other) es peor (que el otro) *es pe·or (ke el o·tro)* □ *adv* to do something worse hacer* algo peor *a·ther al·go pe·or*

worst *adj* □ the worst book el peor libro *el pe·or lee·bro* □ *adv* he did it worst lo hizo peor que todos *lo ee·tho pe·or ke to·dos*

worth *adj* □ to be worth $5 valer* $5 *ba·ler $5*; 1,000 pesetas worth of gas 1,000 pesetas de gasolina *1,000 pe·se·tas de ga·so·lee·na*; it's worth it vale la pena *ba·le la pe·na*

worthwhile *adj* (*activity*) valioso(a) *ba·lyo·so(a)*

would *vi* □ she would come if... ella vendría si... *el·ya ben·dree·a see*; would you like a cup of coffee? ¿le gustaría una taza de café? *le goos·ta·ree·a oo·na ta·tha de ka·fe*

wound *n* (*injury*) la herida *e·ree·da*

wrap *vt* envolver* *en·bol·ber*; to wrap up a parcel envolver* un paquete *en·bol·ber oon pa·ke·te* □ *n* wrap (*shawl*) el chal *chal* S23

wrapper *n* (*paper*) la envoltura *en·bol·too·ra*

wrapping paper *n* el papel de envolver *pa·pel de en·bol·ber*

wreck *n* (*ship*) el barco naufragado *bar·ko now·fra·ga·do* □ *vt* hacer* naufragar *a·ther now·fra·gar*; (*plans*) arruinar *a·rooy·nar*

wrench *n* la llave inglesa *lya·be een·gle·sa*

wrestling *n* la lucha libre *loo·cha lee·bre*

wring *vt* (*clothes*) escurrir *es·koo·rreer*

wrinkle *n* la arruga *a·rroo·ga*

wrist *n* la muñeca *moon·ye·ka*

write *vt/i* escribir* *es·kree·beer*; to write down anotar *a·no·tar*; to write off a

debt cancelar una deuda *kan·the·lar oo·na de·oo·da*

writer *n* el escritor *es·kree·tor* B28

writing *n* la escritura *es·kree·too·ra*; in writing por escrito *por es·kree·to*

writing paper *n* el papel de escribir *pa·pel de es·kree·beer*

wrong *adj* equivocado(a) *e·kee·bo·ka·do(a)*; you're wrong no tiene razón *no tye·ne ra·thon*; that's wrong eso está equivocado *e·so es·ta e·kee·bo·ka·do*; the wrong road el camino equivocado *el ka·mee·no e·kee·bo·ka·do*; what's wrong? ¿pasa algo? *pa·sa al·go*; to go wrong (*machine*) fallar *fal·yar*

X

Xerox *n* la fotocopia *fo·to·ko·pya* □ *vt* fotocopiar *fo·to·ko·pyar*

X-ray *n* (*photo*) la radiografía *ra·dyo·gra·fee·a* □ *vt* hacer* una radiografía *a·ther oo·na ra·dyo·gra·fee·a*

Y

yacht *n* el yate *ya·te*

yachting *n* el deporte de la vela *de·por·te de la be·la*; to go yachting hacer* vela *a·ther be·la*

yard *n* (*of building*) el patio *pa·tyo*; (*measure*) la yarda *yar·da*

yawn *vi* bostezar* *bos·te·thar*

year *n* el año *an·yo*

yearly *adj* anual *a·nwal* □ *adv* anualmente *a·nwal·men·te*

yeast *n* la levadura *le·ba·doo·ra*

yellow *adj* amarillo(a) *a·ma·reel·yo(a)*

yes *adv* sí *see*

yesterday *adv* ayer *a·yer*

yet *adv* todavía *to·da·bee·a*; not yet todavía no *to·da·bee·a no*

yield *n* el rendimiento *ren·dee·myen·to*; (*financial*) el rédito *re·dee·to* □ *vt* (*investment*) rendir* *ren·deer* □ *vi* (*to traffic*) ceder el paso *the·der el pa·so*

yoga *n* el yoga *yo·ga*

yogurt *n* el yogur *yo·goor*

you *pron* (*familiar form*) tú *too*; (*polite form*) Usted (Ud) *oos·ted*; (*plural form*) Ustedes (Uds) *oos·te·des*; he's watching you (*familiar form*) te está mirando *te es·ta mee·ran·do*; (*polite form*) le está mirando (a Ud) *le es·ta mee·ran·do (a oos·ted)*

young *adj* joven *kho·ben*

your *adj* (*familiar form*) tu *too*, tus *toos*; (*plural*) vuestro(a) *bwes·tro(a)*; (*polite form*) su *soo*, sus *soos*; your father tu/su/vuestro padre *too/soo/bwes·tro pa·dre*; your mother tu/su/vuestra madre *too/soo/bwes·tra ma·dre*; your sisters tus/sus/vuestras hermanas *toos/soos/bwes·tras er·ma·nas*

yours *pron* (*familiar form*) el tuyo *el too·yo*, la tuya *la too·ya*; (*polite form*) el suyo *el soo·yo*, la suya *la soo·ya*; (*plural form*) el vuestro *el bwes·tro*, la vuestra *la bwes·tra*; where are yours? ¿dónde están los tuyos/los suyos/los vuestros? *don·de es·tan los too·yos/ soo·yos/los bwes·tros*; these are yours estos son tuyos/ suyos/vuestros *es·tos son too·yos/ soo·yos/bwes·tros*

yourself *pron* (*familiar form*) tú mismo(a) *too mees·mo(a)*; (*polite form*) Usted mismo(a) *oos·ted mees·mo(a)*; you've hurt yourself Ud se ha lastimado *oos·ted se a las·tee·ma·do*; you

did it yourself lo ha hecho Ud mismo *lo a·cho oos·ted mees·mo*

yourselves *pron* Ustedes mismos *oos·te·des mees·mos*; **you've hurt yourselves** Uds se han lastimado *oos·te·des se an las·tee·ma·do*; **you did it yourselves** lo han hecho Uds mismos *lo an e·cho oos·te·des mees·mos*

youth *n* (*period*) la juventud *khoo·ben·tood*

youth club *n* el centro para jovenes *then·tro pa·ra kho·be·nes*

youth hostel *n* el albergue de juventud *al·ber·ge de khoo·ben·tood*

Yugoslavia *n* Yugoslavia (*f*) *yoo·gos·la·bya*

Yugoslav(ian) *adj* yugoslavo(a) *yoo·gos·la·bo(a)*

zebra *n* la cebra

zero *n* el cero *th*

zinc *n* el cinc *th*

zip code *n* el c
pos·tal

zipper *n* la cremallera *kre·*
S75, Sn79

zone *n* la zona *tho·na*; (*postal*) el distrito postal *dees·tree·to pos·tal*

zoo *n* el zoo *tho*

zoom lens *n* el objetivo zoom *ob·khe·tee·bo thoom*

zucchini *pl* los calabacines *ka·la·ba·thee·nes*

Notes

Notes

236

Notes

Notes

Notes